MEDICAL ETHICS

A Reader

MEDICAL ETHICS

A Reader

Arthur Zucker
Donald Borchert
David Stewart

Ohio University

PRENTICE HALL, *Englewood Cliffs, New Jersey 07632*

Library of Congress Cataloging-in-Publication Data

Medical ethics : a reader / [edited by] Arthur Zucker, Donald Borchert,
David Stewart.
  p. cm.
  Reprinted from various sources.
  Includes bibliographical references and index.
  ISBN 0-13-572496-1
  1. Medical ethic. I. Zucker, Arthur (date). II. Borchert,
Donald M. (date).   III. Stewart, David (date).
  [DNLM: 1. Ethics, Medical—collected works.   W 50 M484]
  R724.M29285   1992
  174'.2—dc20
  DNLM/DLC
  for Library of Congress   91-28843
                                                                CIP

Acquisitions editor: *Ted Bolen*
Production editor: *Carolyn Serebreny*
Supervisory editor: *Joan L. Stone*
Copy editor: *Carolyn Serebreny*
Cover design: *20/20 Services Inc.*
Prepress buyer: *Herb Klein*
Manufacturing buyer: *Patrice Fraccio*
Editorial assistant: *Diane Schaible*

Printed in the United States of America
10 9 8 7 6 5 4 3 2 1

ISBN 0-13-572496-1

PRENTICE-HALL INTERNATIONAL (UK) LIMITED, *London*
PRENTICE-HALL OF AUSTRALIA PTY. LIMITED, *Sydney*
PRENTICE-HALL CANADA INC., *Toronto*
PRENTICE-HALL HISPANOAMERICANA, S.A., *Mexico*
PRENTICE-HALL OF INDIA PRIVATE LIMITED, *New Delhi*
PRENTICE-HALL OF JAPAN, INC., *Tokyo*
SIMON & SCHUSTER ASIA PTE. LTD., *Singapore*
EDITORA PRENTICE-HALL DO BRASIL, LTDA., *Rio de Janeiro*

CONTENTS

— 8 —
ETHICAL ISSUES RELATING TO AIDS, 334

PREFACE

This text is not meant to cover all possible medical ethics readings. While it does deal with the traditional issues of medical ethics, there are topics not mentioned. We list a few such areas.

The concepts of disease and normality

Rationality and competence

Professionalism

Minorities in medicine: both as patient and physician

The meaning of suffering and the often-asked question, "What did I do to deserve this?" or the statement, "It's not fair."

Nursing ethics

Moral theory beyond our examples

Alternative concepts of medicine

Comparative bioethics

The role of diagnostic related groups (DRGs) in medical practice

Phenomenological approaches to medical ethics

We do not consider these unimportant, but we did have to choose, given our goal of a relatively short anthology. Our hope is that the bibliography, which includes these topics, will help students and instructors who want to pursue questions in these areas. More than just a hope, however, is our expectation, based on teaching medical ethics in many contexts for many years, that if students master the material in this book, they will be able to think through new issues easily and for themselves.

Why a brief anthology and why just this one?

There are quite a few lengthy anthologies (for some of them, see our bibliography), which is one reason that there is no real need for yet another comprehensive text of medical ethics. But there is another reason: Medical ethics has grown to the point where it is just about impossible to have a comprehensive text—short of another *Encyclopedia of Bioethics.* As with any field, it is impossible for a text to be truly current, but as with any text, we have tried to be as current as possible. Throughout the book we have stressed the timeless philosophical issues underlying medical ethics. No student who reads this book seriously should come away feeling that medical ethics is a discipline that stands alone. We show its interdependence with law in our weaving of philosophy of law into the issues. We do not merely say what the law is, we ask students to ponder the use of law as well as some legal concepts.

The choice of readings was driven by two considerations. The first was to include readings that have become classics in the field, such as Thomson on abortion, Rescher's proposals for allocating exotic therapies, Foot's article on euthanasia, and Rachel's critique of the distinction between active and passive euthanasia. The second was to include such timely materials as the guidelines for medical decisions formulated by The Stanford University Medical Center Committee on Ethics, the "It's Over, Debbie" piece from the *JAMA,* a discussion of Oregon's attempt to allocate medical resources, and recent Supreme Court cases relating to abortion and the "right to die."

This book grew out of our experience teaching medical ethics both to medical students and to undergraduates. To help the latter group, we have presented readings with a minimum of technical terms from medicine and have included a glossary of medical terms, as well as a glossary of philosophical terms. We have kept the size of this book small enough for it to be used in a general course in ethics as a supplementary text. We have also tried to avoid taking the place of the professor in the way we present the materials. There is a minimum of theory; examples, case studies, and hard questions are the core of applied ethics.

This book, we believe, covers enough issues, uses enough cases, and asks enough questions that it can stand alone in a medical ethics course. However, it is brief enough so that it can be supplemented by a set of cases (many of which are available) or an ethics text, depending upon the instructor, students, and level of the course. Moreover, we are convinced that the book, given its length and style, can itself be a supplement to a course in ethics or applied ethics.

We wish to thank the able staff of Prentice Hall for their help: Joe Heider, Caroline Carney, Ted Bolen, Carolyn Serebreny, Joan Stone, and especially Robert Thoresen, whose interest kept this project alive. Our thanks also to colleagues David Patriquin for providing the glossary of medical terms and Marjorie Nelson for reading Chapter 8, and B. J. Wilkus for the literature search, Robert Murphy for typing the bibliography, and to Christina Dalesandry and Alice Donohoe for great care in proofreading.

MEDICAL ETHICS

A Reader

1

ETHICAL THEORY
AND
APPLIED ETHICS

The moral dimension of life is virtually a universal experience of human beings. People in every culture find themselves assessing acts, persons, and institutions in moral terms. They find themselves morally approving of some things and morally disapproving of other things. Some acts they consider right, others they see as wrong. Some people they evaluate as moral, others as immoral.

Occasionally people will take a step back from their daily routines and ask themselves some very general questions in an attempt to understand their moral judgments. What exactly is it that makes right acts right? What is the difference between "good" and "bad" and "evil"? These sorts of questions do not get asked in leisure moments; more often, people begin to reflect on these matters only when they are faced with a moral problem that requires immediate action and yet has no clear answer. In these cases people ask "What should I do?"

Whether people ask "What should I do, now?" or "What is it that makes right actions right?" they are practicing what philosophers call *ethics*. Without fully realizing it, they are trying to develop a moral theory, a systematic approach to understanding the nature of moral problems, an approach that will also yield a procedure for making choices when they encounter moral dilemmas.

Anyone who has ever encountered a moral dilemma knows firsthand how difficult it is to get a satisfactory answer. Anyone who has ever discussed a moral question knows how difficult it can be to reach agreement. It should come as no surprise, therefore, that people of similar intelligence and kindred moral seriousness have developed very different moral theories.

Moral theories have come to be classified under two major categories.

One approach to ethics is found in *teleological* theories, from the Greek word *telos* meaning goal, end, or purpose, according to which the rightness or wrongness of an act depends upon the consequences of the act. Proponents of these theories believe that people should try to attain a certain goal which is regarded by them as good. Some people, like the ancient Greek philosopher Aristotle and the contemporary American psychologist Carl Rogers, believe that the good for which we ought to strive is the actualization of our distinctively human potentialities. Others, such as the utilitarians, declare that the goal of human action ought to be the maximization of human pleasure or happiness. Regardless of how the supreme goal of human action is defined, that goal becomes for these theories the standard, the good, which determines the rightness or wrongness of human actions. If an act maximizes the good, then that act is right; if it inhibits the maximization of the good, it is wrong.

The most prominent teleological approach on the contemporary scene is *utilitarianism,* which, as such, merits additional comment. The founder of utilitarianism was the British social philosopher Jeremy Bentham (1748–1832). Bothered by the dehumanizing consequences of the Industrial Revolution in Britain and desirous of formulating a moral theory that would not only guide legislators in the shaping of a more human society but that would also be rationally warranted and therefore acceptable to all rational persons, Bentham set forth the doctrine of utilitarianism.

Bentham began with the observation that humans are subjected to two "sovereign masters": pain and pleasure. "It is for them alone," says Bentham, "to point out what we ought to do, as well as to determine what we shall do." We humans are pleasure-seeking, pain-avoiding beings. All of us desire the happiness that comes through pleasures obtained and pains avoided. Pleasure is so desirable, so fulfilling, that we really ought to seek it. In contrast, pain is so undesirable and so disruptive that we all ought to avoid it. Indeed, pleasure is so desirable and pain so undesirable that we not only ought to seek the former and avoid the latter, but we do in fact find ourselves doing just that. When the chips are down, pleasure and pain are the incentives that impel us to do what we do.

Because of our pleasure-seeking, pain-avoiding natures, the legislator who is committed to creating a truly happy society replete with pleasures can use pleasures and pains to motivate citizens to do those deeds that will promote that happy, pleasure-rich society. Sometimes pleasurable rewards may be issued; on other occasions painful sanctions may be administered. What justifies the specific pleasure-producing or pain-producing action initiated by a legislator, or by any other person for that matter, is whether or not the chosen act is likely to produce a greater surplus of pleasure over pain for humankind than any other act the agent can select in those circumstances. In other words, an act is morally warranted if it is likely to maximize the pleasure or happiness of humankind in the given circumstances. This principle of maximizing the pleasure or happiness of humankind is Bentham's famous *principle of utility.* "By the principle of utility," writes Bentham, "is meant that principle which approves or disapproves of every action whatsoever, according to the tendency which it appears to have to augment or diminish the happiness of the party whose interest is in question. . . ."

Clearly, Bentham's perspective involves the calculation of the amount of pleasure and/or pain a specific action is likely to generate. To facilitate such calculations, Bentham set forth his so-called hedonistic calculus, which contained seven different categories that the moral agent must take into account in estimating the amount of pleasure and/or pain a proposed action is likely to produce: (1) the intensity of the pleasure or pain; (2) its duration; (3) its certainty or uncertainty; (4) its nearness or remoteness; (5) its fecundity or the likelihood that it will generate additional sensations of the same kind; (6) its purity or the likelihood that it will generate sensations of the opposite kind; and (7) its extent; that is, consideration of all the persons near and far, in the present and in the future, whom the action is likely to impact with pleasure or pain. Having weighed alternative courses of action by means of this strategy, or calculus, Bentham believed the moral agent would be ready to declare which course of action was morally warranted.

Bentham's calculus, however, encountered a number of significant objections, such as: Is there sufficient time to run through the calculus each time you must make a decision? Should one ignore the qualities of pleasures, as Bentham does when he focuses on calculating the quantity of pleasure an act is likely to produce? What should one do if two possible acts yield the same projected amount of pleasure? Flip a coin?

The disciple of Bentham, John Stuart Mill (1806–1873), defended utilitarianism against such objections and in his defense both modified and popularized Bentham's position. Mill argued that the utilitarian need not run through the calculus for each alternative act in the moment of decision; indeed, one can assess types of acts in advance and establish various guidelines or rules that will facilitate speedy responses when necessary. Moreover, Mill claimed that the utilitarian need not ignore the qualities of pleasures; after all, those pleasures that engage the intellect are far more desirable than those that simply gratify the body. Furthermore, if two acts seem to yield equal pleasurable outcomes, then Mill advises us to seek the advice of "competent judges"—people who have experienced such a wide variety of pleasures that they have the basis for deciding such close calls. Through the advocacy of Mill, utilitarianism gained support and flourished.

Not all persons, however, have accepted a teleological approach to ethics. Criticism of and opposition to utilitarianism (and to all teleological positions) is encountered in the other major approach to ethics: the *deontological* point of view (from a Greek word meaning that which is binding, needful, one's duty). According to deontological theories, the rightness or wrongness of an act depends on considerations other than, or in addition to, the consequences of the act. Deontological ethics especially stresses obedience to the call of duty. For example, some people believe that one ought to obey the commands of God regardless of the consequences. Others hold that there are certain moral rules or values that should be obeyed and preserved irrespective of the consequences.

The classic exponent of deontological ethics is Immanuel Kant (1724–1804). For Kant, teleological (or consequentialist) ethics has three major shortcomings. First, because teleological ethics bases the rightness or wrongness of an act on the projected future consequences of the act, and because one can never be sure that the projected consequences will in fact occur, one can never be certain in advance that the act one is about to commit is morally right or wrong. All teleological views suffer from this measure of uncertainty. To use Kant's terms, they lack the universality and necessity that are crucial for ethics. An ethical viewpoint must indicate without uncertainty what is morally right and what is morally wrong for all persons in given situations even before they act and encounter the actual consequences of their deeds.

Second, one could justify on teleological grounds actions that most of us would surely consider to be morally repugnant. For example, slavery was justified in bygone days on the basis that it contributed to the wealth and happiness of the majority, which transcended the poverty and misery of the slaves (who, some argued, were not fully human anyway). Similarly, most of us would surely find it morally offensive to engage in medical experimentation on institutionalized persons (such as prisoners and the mentally incompetent) without their free and informed consent, even if by so doing the experimenters would be able to take giant steps forward in achieving cures for hepatitis, cancer, and AIDS. Yet such teleological justifications were used, no doubt, not only by the German physicians experimenting in the Nazi concentration camps, but also by those physicians and administrators in charge of the Tuskegee Experiment, in which four hundred blacks with syphilis were not told their diagnosis and were denied treatment for forty years in order to trace the natural history of the disease.

Third, Kant would argue that utilitarianism misses the true relation between the moral life and happiness. The utilitarian, bent on maximizing happiness, fails to ask the crucial question: Is the person experiencing pleasure and happiness *worthy* of the experience? Consider, for example, the drug pushers whose lavish pleasures and happy days are procured at the expense of the wasted lives of young addicts. Do those pushers merit happiness? Is not their happiness an offense to reason? How then can the happiness generated by an act be the standard that determines the rightness or wrongness of the act?

For Kant, then, the rightness of an action does not depend at all upon the consequences of the act—upon how much pleasure or happiness the act generates. Instead, the rightness or wrongness of an act depends solely upon the motive of the agent. What matters for Kant is not the quantity of pleasure generated by an act, but the quality of the will that performed the action.

Kant's ethic, accordingly, focuses on the "good will" that is good because it wills with the correct motivation, and correct motivation involves obedience to the commands of reason. For Kant there are two kinds of commands issued by reason.

The first kind of command, called a *hypothetical imperative,* has this type of structure: "If you desire X, then you must do Y." Such commands tell you what to do if you wish to achieve a certain goal or purpose. They do not, however, tell you whether the desired goal is something you should be pursuing. These imperatives, accordingly, have a great deal of "iffyness" embedded in them: You would obey them *if* you desired a certain goal and *if* they in fact lead to that goal. They are, therefore, not an adequate basis for indicating what all humans ought to do.

The second kind of command of reason, the *categorical imperative,* involves no iffyness at all. It does not say "If you desire a certain goal, then do the following." It is a command of reason that you obey irrespective of the consequences of obeying the command. It is a command of reason that is to be obeyed without any reservations. There is only one such categorical (no iffyness) imperative. Kant states it this way: "Act only according to that maxim whereby you can at the same time will that it should become a universal law."

Kant discerned that when one acts deliberately; that is, when one ponders whether or not one ought to do an act before performing it, one's action is based on a principle called a *maxim.* For example, suppose a physician on night duty is called to the bed of a terminally ill cancer patient. Suppose the patient pleads with the doctor for a lethal dose to end the unrelenting agony. If, after deliberating about the matter, the physician ministers the lethal injection, then the principle or maxim he who following would be something like this: "Euthanize a suffering not be wishes to die." Kant would probably argue that such a maxim he preserve universalized because it seems to be a form of self-destr opposed under all circumstances. Kant thought that determining life was fundamental. the euthanizing

Now the categorical imperative provide tive asks whether whether that maxim is morally sound and, h a universal law action is morally allowable. First, the cat the maxim is universalizable: "Could ɪ'

.thout the law becoming self-defeating?" Second,
ive asks whether the maxim is reversible: "Could I
to be a universal law if I were the recipient of the
ne agent of the action?" If scrutinizing the maxim of the
yielded affirmative responses to both of these questions,
nasia would be morally allowable, and the physician would
the characteristics of the good will. Failure of the maxim to
iversalizable and reversible would mean that the euthanasia was
ally permitted.

good will, then, is developed in the person who tests alternative
actions using the categorical imperative and wills to do those actions that
measure up to the criteria of the categorical imperative.

Utilitarians would, however, object to Kant even as he objected to
them. Kant and his followers would usually endorse such maxims as *Keep
your promises* and *Tell the truth* as having measured up to the categorical imperative. It is relatively easy for utilitarians to think of scenarios in which
keeping one's promises or telling the truth would lead to such horrendous
consequences that the Kantian unwillingness to take consequences into account when judging the morality of an action would appear to be morally
problematic. Suppose, for example, I as a Kantian kept my promise to a
dying friend in spite of the fact that I saw that doing so would lead to great
suffering for a number of children. Would not keeping such a promise irrespective of the consequences offend our moral sensibilities?

The debate between utilitarians and Kantians has been extensive,
complex, and at times heated. Can the conflict be resolved?

To be sure, each side seems to have grasped important moral insights.
For example, do not our moral intuitions support the utilitarian affirmation that happiness is a worthy human goal and that consequences really
cannot be totally ignored in assessing the rightness or wrongness of an action? And do not those same moral intuitions agree with the Kantians in
affirming that there seem to be some things like truth-telling and promise-
keeping that humans ought generally to do? Furthermore, do not the Kantian notions of universalizability and reversibility seem to be important
criteria for evaluating actions?

Furthermore, is it perhaps the case that both utilitarianism and Kant-
sla can lead to morally objectionable results (such as morally justifying
the medical experimentation without free and informed consent in
forest utilitarianism, and promise-keeping or truth-telling that leads to
of these man suffering in the case of Kantianism) precisely when one
the oth theories is developed without the benefit of the insights from
develop and be the case, would it not seem advisable to attempt to
anism That story that blended the valuable insights of both utilitari-

xactly what the British philosopher W. D. Ross

(1877–1971) attempted to do in the first half of this century. At the core of his moral theory is a distinction between *prima facie* duties and actual duties that Ross identified. *Prima facie* duties are duties "at first glance," duties that reason recognizes in advance as moral commands, duties that are self-evident and perfectly obvious to all rational persons. Ross notes at least six kinds of such duties.

1. Duties arising from my previous actions.   When I make a promise, I incur a duty of fidelity, an obligation to keep my promise. Also, when I commit a wrongful act, I incur a duty of reparation, an obligation to make amends for my misdeed.
2. Duties arising from the actions of others.   When others perform services for me, I incur a duty of gratitude.
3. Duties of justice.   These duties arise from the fact or possibility that the distribution of pleasure or happiness to persons does not correspond to their merit.
4. Duties of beneficence.   These duties arise from the fact that there are persons whose situation we can improve with respect to virtue, intelligence, or pleasure.
5. Duties of self-improvement.
6. Duties to do no harm to others.

Into a framework of Kantian-type duties, Ross has inserted the utilitarian concern for maximizing the happiness of humankind, particularly within the duties of beneficence. Yet, clearly there is more in Ross's ethical criteria than maximizing humankind's happiness. For Ross, a chief characteristic of a moral problem is that in it obedience to more than one of these *prima facie* duties is at stake and it is impossible to obey all of these duties simultaneously. Obedience to one of the duties involves violating another duty. Consider the scenario of keeping the promise to my dying friend, which would result in harm to some children. I have the duty to keep my promises. But I also have the duty of beneficence and the duty of doing no harm to others, both of which would be violated through the harm brought to the children if I kept my promise. In concrete situations in which duties conflict, I must use my reason and creative imagination, says Ross, to determine which duty I am going to obey when I cannot obey all of them. In so deciding, I determine what my *actual duty* is.

Now, while our *prima facie* duties are self-evident to reason (indeed, their truth shines clearly to all rational beings), that is not the case with our actual duty. Our actual duty is not self-evident. Nor can it be derived logically from our *prima facie* duties so that every rational creature would be compelled rationally to agree on what our actual duty is. Accordingly, people of keen minds and moral seriousness can and do differ on what one's actual duty in a situation might be even though they agree on our *prima facie* duties.

In developing the distinction between *prima facie* duties and actual duties, and by combining the Kantian concern for duties with the utilitarian emphasis on consequences, Ross has described with considerable clarity the nature of moral dilemmas as experienced by many persons. Faced with concrete moral problems, we do frequently find ourselves pulled in opposite directions by duties we affirm but cannot serve simultaneously. And we do frequently find ourselves, as Ross suggests, struggling with the aid of intellect and imagination to determine which duty seems most compelling in the given situation. And we do frequently find ourselves mustering our courage to pursue our actual duty knowing that we could be mistaken.

By focusing attention on resolving the conflicting values in moral problems, Ross prepares the way remarkably for confronting the specific problems in medical ethics where it is commonplace for our moral intuitions to recognize several moral values at stake that we cannot serve simultaneously. Yet this is where Ross's theory is weakest. A common criticism of Ross is that his positive theory is nonexistent: He does not tell us how to choose from among the *prima facie* duties.

Moral theory, like scientific theory, deals in generalities: It raises issues such as what makes acts right or wrong; not whether it is right or wrong for me to support a specific cause, to perform this abortion, to treat this AIDS patient, or to undertake this experimental therapy. When one tries to bring moral theory to bear on concrete, specific human problems, as we do in this book, one is engaging in what has come to be called *applied ethics*. While it might seem logical and appropriate to move from a theoretical study to practical application, in ethics the transition is not always smooth. Two difficulties often inhibit that transition.

First, there is the difficulty of generating a moral theory that is accepted by persons regardless of differing social environments. As we already noted, there are competing moral theories. Now we should add that, despite the cogent arguments of this philosopher and that philosopher, none of these theories has achieved acceptance by everybody. Such a situation might suggest that applied ethics is a flawed enterprise from the outset. After all, if there is no single moral theory that everybody accepts, how can one speak of applying moral theory to concrete situations? Instead, must not one speak of applying this theory or that theory to specific problems? Furthermore, in the absence of a universally accepted moral theory, is not moral assessment thereby contextualized; that is, made legitimate only within a specific social context? If so, that would be a powerful argument against writing a book on applied ethics (such as this one) that seems to presuppose the existence of an official moral theory that everybody would accept.

Things are not as bad as this.

While it is true that moral philosophers have not yet generated a moral theory acceptable to all, it does not follow that there are no generally accepted moral norms or that moral assessment must be contextualized within a specific framework. To pursue applied ethics, to wrestle with the thorny issues of contemporary moral problems, it is not essential for a person to have any moral theory literally in mind.

To be sure, it is helpful to have a clear, consistent, and coherent picture of what one believes to be right and wrong. But once it is realized that other people, for various reasons, may find a different picture more compelling, we see how self-defeating it would be to make agreement on theoretical matters a necessary condition for any attempt to deal with particular moral problems.

The presence of diversity neither precludes nor weakens applied ethics. It would do so only if one expected applied ethics to yield precise, clear, and incontestable solutions to concrete moral problems. Yet if Aristotle's comment that ethics is a study fraught with ambiguities is on target, then we should expect that those ambiguities will invite diverse interpretations, inspire various ethical theories, and permit alternative solutions to moral dilemmas. Each ethical theory presumably has the capacity to help its adherents penetrate and make some moral sense out of confusing concrete moral problems. That capacity is sufficient for the pursuit of applied ethics. Shortly we will try to say more about this task of making sense out of concrete moral problems.

Perhaps the reason that some philosophers have shied away from applied ethics is due to their desire to make ethics scientific after the model of the natural sciences. To place ethics on this kind of scientific foundation would require a moral philosophy that everybody would accept. If such an ethical theory were to be had, (1) it would have to concentrate on abstract generalities that describe the nature of ethical language and ethical judgment, and (2) it would have to avoid contamination from concrete, specific moral problems where moral ambiguity is often so intense that universally accepted solutions are seldom, if ever, reached.

If we expect to have the precision of the natural sciences and want applied ethics to yield single solutions to pressing moral problems that will be convincing to all, then our expectations will forever be frustrated by the ambiguities of real moral problems. Applied ethics will then be seen as either an embarrassment or a domain alien to ethics. These ambiguities, felt by anyone who has wrestled with real-world ethical problems, often result from the limited state of our knowledge of the world as well as from the fact that in moral dilemmas one finds oneself confronted by competing moral values all of which one affirms, but all of which one cannot serve.

If, however, we do not expect applied ethics to yield unquestioned and certain solutions to moral problems, but instead to provide an opportunity for reasonable persons to wrestle with moral problems that often lend themselves to more than one attractive solution, then applied ethics can be seen as important and legitimate work for philosophers.

What, then, is the role of ethical theory in applied ethics? How can theory aid us in making sense out of the ambiguities of concrete moral problems? Part of the answer lies in the nature of ethical theory itself. Most philosophers who have attempted to present a theoretical framework for ethics have looked around them at moral actions and then attempted to give a consistent account of what made those actions moral. The transition, in other words, was from moral actions to a theoretical account of what made such actions moral. Immanuel Kant, for one, described this as the "transition from common sense knowledge of morals to the philosophical."[1] The principal role of philosophers, he thought, was to do this theoretical analysis. We are now seeing, in a way that Kant did not, that philosophers have another role as well, namely, to go from ethical theory back to real-world problems and to use moral theory to help us wrestle with those problems.

Here are just some of the ways ethical theory helps us deal with moral issues.

1. *Ethical theory helps us identify morally relevant factors.*   In this regard theory in ethics is not all that different from theory in the natural sciences. Suppose, for example, that we wish to determine the velocity of a ball rolling down an inclined plane. Newtonian mechanics provides a theory for identifying the relevant factors that we must take into account if we are going to discover the velocity of the ball at the bottom of the plane. Relevant factors would include gravity, friction, the height of the plane, and the mass of the ball. And if we wanted to fine-tune our solution, we would include as relevant such factors as the location of the plane on the earth. At the same time, Newtonian theory would exclude as irrelevant such factors as the color of the plane, the day of the week, and the feelings of the observer.

In a similar fashion, ethical theory can help us to identify the morally relevant issues in a specific moral problem. Consider, for example, a problem pregnancy for which the question to be decided is whether or not to abort the fetus. To determine the morally relevant factors, a teleological ethical theory (such as Mill's utilitarianism) would have us focus on the consequences both of aborting and not aborting. The motives of the agent would be regarded as irrelevant to the rightness or wrongness of the proposed action; the outcomes of the action are decisive. In contrast, motives are crucial to a deontological Kantian, who would direct our attention to the requirements of duty in the situation irrespective of the consequences; duty being discovered by the application of the principles of universaliza-

[1]See the *Foundations of the Metaphysics of Morals* at 393.

bility and reversibility. That is to say that we would cast our choice (to abort or not to abort) in terms of a universal rule and would ask if we would be willing for all others to follow that rule, even if we were the recipients rather than the doers of the action. Accordingly, we would focus on the moral duties that seem to command our obedience in the situation, such as respect for the right of the fetus to life and respect for the right of the mother to privacy regarding her body, and we would screen out as irrelevant the consequences of our choice. By focusing our attention on certain aspects of a moral problem, ethical theory provides us with direction—with a way of investigating the moral problem. The theory may prove to have serious limitations as we try to sort out the complexities and ambiguities of the specific situation, and we shall speak shortly about these limitations. The initial function of an ethical theory in applied ethics is to provide an agenda to attack a concrete moral problem and to sort out the morally relevant features.

2. *Moral theory provides a vocabulary for discussing moral issues.*   Without a shared vocabulary in any field of inquiry, fruitful discussion is impossible. Part of the difficulty people have in discussing issues with which they have only a vague familiarity is due to the lack of a common terminology. Philosophers therefore have an ongoing interest in defining and clarifying terms, the analysis of how terms function in ethical discourse, and the question of whether language functions differently in moral statements from the way it does in nonmoral ones. Without a shared vocabulary, discussion of issues in ethics soon degenerates into vague generalities or subjective preferences.

A vocabulary for discussing ethical issues also allows for the application of ethical insights to contexts which may not at first appear to have ethical ramifications. A common form of business inquiry, for example, is a cost-benefit analysis; yet those familiar with utilitarian theory recognize in it an application of utility principles.

3. *Ethical theories, by being limited, keep us open to alternative interpretations.*   Ethical theories such as Mill's utilitarianism and Kant's ethic of duty are able to penetrate the complexities of a moral problem and provide us with an agenda for making moral sense out of those complexities because those theories possess an artificial simplicity. Those theories abstract a certain feature from the human moral experience—the maximization of happiness, in the case of Mill, and obedience to the universalizable commands of reason, in the case of Kant—and invest that feature with fundamental value and then employ it as the standard for right and wrong. When, however, that standard is brought to bear on the complexities of the concrete human situation, the limitations of that standard and its theory soon become apparent.

Consider, for example, the allocation of scarce life-saving medical resources. Suppose we have ten candidates for a certain life-saving protocol, but our resources are so limited that we can treat only five. If we adopted the utilitarian posture, we would focus on the consequences of allocating the scarce resources. We would identify those conditions that would maximize the happiness of humankind. Presumably we would try to assess the relative benefits to society of prolonging the lives of the various patients. And presumably we would select those five for treatment who were likely to contribute the most to society's happiness. And is it not likely that the rich, the powerful, the gifted, and talented would be favored inevitably over the poor, the weak, and the average every time? But is there not something about that imbalance that offends our moral sensibilities? Furthermore, how certain can we be that the happiness we believe will accrue to society from prolonging the life of one of the patients selected for treatment will really come to pass? What if that patient becomes dominated after treatment by an acquisitive mania that cruelly exploits others in order to accumulate wealth?

For reasons such as these, Kantian deontologists would urge us to consider factors other than consequences as morally relevant. Affirming the equal worth of every human life, they would argue that a lottery was the only way to select those who were to receive treatment. The deontological approach would completely ignore the social utility of each of the patients; it would instead insist on respect for the value of each human life regardless of the consequences. But what if one of the patients selected for treatment was a convicted murderer and rapist and one of the patients not selected at random was one of his raped victims? Would not that eventuality offend our moral sensibilities? And suppose that another one of the patients not randomly selected for treatment was a talented diplomat whose consummate skills had contributed significantly not only to slowing the arms race but also to the release of hostages held by international terrorists? Would it not also be an offense to our moral sensibilities to see the murderer-rapist saved and the diplomat sacrificed? If so, would we not want to take into account consequences as morally relevant in selecting who is to receive treatment? Would we not want to screen out from the beginning the murderer–rapist as likely to contribute little to human well-being? And would we not want to ensure from the outset that the diplomat, whose talents have benefited society so much and are likely to continue to do so, would be included among those who would receive treatment?

Although both consequentialist and deontological ethical theories provide us with an initial agenda for attacking concrete moral problems by helping us to focus on morally relevant issues, those theories exhibit significant limitations as we probe further the complexities of moral problems. Do these limitations suggest, therefore, that ethical theory is actually incapable of dealing with concrete moral problems? Is the business of applied ethics a fatally flawed enterprise after all? The answer is yes only if

one expects applied ethics to generate a single, absolute solution to concrete moral problems. We have already noted that human experience faces
difficult ambiguities that will forever frustrate that expectation.

What, then, can we legitimately expect from ethical theory applied to
specific moral problems? We can expect an initial agenda for investigating
moral problems, an agenda which will in due course exhibit significant limitations. In addition, we can expect that those limitations will generate a
measure of humility about ethical theory that will express itself in our recognition of the limitations of our own theory and in our creative openness
to the insights offered by other ethical theories. Having used a particular
ethical theory to initiate ethical analysis of a specific moral problem, we
can legitimately combine insights from several theories in attempting to
identify *all* the morally relevant features of that problem. When those features are identified, some of them are likely to conflict with each other. We
must then make a judgment call in which some morally relevant features
of this specific moral problem are deemed to take precedence over other
morally relevant features.

There will be disagreement concerning which morally relevant features are to be given priority in a specific case. But disagreement at this
point does not reveal a weakness in applied ethics. On the contrary, disagreement exposes strength by requiring each individual involved in a
moral problem to risk making a decision with all the burden that human
freedom imposes. When careful analysis of specific moral problems results
in different priorities being assigned by different persons to various morally relevant features, that disagreement underscores the reality of human
freedom. Under these circumstances the ambiguities of human moral experience and the inevitable imprecision of ethics cannot be avoided.

As we begin to examine the issues raised by the readings in this book,
it is well to remember that, even though ethical theory makes important
contributions to the analysis of issues in applied ethics, a person does not
need to be an expert in moral theory to think morally. The relation between
moral theory and the moral point of view is similar to that between the
study of grammar and the ability to use a language.[2] Our ability to perform
in a language will be aided by our knowledge of its grammar; anyone who
has struggled with learning a new language knows precisely what this
means. As we work through the thorny issues that confront us in medical
ethics, we will discover that our ability to maintain the moral point of view
will be aided by the insights provided by moral theory. The two readings
in this chapter are from contemporary moral theorists who give a foundation and strategy for assessing concrete moral problems.

---

[2]The importance of this sort of distinction is defended by John Searle in *Speech Acts*.

Moral Rules

Not unlike W. D. Ross, as discussed in the introduction, the contemporary American philosopher Bernard Gert has developed a blend of utilitarianism and Kantianism and attempts to provide additional insight about which actions are morally allowable and justified in concrete situations.

Gert presents his view with carefully reasoned detail in his recently published volume, *Morality: A New Justification of the Moral Rules.* According to Gert, morality is a public system that applies to all rational persons and that has as its goal the minimization of evil. All rational persons, says Gert, would agree that the following things are evils to be avoided: death, pain (both physical and psychological), disabilities, and the loss of freedom, opportunity, or pleasure. Gert identified a set of ten moral rules, related to these evils, that have been the core of the moral experience of humankind throughout the ages and that ought not to be violated without adequate reason.

Do not kill.
Do not cause pain.
Do not disable.
Do not deprive of freedom or opportunity.
Do not deprive of pleasure.
Do not deceive.
Keep your promises.
Do not cheat.
Obey the law.
Do your duty (in your job or profession).

In assessing a proposed course of action, the agent should ask: Does my action entail violating a moral rule? If it doesn't, then the action is morally allowable. If it does involve the violation of a moral rule, then the agent must determine if there are adequate reasons for such a violation. To see if such an adequate reason is present, Gert provides a strategy that blends utilitarian and Kantian features. First of all, one must identify which rules would be violated and ask: What amounts of evils would my action be likely to avoid, prevent, or cause? Furthermore, would all impartial rational persons agree that the evils avoided and prevented greatly outweigh the evils caused? In addition, would all impartial rational persons publicly advocate the universal violation of these moral rules for this kind of case? If all impartial rational persons would estimate that less evil would be suffered if that kind of violation were publicly allowed, then all impartial rational persons would advocate that that kind of violation be publicly allowed and my violation of the moral rules would be strongly justified. When impartial rational persons differ in their estimates of the evils avoided, prevented, or caused, the kind of violation of the moral rules involved in my action might receive only weak justification. Because impartiality, rationality, and irrationality are key terms for Gert's analysis, he spends considerable time defining and clarifying these concepts.

Gert's point of view seems to blend a kind of negative utilitarianism (that is, minimizing evils rather than maximizing goods) with the Kantian principle of universalizability. He developed his thinking with particular concern for the moral problems encountered by health-care professionals. Has he in fact overcome the long-standing disagreement between utilitarians and Kantians? And, at the same time, has he provided a specific, workable strategy for resolving the moral problems in medicine?

Total agreement in answering these questions is unlikely to be reached by those who read the following brief summary of Gert's views entitled "Moral Theory." Most readers, however, are likely to agree that his discussion yields fresh insight about the moral experience of humankind.

MORAL THEORY

Bernard Gert

It is misleading to discuss any moral problem as if it were an isolated problem whose solution did not have implications for all other moral problems. Morality is a system and the acceptability of the answers that this system gives to any particular problem is affected by the acceptability of the answers that it gives to all other problems. One should not trust a moral system that sometimes provides unacceptable answers. Nor should one use a moral system without understanding it. A moral theory is an attempt to explain and, if possible, justify morality. Therefore, before we discuss the moral problems involved in medicine, I shall present an account of the moral theory which explains what morality is, and an account of that moral system.

A Moral Theory

A moral theory consists of the analysis of the concepts necessary to explain and, if possible, to justify morality, viz., rationality, impartiality, and moral-

Source: "Moral Theory," Lecture delivered at the Center for Applied and Professional Ethics, Ohio University, October, 1989. Used by permission. The lecture summarizes the moral theory presented in *Morality: A New Justification of the Moral Rules* by Bernard Gert (Oxford University Press, 1988).

ity itself, together with an account of how they are related to each other. Rationality is the fundamental normative concept. To justify morality, or anything else, requires showing that it is, at least, compatible with rationality. Since everything else depends on rationality, this means that rationality itself must be such that everyone accepts that no one ever ought to act irrationally. A moral theory must provide an account of rationality that has this feature and show how it is related to morality. Impartiality is universally recognized as an essential feature of morality. A moral theory must provide a clear account of the kind of impartiality that morality requires and also of the way in which this kind of impartiality is related to morality. A moral theory must also identify the essential features of morality, i.e., the actual moral system that, in so far as we are concerned with acting morally, we use to guide our conduct and to make judgments on the conduct of others. A moral theory should explain why morality prohibits some behavior, requires other behavior, and allows or encourages still other behavior.

Morality

Morality is a public system for guiding and judging the behavior of all rational persons. A public system is a system (1) that all persons to whom it applies, those whose behavior is to be guided and judged by that system, understand it, i.e., know what behavior the system prohibits, requires, allows and encourages; and (2) that it is not irrational for any of them to accept being guided or judged by. The clearest example of a public system is a game. The rules of the game form a system that is understood by all of the players, i.e., they all know what kind of behavior is prohibited, required, allowed, and encouraged by the rules; and it is not irrational for any player to use the rules to guide his own behavior and to judge the behavior of other players by them. The rules of a game, although they are a public system, apply only to those playing the game. Morality is a public system that applies to all rational persons; a person is subject to morality simply in virtue of being a rational person.

Morality consists of rules which prohibit some kinds of actions, e.g., killing, require others, e.g., keeping promises; and what I call moral ideals, which encourage certain kinds of actions, e.g., preserving life and relieving pain. It also contains a procedure for determining when it is justified to violate a moral rule, e.g., when moral rules conflict or when a moral ideal conflicts with a moral rule. But morality does not provide unique answers to every question, it merely sets the limits to genuine moral disagreement. The content of morality is determined by the content of the rules and ideals that all impartial rational persons would include in a public system that applies to all rational persons. But this content cannot deviate in any significant way from our common conception of morality, for the function of moral philosophy is to clarify, make more precise, and justify, if possible, the common conception of morality, not to put forward some substitute for it.

There are certain kinds of actions that we all regard as being immoral unless one has an adequate justification for doing them. Among these kinds of actions are killing, causing pain, deceiving, and breaking promises. Anyone who kills people, causes them pain, deceives them, or breaks a promise, and does so without an adequate justification, is universally regarded as acting immorally. To say that there is a moral rule prohibiting that kind of act is another way of saying that a certain kind of act is immoral unless it is justified. To say that it is justified to break that moral rule is another way of saying that it is justifiable to act in that way. There are other kinds of actions that we all regard as morally good unless there is a moral rule prohibiting our doing them. Among these kinds of actions are saving lives and relieving pain. Following these moral ideals sometimes even justifies violating a moral rule.

Rationality

My account of rationality, although it accurately describes the way in which we all use the concept, differs radically from that normally provided by philosophers in two important ways. First, it takes irrationality to be more basic than rationality, and second, it defines irrationality by means of a list rather than a formula. The basic definition is as follows: *A person with sufficient knowledge and intelligence to be a moral agent acts irrationally when he acts in a way that he knows, (justifiably believes) or should know, will significantly increase the probability that he will suffer death, pain, disability, loss of freedom or loss of pleasure, and he does not have an adequate reason for so acting.* This list also defines what counts as an evil or harm. *A reason is a conscious belief that one's action will help anyone, not merely oneself, avoid one of these evils, or gain some good, viz., ability, freedom, or pleasure, and this belief is not obviously inconsistent with what one knows.* A reason is adequate if any significant group of rational persons regard the evil avoided or good gained as at least as important as the evil suffered. Any action that is not irrational, is rational.

This account of rationality, and only this account, has the desired result that everyone, who is regarded as sane, always wants himself and his friends to act rationally. Certainly, none of us would ever want ourselves or anyone for whom we are concerned to act irrationally. But if we accept any of the standard philosophical accounts of rationality, e.g., acting rationally is acting so as to maximize the satisfaction of one's desires, it turns out that unless we rule out what I call irrational desires, e.g., desires for anything on the list of evils I have provided, we would not always want those for whom we are concerned to act rationally. If I had a friend who developed an extremely strong desire to kill himself in the most painful possible way, I would not want him to satisfy that desire even if doing so would maximize the satisfaction of his desires; rather I would want him to see a psychiatrist in order to get rid of that desire.

Impartiality

Impartiality, like simultaneity, is usually taken to be a simpler concept than it really is. Einstein showed that one cannot simply ask whether A and B occurred simultaneously, one must also specify something about C, the point of view of the observer. Similarly, one cannot simply ask if someone is impartial, one must specify the group with regard to which the person must be impartial and also in what respects she is required to be impartial with regard to that group. When discussing morality, the minimal group toward which one must be impartial consists of all moral agents, including oneself, and former moral agents who are still persons; and the respect in which one must be impartial toward this group is in using the moral rules to guide one's behavior and to make moral judgments. This requires that one violate a moral rule, or judge a violation to be justified, only when such a violation can be allowed as part of the public system that applies to all rational persons.

This kind of impartiality can be achieved by using only those beliefs that are shared by all rational persons. These include general beliefs such as: we all know some things about the world, but no one knows everything, i.e., people have limited knowledge; also people are mortal, can suffer pain, etc. Scientific beliefs as well as religious beliefs are excluded, e.g., beliefs about the functions of the brain, heart, etc., are excluded, for rational persons do not share a set of common beliefs about these matters. Included are some personal beliefs, viz., beliefs about oneself that all rational persons have about themselves, e.g., beliefs that one can be killed and suffer pain, etc. Excluded are all beliefs about one's race, sex, religion, etc., because these beliefs are not common to all rational persons. Impartiality, however, does not require uniformity, for impartial rational persons may rank the goods and evils differently. Different rankings of the goods and evils, e.g., differences about whether pain of a certain intensity and duration is worse than death, may result in equally informed impartial rational persons disagreeing on how one ought to act.

The Justified Moral System

The moral system that all impartial rational persons would choose as a public system that applies to all rational persons is the justified moral system.

This system includes rules prohibiting each of the five evils that all rational persons want to avoid, thus it includes the following five rules.

> Don't kill.
> Don't cause pain.
> Don't disable.
> Don't deprive of freedom.
> Don't deprive of pleasure.

Morality also includes rules prohibiting those kinds of actions which generally cause evil even though not every act of that kind causes an evil. Thus it includes the following five rules.

> Don't deceive.
> Keep your promise. (Don't break your promise.)
> Don't cheat.
> Obey the law. (Don't break the law.)
> Do your duty. (Don't neglect your duty.) I use the term "duty" in its everyday sense to refer to what is required by one's role in society, primarily one's job, not as philosophers customarily use it, simply as a synonym for "what one morally ought to do."

These rules are not absolute, all of them have justified exceptions. The attitude that all impartial rational persons would take toward these rules when considering them as moral rules, i.e., as rules in a public system applying to all rational persons, is the following: *Everyone is always to obey the rule unless an impartial rational person can advocate that violating it be publicly allowed. Anyone who violates the rule when an impartial rational person cannot advocate that such a violation be publicly allowed may be punished.* (The unless clause only means that when an impartial rational person can advocate that such a violation be publicly allowed, impartial rational persons may disagree on whether one should obey the rule, not that they agree one should not obey.)

In deciding whether or not to advocate that a violation of a moral rule be publicly allowed, an impartial rational person can use only morally relevant features. These features are contained in the answers to the following eight questions.

1. What moral rules are being violated?
2. What evils are being (a) avoided, (b) prevented, (c) caused?
3. What are the relevant desires of the people toward whom the rule is being violated?
4. What are the relevant rational beliefs of the people toward whom the rule is being violated?

5. Does one have a duty to violate moral rules with regard to the person(s), and is one in a unique or almost unique position in this regard?
6. What goods are being promoted?
7. Is an unjustified or weakly justified violation of a moral rule being prevented?
8. Is an unjustified or weakly justified violation of a moral rule being punished?

When considering the evils being avoided, prevented or caused, and the goods being promoted, one must consider not only their intensity, duration, and probability, one must also consider the kind of good or evil involved. If more than one person is affected, one must consider not only how many people will be affected, but also the distribution of the harms and benefits. If two violations are the same in all of their morally relevant features then they count as the same kind of violation, and any impartial rational person who advocates that one of them by publicly allowed must advocate that the other also be publicly allowed. However, this does not mean that two impartial rational persons, who agree that two actions count as the same kind of violation, must always agree on whether or not to advocate that that kind of violation be publicly allowed, for they may differ in their estimate of the consequences of publicly allowing that kind of violation or they may rank the goods and evils involved differently.

An impartial rational person decides whether or not to advocate that a violation be publicly allowed by estimating what effect this kind of violation, if publicly allowed, would have. If all impartial rational persons would estimate that less evil would be suffered if that kind of violation were publicly allowed, then all impartial rational persons would advocate that that kind of violation be publicly allowed and the violation is strongly justified; if all rational persons would estimate that more evil would be suffered, then no rational person would advocate that that kind of violation be publicly allowed and the violation is unjustified. However, impartial rational persons, even if equally informed, may disagree in their estimate of whether more or less evil will result from that kind of violation being publicly allowed. When this happens they will disagree on whether or not to advocate that that kind of violation be publicly allowed and such a violation counts as weakly justified.

Disagreements in the estimates of whether a given kind of violation being publicly allowed will result in more or less evil may stem from two distinct sources. The first is a difference in the rankings of the various kinds of evils. (If governments are involved, rankings of goods are also relevant.) If someone ranks a specified amount of pain and suffering as worse than a specified amount of loss of freedom, and someone else ranks them in the opposite way, then although they agree that a given action is the same kind of violation, they may disagree on whether or not to advocate that that kind of violation be publicly allowed. The second is a difference in estimates of how much evil would result from publicly allowing a given kind of violation, even when there seems to be no difference in the rankings of the different kinds of evils. These differences may stem from differences in beliefs about human nature or about the nature of human societies. In so far as these differences cannot be settled by any universally agreed upon empirical method, I call such differences, ideological. However, I suspect that most ideological differences also involve differences in the rankings of different kinds of evils.

For example, one impartial rational person may estimate that if deception were publicly allowed in order to avoid causing a specified degree of anxiety and other mental suffering, this would result in less overall evil being suffered than if this kind of violation were not publicly allowed, while another person may estimate the opposite. The latter may hold that knowledge that deception of this kind is publicly allowed will actually increase the amount of anxiety suffered, because, e.g., patients will suffer anxiety even when their doctor truthfully tells them that the tests were negative and they have nothing to worry about. She may also hold that deception of this kind may result in loss of freedom, as patients will be deprived of the opportunity to make decisions based upon the facts. The former person may not only claim that publicly allowing the violation will decrease the amount of anxiety, for he does not think that people will be seriously affected by knowing the violation is allowed, he may also not rank the resulting loss of freedom very highly. This disagreement may thus involve either a difference in the rankings of the evils, or ideological differences, or both.

Contrasts with Other Systems for Guiding Conduct

In order to clarify the moral system it may be worthwhile to contrast it with systems similar to those proposed by Kant and Mill. On a Kantian system one should never act in any way that one cannot will to be a universal law. If it would be impossible for everyone to do some kind of action, then everyone is prohibited from doing that same kind of action. On the moral system, one is prohibited from doing a kind of action only if no impartial rational person would advocate that that kind of action be publicly allowed. A Kantian system seems to rule out ever making false promises, whereas the moral system allows the making of false promises in some circumstances, e.g., when the evil to be prevented by doing so is sufficiently great that less overall evil would be suffered even if it were publicly allowed.

On a Utilitarian or consequentialist system one not only may, but should, violate any rule if the forseeable consequences of that particular violation, including the effects on future obedience to the rule, are better than the consequences of not violating the rule. A consequentialist system is concerned only with the forseeable consequences of the particular violation, not with the forseeable consequences of that kind of violation being publicly allowed. But on the moral system, it is precisely the forseeable consequences of that kind of violation being publicly allowed that are decisive in determining whether or not it is morally allowed. The consequences of the particular act are important only in that they help determine the kind of violation under consideration. A consequentialist system favors cheating on an exam if it were extremely unlikely that one would get caught and no harm would result from that particular violation of the rule against cheating. The moral system would not allow this kind of violation of the rule against cheating, for if this kind of violation were publicly allowed, it would eliminate the possibility of even having exams. I am assuming that the exams serve a useful function.

The moral system differs from a Kantian system and resembles a consequentialist system in that it explicitly takes consequences into consideration. It resembles a Kantian system and differs from a consequentialist system in that it takes rules to be an essential feature of morality; it requires impartiality with respect to rules and not merely with respect to consequences. Impartiality with respect to rules is required because of the public nature of morality and the limited knowledge of rational persons. Morality differs from both systems in that it does not require all moral questions to have unique answers, but explicitly allows for disagreements among equally informed impartial rational persons. Morality also includes moral ideals, which cannot possibly be followed by anyone impartially with regard to all other moral agents, and hence need not be followed impartially.

The Virtues

Needless to say, Gert's discussion does not represent the only current attempt to overcome the apparent stalemate that utilitarians and Kantians have reached after decades of debate; others have attempted to do so and to offer direction for dealing with concrete moral problems. An intriguing alternative has been provided by some philosophers who, weary of the prevailing debates in ethics and not interested in attempting to blend utilitarian and Kantian emphases, have turned back to the perspectives of Plato, Aristotle, and Saint Thomas Aquinas in which they discern an emphasis on the nature and traits of the moral person rather than on the nature and foundation of moral rules. This return to such classical philosophers has been led by Elizabeth Anscombe, whose 1958 essay "Modern Moral Philosophy" appearing in *Philosophy* provoked widespread discussion, and by Alasdair MacIntyre, whose subsequent book *After Virtue* advanced further the development of a point of view which has come to be known as *virtue ethics*. An excellent introduction to the concerns of virtue ethicists and the solutions they propose is to be found in an essay by Robert B. Kruschwitz and Robert C. Roberts. Their summary of the analysis and recommendations made by Alasdair MacIntyre in *After Virtue* is given here.

In reviewing the position of virtue ethics, it is helpful to keep in mind that this view asks not so much "What ought I to do?" but rather focuses on "What sort of a person should I become?" Accordingly, when confronted with moral decisions, the question to be answered is, "What sort of person will doing this act tend to make me?"

CONTEMPORARY
VIRTUE ETHICS:
ALASDAIR MACINTYRE'S *AFTER VIRTUE*[1]

Robert B. Kruschwitz and Robert C. Roberts

Our Predicament According to MacIntyre

MacIntyre's point of departure . . . is the bankruptcy of modern moral philosophy, and indeed of the moral consciousness of most of recent Western civilization (which is dominated by what he often refers to as "modern liberal individualism"). In our world, moral debate about central issues tends to go on endlessly, neither side winning by rational argument. Some say that justice is served by forcing richer people, through taxation, to share their wealth with poorer ones, because everyone has a right to basic necessities of life. Others argue this is not just, because it unduly restricts the freedom of the wealthy (and of the poor, to the extent that they may become wealthy) to do as they please with the fruits of their labor, ingenuity, or good fortune. Some say abortion at an early stage of pregnancy is every woman's right, since every person has a right to determine what happens in his or her own body, and an embryo at that stage is a part of its mother's body. Others say that such abortions are almost always wrong, because an embryo, even at that stage, is an innocent, identifiable human individual, and knowingly to kill such an individual is immoral. Valid arguments can be constructed for each of the preceding four positions; the disagreement comes from the different *premises,* or starting points, of the arguments. (Philosophers, just like ordinary people, divide up into such camps as these; the chief difference is that the philosophers' arguments are more careful and detailed.)

Why can't people agree on their moral starting points? The reason, MacIntyre argues, is that we do not belong to any consistent, shared moral tradition. Instead we are the inheritors of fragments, often mutually inconsistent, of moral traditions and philosophies.

For the most part we are unaware of where these parts of traditions came from and indeed of the fact that they are leftover fragments, isolated from the whole systems of moral thought and life to which they originally belonged. Rather we vaguely believe there is something called "morality," a single body of concepts on which all decent people draw when they make moral decisions. And so we are frustrated that we can't terminate our moral debates rationally. Thus our moral mind-set comes to have two sides—one coming from our recognition that our contemporary moral debates are fundamentally unsettleable, the other from the residue of the moral traditions from which we have inherited our fragments, in which moral debates *were* settleable.

On the one side, because there is no way of securing rational agreement in moral debate, we tend to think morality is not a rational affair at all. We see it as a matter of commitments, feeling, individual interpretation, and individual choice. If you can't *rationally* decide whether to make the right to necessities more basic than the right to free disposal of property, then you just "hunker down" over one side or the other, just make a "decision of principle" or consult your feelings. And you realize that the arguments you use in moral debate are ultimately just *rhetoric*. Their purpose is not to find or express truth or enlighten your opponent, but to give expression to your feelings and manipulate your opponent into seeing things your way, like the ads for soft drinks or an arms manufacturer lobbying for a government contract.

Related to the loss of rationality in ethics is the loss of the moral self. MacIntyre sketches contemporary "characters"—that is, personality types that function for us as moral paradigms: the Bureaucratic Manager, the Rich Playperson, and the Therapist. These "characters" have in common that they are all manipulators of other persons, and tend to seek goods external to practices. (Money is a good external to the practice of medicine, while the well-being of one's patients is a good internal to that practice. Fame is a good external to the practice of philosophy, while wisdom is a good internal to it.) This tendency toward the failure of moral rationality and the deterioration of individual moral substance MacIntyre calls "emotivism," naming it after the twentieth-century movement in metaethics that articulates it philosophically.

But, on the other side, we are never completely at ease with emotivism. Even if we often find ourselves taking refuge in "decisions of principle," this remains a desperate move. It is not how things ought to be! We sense that as long as we are only expressing our feelings and manipulating our interlocutors, our stance cannot be called "morality." Candor about emotivist theory is incompatible with emotivist practice: even if we are crass enough to manipulate others in argument, still, we can't let our interlocutor know we are only subjecting him or her to nonrational rhetoric. The rhetoric won't work unless the listener believes we are offering an argument!

We are unhappy emotivists, and our predicament is the result of a long and bumpy history that MacIntyre chronicles in *After Virtue*. His construal of this history is also an argument that a version of a recurring moment in that history—the Aristotelian tradition of the virtues—contains a path out of our predicament. If we can become Aristotelians in a certain sense, we will find ways to settle our moral debates rationally, while at the same time rescuing our moral selfhood from the formlessness and emptiness characteristic of the twentieth-century "characters."

A History of the Virtues

Heroic Societies. The history begins with "heroic societies," the most prominent example being the one in Homer's *Iliad*. In that society the actions required of a person were determined by fixed social roles, which in turn were determined by the person's social status: "Every individual has a given role and status within a well-defined and highly determinate system of roles and statuses. The key structures are those of kinship and of the household. In such a society a man knows who he is by knowing his role in these structures; and in knowing this he knows also what he owes and what is owed to him by the occupant of every other role and status."[2] To fulfill the role of head of household was to protect it in battle, and for this one must be fitted by courage. Such a person would also be bound by ties of kinship and friendship with other households and their heads; these ties would also demand entering into battle, with a consequent need for fidelity and courage. Duties in heroic society were not separable from social roles. To be a friend or brother meant to endeavor to take the life of anyone who took the life of your friend or brother. This meant that a certain storyline, of which the final episode was the violent death of the hero, characterized virtually every inhabiter of the role. Membership in a heroic society ensured the impossibility of moral doubt on the central issues, and ensured that the occupant of the role had a firm personal identity and undoubting sense of his or her identity. According to MacIntyre, the heroic poetry has two things to teach us about ethics: "First that all morality is always to some degree tied to the socially local and particular and that the aspirations of the morality of modernity to a universality freed from all particularity is an illusion; and secondly that there is no way to possess the virtues except as part of a tradition in which we inherit them and our understanding of them from a series of predecessors in which series heroic societies hold first place."[3]

The Sophists and Plato.   By contrast with the society of Homer's poems, the Athens of Socrates (469–399 B.C.) and Plato (427–347 B.C.) showed what we would call moral "pluralism." The Athenians agreed with heroic society that virtues are conditions for personal success within a social fabric, but because of intercourse with the "outside world," the Athenians were vividly aware, as the heroes were not, of the *variety* of customs and of virtue concepts. Furthermore, the social matrix supporting and giving sense to the virtues had shifted from the Homeric family to the city-state. The result was a far less clear and consistent use of the moral vocabulary. For example, it was agreed that *dikaiosune* (justice) is a virtue and that it, like other virtues, is intimately linked with the pursuit of happiness and the fulfillment of desire; but there was much disagreement about what this virtue means.

The sophists concluded from this failure of agreement that there was no such thing as *dikaiosune* in itself, but only *dikaiosune*-as-practiced-in-a-given-city. This extreme "cultural relativism" was difficult to maintain and made some sophists easy prey of Socrates' efforts to trap them in inconsistency. If they claimed there is no *dikaiosune*-in-itself, while nevertheless assuming their own concept of *dikaiosune* in criticizing other conceptions, they seemed to say that there both is, and is not, *dikaiosune*-in-itself. This inconsistency could be avoided, as Callicles did (see Plato's *Gorgias*), by claiming without wavering that the "virtuous" person is one who uses his cunning to dominate others "and who uses his domination to satisfy his desires without limit."[4]

Plato's theory of the virtues tries to avoid both relativism and the ruthless, antisocial character of Callicles' conception of "virtue." His strategy is to present a universal philosophical psychology that entails an idea of happiness and satisfaction of human desire radically different from that of Callicles. The human soul is composed of three parts: the desiring part (bodily appetites), the high spirited part (certain emotions), and the reasoning part. Virtue is the proper functioning and harmonious interaction of these parts. A person has *sophia* ("wisdom") when the reasoning part is in touch with reality and above all with the Form of the Good. This enables it to legislate humanly appropriate behavior. *Sophrosune* ("temperance") occurs when the desiring part is restrained according to what reason declares to be humanly appropriate behavior. *Andreia* ("courage") is a preservative of knowledge of what is good, which functions where fear and pleasure threaten to diminish that knowledge. As the virtue of the high spirited part, courage would seem also to include those emotional dispositions implementing the dictates of reason—for example, feeling repugnance for wrongdoing and joy in good conduct. Finally, *dikaiosune* ("justice") is the presence of the other three virtues; each part of the soul functioning according to its nature and thus appropriately interacting with the other parts. The soul flourishes when it thus realizes its true nature. It is this, argues Plato, that human beings really desire, even though they may think they desire, as Callicles claims, to dominate others and enjoy the fruits of such domination.

The social matrix fitting such a person of virtue is a city-state with a structure analogous to that of a perfected human personality. The guardians (reasoning part) will legislate with wisdom, the warriors (high spirited part) will execute the will of the guardians, and the workers (desiring part) will provide the economic energy in the city. And each part will exemplify *dikaiosune* as it performs its own, and only its own, function with excellence, thus fitting into an organic harmony with the whole. MacIntyre notes that while Plato believed there was no existing political order that supported virtue as he conceived it, "nonetheless the concept of virtue remains a political concept; for Plato's account of the virtuous man is inseparable from his account of the virtuous citizen."[5]

Several points can be made about Plato's conception of the virtues. First, it is in acquiring the virtues that a person achieves the well-being characteristic of humans. Second, what this well-being amounts to is dictated by a culture-transcendent human nature, reflected in Plato's philosophical psychology. But, third, Plato believes that the realization of that nature is tied to a political order or social matrix. Fourth, since no political order adequate to human nature exists on earth, the political order in which Plato embeds the virtuous person is itself transcendent (ideal). This raises the question whether having the virtues is a real possibility. Fifth, Plato does not believe in tragedy, if we mean by tragedy a situation in which a perfectly virtuous person is caught in a ruining conflict. Virtue = harmony = success = happiness: so, if a seemingly virtuous person is caught in a "tragic" situation, he must have a hidden personal flaw. There are no essentially tragic situations. Plato's disbelief in tragedy is tied to his belief in the unity of the virtues. Two virtues cannot conflict because to have any virtue is to have all the virtues. It is not possible, as the tragedian Sophocles believed it was, that exercising "the virtue of doing what is required of a sister (Antigone) or a friend (Odysseus) be at odds with the exercise of the virtues of justice (Creon) or of compassion and truthfulness (Neoptolemus)."[6]

Aristotle. On these points Plato's pupil Aristotle agreed with him on all but the fourth. Aristotle was more optimistic than Plato about the constitution of his own city-state, Athens, as providing a context for the actualization of human nature in the virtues. Thus Aristotle's "sociology" is less idealized and more empirical than Plato's. Indeed his ethics is equally an ethics of the Athenian citizen and a universally human ethics. On the second point, Aristotle agreed that there is a human nature independent of cultures, and that it is the job of the ethical theorist to explicate this nature and thus to show what its full realization in the virtues would look like. But in its details Aristotle's philosophical psychology is much richer than, and in some ways divergent from, Plato's.

As we remarked earlier, Aristotle is the hero in MacIntyre's story. It is the "Aristotelian tradition" in its various forms from which we must learn if we are to extricate ourselves from the confusions and characterlessness of "modern liberal individualism." This tradition includes such predecessors of Aristotle as Sophocles and Plato, and such successors as the Christian theologian Thomas Aquinas (1224–74) and the English novelist Jane Austen (1775–1817); but Aristotle himself is the greatest representative of the tradition.[7] Four aspects of Aristotle's moral philosophy stand out as essential, in MacIntyre's view, to the project of restoring ethical rationality and substance.

First, Aristotle's ethical thought is *teleological.* The basic idea here is that human nature is not just whatever people happen, on the average, to be. It is a built-in *goal,* and one that perhaps few individuals ever reach. There is almost always a difference between the way humans are, and the way they would be if they achieved, or actualized, their nature. (It is conceivable, indeed, that *no* individuals ever achieve their human nature.) The virtues are features of self-actualization, characteristics of the human being who has become what his nature dictates that he should be. Furthermore, this achievement is something that people must themselves undertake. A beet seed contains within it the tendency to become a fully realized beet; and if it is placed in appropriate conditions of soil, moisture, temperature, and the passage of time, it will become the best beet it can, something with all the beet virtues. However, it is no part of beet nature to *undertake* to become a fully actualized beet; it is enough that it be placed in a fitting environment. But an aspect of the human virtues, dictated by human nature, is that the individual become a responsible initiator of the actions characteristic of justice, courage, temperance, and wisdom.

Second, the concept of *pleasure* has a central place in Aristotle's ethical thought. He points out that pleasure naturally accompanies unimpeded excellent activity. When you are doing something well (let us say, building a deck on the back of your house), in conditions that do not hinder you, then you "enjoy yourself" in the activity. But the virtues are capacities for humanly excellent activities. So given unhindering external conditions, the virtues are capacities for pleasure, for leading a life of enjoyment. As the virtuous person enjoys being who he or she is and performing actions characteristic of himself or herself, the individual is directly aware of the goodness of his or her life.

MacIntyre points out how Aristotle differs from the utilitarians in his treatment of pleasure. For them pleasure (some call it happiness) is the good, the goal of all action, while for Aristotle it is a natural accompaniment of the humanly excellent life. For them the amount of pleasure an action produces is what determines the moral goodness or badness of it. For Aristotle the criterion is the much more complex matter of what human nature is, and pleasures are judged good or bad according to what activities they accompany. For the utilitarians pleasure is some single mental state that can in principle be measured and added up. For Aristotle pleasure is activity- and excellence-relative; there are as many different pleasures as there are "faculties" and activities of faculties.

Third, Aristotle gives a central place to the virtue of *friendship*. Indeed he devotes a larger proportion of his *Nicomachean Ethics* to this than to any other single topic. Friendship is important because it is the human bond necessary to the kind of community in which people can flourish (develop the virtues). What is friendship? It is not just liking one another, or enjoying some common hobby or professional pursuit, but sharing with others the aim of realizing the common, or "political" good (that is, the good of the *polis*). Thus friendship is at the same time patriotism.

From our modern individualist perspective, it is hard to conceive of people genuinely bound together by ties of affection in the pursuit of the well-being of their society. Instead we think of "politics" as a factional enterprise engaged in by persons seeking their own individual "political" advancement. MacIntyre states that "from an Aristotelian point of view, a modern liberal political society can appear only as a collection of citizens of nowhere, who have banded together for their common protection. They possess at best that inferior form of friendship that is founded on mutual advantage."[8] Thus we have no real sense of political community and, consequently, lack the social context that, according to Aristotle, is necessary if we are to become human.

Fourth is Aristotle's conception of *practical reasoning*, or reasoning leading to action. Aristotle's picture includes four elements: a want, a major premise, a minor premise, and an action. Anytime a person reasons practically, he or she must want something. Let us say you want to sharpen a pencil neatly and with minimum effort. You believe (major premise) that anyone who wants to sharpen a pencil neatly and easily is well advised to use a pencil sharpener. Through inquiry you learn that (minor premise) there is a pencil sharpener in the next room. Finally (action) you go to that room and sharpen your pencil.

Moral reasoning is a species of practical reasoning. If an agent is to reason about justice to any practical effect, he or she must be the sort of person who wants just states of affairs. In general, the virtues all contain or presuppose a concern about the well-being of the agent and the community. Second, the agent must believe (major premise) propositions of the following sort: job discrimination against persons on the basis of their ethnic background is unjust, taking away a person's property without his or her permission is unjust, and so on. Third, the agent must be able to recognize (minor premise) truths of the following sort: This is a case of ethnic discrimination, this is a case of taking property without permission, and so on.

Practical circumstances, of course, are much more complicated than being just a matter of a single major and a single minor premise presenting themselves in splendid isolation. Consequently, these premises must be ranked in weight relative to other morally (and perhaps nonmorally) relevant beliefs; in other words, the agent must have refined judgment, or what Aristotle calls *phronesis* ("practical wisdom"). Practical wisdom is a virtue pervading all the other virtues, since actions will not properly exemplify the virtues if they are not intelligent. In this connection MacIntyre observes also how Aristotle's conception of the moral life differs from that of most modern philosophers, for whom moral rules are basic. For Aristotle, it is the virtues that are basic; the rules are, necessarily and at their best, embodied in the intelligence of the morally mature individual. As MacIntyre notes, "Knowing how to apply the law is itself possible only for someone who possesses the virtue of justice."[9]

Stoicism and the Middle Ages. The next stage in our history is that of Stoicism (Zeno, fourth century B.C.; Chrysippus, third century B.C.; Epictetus, first century A.D.; Marcus Aurelius, second century A.D.), which arose when the city-state ceased to be the main form of political life and was replaced, first by the Macedonian kingdom and later by the Roman empire. Stoicism, anticipating modern morality, is a philosophy of individualism, a symptom of the individual's being cut off from a close-knit community committed to a social goal of human flourishing. To be a citizen, in Stoic terms, can only mean to be a citizen of the world at large. Stoicism is a morality of law, but not of the positive laws of a political community. Instead the laws are of nature—such as that all humans will die, that pain is a consequence of desire, or that people are in control of nothing that happens but only of their attitudes toward happenings. Virtue is central for the Stoics, but it is virtue in the singular rather than, as in the Aristotelian tradition, the multiple virtues of the good citizen. The one virtue is the submission of one's will to nature, the willing acceptance of the harsh ways reality is. And so virtue is interiorized; it is no longer embodied, as it was in heroic society, in action contributions to the communal welfare. Virtue is practiced, not as a way of securing a healthy social order, but as an end in itself. MacIntyre points out that elements of Stoicism recur regularly in the history of ethics: "whenever the virtues begin to lose their central place, Stoic patterns of thought and action at once reappear"[10]—for example, in the twelfth century in Abelard and in the eighteenth century in Kant.

MacIntyre makes almost no mention of the Christian church fathers, and gives only a sketchy account of the medieval period. The latter was characterized by philosophical conflict and only partially successful efforts to synthesize diverse traditions, which included elements of Stoicism and of course Christianity, as well as Aristotelianism. Saint Thomas Aquinas, as a strict Aristotelian, is "an unexpectedly marginal figure to the history which I am writing."[11] With his theistic framework Aquinas complicates and adds to Aristotle, without essentially altering the scheme: "The table of virtues and vices has to be amended and added to and a concept of sin is added to the Aristotelian concept of error. The law of God requires a new kind of respect and awe. The true end of man can no longer be completely achieved in this world, but only in another. Yet the threefold structure of untutored human-nature-as-it-happens-to-be, human-nature-as-it-could-be-if-it-realized-its-telos and the precepts of rational ethics as means for the transition from one to the other remains central to the theistic understanding of evaluative thought and judgment."[12] Aquinas, then, combines the notion that morality is obedience to the decrees of God with the notion that morality's function is to specify what it will take for humans to actualize their human nature or essence.

The Enlightenment. By the late seventeenth and eighteenth centuries, says MacIntyre, secularization was rooting out the belief that moral precepts could be traced to the will of God, and a new concept of rationality excluded thinking of human nature as something not actual and observable, but as a potentiality to be actualized. This new concept of rationality had roots both in Protestant theology, which claimed that sin had corrupted the mind's capacity to discern true human nature, and in the rising new science, which tended to think of rationality as methodical observation and generalization, and as deductive logic. At the same time, however, the *content* of morality was derived largely from classical Christianity. David Hume (1711–76), for example, believed in the chastity of women, and Immanuel Kant (1724–1804) believed in the absolute prohibition of lying. "Marriage and the family are *au fond* as unquestioned by Diderot's rationalist *philosophe* as they are by Kierkegaard's Judge Wilhelm; promise-keeping and justice are as inviolable for Hume as they are for Kant. Whence did they inherit these shared beliefs? Obviously from their shared Christian past."[13] This combination of retaining belief in morality while undercutting its traditional rational supports posed an urgent challenge to philosophers, namely the challenge to find an alternative foundation for morality. The philosophers' response to this challenge MacIntyre calls "the Enlightenment project of finding a rational justification for morality."

All the participants in the Enlightenment project looked to actual, observable human nature for a justification of traditional moral norms. Hume tried to find it in such supposedly universal feelings as the "sentiment of humanity"—a feeling of sympathy for one another that all human beings supposedly share. The difficulty with this view is that apart from a particular culture and training that inculcates such sentiments, people just don't seem to have these feelings.

Kant argued that morality is founded on "pure practical reason," a kind of rationality essential to human nature. The ultimate principle of this rationality is the Categorical Imperative: So act that you can will the maxim of your action as a universal law. Kant supposed that you could take any immoral maxim, such as "When there's no other way out of a tough situation, lie" or "When your spouse is away for more than a week, you may adulterize with a friendly person." If you then imagine its being made into a principle that holds universally for all human beings, then you will be imagining a contradictory state of affairs. Thus violating the rules of morality has a result similar to that of violating the laws of logic; you do so at the price of logical incoherence. The chief difficulty with Kant's proposal is that it is false: universalizing an immoral maxim almost never yields a contradiction.

According to MacIntyre, the Danish thinker Søren Kierkegaard (1813–55) was addressing the same problem as Hume and Kant. But he looked for the foundation (not quite the justification) of morality neither in the sentiments nor in the rationality characteristic of human nature, but in "the characteristics of fundamental decision-making."[14] Looking back on the earlier, Humean and Kantian versions of the Enlightenment project, Kierkegaard sees clearly that *there is no rational foundation for morality.* Morality belongs to a different order than things that can be decided through reasoned investigation; it is something the individual must simply choose for himself or herself out of the vigor of his or her own will, without reasons. Thus Kierkegaard, in MacIntyre's view, anticipates the emotivism and existentialism of the twentieth century. But Kierkegaard's effort, too, is a failure, since it involves saying at the same time that traditional morality can have authority over us (otherwise it wouldn't be morality), *and* that each individual is the sole and ultimate source of the principles of morality. MacIntyre remarks, "The contradiction in Kierkegaard's doctrine is plain."[15]

It remains for Friedrich Nietzsche (1844–1900) to draw the radical conclusion from the failure of the Enlightenment project: the individual must "raze to the ground the structures of inherited moral belief and argument,"[16] with their communal conceptions of justice, respect for others, and compassion, and rebuild upon the naked ground the honestly self-absorbed, self-glorifying, noncommunicating "great man" whose final authority is his own will to power.

In the last chapter of *After Virtue*, MacIntyre poses the alternatives: Nietzsche *or* Aristotle. The historical argument of the entire book has been that a broadly Aristotelian approach to ethics—which is to say, an ethics of the virtues—is the *only* rational way to avoid the Nietzschean conclusion, which in so many ways (though always half-heartedly) our contemporary culture has drawn. Let us conclude this very sketchy summary of *After Virtue* with a brief account of MacIntyre's own proposed version of Aristotelianism—his account of the nature of the virtues.

MacIntyre's Account of the Virtues

MacIntyre presents his concept of a virtue in terms of three conceptual "stages": the concepts of a *practice*, the *narrative order of a single human life*, and a *moral tradition*.

"Practices," in MacIntyre's sense, are complex and demanding activities with standards of excellence and goods "internal" to them. A few examples are chess, architecture, physics, baseball, historiography, farming, portrait painting, running a household or a city, and playing the violin. All the practices just listed can lead to such *external* goods as money, prestige, and the pleasures of the palate. But, in addition, they all have goods *internal* to them: in physics, say, insight into the relations between physical phenomena, in architecture the design of a beautiful and functional space, in violin playing a near-perfect performance of the Mendelssohn concerto, or in running a household the rearing of healthy and virtuous children. Attaining the goods internal to a practice requires the practitioner to submit to the rules of the practice (for example, the canons of scholarship, the techniques of farming, the rules of baseball), and this, in turn, places the practitioner in a social context. In some practices the immediate social context is very evident: a baseball player cannot play alone, a scholar is necessarily dependent on the work of other scholars, the violinist who plays the Mendelssohn concerto must work with the members of the orchestra, and so on. But every practice has the social dimension of the historical tradition that has given rise to its rules and canons of excellence. Even if the violinist plays only solo performances, he or she can begin to realize the goods internal to violin playing only by aligning himself or herself to the tradition by taking lessons from a teacher, studying the classical violin works, imitating some great violinists, and so forth.

Now MacIntyre argues that a virtue is a learned human quality necessary to attain any goods internal to a practice. "We have to learn to recognize what is due to whom [justice]; we have to be prepared to take whatever self-endangering risks are demanded along the way [courage]; and we have to listen carefully to what we are told about our own inadequacies and to reply with the same carefulness for the facts [truthfulness]."[17] While there are certainly dishonest violinists, cowardly farmers, and cheating baseball players, still, without these virtues the kinds of social involvement that are the necessary background of these practices would not be possible. Furthermore, unless at least some practitioners along the way practice with the virtues, the tradition sustaining the practice is in jeopardy of decaying. If portrait painters began to care only about making money and being interviewed on talk shows, and consequently ceased to listen honestly to the tradition of portrait painting and its judgments upon their work, the practice would be in danger of dying out. One can see how MacIntyre's theory so far is broadly Aristotelian. Without practices, the characteristically human form of life would not exist; without certain virtues, practices could not be learned, carried on, and sustained; so these virtues are essential to any distinctly human form of life.

The second stage in MacIntyre's account of the virtues is "the narrative concept of selfhood."[18] Throughout *After Virtue*, MacIntyre is on the prowl against a particular concept of the human self, with roots in the Enlightenment, which is incompatible with the Aristotelian virtues. The emotivist or existentialist self is a being who has a past and a future only incidentally; its "character" (if you want to glorify it with that name) is determined by what it happens at the moment to be choosing or by the role that it happens at the moment to be playing. "Authenticity" is procured by forthrightly owning up to one's choices and to the fluidity with which the self moves from role to role. Authenticity so understood is the only human virtue.

Against this radically disjointed and nonhistorical concept of selfhood, MacIntyre contrasts "a concept of a self whose unity resides in the unity of a narrative which links birth to life to death as narrative beginning to middle to end."[19] This, then, is the concept of a self with continuity, with personal identity—a self that can be "characterized" not just by its present role or decision, or even by the chronological listing of its life-episodes, its decisions and its evolution through roles, but by the unity that is its biography, both retrospective and prospective. MacIntyre invites us to notice that biographical narrative is what makes sense of the individual episodes—the actions and decisions—of a human life. Without their setting-in-the-story, these actions and decisions do not present themselves as intelligible.

The individual person must be a self whose actions make sense as parts of a narrative whole stretching back into his or her past and forward into the future. The details of this story are largely determined by factors other than the individual's decisions—that is, the persons the individual finds himself or herself related to, the nation and culture he or she is born into, and the individual's status within these. By virtue of being placed, and taking one's place, in such a setting, the individual has a personal identity and comes to know what that identity is.

But not just any narrative form shapes a self capable of possessing justice, truthfulness, courage, and friendship; not all narratives are such that the protagonist needs the *virtues* for successful pursuit of the story line. What, then, is the required narrative form? It is the form of a quest for *the human good.* An individual life must be the story of a search to know and achieve his or her human well-being or flourishing. But where shall we seek a conception of the human good? We start, says MacIntyre, with our knowledge of the goods internal to human practices and with the recognition that these goods need to be *ordered.* The goods internal to chess are surely on a different plane of importance than the goods internal to structuring a society. In the process of seeking to rank things that we already know to be good, and to order our lives with respect to this ranking, we will come to a clearer understanding both of what the human good is, and of ourselves. And the virtues will be qualities required of us in this quest for the human good: "The virtues therefore are to be understood as those dispositions which will not only sustain practices and enable us to achieve the goods internal to practices, but which will also sustain us in the relevant kind of quest for the good, by enabling us to overcome the harms, dangers, temptations and distractions which we encounter and which will furnish us with increasing self-knowledge and increasing knowledge of the good."[20]

The third stage in MacIntyre's account of the nature of the virtues is the concept of a moral tradition. There is no such thing as abstract, universal morality. Each of us must launch the quest for our human good from the vantage point of some *particular* moral tradition, indeed from our own particular place within that tradition. If you are an American, your moral tradition unavoidably includes certain democratic ideals, an individualistic conception of political freedom, and, in its history, the institution of black slavery and the bombing of Hiroshima. Even if you stand in rebellion against certain elements of this tradition, the terms and issues of your rebellion are set by the tradition. The values to which you appeal in your rebellion must initially be found in the tradition. Furthermore, the particular dimensions of your quest for the human good are determined by such things as the period in that history in which you were born, the moral and political persuasions and powers of your family, and your race. Your moral tradition is neither a straitjacket nor a dispensable outer garment: "Without those moral particularities to begin from there would never be anywhere to begin; but it is in moving forward from such particularity that the search for the good, for the universal, consists. Yet particularity can never be simply left behind or obliterated. The notion of escaping from it into a realm of entirely universal maxims which belong to man as such, whether in its eighteenth-century Kantian form or in the presentation of some modern analytical moral philosophies, is an illusion."[21]

If a moral tradition is a necessary background for an individual's life to have the narrative form of a pursuit of the good amid the goods internal to human practices, a moral tradition itself requires the historical background of courageous, truthful, and just individuals who inhabit it. Moral traditions are subject to decay, disintegration, and disappearance, and they are sustained, ultimately, only if there are persons who practice them with integrity. This is the third way in which the virtues are necessary for the prosecution of a fully human life. MacIntyre nicely summarizes: "The virtues find their point and purpose not only in sustaining those relationships necessary if the variety of goods internal to practices are to be achieved and not only in sustaining the form of an individual life in which that individual may seek out his or her good as the good of his or her whole life, but also in sustaining those traditions which provide both practices and individual lives with their necessary historical context."[22]

The Virtues and Contemporary Moral Debate

How can reckoning with these very general truths about the nature of the virtues help us to resolve the interminable moral debates of our day and to escape the emotivist self that we are all threatening to become? Obviously MacIntyre's theory of the virtues is not directly a solution to the question of whether early abortions are permissible, or whether building weapons capable of destroying the earth is an acceptable strategy in international politics, or whether it is just for government to tax the rich to support the poor. It is not a formula for resolving moral debates. Rather, it is an invitation to adopt a different conception of the nature of morality, and thus of moral debate, than the one presupposed by the parties to the previously mentioned debates.

MacIntyre's book is an argument that our incapacity to resolve such moral debates is the result of a mind-set that has evolved historically from abandoning the Aristotelian perspective in ethics. If we recognize that morality is always bound to a social tradition, we will not expect conclusive resolutions of moral debates unless these are carried on within a sufficiently rich and coherent tradition. And if we reckon that moral thinking requires a notion of human nature not just as it is, but as it would be if it realized its *telos*, or ultimate end, then we shall seek to recapture a tradition in which inquiry into our *telos* is a basic and legitimate exercise of human rationality. The questions these debates raise cannot be answered rationally in our secular and "pluralistic" situation ("modern liberal individualism"), which is one of a moral noncommunity not focused on human-nature-as-*telos* but seeking instead, with only confused fragmented remnants of traditions, abstract community- and tradition-free moral principles. But the questions can be answered rationally within a concrete moral community in which the human *telos* is concertedly sought.

MacIntyre's optimism about finding rational answers to the moral questions besetting us is due in large part to his rejection of the Enlightenment belief in rationality with a big *R*. Part of the restoration of morality in our day must be a liberation from this false and constricting picture. Rationality is far more faceted, historical, community-centered, and infused with human needs and yearnings than the Enlightenment would have us believe. And because rationality is good for more than just figuring out how things "tick," there is a place in it for Aristotle's project of debating and envisioning the human good.

Notes

[1]Notre Dame University Press, 1981; 2d ed., 1984. Page references are to the pages in the first edition, followed by the pages in the second edition in square brackets.

[2]*After Virtue*, 115 [122].

[3]Ibid., 119 [126–27].

[4]Ibid., 131 [140].

[5]Ibid., 132 [141].

[6]Ibid., 133 [142].

[7]For comments on the relations Aristotle bears to this tradition, see 154 [165].

[8]Ibid., 147 [157].

[9]Ibid., 143 [152].

[10]Ibid., 158 [170].

[11]Ibid., 166 [178].

[12]Ibid., 51 [53].

[13]Ibid., 49 [51].

[14]Ibid., 50 [52].

[15]Ibid., 41. MacIntyre's interpretation of Kierkegaard is more plausible as an account of how Kierkegaard has been *read* in the twentieth century, than as a reading of Kierkegaard himself. As MacIntyre admits, his reading goes against both Kierkegaard's self-interpretation and that of "the best Kierkegaard scholars of our own time, such as Louis Mackey and Gregor Malantschuk"(40). The editors believe that Kierkegaard's thought about the human condition has far more in common with Aristotle's than with that of C. L. Stevenson, R. M. Hare, and J-P. Sartre. He should be read as in some respects like Aquinas—as a relatively lonely figure trying to restore the tradition of the virtues in his own day.

[16]Ibid., 238 [256].

[17]Ibid., 178 [191].

[18]Ibid., 202 [217].

[19]Ibid., 191 [205].

[20]Ibid., 204 [219].

[21]Ibid., 205f [221]. MacIntyre is referring in this last line to such philosophers as Alan Gewitch, whose work he discusses on 64–65 [66–67].

[22]Ibid., 207 [223].

2

ABORTION

Gayle Berger and Cindy Gore, students attending college in the Boston area, had spent a pleasant evening listening to the Boston Symphony, after which they paused for a snack in a nearby restaurant. As they waited on a dimly lit corner for the midnight bus that would take them back to their campus, a car pulled up to the curb, and two gun-wielding young males leaped out and forced the two women into the car. When the car stopped for a red light, Gayle was able to escape into the night. Cindy, however, was abandoned in a wooded area in one of the western suburbs after she had been raped by all the male occupants of the car. While recovering from the emotional duress of her experience, Cindy discovered she was pregnant and immediately asked the physician in the college's infirmary to assist her in securing an abortion.

Mrs. Harry J. Spencer III, aged 24, was pregnant for the second time. Her previous pregnancy resulted in the birth of a healthy, normal baby boy. Mr. and Mrs. Spencer planned to have a balanced family: one son and one daughter, and that's all. Amniocentesis performed on Mrs. Spencer at the State University's Medical Center revealed that she was carrying a male fetus. With little hesitation, the Spencers asked their obstetrician to perform an abortion immediately.

Chorionic villi biopsy, a procedure in which fetal membranes are examined, performed on Susan George revealed the presence of trisomy 21 in her fetus. If carried to term, the pregnancy would result in the birth of an infant with Down's syndrome. Anti-abortion friends of Mrs. George advised her and her husband to carry the baby to term, citing the moral and spiritual strength developed in parents who have had the privilege of bestowing their affection upon a special child. Other friends of Mr. and Mrs. George advised them to seek an abortion because, they argued, the added care and stress to their household created by an abnormal child would jeopardize Mr. George's ability to finish his doctoral program in creative writing at the university, would drain time away from their normal two-year-old daughter, and would probably lead to friction in their marriage, which could result in divorce. Mr. and Mrs. George were bewildered.

Grace and Thomas Sullivan, married for 21 years, already had three children, aged 20, 18, and 15. Financial hardships were not foreign to the Sullivans; but hard work and frugal management of resources had enabled them to live comfortably and to plan a college education for each of their children. Grace became pregnant unexpectedly despite the contraceptive measures she and her husband had practiced. At first, Grace and Thomas accepted the unexpected pregnancy, with resignation. Thomas, however, began to be troubled about the deteriorating financial situation that a fourth child would occasion for the family and suggested they seek an abortion. Grace, who was about to enter her seventh month of pregnancy, cited the teachings of her church against abortion and wondered if abortion would be immoral and sinful. After serious and painful hours of debating the issue, Grace and Thomas decided to seek the advice of their family physician.

It was Jennifer's first pregnancy, and it was ectopic: implantation had taken place outside the uterus in one of the fallopian tubes. Shortly after missing her first menstrual period, she noticed some spotting and cramping pain. About eight weeks into her pregnancy, she experienced an episode of sudden severe lower abdominal pain, followed by fainting. Her obstetrician prescribed ultrasonography, through which he diagnosed her pregnancy as ectopic. Untreated, her pregnancy would prove fatal. Jennifer and her husband asked the physician to proceed immediately with corrective surgery.

Every problem pregnancy that seems to be resolvable through an abortion, such as the five cases just cited, forces us to face the question: Is it morally right to perform this abortion? Clearly, the landmark decision of the Supreme Court of the United States on January 22, 1973, in *Roe v. Wade*, legalized virtually all abortions. But that which is legal is not necessarily moral. Indeed, immoral laws have been enacted that exploit the masses, establish apartheid, censor freedom of the press, and deny voting rights to women, just to name a few. Such laws have been challenged on moral grounds and have often been modified or repealed. Accordingly, the legalization of abortion has by no means silenced the debate over the morality of the issue.

To engage in this debate, how does one go about determining whether or not an abortion is morally justified? As a starter, we could try to decide what an abortion is. Suppose we were to say that an abortion is the induced termination of a pregnancy that results in the destruction of _____. How should we fill in the blank? A great deal seems to depend on our answer. For example, if we put "living tissue" in the blank, then presumably an abortion would be in the same class of actions as cutting one's hair, clipping one's nails, and removing a cancerous tumor. If those acts do not present a particular moral problem, then neither should abortion. If, however, we fill in the blank with "human being," then an abortion would be significantly different from trimming hair or nails or removing tumors. Indeed, it would be the destruction of a human being, and such an act in the eyes of most of us would require weighty moral justification.

Consider the five cases we have cited. Would Cindy's rape and resulting pregnancy be sufficient grounds for destroying another human being? Is perhaps her fetus simply an innocent bystander? Would the Spencer's desire to have a "balanced family" constitute sufficient grounds for killing a human being? Would Down's Syndrome be sufficient basis for the Georges' abortion? If so, does that entail the conclusion that it is morally permissible to destroy other deformed human beings who are living in our midst? Would the economic hardship of raising a child, as in the case of the Sullivan's, be sufficient grounds for killing a human being? What about Jennifer's ectopic pregnancy? Is it permissible to kill another human being to save one's own life?

When we fill in the blank with "human being" instead of "living tissue" the moral justification of abortion becomes far more problematic. Suppose, however, we were to say that the gametes (the egg and the sperm cells) are not human beings, but that the postbirth infant is a human being. Then we might try to identify the point between conception and birth at which the unborn human tissue becomes a human being. The ability to determine when life in the womb becomes a human being would appear to be very helpful because, presumably, the dividing line between nonhuman being and human being would also be a dividing line between morally unproblematic and morally problematic (and some people would add "not morally permissible") abortions. It is, however, difficult (if not impossible) to draw that line with a high degree of certainty. Whatever point we select for the emergence of the human being in the womb—whether it be viability, quickening, the appearance of brain activity, or the appearance of infant-like form—our selection will prove to be somewhat arbitrary, because other points can be selected with equally good reasons. We are left with a puzzle, in that a human being seems to develop in the womb, but we are not able to say precisely when.

Perhaps the morally safe thing to do, then, is to say that the content of a pregnant womb is a human being. If so, should we not invest that *in utero* human being with the same right to life that we would grant to any other human being? If we do so, then each problematic pregnancy, such as the five described earlier, becomes invested with competing moral values that most of us would probably respect, but all of which we cannot possibly serve in a particular case. The presence of competing moral values, all of which cannot be served simultaneously, is at the heart of the problem of morally justifying abortion. Whether a particular abortion would be morally justified, accordingly, would depend on whether the preciousness of human life with its companion right to life could be overridden by the competing values with their accompanying rights and demands. Each thoughtful and morally sensitive person must make that decision in morally assessing an abortion.

But before one makes such a decision, one must identify clearly the moral issues at stake in a particular abortion. The readings included in this chapter will provide background to aid you in identifying those issues. The first reading provides excerpts from the 1973 Supreme Court decision in the case of *Roe v. Wade.* The next two readings give intimate views of abortion, from a woman who had an abortion and from a surgeon who witnessed an abortion for the first time. Judith Jarvis Thomson's article is a compelling argument for a woman's right to have an abortion.

KINDS OF ABORTIONS AND TYPES OF PROCEDURES

Two major kinds of abortions can be identified. Some abortions are *spontaneous;* others are *induced.* A spontaneous abortion occurs when natural human processes expel the embyo or fetus from the womb. Such an abortion is commonly called a "miscarriage." An induced abortion occurs when human action intrudes upon *in utero* development and causes the embryo or fetus to be expelled. Induced abortions may be either *intentional* (when humans knowlingly and willingly seek to abort the embryo or fetus) or *unintentional* (when the human actions causing the abortion did not have abortion as their goal). Unintentional abortions can be either *accidental* or *indirect.* Accidentally induced abortions occur when humans by chance do something that results in an abortion: for exmple, inadvertently causing a pregnant woman to stumble. Indirectly induced abortions are said to occur when procedures are pursued either to save the life or to promote the health of the mother, with the accompanying risk of abortion, and abortion does in fact take place but not as the goal of those procedures.

It is induced abortions which are either intentional or indirect that are at issue in the current national debate on abortion. . . .

Several standard procedures are used for intentional abortions depending upon the stage of fetal development. During the first trimester the uterine contents are usually small enough that they can be conveniently removed by dilating the cervix and evacuating the contents of the womb (using either suction or scraping). Dilation and curettage (scraping the uterus with a surgical instrument shaped like a spoon), the procedure commonly referred to as "D and C" is somewhat more hazardous than suction because the steel curette might puncture the wall of the uterus. RU 486, an abortion drug recently developed in France, is being hailed in many quarters an an important breakthrough. It is inexpensive, easy to use, very safe and remarkably effective. Taken in the form of a pill, the drug when followed in two days with prostaglandin, is about 95% effective in terminating pregnancies within their first seven weeks.

During the second trimester the fetus usually develops to a size that the rapid evacuation procedures described above become more hazardous for the woman. Accordingly, procedures are used which resemble a birth event. On the one hand, an incision can be made through the wall of the uterus (called an hysterotomy) and the fetus can then be removed in a fashion similar to a Caesarean section. On the other hand, uterine contractions can be induced so that the fetus will be expelled through the dilated cervix very much like a natural birth. Various procedures are used to induce the contractions, such as injection of a saline solution into the amniotic fluid (which kills the fetus), or injection also into the amniotic fluid of the hormone prostaglandin (which triggers contractions), or intravenous injection into the mother's circulatory system of a substance derived from the pituitary gland called pitocin (which also initiates contractions).

The procedures used in indirect abortions may be the same as those used in intentional abortions with the important distinguishing feature that the goal of those procedures is the preservation of the life and health of the mother rather than the destruction of the embryo or fetus. Additional procedures may also be deployed in indirect abortions, such as chemotherapy, the surgical removal of a cancerous uterus, etc. which are pursued as beneficial to the mother but with attendant hazards for the fetus.

Source: Adapted from Donald M. Borchert and J. Phillip Jones. "Abortion: Morally Right or Wrong?" *Listening.* Vol. 22, no. 1, 22–35 (Winter, 1987).

Abortion and Legality

The key document for understanding the legality of abortion in the United States is the ruling of the Supreme Court of the United States on January 22, 1973 in the case of *Roe* v. *Wade.* A single woman who was residing in Dallas County, Texas, instituted a federal class-action suit in the United

States District Court for the Northern District of Texas against Henry Wade, the District Attorney of Dallas County. Using the pseudonym of Jane Roe, she challenged the constitutionality of the Texas criminal abortion statutes, which allowed abortions only for the purpose of saving the life of the mother.

Roe alleged (1) that she was unmarried and pregnant; (2) that she wished to have an abortion performed by a competent, licensed physician under safe, clinical conditions; (3) that she could not secure a legal abortion in Texas because her life did not appear to be threatened by her pregnancy; (4) that she could not afford to travel to another jurisdiction to secure a legal, safe abortion; and (5) that the Texas statutes were unconstitutionally vague and that they abridged her right of personal privacy, protected by several Amendments to the Constitution.

The District Court ruled in Roe's favor. Wade appealed the decision directly to the Supreme Court of the United States. By a margin of seven to two the Supreme Court ruled in favor of Roe, basing its judgment on the right of privacy it saw protected by the Fourteenth Amendment. The majority opinion, delivered by Mr. Justice Blackmun, divides a pregnancy into three stages which approximate the three trimesters of a typical nine-month pregnancy. The Court ruled that during the first trimester, "the abortion decision and its effectuation must be left to the medical judgment of the pregnant woman's attending physician." During the second trimester, the State may regulate abortion procedures to insure maternal health. Finally, during the third trimester, the State ("in promoting its interest in the potentiality of human life") may "regulate, and even proscribe, abortion except where it is necessary, in appropriate medical judgment, for the preservation of the life or health of the mother."

Does this ruling, as some would claim, virtually make any proposed abortion legal? Clearly, the State is not allowed to outlaw abortions during the first and second trimesters. During those periods, is it not the case that all that a pregnant woman need do to have a legal abortion is find an attending physician to support her request? And is it not altogether likely that a pregnant woman seeking an abortion during the third trimester could claim with good cause that the continuation of her pregnancy threatened at least her mental and emotional health? If so, is it not the case that a pregnant woman could quite easily fulfill the criteria for a legal abortion even in the third trimester? Are we then not forced to the conclusion that virtually any abortion, with little difficulty, could be shown to be legal according to the Supreme Court's ruling?

But is the Court's ruling warranted? Mr. Justice Rehnquist dissented from the majority, claiming among other things that the Court had misinterpreted the notion of privacy in the Fourteenth Amendment. A question we should also ask is whether the Court's legalizing of abortion makes it morally right.

These are some of the issues that one should ponder in studying the abridged text of the Court's ruling and Mr. Justice Rehnquist's dissent, reproduced in the following pages. The Court's ruling contained a number of items—such as a well-documented historical review of human attitudes and laws relating to abortion—which space limitations prevent us from including.

JANE ROE ET AL., APPELLANTS

v.

HENRY WADE
No. 70–18
ON APPEAL FROM THE UNITED STATES
DISTRICT COURT FOR THE NORTHERN
DISTRICT OF TEXAS
Supreme Court of the United States
January 22, 1973

MR. JUSTICE BLACKMUN delivered the opinion of the Court....

The Texas statutes under attack here are typical of those that have been in effect in many States for approximately a century....

We forthwith acknowledge our awareness of the sensitive and emotional nature of the abortion controversy, of the vigorous opposing views, even among physicians, and of the deep and seemingly absolute convictions that the subject inspires. One's philosophy, one's experiences, one's exposure to the raw edges of human existence, one's religious training, one's attitudes toward life and family and their values, and the moral standards one establishes and seeks to observe, are all likely to influence and to color one's thinking and conclusions about abortion.

In addition, population growth, pollution, poverty, and racial overtones tend to complicate and not to simplify the problem.

Our task, of course, is to resolve the issue by constitutional measurement free of emotion and of predilection....

I

The Texas statutes that concern us here are Arts. 1191–1194 and 1196 of the State's Penal Code. These make it a crime to "procure an abortion," as therein defined, or to attempt one, except with respect to "an abortion procured or attempted by medical advice for the purpose of saving the life of the mother." Similar statutes are in existence in a majority of the States ...

II

Jane Roe, a single woman who was residing in Dallas County, Texas, instituted this federal action in March 1970 against the District Attorney of the county. She sought a declaratory judgment that the Texas criminal abortion statutes were unconstitutional on their face, and an injunction restraining the defendant from enforcing the statutes.

Roe alleged that she was unmarried and pregnant; that she wished to terminate her pregnancy by an abortion "performed by a competent, licensed physician, under safe, clinical conditions"; that she was unable to get a "legal" abortion in Texas because her life did not appear to be threatened by the continuation of her pregnancy; and that she could not afford to travel to another jurisdiction in order to secure a legal abortion under safe conditions. She claimed that the Texas statutes were unconstitutionally vague and that they abridged her right of personal privacy, protected by the First, Fourth, Fifth, Ninth, and Fourteenth Amendments. By an amendment to her complaint Roe purported to sue "on behalf of herself and all other women" similarly situated....

V

The principal thrust of appellant's attack on the Texas statutes is that they improperly invade a right, said to be possessed by the pregnant woman, to choose to terminate her pregnancy. Appellant would discover this right in the concept of personal "liberty" embodied in the Fourteenth Amendment's Due Process Clause; or in personal, marital, familial, and sexual privacy said to be protected by the Bill of Rights or its penumbras, see *Griswold* v. *Connecticut,* 381 U.S. 479 (1965); *Eisenstadt* v. *Baird,* 405 U.S. 438 (1972); *id.,* at 460 (WHITE, J., Concurring); or among those rights reserved to the people by the Ninth Amendment, *Griswold* v. *Connecticut,* 381 U.S., at 486 (Goldberg, J., concurring). Before addressing this claim, we feel it desirable briefly to survey, in several aspects, the history of abortion, for such insight as that history may afford us, and then to examine the state purposes and interests behind the criminal abortion laws.

VI

It perhaps is not generally appreciated that the restrictive criminal abortion laws in effect in a majority of States today are of relatively recent vintage. Those laws, generally proscribing abortion or its attempt at any time during pregnancy except when necessary to preserve the pregnant woman's life, are not of ancient or even of common law origin. Instead, they derive from statutory changes effected, for the most part, in the latter half of the 19th century. . . .

VII

Three reasons have been advanced to explain historically the enactment of criminal abortion laws in the 19th century and to justify their continued existence.

It has been argued occasionally that these laws were the product of a Victorian social concern to discourage illicit sexual conduct. Texas, however, does not advance this justification in the present case, and it appears that no court or commentator has taken the argument seriously. The appellants and *amici* contend, moreover, that this is not a proper state purpose at all and suggest that, if it were, the Texas statutes are overbroad in protecting it since the law fails to distinguish between married and unwed mothers.

A second reason is concerned with abortion as a medical procedure. When most criminal abortion laws were first enacted, the procedure was a hazardous one for the woman. This was particularly true prior to the development of antisepsis. Antiseptic techniques, of course, were based on discoveries by Lister, Pasteur, and others first announced in 1867, but were not generally accepted and employed until about the turn of the century. Abortion mortality was high. Even after 1900, and perhaps until as late as the development of antibiotics in the 1940's, standard modern techniques such as dilation and curettage were not nearly so safe as they are today. Thus it has been argued that a State's real concern in enacting a criminal abortion law was to protect the pregnant woman, that is, to restrain her from submitting to a procedure that placed her life in serious jeopardy.

Modern medical techniques have altered this situation. Appellants and various *amici* refer to medical data indicating that abortion in early pregnancy, that is, prior to the end of first trimester, although not without its risk, is now relatively safe. Mortality rates for women undergoing early abortions, where the procedure is legal, appear to be as low as or lower than the rates for normal childbirth. Consequently, any interest of the State in protecting the woman from an inherently hazardous procedure, except when it would be equally dangerous for her to forgo it, has largely disappeared. Of course, important state interests in the area of health and medical standards do remain. The State has a legitimate interest in seeing to it that abortion, like any other medical procedure, is performed under circumstances that insure maximum safety for the patient. This interest obviously extends at least to the performing physician and his staff, to the facilities involved, to the availability of after-care, and to adequate provision for any complication or emergency that might arise. The prevalence of high mortality rates at illegal "abortion mills" strengthens, rather than weakens, the State's interest in regulating the conditions under which abortions are performed. Moreover, the risk to the woman increases as her pregnancy continues. Thus the State retains a definite interest in protecting the woman's own health and safety when an abortion is proposed at a late stage of pregnancy.

The third reason is the State's interest—some phrase it in terms of duty—in protecting prenatal life. Some of the argument for this justification rests on the theory that a new human life is present from the moment of conception. The State's interest and general obligation to protect life then extends, it is argued, to prenatal life. Only when the life of the pregnant mother herself is at stake, balanced against the life she carries within her, should the interest of the embryo or fetus not prevail. Logically, of course, a legitimate state interest in this area need not stand or fall on acceptance of the belief that life begins at conception or at some other point prior to live birth. In assessing the State's interest, recognition may be given to the less rigid claim that as long as at least *potential* life is involved, the State may assert interests beyond the protection of the pregnant woman alone.

Parties challenging state abortion laws have sharply disputed in some courts the contention that a purpose of these laws, when enacted, was to protect prenatal life. Pointing to the absence of legislative history to support the contention, they claim that most state laws were designed solely to protect the woman. Because medical advances have lessened this concern, at least with respect to abortion in early pregnancy, they argue that with respect to such abortions the laws can no longer be justified by any state interest. There is some scholarly support for this view of original purpose. The few state courts called upon to interpret their laws in the late 19th and early 20th centuries did focus on the State's interest in protecting the woman's health rather than in preserving the embryo and fetus. Proponents of this view point out that in many States, including Texas, by statute or judicial interpretation, the pregnant woman herself could not be prosecuted for self-abortion or for cooperating in an abortion performed upon her by another. They claim that adoption of the "quickening" distinction through received common law and state statutes tacitly recognizes the greater health hazards inherent in late abortion and impliedly repudiates the theory that life begins at conception.

It is with these interests, and the weight to be attached to them, that this case is concerned.

VIII

The Constitution does not explicitly mention any right of privacy. In a line of decisions, however, going back perhaps as far as *Union Pacific R. Co.* v.

Botsford, 141 U.S. 250, 251 (1891), the Court has recognized that a right of personal privacy, or a guarantee of certain areas or zones of privacy, does exist under the Constitution. . . .

This right of privacy, whether it be founded in the Fourteenth Amendment's concept of personal liberty and restrictions upon state action, as we feel it is, or, as the District Court determined, in the Ninth Amendment's reservation of rights to the people, is broad enough to encompass a woman's decision whether or not to terminate her pregnancy. The detriment that the State would impose upon the pregnant woman by denying this choice altogether is apparent. Specific and direct harm medically diagnosable even in early pregnancy may be involved. Maternity, or additional offspring, may force upon the woman a distressful life and future. Psychological harm may be imminent. Mental and physical health may be taxed by child care. There is also the distress, for all concerned, associated with the unwanted child, and there is the problem of bringing a child into a family already unable, psychologically and otherwise, to care for it. In other cases, as in this one, the additional difficulties and continuing stigma of unwed motherhood may be involved. All these are factors the woman and her responsible physician necessarily will consider in consultation.

On the basis of elements such as these, appellants and some *amici* argue that the woman's right is absolute and that she is entitled to terminate her pregnancy at whatever time, in whatever way, and for whatever reason she alone chooses. With this we do not agree. Appellants' arguments that Texas either has no valid interest at all in regulating the abortion decision, or no interest strong enough to support any limitation upon the woman's sole determination, is unpersuasive. The Court's decisions recognizing a right of privacy also acknowledge that some state regulation in areas protected by that right is appropriate. As noted above, a state may properly assert important interests in safeguarding health, in maintaining medical standards, and in protecting potential life. At some point in pregnancy, these respective interests become sufficiently compelling to sustain regulation of the factors that govern the abortion decision. The privacy right involved, therefore, cannot be said to be absolute. In fact, it is not clear to us that the claim asserted by some *amici* that one has an unlimited right to do with one's body as one pleases bears a close relationship to the right of privacy previously articulated in the Court's decisions. The Court has refused to recognize an unlimited right of this kind in the past. *Jacobson* v. *Massachusetts,* 197 U.S. 11 (1905) (vaccination); *Buck* v. *Bell,* 274 U.S. 200 (1927) (sterilization).

We therefore conclude that the right of personal privacy includes the abortion decision, but that this right is not unqualified and must be considered against important state interests in regulation.

We note that those federal and state courts that have recently considered abortion law challenges have reached the same conclusion. A majority, in addition to the District Court in the present case, have held state laws unconstitutional, at least in part, because of vagueness or because of over-breadth and abridgement of rights. . . .

Although the results are divided, most of these courts have agreed that the right of privacy, however based, is broad enough to cover the abortion decision; that the right, nonetheless, is not absolute and is subject to some limitations; and that at some point the state interests as to protection of health, medical standards, and prenatal life, become dominant. We agree with this approach.

Where certain "fundamental rights" are involved, the Court has held that regulation limiting these rights may be justified only by a "compelling state interest," . . . and that legislative enactments must be narrowly drawn to express only the legitimate state interests at stake. . . .

In the recent abortion cases, . . . courts have recognized these princi-ples. Those striking down state laws have generally scrutinized the State's interest in protecting health and potential life and have concluded that neither interest justified broad limitations on the reasons for which a physi-cian and his pregnant patient might decide that she should have an abor-tion in the early stages of pregnancy. Courts sustaining state laws have held that the State's determinations to protect health or prenatal life are domi-nant and constitutionally justifiable.

IX

The District Court held that the appellee failed to meet his burden of dem-onstrating that the Texas statute's infringement upon Roe's rights was nec-essary to support a compelling state interest, and that, although the defen-dant presented "several compelling justifications for state presence in the area of abortions," the statutes outstripped these justifications and swept "far beyond any areas of compelling state interest." Appellant and appellee both contest that holding. Appellant, as has been indicated, claims an abso-lute right that bars any state imposition of criminal penalties in the area. Appellee argues that the State's determination to recognize and protect prenatal life from and after conception constitutes a compelling state inter-est. As noted above, we do not agree fully with either formulation.

A. The appellee and certain *amici* argue that the fetus is a "person" within the language and meaning of the Fourteenth Amendment. In sup-port of this they outline at length and in detail the well-known facts of fetal development. If this suggestion of personhood is established, the appel-lant's case, of course, collapses, for the fetus' right to life is then guaranteed specifically by the Amendment. The appellant conceded as much on reargu-ment. On the other hand, the appellee conceded on reargument that no case could be cited that holds that a fetus is a person within the meaning of the Fourteenth Amendment.

The Constitution does not define "person" in so many words. Section 1 of the Fourteenth Amendment contains three references to "person." The first, in defining "citizens," speaks of "persons born or naturalized in the United States." The word also appears both in the Due Process Clause and in the Equal Protection Clause. "Person" is used in other places in the Constitution.... But in nearly all these instances, the use of the word is such that it has application only postnatally. None indicates, with any assurance, that it has any possible pre-natal application.

All this, together with our observation, *supra,* that throughout the major portion of the 19th century prevailing legal abortion practices were far freer than they are today, persuades us that the word "person," as used in the Fourteenth Amendment, does not include the unborn....

This conclusion, however, does not of itself fully answer the contentions raised by Texas, and we pass on to other considerations.

B. The pregnant woman cannot be isolated in her privacy. She carries an embryo and, later, a fetus, if one accepts the medical definitions of the developing young in the human uterus. See Dorland's Illustrated Medical Dictionary, 478–479, 547 (24th ed. 1965). The situation therefore is inherently different from marital intimacy, or bedroom possession of obscene material, or marriage, or procreation, or education, with which *Eisenstadt, Giswold, Stanley, Loving, Skinner, Pierce,* and *Meyer* were respectively concerned. As we have intimated above, it is reasonable and appropriate for a State to decide that at some point in time another interest, that of health of the mother or that of potential human life, becomes significantly involved. The woman's privacy is no longer sole and any right of privacy she possesses must be measured accordingly.

Texas urges that, apart from the Fourteenth Amendment, life begins at conception and is present throughout pregnancy, and that, therefore, the State has a compelling interest in protecting that life from and after conception. We need not resolve the difficult question of when life begins. When those trained in the respective disciplines of medicine, philosophy, and theology are unable to arrive at any consensus, the judiciary, at this point in the development of man's knowledge, is not in a position to speculate as to the answer.

It should be sufficient to note briefly the wide divergence of thinking on this most sensitive and difficult question. There has always been strong support for the view that life does not begin until live birth. This was the belief of the Stoics. It appears to be the predominant, though not the unanimous, attitude of the Jewish faith. It may be taken to represent also the position of a large segment of the Protestant community, insofar as that can be ascertained; organized groups that have taken a formal position on the abortion issue have generally regarded abortion as a matter for the conscience of the individual and her family. As we have noted, the common law found greater significance in quickening. Physicians and their scientific colleagues have regarded that event with less interest and have tended to focus either upon conception or upon live birth or upon the interim point at which the fetus becomes "viable," that is, potentially able to live outside the mother's womb, albeit with artificial aid. Viability is usually placed at about seven months (28 weeks) but may occur earlier, even at 24 weeks. The Aristotelian theory of "mediate animation," that held sway throughout the Middle Ages and the Renaissance in Europe, continued to be official Roman Catholic dogma until the 19th century, despite opposition to this "ensoulment" theory from those in the Church who would recognize the existence of life from the moment of conception. The latter is now, of course, the official belief of the Catholic Church. As one of the briefs *amicus* discloses, this is a view strongly held by many non-Catholics as well, and by many physicians. Substantial problems for precise definition of this view are posed, however, by new embryological data that purport to indicate that conception is a "process" over time, rather than an event, and by new medical techniques such as menstrual extraction, the "morning-after" pill, implantation of embryos, artificial insemination, and even artificial wombs.

In areas other than criminal abortion the law has been reluctant to endorse any theory that life, as we recognize it, begins before live birth or to accord legal rights to the unborn except in narrowly defined situations and except when the rights are contingent upon live birth. For example, the traditional rule of tort law had denied recovery for prenatal injuries even though the child was born alive. That rule has been changed in almost every jurisdiction. In most States recovery is said to be permitted only if the fetus was viable, or at least quick, when the injuries were sustained, though few courts have squarely so held. In a recent development, generally opposed by the commentators, some States permit the parents of a stillborn child to maintain an action for wrongful death because of prenatal injuries. Such an action, however, would appear to be one to vindicate the parents' interest and is thus consistent with the view that the fetus, at most, represents only the potentiality of life. Similarly, unborn children have been recognized as acquiring rights or interests by way of inheritance or other devolution of property, and have been represented by guardians *ad litem*. Perfection of the interests involved, again, has generally been contingent upon live birth. In short, the unborn have never been recognized in the law as persons in the whole sense.

X

In view of all this, we do not agree that, by adopting one theory of life, Texas may override the rights of the pregnant woman that are at stake. We repeat, however, that the State does have an important and legitimate interest in preserving and protecting the health of the pregnant woman, whether she be a resident of the State or a nonresident who seeks medical consultation and treatment there, and that it has still *another* important and legitimate interest in protecting the potentiality of human life. These interests are separate and distinct. Each grows in substantiality as the woman approaches term and, at a point during pregnancy, each becomes "compelling."

With respect to the State's important and legitimate interest in the health of the mother, the "compelling" point, in the light of present medical knowledge, is at approximately the end of the first trimester. This is so because of the now established medical fact, referred to above, that until the end of the first trimester mortality in abortion is less than mortality in normal childbirth. It follows that, from and after this point, a State may regulate the abortion procedure to the extent that the regulation reasonably relates to the preservation and protection of maternal health. Examples of permissible state regulation in this area are requirements as to the qualifications of the person who is to perform the abortion; as to the licensure of that person; as to the facility in which the procedure is to be performed, that is, whether it must be a hospital or may be a clinic or some other place of less-than-hospital status; as to the licensing of the facility; and the like.

This means, on the other hand, that, for the period of pregnancy prior to this "compelling" point, the attending physician, in consultation with his patient, is free to determine, without regulation by the State, that in his medical judgment the patient's pregnancy should be terminated. If that decision is reached, the judgment may be effectuated by an abortion free of interference by the State.

With respect to the State's important and legitimate interest in potential life, the "compelling" point is at viability. This is so because the fetus then presumably has the capability of meaningful life outside the mother's womb. State regulation protective of fetal life after viability thus has both logical and biological justifications. If the State is interested in protecting fetal life after viability, it may go so far as to proscribe abortion during that period except when it is necessary to preserve the life or health of the mother.

Measured against these standards, Art. 1196 of the Texas Penal Code, in restricting legal abortions to those "procured or attempted by medical advice for the purpose of saving the life of the mother," sweeps too broadly. The statute makes no distinction between abortions performed early in pregnancy and those performed later, and it limits to a single reason, "saving" the mother's life, the legal justification for the procedure. The statute, therefore, cannot survive the constitutional attack made upon it here.

This conclusion makes it unnecessary for us to consider the additional challenge to the Texas statute asserted on grounds of vagueness. See *United States* v. *Vuitch,* 402 U.S. 62, 67–72, (1971).

XI

To summarize and to repeat:

1. A state criminal abortion statute of the current Texas type, that excepts from criminality only a *life saving* procedure on behalf of the mother, without regard to pregnancy stage and without recognition of the other interests involved, is violative of the Due Process Clause of the Fourteenth Amendment.

(a) For the stage prior to approximately the end of the first trimester, the abortion decision and its effectuation must be left to the medical judgment of the pregnant woman's attending physician.

(b) For the stage subsequent to approximately the end of the first trimester, the State, in promoting its interest in the health of the mother, may, if it chooses, regulate the abortion procedure in ways that are reasonably related to maternal health.

(c) For the stage subsequent to viability the State, in promoting its interest in the potentiality of human life, may, if it chooses, regulate, and even proscribe, abortion except where it is necessary, in appropriate medical judgment, for the preservation of the life or health of the mother.

2. The State may define the term "physician," as it has been employed in the preceding numbered paragraphs of this Part XI of this opinion, to mean only a physician currently licensed by the State, and may proscribe any abortion by a person who is not a physician as so defined.

In *Doe* v. *Bolton, post,* procedural requirements contained in one of the modern abortion statutes are considered. That opinion and this one, of course, are to be read together.

This holding, we feel, is consistent with the relative weights of the respective interests involved, with the lessons and example of medical and legal history, with the lenity of the common law, and with the demands of the profound problems of the present day. The decision leaves the State free to place increasing restrictions on abortion as the period of pregnancy lengthens, so long as those restrictions are tailored to the recognized state interests. The decision vindicates the right of the physician to administer medical treatment according to his professional judgment up to the points where important state interests provide compelling justifications for intervention. Up to those points the abortion decision in all its aspects is inherently, and primarily, a medical decision, and basic responsibility for it must rest with the physician. If an individual practitioner abuses the privilege of exercising proper medical judgment, the usual remedies, judicial and intraprofessional, are available.

XII

Our conclusion that Art. 1190 is unconstitutional means, of course, that the Texas abortion statutes, as a unit must fall . . .

It is so ordered.

MR. JUSTICE WHITE, with whom MR. JUSTICE REHNQUIST joins, dissenting.

At the heart of the controversy in these cases are those recurring pregnancies that pose no danger whatsoever to the life or health of the mother but are nevertheless unwanted for any one or more of a variety of reasons—convenience, family planning, economics, dislike of children, the embarrassment of illegitimacy, etc. The common claim before us is that for any one of such reasons, or for no reason at all, and without asserting or claiming any threat to life or health, any woman is entitled to an abortion at her request if she is able to find a medical advisor willing to undertake the procedure.

The Court for the most part sustains this position: During the period prior to the time the fetus becomes viable, the Constitution of the United States values the convenience, whim or caprice of the putative mother more than the life or potential life of the fetus; the Constitution, therefore, guarantees the right to an abortion as against any state law or policy seeking to protect the fetus from an abortion not prompted by more compelling reasons of the mother.

With all due respect, I dissent. I find nothing in the language or history of the Constitution to support the Court's judgment. The Court simply fashions and announces a new constitutional right for pregnant mothers and, with scarcely any reason or authority for its action, invests that right with sufficient substance to override most existing state abortion statutes. The upshot is that the people and the legislatures of the 50 States are constitutionally disentitled to weigh the relative importance of the continued existence and development of the fetus on the one hand against a spectrum of possible impacts on the mother on the other hand. As an exercise of raw judicial power, the Court perhaps has authority to do what it does today; but in my view its judgment is an improvident and extravagant exercise of the power of judicial review which the Constitution extends to this Court.

The Court apparently values the convenience of the pregnant mother more than the continued existence and development of the life or potential life which she carries. Whether or not I might agree with that marshalling of values, I can in no event join the Court's judgment because I find no constitutional warrant for imposing such an order of priorities on the people and legislatures of the States. In a sensitive area such as this, involving as it does issues over which reasonable men may easily and heatedly differ, I cannot accept the Court's exercise of its clear power of choice by interposing a constitutional barrier to state efforts to protect human life and by investing mothers and doctors with the constitutionally protected right to exterminate it. This issue, for the most part, should be left with the people and to the political processes the people have devised to govern their affairs.

It is my view, therefore, that the Texas statute is not constitutionally infirm because it denies abortions to those who seek to serve only their convenience rather than to protect their life or health. Nor is this plaintiff, who claims no threat to her mental or physical health, entitled to assert the possible rights of those women whose pregnancy assertedly implicates their health. This, together with *United States* v. *Vuitch,* 402 U.S. 62 (1971), dictates reversal of the judgment of the District Court . . .

MR. JUSTICE REHNQUIST, dissenting.

The Court's opinion brings to the decision of this troubling question both extensive historical fact and a wealth of legal scholarship. While its opinion thus commands my respect, I find myself nonetheless in fundamental disagreement with those parts of it which invalidate the Texas statute in question, and therefore dissent.

I

The Court's opinion decides that a State may impose virtually no restriction on the performance of abortions during the first trimester of pregnancy. Our previous decisions indicate that a necessary predicate for such an opinion is a plaintiff who was in her first trimester of pregnancy at some time during the pendency of her law suit. While a party may vindicate his own constitutional rights, he may not seek vindication for the rights of others. *Moose Lodge* v. *Irvis,* 407 U.S. 163 (1972); *Sierra Club* v. *Morton,* 405 U.S. 727 (1972). The Court's statement of facts in this case makes clear, however, that the record in no way indicates the presence of such a plaintiff. We know only that plaintiff Roe at the time of filing her complaint was a pregnant woman; for aught that appears in this record, she may have been in her *last* trimester of pregnancy as of the date the complaint was filed . . .

Even if there were a plaintiff in this case capable of litigating the issue which the Court decides, I would reach a conclusion opposite to that reached by the Court. I have difficulty in concluding, as the Court does, that the right of "privacy" is involved in this case. Texas by the statute here challenged bars the performance of a medical abortion by a licensed physician on a plaintiff such as Roe. A transaction resulting in an operation such as this is not "private" in the ordinary usage of that word. Nor is the "privacy" which the Court finds here even a distant relative of the freedom from searches and seizures protected by the Fourth Amendment to the Constitution which the Court has referred to as embodying a right to privacy. *Katz* v. *United States,* 389 U.S. 347 (1967) ...

To reach its result the Court necessarily has had to find within the scope of the Fourteenth Amendment a right that was apparently completely unknown to the drafters of the Amendment. As early as 1821, the first state law dealing directly with abortion was enacted by the Connecticut legislature. Conn. Stat. Tit. 22, §§14, 16 (1821). By the time of the adoption of the Fourteenth Amendment in 1868 there were at least 36 laws enacted by state or territorial legislatures limiting abortion. While many States have amended or updated their laws, 21 of the laws on the books in 1868 remain in effect today. Indeed, the Texas statute struck down today was, as the majority notes, first enacted in 1857 and "has remained substantially unchanged to the present time." ...

There apparently was no question concerning the validity of this provision or of any of the other state statutes when the Fourteenth Amendment was adopted. The only conclusion possible from this history is that the drafters did not intend to have the Fourteenth Amendment withdraw from the States the power to legislate with respect to this matter ...

For all of the foregoing reasons, I respectfully dissent.

A Patient's View
of Abortion

In the same year that the Supreme Court rendered its landmark decision concerning abortion, Linda Bird Francke had an abortion. She was already the mother of three children, was just beginning a full-time job in publishing, and was supportive of her husband's plans for a career change. It was an enormously inconvenient time to have a baby. She and her husband agreed that an abortion was called for.

The speed with which the abortion of a fetus in the early weeks of the first trimester could be scheduled and performed stands in sharp contrast to the moral ambivalence and anxiety that can invade and linger in such a sensitive person as Ms. Francke. An outspoken advocate of a woman's right to have an abortion, Ms. Francke discovered that when she herself decided to undergo an abortion, she was not, in her words, "the modern woman" she thought she was. What may have seemed so clearly justified in the abstract became exceedingly problematic in the concrete situation.

Without surrendering her support for a woman's right to have an abortion, and believing that it would prove helpful to other women going through the intellectual uncertainties and emotional duress associated with an abortion, Ms. Francke decided several years after her abortion to publish the thoughts she had penned shortly after her abortion. Her reflections, presented under a pseudonym, appeared on the Op-Ed page of the *New York Times* in May 1976. The article in the *Times* was cited (in various edited versions) both by proabortionists and by antiabortionists to support their positions. Ms. Francke herself, as the following material seems to indicate, wishes her experience to display not the clear-cut correctness of one side or the other in the debate over abortion, but rather the moral ambiguities and perplexities that can accompany an abortion.

THE AMBIVALENCE OF ABORTION

Linda Bird Francke

"Jane Doe," thirty-eight, had an abortion in New York City in 1973. The mother of three children, then three, five, and eleven, Jane had just started a full-time job in publishing. She and her husband, an investment banker, decided together that another baby would add an almost unbearable strain to their lives, which were already overfull. What Jane had not anticipated was the guilt and sadness that followed the abortion. She wrote about the experience shortly thereafter and filed the story away. Three years later she reread it and decided it might be helpful to other women who experience the ambivalence of abortion. The *New York Times* ran it on their Op-Ed page in May 1976. This is what she wrote:

> We were sitting in a bar on Lexington Avenue when I told my husband I was pregnant. It is not a memory I like to dwell on. Instead of the champagne and hope which had heralded the impending births of the first, second and third child, the news of this one was greeted with shocked silence and Scotch. "Jesus," my husband kept saying to himself, stirring the ice cubes around and around. "Oh, Jesus."
>
> Oh, how we tried to rationalize it that night as the starting time for the movie came and went. My husband talked about his plans for a career change in the next year, to stem the staleness that fourteen years with the same investment-banking firm had brought him. A new baby would preclude that option.
>
> The timing wasn't right for me either. Having juggled pregnancies and child care with what freelance jobs I could fit in between feedings, I had just taken on a full-time job. A new baby would put me right back in the nursery just when our youngest child was finally school age. It was time for *us*, we tried to rationalize. There just wasn't room

Source: The Ambivalence of Abortion by Linda Bird Francke (Random House, 1978). Used by permission of Random House and *The New York Times*.

in our lives now for another baby. We both agreed. And agreed. And agreed.

How very considerate they are at the Women's Services, known formally as the Center for Reproductive and Sexual Health. Yes, indeed, I could have an abortion that very Saturday morning and be out in time to drive to the country that afternoon. Bring a first morning urine specimen, a sanitary belt and napkins, a money order or $125 cash—and a friend.

My friend turned out to be my husband, standing awkwardly and ill at ease as men always do in places that are exclusively for women, as I checked in at nine A.M. Other men hovered around just as anxiously, knowing they had to be there, wishing they weren't. No one spoke to each other. When I would be cycled out of there four hours later, the same men would be slumped in their same seats, locked downcast in their cells of embarrassment.

The Saturday morning women's group was more dispirited than the men in the waiting room. There were around fifteen of us, a mixture of races, ages and backgrounds. Three didn't speak English at all and a fourth, a pregnant Puerto Rican girl around eighteen, translated for them.

There were six black women and a hodge-podge of whites, among them a T-shirted teenager who kept leaving the room to throw up and a puzzled middle-aged woman from Queens with three grown children.

"What form of birth control were you using?" the volunteer asked each one of us. The answer was inevitably "none." She then went on to describe the various forms of birth control available at the clinic, and offered them to each of us.

The youngest Puerto Rican girl was asked through the interpreter which she'd like to use: the loop, diaphragm, or pill. She shook her head "no" three times. "You don't want to come back here again, do you?" the volunteer pressed. The girl's head was so low her chin rested on her breastbone. "Si," she whispered.

We had been there two hours by that time, filling out endless forms, giving blood and urine, receiving lectures. But unlike any other group of women I've been in, we didn't talk. Our common denominator, the one which usually floods across language and economic barriers into familiarity, today was one of shame. We were losing life that day, not giving it.

The group kept getting cut back to smaller, more workable units, and finally I was put in a small waiting room with just two other women. We changed into paper bathrobes and paper slippers, and we rustled whenever we moved. One of the women in my room was shivering and an aide brought her a blanket.

"What's the matter?" the aide asked her. "I'm scared," the woman said. "How much will it hurt?" The aide smiled. "Oh, nothing worse than a couple of bad cramps," she said. "This afternoon you'll be dancing a jig."

I began to panic. Suddenly the rhetoric, the abortion marches I'd walked in, the telegrams sent to Albany to counteract the Friends of the Fetus, the Zero Population Growth buttons I'd worn, peeled away, and I was all alone with my microscopic baby. There were just the two of us there, and soon, because it was more convenient for me and my husband, there would be one again.

How could it be that I, who am so neurotic about life that I step over bugs rather than on them, who spend hours planting flowers and vegetables in the spring even though we rent out the house and never see them, who make sure the children are vaccinated and inoculated and filled with vitamin C, could so arbitrarily decide that this life shouldn't be?

"It's not a life," my husband had argued, more to convince himself than me. "It's a bunch of cells smaller than my fingernail."

But any woman who has had children knows that certain feeling in her taut, swollen breasts, and the slight but constant ache in her uterus that signals the arrival of a life. Though I would march myself into blisters for a woman's right to exercise the option of motherhood, I discovered there in the waiting room that I was not the modern woman I thought I was.

When my name was called, my body felt so heavy the nurse had to help me into the examining room. I waited for my husband to burst through the door and yell "stop," but of course, he didn't. I concentrated on three black spots in the acoustic ceiling until they grew in size to the shape of saucers, while the doctor swabbed my insides with antiseptic.

"You're going to feel a burning sensation now," he said, injecting Novocaine into the neck of the womb. The pain was swift and severe, and I twisted to get away from him. He was hurting my baby, I reasoned, and the black saucers quivered in the air. "Stop," I cried. "Please stop." He shook his head, busy with his equipment. "It's too late to stop now," he said. "It'll just take a few more seconds."

What good sports we women are. And how obedient. Physically the pain passed even before the hum of the machine signaled that the vacuuming of my uterus was completed, my baby sucked up like ashes after a cocktail party. Ten minutes start to finish. And I was back on the arm of the nurse.

There were twelve beds in the recovery room. Each one had a gaily flowered draw sheet and a soft green or blue thermal blanket. It was all very feminine. Lying on these beds for an hour or more were the shocked victims of their sex, their full wombs now stripped clean, their futures less encumbered.

It was very quiet in that room. The only voice was that of the nurse, locating the new women who had just come in so she could monitor their blood pressure, and checking out the recovered women who were free to leave.

Juice was being passed about, and I found myself sipping a Dixie cup of Hawaiian Punch. An older woman with tightly curled bleached hair was just getting up from the next bed, "That was no goddamn snap," she said, resting before putting on her miniskirt and high white boots. Other women came and went, some walking out as dazed as they had entered, others with a bounce that signaled they were going right back to Bloomingdale's.

Finally then, it was time for me to leave. I checked out, making an appointment to return in two weeks for an IUD insertion. My husband was slumped in the waiting room, clutching a single yellow rose wrapped in a wet paper towel and stuffed into a baggie.

We didn't talk the whole way home, but just held hands very tightly. At home there were more yellow roses and a tray in bed for me and the children's curiosity to divert.

It had certainly been a successful operation. I didn't bleed at all for two days just as they had predicted, and then I bled only moderately for another four days. Within a week my breasts had subsided and the tenderness vanished, and my body felt mine again instead of the egg-shell it becomes when it's protecting someone else.

My husband and I are back to planning our summer vacation and his career switch.

And it certainly does make more sense not to be having a baby right now—we say that to each other all the time. But I have this ghost now. A very little ghost that only appears when I'm seeing something beautiful, like the full moon on the ocean last weekend. And the baby waves at me. And I wave at the baby. "Of course, we have room," I cry to the ghost. "Of course, we do."

I am "Jane Doe." Using a pseudonym was not the act of cowardice some have said it was, but rather an act of sympathy for the feelings of my family. My daughters were too young then to understand what an abortion was, and my twelve-year-old son (my husband's stepson) reacted angrily when I even broached the subject of abortion to him. Andrew was deeply moralistic, as many children are at that age, and still young enough to feel threatened by the actions of adults; his replies to my "suppose I had an abortion" queries were devastating. "I think abortion is okay if the boy and girl aren't married, and they just made a mistake," he said. "But if you had an abortion, that would be different. You're married, and there is no reason for you not to have another baby. How could you just kill something—no matter how little it is—that's going to grow and have legs and wiggle its fingers?

"I would be furious with you if you had an abortion. I'd lose all respect for you for being so selfish. I'd make you suffer and remind you of it all the time. I would think of ways to be mean. Maybe I'd give you the silent treatment or something.

"If God had meant women to have abortions, He would have put buttons on their stomachs."

I decided to wait until he was older before we discussed it again.

There were other considerations as well. My husband and I had chosen not to tell our parents about the abortion. My mother was very ill at the time and not up to a barrage of phone calls from her friends about "what Linda had written in the newspaper." And there were my parents-in-law, who had always hoped for a male grandchild to carry on the family name. So I avoided the confessional and simply wrote what I thought would be a helpful piece for other women who might have shared my experience.

The result was almost great enough to be recorded on a seismograph. Interpreting the piece as anti-abortion grist, the Right-to-Lifers reproduced it by the thousands and sent it to everyone on their mailing lists. In one Catholic mailing, two sentences were deleted from the article: one that said I was planning to return to the clinic for an IUD insertion, and the other the quote from a middle-aged woman, "That was no goddamn snap." Papers around the country and in Canada ran it, culminating in its appearance in the Canadian edition of the *Reader's Digest,* whose staff took it upon their editorial selves to delete the last paragraph about the "little ghost" because they considered it "mawkish." They also changed the title from "There Just Wasn't Room in Our Lives for Another Baby" to "A Successful Operation" in the hopes that it would change their magazine's pro-abortion image.

Hundreds of letters poured into the *New York Times,* some from Right-to-Lifers, who predictably called me a "murderer," and others from pro-choice zealots who had decided the article was a "plant" and might even have been written by a man. Women wrote about their own abortions, some of which had been positive experiences and some disastrous. One woman even wrote that she wished her own mother had had an abortion instead of subjecting her to a childhood that was "brutal and crushing." Many of the respondents criticized me, quite rightly, for not using birth control in the first place. I was stunned, and so was the *New York Times.* A few weeks later they ran a sampling of the letters and my reply, which follows:

> The varied reactions to my abortion article do not surprise me at all. They are all right. And they are all wrong. There is no issue so fundamental as the giving of life, or the cessation of it. These decisions are the most personal one can ever make and each person facing them

reacts in her own way. It is not black-and-white as the laws governing abortion are forced to be. Rather it is the gray area whose core touches our definition of ourselves that produces "little ghosts" in some, and a sense of relief in others.

I admire the woman who chose not to bear her fourth child because she and her husband could not afford to give that child the future they felt necessary. I admire the women who were outraged that I had failed to use any form of contraception. And I ache for the woman whose mother had given birth to her even though she was not wanted, and thus spent an empty, lonely childhood. It takes courage to take the life of someone else in your own hands, and even more courage to assume responsibility for your own.

I had my abortion over two years ago. And I wrote about it shortly thereafter. It was only recently, however, that I decided to publish it. I felt it was important to share how one person's abortion had affected her, rather than just sit by while the pro and con groups haggled over legislation.

The effect has indeed been profound. Though my husband was very supportive of me, and I, I think, of him, our relationship slowly faltered. As our children are girls, my husband anguished at the possibility that I had been carrying a son. Just a case of male macho, many would argue. But still, that's the way he feels, and it is important. I hope we can get back on a loving track again.

Needless to say, I have an IUD now, instead of the diaphragm that is too easily forgotten. I do not begrudge my husband his lack of contraception. Condoms are awkward. Neither do I feel he should have a vasectomy. It is profoundly difficult for him to face the possibility that he might never have that son. Nor do I regret having the abortion. I am just as much an avid supporter of children by choice as I ever was.

My only regret is the sheer irresponsibility on my part to become pregnant in the first place. I pray to God that it will never happen again. But if it does, I will be equally thankful that the law provides women the dignity to choose whether to bring a new life into the world or not.

A Doctor's View of Abortion

Even as a patient's personal encounter with her own abortion can raise ambiguities and uncertainties about abortion, a physician's first encounter with an abortion can also make the doctor uneasy. Such was the case with Dr. Richard Selzer.

Dr. Selzer, when he wrote the following article, "Abortion," was a surgeon affiliated with Yale University and also a professional writer. Although he was well advanced in his career as a surgeon, he had never witnessed an abortion. Curiosity apparently led him to observe one. What he saw he reported with the seasoned pen of an experienced journalist. His description, which appeared in the January 1976 issue of *Esquire*, is presented in emotively provocative language and with a dramatic flair clearly intended to evoke in us the feelings that he felt and the thoughts that he thought on that day in the operating room on the fourth floor of a great university hospital. Selzer's intense involvement in and unsettling questions about the abortion stand in sharp contrast to the rather detached, matter-of-fact approach of the attending physician, for whom the whole affair was simply a "routine procedure."

But is abortion nothing more than a routine procedure? For Dr. Selzer, as for Ms. Francke, something happened during the abortion that infused the event with a moral ambiguity that rendered it less routine and more problematic. For Selzer, that "something" was centered in the "flick of a needle." What does that "flick" represent? Is that "flick" morally relevant for determining the rightness or wrongness of abortion? Is perhaps Selzer's description the emotionally packed report of a first-time observer whose passions will cool with additional encounters with abortion, and whose initial reactions must accordingly be discounted? These are some of the questions to be kept in mind when reading Selzer's account.

WHAT I SAW
AT THE
ABORTION

Richard Selzer

I am a surgeon. Particularities of sick flesh is everyday news. Escaping blood, all the outpourings of disease—phlegm, pus, vomitus, even those occult meaty tumors that terrify—I see as blood, disease, phlegm, and so on. I touch them to destroy them. But I do not make symbols of them.

What I am saying is that I have seen and I am used to seeing. We are talking about a man who has a trade, who has practiced it long enough to see no news in any of it. Picture this man, then. A professional. In his forties. Three children. Lives in a university town—so, necessarily, well—enlightened? Enough, anyhow. Successful in his work, yes. No overriding religious posture. Nothing special, then, your routine fellow, trying to do his work and doing it well enough. Picture him, this professional, a sort of scientist, if you please, in possession of the standard admirable opinions, positions, convictions, and so on—on this and that matter—on *abortion*, for example.

All right.

Now listen.

It is the western wing of the fourth floor of a great university hospital. I am present because I asked to be present. I wanted to see what I had never seen. An abortion.

The patient is Jamaican. She lies on the table in that state of notable submissiveness I have always seen in patients. Now and then she smiles at one of the nurses as though acknowledging a secret.

A nurse draws down the sheet, lays bare the abdomen. The belly mounds gently in the twenty-fourth week of pregnancy. The chief surgeon paints it with a sponge soaked in red antiseptic. He does this three times, each time a fresh sponge. He covers the area with a sterile sheet, an aperture in its center. He is a kindly man who teaches as he works, who pauses to reassure the woman.

He begins.

A little pinprick, he says to the woman.

He inserts the point of a tiny needle at the midline of the lower portion of her abdomen, on the downslope. He infiltrates local anesthetic into the skin, where it forms a small white bubble.

The woman grimaces.

That is all you will feel, the doctor says. Except for a little pressure. But no more pain.

She smiles again. She seems to relax. She settles comfortably on the table. The worst is over.

The doctor selects a three-and-one-half-inch needle bearing a central stylet. He places the point at the site of the previous injection. He aims it straight up and down, perpendicular. Next he takes hold of her abdomen with his left hand, palming the womb, steadying it. He thrusts with his right hand. The needle sinks into the abdominal wall.

Oh, says the woman quietly.

But I guess it is not pain that she feels. It is more a recognition that the deed is being done.

Another thrust and he has speared the uterus.

We are in, he says.

He has felt the muscular wall of the organ gripping the shaft of his needle. A further slight pressure on the needle advances it a bit more. He takes his left hand from the woman's abdomen. He retracts the filament of the stylet from the barrel of the needle. A small geyser of pale yellow fluid erupts.

We are in the right place, says the doctor. Are you feeling any pain? he says.

She smiles, shakes her head. She gazes at the ceiling.

In the room we are six: two physicians, two nurses, the patient, and me.

The participants are busy, very attentive. I am not at all busy—but I am no less attentive. I want to see.

I see something!

It is unexpected, utterly unexpected, like a disturbance in the earth, a tumultuous jarring. I see something other than what I expected here. I see a movement—a small one. But I have seen it.

And then I see it again. And now I see that it is the hub of the needle in the woman's belly that has jerked. First to one side. Then to the other side. Once more it wobbles, is *tugged*, like a fishing line nibbled by a sunfish.

Again! And I *know!*

It is the *fetus* that worries thus. It is the fetus struggling against the needle. Struggling? How can that be? I think: *that cannot be.* I think: the fetus feels no pain, cannot feel fear, has no *motivation*. It is merely reflex.

I point to the needle.

It is a reflex, says the doctor.

By the end of the fifth month, the fetus weighs about one pound, is about twelve inches long. Hair is on the head. There are eyebrows, eye-lashes. Pale pink nipples show on the chest. Nails are present, at the finger-tips, at the toes.

At the beginning of the sixth month, the fetus can cry, can suck, can make a fist. He kicks, he punches. The mother can feel this, can *see* this. His eyelids, until now closed, can open. He may look up, down, sideways. His grip is very strong. He could support his weight by holding with one hand.

A reflex, the doctor says.

I hear him. But I saw something. I saw *something* in that mass of cells *understand* that it must bob and butt. And I see it again! I have an impulse to shove to the table—it is just a step—seize that needle, pull it out.

We are not six, I think. I think we are *seven.*

Something strangles *there.* An effort, its effort, binds me to it.

I do not shove to the table. I take no little step. It would be ... well, madness. Everyone here wants the needle where it is. Six do. No, *five* do.

I close my eyes. I see the inside of the uterus. It is bathed in ruby gloom. I see the creature curled upon itself. Its knees are flexed. Its head is bent upon its chest. It is in fluid and gently rocks to the rhythm of the distant heartbeat.

It resembles . . . a sleeping infant.

Its place is entered by something. It is sudden. A point coming. A needle!

A spike of *daylight* pierces the chamber. Now the light is extinguished. The needle comes closer in the pool. The point grazes the thigh, and I stir. Perhaps I wake from dozing. The light is there again. I twist and straighten. My arms and legs *push*. My hand finds the shaft—grabs! I *grab*. I bend the needle this way and that. The point probes, touches on my belly. My mouth opens. Could I cry out? All is a commotion and a churning. There is a presence in the pool. An activity! The pool colors, reddens, darkens.

I open my eyes to see the doctor feeding a small plastic tube through the barrel of the needle into the uterus. Drops of pink fluid overrun the rim and spill onto the sheet. He withdraws the needle from around the plastic tubing. Now only the little tube protrudes from the woman's body. A nurse hands the physician a syringe loaded with a colorless liquid. He attaches it to the end of the tubing and injects it.

Prostaglandin, he says.

Ah, well, prostaglandin—a substance found normally in the body. When given in concentrated dosage, it throws the uterus into vigorous contraction. In eight to twelve hours, the woman will expel the fetus.

The doctor detaches the syringe but does not remove the tubing.

In case we must do it over, he says.

He takes away the sheet. He places gauze pads over the tubing. Over all this he applies adhesive tape.

I know. We cannot feed the great numbers. There is no more room. I know, I know. It is woman's right to refuse the risk, to decline the pain of childbirth. And an unwanted child is a very great burden. An unwanted child is a burden to himself. I know.

And yet . . . there is the flick of that needle. I *saw* it. I saw . . . I *felt*—in that room, a pace away, life prodded, life fending off. I saw life avulsed—swept by flood, blackening—then *out*.

There, says the doctor. It's all over. It wasn't too bad, was it? he says to the woman.

She smiles. It is all over. Oh, yes.

And who would care to imagine that from a moist and dark commencement six months before there would ripen the cluster and globule, the sprout and pouch of man?

And who would care to imagine that trapped within the laked pearl and a dowry of yolk would lie the earliest stuff of dream and memory?

It is a persona carried here as well as person, I think. I think it is a signed piece, engraved with a hieroglyph of human genes.

I did not think this until I saw. The flick. The fending off.

We leave the room, the three of us, the doctors.

"Routine procedure," the chief surgeon says.

"All right," I say.

"Scrub nurse says first time you've seen one, Dick. First look at a purge," the surgeon says.

"That's right," I say. "First look."

"Oh, well," he says, "I guess you've seen everything else."

"Pretty much," I say.

"I'm not prying, Doctor," he says, "but was there something on your mind? I'd be delighted to field any questions. . . ."

"No," I say. "No, thanks. Just simple curiosity."

"Okay," he says, and we all shake hands, scrub, change, and go to our calls.

I know, I know. The thing is normally done at sixteen weeks. Well, I've since seen it performed at that stage, too. And seen . . . the flick. But I also know that in the sovereign state of my residence it is hospital policy to warrant the procedure at twenty-four weeks. And that in the great state that is adjacent, policy is enlarged to twenty-eight weeks.

Does this sound like argument? I hope not. I am not trying to argue. I am only saying I've *seen.* The flick. Whatever else may be said in abortion's defense, the vision of that other defense will not vanish from my eyes.

What I saw I saw as that: a *defense,* a motion *from,* an effort *away.* And it has happened that you cannot reason with me now. For what can language do against the truth of what I saw?

Abortion Defended

For a number of years prior to the Supreme Court's 1973 decision in *Roe* v. *Wade* a vigorous national debate was in progress concerning the moral justification of abortion. The debate had its roots deep in Jewish and Christian religious traditions as well as in ancient Greek philosophy. Clearly, the Supreme Court was aware of this debate: The majority opinion delivered by Mr. Justice Blackmun refers to some of the pertinent literature of the debate, including citations from such ancient sources as Aristotle and Augustine, and from such contemporary writers as J. Noonan and G. Williams.

Judith Jarvis Thomson's article, "A Defense of Abortion," reproduced next, has become a classic in the ongoing discussion, which the Supreme Court's ruling by no means silenced. Thomson begins by stating the position of the opponents of abortion, who argue that because the fetus is a human being (a person) from the moment of conception, the fetus is accordingly invested with a right to life which is stronger and more stringent than the mother's right to decide what happens to her body (viz., the right to privacy). Thomson proceeds to attack this position by conjuring up a powerful scenario in which she supposes that you awaken one morning to discover that you are back-to-back in bed with an unconscious famous violinist who has a fatal kidney ailment and who is now plugged into your circulatory system. You are informed that the Society of Music Lovers did this to you, but that it will only be for nine months.

This illustration is not just a silly story. Rather, it is a relevant experiment—not a laboratory experiment, but a thought experiment of the kind philosophers use to test ideas, claims, and points of view. The experimenter seeks to expose any ambiguities and inconsistencies that may exist in those ideas, claims, or points of view that would render them far less acceptable than they were at first glance.

Most of us would be outraged by the thought of being kidnapped so that someone might use our bodies temporarily without our consent. But how different is that situation from a pregnancy? Is not the fetus using the mother's body? Did the mother give her consent to the fetus' use of her womb? If she gave her consent, can she later withdraw it? Are there any circumstances under which the mother's right to use her body as she sees fit outweighs the fetus' right to life? And are there any circumstances under which the mother's right to life outweighs the fetus' right to life? But what does right to life mean? Does it mean the right to the bare minimum of resources required to keep one alive (even if it means being plugged into the mother without her consent)? Or does it mean the right not to be killed by anybody unjustly?

After exploring a series of such questions, Thomson focuses on what she considers to be the crucial flaw in the argument against abortion: Opponents of abortion need to show (as they have not) that abortion is always the *unjust* killing of the fetus. Thomson explores the difference between just and unjust killing and concludes with her own case for the permissibility of some, but not necessarily all, abortions.

A DEFENSE
OF ABORTION[1]

Judith Jarvis Thomson

Most opposition to abortion relies on the premise that the fetus is a human being, a person, from the moment of conception. The premise is argued for, but, as I think, not well. Take, for example, the most common argument. We are asked to notice that the development of a human being from conception through birth into childhood is continuous; then it is said that to draw a line, to choose a point in this development and say "before this point the thing is not a person, after this point it is a person" is to make an arbitrary choice, a choice for which in the nature of things no good reason can be given. It is concluded that the fetus is, or anyway that we had better say it is, a person from the moment of conception. But this conclusion does not follow. Similar things might be said about the development of an acorn into an oak tree, and it does not follow that acorns are oak trees, or that we had better say they are. Arguments of this form are sometimes called "slippery slope arguments"—the phrase is perhaps self-explanatory—and it is dismaying that opponents of abortion rely on them so heavily and uncritically.

I am inclined to agree, however, that the prospects for "drawing a line" in the development of the fetus look dim. I am inclined to think also that we shall probably have to agree that the fetus has already become a human person well before birth. Indeed, it comes as a surprise when one first learns how early in its life it begins to acquire human characteristics. By the tenth week, for example, it already has a face, arms and legs, fingers and toes; it has internal organs, and brain activity is detectable.[2] On the other hand, I think that the premise is false, that the fetus is not a person from the moment of conception. A newly fertilized ovum, a newly implanted clump of cells, is no more a person than an acorn is an oak tree. But I shall not discuss any of this. For it seems to me to be of great interest to ask what happens if, for the sake of argument, we allow the premise. How, precisely, are we supposed to get from there to the conclusion that abortion is morally impermissible? Opponents of abortion commonly spend most of their time establishing that the fetus is a person, and hardly any time explaining the step from there to the impermissibility of abortion. Perhaps they think the step too simple and obvious to require much comment. Or perhaps instead they are simply being economical in argument. Many of those who defend abortion rely on the premise that the fetus is

Source: "A Defense of Abortion" by Judith Jarvis Thomson. *Philosophy and Public Affairs,* vol. 1, no. 1 (Fall 1971). Copyright © 1971 by Princeton University Press. Reprinted with permission of Princeton University Press.

not a person, but only a bit of tissue that will become a person at birth; and why pay out more arguments than you have to? Whatever the explanation, I suggest that the step they take is neither easy nor obvious, that it calls for closer examination than it is commonly given, and that when we do give it this closer examination we shall feel inclined to reject it.

I propose, then, that we grant that the fetus is a person from the moment of conception. How does the argument go from here? Something like this, I take it. Every person has a right to life. So the fetus has a right to life. No doubt the mother has a right to decide what shall happen in and to her body; everyone would grant that. But surely a person's right to life is stronger and more stringent than the mother's right to decide what happens in and to her body, and so outweighs it. So the fetus may not be killed; an abortion may not be performed.

It sounds plausible. But now let me ask you to imagine this. You wake up in the morning and find yourself back to back in bed with an unconscious violinist. A famous unconscious violinist. He has been found to have a fatal kidney ailment, and the Society of Music Lovers has canvassed all the available medical records and found that you alone have the right blood type to help. They have therefore kidnapped you, and last night the violinist's circulatory system was plugged into yours, so that your kidneys can be used to extract poisons from his blood as well as your own. The director of the hospital now tells you, "Look, we're sorry the Society of Music Lovers did this to you—we would never have permitted it if we had known. But still, they did it, and the violinist now is plugged into you. To unplug you would be to kill him. But never mind, it's only for nine months. By then he will have recovered from his ailment, and can safely be unplugged from you." Is it morally incumbent on you to accede to this situation? No doubt it would be very nice of you if you did, a great kindness. But do you *have* to accede to it? What if it were not nine months, but nine years? Or longer still? What if the director of the hospital says, "Tough luck, I agree, but you've now got to stay in bed, with the violinist plugged into you, for the rest of your life. Because remember this. All persons have a right to life, and violinists are persons. Granted you have a right to decide what happens in and to your body, but a person's right to life outweighs your right to decide what happens in and to your body. So you cannot ever be unplugged from him." I imagine you would regard this as outrageous, which suggests that something really is wrong with that plausible-sounding argument I mentioned a moment ago.

In this case, of course, you were kidnapped; you didn't volunteer for the operation that plugged the violinist into your kidneys. Can those who oppose abortion on the ground I mentioned make any exception for a pregnancy due to rape? Certainly. They can say that persons have a right to life only if they didn't come into existence because of rape; or they can say that all persons have a right to life, but that some have less of a right to life than

others, in particular, that those who came into existence because of rape
have less. But these statements have a rather unpleasant sound. Surely the
question of whether you have a right to life at all, or how much of it you
have, shouldn't turn on the question of whether or not you are the product
of a rape. And in fact the people who oppose abortion on the ground I
mentioned do not make this distinction, and hence do not make an exception in case of rape.

Nor do they make an exception for a case in which the mother has to
spend the nine months of her pregnancy in bed. They would agree that
would be a great pity, and hard on the mother; but all the same, all persons
have a right to life, the fetus is a person, and so on. I suspect, in fact, that
they would not make an exception for a case in which, miraculously
enough, the pregnancy went on for nine years, or even the rest of the mother's life.

Some won't even make an exception for a case in which continuation
of the pregnancy is likely to shorten the mother's life; they regard abortion
as impermissible even to save the mother's life. Such cases are nowadays
very rare, and many opponents of abortion do not accept this extreme view.
All the same, it is a good place to begin: a number of points of interest
come out in respect to it.

1. Let us call the view that abortion is impermissible even to save the
mother's life "the extreme view." I want to suggest first that it does not issue
from the argument I mentioned earlier without the addition of some fairly
powerful premises. Suppose a woman has become pregnant, and now
learns that she has a cardiac condition such that she will die if she carries
the baby to term. What may be done for her? The fetus, being a person, has
a right to life, but as the mother is a person too, so has she a right to life.
Presumably they have an equal right to life. How is it supposed to come out
that an abortion may not be performed? If mother and child have an equal
right to life, shouldn't we perhaps flip a coin? Or should we add to the
mother's right to life her right to decide what happens in and to her body,
which everybody seems to be ready to grant—the sum of her rights now
outweighing the fetus' right to life?

The most familiar argument here is the following. We are told that
performing the abortion would be directly killing[3] the child, whereas doing
nothing would not be killing the mother, but only letting her die. Moreover,
in killing the child, one would be killing an innocent person, for the child
has committed no crime, and is not aiming at his mother's death. And then
there are a variety of ways in which this might be continued. (1) But as
directly killing an innocent person is always and absolutely impermissible,
an abortion may not be performed. Or, (2) as directly killing an innocent
person is murder, and murder is always and absolutely impermissible, an
abortion may not be performed.[4] Or, (3) as one's duty to refrain from directly killing an innocent person is more stringent than one's duty to keep

a person from dying, an abortion may not be performed. Or, (4) if one's only options are directly killing an innocent person or letting a person die, one must prefer letting the person die, and thus an abortion may not be performed.[5]

Some people seem to have thought that these are not further premises which must be added if the conclusion is to be reached, but that they follow from the very fact that an innocent person has a right to life.[6] But this seems to me to be a mistake, and perhaps the simplest way to show this is to bring out that while we must certainly grant that innocent persons have a right to life, the theses in (1) through (4) are all false. Take (2), for example. If directly killing an innocent person is murder, and thus is impermissible, then the mother's directly killing the innocent person inside her is murder, and thus is impermissible. But it cannot seriously be thought to be murder if the mother performs an abortion on herself to save her life. It cannot seriously be said that she *must* refrain, that she *must* sit passively by and wait for her death. Let us look again at the case of you and the violinist. There you are, in bed with the violinist, and the director of the hospital says to you, "It's all most distressing, and I deeply sympathize, but you see this is putting an additional strain on your kidneys, and you'll be dead within the month. But you *have* to stay where you are all the same. Because unplugging you would be directly killing an innocent violinist, and that's murder, and that's impermissible." If anything in the world is true, it is that you do not commit murder, you do not do what is impermissible, if you reach around to your back and unplug yourself from that violinist to save your life.

The main focus of attention in writings on abortion has been on what a third party may or may not do in answer to a request from a woman for an abortion. This is in a way understandable. Things being as they are, there isn't much a woman can safely do to abort herself. So the question asked is what a third party may do, and what the mother may do, if it is mentioned at all, is deduced, almost as an afterthought, from what it is concluded that third parties may do. But it seems to me that to treat the matter in this way is to refuse to grant to the mother that very status of person which is so firmly insisted on for the fetus. For we cannot simply read off what a person may do from what a third party may do. Suppose you find yourself trapped in a tiny house with a growing child. I mean a very tiny house, and a rapidly growing child—you are already up against the wall of the house and in a few minutes you'll be crushed to death. The child on the other hand won't be crushed to death; if nothing is done to stop him from growing he'll be hurt, but in the end he'll simply burst open the house and walk out a free man. Now I could well understand it if a bystander were to say, "There's nothing we can do for you. We cannot choose between your life and his, we cannot be the ones to decide who is to live, we cannot intervene." But it cannot be concluded that you too can do nothing, that you cannot attack it to save your life. However innocent the child may be, you do not have to wait passively while it crushes you to death. Perhaps a pregnant woman is vaguely felt to have the status of house, to which we don't allow the right of self-defense. But if the woman houses the child, it should be remembered that she is a person who houses it.

I should perhaps stop to say explicitly that I am not claiming that people have a right to do anything whatever to save their lives. I think, rather, that there are drastic limits to the right of self-defense. If someone threatens you with death unless you torture someone else to death, I think you have not the right, even to save your life, to do so. But the case under consideration here is very different. In our case there are only two people involved, one whose life is threatened, and one who threatens it. Both are innocent: the one who is threatened is not threatened because of any fault, the one who threatens does not threaten because of any fault. For this reason we may feel that we bystanders cannot intervene. But the person threatened can.

In sum, a woman surely can defend her life against the threat to it posed by the unborn child, even if doing so involves its death. And this shows not merely that the theses in (1) through (4) are false; it shows also that the extreme view of abortion is false, and so we need not canvass any other possible ways of arriving at it from the argument I mentioned at the outset.

2. The extreme view could of course be weakened to say that while abortion is permissible to save the mother's life, it may not be performed by a third party, but only by the mother herself. But this cannot be right either. For what we have to keep in mind is that the mother and the unborn child are not like two tenants in a small house which has, by an unfortunate mistake, been rented to both: the mother *owns* the house. The fact that she does adds to the offensiveness of deducing that the mother can do nothing from the supposition that third parties can do nothing. But it does more than this: it casts a bright light on the supposition that third parties can do nothing. Certainly it lets us see that a third party who says "I cannot choose between you" is fooling himself if he thinks this is impartiality. If Jones has found and fastened on a certain coat, which he needs to keep him from freezing, but which Smith also needs to keep him from freezing, then it is not impartiality that says "I cannot choose between you" when Smith owns the coat. Women have said again and again "This body is *my* body!" and they have reason to feel angry, reason to feel that it has been like shouting into the wind. Smith, after all, is hardly likely to bless us if we say to him, "Of course it's your coat, anybody would grant that it is. But no one may choose between you and Jones who is to have it."

We should really ask what it is that says "no one may choose" in the face of the fact that the body that houses the child is the mother's body. It may be simply a failure to appreciate this fact. But it may be something more interesting, namely the sense that one has a right to refuse to lay hands on people, even where it would be just and fair to do so, even where justice seems to require that somebody do so. Thus justice might call for somebody to get Smith's coat back from Jones, and yet you have a right to refuse to be the one to lay hands on Jones, a right to refuse to do physical violence to him. This, I think, must be granted. But then what should be said is not "no one may choose," but only "*I* cannot choose," and indeed not even this, but "*I* will not *act*," leaving it open that somebody else can or should, and in particular that anyone in a position of authority, with the job of securing people's rights, both can and should. So this is no difficulty. I have not been arguing that any given third party must accede to the mother's request that he perform an abortion to save her life, but only that he may.

I suppose that in some views of human life the mother's body is only on loan to her, the loan not being one which gives her any prior claim to it. One who held this view might well think it impartiality to say "I cannot choose." But I shall simply ignore this possibility. My own view is that if a human being has any just, prior claim to anything at all, he has a just, prior claim to his own body. And perhaps this needn't be argued for here anyway, since, as I mentioned, the arguments against abortion we are looking at do grant that the woman has a right to decide what happens in and to her body.

But although they do grant it, I have tried to show that they do not take seriously what is done in granting it. I suggest the same thing will reappear even more clearly when we turn away from cases in which the mother's life is at stake, and attend, as I propose we now do, to the vastly more common cases in which a woman wants an abortion for some less weighty reason than preserving her own life.

3. Where the mother's life is not at stake, the argument I mentioned at the outset seems to have a much stronger pull. "Everyone has a right to life, so the unborn person has a right to life." And isn't the child's right to life weightier than anything other than the mother's own right to life, which she might put forward as ground for an abortion?

This argument treats the right to life as if it were unproblematic. It is not, and this seems to me to be precisely the source of the mistake.

For we should now, at long last, ask what it comes to, to have a right to life. In some views having a right to life includes having a right to be given at least the bare minimum one needs for continued life. But suppose that what in fact *is* the bare minimum a man needs for continued life is something he has no right at all to be given? If I am sick unto death, and the only thing that will save my life is the touch of Henry Fonda's cool hand on my fevered brow, then all the same, I have no right to be given the touch of Henry Fonda's cool hand on my fevered brow. It would be frightfully nice of him to fly in from the West Coast to provide it. It would be less nice, though no doubt well meant, if my friends flew out to the West Coast and carried Henry Fonda back with them. But I have no right at all against anybody that he should do this for me. Or again, to return to the story I told earlier, the fact that for continued life that violinist needs the continued use of your kidneys does not establish that he has a right to be given the continued use of your kidneys. He certainly has no right against you that *you* should give him continued use of your kidneys. For nobody has any right to use your kidneys unless you give him such a right; and nobody has the right against you that you shall give him this right—if you do allow him to go on using your kidneys, this is a kindness on your part, and not something he can claim from you as his due. Nor has he any right against anybody else that *they* should give him continued use of your kidneys. Certainly he had no right against the Society of Music Lovers that they should plug him into you in the first place. And if you now start to unplug yourself, having learned that you will otherwise have to spend nine years in bed with him, there is nobody in the world who must try to prevent you, in order to see to it that he is given something he has a right to be given.

Some people are rather stricter about the right to life. In their view, it does not include the right to be given anything, but amounts to, and only to, the right not to be killed by anybody. But here a related difficulty arises. If everybody is to refrain from killing that violinist, then everybody must refrain from doing a great many different sorts of things. Everybody must refrain from slitting his throat, everybody must refrain from shooting him—and everybody must refrain from unplugging you from him. But does he have a right against everybody that they shall refrain from unplugging you from him? To refrain from doing this is to allow him to continue to use your kidneys. It could be argued that he has a right against us that *we* should allow him to continue to use your kidneys. That is, while he has no right against us that we should give him the use of your kidneys, it might be argued that he anyway has a right against us that we shall not now intervene and deprive him of the use of your kidneys. I shall come back to third-party interventions later. But certainly the violinist has no right against you that *you* shall allow him to continue to use your kidneys. As I said, if you do allow him to use them, it is a kindness on your part, and not something you owe him.

The difficulty I point to here is not peculiar to the right to life. It reappears in connection with all the other natural rights; and it is something which an adequate account of rights must deal with. For present purposes it is enough just to draw attention to it. But I would stress that I am not arguing that people do not have a right to life—quite to the contrary, it seems to me that the primary control we must place on the acceptability of an account of rights is that it should turn out in that account to be a truth that all persons have a right to life. I am arguing only that having a right to life does not guarantee having either a right to be given the use of or a right to be allowed continued use of another person's body—even if one needs it for life itself. So the right to life will not serve the opponents of abortion in the very simple and clear way in which they seem to have thought it would.

4. There is another way to bring out the difficulty. In the most ordinary sort of case, to deprive someone of what he has a right to is to treat him unjustly. Suppose a boy and his small brother are jointly given a box of chocolates for Christmas. If the older boy takes the box and refuses to give his brother any of the chocolates, he is unjust to him, for the brother has been given a right to half of them. But suppose that, having learned that otherwise it means nine years in bed with that violinist, you unplug yourself from him. You surely are not being unjust to him, for you gave him no right to use your kidneys, and no one else can have given him any such right. But we have to notice that in unplugging yourself, you are killing him; and violinists, like everybody else, have a right to life, and thus in the view we were considering just now, the right not to be killed. So here you do what he supposedly has a right you shall not do, but you do not act unjustly to him in doing it.

The emendation which may be made at this point is this: the right to life consists not in the right not to be killed, but rather in the right not to be killed unjustly. This runs a risk of circularity, but never mind: it would enable us to square the fact that the violinist has a right to life with the fact that you do not act unjustly toward him in unplugging yourself, thereby killing him. For if you do not kill him unjustly, you do not violate his right to life, and so it is no wonder you do him no injustice.

But if this emendation is accepted, the gap in the argument against abortion stares us plainly in the face: it is by no means enough to show that the fetus is a person, and to remind us that all persons have a right to life— we need to be shown also that killing the fetus violates its right to life, i.e., that abortion is unjust killing. And is it?

I suppose we may take it as a datum that in a case of pregnancy due to rape the mother has not given the unborn person a right to the use of her body for food and shelter. Indeed, in what pregnancy could it be supposed that the mother has given the unborn person such a right? It is not as if there were unborn persons drifting about the world, to whom a woman who wants a child says "I invite you in."

But it might be argued that there are other ways one can have acquired a right to the use of another person's body than by having been invited to use it by that person. Suppose a woman voluntarily indulges in intercourse, knowing of the chance it will issue in pregnancy, and then she does become pregnant; is she not in part responsible for the presence, in fact the very existence, of the unborn person inside her? No doubt she did not invite it in. But doesn't her partial responsibility for its being there itself give it a right to the use of her body?[7] If so, then her aborting it would be more like the boy's taking away the chocolates, and less like your unplugging yourself from the violinist—doing so would be depriving it of what it does have a right to, and thus would be doing it an injustice.

And then, too, it might be asked whether or not she can kill it even to save her own life: If she voluntarily called it into existence, how can she now kill it, even in self-defense?

The first thing to be said about this is that it is something new. Opponents of abortion have been so concerned to make out the independence of the fetus, in order to establish that it has a right to life, just as its mother does, that they have tended to overlook the possible support they might gain from making out that the fetus is *dependent* on the mother, in order to establish that she has a special kind of responsibility for it, a responsibility that gives it rights against her which are not possessed by any independent person—such as an ailing violinist who is a stranger to her.

On the other hand, this argument would give the unborn person a right to its mother's body only if her pregnancy resulted from a voluntary act, undertaken in full knowledge of the chance a pregnancy might result from it. It would leave out entirely the unborn person whose existence is due to rape. Pending the availability of some further argument, then, we would be left with the conclusion that unborn persons whose existence is due to rape have no right to the use of their mothers' bodies, and thus that aborting them is not depriving them of anything they have a right to and hence is not unjust killing.

And we should also notice that it is not at all plain that this argument really does go even as far as it purports to. For there are cases and cases, and the details make a difference. If the room is stuffy, and I therefore open a window to air it, and a burglar climbs in, it would be absurd to say, "Ah, now he can stay, she's given him a right to the use of her house—for she is partially responsible for his presence there, having voluntarily done what enabled him to get in, in full knowledge that there are such things as burglars, and that burglars burgle." It would be still more absurd to say this if I had had bars installed outside my windows, precisely to prevent burglars from getting in, and a burglar got in only because of a defect in the bars. It remains equally absurd if we imagine it is not a burglar who climbs in, but an innocent person who blunders or falls in. Again, suppose it were like this: people-seeds drift about in the air like pollen, and if you open your windows, one may drift in and take root in your carpets or upholstery. You don't want children, so you fix up your windows with fine mesh screens, the very best you can buy. As can happen, however, and on very, very rare occasions does happen, one of the screens is defective; and a seed drifts in and takes root. Does the person-plant who now develops have a right to the use of your house? Surely not—despite the fact that you voluntarily opened your windows, you knowingly kept carpets and upholstered furniture, and you knew that screens were sometimes defective. Someone may argue that you are responsible for its rooting, that it does have a right to your house, because after all you *could* have lived out your life with bare floors and furniture, or with sealed windows and doors. But this won't do—for by the same token anyone can avoid a pregnancy due to rape by having a hysterectomy, or anyway by never leaving home without a (reliable!) army.

It seems to me that the argument we are looking at can establish at most that there are *some* cases in which the unborn person has a right to the use of its mother's body, and therefore *some* cases in which abortion is unjust killing. There is room for much discussion and argument as to precisely which, if any. But I think we should sidestep this issue and leave it open, for at any rate the argument certainly does not establish that all abortion is unjust killing.

5. There is room for yet another argument here, however. We surely must all grant that there may be cases in which it would be morally indecent to detach a person from your body at the cost of his life. Suppose you learn that what the violinist needs is not nine years of your life, but only one hour: all you need do to save his life is to spend one hour in that bed with him. Suppose also that letting him use your kidneys for that one hour would not affect your health in the slightest. Admittedly you were kidnapped. Admittedly you did not give anyone permission to plug him into you. Nevertheless it seems to me plain you *ought* to allow him to use your kidneys for that hour—it would be indecent to refuse.

Again, suppose pregnancy lasted only an hour, and constituted no threat to life or health. And suppose that a woman becomes pregnant as a result of rape. Admittedly she did not voluntarily do anything to bring about the existence of a child. Admittedly she did nothing at all which would give the unborn person a right to the use of her body. All the same it might well be said, as in the newly emended violinist story, that she *ought* to allow it to remain for that hour—that it would be indecent of her to refuse.

Now some people are inclined to use the term "right" in such a way that it follows from the fact that you ought to allow a person to use your body for the hour he needs, that he has a right to use your body for the hour he needs, even though he has not been given that right by any person or act. They may say that it follows also that if you refuse, you act unjustly toward him. This use of the term is perhaps so common that it cannot be called wrong; nevertheless it seems to me to be an unfortunate loosening of what we would do better to keep a tight rein on. Suppose that box of chocolates I mentioned earlier had not been given to both boys jointly, but was given only to the older boy. There he sits, stolidly eating his way through the box, his small brother watching enviously. Here we are likely to say "You ought not to be so mean. You ought to give your brother some of those chocolates." My own view is that it just does not follow from the truth of this that the brother has any right to any of the chocolates. If the boy refuses to give his brother any, he is greedy, stingy, callous—but not unjust. I suppose that the people I have in mind will say it does follow that the brother has a right to some of the chocolates, and thus that the boy does act unjustly if he refuses to give his brother any. But the effect of saying this is to obscure what we should keep distinct, namely the difference between the boy's refusal in this case and the boy's refusal in the earlier case, in which the box was given to both boys jointly, and in which the small brother thus had what was from any point of view clear title to half.

A further objection to so using the term "right" that from the fact that A ought to do a thing for B, it follows that B has a right against A that A do it for him, is that it is going to make the question of whether or not a man has a right to a thing turn on how easy it is to provide him with it; and this seems not merely unfortunate, but morally unacceptable. Take the case of Henry Fonda again. I said earlier that I had no right to the touch of his cool hand on my fevered brow, even though I needed it to save my life. I said it would be frightfully nice of him to fly in from the West Coast to provide me with it, but that I had no right against him that he should do so. But suppose he isn't on the West Coast. Suppose he has only to walk across the room, place a hand briefly on my brow—and lo, my life is saved. Then surely he ought to do it, it would be indecent to refuse. Is it to be said "Ah, well, it follows that in this case she has a right to the touch of his hand on her brow, and so it would be an injustice to him to refuse?" So that I have a right to it when it is easy for him to provide it, though no right when it's hard? It's rather a shocking idea that anyone's rights should fade away and disappear as it gets harder and harder to accord them to him.

So my own view is that even though you ought to let the violinist use your kidneys for the one hour he needs, we should not conclude that he has a right to do so—we should say that if you refuse, you are, like the boy who owns all the chocolates and will give none away, self-centered and callous, indecent in fact, but not unjust. And similarly, that even supposing a case in which a woman pregnant due to rape ought to allow the unborn person to use her body for the hour he needs, we should not conclude that he has a right to do so; we should conclude that she is self-centered, callous, indecent, but not unjust, if she refuses. The complaints are no less grave; they are just different. However, there is no need to insist on this point. If anyone does wish to deduce "he has a right" from "you ought," then all the same he must surely grant that there are cases in which it is not morally required of you that you allow that violinist to use your kidneys, and in which he does not have a right to use them, and in which you do not do him an injustice if you refuse. And so also for mother and unborn child. Except in such cases as the unborn person has a right to demand it—and we were leaving open the possibility that there may be such cases—nobody is morally *required* to make large sacrifices, of health, of all other interests and concerns, of all other duties and commitments, for nine years, or even for nine months, in order to keep another person alive.

6. We have in fact to distinguish between two kinds of Samaritan: the Good Samaritan and what we might call the Minimally Decent Samaritan. The story of the Good Samaritan, you will remember, goes like this:

> A certain man went down from Jerusalem to Jericho, and fell among thieves, which stripped him of his raiment, and wounded him, and departed, leaving him half dead.
>
> And by chance there came down a certain priest that way; and when he saw him, he passed by on the other side.
>
> And likewise a Levite, when he was at the place, came and looked on him, and passed by on the other side.
>
> But a certain Samaritan, as he journeyed, came where he was; and when he saw him he had compassion on him.
>
> And went to him, and bound up his wounds, pouring in oil and wine, and set him on his own beast, and brought him to an inn, and took care of him.
>
> And on the morrow, when he departed, he took out two pence, and gave them to the host, and said unto him, "Take care of him; and whatsoever thou spendest more, when I come again, I will repay thee."

(Luke 10:30–35)

The Good Samaritan went out of his way, at some cost to himself, to help one in need of it. We are not told what the options were, that is, whether or not the priest and the Levite could have helped by doing less than the Good Samaritan did, but assuming they could have, then the fact they did nothing at all shows they were not even Minimally Decent Samaritans, not because they were not Samaritans, but because they were not even minimally decent.

These things are a matter of degree, of course, but there is a difference, and it comes out perhaps most clearly in the story of Kitty Genovese, who, as you will remember, was murdered while thirty-eight people watched or listened, and did nothing at all to help her. A Good Samaritan would have rushed out to give direct assistance against the murderer. Or perhaps we had better allow that it would have been a Splendid Samaritan who did this, on the ground that it would have involved a risk of death for himself. But the thirty-eight not only did not do this, they did not even trouble to pick up a phone to call the police. Minimally Decent Samaritanism would call for doing at least that, and their not having done it was monstrous.

After telling the story of the Good Samaritan, Jesus said "Go, and do thou likewise." Perhaps he meant that we are morally required to act as the Good Samaritan did. Perhaps he was urging people to do more than is morally required of them. At all events it seems plain that it was not morally required of any of the thirty-eight that he rush out to give direct assistance at the risk of his own life, and that it is not morally required of anyone that he give long stretches of his life—nine years or nine months—to sustaining the life of a person who has no special right (we were leaving open the possibility of this) to demand it.

Indeed, with one rather striking class of exceptions, no one in any country in the world is *legally* required to do anywhere near as much as this for anyone else. The class of exceptions is obvious. My main concern here is not the state of the law in respect to abortion, but it is worth drawing attention to the fact that in no state in this country is any compelled by law to be even a Minimally Decent Samaritan to any person; there is no law under which charges could be brought against the thirty-eight who stood by while Kitty Genovese died. By contrast, in most states in this country women are compelled by law to be not merely Minimally Decent Samaritans, but Good Samaritans to unborn persons inside them. This doesn't by itself settle anything one way or the other, because it may well be argued that there should be laws in this country—as there are in many European countries—compelling at least Minimally Decent Samaritanism.[8] But it does show that there is a gross injustice in the existing state of the law. And it shows also that the groups currently working against liberalization of abortion laws, in fact working toward having it declared unconstitutional for a state to permit abortion, had better start working for the adoption of Good Samaritan laws generally, or earn the charge that they are acting in bad faith.

I should think, myself, that Minimally Decent Samaritan laws would be one thing, Good Samaritan laws quite another, and in fact highly improper. But we are not here concerned with the law. What we should ask is not whether anybody should be compelled by law to be a Good Samaritan, but whether we must accede to a situation in which somebody is being compelled—by nature, perhaps—to be a Good Samaritan. We have, in other words, to look. now at third-party interventions. I have been arguing that no person is morally required to make large sacrifices to sustain the life of another who has no right to demand them, and this even where the sacrifices do not include life itself; we are not morally required to be Good Samaritans or anyway Very Good Samaritans to one another. But what if a man cannot extricate himself from such a situation? What if he appeals to us to extricate him? It seems to me plain that there are cases in which we can, cases in which a Good Samaritan would extricate him. There you are, you were kidnapped, and nine years in bed with that violinist lie ahead of you. You have your own life to lead. You are sorry, but you simply cannot see giving up so much of your life to the sustaining of his. You cannot extricate yourself, and ask us to do so. I should have thought that—in light of his having no right to the use of your body—it was obvious that we do not have to accede to your being forced to give up so much. We can do what you ask. There is no injustice to the violinist in our doing so.

7. Following the lead of the opponents of abortion, I have throughout been speaking of the fetus merely as a person, and what I have been asking is whether or not the argument we began with, which proceeds only from the fetus' being a person, really does establish its conclusion. I have argued that it does not.

But of course there are arguments and arguments, and it may be said that I have simply fastened on the wrong one. It may be said that what is important is not merely the fact that the fetus is a person, but that it is a person for whom the woman has a special kind of responsibility issuing from the fact that she is its mother. And it might be argued that all my analogies are therefore irrelevant—for you do not have that special kind of responsibility for that violinist, Henry Fonda does not have that special kind of responsibility for me. And our attention might be drawn to the fact that men and women both *are* compelled by law to provide support for their children.

I have in effect dealt (briefly) with this argument in section 4 above; but a (still briefer) recapitulation now may be in order. Surely we do not have any such "special responsibility" for a person unless we have assumed it, explicitly or implicitly. If a set of parents do not try to prevent pregnancy, do not obtain an abortion, and then at the time of birth of the child do not put it out for adoption, but rather take it home with them, then they have assumed responsibility for it, they have given it rights, and they cannot *now* withdraw support from it at the cost of its life because they now find it difficult to go on providing for it. But if they have taken all reasonable precautions against having a child, they do not simply by virtue of their biological relationship to the child who comes into existence have a special responsibility for it. They may wish to assume responsibility for it, or they may not wish to. And I am suggesting that if assuming responsibility for it would require large sacrifices, then they may refuse. A Good Samaritan would not refuse—or anyway, a Splendid Samaritan, if the sacrifices that had to be made were enormous. But then so would a Good Samaritan assume responsibility for that violinist; so would Henry Fonda, if he is a Good Samaritan, fly in from the West Coast and assume responsibility for me.

8. My argument will be found unsatisfactory on two counts by many of those who want to regard abortion as morally permissible. First, while I do argue that abortion is not impermissible, I do not argue that it is always permissible. There may well be cases in which carrying the child to term requires only Minimally Decent Samaritanism of the mother, and this is a standard we must not fall below. I am inclined to think it a merit of my account precisely that it does *not* give a general yes or a general no. It allows for and supports our sense that, for example, a sick and desperately frightened fourteen-year-old schoolgirl, pregnant due to rape, may *of course* choose abortion, and that any law which rules this out is an insane law. And it also allows for and supports our sense that in other cases resort to abor-

tion is even positively indecent. It would be indecent in the woman to request an abortion, and indecent in a doctor to perform it, if she is in her seventh month, and wants the abortion just to avoid the nuisance of postponing a trip abroad. The very fact that the arguments I have been drawing attention to treat all cases of abortion, or even all cases of abortion in which the mother's life is not at stake, as morally on a par ought to have made them suspect at the outset.

Secondly, while I am arguing for the permissibility of abortion in some cases, I am not arguing for the right to secure the death of the unborn child. It is easy to confuse these two things in that up to a certain point in the life of the fetus it is not able to survive outside the mother's body; hence removing it from her body guarantees its death. But they are importantly different. I have argued that you are not morally required to spend nine months in bed, sustaining the life of that violinist; but to say this is by no means to say that if, when you unplug yourself, there is a miracle and he survives, you then have a right to turn round and slit his throat. You may detach yourself even if this costs him his life; you have no right to be guaranteed his death, by some other means, if unplugging yourself does not kill him. There are some people who will feel dissatisfied by this feature of my argument. A woman may be utterly devastated by the thought of a child, a bit of herself, put out for adoption and never seen or heard of again. She may therefore want not merely that the child be detached from her, but more, that it die. Some opponents of abortion are inclined to regard this as beneath contempt—thereby showing insensitivity to what is surely a powerful source of despair. All the same, I agree that the desire for the child's death is not one which anybody may gratify, should it turn out to be possible to detach the child alive.

At this place, however, it should be remembered that we have only been pretending throughout that the fetus is a human being from the moment of conception. A very early abortion is surely not the killing of a person, and so is not dealt with by anything I have said here.

Notes

[1] I am very much indebted to James Thomson for discussion, criticism, and many helpful suggestions.

[2] Daniel Callahan, *Abortion: Law, Choice, and Morality* (New York, 1970), p. 373. This book gives a fascinating survey of the available information on abortion. The Jewish tradition is surveyed in David M. Feldman, *Birth Control in Jewish Law* (New York, 1968), Part 5, the Catholic tradition in John T. Noonan, Jr., "An Almost Absolute Value in History," in *The Morality of Abortion*, ed. John T. Noonan, Jr. (Cambridge, Mass., 1970).

[3] The term "direct" in the arguments I refer to is a technical one. Roughly, what is meant by "direct killing" is either killing as an end in itself, or killing as a means to some end, for example, the end of saving someone else's life. See note 6, below, for an example of its use.

[4] Cf. *Encyclical Letter of Pope Pius XI on Christian Marriage*, St. Paul Editions (Boston, n.d.),

p. 32: "however much we may pity the mother whose health and even life is gravely imperiled in the performance of the duty allotted to her by nature, nevertheless what could ever be a sufficient reason for excusing in any way the direct murder of the innocent? This is precisely what we are dealing with here." Noonan (*The Morality of Abortion*, p. 43) reads this as follows: "What cause can ever avail to excuse in any way the direct killing of the innocent? For it is a question of that."

[5]The thesis in (4) is in an interesting way weaker than those in (1), (2), and (3): they rule out abortion even in cases in which both mother *and* child will die if the abortion is not performed. By contrast, one who held the view expressed in (4) could consistently say that one needn't prefer letting two persons die to killing one.

[6]Cf. the following passage from Pius XII, *Address to the Italian Catholic Society of Midwives:* "The baby in the maternal breast has the right to life immediately from God.—Hence there is no man, no human authority, no science, no medical, eugenic, social, economic or moral 'indication' which can establish or grant a valid juridical ground for a direct deliberate disposition of an innocent human life, that is a disposition which looks to its destruction either as an end or as a means to another end perhaps in itself not illicit.—The baby, still not born, is a man in the same degree and for the same reason as the mother" (quoted in Noonan, *Morality of Abortion*, p. 45).

[7]The need for a discussion of this argument was brought home to me by members of the Society for Ethical and Legal Philosophy, to whom this paper was originally presented.

[8]For a discussion of the difficulties involved, and a survey of the European experience with such laws, see *The Good Samaritan and the Law*, ed. James M. Ratcliffe (New York, 1966).

Another Abortion Ruling

A State of Missouri statute says in its preamble that the life of each human being begins at conception. The statute goes on to stipulate that

1. Unborn children must be provided all the rights of (adult) persons
2. Prior to performing an abortion, a physician must make every effort to ascertain the viability of the fetus if that physician has reason to believe that the fetus may be 20 weeks or more old
3. Public employees and public facilities may not be used to performing or assist in the performing of abortions unless they are necessary to save the life of the mother
4. The use of public funds, facilities, and employees to counsel or to encourage a woman to have an abortion unless it is necessary to save her life is forbidden

The Eighth Circuit Court of Appeals struck down this statute on the grounds that it violated the rights created by *Roe* v. *Wade*. The state, in the person of William Webster, the Attorney General of Missouri, appealed to the Supreme Court. In its decision, the Court found that the statute does not violate *Roe* v. *Wade*. It, therefore, overturned the Court of Appeals decision.

The Supreme Court examines each aspect of the Missouri statute and shows why it thinks it is consistent with previous findings. The way the Court argues can be referred to as "narrow"—it makes few, if any, inferences from the actual statements of the previous decisions. One might, for example, think that if *Roe* v. *Wade* made abortion a private decision between woman and physician, then her reasons for it should not matter. If this is so, then the restriction on abortions performed in public facilities and by public employees seems to conflict with that privacy, for the Missouri statute rules out all reasons except danger to the life of the mother. It is difficult to see clearly how the Court justifies this restriction on abortion rights.

Does this decision violate the spirit of privacy mentioned in *Roe*? Should one even try to find the "spirit" of a law? Ask yourself if the two decisions contradict each other. Justice O'Connor said they do not. Conversely, Justice Scalia said that there is a clear contradiction, because the *Webster* finding allowed "legislative imposition on the judgment of the physician."

WILLIAM L. WEBSTER, ATTORNEY GENERAL OF MISSOURI, ET AL., APPELLANTS

v.

REPRODUCTIVE HEALTH SERVICES ET AL.

No. 88-505
Argued April 26, 1989
Decided July 3, 1989
ON APPEAL FROM THE UNITED STATES
COURT OF APPEALS
FOR THE EIGHTH CIRCUIT
Citation
—S.Ct.—
1989 WL 70950 (U.S.)

THE CHIEF JUSTICE delivered the opinion of the Court ...

II

Decision of this case requires us to address four sections of the Missouri Act: (a) the preamble; (b) the prohibition on the use of public facilities or employees to perform abortions; (c) the prohibition on public funding of abortion counseling; and (d) the requirement that physicians conduct viability tests prior to performing abortions. We address these seriatim.

A

The Act's preamble, as noted, sets forth "findings" by the Missouri legisla-ture that "[t]he life of each human being begins at conception," and that "[u]nborn children have protectable interests in life, health, and well-being" ...

In our view, the preamble does not by its terms regulate abortion or any other aspect of appellees' medical practice. The Court has emphasized that *Roe* v. *Wade* implies no limitation on the authority of a State to make a value judgment favoring childbirth over abortion ... The preamble can be read simply to express that sort of value judgment ...

B

Section 188.210 provides that "[i]t shall be unlawful for any public em-ployee within the scope of his employment to perform or assist an abortion, not necessary to save the life of the mother," while section 188.215 makes it "unlawful for any public facility to be used for the purpose of performing or assisting an abortion not necessary to save the life of the mother," ...

Due Process Clauses generally confer no affirmative right to govern-mental aid, even where such aid may be necessary to secure life, liberty, or property interests of which the government itself may not deprive the individual ... the Court upheld a Connecticut welfare regulation under which Medicaid recipients received payments for medical services related to childbirth, but not for nontherapeutic abortions ...

The State may have made childbirth a more attractive alternative, thereby influencing the woman's decision, but it has imposed no restriction on access to abortions that was not already there. The indigency that may make it difficult—and in some cases, perhaps, impossible—for some women to have abortions is neither created nor in any way affected by the Connecticut regulation ...

The State's decision here to use public facilities and staff to encourage childbirth over abortion places no governmental obstacle in the path of a woman who chooses to terminate her pregnancy ...

Missouri's refusal to allow public employees to perform abortions in public hospitals leaves a pregnant woman with the same choices as if the State had chosen not to operate any public hospitals at all ...

Having held that the State's refusal to fund abortion does not violate *Roe* v. *Wade,* it strains logic to reach a contrary result for the use of public facilities and employees. If the State may "make a value judgment favoring childbirth over abortion and ... implement that judgment by the allocation of public funds," surely it may do so through the allocation of other public resources, such as hospitals and medical staff . . .

Nothing in the Constitution requires States to enter or remain in the business of performing abortions. Nor, as appellees suggest, do private physicians and their patients have some kind of constitutional right of access to public facilities for the performance of abortions . . .

Thus we uphold the Act's restrictions on the use of public employees and facilities for the performance or assistance of non-therapeutic abortions.

C

Appellees contend that they are not "adversely" affected under the State's interpretation of section 188.205, and therefore that there is no longer a case or controversy before us on this question.

D

Section 188.029 of the Missouri Act provides:
"Before a physician performs an abortion on a woman he has reason to believe is carrying an unborn child of twenty or more weeks gestational age, the physician shall first determine if the unborn child is viable by using and exercising that degree of care, skill, and proficiency commonly exercised by the ordinarily skillful, careful, and prudent physician engaged in similar practice under the same or similar conditions. In making this determination of viability, the physician shall perform or cause to be performed such medical examinations and tests as are necessary to make a finding of the gestational age, weight, and lung maturity of the unborn child and shall enter such findings and determination of viability in the medical record of the mother . . ."

As with the preamble, the parties disagree over the meaning of this statutory provision. The State emphasizes the language of the first sentence, which speaks in terms of the physician's determination of viability being made by the standards of ordinary skill in the medical profession . . . Appellees stress the language of the second sentence, which prescribes such "tests as are necessary" to make a finding of gestational age, fetal weight, and lung maturity . . .

We think the viability-testing provision makes sense only if the second sentence is read to require only those tests that are useful to making subsidiary findings as to viability. If we construe this provision to require a physician to perform those tests needed to make the three specified findings in all circumstances, including when the physician's reasonable professional judgment indicates that the tests would be irrelevant to determining viability or even dangerous to the mother and the fetus, the second sentence of section 188.029 would conflict with the first sentence's requirement that a physician apply his reasonable professional skill and judgment . . .

The viability-testing provision of the Missouri Act is concerned with promoting the State's interest in potential human life rather than in maternal health. Section 188.029 creates what is essentially a presumption of viability at 20 weeks, which the physician must rebut with tests indicating that the fetus is not viable prior to performing an abortion. It also directs the physician's determination as to viability by specifying consideration, if feasible, of gestational age, fetal weight, and lung capacity . . .

In *Roe* v. *Wade,* the Court recognized that the State has "important and legitimate" interests in protecting maternal health and in the potentiality of human life . . . During the second trimester, the State "may, if it chooses, regulate the abortion procedure in ways that are reasonably related to maternal health" . . . After viability, when the State's interest in potential human life was held to become compelling, the State "may, if it chooses, regulate, and even proscribe, abortion except where it is necessary, in appropriate medical judgment, for the preservation of the life or health of the mother" . . .

The rigid Roe framework is hardly consistent with the notion of a Constitution cast in general terms, as ours is, and usually speaking in general principles, as ours does. The key elements of the Roe framework—trimesters and viability—are not found in the text of the Constitution or in any place else one would expect to find a constitutional principle. Since the bounds of the inquiry are essentially indeterminate, the result has been a web of legal rules that have become increasingly intricate, resembling a code of regulations rather than a body of constitutional doctrine . . . As JUSTICE WHITE has put it, the trimester framework has left this Court to serve as the country's "ex officio medical board with powers to approve or disapprove medical and operative practices and standards throughout the United States" . . .

We do not see why the State's interest in protecting potential human life should come into existence only at the point of viability, and that there should therefore be a rigid line allowing state regulation after viability but prohibiting it before viability . . .

The tests that section 188.029 requires the physician to perform are designed to determine viability. The State here has chosen viability as the point at which its interest in potential human life must be safeguarded . . .

It is true that the tests in question increase the expense of abortion, and regulate the discretion of the physician in determining the viability of the fetus. Since the tests will undoubtedly show in many cases that the fetus is not viable, the tests will have been performed for what were in fact second-trimester abortions. But we are satisfied that the requirement of these tests permissibly furthers the State's interest in protecting potential human life, and we therefore believe section 188.029 to be constitutional ...

Roe v. *Wade* sought to establish a constitutional framework for judging state regulation of abortion during the entire term of pregnancy. That framework sought to deal with areas of medical practice traditionally sub-ject to state regulation, and it sought to balance once and for all by refer-ence only to the calendar the claims of the State to protect the fetus as a form of human life against the claims of a woman to decide for herself whether or not to abort a fetus she was carrying. The experience of the Court in applying Roe v. Wade in later cases, suggests to us that there is wisdom in attempting to elaborate the abstract differences between a "fun-damental right" to abortion, ... [a] limited fundamental constitutional right, ... or a liberty interest protected by the Due Process Clause, which we believe it to be. The Missouri testing requirement here is reasonably designed to ensure that abortions are not performed where the fetus is viable—an end which all concede is legitimate—and that is sufficient to sustain its constitutionality.

Because none of the challenged provisions of the Missouri Act prop-erly before us conflict with the Constitution, the judgment of the Court of Appeals is reversed.

A group of bioethicists filed a brief on behalf of Reproductive Services. They argued that the Missouri statute conflicts with *Roe* and with the ethical practice of medicine, and that the Court, therefore, ought not to overturn the original decision made by the Eighth Court of Appeals. The bioethicists' claims are simple and straightforward:

The statute violates the right to privacy.
The right to privacy insures a doctor–patient relationship free of gov-ernmental influences.
The statute censures the free speech of physicians by restricting what they may counsel patients.
If privacy is eroded by a finding for Webster, then what will prevent any state from prohibiting any medical procedure its legislature finds distasteful?

Did the Court address these issues? Are these arguments "narrow" or "wide" in the previous sense given these terms in the introduction to this reading?

IN THE
SUPREME COURT OF THE UNITED STATES
October Term, 1988

No. 88-605

WILLIAM L. WEBSTER, et al.,
APPELLANTS,

v.

REPRODUCTIVE HEALTH SERVICES, et al.,
APPELLEES.

On Appeal from the United States Court of Appeals
For the Eighth Circuit

BRIEF FOR BIOETHICISTS FOR PRIVACY
AS AMICUS CURIAE SUPPORTING APPELLEES

Interest of Amicus

Amicus is an ad hoc group of 57 philosophers, theologians, attorneys, and physicians from 20 states and the District of Columbia who teach medical ethics to medical students and/or physicians, or who have a major professional interest in medical ethics. Although the precise beliefs and practices of the members of this group vary, as do their professional and religious backgrounds, the members believe that permitting competent adults to make important, personal medical decisions in consultation with their physician is a fundamental principle of medical ethics, and that the doctor-patient relationship deserves the constitutional protection this Court has afforded it under the right of privacy. Medical ethics, individual autonomy, and professional accountability will all be fostered by preserving the right of privacy. Compromising the right of privacy, and substituting the state as the decision-maker in the doctor-patient relationship, would undermine principles of medical ethics and compromise principles of good patient care and good medical practice to the detriment of physicians and patients alike.

Summary of Argument

I

Missouri asks this Court to renounce a right of privacy which this Court has described as "older than the Bill of Rights." This Court has provided lawmakers with a consistent and coherent set of parameters for identifying what the right of privacy protects, especially with respect to decisions about abortion. Abandonment of the right of privacy would permit state legislatures to control personal decisions that are now made in the doctor-patient relationship. Without the protection of the right of privacy, each legislature would be free to impose its values by dictating the outcome of what are and should be personal medical care decisions.

II

A. As this Court has recognized, a woman's right to decide to terminate a pregnancy is exercised within the context of the doctor-patient relationship. The ancient tradition of safeguarding the privacy and freedom of unfettered communication between doctor and patient is embodied in ethical precepts which the law recognizes and supports. The Missouri legislation is a direct, governmental attack on this relationship, thereby jeopardizing patients' rights, and compromising physicians' ethical obligations to their patients.

B. Both legal and ethical principles require physicians to discuss health risks that are caused or exacerbated by pregnancy and information concerning possible fetal genetic or congenital disorders. The Missouri statutes prohibit such discussions by publicly-funded physicians if they may lead to a decision to abort. Physicians' speech is censored and patients are deprived by the state of critical information on which to base decisions about pregnancy. The ethical practice of medicine is made unlawful and the health and well-being of pregnant patients is likely to be seriously jeopardized as a result. Missouri gives "any taxpayer" of the state standing to enforce its restrictions in the courts. Thus, whatever is said or done in the privacy of the doctor-patient relationship is subject to public scrutiny at any time.

C. Without the constitutional right of privacy, there would be no constitutional principle that would prevent a state from prohibiting patients from using *any* medically recognized and accepted treatments which a majority of the legislature happens to disfavor. Worse, a state would be free to prevent physicians from even telling their patients about such treatment. This differs dramatically from a state's merely refusing to pay for certain treatments.

Advances in medical science have made possible new methods of treatment for a wide variety of medical conditions, often controversial, and with the potential for profound consequences for the patient. Scientific progress has increased the importance of the doctor-patient relationship, for it is only in this context that difficult personal medical decisions can be made taking into consideration all of the medical and personal consequences that may ensue. Thus there is even more reason today to uphold the constitutional protection of decisions made in the privacy of the doctor-patient relationship than when *Roe* v. *Wade* was decided. For these reasons the decision of the court of appeals should be affirmed.

3

EUTHANASIA

Joseph Dohr, a seventy-eight year-old man, was in the hospital being kept alive by machines. That part of his nervous system that controlled all vital functions was not working. The attending physician had told Mr. Dohr's wife and his daughters that the condition was irreversible and that he would die. Mr. Dohr was being kept alive by machines that were feeding him, breathing for him, and draining his body of wastes. Given that information, the family asked the attending physician to disconnect the life-support systems that were keeping Mr. Dohr alive. The physician refused. A nurse who was caring for Mr. Dohr disconnected his oxygen supply. In fewer than ten minutes, there was no heartbeat, and Mr. Dohr was pronounced dead. When defending his action, the nurse stated that he had taken the action because the support systems used with the patient were "maintaining his existence but not his life."

Harriet Shulan, 82 years old, had refused a heart-bypass operation on the grounds that she was "too old for such things." Finally she relented and underwent the surgery. After the operation, her condition steadily worsened; she would not eat and could not cough out body fluids. Her daughter agreed to her mother's being temporarily placed on a respirator in spite of Ms. Shulan's objections. Ms. Shulan said, "I am 82 years old, and I don't want this done." Yet tubes were placed in her nose and into her throat and into her arms. Once she was placed on a respirator, it was illegal according to the state's laws to disconnect Ms. Shulan from the life-saving support systems. Although she could not talk because of the tubes in her throat, Ms. Shulan repeatedly wrote notes to her daughter asking to be freed from the systems that were keeping her alive. "Please let me die," she wrote.

Roswell Gilbert's wife was dying slowly from degenerative and incurable diseases. Mr. Gilbert and his wife had been married 51 years, and he could not bear to see her in such misery. To end his wife's worsening suffering, Mr. Gilbert obtained a gun and fired two shots into his wife's head. For this act he was convicted of first-degree murder.

All these are actual cases. Each raises a distinctive issue relating to the question of euthanasia, a word derived from two Greek words meaning "pleasant death." Regardless of their differences, all these cases contain several common themes.

First there is the issue of individual *autonomy;* that is, the right of individuals to decide important issues for themselves and not have these issues decided for them by others. Where decisions are made for others, often for their benefit, we say that these decisions are *paternalistic.*

Cases of euthanasia in which the patient decides are classified as *voluntary.* If the patient cannot decide, such as an infant or a comatose person, a decision for euthanasia is classified as *nonvoluntary* to signify that the decision was made by others. The expression *nonvoluntary* is used to avoid the connotation of *in*voluntary; namely, that the decision was made *against* the will of another, as opposed to being made without full knowledge or the will of another.

Notice that there are some differences depending on cases. An infant cannot make decisions; we always act in a paternalistic way toward infants. A comatose patient cannot make decisions, but may have left clear instructions concerning euthanasia. An act of euthanasia, if requested by such a person, would be termed voluntary and not paternalistic. With a comatose stranger, a decision for euthanasia would have to be considered paternalistic and nonvoluntary with the hope that it would not have been involuntary if the person had been conscious.

Keeping Ms. Shulan on the respirator (as well as placing her on it initially) is an example of a paternalistic action done against Ms. Shulan's will. She wanted to have the treatment withdrawn so she could die. If the respirator had been withdrawn, it would have been a case of voluntary euthanasia. This exercise in clarifying terms shows the importance of definitions in helping achieve the clarity needed for moral judgments.

The case of Ms. Gilbert raises the issue of the right of individuals to terminate their own lives or to seek assistance in doing so. Mr. Dohr was not in a position to make decisions for himself, so the question is: Who has the right to decide in cases when the patient cannot? This question also emerges with considerable force in those cases when infants are born with life-threatening disabilities and require extensive, and expensive, therapies to prolong their lives even when death from the disabilities is assured. Cases involving the very young and the very old force us to consider whether age is a morally relevant factor in decision making.

A second set of issues surrounds the distinction between active and passive euthanasia. In *active* euthanasia, someone (the physician, a friend the patient) commits an act that produces death, usually sooner and in a manner that would not have occurred had nothing or something else been done. In *passive* euthanasia, something not done results in a death, usually sooner and in a manner that would not have occurred had something been done. Often with passive euthanasia a treatment is *withheld*. Some medical ethicists also characterize *withdrawing* treatment as passive euthanasia, because it seems to be more akin to the notion of letting someone die, which is basic to passive euthanasia, and quite different from the deliberate taking of a life, which characterizes active euthanasia. At first glance, there seems to be a major difference between active and passive euthanasia, but does this distinction really stand up under analysis?

Combining the foregoing distinctions gives us four possibilities: active voluntary and active nonvoluntary euthanasia; passive voluntary; and passive nonvoluntary euthanasia. (Notice that active involuntary euthanasia is, on the face of it, always wrong, seemingly bordering on murder.) Mr. Gilbert did something that was active (he pulled the trigger). Ms. Shulan voluntarily asked not to be connected to life-sustaining machinery, preferring the passive approach to treatment. Mr. Dohr's nurse made a decision for his patient, a decision he concluded Mr. Dohr would have made for himself, and disconnected Mr. Dohr's oxygen supply. This was certainly an example of involuntary euthanasia; whether it is active or passive depends on how you classify the withdrawing of lifesaving treatment once it has been given.

There appears to be a major ethical difference between active nonvoluntary euthanasia (deciding for others to terminate their lives) and passive voluntary euthanasia (withholding treatment at a patient's request). Ranking these four possibilities in order of their moral acceptability (from most acceptable to least acceptable) might give us the following list:

Passive voluntary euthanasia
Passive nonvoluntary euthanasia
Active voluntary euthanasia
Active nonvoluntary euthanasia

But do these distinctions really stand up? The article by James Rachels in this section explores the distinction between active and passive euthanasia, and his conclusion may surprise you.

A third issue relates to the morality of suicide. From autonomy, the right of individuals to make decisions about things affecting their lives and, in these cases, their own deaths, it seems to follow that each of us has the right to commit suicide. But are there limits to autonomy? Does a person have the right to suicide? Many ethical theories have denied that there is such a right. Even so, some philosophers, who deny that there is a right to suicide, say that a voluntary decision on a patient's part to refuse medical treatment is not an act of suicide.

A fourth issue involves the competence of the patient to decide for or against one's own life. The notion of autonomy presupposes at least that a person is capable of making a decision, is not mentally impaired, and understands the relevant facts. Because these requirements for autonomy are often difficult to meet in the face of serious problems, some have argued that the time to make the decision not to have one's life sustained by mechanical means is long before the need for such a decision arrives. Some people execute a document known as a living will to guarantee that their autonomy will be respected in the future. Some states, however, do not accept living wills as legally binding, and in other jurisdictions their status is dubious unless supplemented with additional legal documentation.

A fifth set of issues relates to the professional obligations of health-care providers. Physicians have many duties toward patients, the duty to sustain life being a principal one. But this duty often conflicts with the principle of patient autonomy, and we have already seen how the autonomy of the patient who decides to refuse medical treatment can conflict with a medical decision to apply life-sustaining therapies to the terminally ill.

Another important moral principle is to apply a rule universally and treat all persons alike. This is especially difficult to do in cases involving terminally ill patients, since each case varies so much from the others, unless one takes as the principal rule the duty to sustain life. This seems to be a principle that can be applied universally regardless of circumstances, and physicians are attracted to it for other reasons as well. Their training emphasizes the prolonging of life. To assist someone in dying or to refrain from using all available means to sustain life violates the commitment to life basic to a physician's training.

The medical profession is committed to the principle of beneficence: Maximize benefits and minimize harm. Although it has been claimed that the primary guiding principle is "Above all, do no harm," this is a principle whose actual use is limited to relatively rare situations, in which benefits are few, unknown, or unlikely. In general, almost any medical treatment will produce some possible benefit, which will then be weighed against possible harm. But does it really benefit a terminally ill patient to be kept alive, to be sustained in pain and suffering, when there is no hope for recovery? Isn't it really harmful to do things that cause extreme pain to patients? Would it not be less harmful to help them die by either withholding or withdrawing mechanical means of supporting life?

Physicians reply that it would cause more harm *in the long run* to expect physicians to cooperate in promoting someone's death. It is much better for society, they say, if physicians use every means possible to sustain life. Especially is this true in emergency situations when decisions have to be made immediately and there is no time for a philosophical discussion. The best rule in such circumstances, they argue, is to do everything possible to keep the patient alive.

A final set of issues pertains to rules for behavior based on the consideration of consequences. What rules regarding euthanasia should we have? It is not so easy to answer this question. Consider: One could argue that the best rule is always to try to keep patients alive. But when the consequences of this decision prolong the patient's suffering and pain, should we not also have a rule that says it is wrong to cause unnecessary suffering?

Another consequence to be considered is the effect the medical decision has on the patient's family. But how do we balance the patient's welfare with the concerns of the patient's family? Suppose the patient preferred death, even though this would cause suffering, guilt, and general unhappiness for the family. Whose interests should take precedence in cases like this, the patient's or the family's?

Sometimes medical practitioners speak of "treating the family" by allowing a comatose patient to be sustained by life-saving therapies even when the patient is not conscious and will never recover. What can treating the family mean if not that the interests of the patient are being sacrificed for the interest of the family? This is in conflict with the moral principle that holds that the rights of an individual may never be sacrificed for the happiness of a greater number of people.

The legal right to die was challenged by the state of Missouri when it refused to allow life-preserving treatment to be removed from Nancy Cruzan, who had been in a persistent vegetative state since 1983. Her parents and sister wanted her to be allowed to die. The case was decided by the U.S. Supreme Court in 1990. The court held that if there is clear evidence that a patient does not want, or never would have wanted, treatment to begin or to be continued, then that treatment may not be started or must be discontinued. The court held that it is up to each state to decide what will count as sufficient evidence of this desire. Thus, while the court was seen to uphold a right to die, it did so in the decision where it held that Missouri's refusal to allow the withdrawal of artificial feeding of Nancy Cruzan was constitutional because it was based on what Missouri took to be reasonable grounds for sufficient evidence in such cases. The State of Missouri subsequently withdrew its opposition, and a probate court judge in the state authorized the removal of Nancy Cruzan's feeding tube. She died late in 1990, twelve days after the removal of the tube.

In its decision, the Supreme Court explicitly held that this right to die was a liberty right (under the Fourteenth Amendment) and not a right to privacy. Liberty rights are those which can be seen as maximizing freedom by minimizing outside interference in our actions, except where such interference would clearly promote the greatest amount of liberty for each (this should remind you of a version of utilitarianism). Examples of liberty are freedom from unlawful arrest or restraint; freedom to own, control, and use property; freedom to move around from place to place except where this is legally restricted, such as by a court order to keep a certain distance from a person you may have been threatening. The right to privacy is often seen as an integral part of the concept of liberty. The right to privacy is meant to guarantee little or no interference in personal relationships or personal and fundamental choices.

Remember that in *Roe* v. *Wade* abortion was seen as a right to privacy. Why would the court not see the right to die under the rubric of a right to privacy? Notice that freedom of speech would seem to fall under liberty rights and not a right to privacy.

As is the case with many topics in ethics, euthanasia often raises more questions than answers. But knowing which questions to ask can sometimes point us in the direction of answers. Added to the difficulty of assessing the ethical implications of a medical issue is the problem that while one is living through the issue there may not be time, or the inclination, to attempt to sort out the ethical issues involved. This sort of analysis comes after the fact and is much like quarterbacking a football game on Monday morning. It is much easier to decide what should have been done when the outcome is known, less easy to know what action is the best when the outcome is in doubt.

The following essays probe the issues surrounding euthanasia and can help us discover what the important issues are arising from a consideration of this difficult topic. To avoid being kept alive by artificial means when all hope of recovery is gone, some people execute a "living will" such as the one shown on the opposite page. Not all states recognize the legitimacy of such documents, however.

Do We Have a Right to Die?

Several articles in medical ethics have already become classics. This essay by Philippa Foot is one of these. Its contribution lies in clarifying a number of important terms and concepts that appear again and again in discussions of medical ethics.

For example, it is frequently said that one has a right to die. Usually the term "right" is used to refer to something that is a good. As Foot observes, we don't say that we have a right to garbage or polluted air. Since

To My Family, My Physician, My Lawyer
And All Others Whom It May Concern

Death is as much a reality as birth, growth, and aging—it is the one certainty of life. In anticipation of decisions that may have to be made about my own dying and as an expression of my right to refuse treatment, I, _____, being of sound mind, make this statement of my wishes and instructions concerning treatment.   (print name)

By means of this document, which I intend to be legally binding, I direct my physician and other care providers, my family, and any surrogate designated by me or appointed by a court, to carry out my wishes. If I become unable, by reason of physical or mental incapacity, to make decisions about my medical care, let this document provide the guidance and authority needed to make any and all such decisions.

If I am permanently unconscious or there is no reasonable expectation of my recovery from a seriously incapacitating or lethal illness or condition, I do not wish to be kept alive by artificial means. I request that I be given all care necessary to keep me comfortable and free of pain, even if pain-relieving medications may hasten my death, and I direct that no life-sustaining treatment be provided except as I or my surrogate specifically authorize.

This request may appear to place a heavy responsibility upon you, but by making this decision according to my strong convictions, I intend to ease that burden. I am acting after careful consideration and with understanding of the consequences of your carrying out my wishes. *List optional specific provisions in the space below. (See other side.)*

───── **Durable Power of Attorney for Health Care Decisions** (Cross out if you do not wish to use this section) ─────

To effect my wishes, I designate _____, residing at _____
_____, (phone #) _____, (or if he or she shall
for any reason fail to act, _____, residing at _____
_____, (phone #) _____) as my health care
surrogate—that is, my attorney-in-fact regarding any and all health care decisions to be made for me, including the decision
to refuse life-sustaining treatment—if I am unable to make such decisions myself. This power shall remain effective during
and not be affected by my subsequent illness, disability or incapacity. My surrogate shall have authority to interpret my
Living Will, and shall make decisions about my health care as specified in my instructions or, when my wishes are not clear,
as the surrogate believes to be in my best interests. I release and agree to hold harmless my health care surrogate from any
and all claims whatsoever arising from decisions made in good faith in the exercise of this power.

I sign this document knowingly, voluntarily, and after care-   Witness _____
ful deliberation, this _____ day of _____,   Printed Name _____
19____.   Address _____
                                                                      _____
_____
(signature)
Address _____   Witness _____
_____   Printed Name _____
                                                                      Address _____
I do hereby certify that the within document was executed and   _____
acknowledged before me by the principal this _____ day of
_____, 19____.

_____   Copies of this document have been given to:
Notary Public

This Living Will expresses my personal treatment preferences. The fact that I may have also executed a declaration in the form recommended by state law should not be construed to limit or contradict this Living Will, which is an expression of my common-law and constitutional rights.

(Optional) my Living Will is registered with Concern for Dying (Registry No. _____)

Distributed by Concern for Dying, 250 West 57th Street, New York, NY 10107 (212) 246-6962

Figure 1
Reprinted by permission of Concern for Dying, 250 West 57th Street, New York, NY 10107.

life is a good thing, and death is viewed as a bad thing, it is at first difficult to know what sense could be made out of the claim that we have a right to die. It would only be in those cases in which death is a good or happy event that one could talk about a right to such a death. But what conditions make death preferable to life? Or, to put the questions differently, when does life—which is usually a good thing—become a bad thing? Is there ever a time when life becomes not worth living? One possible answer might be when consciousness has sunk to a very low level, as in extreme senility or severe brain damage. But even in these cases we come up against human fallibility. Mistakes can be made, and there could be highly undesirable side effects of making euthanasia legal. Additionally, we have great moral reluctance to say that euthanasia is justifiable when the person cannot voluntarily agree to it.

One conclusion emerges from Foot's analysis: Euthanasia is not justified as long as the person wishes to be kept alive. But it is not so clear that a person should be kept alive if that individual wishes to die. It is even more difficult to justify euthanasia when patients are not in a position to make their wishes known. Even if there are some cases when euthanasia could be considered an act of charity, a major stumbling block to making it legal is the possibility of abuse. This continues to form a powerful barrier to legalization of euthanasia.

Throughout her discussion Foot refers to the distinction between *active* and *passive* euthanasia. So important is this distinction to a clear understanding of the issues raised that the second reading is devoted entirely to this topic.

EUTHANASIA

Philippa Foot

The widely used *Shorter Oxford English Dictionary* gives three meanings for the word "euthanasia": the first, "a quiet and easy death"; the second, "the means of procuring this"; and the third, "the action of inducing a quiet and easy death." It is a curious fact that no one of the three gives an adequate definition of the word as it is usually understood. For "euthanasia" means much more than a quiet and easy death, or the means of procuring it, or the action of inducing it. The definition specifies only the manner of death, and if this were all that was implied a murderer, careful to drug his victim, could claim that his act was an act of euthanasia. We find this ridiculous because we take it for granted that in euthanasia it is death itself, not just the manner of death, that must be kind to the one who dies. . . .

Source: "Euthanasia" by Philippa Foot. *Philosophy and Public Affairs*, vol. 6, no. 2, 1977. Used by permission of the author.

Let us insist, then, that when we talk about euthanasia we are talking about a death understood as a good or happy event for the one who dies. This stipulation follows etymology, but is itself not exactly in line with current usage, which would be captured by the condition that the death should *not* be an evil rather than that it *should* be a good. That this is how people talk is shown by the fact that the case of Karen Ann Quinlan and others in a state of permanent coma is often discussed under the heading of "euthanasia." Perhaps it is not too late to object to the use of the word "euthanasia" in this sense. Apart from the break with the Greek origins of the word there are other unfortunate aspects of this extension of the term. For if we say that the death must be supposed to be a good to the subject we can also specify that it shall be for his sake that an act of euthanasia is performed. If we say merely that death shall not be an evil to him, we cannot stipulate that benefiting him shall be the motive where euthanasia is in question. Given the importance of the question, For whose sake are we acting? it is good to have a definition of euthanasia which brings under this heading only cases of opting for death for the sake of the one who dies. Perhaps what is most important is to say either that euthanasia is to be for the good of the subject or at least that death is to be no evil to him, thus refusing to talk Hitler's language. However, in this paper it is the first condition that will be understood, with the additional proviso that by an act of euthanasia we mean one of inducing or otherwise opting for death for the sake of the one who is to die.

One [problem] that is dauntingly difficult has been passed over in this discussion of the definition, and must now be faced. It is easy to say, as if this raised no problems, that an act of euthanasia is by definition one aiming at the *good* of the one whose death is in question, and that it is *for his sake* that his death is desired. But how is this to be explained? Presumably we are thinking of some evil already with him or to come on him if he continues to live, and death is thought of as a release from this evil. But this cannot be enough. Most people's lives contain evils such as grief or pain, but we do not therefore think that death would be a blessing to them. On the contrary, life is generally supposed to be a good even for someone who is unusually unhappy or frustrated. How is it that one can ever wish for death for the sake of the one who is to die? This difficult question is central to the discussion of euthanasia, and we shall literally not know what we are talking about if we ask whether acts of euthanasia defined as we have defined them are ever morally permissible without first understanding better the reason for saying that life is a good, and the possibility that it is not always so.

If a man should save my life he would be my benefactor. In normal circumstances this is plainly true; but does one always benefit another in saving his life? It seems certain that he does not. Suppose, for instance, that a man were being tortured to death and was given a drug that lengthened his sufferings; this would not be a benefit but the reverse. Or suppose that in a ghetto in Nazi Germany a doctor saved the life of someone threatened by disease, but that the man once cured was transported to an extermination camp; the doctor might wish for the sake of the patient that he had died of the disease. Nor would a longer stretch of life always be a benefit to the person who was given it. Comparing Hitler's camps with those of Stalin, Dmitri Panin observes that in the latter the method of extermination was made worse by agonies that could stretch out over months.

> Death from a bullet would have been bliss compared with what many millions had to endure while dying of hunger. The kind of death to which they were condemned has nothing to equal it in treachery and sadism.[1]

These examples show that to save or prolong a man's life is not always to do him a service: it may be better for him if he dies earlier rather than later. It must therefore be agreed that while life is normally a benefit to the one who has it, this is not always so.

The judgment is often fairly easy to make—that life is or is not a good to someone—but the basis for it is very hard to find. When life is said to be a benefit or a good, on what grounds is the assertion made?

The difficulty is underestimated if it is supposed that the problem arises from the fact that one who is dead has nothing, so that the good someone gets from being alive cannot be compared with the amount he would otherwise have had. For why should this particular comparison be necessary? Surely it would be enough if one could say whether or not someone whose life was prolonged had more good than evil in the extra stretch of time. Such estimates are not always possible, but frequently they are; we say, for example, "He was very happy in those last years," or, "He had little but unhappiness then." If the balance of good and evil determined whether life was a good to someone we would expect to find a correlation in the judgments. In fact, of course, we find nothing of the kind. First, a man who has no doubt that existence is a good to him may have no idea about the balance of happiness and unhappiness in his life, or of any other positive and negative factors that may be suggested. So the supposed criteria are not always operating where the judgment is made. And secondly the application of the criteria gives an answer that is often wrong. Many people have more evil than good in their lives; we do not, however, conclude that we would do these people no service by rescuing them from death ...

The problem remains, and it is hard to know where to look for a solution. Is there a conceptual connection between *life* and *good*? Because life is not always a good we are apt to reject this idea, and to think that it must be a contingent fact that life is usually a good, as it is a contingent matter that legacies are usually a benefit, if they are. Yet it seems not to be a contingent matter that to save someone's life is ordinarily to benefit him. The problem is to find where the conceptual connection lies. . . .

Might it not be counted as a necessary condition of life's being a good to a man that he should see it as such? Is there not some difficulty about the idea that a benefit might be done to him by the saving or prolonging of his life even though he himself wished for death? Of course he might have a quite mistaken view of his own prospects, but let us ignore this and think only of cases where it is life as he knows it that is in question. Can we think that the prolonging of this life would be a benefit to him even though he would rather have it end than continue? It seems that this cannot be ruled out. That there is no simple incompatibility between life as a good and the wish for death is shown by the possibility that a man should wish himself dead, not for his own sake, but for the sake of someone else. And if we try to amend the thesis to say that life cannot be a good to one who wishes *for his own sake* that he should die, we find the crucial concept slipping through our fingers. As Bishop Butler pointed out long ago not all ends are either benevolent or self-interested. Does a man wish for death for his own sake in the relevant sense if, for instance, he wishes to revenge himself on another by his death? Or what if he is proud and refuses to stomach dependence or incapacity even though there are many good things left in life for him? The truth seems to be that the wish for death is sometimes compatible with life's being a good and sometimes not, which is possible because the description "wishing for death" is one covering diverse states of mind from that of the determined suicide, pathologically depressed, to that of one who is surprised to find that the thought of a fatal accident is viewed with relief . . .

When are we to say that life is a good or a benefit to a man? The dilemma that faces us is this. If we say that life as such is a good we find ourselves refuted by the examples given at the beginning of this discussion. We therefore incline to think that it is as bringing good things that life is a good, where it is a good. But if life is a good only because it is the condition of good things why is it not equally an evil when it brings bad things? And how can it be a good even when it brings more evil than good? . . .

It seems . . . that merely being alive even without suffering is not a good, and that we must distinguish this from normal life. But how is the line to be drawn . . . ? What is to count as ordinary human life in the relevant sense? If it were only the very senile or very ill who were said not to have this life it might seem right to describe it in terms of *operation*. But it will be hard to find the sense in which the men described by Panin were not operating, given that they dragged themselves out to the forest to work. What is it about the life that the prisoners were living that makes us put it on the other side of the dividing line from that of most of the physically or mentally handicapped and of some severely ill or suffering patients? It is not that they were in captivity, for life in captivity can certainly be a good.

Nor is it merely the unusual nature of their life. In some ways the prisoners were living more as other men do than the patient in the iron lung.

The idea we need seems to be that of life which is ordinary human life in the following respect—that it contains a minimum of basic human goods. What is ordinary in human life—even in very hard lives—is that a man is not driven to work far beyond his capacity; that he has the support of a family or community; that he can more or less satisfy his hunger; that he has hopes for the future; that he can lie down to rest at night . . .

The suggested solution to the problem is, then, that there is a certain conceptual connection between *life* and *good* in the case of human beings as in that of animals and even plants. Here, as there, however, it is not the mere state of being alive that can determine, or itself count as, a good, but rather life coming up to some standard of normality. It was argued that it is as part of ordinary life that the elements of good that a man may have are relevant to the question of whether saving his life counts as benefiting him. Ordinary human lives, even very hard lives, contain a minimum of basic goods, but when these are absent the idea of life is no longer linked to that of good. And since it is in this way that the elements of good contained in a man's life are relevant to the question of whether he is benefited if his life is preserved, there is no reason why it should be the balance of good and evil that counts.

It should be added that evils are relevant in one way when, as in the examples discussed above, they destroy the possibility of ordinary goods, but in a different way when they invade a life from which the goods are already absent for a different reason. So, for instance, the connection between *life* and *good* may be broken because consciousness has sunk to a very low level, as in extreme senility or severe brain damage. In itself this kind of life seems to be neither good nor evil, but if suffering sets in one would hope for a speedy end.

This, admittedly inadequate, discussion of the sense in which life is normally a good, and of the reasons why it may not be so in some particular case, completes the account of what euthanasia is here taken to be. An act of euthanasia, whether literally act or rather omission, is attributed to an agent who opts for the death of another because in his case life seems to be an evil rather than a good. The question now to be asked is whether acts of euthanasia are ever justifiable. But there are two topics here rather than one. For it is one thing to say that some acts of euthanasia considered only in themselves and their results are morally unobjectionable, and another to say that it would be all right to legalise them. Perhaps the practice of euthanasia would allow too many abuses, and perhaps there would be too many mistakes. Moreover the practice might have very important and highly undesirable side effects, because it is unlikely that we could change our principles about the treatment of the old and the ill without changing fundamental emotional attitudes and social relations. The topics must, therefore, be treated separately. In the next part of the discussion, nothing will be said about the social consequences and possible abuses of the practice of euthanasia, but only about acts of euthanasia considered in themselves.

What we want to know is whether acts of euthanasia, defined as we have defined them, are ever morally permissible. To be more accurate, we want to know whether it is ever sufficient justification of the choice of death for another that death can be counted a benefit rather than harm, and that this is why the choice is made.

It will be impossible to get a clear view of the area to which this topic belongs without first marking the distinct grounds on which objection may lie when one man opts for the death of another. There are two different virtues whose requirements are, in general, contrary to such actions. An unjustified act of killing, or allowing to die, is contrary to justice or to charity, or to both virtues, and the moral failings are distinct. Justice has to do with what men *owe* each other in the way of noninterference and positive service. When used in this wide sense, which has its history in the doctrine of the cardinal virtues, justice is not especially connected with, for instance, law courts but with the whole area of rights, and duties corresponding to rights. Thus murder is one form of injustice, dishonesty another, and wrongful failure to keep contracts a third; chicanery in a law court or defrauding someone of his inheritance are simply other cases of injustice. Justice as such is not directly linked to the good of another, and may require that something be rendered to him even where it will do him harm, as Hume pointed out when he remarked that a debt must be paid even to profligate debauchee who "would rather receive harm than benefit from large possessions." Charity, on the other hand, is the virtue which attaches us to the good of others. An act of charity is in question only where something is not demanded by justice, but a lack of charity and of justice can be shown where a man is denied something which he both needs and has a right to; both charity and justice demand that widows and orphans are not defrauded, and the man who cheats them is neither charitable nor just.

It is easy to see that the two grounds of objection to inducing death are distinct. A murder is an act of injustice. A culpable failure to come to the aid of someone whose life is threatened is normally contrary, not to justice, but to charity. But where one man is under contract, explicit or implicit, to come to the aid of another injustice too will be shown. Thus injustice may be involved either in an act or an omission, and the same is true of a lack of charity; charity may demand that someone be aided, but also that an unkind word not be spoken.

The distinction between charity and justice will turn out to be of first importance when voluntary and nonvoluntary euthanasia are distinguished later on. This is because of the connection between justice and rights, and something should now be said about this. I believe it is true to say that wherever a man acts unjustly he has infringed a right, since justice has to do with whatever a man is owed, and whatever he is owed is his as a matter of right. Something should therefore be said about the different kinds of rights. The distinction commonly made is between having a right in the sense of having a liberty, and having a "claim-right" or "right of recipience." The best way to understand such a distinction seems to be as follows. To say that a man has a right in the sense of liberty is to say that no one can demand that he does not do a thing which he has the right to do. The fact that he has a right to do it consists in the fact that a certain kind of objection does not lie against his doing it. Thus a man has a right in this sense to walk down a public street or park his car in a public parking space. It does not follow that no one else may prevent him from doing so. If for some reason I want a certain man not to park in a certain place I may lawfully park there myself or get my friends to do so, thus preventing him from doing what he has a right (in the sense of a liberty) to do. It is different, however, with a claim-right. This is the kind of right which I have in addition to a liberty when, for example, I have a private parking space; now others have duties in the way of noninterference, as in this case, or of service, as in the case where my claim-right is to goods or services promised to me. Sometimes one of these rights gives other people the duty of securing to me that to which I have a right, but at other times their duty is merely to refrain from interference. If a fall of snow blocks my private parking space there is normally no obligation for anyone else to clear it away. Claim rights generate duties; sometimes these duties are duties of noninterference; sometimes they are duties of service. If your right gives me the duty not to interfere with you I have "no right" to do it; similarly, if your right gives me the duty to provide something for you I have "no right" to refuse to do it. What *I* lack is the right which is a liberty: I am not 'at liberty' to interfere with you or to refuse the service.

Where in this picture does the right to life belong? No doubt people have the right to live in the sense of a liberty, but what is important is the cluster of claim-rights brought together under the title of the right to life. The chief of these is, of course, the right to be free from interferences that threaten life. . . .

Let us now ask how the right to life affects the morality of acts of euthanasia. Are such acts sometimes or always ruled out by the right to life? This is certainly a possibility; for although an act of euthanasia is, by our definition, a matter of opting for death for the good of the one who is to die, there is, as we noted earlier, no simple connection between that to which a man has a right and that which is for his good. It is true that men have the right only to the kind of thing that is, in general, a good: we do not think that people have the right to garbage or polluted air. Nevertheless, a man may have the right to something which he himself would be better off without; where rights exist it is a man's will that counts not his or anyone else's estimate of benefit or harm. So the duties complementary to the right to life—the general duty of noninterference and the duty of service incurred by certain persons—are not affected by the quality of a man's life or by his prospects. Even if it is true that he would be, as we say, "better off dead," so long as he wants to live this does not justify us in killing him and may not justify us in deliberately allowing him to die. All of us have the duty of noninterference, and some of us may have the duty to sustain his life . . .

Interestingly enough we have arrived by way of a consideration of the right to life at the distinction normally labelled "active" versus "passive" euthanasia, and often thought to be irrelevant to the moral issue. Once it is seen that the right to life is a distinct ground of objection to certain acts of euthanasia, and that this right creates a duty of noninterference more widespread than the duties of care there can be no doubt about the relevance of the distinction between passive and active euthanasia. Where everyone may have the duty to leave someone alone, it may be that no one has the duty to maintain his life, or that only some people do.

Where then do the boundaries of the "active" and "passive" lie? In some ways the words are themselves misleading, because they suggest the difference between act and omission which is not quite what we want. Certainly the act of shooting someone is the kind of thing we were talking about under the heading of "interference," and omitting to give him a drug a case of refusing care. But the act of turning off a respirator should surely be thought of as no different from the decision not to start it; if doctors had decided that a patient should be allowed to die, either course of action might follow, and both should be counted as passive rather than active euthanasia if euthanasia were in question. The point seems to be that interference in a course of treatment is not the same as other interference in a man's life, and particularly if the same body of people are responsible for the treatment and for its discontinuance. In such a case we could speak of the disconnecting of the apparatus as killing the man, or of the hospital as allowing him to die. By and large, it is the act of killing that is ruled out under the heading of noninterference, but not in every case.

Doctors commonly recognize this distinction, and the grounds on which some philosophers have denied it seem untenable. James Rachels, for instance, believes that if the difference between active and passive is relevant anywhere, it should be relevant everywhere, and he has pointed to an example in which it seems to make no difference which is done. If someone saw a child drowning in a bath it would seem just as bad to let it drown as to push its head under water. If "it makes no difference" means that one act would be as iniquitous as the other this is true. It is not that killing is *worse* than allowing to die, but that the two are contrary to distinct virtues, which gives the possibility that in some circumstances one is impermissible and the other permissible. In the circumstances invented by Rachels, both are wicked: it is contrary to justice to push the child's head under the water—something one has no right to do. To leave it to drown is not contrary to justice, but is a particularly glaring example of lack of charity. Here it makes no practical difference because the requirements of justice and charity coincide; but in the case of the retreating army they did not: charity would have required that the wounded soldier be killed had not justice required that he be left alive. In such a case it makes all the difference whether a man opts for the death of another in a positive action, or whether he allows him to die . . .

We see then that the distinction between active and passive, importance as it is elsewhere, has a special importance in the area of euthanasia . . .

So far we have said very little about the right to service as opposed to the right to noninterference, though it was agreed that both might be brought under the heading of "the right to life." What about the duty to preserve life that may belong to special classes of persons such as bodyguards, firemen, or doctors? Unlike the general public they are not within their rights if they merely refrain from interfering and do not try to sustain life. The subject's claim-rights are two-fold as far as they are concerned and passive as well as active euthanasia may be ruled out here if it is against his will. This is not to say that he had the right to any and every service needed to save or prolong his life; the rights of other people set limits to what may be demanded, both because they have the right not to be interfered with and because they may have a competing right to services. Furthermore one must enquire just what the contract or implicit agreement amounts to in each case. Firemen and bodyguards presumably have a duty which is simply to preserve life, within the limits of justice to others and of reasonableness to themselves. With doctors it may however be different, since their duty relates not only to preserving life but also to the relief of suffering. It is not clear what a doctor's duties are to his patient if life can be prolonged only at the cost of suffering or suffering relieved only by measures that shorten life. George Fletcher has argued that what the doctor is under contract to do depends on what is generally done, because this is what a patient will reasonably expect. This seems right. If procedures are part of normal medical practice then it seems that the patient can demand them however much it may be against his interest to do so. Once again it is not a matter of what is "most humane."

That the patient's right to life may set limits to permissible acts of euthanasia seems undeniable. If he does not want to die no one has the right to practice active euthanasia on him, and passive euthanasia may also be ruled out where he has a right to the services of doctors or others.

Perhaps few will deny what has so far been said about the impermissibility of acts of euthanasia, simply because we have so far spoken about the case of one who positively wants to live, and about his rights; whereas those who advocate euthanasia are usually thinking either about those who wish to die or about those whose wishes cannot be ascertained either because they cannot properly be said to have wishes or because, for one reason or another, we are unable to form a reliable estimate of what they are. The question that must now be asked is whether the latter type of case, where euthanasia though not *in*voluntary would again be *non*voluntary, is different from the one discussed so far. Would we have the right to kill someone for his own good so long as we had no idea that he positively wished to live? And what about the life-prolonging duties of doctors in the same circumstances? This is a very difficult problem. On the one hand, it seems ridiculous to suppose that a man's right to life is something which generates duties only where he has signalled that he wants to live; as a borrower does indeed have a duty to return something lent on indefinite loan only if the lender indicates that he wants it back. On the other hand, it might be argued that there is something illogical about the idea that a right has been infringed if someone incapable of saying whether he wants it or not is deprived of something that is doing him harm rather than good . . . Perhaps if we could make confident judgments about what anyone in such circumstances would wish, or what he would have wished beforehand had he considered the matter, we could agree to consider the right to life as "dormant," needing to be asserted if the normal duties were to remain. But as things are we cannot make any such assumption; we simply do not know what most people would want, or would have wanted, us to do unless they tell us. This is certainly the case so far as active measures to end life are concerned. Possibly it is different, or will become different, in the matter of being kept alive, so general is the feeling against using sophisticated procedures on moribund patients, and so much is this dreaded by people who are old or terminally ill. Once again the distinction between active and passive euthanasia has come on the scene, but this time because most people's attitudes to the two are so different. It is just possible that we might presume, in the absence of specific evidence, that someone would not wish, beyond a certain point to be kept alive; it is certainly not possible to assume that he would wish to be killed.

In the last paragraph we have begun to broach the topic of voluntary euthanasia, and this we must now discuss. What is to be said about the case in which there is no doubt about someone's wish to die? Either he has told us beforehand that he would wish it in circumstances such as he is now in, and has shown no sign of a change of mind, or else he tells us now, being in possession of his faculties and of a steady mind. We should surely say that the objections previously urged against acts of euthanasia, which it must be remembered were all on the grounds of rights, had disappeared. It does not seem that one would infringe someone's right to life in killing him with his permission and in fact at his request. Why should someone not be able to waive his right to life, or rather, as would be more likely to happen, to cancel some of the duties of noninterference that this right entails? . . . Reli-

gion apart, there seems to be no case to be made out for an infringement
of rights if a man who wishes to die is allowed to die or even killed. But of
course it does not follow that there is no moral objection to it. Even with
property, which is after all a relatively small matter, one might be wrong to
destroy what one had the right to destroy. For, apart from its value to other
people, it might be valuable to the man who wanted it destroyed, and charity might require us to hold our hand where justice did not . . .

Turning now to the other objection that normally holds against inducing the death of another, that it is against charity, or benevolence, we must
tell a very different story. Charity is the virtue that gives attachment to the
good of others, and because life is normally a good, charity normally demands that it should be saved or prolonged. But as we so defined an act of
euthanasia that it seeks a man's death for his own sake—for his good—
charity will normally speak in favor of it. This is not, of course, to say that
charity can require an act of euthanasia which justice forbids, but if an act
of euthanasia is not contrary to justice—that is, it does not infringe rights—
charity will rather be in its favor than against.

Once more the distinction between nonvoluntary and voluntary euthanasia must be considered. Could it ever be compatible with charity to
seek a man's death although he wanted to live, or at least had not let us
know that he wanted to die? I have argued that in such circumstances active
euthanasia would infringe his right to life, but passive euthanasia would
not do so, unless he had some special right to life-preserving service from
the one who allowed him to die. What would charity dictate? Obviously
when a man wants to live there is a presumption that he will be benefited
if his life is prolonged, and if it is so the question of euthanasia does not
arise . . .

So much for the relation of charity to nonvoluntary passive euthanasia, which was not, like nonvoluntary active euthanasia, ruled out by the
right to life. Let us now ask what charity has to say about voluntary euthanasia both active and passive. It was suggested in the discussion of justice that
if of sound mind and steady desire a man might give others the *right* to
allow him to die or even to kill him, where otherwise this would be ruled
out. But it was pointed out that this would not settle the question of whether
the act was morally permissible, and it is this that we must now consider.
Could not charity speak against what justice allowed? Indeed it might do
so. For while the fact that a man wants to die suggests that his life is
wretched, and while his rejection of life may itself tend to take the good
out of things he might have enjoyed, nevertheless his wish to die might here
be opposed for his own sake just as it might be if suicide were in question.
Perhaps there is hope that his mental condition will improve. Perhaps he
is mistaken in thinking his disease is incurable. Perhaps he wants to die for
the sake of someone else on whom he feels he is a burden, and we are not
ready to accept this sacrifice whether for ourselves or others. In such cases,
and there will surely be many of them, it could not be for his own sake that

we kill him or allow him to die, and therefore euthanasia as defined in this paper would not be in question. But this is not to deny that there could be acts of voluntary euthanasia both passive and active against which neither justice nor charity would speak.

We have now considered the morality of euthanasia both voluntary and nonvoluntary, and active and passive. The conclusion has been the non-voluntary active euthanasia (roughly, killing a man against his will or without his consent) is never justified; that is to say, that a man's being killed for his own good never justifies the act unless he himself has consented to it. A man's rights are infringed by such an action, and it is therefore contrary to justice. However, all the other combinations, nonvoluntary passive euthanasia, voluntary active euthanasia, and voluntary passive euthanasia are sometimes compatible with both justice and charity. But the strong condition carried in the definition of euthanasia adopted in this paper must not be forgotten; an act of euthanasia as here understood is one whose purpose is to benefit the one who dies.

In the light of this discussion let us look at our present practices. Are they good or are they bad? And what changes might be made, thinking now not only of the morality of particular acts of euthanasia but also of the indirect effects of instituting different practices, of the abuses to which they might be subject and of the changes that might come about if euthanasia became a recognized part of the social scene?

The first thing to notice is that it is wrong to ask whether we should introduce the practice of euthanasia as if it were not something we already had. In fact we do have it. For instance it is common, where the medical prognosis is very bad, for doctors to recommend against measures to pro-long life, and particularly where a process of degeneration producing one medical emergency after another has already set in. If these doctors are not certainly within their legal rights this is something that is apt to come as a surprise to them as to the general public. It is also obvious that euthanasia is often practiced where old people are concerned. If someone very old and soon to die is attacked by a disease that makes his life wretched, doctors do not always come in with life-prolonging drugs. Perhaps poor patients are more fortunate in this respect than rich patients, being more often left to die in peace; but it is in any case a well recognized piece of medical practice, and a form of euthanasia.

No doubt, the case of infants with mental or physical defects will be suggested as another example of the practice of euthanasia as we already have it, since such infants are sometimes deliberately allowed to die. That they are deliberately allowed to die is certain ... We must ask the crucial question, "Is it for the sake of the child himself that the doctors and parents choose his death?" In some cases the answer may really be yes, and what is more important it may really be true that the kind of life which is a good is not possible or likely for this child, and that there is little but suffering and frustration in store for him. ... The fact is, however, that the doctors who recommend against life-saving procedures for handicapped infants are usually thinking not of them but rather of their parents and of other children in the family or of the "burden on society" if the children survive. So it is not for their sake but to avoid trouble to others that they are allowed to die. When brought out into the open this seems unacceptable; at least we do not easily accept the principle that adults who need special care should be counted as too burdensome to be kept alive ...

Nevertheless if it is ever right to allow deformed children to die because life will be a misery to them, or not to take measures to prolong for a little the life of a newborn baby whose life cannot extend beyond a few months of intense medical intervention, there is a genuine problem about active as opposed to passive euthanasia. There are well-known cases in which the medical staff has looked on wretchedly while an infant died slowly from starvation and dehydration because they did not feel able to give a lethal injection. According to the principles discussed in the earlier part of this paper they would indeed have had no right to give it, since an infant cannot ask that it should be done. The only possible solution— supposing that voluntary active euthanasia were to be legalized—would be to appoint guardians to act on the infant's behalf. In a different climate of opinion this might not be dangerous, but at present, when people so readily assume that the life of a handicapped baby is of no value, one would be loath to support it.

Finally, on the subject of handicapped children, another word should be said about those with severe mental defects. For them too it might sometimes be right to say that one would wish for death for their sake. But not even severe mental handicap automatically brings a child within the scope even of a possible act of euthanasia. If the level of consciousness is low enough it could not be said that life is a good to them, any more than in the case of those suffering from extreme senility. Nevertheless if they do not suffer it will not be an act of euthanasia by which someone opts for their death. Perhaps charity does not demand that strenuous measures are taken to keep people in this state alive, but euthanasia does not come into the matter, any more than it does when someone is, like Karen Ann Quinlan, in a state of permanent coma. Much could be said about this last case. It might even be suggested that in the case of unconsciousness this "life" is not the life to which "the right to life" refers. But that is not our topic here.

What we must consider, even if only briefly, is the possibility that euthanasia, genuine euthanasia, and not contrary to the requirements of justice or charity, should be legalized over a wider area. Here we are up against the really serious problem of abuse. Many people want, and want very badly, to be rid of their elderly relatives and even of their ailing husbands or wives. Would any safeguards ever be able to stop them describing as euthanasia what was really for their own benefit? And would it be possible to prevent the occurrence of acts which were genuinely acts of euthanasia but morally impermissible because infringing the rights of a patient who wished to live or whose wishes were unknown?

Perhaps the furthest we should go is to encourage patients to make their own contracts with a doctor by making it known whether they wish him to prolong their lives in case of painful terminal illness or of incapacity. A document such as the Living Will seems eminently sensible, and should surely be allowed to give a doctor following the previously expressed wishes of the patient immunity from legal proceedings by relatives. Legalizing active euthanasia is, however, another matter. Apart from the special repugnance doctors feel towards the idea of a lethal injection, it may be of the very greatest importance to keep a psychological barrier up against killing. Moreover it is active euthanasia which is the most liable to abuse. Hitler would not have been able to kill 275,000 people in his "euthanasia" program if he had had to wait for them to need life-saving treatment. But there are other objections to active euthanasia, even voluntary active euthanasia. In the first place it would be hard to devise procedures that would protect people from being persuaded into giving their consent. And secondly the possibility of active voluntary euthanasia might change the social scene in ways that would be very bad. As things are, people do, by and large, expect to be looked after if they are old or ill. This is one of the good things that we have, but we might lose it, and be much worse off without it. It might come to be expected that someone likely to need a lot of looking after should call for the doctor and demand his own death. Something comparable could be good in an extremely poverty-stricken community where the children genuinely suffered from lack of food; but in rich societies such as ours it would surely be a spiritual disaster. Such possibilities should make us very wary of supporting large measures of euthanasia, even where moral principle applied to the individual act does not rule it out.

Note

[1]Dmitri Panin, *The Notebooks of Sologdin* (London, 1976).

Killing or Letting Die?

The 1973 policies of the American Medical Association distinguish between the "intentional termination of the life of one human being by another" and the decision to cease using "extraordinary means to prolong the life of the body when there is irrefutable evidence that biological death is imminent." The former, sometimes calls mercy killing, is not to be allowed, but the latter is the decision of the patient or the patient's immediate family. Taking this policy statement as his starting point, Rachels characterizes "intentional termination of the life of one human being by another" as active euthanasia and the decision to cease using "extraordinary means to prolong the life of the body when there is irrefutable evidence that biological death is imminent" as passive euthanasia. He then offers a careful analysis of the distinction between active and passive forms of euthanasia.

Rachels attacks this distinction first by pointing out that if the goal of passive euthanasia is to help the patient avoid pain, it would be much kinder to administer a lethal injection than to let the individual live in prolonged agony while the disease runs its course. His second argument against the distinction between active and passive euthanasia is that it leads to decisions in which true moral focus is clouded. For example, consider the case of a child born with Down's syndrome who also has a medical condition that will cause the child to die unless an operation is performed. According to Rachels, letting the baby die from the medical condition is a subterfuge forced on us because of our desire to find a way for letting the baby die. We should be able to face the reality of the situation. If a child's life is judged not worth living, then all children like it ought not to live. Allowing only some children with a certain kind of medical condition to live while denying life to others with the same condition is not in keeping with reasonable moral judgments.

Rachels concludes that there is no substantial difference between killing and letting die. "If a doctor lets a patient die, for humane reasons, he is in the same moral position as if he had given the patient a lethal injection for humane reasons." If Rachels is correct in his conclusion, there are two inferences that can be drawn from it. The first is that if we object to active euthanasia, we must object to passive euthanasia as well. The second is that if we do not object to passive euthanasia ("letting the patient die") physicians should also be prepared actively to end the life of a terminally ill patient. If these inferences present us with a dilemma, the way to avoid it is to reject euthanasia entirely as a morally acceptable practice. Does the criticism that Rachels offers of the distinction between active and passive euthanasia imply that he supports or that he rejects euthanasia?

ACTIVE AND PASSIVE EUTHANASIA

James Rachels

The distinction between active and passive euthanasia is thought to be crucial for medical ethics. The idea is that it is permissible, at least in some

Source: "Active and Passive Euthanasia" by James Rachels. *The New England Journal of Medicine*, vol. 292 (January 9, 1975), pp. 78–80. Used by permission.

cases, to withhold treatment and allow a patient to die, but it is never permissible to take any direct action designed to kill the patient. This doctrine seems to be accepted by most doctors, and it is endorsed in a statement adopted by the House of Delegates of the American Medical Association on December 4, 1973:

> The intentional termination of the life of one human being by another—mercy killing—is contrary to that for which the medical profession stands and is contrary to the policy of the American Medical Association.
>
> The cessation of the employment of extraordinary means to prolong the life of the body when there is irrefutable evidence that biological death is imminent is the decision of the patient and/or his immediate family. The advice and judgment of the physician should be freely available to the patient and/or his immediate family.

However, a strong case can be made against this doctrine. In what follows I will set out some of the relevant arguments, and urge doctors to reconsider their views on this matter.

To begin with a familiar type of situation, a patient who is dying of incurable cancer of the throat is in terrible pain, which can no longer be satisfactorily alleviated. He is certain to die within a few days, even if present treatment is continued, but he does not want to go on living for those days since the pain is unbearable. So he asks the doctor for an end to it, and his family joins in the request.

Suppose the doctor agrees to withhold treatment, as the conventional doctrine says he may. The justification for his doing so is that the patient is in terrible agony, and since he is going to die anyway, it would be wrong to prolong his suffering needlessly. But now notice this. If one simply withholds treatment, it may take the patient longer to die, and so he may suffer more than he would if more direct action were taken and a lethal injection given. This fact provides strong reason for thinking that, once the initial decision not to prolong his agony has been made, active euthanasia is actually preferable to passive euthanasia, rather than the reverse. To say otherwise is to endorse the option that leads to more suffering rather than less, and is contrary to the humanitarian impulse that prompts the decision not to prolong his life in the first place.

Part of my point is that the process of being "allowed to die" can be relatively slow and painful, whereas being given a lethal injection is relatively quick and painless. Let me give a different sort of example. In the United States about one in 600 babies is born with Down's syndrome. Most of these babies are otherwise healthy—that is, with only the usual pediatric care, they will proceed to an otherwise normal infancy. Some, however, are born with congenital defects such as intestinal obstructions that require operations if they are to live. Sometimes, the parents and the doctor will decide not to operate, and let the infant die. Anthony Shaw describes what happens then:

> When surgery is denied [the doctor] must try to keep the infant from suffering while natural forces sap the baby's life away. As a surgeon whose natural inclination is to use the scalpel to fight off death, standing by and watching a salvageable baby die is the most emotionally exhausting experience I know. It is easy at a conference, in a theoretical discussion to decide that such infants should be allowed to die. It is altogether different to stand by in the nursery and watch as dehydration and infection wither a tiny being over hours and days. This is a terrible ordeal for me and the hospital staff—much more so than for the parents who never set foot in the nursery.[1]

I can understand why some people are opposed to all euthanasia, and insist that such infants must be allowed to live. I think I can also understand why other people favor destroying these babies quickly and painlessly. But why should anyone favor letting "dehydration and infection wither a tiny being over hours and days"? The doctrine that says that a baby may be allowed to dehydrate and wither, but may not be given an injection that would end its life without suffering, seems so patently cruel as to require no further refutation. The strong language is not intended to offend, but only to put the point in the clearest possible way.

My second argument is that the conventional doctrine leads to decisions concerning life and death made on irrelevant grounds.

Consider again the case of the infants with Down's syndrome who need operations for congenital defects unrelated to the syndrome to live. Sometimes, there is no operation, and the baby dies, but when there is no such defect, the baby lives on. Now, an operation such as that to remove an intestinal obstruction is not prohibitively difficult. The reason why such operations are not performed in these cases is, clearly, that the child has Down's syndrome and the parents and the doctor judge that because of that fact it is better for the child to die.

But notice that this situation is absurd, no matter what view one takes of the lives and potentials of such babies. If the life of such an infant is worth preserving what does it matter if it needs a simple operation? Or, if one thinks it better that such a baby should not live on, what difference does it make that it happens to have an unobstructed intestinal tract? In either case, the matter of life and death is being decided on irrelevant grounds. It is the Down's syndrome, and not the intestines, that is the issue. The matter should be decided, if at all, on that basis, and not be allowed to depend on the essentially irrelevant question of whether the intestinal tract is blocked.

What makes this situation possible, of course, is the idea that when there is an intestinal blockage, one can "let the baby die," but when there is no such defect there is nothing that can be done, for one must not "kill" it. The fact that this idea leads to such results as deciding life or death on irrelevant grounds is another good reason why the doctrine would be rejected.

One reason why so many people think that there is an important moral difference between active and passive euthanasia is that they think killing someone is morally worse than letting someone die. But is it? Is killing, in itself, worse than letting die? To investigate this issue, two cases may be considered that are exactly alike except that one involves killing whereas the other involves letting someone die. Then, it can be asked whether this difference makes any difference to the moral assessments. It is important that the cases be exactly alike, except for this one difference, since otherwise one cannot be confident that it is this difference and not some other that accounts for any variation in the assessments of the two cases. So, let us consider this pair of cases:

In the first, Smith stands to gain a large inheritance if anything should happen to his six-year-old cousin. One evening while the child is taking his bath, Smith sneaks into the bathroom and drowns the child, and then arranges things so that it will look like an accident.

In the second, Jones also stands to gain if anything should happen to his six-year-old cousin. Like Smith, Jones sneaks in planning to drown the child in his bath. However, just as he enters the bathroom Jones sees the child slip and hit his head, and fall face down in the water. Jones is delighted; he stands by, ready to push the child's head back under if it is necessary, but it is not necessary. With only a little thrashing about, the child drowns all by himself, "accidentally," as Jones watches and does nothing.

Now Smith killed the child, whereas Jones "merely" let the child die. That is the only difference between them. Did either man behave better, from a moral point of view? If the difference between killing and letting die were in itself a morally important matter, one should say that Jones's behavior was less reprehensible than Smith's. But does one really want to say that? I think not. In the first place, both men acted from the same motive, personal gain, and both had exactly the same end in view when they acted. It may be inferred from Smith's conduct that he is a bad man, although that judgment may be withdrawn or modified if certain further facts are learned about him—for example, that he is mentally deranged. But would not the very same thing be inferred about Jones from his conduct? And would not the same further considerations also be relevant to any modification of this judgment? Moreover, suppose Jones pleaded, in his own defense, "After all, I didn't do anything except just stand there and watch the child drown. I didn't kill him; I only let him die." Again, if letting die were in itself less bad than killing, this defense should have at least some weight. But it does not. Such a "defense" can only be regarded as a grotesque perversion of moral reasoning. Morally speaking, it is no defense at all.

Now, it may be pointed out, quite properly, that the cases of euthanasia with which doctors are concerned are not like this at all. They do not involve personal gain or the destruction of normal healthy children. Doctors are concerned only with cases in which the patient's life is of no further use to him, or in which the patient's life has become or will soon become a terrible burden. However, the point is the same in these cases: the bare difference between killing and letting die does not, in itself, make a moral difference. If a doctor lets a patient die, for humane reasons, he is in the same moral position as if he had given the patient a lethal injection for humane reasons. If his decision was wrong—if, for example, the patient's illness was in fact curable—the decision would be equally regrettable no matter which method was used to carry it out. And if the doctor's decision was the right one, the method used is not in itself important.

The AMA policy statement isolates the crucial issue very well; the crucial issue is "the intentional termination of the life of one human being by another." But after identifying this issue, and forbidding "mercy killing," the statement goes on to deny that the cessation of treatment is the intentional termination of a life. This is where the mistake comes in, for what is the cessation of treatment, in these circumstances, if it is not "the intentional termination of the life of one human being by another"? Of course it is exactly that, and if it were not, there would be no point to it.

Many people will find this judgment hard to accept. One reason, I think, is that it is very easy to conflate the question of whether killing is, in itself, worse than letting die, with the very different question of whether most actual cases of killing are more reprehensible than most actual cases of letting die. Most actual cases of killing are clearly terrible (think, for example, of all the murders reported in the newspapers), and one hears of such cases every day. On the other hand, one hardly ever hears of a case of letting die, except for the actions of doctors who are motivated by humanitarian reasons. So one learns to think of killing in a much worse light than of letting die. But this does not mean that there is something about killing that makes it in itself worse that letting die, for it is not the bare difference between killing and letting die that makes the difference in these cases. Rather, the other factors—the murderer's motive of personal gain, for example, contrasted with the doctor's humanitarian motivation—account for different reactions to the different cases.

I have argued that killing is not in itself any worse than letting die; if my contention is right, it follows that active euthanasia is not any worse than passive euthanasia. What arguments can be given on the other side? The most common, I believe, is the following:

> The important difference between active and passive euthanasia is that, in passive euthanasia, the doctor does not do anything to bring

about the patient's death. The doctor does nothing, and the patient dies of whatever ills already afflict him. In active euthanasia, however, the doctor does something to bring about the patient's death: he kills him. The doctor who gives the patient with cancer a lethal injection has himself caused his patient's death; whereas if he merely ceases treatment, the cancer is the cause of the death.

A number of points need to be made here. The first is that it is not exactly correct to say that in passive euthanasia the doctor does nothing, for he does do one thing that is very important: he lets the patient die. "Letting someone die" is certainly different, in some respects, from other types of action—mainly in that it is a kind of action that one may perform by way of not performing certain other actions. For example, one may let a patient die by way of not giving medication, just as one may insult someone by way of not shaking his hand. But for any purpose of moral assessment, it is a type of action nonetheless. The decision to let a patient die is subject to moral appraisal in the same way that a decision to kill him would be subject to moral appraisal: it may be assessed as wise or unwise, compassionate or sadistic, right or wrong. If a doctor deliberately let a patient die who was suffering from a routinely curable illness, the doctor would certainly be to blame if he had needlessly killed the patient. Charges against him would be appropriate. If so, it would be no defense at all for him to insist that he didn't "do anything." He would have done something very serious indeed, for he let his patient die.

Fixing the cause of death may be very important from a legal point of view, for it may determine whether criminal charges are brought against the doctor. But I do not think that this notion can be used to show a moral difference between active and passive euthanasia. The reason why it is considered bad to be the cause of someone's death is that death is regarded as a great evil—and so it is. However, if it has been decided that euthanasia—even passive euthanasia—is desirable in a given case, it has also been decided that in this instance death is no greater an evil than the patient's continued existence. And if this is true, the usual reason for not wanting to be the cause of someone's death simply does not apply.

Finally, doctors may think that all of this is only of academic interest—the sort of thing that philosophers may worry about but that has no practical bearing on their own work. After all, doctors must be concerned about the legal consequences of what they do, and active euthanasia is clearly forbidden by the law. But even so, doctors should also be concerned with the fact that the law is forcing upon them a moral doctrine that may be indefensible, and has a considerable effect on their practices. Of course, most doctors are not now in the position of being coerced in this matter, for they do not regard themselves as merely going along with what the law requires. Rather, in statements such as the AMA policy statement that I have quoted they are endorsing this doctrine as a central point of medical ethics. In that statement, active euthanasia is condemned not merely as illegal but as "contrary to that for which the medical profession stands," whereas passive euthanasia is approved. However, the preceding considerations suggest that there is really no moral difference between the two, considered in themselves (there may be important moral differences in some cases in their *consequences,* but, as I pointed out, these differences may make active euthanasia, and not passive euthanasia, the morally preferable option). So, whereas doctors may have to discriminate between active and passive euthanasia to satisfy the law, they should not do any more than that. In particular, they should not give the distinction any added authority and weight by writing it into official statements of medical ethics.

Note

[1]Anthony Shaw, "Doctor, Do We Have a Choice?" *The New York Times Magazine,* 30 January 1972, 54.

A Physician's Challenge

It is easy to talk about life and death issues when one is sitting comfortably in a classroom discussing the pros and cons of active versus passive euthanasia, ordinary versus extraordinary therapies, and the subtleties of distinguishing between voluntary, involuntary, and nonvoluntary euthanasia. It is quite different to be faced with real-world choices and to see the limited options available to physicians practicing their art in restricted settings. The following reading, by a physician, gives us a glimpse into the day-to-day challenges of deciding what kinds of therapies are appropriate for patients who, by reason of age or illness, are debilitated. Without offering his judgment of the ethics of the situation, the author reports that, as an empirical fact, "the old, chronically ill, debilitated, or mentally impaired do not receive the same level of aggressive medical evaluation and treatment as do the young, acutely ill, and mentally normal."

How should the physician be guided when faced with agonizing choices? It is certainly easier if patients, while still in possession of vigor and rationality, have discussed with their physicians their wishes regarding prolongation of life by extraordinary means. It is also useful if they have executed a living will as mentioned in the introduction to this chapter. But there are two problems with this. The first is that most people do not like to think about their own aging and death and will not take the time to execute a living will. The second factor working against this solution is the sheer mobility of our society. Who knows if their final treatment will be from a physician familiar with the patient's wishes or from a stranger?

The final problem for a physician is the sheer complexity of the variety of cases demanding a decision. The conclusion the author reaches is that a physician will have to face difficult decisions alone, for the courts have reached no consensus on basic issues in euthanasia, and writers in ethics likewise disagree on fundamental values in euthanasia. While the situation is certainly far from easy, it may not be as confused as the author suggests. As you read through the following reading, see if you can suggest areas of constructive agreement based on previous selections in this chapter that might be of benefit to the practicing physician.

ALLOWING THE DEBILITATED
TO DIE

David Hilfiker

The phone wakes me; it is 3 a.m.

"Hello, Dr. Hilfiker? This is Ginger at the nursing home. Mrs. Toivonen has a fever."

Despite my tiredness my mind is immediately clear. Elsa Toivonen, 83 years old. Confined to the nursing home ever since her stroke three years ago. Bedridden. Aphasic. In an instant I remember her as she was before her stroke: her dislike and distrust of doctors and hospitals, her staunch pride and independence despite her severe scoliosis, her wry grin every time I suggested hospitalization for some problem. I remember admitting her to the hospital after her stroke, one side completely paralyzed, globally aphasic, incontinent, and reduced to helplessness. And I remember those first few hospital days in which I aggressively treated the pneumonia that developed as a complication, giving her intravenous antibiotics despite her apparent desire to die. "Depressed," I had thought. "She'll get over it. Besides, she may recover substantially in the next few weeks." She recovered from the pneumonia, but she remained paralyzed and aphasic. For the past three years she had lain curled in her nursing-home bed, a grim reminder of the "power" of modern medicine.

"David?" Ginger's voice brings me back to my tired body.

"Oh ... yes. Any other symptoms?" I know already that I'm going to have to go in, but I try to postpone the decision for a few minutes.

Source: "Allowing the Debilitated to Die" by David Hilfiker. *The New England Journal of Medicine,* vol. 308 (March 24, 1983), pp. 716–19. Used by permission.

"Well, it's hard to tell. She hasn't been eating much the last few days, and she's had a little cough. Her temp started during the evening."

"What's her temperature now?"

"One hundred three point five, rectally."

"Oh . . . all right," I say reluctantly. "I'll be right in."

Ginger is waiting for me in the dark hall of the nursing home, just outside Mrs. Toivonen's room, chart in hand. "She looks pretty sick, David."

She does, indeed! Wasted away to 69 lb., decubitus ulcers on her back and hip, peering at me from behind her blank face—I'm used to all that from my monthly rounds. But this morning there is no movement of her eyes, no resistance to my examination, nothing to indicate that she is really there. There is little more to the history of Mrs. Toivonen's fever than what I gathered over the phone, and her aphasia precludes much of an interview. My examination is brief, directed pointedly toward the usual causes of fever in the elderly. (I remember the *Journal* article[1] suggesting that nursing-home patients received less thorough attention simply because they were debilitated. It's true, of course, and I can't defend it, but I know that if Joe Blow, 47-year-old schoolteacher, were in the emergency room with a fever I would be spending an hour talking with him and examining him thoroughly.) I try to assuage my guilt with the thought that I can't exhaust myself now in the middle of the night if I'm going to be able to give decent care to all the other patients, beginning at eight in the morning.

Listening to Mrs. Toivonen's chest, I hear the expected rales, and I complete the rest of the examination without finding anything else.

"I think she's got pneumonia," I say to Ginger, and we both look down at Mrs. Toivonen's withered body. I wonder to myself what I'm going to do now.

I ask Ginger to call the technician out of bed for a chest x-ray, and I write orders for a urine culture. While waiting for the x-ray, Ginger and I sit at the nurses' station, writing our respective reports.

Ginger looks up. "Mabel Lundberg said she hoped there wouldn't be any heroics if Mrs. Toivonen got sick again."

"I know," I answer. "She talked with me. What does she mean by 'heroics'?" Mabel is the only friend Mrs. Toivonen has, her only visitor; she probably knows better than anyone what Mrs. Toivonen would really want. But the only relative, a distant niece living in another state, has called some months ago asking that "everything possible" be done for her aunt. "Everything possible," "heroics": it all depends on the words you choose.

Essentially alone, foggy from tiredness in the middle of the night, I will make decisions that will probably mean life or death for this poor old woman. I think back to medical school and university hospital, where $1,000 worth of laboratory and x-ray studies would have been done to make sure she really did have pneumonia: several views of the chest, urine cultures, blood cultures, throat cultures, sputum for stain and culture (obtained by inducing this 69-lb, 83-year-old lady to expectorate or by transtracheal aspiration), blood counts, Mantoux test, lung scans to rule out emboli—the list is only as limited as one's imagination. And each study is "reasonable" if we really mean to be thorough; I can almost hear the residents suggesting obscure possibilities to demonstrate their erudition. (And they are not wrong, either. Can any price be put on a human life? Is it not worth anything to discover a rare, potentially fatal, but curable illness?)

There in the middle of the night I consider "doing everything possible" for Mrs. Toivonen: transfer to the hospital, intravenous lines for hydration and antibiotics, thorough laboratory and x-ray evaluation, twice-daily rounds to be sure she is recovering, more toxic antibiotics, and even transfer to our regional hospital for evaluation and care by a specialist. None of it is unreasonable, and another night I might choose just such a course. But tonight my human sympathies lie with Mrs. Toivonen and what I perceive as her desire to die. Perhaps it's because Ginger is working, and I know how impatient she is with technologic heroics; perhaps it's because I've been feeling a little depressed myself in the past few days; perhaps, I think to myself, it's because I'm tired and lazy and don't want to bother. In any event I decide against the heroics.

But I can't just do nothing, either. My training and background are too strong. I do not allow myself to be consistent and just go home. Compromising (and ultimately making a decision that makes no medical or ethical sense at all), I write orders instructing the nursing staff to administer liquid penicillin, to encourage fluid intake, and to make an appointment with my office so I can reexamine Mrs. Toivonen in 36 hours. On my way out of the dark hospital, I talk with the x-ray technician and check the x-ray film: It is questionable at best. With her severe scoliosis Mrs. Toivonen is always difficult to x-ray, and the chronic changes in her lungs make early inflammation difficult to detect. I thank the technician for the x-ray, wondering to myself why I ordered it. Driving home, I wonder why practicing medicine is so often dissatisfying; as usual it takes me an hour to get back to sleep.

In my own practice and in the physician practices I see around me, the old, chronically ill, debilitated, or mentally impaired do not receive the same level of aggressive medical evaluation and treatment as do the young, acutely ill, and mentally normal. We do not discuss this reality or debate its ethics, but the fact remains that many patients are allowed to die by the withholding of "all available care." There seems to be, however, a general denial of this reality: A widespread misperception exists that all patients receive (or at the very least should receive) the maximal possible care for any given medical problem. In medical schools, in medical literature, even in conversations between physicians it is assumed that all patients (with the possible exception of the "terminally ill" who have requested no heroics) receive the maximal possible care. Because the reality is so grossly different from the perception, there is little discussion of this extraordinarily common, deeply profound ethical problem. Practicing physicians are left to fly by the seat of their pants.

I will not pretend in this brief space to advance a particular solution to this ethical dilemma; my purpose is rather to sketch its outlines and to stimulate discussion about a situation that seems to have been ignored.

Although some persons may be tempted to dismiss the problem with the simple assertion that all patients deserve maximal care, that assertion would only heighten the relevance of this discussion, since current practice is so different from what it describes. In our nursing home, for example, there is a middle-aged woman who has been comatose for five years as a result of an accident. Although there is no meaningful chance that she will ever improve, she is certainly not "brain dead" and is supported only by routine nursing care that consists of tube feedings, regular turnings, urinary catheters, and good hygiene; she is on no respirator or other machine. If her physician were somehow to discover on routine examination that she was in imminent danger of a myocardial infarction, few persons would, I think, recommend full-scale evaluation for possible coronary-artery bypass surgery. The decision not to offer her maximal care might be justified in any one of several ways, but most often the question would simply not arise. It would simply seem obvious to the practicing physician that this particular patient should not receive such heroic treatment.

I think few would quarrel with the decision to withhold such evaluation and treatment. But once we have allowed that some persons should not receive some treatments that might prolong their lives, we must then begin the thorny ethical process of drawing lines: which patients, which treatments? Once we have allowed that our comatose patient should not receive bypass surgery, we must decide what kinds of treatment we should be prepared to offer her: aneurysmectomy for a dissecting aortic aneurysm? appendectomy? hospitalization for pneumonia? intravenous infusions for fluid loss with diarrhea? oral antibiotics for a bladder infection? tube feedings? routine nursing care? Each person may draw the line differently, but once it is accepted that heroic treatment will not be offered, we must decide what we will then do.

Because of our expertise, we physicians ordinarily have the responsibility and the power to make such decisions. As good physicians we must of course try to include the patient and the family in such important deliberations, but our ability to phrase options, stress information, and present our own advice gives us tremendous power. This power becomes for all practical purposes absolute when we are dealing with incapacitated patients, especially if family members are far away or otherwise not closely involved.

One would expect, then, that we would have special training or at least some resources to which we might turn when such common problems arise. But our collective denial that we make such decisions has left us without resources. There has certainly been a great deal published about the termination of life-support measures for persons with brain death, but that problem is both simple and uncommon compared with the one we are discussing; the solutions there are primarily technical rather than ethical. There has also been much discussion about the care of the terminally ill (cancer) patient, but that situation is also much more clear-cut than the usual one of the debilitated elderly patient, because the cancer patient and his or her physician can know that the illness is terminal within a certain period of time. We physicians therefore reassure ourselves that we are not so much "withholding available treatment" as "allowing the person to die with dignity." (The professional ethicist may see little distinction between the terminally ill cancer patient and Mrs. Toivonen, but the certainty of the former's death within a very short time compared with the possibility of the latter's living for years creates an important distinction for the practicing physician.) Also, the relatively rapid course of terminal cancer allows the patient to know, while still completely lucid, that the illness is terminal; the patient can thus participate fully in the discussion of the matter before decisions are made. Although there has been much energy devoted to the ethics of treating the brain-dead and the terminally ill patient, the much more common situation of the elderly, debilitated patient who contracts an acute illness seems to have been left relatively unaddressed.

Ethicists have advanced two seemingly helpful suggestions. Some have suggested that the practicing physician sit down with his patients to discuss, in advance, what the patient might like done under certain circumstances. Others have suggested a "living will," that would direct the physician to a particular course of action if the patient became disabled. Although these are helpful ideas, they suffer from some serious problems.

First of all, few in our society want to think seriously about their aging and death. Apart from offhand comments ("I hope they don't let me linger on like that!"), most persons do not wish to confront the eventual loss of their powers. Few are likely to make out a living will or pay their physician for the privilege of discussing the possibility of their own incapacity.

Secondly, in our mobile society a patient who has discussed such issues with his personal physician will probably be attended by someone else when these issues arise.

Furthermore, persons' ideas about the quality of life change drastically as they age, especially in the last years of their lives. The 21-year-old who wants to be shot rather than suffer the imagined ignominy of a nursing home is only too grateful to accept the nursing-home bed and warm meals when he turns 85. A living will or a frank conversation with one's physician even at age 55 would rarely reflect what one's wishes would be at age 70.

Finally, and most important, it is simply too difficult to define all the varieties of illness, suffering, prognosis, and treatment with sufficient precision for the definitions to be of much help in the actual situation. A physician may know, for instance, that the patient does not want to be "kept alive" "unnecessarily" "if I'm a vegetable" and there is "no hope of improvement." The real-life situation is, unfortunately, much more complex. What constitutes keeping a person alive? Is it giving him a warm room and regular meals rather than allowing him to lie at home paralyzed and with no heat? Is it giving him an intravenous infusion? Routine antibiotics? And what quality of life constitutes "being a vegetable"? Furthermore, in real life there is rarely any certainty about prognosis. Improvement may be unlikely, but it is often possible. So, even in the best case, in which a self-aware person had talked with his physician or made out a recent living will, the complexities of the actual situation would probably render those efforts of little practical use to the physician. And because of his debilities or the seriousness of his acute illness, the patient himself is rarely fully available to the physician at the needed moment.

If the professional ethicists have not yet provided much help in this most difficult situation, the law has been positively confusing. As I understand it, many recent court decisions have suggested that the courts must authorize the withholding of treatment in any particular case. Although I would not argue with the attempt to relieve the physician of this responsibility, the facts are that these decisions usually need to be made quickly (within hours or days), repeatedly (options with respect to quality of life, prognosis, and treatment may vary from day to day), and with a considerable degree of medical expertise. In my opinion, it is ridiculous to believe that the courts could (even if we thought they should) decide such matters promptly. It will be interesting to see how the courts finally settle this issue, but I expect that physicians will get little help, regardless.

In fact, then, the primary-care physician faces this complex dilemma alone. Because we have ignored the frequency with which such situations arise and their tremendous ethical importance, we force the physician into making profound ethical choices unprepared. He or she may try to share the decision with the family (who may know how the patient would decide in such a situation), but most often the family has even less idea of what to do than the physician on whom they rely for guidance. (And even when someone in the family does have a definite idea of what should be done, the physician needs to judge the ethics of that decision anyway, because our society does not indiscriminately assign the right to refuse treatment to any relative who might think he knows what is best.) For better or for worse, the decision returns to the physician.

What does one do, then? We have developed no rational way to decide what treatment to give and what to withhold once it has been decided to withhold "heroics." Perhaps my own most frequent response (and I do not admit this easily) is not to make a conscious decision at all. Aware that Mrs. Toivonen has a fever, I may decide to see her at the end of office hours and hen, in the rush of late-afternoon appointments, "forget" to drop by the nursing home until the next morning, by which time she will be either better or so much worse that "it won't help much to put her in the hospital, anyway." Or if I do examine her promptly, my examination will not be so thorough as it might be, and I will decide that the fever is "only a virus" when I really haven't excluded all the likely possibilities. Or, as I did this time, I will give some treatment that will probably help but that is not as aggressive as it could be.

The problem is simply too difficult for me as a single human being to face in a conscious way. How do I consciously decide to let this person die when everything in my being says that life has the ultimate value? How can I make a decision about the quality of this life? How can I know what the patient would want? Yet, on the other hand, how can I inflict the pain of aggressive treatment, and the suffering of further living, and spend the scarce resources of time and money on this person who is so obviously "trying" to die? And so, all too often, I don't make a conscious decision at all. I simply act, do something, make a decision without really considering the meaning of what I do, for the real meaning is too painful.

At other times, I do my best to make a conscious, rational decision, but this is little better. Since I am operating in a vacuum and have no reliable criteria on which to base a decision, my choice is ultimately guided by my feelings, prejudices, and mood more than by my reason.

Physicians have been making these decisions routinely, of course, ever since we acquired the power actually to influence the course of disease. As far as I can determine, however, we have not yet admitted to ourselves the awesomeness of our situation. We have been forced into the role of God, yet we hardly seem to have recognized it. For my part, the underlying irrationality of my decisions has gnawed at me; the life-and-death importance of my actions has kept me awake at night; the guilt and depression of never really knowing whether I have acted properly have been overwhelming. I would suggest that it is time we publicly examined our role in these situations, offered each other some guidelines, and came to some consensus about our responsibility. There is clearly no way to avoid these awesome decisions; let us at least come to them better prepared and with a clearer understanding of what we do.

Note

[1]Brown, N. K., and Thompson, D. J. "Nontreatment of Fever in Extended-Care Facilities." *New England Journal of Medicine* (1979), vol. 300: pp. 1246–50.

Guidelines
for Medical Decisions

The previous reading showed an individual physician's lament over the difficulty of making decisions when faced with the difficult choices that form a part of medical practice when dealing with the terminally ill. Part of the difficulty here is the fact that physicians face these decisions alone so often. Another complicating factor is that when families are faced with a difficult decision, they have no guidelines to help them work through the emotional decisions they must make. Guilt, desire to do the right thing, and ignorance of medical alternatives all cloud their ability to choose a proper treatment.

But what is a *proper* treatment? The literature surrounding euthanasia makes reference to using "extraordinary means" to sustain life, supporting life by "mechanical devices" or "exotic therapies." All these terms suggest that interfering with the natural course of a terminal illness to keep the body alive long after there is any hope of restoration of an enjoyable, conscious life is somehow unnatural. And who is to make the decision to withhold a treatment, or to remove it once begun?

A now-famous, or perhaps infamous, account that appeared in *The Journal of the American Medical Association* dealt with the decision of a hospital resident and brought to public discussion an example embodying the worst fears of all those opposed to euthanasia. Those fears are that, once the barriers against euthanasia are toppled, individual physicians will be encouraged to make snap decisions on their own that are against the patient's or family's wishes. The article entitled "It's Over, Debbie," has been attacked as not even a real event, just a hypothetical story written to provoke controversy. Whatever its origins, it is thought provoking.

IT'S OVER, DEBBIE

The call came in the middle of the night. As a gynecology resident rotating through a large private hospital, I had come to detest telephone calls, because invariably I would be up for several hours and would not feel good the next day. However, duty called, so I answered the phone. A nurse informed me that a patient was having difficulty getting rest, could I please see her. She was on 3 North.

That was the gynecologic-oncology unit, not my usual duty station. As

Source: "It's Over, Debbie." *The Journal of the American Medical Association,* vol. 259 (January 8, 1988), p. 272. Copyright © 1988, American Medical Association. Used by permission.

I trudged along bumping sleepily against walls and corners and not believing I was up again, I tried to imagine what I might find at the end of my walk. Maybe an elderly woman with an anxiety reaction, or perhaps something particulary horrible.

I grabbed the chart from the nurses station on my way to the patient's room, and the nurse gave me some hurried details: a 20-year-old girl named Debbie was dying of ovarian cancer. She was having unrelenting vomiting, apparently as the result of an alcohol drip administered for sedation. Hmmm, I thought. Very sad. As I approached the room I could hear loud, labored breathing.

I entered and saw an emaciated, dark-haired woman who appeared much older than 20. She was receiving nasal oxygen, had an IV and was sitting in bed suffering from what was obviously severe air hunger. The chart noted her weight at 80 pounds. A second woman, also dark-haired but of middle age, stood at her right, holding her hand. Both looked up as I entered. The room seemed filled with the patient's desperate effort to survive. Her eyes were hollow, and she had suprasternal and intercostal retractions with her rapid inspirations.

She had not eaten or slept in two days. She had not responded to chemotherapy and was being given supportive care only. It was a gallows scene, a cruel mockery of her youth and unfulfilled potential. Her only words to me were, "Let's get this over with."

I retreated with my thoughts to the nurses station. The patient was tired and needed rest. I could not give her health, but I could give her rest. I asked the nurse to draw 20mg. of morphine sulfate into a syringe. Enough, I thought, to do the job. I took the syringe into the room and told the two women I was going to give Debbie something that would let her rest and to say goodbye.

Debbie looked at the syringe, then laid her head on the pillow with her eyes open, watching what was left of the world. I injected the morphine intravenously and watched to see if my calculations on its effects would be correct. Within seconds her breathing slowed to a normal rate, her eyes closed, and her features softened as she seemed restful at last. The older woman stroked the hair of the now-sleeping patient. I waited for the inevitable next effect of depressing the respiratory drive. With clocklike certainty, within four minutes the breathing rate slowed even more, then became irregular, then ceased. The dark-haired woman stood erect and seemed relieved.

It's over, Debbie.

Name Withheld by Request

Using the distinctions noted in the introductory section of this chapter, the Debbie example is an instance of active euthanasia; whether it is voluntary or involuntary depends on how one interprets the ambiguous statement from Debbie, "Let's get this over with." Those who defend the right of a patient to refuse extended medical treatment would argue that the Debbie story is an example of the logical fallacy known as *straw man,* the strategy of offering an easily refuted example as evidence of the weakness of your opponent's position.

More serious discussion surrounds the issue of when to initiate and when to withdraw life support systems for the terminally ill. While technically still euthanasia, the issues surrounding these concerns focus more on allowing the patient, or the patient's representative, the right to refuse a prolonged, painful, and futile death. In an attempt to come to terms with this issue, the Stanford University Medical Center Committee on Ethics unanimously adopted a set of guidelines for initiating and withdrawing life support. The committee comprised representatives from many medical specialties, the clergy, medical administrators, and academic representatives from philosophy, sociology, and religious studies. That part of the document dealing with general ethical fundamentals and practical principles to guide physicians is reprinted here. As you read through this document, see if you think it would help a physician through the difficult decisions described in the previous reading. Also ask whether the intern's actions might have been different had the hospital where Debbie was dying adopted the Stanford Medical Center guidelines.

THE STANFORD UNIVERSITY MEDICAL CENTER COMMITTEE ON ETHICS

General Ethical Fundamentals

The fundamental principles underlying the ethics of medical intervention in all settings are discussed exhaustively in various books.[1] Therefore, although some basic principles are listed here, only the practical principles will be considered in detail. A basic principle of medical ethics is obviously the preservation of life, which is frequently tempered by the second principle, the alleviation of suffering. A third is the injunction that physicians "first do no harm" (*primum non nocere*). A fourth principle, respect for the autonomy of the individual patient, finds a lively expression in the current surge of medical consumerism. A fifth fundamental principle is the concept of justice, exemplified by the effort to ensure that medical resources are allocated fairly.[2] The final principle is truth telling, well discussed recently

Source: "Initiating and Withdrawing Life Support: Principles and Practice in Adult Medicine," by John Edward Ruark, Thomas Alfred Raffin, and the Stanford University Medical Center Committee on Ethics. *The New England Journal of Medicine,* vol. 318 (January 7, 1988), pp. 25–30. Used by permission.

by Bok.[3] Because medical practice often brings these principles into conflict, resolving such conflicts is central to the art of medicine.

Underlying Practical Principles

Establishment of the Source of Authority

The most important key to appropriate ethical management of the initiation and withdrawal of life support is constant awareness of the true source of authority. Although physicians must often be authoritative about the options available to patients, all involved should recognize that the actual authority over the patient never resides with the physician. Patients alone, or their legal surrogates, have the right to control what happens to them. Many of the ethical dilemmas in critical care situations derive from overt or tacit violations of this principle. Physicians should act as consultants engaged to evaluate their patients' problems, present reasonable options for treatment in understandable language, and facilitate decision making. Except in emergencies, doctors should feel permitted to proceed with treatments only after those with the true authority have clearly decided.

Effective Communication with Patients and Families

The ability to communicate effectively with patients and families or legal surrogates is one of the most vital professional skills in appropriate decision making. Especially in critical care situations, stress, fear, intimidation, and unfamiliarity with the setting can overwhelm even sophisticated patients and families. Health professionals are responsible not merely for attempting to communicate, but for ensuring that effective communication takes place.

Certainly, some physicians communicate better than others. When physicians are made aware of communication problems by patients, families, or members of the health care team, they should promptly enlist a proven facilitator—a social worker, chaplain, or psychotherapist, for example. There are several reasons why communication in this setting is difficult for doctors. First, each case is stressful and emotionally wrenching, taking a major physical and psychological toll on physicians. Second, the cumulation of many such cases exacts a high price from physicians in terms of emotional fatigue and distance, personal fear of death, guilt, insecurity, and anxiety. Third, effective communication in catastrophic situations requires time, a scarce commodity among doctors. Outside facilitators can be valuable on the health care team because they have the communication skills and the time to exercise them.

The following are some guidelines for effective communication. First, create an environment that fosters communication. Rushed or chaotic settings such as a hospital corridor hinder effective decision making. Second, remember that stress often impairs the reasoning ability of patients and families. Keep communication simple until it is clear that more detail will be helpful rather than overwhelming. Third, encourage patients and families to ask questions and express feelings. This helps to counteract the intimidation that many people experience when dealing with physicians.

In addition, present information in the language and at the level of detail that best enables patients or surrogates to decide. It is not useful to speak honestly about a situation if you are intimidating people with an esoteric vocabulary, unnecessary details, or an inappropriate emotional tone. Ask patients and families to summarize what has been said in order to check the accuracy of vital communications, provide a chance to correct misunderstandings, and assess their level of sophistication and reasoning. Finally, make a specific effort to sharpen your communication skills. Ivey and Authier,[4] for example, describe a useful model for effective communication by physicians. Various resources[5] offer more detailed advice on communication in the presence of life-threatening illness.

Early Determination and Ongoing Review of Individual Quality-of-Life Values

The ethics of life support require physicians to ascertain, whenever possible, the views of each patient or representative on the balance between quality and mere prolongation of life—the concept of proportionality. Professionals should diligently avoid making assumptions in this area, especially with patients of different religious or ethnic backgrounds. The balance between the probable extension of life and the reduction in quality of life resulting from any treatment must be explicitly described and discussed with each patient. Absolute candor about the level of discomfort associated with any anticipated treatment is essential, but emotional coldness or brutal abruptness should be avoided.

On the other hand, there is no evidence that any worthwhile end is accomplished by painting an unduly optimistic picture. Physicians who do so may unintentionally appear untrustworthy at a time when the ability to trust one's doctor is particularly critical. Specific treatment options for probable complications should be explored as early as possible, to avoid unnecessary guilt in surrogates who are forced to decide for incompetent patients. With permission from patients, family members should be included in anticipatory decision making so that they have no doubt about the patient's wishes.

As an illness progresses, patients commonly reassess the relative costs and benefits of treatments as they gain familiarity with various therapies and as their energy wanes with advancing debilitation. Thus, at a minimum, every important change in a patient's condition demands that decisions about proportionality be reevaluated. Such reassessment requires carefully exploring the ambiguous feelings of families as they make decisions or attempt to influence those of the patient.

Any medical intervention should be oriented toward the patient's goals—for example, to spend some time at home—as well as toward solving a clinical problem. In many cases there is a critical point beyond which medical interventions may act less to prolong acceptable life than to extend a miserable dying process.[6] Professionals cannot expect patients or families to take the lead in raising these questions.

Recognition of Patients' Rights

The final basis for appropriate decision making about life support is the code of patients' rights as articulated by the American Hospital Association and enacted into law in many states. If these rights are observed in spirit as well as in letter, it is difficult to go wrong in initiating or withdrawing medical treatments. In many states, the law requires posting these rights in appropriate places within every hospital. The following patients' rights[7] are particularly relevant: to receive considerate and respectful care; to receive information about the illness, the course of treatment, and the prospects for recovery in terms that the patient can understand; to receive as much information about any proposed treatment or procedure as the patient may need in order to give informed consent or to refuse this course of treatment (except in emergencies, this information should include a description of the procedure or treatment, and medically important risks involved in this treatment, alternative courses of treatment or nontreatment and the risks involved in each, and the name of the person who will carry out the treatment or procedure); to participate actively in decisions regarding medical care (to the extent permitted by law, this includes the right to refuse treatment); and to have all patients' rights apply to the person who may have legal responsibility to make decisions about medical care on behalf of the patient.

Specific Applications

Initiation of Basic Life-Support Measures

Basic life-support measures—providing food, water, and supplementary oxygen—are among the most difficult to forgo in medical practice because of their high emotional content. Although few of us may know what it feels like to undergo cardiopulmonary resuscitation or heart transplantation, we all know what it is like to be hungry, thirsty, or short of breath. Health care professionals may provide these basics of care almost as a reflex, without fully considering whether they are performing a truly caring act.

In critical illness, thoughtful clinicians need to replace such impulses with a careful decision-making process that takes into account several major points. First of all, every medical intervention should serve what patients consider to be their best interests as determined in an active dialogue with their families and their physicians. Second, as in most cases involving the initiation or withdrawal of life support (or any major medical intervention), it is wise to include close family members in the decision-making process whenever possible. This enlists the family on the side of the eventual treatment course, minimizing the possibility of harrowing conflicts at times of great stress. Third, physicians should anticipate the likely medical course and elicit clearly—in advance—the specific choices the patient wishes to make for each possible situation.

Fourth, once any medical intervention is begun in grave illness, withdrawing it in order to avoid an agonizing dying process requires a direct action that may result in a death. However necessary and humane such an action may be, those forced to make such decisions and those who carry them out are inevitably left with disturbing feelings. Furthermore, medications need to be evaluated carefully. In particular, problems may arise from the use of antibiotics or steroids to treat infections or cerebral edema. Comatose, hopelessly ill people may be pulled back needlessly from a painless death to live out an extra few days or weeks in pain and indignity. Perhaps some physicians, frustrated by underlying illnesses that defy medical intervention, gain a sense of control by treating conditions they can treat. In addition, if those responsible for the patient want every possible measure taken to keep the patient alive, professionals should comply with this request at first. If the desire to persist in treatment seems inappropriate, a direct, logical challenge by the professional will often fail, whereas a nonjudgmental exploration of underlying feelings can result in sounder decision making.

Also, physicians need to clarify the purpose of placing intravenous lines. Unless a patient-oriented goal has been defined, it is not acceptable to begin intravenous therapy for "hydration and nutrition." Once an intravenous line is in place, it becomes harder to refrain from treating the infections and chemical imbalances that might provide a humane release. This same reasoning applies to ordering laboratory tests or assessing vital signs: once it is demonstrated that a treatable problem exists, it becomes much harder not to act. Finally, similar cautions apply to the placement of feeding tubes, especially in patients in chronic vegetative states.

Instituting Advanced Life-Support Measures

Cardiopulmonary resuscitation raises many ethical questions. A patient in cardiac or pulmonary arrest presents professionals with a medical emergency that requires a set of automatic responses if function is to be restored before severe organ damage occurs. Unless they are aware of the patient's previously expressed wishes about resuscitation, physicians must act first and evaluate later.

One recent study[8] of all the resuscitations at a major medical center in one year showed that only 14 percent of those who received cardiopulmonary resuscitation survived to leave the hospital. Only 19 percent of all patients discussed the procedure with their physicians, and in only 33 percent of the cases was the family consulted about resuscitation, even though more than 95 percent of the physicians claimed to believe such consultations appropriate. In a related study involving do-not-resuscitate orders,[9] 22 percent of patients and 86 percent of families were involved in decisions not to resuscitate. The families identified the attending physician as the best source of help with their decisions. Other useful factors included the presence of coma or brain death, indicating a hopeless prognosis; support and reassurance from physicians and nurses that the decision was appropriate; assurances from staff that care and comfort would be maintained; and previous conversations with the patient about resuscitation.

These studies underscore the ethical dilemma presented by cardiopulmonary resuscitation. Given the invasive and at times almost brutal nature of the procedure, it is hard to reconcile the relatively small chance of a successful outcome with the loss of a more dignified death—particularly in the setting of chronic, severely debilitating, or terminal conditions. In attempting to resolve this dilemma, there are some important points the physician should take into account. First, since cardiopulmonary arrest is likely to occur during the hospitalization of an elderly, chronically ill, or terminally ill person, there is little ethical justification for not discussing it in advance. This imperative also applies to similar patients who remain at home or in nursing homes. The code status of patients should be identified early and officially conveyed to patients, families, and all health care providers. Prominent signs on the front of medical charts or records are useful.

Attending physicians must take the lead in bringing up this matter. If they neglect to do so, family members or nurses (who are likely to be first on the scene) pay a high price. Physicians who feel uneasy with such decision making or who are poorly prepared to facilitate it have an obligation to seek education or counseling to prepare them to perform this duty effectively. When there is any doubt or a persistent lack of unanimity on the health care team, they should enlist the aid of a facilitator, as discussed above.

Finally, one aspect of this question that is seldom adequately considered is that successful resuscitation almost inevitably results in admission to an intensive care unit or a cardiac care unit. Few patients who have not received intensive care can comprehend the general unpleasantness of even the most humane intensive care unit—the invasive monitoring and treatment, the noise and activity around the clock, and the necessary restrictions on visitors. In particular, mechanical ventilators virtually preclude communication with family members at times when emotional support is most needed. These realities must be clearly communicated when physicians seek informed consent. Given that an average of less than 10 percent of patients with hematologic cancers who receive intensive care survive to leave the hospital,[10] special caution should be employed in deciding to intubate or resuscitate them.

Renal dialysis is another intensive treatment that is difficult to withdraw once it has been started. Its withdrawal, like that of mechanical ventilation, leads directly and observably to the death of patients depending on it. Thus, in order to avoid the emotional distress and long-term guilt connected with "pulling the plug," careful informed consent, perhaps including a chance to talk to a patient on dialysis, should be obtained before dialysis is started. Similar reasoning can be applied to more aggressive interventions such as renal, cardiac, lung, and bone marrow transplantation.

Withdrawing Advanced Life Support

The decision to withdraw advanced life-support measures can be one of the most difficult for professionals and family members to face. Ideally, if such measures are initiated as outlined above, the guidelines for their withdrawal will have been well defined by patients or surrogates. In reality, such clear definition is more the exception than the rule. The following are some suggestions for physicians:

Exercise reasonable clinical judgment about the likelihood of medical benefit from further treatment. Studies such as APACHE (Acute Physiologic Assessment and Chronic Health Evaluation) II[11] provide valuable prognostic guidelines.

Assess the patient's competence. A sound evaluation of mental status is vital to decision making, and psychiatric consultation should be sought when the state of competence cannot be clearly identified.

Seek unanimity among members of the health care team. Problems may arise when any professional feels excluded from the decision-making process. Because nurses provide most of the intensive care, they often have information about patients and families that is available only to those who have spent hours at the bedside.

Vigorously solicit the patient's judgment regarding withdrawal of treatment. Although most persons on life support will be legally incompe-tent, any shred of evidence about what the patient wants will be enormously valuable to those who must decide. Competent patients who request that their life support be stopped must be carefully evaluated. Such patients have a legal right to control their health care, and professionals who do not comply may be committing battery.

Do not rush decision making with families. These negotiations must be regarded as delicate processes with their own timing. Facilitation by non-physician experts, especially chaplains, is often invaluable. The health care team should work with the family toward unanimous decisions regarding the life support of incompetent patients.

Establish time-limited goals, based on clinical judgment and informa-tion such as the APACHE II data. After being advised that life support should be discontinued, families are often overwhelmed with confusion and guilt and may resist the advice. They can be helped in their decision making if concrete temporal milestones can be identified that herald improvement or failure. For example, the doctor might say to the adult children of a man who had been on a ventilator with respiratory and renal failure for two weeks, "If we see no signs that your father has improved over the next 72 hours, then we believe you should consider withdrawing life support. We believe your father is suffering and has essentially no chance to regain any reasonable quality of life, and to withdraw life support would allow him a more peaceful and dignified death."

The interlude provided by these time-based goals is a time for families to let go of the patient emotionally. Able facilitation of this process can be invaluable. Often, patients and family members have agreed to inter-ventions on the basis of unrealistic expectations—of both eventual benefits and quality of life during the treatments. Before they can make rational decisions, they may need to express the anger and mistrust generated by suboptimal informed consent. Here physicians must tolerate expressions of hostility without becoming defensive, but anger usually subsides once patients and families feel that their doctors are truly understanding and supportive. Even if patients or families do not express this anger, look for it in situations where it should reasonably be present. Statements such as, "This may have turned out to be a lot more than you bargained for. It wouldn't surprise me if you were angry about it," can open the way to the expression and resolution of feelings.

An effective way of telling patients or families that you believe life support should be withdrawn is to say, "It is my best judgment, and that of the other doctors and nurses, that your relative has essentially no chance to regain a reasonable quality of life. We believe that life support should be withdrawn, which means that your relative will probably die." There are two important components to this statement. First, the statement is realistically qualified, in a way that implies that the decision must be shared. Second, it is made clear that death is the probable result of the recommended course. Without this knowledge, there is no true informed consent, and potential liability (both emotional and legal) looms.

Grief-stricken or guilty family members may attempt to relieve their distress at the patient's expense by pressing for disproportionate treatment. Such insistence usually dissolves once the underlying feelings are acknowledged and understood.

Professionals should avoid involving themselves with cases that are inconsistent with their ethical principles. The tension and resentment inevitably arising under such circumstances may compromise clinical judgment. If such involvement cannot be avoided, frequent ventilation of feelings with understanding colleagues will make optimal care more likely.

If patients are judged incompetent and no written or oral communication about withdrawal of treatment exists, the problem is greater. The most satisfactory resolution of such cases occurs when professionals and families painstakingly explore the quality-of-life values previously held by the patient. Once family members have agreed that the patient would not have wanted to go on, consent to withdraw treatment usually follows. If no one knows the patient well enough to provide information about his or her quality-of-life values, professionals can establish a group composed of physicians, nurses, family or friends, and two patient advocates (at least one of whom represents an organized religion, preferably that of the patient). This group identifies what it believes to be the most thoughtful "substituted judgment." Decisions should be made by family, friends, health care providers, and facilitators. Only rarely is legal assistance necessary.

Withdrawal of Basic Life Support

The withdrawal of basic life support, such as hydration or nutrition by intravenous lines or feeding tubes, is ethically controversial and complex. Although most people eventually feel at peace with stopping more technical medical interventions, these basic measures are regarded more as signs of caring than as treatment. No one is comfortable with the thought that a loved one may "die of thirst" or "starve to death." Indeed, legal sanction notwithstanding, families will feel guilty if these feelings are not explored and resolved.

The three states whose courts have addressed the question of withdrawal of nutrition and hydration from incompetent patients have treated it in the same manner as the withdrawal of advanced life support. As additional cases are adjudicated, broader judicial support is expected for withdrawing these treatments when they are not clearly benefiting patients.

The key to resolving ethical problems in this area lies in clarifying the patient's interests. In the presence of truly informed consent and sensitive psychosocial management of decision making, most painful ambiguities can be resolved. The patient's wishes regarding withdrawal of the whole array of treatments should be detailed in writing. If possible, conflicts between the patient's wishes and those of the family should be mediated toward a consensus, although the patient's wishes must be controlling. Families need assurances that comfort and caring will be maintained and that doctors will not abandon them.

Conclusions

Most of the ethical dilemmas involved in life support can be avoided with careful attention to certain important points. Recognize that authority in medical care rests with patients or their legal surrogates. Support them in exercising this authority. Support patients' rights, particularly the right to give informed consent. Emphasize effective communication, and be aware of and avoid the circumstances that tend to impair it. Enlist a proven facilitator rapidly if communication becomes less than optimal. Review proportionality decisions early in each treatment course and with each major change in clinical status. Recognize that once an intervention is started, its withdrawal can cause problems; nevertheless, in many settings life support should be thoughtfully withdrawn. And finally, besides being aware of your own feelings, provide emotional support to the other members of the health care team in these difficult cases.

Notes

[1]E.g., Brody H. Ethical decisions in medicine. Boston: Little, Brown, 1976.

[2]Fuchs VR. The "rationing" of medical care. N Engl J Med 1984; 311:1572–73.

[3]Bok S. Lying: moral choice in public and private life. New York: Pantheon, 1978.

[4]Ivey AE, Authier J. Microcounseling: innovations in interviewing, counseling, psychotherapy, and psychoeducation. 2nd ed. Springfield, Ill.: Charles C Thomas, 1978.

[5]Gonda TA, Ruark JE, Dying dignified: the health professional's guide to care. Menlo Park, Calif.: Addison-Wesley, 1984.

[6]Young EWD. Reflections on life and death. Stanford MD 1976; 15:20–4.

[7]Title 22, Section 70707, California Administrative Code.

[8]Bedell SE, Delbanco TL, Cook EF, Epstein FH. Survival after cardiopulmonary resuscitation in the hospital. N Engl J Med 1983; 309:569–76.

[9]Bedell SE, Pelle D, Maher PL, Cleary PD. Do-not-resuscitate orders for critically ill patients in the hospital: How are they used and what is their impact? JAMA 1986; 256:233–7.

[10]Schuster DP, Marion JM, Precedents for meaningful recovery during treatment in a medical intensive care unit: outcomes in patients with hematologic malignancy. Am J Med 1983; 75:402–8.

[11]Knaus WA, Draper EA, Wagner DP, Zimmerman JE. Prognosis in acute organ-system failure. Ann Surg 1985; 202:685–93.

When Is Suicide Rational?

Instances of voluntary euthanasia, whether active or passive, are cases of suicide. We normally think of suicide in terms of a life gone sour: a love lost, a business in bankruptcy, a career stymied. Perhaps what all of these sorts of cases have in common is that they hold out a life of despair. This is true of many of the typical cases of euthanasia, suicide in a medical context.

A diagnosis of Lou Gehrig's disease or Alzheimer's disease means a future of degeneration, mental and physical, with no real hope of cure. Both of these conditions leave one totally helpless and, therefore, dependent on others. Other conditions promise almost uncontrollable pain until death. Death from AIDS is often extremely unpleasant, coming from pneumonias and cancers that are difficult to handle. Elephant man's disease leads to various degrees of disfigurement. Unfortunately, it is not difficult to continue the list.

Suicide seems a reasonable option when life holds so little. That is the assumption behind much argument in favor of euthanasia.

Joseph Margolis, a philosopher, argued in his book, *Negativities: The Limits of Life,* that a life felt to have no meaning at all was a life justifiably ended. It is easy to see how a person diagnosed with Alzheimer's disease or AIDS or a cancer with a poor prognosis might feel that life had from that point lost all meaning. On Margolis's view, such a person would be justified in committing suicide.

H. A. Nielsen challenges Margolis on this point. In doing so Nielsen also challenges a prime driving assumption behind arguments in favor of euthanasia. Nielsen does not offer sophisticated philosophical analysis. Rather, he offers a case and asks us to decide with the person affected. The point Nielsen stresses (and which he thinks Margolis and others have overlooked) is that the *process* of reaching a decision is important in deciding whether or not that suicide can be regarded as rational.

MARGOLIS ON RATIONAL SUICIDE:
AN ARGUMENT
FOR CASE STUDIES IN ETHICS

H. A. Nielsen

To the Socratic question, "Can virtue be taught?" it would seem equally Socratic to reply, "If so, only by example." Yet in books on ethics one rarely sees exploited the illustrative power of a careful individual's full-dress moral reflections. In this paper I want to present an example of someone actually forming moral judgments.

The year 1975 brought forth a small book called *Negativities: The Limits of Life,* whose author, Joseph Margolis, claims to have "provided a sense in which a man may be a rational suicide, the sense in which a man has as his overriding concern the ending of his life."[1] He speaks of persons who "simply wish to put an end to their lives because life has ceased to have a sufficiently favorable significance or because taking one's life, under the circumstances (e.g., a painful terminal illness), does have a sufficiently favorable significance."[2] According to Margolis one could justify suicide even more convincingly if the person "decided that life was utterly meaningless" or "sincerely believed life to have no point at all."[3] We are speaking now, as Margolis insists, of persons with all their faculties intact. Following the author's hints, we need not bind ourselves to the orthodox Freudian view that suicide is invariably triggered by an episode of severe mental illness.

Let our subject then be Margolis's rational suicide, and let us give him a name and some features. Damon K., thirty-eight, a childless widower, modest savings, a supervisor of hospital orderlies who will soon be out of a job because of a muscular disease that cripples its victims by slow degrees. Life expectancy: three to five years. There is no cure in sight. At this point in the description, according to Margolis, we need only add that Damon has "decided that life is utterly meaningless" in order for him to conclude—rationally—that suicide is the path for him.

At this point a reader might understandably raise his hand in protest. "Not so fast. Some of Margolis's expressions bewilder me. For the sake of discussion I agree that if Damon decides his life is utterly meaningless, then as a fellow human being I can at least appreciate his saying next, 'Suicide is for me.' But Margolis's whole point is that this is to be a rational suicide. What will make it rational? Surely not the mere fact that Damon's last inference, the one just cited, happens to strike a lot of people as logically tolera-

Source: "Margolis on Rational Suicide: An Argument for Case Studies in Ethics" by H. A. Nielsen. *Ethics,* vol. 89, no. 4, pp. 195–201. © 1979 by The University of Chicago. 0014-1704/79/8904-0006$00.75 Used by permission of the University of Chicago Press and the author.

ble. Does a single inference make such an irreversible decision rational? Even if Damon shows no sign of mental illness, this fact will hardly guarantee the validity of his reasonings from start to finish. He might well be rational in the sense of possessing all his wits, yet in practice be a muddled or careless reasoner.

"What we must have," our objector continues, "in order to count this a rational suicide in Margolis's sense, is nothing more or less than an account of how Damon arrived at his premise. In short, let Margolis tell us: what is this thing he calls '*deciding* that life is utterly meaningless'? How did Damon decide that? If by inference, from what premises did it follow? If not by inference, then by what other route?"

Faced with potential objections of this sort, it is plain that we need to say more about Damon's prowess and exertions as a thinker before we can test Margolis's claim by trying to construct a rationale for Damon's suicide. To begin, assume further that Damon's mind does not operate on a hair trigger, that he knows he has fallen hard in the past for this or that halftruth or unclear notion, and that he has the diarist's habit of keeping track of his reflections. That diary is what we want.

FROM THE DIARY OF DAMON K.

Feb. 17.—It is a week now since they double-checked that diagnosis with a second battery of tests. I really miss Vivian's willing ear. The doctors listen, yes, but Viv would have listened for free.

I am lucky, though, to have nobody depending on me. Not a worry in the world. With my pension plan paid up I won't be much of a social burden even if it stretches out for quite a long time. By opting for cremation I can even spare someone the labor of digging a hole.

But why stretch it out? There are neat ways of ending it. Why try to wring the last tasteless drop out of a life that makes no sense? Is this cowardly?—I am long past caring what others think of me.

Feb. 18.—Relaxed and in high spirits since the plan came to me yesterday. It is not as if I had to fill up all the blank pages in this diary.

At work I think a lot, and I have been thinking off and on about the *method.* It gives me something hard to gnaw on.

Gave my Sony radio to Mrs. Cavanaugh when hers went on the fritz. She is seventy-nine. She couldn't believe I hadn't switched it on for weeks, not even for news and weather, but it's the truth. Talk shows used to interest me, but no more. Nothing does. I mean nothing except my new plan. Bought a pocket notebook today to jot down ideas at work. Surprising how many things come to mind once you set your sights.

In case I lose the notebook I pasted a name and address sticker inside. Everything else is in a simple code I made up on the bus.

Feb. 19.—My plan is simple. The end is all I want. Do a clean, quick job on a life that makes no more sense than a chain of empty sausage skins. It made no sense from the beginning, though as a boy I couldn't put a question to it. Today I filled in for Baker upstairs in the children's ward. Death grins out of those doorways, too.

End it, and by this I don't mean I expect to *feel* the relief like a couple of aspirins working, or be around in any form to enjoy it. Yet when I was wheeling a child's body from the autopsy room to the morgue a thought pinched me. What *would* give sense to my life? A religion like Mrs. Cavanaugh's? Beliefs like those look and feel to me like wads of foreign money that I can't even read the numbers on and no stores around here will accept as legal tender. Would health give it sense? Or health plus cash? Plus a challenge and the education to meet it, like an engineer's commission to complete a Dover-to-Calais tunnel? Plus a second helping of love and a family? Most people, I know, ask no more than modest helpings of such things. Well, let them. I'm not out to spread melancholy. Anyway, for me those chances are stone dead.

The question kept troubling me on my coffee break. What does it mean to say my life makes no sense? Well, that it *lacks* something. Fine, if it lacks something I should at least be able to name the ingredient that would pep it up, like a dash of paprika in the goulash! If I say *meaning* is the thing it lacks, what am I talking about? Hope? A future? Fun?

The truth is, I don't know what *could* give my life meaning *now*. If the doctor rang me up and said, "There was a mix-up, Damon. Your tests came out normal, you're in fine shape"—how would I feel? Stunned, like a lottery winner. But afterward? Is "meaning" the same as "a clear track ahead into old age?" If you multiply five meaningless years by ten, what do you get? Meaning?

Yet if I can't say what *could* give my life meaning, what sense do I make when I complain that it *lacks* meaning? What is meaning? My head is spinning.

Feb. 20.—Today as I made my rounds part of the answer came to me. Saying my life makes no sense was like Vivian in some of her moods. "You don't love me," she'd say no matter what I did, including cartwheels back when I could do them. Buy her a dress, romance her, take her out, flatter her, rack my brains to figure out what she would *count* as a sign that I loved her. Nothing. Once when the mood was on her for a solid week and I ran clean out of honey and money, I finally said to myself, "There *is* no sign. When she says 'You don't love me' she's not describing *me*. She's saying, 'Damon, I'm in a funk.' "

In the same way, when I call my life senseless maybe I'm not describing my *life* at all, except as far as to say I flew my crate into a cloud and can't be sure yet which way the ground is.

But there must be a kernel of clearness somewhere in the verdict that my life is senseless. It means that life has starved me out of possibilities, left me with no bright prospects, no *reason* to keep living. My horizon is flat, bleak, treeless, with a dead black sea out beyond. Every path leads to that unfeeling shore, but now I spy a blessed shortcut. Except for a few yellowing memories I have nothing to rejoice over. All is vanity, says the only preacher I trust.

Feb. 21.—One-thirty A.M. First time I ever got out of bed to write. I feel a need to be clear about this plan, even if life itself is far from clear. At the moment I sink into endless sleep I don't want a voice to scream in my head, "Damon, you suckered yourself into this!"

No *reason,* I wrote yesterday, to keep living. *What could be clearer ground for ending it?* Yet exactly at this point, when the basis for suicide seems so transparent, and when I have picked out the gas oven as the last place to lay my living head, a tiny airborne spider of uncertainty floats into the lucid air. And gets me out of bed.

Still, if the end is really the end, what should one shattering moment matter? It will take the place of years of misery.

I suppose it matters because I don't want my *last* words in this life to be words of accusation against myself. I don't think I deserve that.

2:30 A.M. Sitting here barren for over an hour. Now it occurs to me to wonder what it means to demand *reasons* for living another year or three or possibly five? I mean, what does this demand tell me about myself? On the face of it, that I don't find myself *interesting* enough to be worth keeping company with over that stretch of time. This is not to forget that I have a disease that will gradually whittle me down, a hard thing to forget when I can already feel it in my back and legs, but it is not an acutely painful sickness, and it doesn't impair the mind. No, I can't get away from it, my interest in being the one I am is gutteringly low.

Thoughts are coming faster now. This unfriendliness towards myself, this idea that my own company is so poor a dish that I require extra *reasons* for putting up with it—whose portrait am I sketching? An hour ago would I have recognized it as my own?

What if my gas oven plan turns out to be an expression—the ultimate expression—of my dislike of myself? Is it too far-fetched to guess that *some* suicides are of that kind?

"What's it worth to be Damon K?" Answer: You wouldn't care for it. It's a tiresome existence to begin with and promises to get more unpleasant on a steady downgrade. Yes, in fact I'm drawing up plans to scotch it for good, but a couple of minor matters have to be cleared

up before I turn back to that. First, does my estimate of a human existence *mirror the facts?* Oh, yes, no question about it. It mirrors the facts
of *my* life. But isn't there something wrong with thinking of this as a
burdensome, disappointing *life,* even though every single day of it fits
that description? In other words, who says it's the *life* that's at fault?

If I were a Jew I would believe that my life belonged to a God, and
if a Christian that this God went somewhat out of his way to save me.
Either way, disliking the creature called Damon K. would be a kind of
impudence those people no doubt reserve a special name for. All the
more reason to play my cards close to the vest. As a religionless man
I am not helped by their pieties, and it would only sour people use-
lessly if I paraded these thoughts. What surprises me is how much I
can unpack from just the fact that I demand *reasons* for living. It's as
if a whole philosophy (which may be too highfalutin a word for it) is
coiled up in that demand. Right or wrong, its *voltage* amazes me.
Who'd expect to step on an electric eel in his own innocent bathtub?
On one point, it seems, I could be entirely wrong. I mean in thinking
I'm not very interesting.

Feb. 22.—Reading about suicide. Hard to see it as a crime from my
personal angle, but why clutter up the picture with legalities? If someone declared it an unnatural act, I guess I would smile. I don't feel
one bit like a part of Nature. Yes, the animal kingdom and the nitro-
gen cycle. I'm involved in all that, but the part of me that cries
"enough of this!"—is it animal, vegetable or mineral?

Feb. 23.—"Enough of this!"—a war cry or a whimper?

This belief of mine that there is nothing in me *worth* drawing close
to, no bright glowing filament—it has to be called a superstition. First
of all an uneasiness haunts it, and secondly I have treated it as a
"truth" when I had only the most hazardous grounds for believing it.
Kind of shabby all around.

What's it worth to *me* to be Damon K. and nobody else? An eerie
question. The first real clue came in the midst of plans to close out
my life. It told me I'm only *conditionally* attached to myself, unwilling
to keep on being Damon K. unless life meets my *conditions*—and what
are those? Fillips, extras to keep my days interesting, since I find no
relish in my own companionship. These sentiments have a slightly
"off" odor about them, but when I ask myself what the alternative is,
the *un*conditional kind of existence, I draw a blank.

Feb. 24.—I feel a strong urge to search myself for further surprises,
to take a close look at my conditional kind of life and the beliefs—like
that superstition of yesterday—that cling to it like a cheap cologne. No
doubt about it, I caught myself just in time, arm cocked like a Goth
about to smash a statue of unknown value. The point is, I am in no

position *yet* to judge that my life is senseless. Even if my guess proved right, the flimsiness, the impatience, the *guesswork* of my earlier judgment makes me shudder.

Feb. 26.—The more intently I looked at that demand for *reasons* to keep going, the more its face changed. On the other side of the same coin it says, "I don't find *myself* interesting." How well, I wonder, do I know Damon K.?

If I had turned on the gas before looking hard at my "conditional" mode of existence (a life which might very well be senseless and savorless *because* it is conditional) it would have to be called an act of confused petulance, a quiet tantrum, shamefully unadult. So it becomes important to me to compare my kind of existence with what I can only call the *other* kind.

I'm not interesting to myself, I'm a dull burden. I do not identify with this existence, I want to cut it short. That is, I identify with the conditions I lay down for it, not with the Damon K. who can possess them or not possess them. The Damon without them is a satchel I drag around, stuffed with worthless rocks. But this, as I said, is my *feeling*, not something known. How do I check out and confirm the feeling, so that I can make my exit with serenity, not stabbing the finger of shame at myself?

Think of the things I've treated as *conditions* for willing to go on:
 my looks (when younger);
 my athletic ability (ditto);
 my decent job;
 my loving relationship with Viv;
 my reputation;
 my mobility and the jazzy things I could do with it;
 my nice home and belongings;
 my health . . .

A glance reveals that every one of these can be washed away overnight. Some have already vanished, and floodwaters are creeping up on the rest.

Now a voice speaks up in me. "You put *top* value on what you *know* can vanish in a wink—isn't something fishy here?"

"If you know so much," I answer, "name something that *can't* vanish in a wink." No reply. Silence, though, is ambiguous. It can mean nobody's there. Or *we're not speaking*, and that spells war. A house divided. The voice that jogs me about my fishy thinking and my iffy kind of existence belongs to a quality-minded side of me, a Damon who worries about me even though my sands are trickling out. It's that side of my consciousness that the rest is divided from, that I'm not entirely on speaking terms with. Damon my would-be preceptor, I judge from those growls that yours is as genuine as any other voice down there.

Tell me, how is it that *you* find me interesting enough to worry about? Or perhaps you're thinking, "If he turns on the gas, he takes me with him," is that it?—No, I know better than to imagine you as a separate little manikin in a fifth chamber of my heart.

Feb. 27.—The side of me that cares about being Damon, that actually *warms* to the idea—what is it like? For one thing it's critical of sloppy judgments and superstitions. Does everyone, I wonder, have a side that's fond of the life it belongs to, criticizes the person (or would if he let it speak), hankers to be consulted, and *splits a man in two* if he ignores it?

War. That comes as another surprise.

Possibly, just possibly, that elusive *other* kind of existence, the unconditional kind, consists in nothing more than giving that warm and willing side of me its fair share of the microphone.

Feb. 28.—One way of stopping the war, I suppose, is by gassing to death the side of me that cares. How much cruder, more Nazi this sounds now than it did before.—Yet psychology has its own names for "the side of me that cares." Practically everybody, I'm told, has a super-ego that guards him, watches out for his interests, his image, his self-esteem.

—But why should I get anxious about "a side of me that cares"?

What does it matter when the whole man dies?

March 1.—The tone of last night's entry jars me like a cracked bell. There's nothing *personal*, when all is said, in a theory of the human psyche that tells us, "Everybody has an id, an ego, and a superego." Even if it's correct it doesn't—it can't—teach a man how to feel toward *his own*.

If there is a side of me grieved in a personal way by my half-hearted attachment to Damon K., then no matter what germ-free scientific name I give it, it remains part of my personal consciousness, and I remain in a state of war against it. Where it speaks out against my conditional kind of life, the hint is that it knows of another kind of life, one in which I *identify* with the side of me that chafes at my present way of living.

And now I sense a stymie, a genuine dilemma. I can't stick my head in the oven without first *trying* the alternative to my present kind of life. That would be mindless, and I'd go under the gas raging at myself. But look at the alternative. It comes to nothing less than upending my whole table of priorities and writing "Stop the war" at the top—with no assurance at all that I'll get anything substantive out of the deal. My old maxim, "Do as you please," drops to a lower rank. More than that, I have to follow the new maxim as singlemindedly as I planned my death, and with just as terminal an intent. Otherwise I would have to fault myself for not really trying.

It's too much. There has to be some crazy kink in the logic that brought me to this fork in the road.

Too soon to judge that. Anyway there's time to check it over. A strange current of pity runs through me for people who take their lives without a pause like mine. Not that it matters to them now, but I hope the interval was brief for the ones who *realized* too late that their conditional way of existing might have set them up for it. Those are the poor patsies of suicide. Most of them (I can't speak for the mentally unsound ones and those desperate with pain) could have put if off for a week and realized this a lot faster than I did.

March 4.—I let a weekend go by for my dilemma to jell. Now I want to reconstruct it.

1. Plans to lop a few downhill years off my life reveal that I find my own company more a burden than anything else;

2. and they reveal, too, that I am not so attached to myself as to want to exist except on specific terms that will enable me to keep my days "interesting."

3. The apparent sallowness of this kind of life is deceiving. In fact, where my terms are not met I prepare to raise a violent hand against myself. A warlike hand.

4. Still, it takes two to make a war. Well, one side of my understanding smells something contemptible in this hemming and hawing about my "terms," my "reasons for living," while to my other side the days remain doughy and flavorless. So my halves have come unstuck, and although no shrink would pronounce me psychotic, here are the makings of a one-man conflict.

5. Then a possibility opened up. Perhaps that fissure within is the *reason why* my own company hangs so heavy on me. I'm drained by the costs of war.

6. Once I acknowledge this possibility, it would be muddleheaded and querulous to cut short my years before checking it out. Very well, check it out. Put those pieces of yourself together and see if the result makes music. And peace.

7. But how does a man really do that? How, I want to ask, does he will unconditionally to be the one he is? So there can be no sham about it, he wills it for as long as he lives. And the furled white flag he's been carrying in his knapsack gets a ceremonial burning.

8. And he gives that critical and caring side of himself a full say in all the decisions that count for anything. A costly move, this, because that side won't let me do less than my best at any task that has my name on it.

9. The *cost* of trying that alternative! Disarm myself and get on speaking terms with the Damon who seems to find more than a Cracker Jack prize in his lifepackage. Get on friendly terms with the

side of me that's already warm toward Damon and would monitor my life in that warmth. I may act against its advice on this or that, but this won't be the same as carrying it out of existence—against its will. (I'll be pretty shamefaced, I suppose, if that side of me turns out to be *interesting company.*)

One thing this pause has taught me. In the first rush of thoughts I was of one mind: end it. But what was the hurry? Well, I had to end it before the other side could get a word in. So ending it meant smothering and brutalizing the side of me that would be Damon K. with a passion if it had its way. Suffocate it and scatter its ashes—what a formula for generating myths about restless spirits!

Comment. It is risky to generalize from a single example, but one may be enough to raise a few suspicions about Margolis's position. The unclearness of his proposed basis for suicide—a person's deciding that life is utterly meaningless—infects any inference drawn from it.[4] Rhetorically it fluctuates anywhere between a pessimist's cliché and a moan of despair. To suppose that someone can believe the sentence "sincerely" does nothing to remove its unclearness or make it more like a bona fide description of "life," its grammatical subject. As Damon begins to notice in the entry dated February 19, this is where the confusion lies in Margolis's formula for a rational suicide.

Classroom use of such extended examples, at least in my own experience, provides a helpful balance to the often abstruse and rarefied literature of value theory.

Notes

[1] J. Margolis, *Negativities: The Limits of Life* (Columbus, Ohio, 1975), p. 34.

[2] Ibid., p. 28.

[3] Ibid., p. 24.

[4] For a more systematic discussion of this point, see Erwin Stengel, *Suicide and Attempted Suicide* (New York, 1964), pp. 112–14.

4

ALLOCATION

The Ethics Committee of a major university medical center had been convened hastily to help decide which two of six possible patients should be the recipients of the hearts that had just become available through the accidental deaths of two donors. The Committee was informed that none of the six patients was likely to survive longer than six months without a transplant, that each patient had a reasonably good chance of surviving the operation without rejecting the transplanted heart, and that the postoperative prognosis was equally good for all six. The Committee was given the following patient biographical briefs on the basis of which to make its recommendation.

Thomas: White, male, American, age 48. Married for 24 years. Two children (boy 21, girl 19), both in college. Spouse: high school English teacher. Education: Ph.D and M.D. Holds joint professorships in the University's College of Medicine and College of Arts and Sciences. Researcher in molecular and cellular biology with a focus on cancer immunization. Regarded by his colleagues as one of the world's leading experts on cancer research and is on the verge of an important breakthrough. Member of a local Presbyterian church and several service organizations.

Robert: White, male, American, age 31. Married for 6 years. One child (girl, 5). Spouse: domestic servant, three months pregnant. Education: high school drop-out, but has been attending night school to learn a trade in electronics. Has been working as a laborer for a local construction firm. No religious affiliation or community service organizations listed.

Ahmir: White, male, Saudi Arabian, age 25. Single. Education: enrolled in Ph.D. program in Computer Science in the University. His father, a wealthy sheik and alumnus of the University, is seriously considering a donation of ten million dollars to the University for support of research in organ transplantation and clinical services for the indigent. A devout Muslim. Member of several international student groups.

Yvonne: Black, female, American, age 34. Single. Education: graduate of selective liberal arts college and the University's Law School. Recently admitted as a partner in one of the state's small but prestigious law firms. One of the state's outstanding civil rights leaders. Regarded by many as having a strong future in politics. Member of local Baptist church and many service and professional organizations.

Edward: White, male, naturalized American citizen, age 40. Divorced, no children. Education: high school graduate with community college certificate in criminology. Has just been paroled from the state penitentiary, where he was serving a sentence for rape. Prior to his incarceration he was a law-enforcement officer.

Jill: White, female, American, age 30. Married for 11 years. Four children (boy 10, boy 8, girl 5, girl 11 months). Education: high school graduate, enrolled in night school at local community college to learn interior design. Husband owns a fashionable clothing store. President of the local Hadassah organization and member of several charitable and service organizations in the community.

Clearly, at the core of the moral problem of allocation is a scarcity of medical resources coupled with a heavy demand that exceeds the supply. Which of those demands should be honored? If you were a member of the Committee, which two would you select? Before you decided, would you want additional information about the candidates? If so, what kind of information? Would you have any qualms about the kind of information or the way it was reported in the bio-briefs? Perhaps most importantly, what strategy do you think the Committee should use in reaching its recommendation?

An attractive point of departure in making the hard choices associated with allocation might be to identify the morally relevant features that ought to be taken into account. For example, most of us would not consider race and sex as morally relevant. Consider the following factors.

Citizenship. At first glance this category might seem just as irrelevant as race and sex. But should not a medical center supported by taxpayers give priority to its citizens? Do they not have a right to the medical resources of their society that outweighs any claims that outsiders might have?

Previous Contributions to Society. Thomas, Yvonne, and, to some extent, Jill seem to have been significantly beneficial to society. Ought they to be rewarded for their past performance? Ought Edward, the rapist, to be punished by being excluded from further consideration?

Future Contributions to Society. Would not this factor give the edge to the cancer research of Thomas and the political potentiality of Yvonne? But how can we be certain that projected future benefits will actually occur?

Finances. It might offend our moral sensibilities to suggest that those who can pay their way should receive priority in the allocation of scarce medical resources. Yet is it not altogether likely that some of the patients would be unable to pay fully for the enormous costs associated with the operation and postoperative therapy? If so, shouldn't we favor those who will cause the least drain on the hospital's hard-pressed resources? Accordingly, shouldn't we give preference to Ahmir, whose father clearly can pay for his son's expenses and whose pending gift to the medical center would enable the hospital not only to service more of society's economically disadvantaged, but also to advance the course of research?

Religious Affiliation. Once again, this feature at first glance might seem morally irrelevant. But is not religious seriousness coupled with past beneficial service to society an important predictor of future performance?

Dependents. Should we perhaps give preference to married persons as opposed to singles? To parents with the greatest number of children? To parents with the youngest children?

Would you wish to exclude any of these factors because they are morally irrelevant? Clearly some of the factors favor some of the patients while other factors favor other patients. Does that present a problem? Is that fair? Are there any other factors, not already mentioned, that you think the Committee should consider in its decision-making? If after weighing all of the morally relevant features the Committee feels that its judgment is still clouded with uncertainty, what should the Committee do?

There are some people who would object to the very way we have been proceeding so far. They would point out that we have been trying to place a value on each of these six human lives. But how can we, or anyone else, do that with any measure of accuracy? Furthermore, can we *really* predict the benefits a human being is likely to produce for society in the future? Can we *really* foresee with precision the harm to others a particular individual might cause? Acknowledging ambiguities and uncertainties in human affairs, should we perhaps abandon the attempt to determine the relative social worth of the patients? Should we perhaps consider them all to be precious human beings of incalculable worth and dignity? If so, what decision strategy should we adopt to identify which of the two shall live when not all six can? One answer is that a purely random selection process—a lottery—is the only truly moral decision procedure.

It is easy to think that this set of examples is totally trumped-up, that the medical profession would never allow such a choice based on such facts. But in the 1960s at the Swedish Hospital in Seattle, Washington, there was a committee whose job it was to choose who would be given kidney dialysis, and live, and who would not, and die. This committee made the final decision after patients had been winnowed by a medical panel.

In 1962 there were thirty applicants for ten positions. The medical panel narrowed the thirty to seventeen. A lay committee (lawyer, clergyperson, housewife, banker, labor leader, and two physicians—all anonymous) made the final decision. The factors they considered and used were "age and sex; marital status and number of dependents; income; net worth; emotional stability, with particular reference to the patient's ability to accept treatment; educational background; nature of occupation; past performance and future potential; and the names of people who could serve as references. . . . Concerning a small businessman . . . [a person on the committee] was impressed with the fact that 'this man is active in church work.'"[1]

In the readings that follow, Nicholas Rescher proposes a strategy to determine, albeit imprecisely, the relative social worth of patients. James Childress, however, is critical of that approach and suggests an alternative. Daniel Callahan focuses on the increasingly important issue of whether *age* is a morally relevant feature in the allocation of medical resources for the elderly. Finally, we offer a look a how the state of Oregon recently tried to handle its allocation of health-care payments.

Calculating Social Worth

One of the most popular ethical perspectives on the contemporary scene is the teleological approach, which assesses acts as right or wrong on the basis of their consequences. When applied to the moral problem of allocating scarce medical resources, such as selecting two patients out of six for heart transplants, one version of this approach attempts (1) to predict what benefits will accrue from giving a heart to each of the prospective recipients, and (2) to select the two recipients whose lives, if saved, are likely to generate the greatest benefit to society.

[1]Paul Ramsey, *The Patient As Person* (New Haven: Yale University Press, 1970), pp. 245–46.

If one is going to calculate the relative social worth of individuals in this fashion, then one must be very sure that one's calculations take into account all relevant data, are accurately done, and are not only inherently fair but are also perceived to be fair by independent observers. In the article that follows, "The Allocation of Exotic Medical Lifesaving Therapy," Nicholas Rescher describes a teleological approach that he believes is rationally sound and fair. Crucial to his method is identifying two sets of appropriate criteria. The first set is used to select from all possible candidates a smaller group who will be given serious consideration for the exotic therapy. The second set is used to single out the particular individuals to whom the therapy will be given.

Questions to keep in mind as you read Rescher's discussion include the following. Has Rescher included all the morally relevant factors in his sets of criteria? How would Thomas, Robert, Ahmir, Yvonne, Edward, and Jill fare in Rescher's decision-making system? How would your own mother, father, brother, or sister fare in his system? Would his system favor the bright, the wealthy, the successful, and the powerful every time? If so, is this procedure morally defensible?

THE ALLOCATION OF EXOTIC
MEDICAL LIFESAVING THERAPY

Nicholas Rescher

I. The Problem

Technological progress has in recent years transformed the limits of the possible in medical therapy. However, the elevated state of sophistication of modern medical technology has brought the economists' classic problem of scarcity in its wake as an unfortunate side product. The enormously sophisticated and complex equipment and the highly trained teams of experts requisite for its utilization are scarce resources in relation to potential demand. The administrators of the great medical institutions that preside over these scarce resources thus come to be faced increasingly with the awesome choice: *Whose life to save?*

A (somewhat hypothetical) paradigm example of this problem may be sketched within the following set of definitive assumptions: We suppose that persons in some particular medically morbid condition are "mortally afflicted": It is virtually certain that they will die within a short time period (say ninety days). We assume that some very complex course of treatment

Source: "The Allocation of Exotic Medical Lifesaving Therapy" by Nicholas Rescher. *Ethics*, vol. 79, no. 3 (April 1969), pp. 173–86. Used by permission of the University of Chicago Press and the author.

(e.g., a heart transplant) represents a substantial probability of life prolongation for persons in this mortally afflicted condition. We assume that the facilities available in terms of human resources, mechanical instrumentalities, and requisite materials (e.g., hearts in the case of a heart transplant) make it possible to give a certain treatment—this "exotic (medical) lifesaving therapy," or ELT for short—to a certain, relatively small number of people. And finally we assume that a substantially greater pool of people in the mortally afflicted condition is at hand. The problem then may be formulated as follows: How is one to select within the pool of afflicted patients the ones to be given the ELT treatment in question; how to select those "whose lives are to be saved"? Faced with many candidates for an ELT process that can be made available to only a few, doctors and medical administrators confront the decision of who is to be given a chance at survival and who is, in effect, to be condemned to die.

As has already been implied, the "heroic" variety of spare-part surgery can pretty well be assimilated to this paradigm. One can foresee the time when heart transplantation, for example, will have become pretty much a routine medical procedure, albeit on a very limited basis, since a cardiac surgeon with the technical competence to transplant hearts can operate at best a rather small number of times each week and the elaborate facilities for such operations will most probably exist on a modest scale. Moreover, in "spare-part" surgery there is always the problem of availability of the "spare parts" themselves. A report in one British newspaper gives the following picture: "Of the 150,000 who die of heart disease each year [in the U.K.], Mr. Donald Longmore, research surgeon at the National Heart Hospital [in London] estimates that 22,000 might be eligible for heart surgery. Another 30,000 would need heart and lung transplants. But there are probably only between 7,000 and 14,000 potential donors a year."[1] Envisaging this situation in which at the very most something like one in four heart-malfunction victims can be saved, we clearly confront a problem in ELT allocation.

A perhaps even more drastic case in point is afforded by long-term haemodialysis, an ongoing process by which a complex device—an "artificial kidney machine"—is used periodically in cases of chronic renal failure to substitute for a non-functional kidney in "cleaning" potential poisons from the blood. Only a few major institutions have chronic haemodialysis units, whose complex operation is an extremely expensive proposition. For the present and the foreseeable future the situation is that "the number of places available for chronic haemodialysis is hopelessly inadequate."[2]

The traditional medical ethos has insulated the physician against facing the very existence of this problem. When swearing the Hippocratic Oath, he commits himself to work for the benefit of the sick in "whatsoever house I enter."[3] In taking this stance, the physician substantially renounces the explicit choice of saving certain lives rather than others. Of course, doctors have always in fact had to face such choices on the battlefield or in times of disaster, but there the issue had to be resolved hurriedly, under pressure, and in circumstances in which the very nature of the case effectively precluded calm deliberation by the decision maker as well as criticism by others. In sharp contrast, however, cases of the type we have postulated in the present discussion arise predictably, and represent choices to be made deliberately and "in cold blood."

It is, to begin with, appropriate to remark that this problem is not fundamentally a medical problem. For when there are sufficiently many afflicted candidates for ELT then—so we may assume—there will also be more than enough for whom the purely medical grounds for ELT allocation are decisively strong in any individual case, and just about equally strong throughout the group. But in this circumstance a selection of some afflicted patients over and against others cannot *ex hypothesi* be made on the basis of purely medical considerations.

The selection problem, as we have said, is in substantial measure not a medical one. It is a problem *for* medical men, which must somehow be solved by them, but that does not make it a medical issue—any more than the problem of hospital building is a medical issue. As a problem it belongs to the category of philosophical problems—specifically a problem of moral philosophy or ethics. Structurally, it bears a substantial kinship with those issues in this field that revolve about the notorious whom-to-save-on-the-lifeboat and whom-to-throw-to-the-wolves-pursuing-the-sled questions. But whereas questions of this just-indicated sort are artificial, hypothetical, and far-fetched, the ELT issue poses a *genuine* policy question for the responsible administrators in medical institutions, indeed a question that threatens to become commonplace in the foreseeable future.

Now what the medical administrator needs to have, and what the philosopher is presumably *ex officio* in a position to help in providing, is a body of *rational guidelines* for making choices in these literally life-or-death situations. This is an issue in which many interested parties have a substantial stake, including the responsible decision maker who wants to satisfy his conscience that he is acting in a reasonable way. Moreover, the family and associates of the man who is turned away—to say nothing of the man himself—have the right to an acceptable explanation. And indeed even the general public wants to know that what is being done is fitting and proper. All of these interested parties are entitled to insist that a reasonable code of operating principles provides a defensible rationale for making the life-and-death choices involved in ELT.

II. The Two Types of Criteria

Two distinguishable types of criteria are bound up in the issue of making ELT choices. We shall call these *Criteria of Inclusion* and *Criteria of Comparison*, respectively. The distinction at issue here requires some explanation. We can think of the selection as being made by a two-stage process: (1) the selection from among all possible candidates (by a suitable screening process) of a group to be taken under serious consideration as candidates for therapy, and then (2) the actual singling out within this group, of the particular individuals to whom therapy is to be given. Thus the first process narrows down the range of comparative choice by eliminating *en bloc* whole categories of potential candidates. The second process calls for a more refined, case-by-case comparison of those candidates that remain. By means of the first set of criteria one forms a selection group; by means of the second set, an actual selection is made within this group.

Thus what we shall call a "selection system" for the choice of patients to receive therapy of the ELT type will consist of criteria of these two kinds. Such a system will be acceptable only when the reasonableness of its component criteria can be established.

III. Essential Features of an Acceptable ELT Selection System

To quality as reasonable, an ELT selection must meet two important "regulative" requirements: it must be *simple* enough to be readily intelligible, and it must be *plausible*, that is, patently reasonable in a way that can be apprehended easily and without involving ramified subtleties. Those medical administrators responsible for ELT choices must follow a modus operandi that virtually all the people involved can readily understand to be acceptable (at a reasonable level of generality, at any rate). Appearances are critically important here. It is not enough that the choice be made in a *justifiable* way; it must be possible for people—*plain* people—to "see" (i.e., understand without elaborate teaching or indoctrination) that *it is justified,* insofar as any mode of procedure can be justified in cases of this sort.

One "constitutive" requirement is obviously an essential feature of a reasonable selection system: all of its component criteria—those of inclusion and those of comparison alike—must be reasonable in the sense of being *rationally defensible.* The ramifications of this requirement call for detailed consideration. But one of its aspects should be noted without further ado: it must be *fair*—it must treat relevantly like cases alike, leaving no room for "influence" or favoritism, etc.

IV. The Basic Screening Stage: Criteria of Inclusion (and Exclusion)

Three sorts of considerations are prominent among the plausible criteria of inclusion/exclusion at the basic screening stage: the constituency factor, the progress-of-science factor, and the prospect-of-success factor.

A. The Constituency Factor

It is a "fact of life" that ELT can be available only in the institutional setting of a hospital or medical institute or the like. Such institutions generally have normal clientele boundaries. A veterans' hospital will not concern itself primarily with treating nonveterans, a children's hospital cannot be expected to accommodate the "senior citizen," an army hospital can regard college professors as outside its sphere. Sometimes the boundaries are geographic—a state hospital may admit only residents of a certain state. (There are, of course, indefensible constituency principles—say race or religion, party membership, or ability to pay; and there are cases of borderline legitimacy, e.g., sex.[4]) A medical institution is justified in considering for ELT only persons within its own constituency, provided this constituency is constituted upon a defensible basis. Thus the haemodialysis selection committee in Seattle "agreed to consider only those applications who were residents of the state of Washington. . . . They justified this stand on the grounds that since the basic research . . . had been done at . . . a state-supported institution—the people whose taxes had paid for the research should be its first beneficiaries."[5]

While thus insisting that constituency considerations represent a valid and legitimate factor in ELT selection, I do feel there is much to be said for minimizing their role in life-or-death cases. Indeed a refusal to recognize them at all is a significant part of medical tradition, going back to the very oath of Hippocrates. They represent a departure from the ideal arising with the institutionalization of medicine, moving it away from its original status as an art practiced by an individual practitioner.

B. The Progress-of-Science Factor

The needs of medical research can provide a second valid principle of inclusion. The research interests of the medical staff in relation to the specific nature of the cases at issue is a significant consideration. It may be important for the progress of medical science—and thus of potential benefit to many persons in the future—to determine how effective the ELT at issue is with diabetics or persons over sixty or with a negative RH factor. Considerations of this sort represent another type of legitimate factor in ELT selection.

A very definitely *borderline* case under this head would revolve around the question of a patient's willingness to pay, not in monetary terms, but in offering himself as an experimental subject, say by contracting to return at designated times for a series of tests substantially unrelated to his own health, but yielding data of importance to medical knowledge in general.

C. The Prospect-of-Success Factor

It may be that while the ELT at issue is not without *some* effectiveness in general, it has been established to be highly effective only with patients in certain specific categories (e.g., females under forty of a specific blood type). This difference in effectiveness—in the absolute or in the probability of success—is (we assume) so marked as to constitute virtually a difference in kind rather than in degree. In this case, it would be perfectly legitimate to adopt the general rule of making the ELT at issue available only or primarily to persons in this substantial-promise-of-success category. (It is on grounds of this sort that young children and persons over fifty are generally ruled out as candidates for haemodialysis.)

We have maintained that the three factors of constituency, progress of science, and prospect of success represent legitimate criteria of inclusion for ELT selection. But it remains to examine the considerations which legitimate them. The legitimating factors are in the final analysis practical or pragmatic in nature. From the practical angle it is advantageous—indeed to some extent necessary—that the arrangements governing medical institutions should embody certain constituency principles. It makes good pragmatic and utilitarian sense that progress-of-science considerations should be operative here. And, finally, the practical aspect is reinforced by a whole host of other considerations—including moral ones—in supporting the prospect-of-success criterion. The workings of each of these factors are of course conditioned by the ever-present element of limited availability. They are operative only in this context, that is, prospect of success is a legitimate consideration at all only because we are dealing with a situation of scarcity.

V. The Final Selection Stage: Criteria of Selection

Five sorts of elements must, as we see it, figure primarily among the plausible criteria of selection that are to be brought to bear in further screening the group constituted after application of the criteria of inclusion: the relative-likelihood-of-success factor, the life-expectancy factor, the family role factor, the potential-contributions factor, and the services-rendered factor. The first two represent the *biomedical* aspect, the second three the *social* aspect.

A. The Relative-Likelihood-of-Success Factor

It is clear that the relative likelihood of success is a legitimate and appropriate factor in making a selection within the group of qualified patients that are to receive ELT. This is obviously one of the considerations that must count very significantly in a reasonable selection procedure.

The present criterion is of course closely related to item C of the preceding section. There we were concerned with prospect-of-success considerations categorically and *en bloc*. Here at present they come into play in a particularized case-by-case comparison among individuals. If the therapy at issue is not a once-and-for-all proposition and requires ongoing treatment, cognate considerations must be brought in. Thus, for example, in the case of a chronic ELT procedure such as haemodialysis it would clearly make sense to give priority to patients with a potentially reversible condition (who would thus need treatment for only a fraction of their remaining lives).

B. The Life-Expectancy Factor

Even if the ELT is "successful" in the patient's case he may, considering his age and/or other aspects of his general medical condition, look forward to only a very short probable future life. This is obviously another factor that must be taken into account.

C. The Family Role Factor

A person's life is a thing of importance not only to himself but to others—friends, associates, neighbors, colleagues, etc. But his (or her) relationship to his immediate family is a thing of unique intimacy and significance. The nature of his relationship to his wife, children, and parents, and the issue of their financial and psychological dependence upon him, are obviously matters that deserve to be given weight in the ELT selection process. Other things being anything like equal, the mother of minor children must take priority over the middle-aged bachelor.

D. The Potential Future-Contributions Factor (Prospective Service)

In "choosing to save" one life rather than another, "the society," through the mediation of the particular medical institution in question—which should certainly look upon itself as a trustee for the social interest—is clearly warranted in considering the likely pattern of future *services to be rendered* by the patient (adequate recovery assumed), considering his age, talent, training, and past record of performance. In its allocations of ELT, society "invests" a scarce resource in one person as against another and is thus entitled to look to the probable prospective "return" on its investment.

It may well be that a thoroughly egalitarian society is reluctant to put someone's social contribution into the scale in situations of the sort at issue. One popular article states that "the most difficult standard would be the candidate's value to society," and goes on to quote someone who said: "You can't just pick a brilliant painter over a laborer. The average citizen would be quickly eliminated."[6] But what if it were not a brilliant painter but a brilliant surgeon or medical researcher that was at issue? One wonders if the author of the *obiter dictum* that one "can't just pick" would still feel equally sure of his ground. In any case, the fact that the standard is difficult to apply is certainly no reason for not attempting to apply it. The problem of ELT selection is inevitably burdened with difficult standards.

Some might feel that in assessing a patient's value to society one should ask not only who if permitted to continue living can make the greatest contribution to society in some creative or constructive way, but also who by dying would leave behind the greatest burden on society in assuming the discharge of their residual responsibilities.[7] Certainly the philosophical utilitarian would give equal weight to both these considerations. Just here is where I would part ways with orthodox utilitarianism. For—though this is not the place to do so—I should be prepared to argue that a civilized society has an obligation to promote the furtherance of positive achievements in cultural and related areas even if this means the assumption of certain added burdens.[8]

E. The Past Services-Rendered Factor (Retrospective Service)

A person's services to another person or group have always been taken to constitute a valid basis for a claim upon this person or group—of course a moral and not necessarily a legal claim. Society's obligation for the recognition and reward of services rendered—an obligation whose discharge is also very possibly conducive to self-interest in the long run—is thus another factor to be taken into account. This should be viewed as a morally necessary correlative of the previously considered factor of *prospective* service. It would be morally indefensible of society in effect to say: "Never mind about services you rendered yesterday—it is only the services to be rendered tomorrow that will count with us today." We live in very future-oriented times, constantly preoccupied in a distinctly utilitarian way with future satisfactions. And this disinclines us to give much recognition to past services. But parity considerations of the sort just adduced indicate that such recognition should be given *on grounds of equity*. No doubt a justification for giving weight to services rendered can also be attempted along utilitarian lines. ("The reward of past services rendered spurs people on to greater future efforts and is thus socially advantageous in the long-run future.") In saying that past services should be counted "on grounds of equity"—rather than "on grounds of utility"—I take the view that even if this utilitarian defense could somehow be shown to be fallacious, I should still be prepared to maintain the propriety of taking services rendered into account. The position does not rest on a utiliarian basis and so would not collapse with the removal of such a basis.[9]

As we have said, these five factors fall into three groups: the biomedical factors *A* and *B*, the familial factor *C*, and the social factors *D* and *E*. With items *A* and *B* the need for a detailed analysis of the medical considerations comes to the fore. The age of the patient, his medical history, his physical and psychological condition, his specific disease, etc., will all need to be taken into exact account. These biomedical factors represent technical issues: they call for the physicians' expert judgment and the medical statisticians' hard data. And they are ethically uncontroversial factors—their legitimacy and appropriateness are evident from the very nature of the case.

Greater problems arise with the familial and social factors. They involve intangibles that are difficult to judge. How is one to develop subcriteria for weighing the relative social contributions of (say) an architect or a librarian or a mother of young children? And they involve highly problematic issues. (For example, should good moral character be rated a plus and bad a minus in judging services rendered?) And there is something strikingly unpleasant in grappling with issues of this sort for people brought up in times greatly inclined towards maxims of the type "Judge not!" and "Live and let live!" All the same, in the situation that concerns us here such distasteful problems must be faced, since a failure to choose to save some is tantamount to sentencing all. Unpleasant choices are intrinsic to the problem of ELT selection; they are of the very essence of the matter.[10]

But is reference to all these factors indeed inevitable? The justification for taking account of the medical factors is pretty obvious. But why should the social aspect of services rendered and to be rendered be taken into account at all? The answer is that they must be taken into account not from the *medical* but from the *ethical* point of view. Despite disagreement on many fundamental issues, moral philosophers of the present day are pretty well in consensus that the justification of human actions is to be sought largely and primarily—if not exclusively—in the principles of utility and of justice.[11] But utility requires reference of services to be rendered and justice calls for a recognition of services that have been rendered. Moral considerations would thus demand recognition of these two factors. (This, of course, still leaves open the question of whether the point of view provides a valid basis of action: Why base one's actions upon moral principles?—or, to put it bluntly—Why be moral? The present paper is, however, hardly the place to grapple with so fundamental an issue, which has been canvassed in the literature of philosophical ethics since Plato.)

VI. More Than Medical Issues Are Involved

An active controversy has of late sprung up in medical circles over the question of whether non-physician laymen should be given a role in ELT selection (in the specific context of chronic haemodialysis). One physician writes: "I think that the assessment of the candidates should be made by a senior doctor on the [dialysis] unit, but I am sure that it would be helpful to him—both in sharing responsibility and in avoiding personal pressure— if a small unnamed group of people [presumably including laymen] officially made the final decision. I visualize the doctor bringing the data to the group, explaining the points in relation to each case, and obtaining their approval of his order of priority.[12]

Essentially this procedure of a selection committee of laymen has for some years been in use in one of the most publicized chronic dialysis units, that of the Swedish Hospital of Seattle, Washington.[13] Many physicians are apparently reluctant to see the choice of allocation of medical therapy pass out of strictly medical hands. Thus in a recent symposium on the "Selection of Patients for Haemodialysis,"[14] Dr. Ralph Shakman writes: "Who is to implement the selection? In my opinion it must ultimately be the responsibility of the consultants in charge of the renal units ... I can see no reason for delegating this responsibility to lay persons. Surely the latter would be better employed if they could be persuaded to devote their time and energy to raise more and more money for us to spend on our patients."[15] Other contributors to this symposium strike much the same note. Dr. F. M. Parsons writes: "In an attempt to overcome ... difficulties in selection some have advocated introducing certain specified lay people into the discussions. Is it wise? I doubt whether a committee of this type can adjudicate as satisfactorily as two medical colleagues, particularly as successful therapy involves close cooperation between doctor and patient."[16] And Dr. M. A. Wilson writes in the same symposium: "The suggestion has been made that lay panels should select individuals for dialysis from among a group who are medically suitable. Though this would relieve the doctor-in-charge of a heavy load of responsibility, it would place the burden on those who have no personal knowledge and have to base their judgments on medical or social reports. I do not believe this would result in better decisions for the group or improve the doctor-patient relationship in individual cases."[17]

But no amount of flag waving about the doctor's facing up to his responsibility—or prostrations before the idol of the doctor-patient relationship and reluctance to admit laymen into the sacred precincts of the conference chambers of medical consultations—can obscure the essential fact that ELT selection is not a wholly medical problem. When there are more than enough places in an ELT program to accommodate all who need it, then it will clearly be a medical question to decide who does have the need and which among these would successfully respond. But when an admitted gross insufficiency of places exists, when there are ten or fifty or one hundred highly eligible candidates for each place in the program, then it is unrealistic to take the view that purely medical criteria can furnish a sufficient basis for selection. The question of ELT selection becomes serious as a phenomenon of scale—because, as more candidates present themselves, strictly medical factors are increasingly less adequate as a selection criterion precisely because by numerical category-crowding there will be more and more cases whose "status is much the same" so far as purely medical considerations go.

The ELT selection problem clearly poses issues that transcend the medical sphere because—in the nature of the case—many residual issues remain to be dealt with once *all* of the medical questions have been faced. Because of this there is good reason why laymen as well as physicians should be involved in the selection process. Once the medical considerations have been brought to bear, fundamental social issues remain to be resolved. The instrumentalities of ELT have been created through the social investment of scarce resources, and the interests of the society deserve to play a role in their utilization. As representatives of their social interests, lay opinions should function to complement and supplement medical views once the proper arena of medical considerations is left behind.[18] Those physicians who have urged the presence of lay members on selection panels can, from this point of view, be recognized as having seen the issue in proper perspective.

One physician has argued against lay representation on selection panels for haemodialysis as follows: "If the doctor advises dialysis and the lay panel refuses, the patient will regard this as a death sentence passed by an anonymous court from which he has no right of appeal."[19] But this drawback is not specific to the use of a lay panel. Rather, it is a feature inherent in every *selection* procedure, regardless of whether the selection is done by the head doctor of the unit, by a panel of physicians, etc. No matter who does the selecting among patients recommended for dialysis, the feelings of the patient who has been rejected (and knows it) can be expected to be much the same, provided that he recognizes the actual nature of the choice (and is not deceived by the possibly convenient but ultimately poisonous fiction that because the selection was made by physicians it was made entirely on medical grounds).

In summary, then, the question of ELT selection would appear to be one that is in its very nature heavily laden with issues of medical research, practice, and administration. But it will not be a question that can be resolved on solely medical grounds. Strictly social issues of justice and utility will invariably arise in this area—questions going outside the medical area in whose resolution medical laymen can and should play a substantial role.

VII. The Inherent Imperfection (Non-Optimality) of Any Selection System

Our discussion to this point of the design of a selection system for ELT has left a gap that is a very fundamental and serious omission. We have argued that five factors must be taken into substantial and explicit account:

A. *Relative likelihood of success.*—Is the chance of the treatment's being "successful" to be rated as high, good, average, etc.?[20]

B. *Expectancy of future life.*—Assuming the "success" of the treatment, how much longer does the patient stand a good chance (75 per cent or better) of living—considering his age and general condition?

C. *Family role.*—To what extent does the patient have responsibilities to others in his immediate family?

D. *Social contributions rendered.*—Are the patient's past services to his society outstanding, substantial, average, etc.?

E. *Social contributions to be rendered.*—Considering his age, talents, training, and past record of performance, is there a substantial probability that the patient will—*adequate recovery being assumed*—render in the future services to his society that can be characterized as outstanding, substantial, average, etc.?

This list is clearly insufficient for the construction of a reasonable selection system, since that would require not only *that these factors be taken into account* (somehow or other), but—going beyond this—would specify *a specific set of procedures for taking account of them.* The specific procedures that would constitute such a system would have to take account of the interrelationship of these factors (e.g., *B* and *E*), and to set out exact guidelines as to the relevant weight that is to be given to each of them. This is something our discussion has not as yet considered.

In fact, I should want to maintain that there is no such thing here as a single rationally superior selection system. The position of affairs seems to me to be something like this: (1) It is necessary (for reasons already canvassed) to *have* a system, and to have a system that is rationally defensible, and (2) to be rationally defensible, this system must take the factors *A–E* into substantial and explicit account. But (3) the exact manner in which a rationally defensible system takes account of these factors cannot be fixed in any one specific way on the basis of general considerations. Any of the variety of ways that give *A–E* "their due" will be acceptable and viable. One cannot hope to find within this range of workable systems some one that is *optimal* in relation to the alternatives. There is no one system that does "the (uniquely) best"—only a variety of systems that do "as well as one can expect to do" in cases of this sort.

The situation is structurally very much akin to that of rules of partition of an estate among the relations of a decedent. It is important *that there be* such rules. And it is reasonable that spouse, children, parents, siblings, etc., be taken account of in these rules. But the question of the exact method of division—say that when the decedent has neither living spouse nor living children then his estate is to be divided, dividing 60 per cent between parents, 40 per cent between siblings versus dividing 90 per cent between parents, 10 per cent between siblings—cannot be settled on the basis of any general abstract considerations of reasonableness. Within broad limits, a *variety* of resolutions are all perfectly acceptable—so that no one procedure can justifiably be regarded as "the (uniquely) best" because it is superior to all others.[21]

VIII. A Possible Basis for a Reasonable Selection System

Having said that there is no such thing as *the optimal* selection system for ELT, I want now to sketch out the broad features of what I would regard as *one acceptable* system.

The basis for the system would be a point rating. The scoring here at issue would give roughly equal weight to the medical considerations (*A* and *B*) in comparison with the extramedical considerations (*C* = family role, *D* = services rendered, and *E* = services to be rendered), also giving roughly equal weight to the three items involved here (*C*, *D*, and *E*). The result of such a scoring procedure would provide the essential *starting point* of our ELT selection mechanism. I deliberately say "starting point" because it seems to me that one should not follow the results of this scoring in an *automatic* way. I would propose that the actual selection should only be guided but not actually be dictated by this scoring procedure, along lines now to be explained.

IX. The Desirability of Introducing an Element of Chance

The detailed procedure I would propose—not of course as optimal (for reasons we have seen), but as eminently acceptable—would combine the scoring procedure just discussed with an element of chance. The resulting selection system would function as follows:

1. First the criteria of inclusion of Section IV above would be applied to constitute a *first phase selection group*—which (we shall suppose) is substantially larger than the number *n* of persons who can actually be accommodated with ELT.

2. Next the criteria of selection of Section V are brought to bear via a scoring procedure of the type described in Section VIII. On this basis a *second phase selection group* is constituted which is only *somewhat* larger—say by a third or a half—than the critical number *n* at issue.

3. If this second phase selection group is relatively homogeneous as regards rating by the scoring procedure—that is, if there are no really major disparities within this group (as would be likely if the initial group was significantly larger than *n*)—then the final selection is made by *random* selection of *n* persons from within this group.

This introduction of the element of chance—in what could be dramatized as a "lottery of life and death"—must be justified. The fact is that such a procedure would bring with it three substantial advantages.

First, as we have argued above (in Section VII), any acceptable selection system is inherently non-optimal. The introduction of the element of chance prevents the results that life-and-death choices are made by the automatic application of an admittedly imperfect selection method.

Second, a recourse to chance would doubtless make matters easier for the rejected patient and those who have a specific interest in him. It would surely be quite hard for them to accept his exclusion by relatively mechanical application of objective criteria in whose implementation subjective judgment is involved. But the circumstances of life have conditioned us to accept the workings of chance and to tolerate the element of luck (good or bad): human life is an inherently contingent process. Nobody, after all, has an absolute right to ELT—but most of us would feel that we have "every bit as much right" to it as anyone else in significantly similar circumstances. The introduction of the element of chance assures a like handling of like cases over the widest possible area that seems reasonable in the circumstances.

Third (and perhaps least), such a recourse to random selection does much to relieve the administrators of the selection system of the awesome burden of ultimate and absolute responsibility.

These three considerations would seem to build up a substantial case for introducing the element of chance into the mechanism of the system for ELT selection in a way limited and circumscribed by other weightier considerations, along some such lines as those set forth above.[22]

It should be recognized that this injection of *man-made* chance supplements the element of *natural* chance that is present inevitably and in any case (apart from the role of chance in singling out certain persons as victims for the affliction at issue). As F. M. Parsons has observed: "any vacancies [in an ELT program—specifically haemodialysis] will be filled immediately by the first suitable patients, even though their claims for therapy may subsequently prove less than those of other patients refused later."[23] Life is a chancy business and even the most rational of human arrangements can cover this over to a very limited extent at best.

Notes

[1]Christine Doyle, "Spare-Part Heart Surgeons Worried by Their Success," *Observer,* May 12, 1968.

[2]J. D. N. Nabarro, "Selection of Patients for Haemodialysis," *British Medical Journal* (March 11, 1967), p. 623. Although several thousand patients die in the U.K. each year from renal failure—there are about thirty new cases per million of population—only 10 per cent of these can for the foreseeable future be accommodated with chronic haemodialysis. Kidney transplantation—itself a very tricky procedure—cannot make a more than minor contribution

here. As this article goes to press, I learn that patients can be maintained in home dialysis at an operating cost about half that of maintaining them in a hospital dialysis unit (roughly an $8,000 minimum). In the United States, around 7,000 patients with terminal uremia who could benefit from haemodialysis evolve yearly. As of mid-1968, some 1,000 of these can be accommodated in existing hospital units. By June 1967, a world-wide total of some 120 patients were in treatment by home dialysis. (Data from a forthcoming paper, "Home Dialysis," by C. M. Conty and H. V. Murdaugh. See also R. A. Baillod et al., "Overnight Haemodialysis in the Home," *Proceedings of the European Dialysis and Transplant Association*, VI [1965], 90 ff.).

[3]For the Hippocratic Oath see *Hippocrates: Works* (Loeb ed.; London, 1959), I, p. 298.

[4]Another example of borderline legitimacy is posed by an endowment "with strings attached," e.g., "In accepting this legacy the hospital agrees to admit and provide all needed treatment for any direct descendant of myself, its founder."

[5]Shana Alexander, "They Decide Who Lives, Who Dies," *Life*, LIII (November 9, 1962), 102-25 (see p. 107).

[6]Lawrence Lader, "Who Has the Right To Live?" *Good Housekeeping* (January 1968), p. 144.

[7]This approach could thus be continued to embrace the previous factor, that of family role, the preceding item (C).

[8]Moreover a doctrinaire utilitarian would presumably be willing to withdraw a continuing mode of ELT such as haemodialysis from a patient to make room for a more promising candidate who came to view at a later stage and who could not otherwise be accommodated. I should be unwilling to adopt this course, partly on grounds of utility (with a view to the demoralization of insecurity), partly on the non-utilitarian ground that a "moral commitment" has been made and must be honored.

[9]Of course the difficult question remains of the relative weight that should be given to prospective and retrospective service in cases where these factors conflict. There is good reason to treat them on a par.

[10]This in the symposium on "Selection of Patients for Haemodialysis," *British Medical Journal* (March 11, 1967), pp. 622-24. F. M. Parsons writes: "But other forms of selecting patients [distinct from first come, first served] are suspect in my view if they imply evaluation of man by man. What criteria could be used? Who could justify a claim that the life of a mayor would be more valuable than that of the humblest citizen of his borough? Whatever we may think as individuals none of us is indispensable." But having just set out this hard-line view he immediately backs away from it: "On the other hand, to assume that there was little to choose between Alexander Fleming and Adolf Hitler ... would be nonsense, and we should be naive if we were to pretend that we could not be influenced by their achievements and characters if we had to choose between the two of them. Whether we like it or not we cannot escape the fact that this kind of selection for long-term haemodialysis will be required until very large sums of money become available for equipment and services [so that *everyone* who needs treatment can be accommodated]."

[11]The relative fundamentality of these principles is, however, a substantially disputed issue.

[12]J. D. N. Nabarro, op. cit., p. 622.

[13]See Shana Alexander, op. cit.

[14]*British Medical Journal* (March 11, 1967), pp. 622-24.

[15]*Ibid.*, p. 624. Another contributor writes in the same symposium, "The selection of the few [to receive haemodialysis] is proving very difficult—a true 'Doctor's Dilemma'—for almost everybody would agree that this must be a medical decision, preferably reached by consultation among colleagues" (Dr. F. M. Parsons, *ibid.*, p. 623).

[16]"The Selection of Patients for Haemodialysis," op. cit. (n. 10 above), p. 623.

[17]Dr. Wilson's article concludes with the perplexing suggestion—wildly beside the point given the structure of the situation at issue—that "the final decision will be made by the patient." But this contention is only marginally more ludicrous than Parson's contention that in selecting patients for haemodialysis "gainful employment in a well chosen occupation is necessary to achieve the best results" since "only the minority wish to live on charity" (*ibid.*).

[18]To say this is of course not to deny that such questions of applied medical ethics

will invariably involve a host of medical considerations—it is only to insist that extramedical considerations will also invariably be at issue.

[19]M. A. Wilson, "Selection of Patients for Haemodialysis," *op. cit.*, p. 624.

[20]In the case of an ongoing treatment involving complex procedure and dietary and other mode-of-life restrictions—and chronic haemodialysis definitely falls into this category—the patient's psychological makeup, his willpower to "stick with it" in the face of substantial discouragements—will obviously also be a substantial factor here. The man who gives up, takes not his life alone, but (figuratively speaking) also that of the person he replaced in the treatment schedule.

[21]To say that acceptable solutions can range over broad limits is *not* to say that there are no limits at all. It is an obviously intriguing and fundamental problem to raise the question of the factors that set these limits. This complex issue cannot be dealt with adequately here. Suffice it to say that considerations regarding precedent and people's expectations, factors of social utility, and matters of fairness and sense of justice all come into play.

[22]One writer has mooted the suggestion that: "Perhaps the right thing to do, difficult as it may be to accept, is to select [for haemodialysis] from among the medical and psychologically qualified patients on a strictly random basis" (S. Gorovitz, "Ethics and the Allocation of Medical Resources," *Medical Research Engineering*, V [1966], p. 7). Outright random selection would, however, seem indefensible because of its refusal to give weight to considerations which, under the circumstances, *deserve* to be given weight. The proposed procedure of superimposing a certain degree of randomness upon the rational-choice criteria would seem to combine the advantages of the two without importing the worst defects of either.

[23]"Selection of Patients for Haemodialysis," *op. cit.*, p. 623. The question of whether a patient for chronic treatment should ever be terminated from the program (say if he contracts cancer) poses a variety of difficult ethical problems with which we need not at present concern ourselves. But it does seem plausible to take the (somewhat antiutilitarian) view that a patient should not be terminated simply because a "better qualified" patient comes along later on. It would seem that a quasi-contractual relationship has been created through established expectations and reciprocal understandings, and that the situation is in this regard akin to that of the man who, having undertaken to sell his house to one buyer, cannot afterward unilaterally undo this arrangement to sell it to a higher bidder who "needs it worse" (thus maximizing the overall utility).

[24]I acknowledge with thanks the help of Miss Hazel Johnson, Reference Librarian at the University of Pittsburgh Library, in connection with the bibliography.

Randomizing Persons

Suppose that the Ethics Committee of the University's Medical Center had been summoned not to select organ transplant recipients, but rather to recommend a policy for using the new neonatal intensive care facilities. Through the gift of a generous donor the Medical Center has secured equipment and personnel to support twenty stations. The new unit, scheduled to open in a month, will enhance the likelihood that profoundly sick newborn infants will survive. The cost of treating just one of these neonates in the facility will exceed one thousand dollars per day. The Medical Center's staff has projected that within one month of its opening, all twenty stations will be in use and that requests for access to the facilities will exceed their availability.

If you were on the Committee, what policy do you think the Commit-

tee should recommend to the Medical Center? Suppose the Committee
were to adopt Rescher's approach. Clearly it would be difficult to apply
several of his criteria of selection to neonates. Neonates have neither family
responsibilities nor previous contributions to society which could be fac-
tored into deciding which of them should have access to the exotic therapy.
Furthermore, how accurately can one project the future contributions to
society of a neonate? Perhaps Rescher would say that because among neonates there are no really major disparities which would lead us to prefer
one medically appropriate neonate above another, we should take his fall-
back position of randomization. In the following article, James Childress
argues that the strategy of randomization, rather than being just a backup
position, should be seen as the most morally justified approach for allocating scarce lifesaving medical resources.

Like Rescher, Childress suggests a two-stage strategy for allocating
scarce resources. His first stage singles out the candidates for treatment
who are "medically acceptable" (a term which seems to signify that the patient has some reasonable prospect of responding favorably to the proposed treatment). The second stage involves selection, from this group of
the medically acceptable, those to whom resources will be allocated. In discussing this stage Childress provides an unrelenting attack on the criteria
used by consequentialists, such as Rescher, and presents his own case for
randomization. In brief, he claims that consequentialism (the view that
judges the rightness or wrongness of an act on the basis of its consequences)
is flawed by its threefold inability to establish criteria for determining the
social worth of individuals, to predict accurately the future outcomes of
human acts, and to safeguard the dignity of human beings, who are so easily
violated when viewed as means for achieving social ends. In winding up his
case for randomization, Childress allows for the possibility that some
people might, on consequentialist grounds, be given preferential treatment;
but he makes the conditions for such preference so stringent that it is difficult to conceive of anyone actually qualifying.

Suppose we adopted Childress's approach in allocating the two hearts
in our opening scenario, and suppose that the lottery selected Edward (the
paroled rapist) as one of the transplant recipients and excluded Thomas
(the cancer researcher). Would your moral sensitivities be offended by such
an outcome? How do you think Childress would assess such as eventuality?

WHO SHALL LIVE WHEN NOT ALL CAN LIVE?

James F. Childress

Who shall live when not all can live? Although this question has been ur-
gently forced upon us by the dramatic use of artificial internal organs and

Source: "Who Shall Live When Not All Can Live?" by James F. Childress.
Soundings, vol. 53, no. 4 (Winter 1970), pp. 339-55. Used by permission.

organ transplantations, it is hardly new. George Bernard Shaw dealt with it in "The Doctor's Dilemma":

> SIR PATRICK. Well, Mr. Savior of Lives: which is it to be? that honest decent man Blenkinsop, or that rotten blackguard of an artist, eh?
> RIDGEON. It's not an easy case to judge, is it? Blenkinsop's an honest decent man; but is he any use? Dubedat's a rotten blackguard; but he's a genuine source of pretty and pleasant and good things.
> SIR PATRICK. What will he be a source of for that poor innocent wife of his, when she finds him out?
> RIDGEON. That's true. Her life will be a hell.
> SIR PATRICK. And tell me this. Suppose you had this choice put before you: either to go through life and find all the pictures bad but all the men and women good, or go through life and find all the pictures good and all the men and women rotten. Which would you choose?[1]

A significant example of the distribution of scarce medical resources is seen in the use of penicillin shortly after its discovery. Military officers had to determine which soldiers would be treated—those with venereal disease or those wounded in combat?[2] In many respects such decisions have become routine in medical circles. Day after day physicians and others make judgments and decisions "about allocations of medical care to various segments of our population, to various types of hospitalized patients, and to specific individuals,"[3] for example, whether mental illness or cancer will receive the higher proportion of available funds. Nevertheless, the dramatic forms of "Scarce Life-Saving Medical Resources" (hereafter abbreviated as SLMR) such as hemodialysis and kidney and heart transplants have compelled us to examine the moral questions that have been concealed in many routine decisions. I do not attempt in this paper to show how a resolution of SLMR cases can help us in the more routine ones which do not involve a conflict of life with life. Rather I develop an argument for a particular method of determining who shall live when not all can live. No conclusions are implied about criteria and procedures for determining who shall receive medical resources that are not directly related to the preservation of life (e.g., corneal transplants) or about standards for allocating money and time for studying and treating certain diseases.

Just as current SLMR decisions are not totally discontinuous with other medical decisions, so we must ask whether some other cases might, at least by analogy, help us develop the needed criteria and procedures. Some have looked at the principles at work in our responses to abortion, euthanasia, and artificial insemination.[4] Usually they have concluded that these cases do not cast light on the selection of patients for artificial and transplanted organs. The reason is evident: in abortion, euthanasia, and artificial insemination, there is no conflict of life with life for limited but indispensable resources (with the possible exception of therapeutic abortion). In current SLMR decisions, such a conflict is inescapable, and it makes them so morally perplexing and fascinating. If analogous cases are to be found, I think that we shall locate them in moral conflict situations.

Analogous Conflict Situations

An especially interesting and pertinent one is *U.S.* v. *Holmes.*[5] In 1841 an American ship, the *William Brown,* which was near Newfoundland on a trip from Liverpool to Philadelphia, struck an iceberg. The crew and half the passengers were able to escape in the two available vessels. One of these, a longboat, carrying too many passengers and leaking seriously, began to founder in the turbulent sea after about twenty-four hours. In a desperate attempt to keep it from sinking, the crew threw overboard fourteen men. Two sisters of one of the men either jumped overboard to join their brother in death or instructed the crew to throw them over. The criteria for determining who should live were "not to part man and wife, and not to throw over any women." Several hours later the others were rescued. Returning to Philadelphia, most of the crew disappeared, but one, Holmes, who had acted upon orders from the mate, was indicted, tried, and convicted on the charge of "unlawful homicide."

We are interested in this case from a moral rather than a legal standpoint, and there are several possible responses to and judgments about it. Without attempting to be exhaustive I shall sketch a few of these. The judge contended that lots should have been cast, for in such conflict situations, there is no other procedure "so consonant both to humanity and to justice." Counsel for Holmes, on the other hand, maintained that the "sailors adopted the only principle of selection which was possible in an emergency like theirs,—a principle more humane than lots."

Another version of selection might extend and systematize the maxims of the sailors in the direction of "utility"; those are saved who will contribute to the greatest good for the greatest number. Yet another possible option is defended by Edmond Cahn in *The Moral Decision.* He argues that in this case we encounter the "morals of the last days." By this phrase he indicates that an apocalyptic crisis renders totally irrelevant the normal differences between individuals. He continues,

> In a strait of this extremity, all men are reduced—or raised, as one may choose to denominate it—to members of the genus, mere congeners and nothing else. Truly and literally, all were "in the same boat," and thus none could be saved separately from the others. I am driven to conclude that otherwise—that is, if none sacrifice themselves of free will to spare the others—they must all wait and die together. For where

all have become congeners, pure and simple, no one can save himself by killing another.[6]

Cahn's answer to the question "who shall live when not all can live" is "none" unless the voluntary sacrifice by some persons permits it.

Few would deny the importance of Cahn's approach although many, including this writer, would suggest that it is relevant mainly as an affirmation of an elevated and, indeed, heroic or saintly morality which one hopes would find expression in the voluntary actions of many persons trapped in "borderline" situations involving a conflict of life with life. It is a maximal demand which some moral principles impose on the individual in the recognition that self-preservation is not a good which is to be defended at all costs. The absence of this saintly or heroic morality should not mean, however, that everyone perishes. Without making survival an absolute value and without justifying all means to achieve it, we can maintain that simply letting everyone die is irresponsible. This charge can be supported from several different standpoints, including society at large as well as the individuals involved. Among a group of self-interested individuals, none of whom volunteers to relinquish his life, there may be better and worse ways of determining who shall survive. One task of social ethics, whether religious or philosophical, is to propose relatively just institutional arrangements within which self-interested and biased men can live. The question then becomes: which set of arrangements—which criteria and procedures of selection—is most satisfactory in view of the human condition (man's limited altruism and inclination to seek his own good) and the conflicting values that are to be realized?

There are several significant differences between the *Holmes* and SLMR cases, a major one being that the former involves *direct* killing of another person, while the latter involves only *permitting* a person to die when it is not possible to save all. Furthermore, in extreme situations such as *Holmes*, the restraints of civilization have been stripped away, and something approximating a state of nature prevails, in which life is "solitary, poor, nasty, brutish and short." The state of nature does not mean that moral standards are irrelevant and that might should prevail, but it does suggest that much of the matrix which normally supports morality has been removed. Also, the necessary but unfortunate decisions about who shall live and die are made by men who are existentially and personally involved in the outcome. Their survival too is at stake. Even though the institutional role of sailors seems to require greater sacrificial actions, there is obviously no assurance that they will adequately assess the number of sailors required to man the vessel or that they will impartially and objectively weigh the common good at stake. As the judge insisted in his defense of casting lots in the *Holmes* case: "In no other than this [casting lots] or some like way are those having equal rights put upon an equal footing, and in no other way is it possible to guard against partiality and oppression, violence, and conflict." This difference should not be exaggerated since self-interest, professional pride, and the like obviously affect the outcome of many medical decisions. Nor do the remaining differences cancel *Holmes'* instructiveness.

Criteria of Selection for SLMR

Which set of arrangements should be adopted for SLMR? Two questions are involved: Which standards and criteria should be used? and, Who should make the decision? The first question is basic, since the debate about implementation, e.g., whether by a lay committee or physician, makes little progress until the criteria are determined.

We need two sets of criteria which will be applied at two different stages in the selection of recipients of SLMR. First, medical criteria should be used to exclude those who are not "medically acceptable." Second, from this group of "medically acceptable" applicants, the final selection can be made. Occasionally in current American medical practice, the first stage is omitted, but such an omission is unwarranted. Ethical and social responsibility would seem to require distributing these SLMR only to those who have some reasonable prospect of responding to the treatment. Furthermore, in transplants such medical tests as tissue and blood typing are necessary, although they are hardly fully developed.

"Medical acceptability" is not as easily determined as many non-physicians assume since there is considerable debate in medical circles about the relevant factors (e.g., age and complicating diseases). Although ethicists can contribute little or nothing to this debate, two proposals may be in order. First, "medical acceptability" should be used only to determine the group from which the final selection will be made, and the attempt to establish fine degrees of prospective response to treatment should be avoided. Medical criteria, then, would exclude some applicants but would not serve as a basis of comparison between those who pass the first stage. For example, if two applicants for dialysis were medically acceptable, the physicians would *not* choose the one with the *better* medical prospects. Final selection would be made on other grounds. Second, psychological and environmental factors should be kept to an absolute minimum and should be considered only when they are without doubt critically related to medical acceptability (e.g., the inability to cope with the requirements of dialysis which might lead to suicide).[7]

The most significant moral questions emerge when we turn to the final selection. Once the pool of medically acceptable applicants has been defined and still the number is larger than the resources, what other criteria should be used? How should the final selection be made? First, I shall examine some of the difficulties that stem from efforts to make the final selection in terms of social value; these difficulties raise serious doubts about the feasibility and justifiability of the utilitarian approach. Then I shall consider the possible justification for random selection or chance.

Occasionally criteria of social worth focus on past contributions but most often they are primarily future-oriented. The patient's potential and probable contribution to the society is stressed. Although this obviously cannot be abstracted from his present web of relationships (e.g., dependents) and occupational activities (e.g., nuclear physicist). Indeed, the magnitude of his contribution to society (as an abstraction) is measured in terms of these social roles, relations, and functions. Enough has already been said to suggest the tremendous range of factors that affect social value or worth.[8] Here we encounter the first major difficulty of this approach: How do we determine the relevant criteria of social value?

The difficulties of quantifying various social needs are only too obvious. How does one quantify and compare the needs of the spirit (e.g., education, art, religion), political life, economic activity, technological development? Joseph Fletcher suggests that "some day we may learn how to 'quantify' or 'mathematicate' or 'computerize' the value problem in selection, in the same careful and thorough way that diagnosis has been."[9] I am not convinced that we can ever quantify values, or that we should attempt to do so. But even if the various social and human needs, in principle, could be quantified, how do we determine how much weight we will give to each one? Which will have priority in case of conflict? Or even more basically, in the light of which values and principles do we recognize social "needs"?

One possible way of determining the values which should be emphasized in selection has been proposed by Leo Shatin.[10] He insists that our medical decisions about allocating resources are already based on an unconscious scale of values (usually dominated by material worth). Since there is really no way of escaping this, we should be self-conscious and critical about it. How should we proceed? He recommends that we discover the values that most people in our society hold and then use them as criteria for distributing SLMR. These values can be discovered by attitude or opinion surveys. Presumably if fifty-one percent in this testing period put a greater premium on military needs than technological development, military men would have a greater claim on our SLMR than experimental researchers. But valuations of what is significant change, and the student revolutionary who was denied SLMR in 1970 might be celebrated in 1990 as the greatest American hero since George Washington.

Shatin presumably is seeking criteria that could be applied nationally, but at the present, regional and local as well as individual prejudices tincture the criteria of social value that are used in selection. Nowhere is this more evident than in the deliberations and decisions of the anonymous selection committee of the Seattle Artificial Kidney Center where such factors as church membership and Scout leadership have been deemed significant for determining who shall live.[11] As two critics conclude after examining these criteria and procedures, they rule out "creative non-conformists, who rub the bourgeoisie the wrong way but who historically have contributed so much to the making of America. The Pacific Northwest is no place for a Henry David Thoreau with bad kidneys."[12]

Closely connected to this first problem of determining social values is a second one. Not only is it difficult if not impossible to reach agreement on social values, but it is also rarely easy to predict what our needs will be in a few years and what the consequences of present actions will be. Furthermore it is difficult to predict which persons will fulfill their potential function in society. Admissions committees in colleges and universities experience the frustrations of predicting realization of potential. For these reasons, as someone has indicated, God might be a utilitarian, but we cannot be. We simply lack the capacity to predict very accurately the consequences which we then must evaluate. Our incapacity is never more evident than when we think in societal terms.

Other difficulties make us even less confident that such an approach to SLMR is advisable. Many critics raise the spectre of abuse, but this should not be overemphasized. The fundamental difficulty appears on another level: the utiliarian approach would in effect reduce the person to his social role, relations, and functions. Ultimately it dulls and perhaps even eliminates the sense of the person's transcendence, his dignity as a person which cannot be reduced to his past or future contribution to society. It is not at all clear that we are willing to live with these implications of utilitarian selection. Wilhelm Kolff, who invented the artificial kidney, has asked: "Do we really subscribe to the principle that social standing should determine selection? Do we allow patients to be treated with dialysis only when they are married, go to church, have children, have a job, a good income and give to the Community Chest?"[13]

The German theologian Helmut Thielicke contends that any search for "objective criteria" for selection is already a capitulation to the utilitarian point of view which violates man's dignity.[14] The solution is not to let all die, but to recognize that SLMR cases are "borderline situations" which inevitably involve guilt. The agent, however, can have courage and freedom (which, for Thielicke, come from justification by faith) and can

> go ahead anyway and seek for criteria for deciding the question of life or death in the matter of the artificial kidney. Since these criteria are ... questionable, necessarily alien to the meaning of human existence, the decision to which they lead can be little more than that arrived at by casting lots.[15]

The resulting criteria, he suggests, will probably be very similar to those already employed in American medical practice.

He is most concerned to preserve a certain *attitude* or *disposition* in SLMR—the sense of guilt which arises when man's dignity is violated. With this sense of guilt, the agent remains "sound and healthy where it really counts."[16] Thielicke uses man's dignity only as a judgmental, critical, and negative standard. It only tells us how all selection criteria and procedures (and even the refusal to act) implicate us in the ambiguity of the human condition and its metaphysical guilt. This approach is consistent with his view of the task of theological ethics: "to teach us how to understand and endure—not 'solve'—the borderline situation."[17] But ethics, I would contend, can help us discern the factors and norms in whose light relative, discriminate judgments can be made. Even if all actions in SLMR should involve guilt, some may preserve human dignity to a greater extent than others. Thielicke recognizes that a decision based on any criteria is "little more than that arrived at by casting lots." But perhaps selection by chance would come the closest to embodying the moral and nonmoral values that we are trying to maintain (including a sense of man's dignity).

The Values of Random Selection

My proposal is that we use some form of randomness or chance (either natural, such as "first come, first served," or artificial, such as a lottery) to determine who shall be saved. Many reject randomness as a surrender to nonrationality when responsible and rational judgments can and must be made. Edmond Cahn criticizes "Holmes' judge" who recommended the casting of lots because, as Cahn puts it, "the crisis involves stakes too high for gambling and responsibilities too deep for destiny."[18] Similarly, other critics see randomness as a surrender to "non-human" forces which necessarily vitiates human values. Sometimes these values are identified with the process of decision-making (e.g., it is important to have persons rather than impersonal forces determining who shall live). Sometimes they are identified with the outcome of the process (e.g., the features such as creativity and fullness of being which make human life what it is are to be considered and respected in the decision). Regarding the former, it must be admitted that the use of chance seems cold and impersonal. But presumably the defenders of utilitarian criteria in SLMR want to make their application as objective and impersonal as possible so that subjective bias does not determine who shall live.

Such criticisms, however, ignore the moral and nonmoral values which might be supported by selection by randomness or chance. A more important criticism is that the procedure that I develop draws the relevant moral context too narrowly. That context, so the argument might run, includes the society and its future and not merely the individual with his illness and claim upon SLMR. But my contention is that the values and prin-

ciples at work in the narrower context may well take precedence over those
operative in the broader context both because of their weight and significance and because of the weaknesses of selection in terms of social worth.
As Paul Freund rightly insists, "The more nearly total is the estimate to be
made of an individual, and the more nearly the consequence determines
life and death, the more unfit the judgment becomes for human reckoning.
... Randomness as a moral principle deserves serious study."[19] Serious
study would, I think, point toward its implementation in certain conflict
situations, primarily because it preserves a significant degree of *personal
dignity* by providing *equality* of opportunity. Thus it cannot be dismissed as
a "non-rational" and "non-human" procedure without an inquiry into the
reasons, including human values, which might justify it. Paul Ramsey
stresses this point about the *Holmes* case:

> Instead of fixing our attention upon "gambling" as the solution—with
> all the frivolous and often corrupt associations the word raises in our
> minds—we should think rather of *equality* of opportunity as the ethical
> substance of the relations of those individuals to one another that
> might have been guarded and expressed by casting lots.[20]

The individual's personal and transcendent dignity, which on the utilitarian approach would be submerged in his social role and function, can
be protected and witnessed to by a recognition of his equal right to be
saved. Such a right is best preserved by procedures which establish equality
of opportunity. Thus selection by chance more closely approximates the
requirements established by human dignity than does utilitarian calculation. It is not infallibly just, but it is preferable to the alternatives of letting
all die or saving only those who have the greatest social responsibilities and
potential contribution.

This argument can be extended by examining values other than individual dignity and equality of opportunity. Another basic value in the medical sphere is the relationship of trust between physician and patient. Which
selection criteria are most in accord with this relationship of trust? Which
will maintain, extend, and deepen it? My contention is that selection by
randomness or chance is preferable from this standpoint too.

Trust, which is inextricably bound to respect for human dignity, is an
attitude of expectation about another. It is not simply the expectation that
another will perform a particular act, but more specifically that another
will act toward him in certain ways—which will respect him as a person. As
Charles Fried writes:

> Although trust has to do with reliance on a disposition of another
> person, it is reliance on a disposition of a special sort: the disposition
> to act morally, to deal fairly with others, to live up to one's undertak-

ings, and so on. Thus to trust another is first of all to expect him to accept the principle of morality in his dealings with you, to respect your status as a person, your personality.[21]

This trust cannot be preserved in life-and-death situations when a person expects decisions about him to be made in terms of his social worth, for such decisions violate his status as a person. An applicant rejected on grounds of inadequacy in social value or virtue would have reason for feeling that his "trust" had been betrayed. Indeed, the sense that one is being viewed not as an end in himself but as a means in medical progress or the achievement of a greater social good is incompatible with attitudes and relationships of trust. We recognize this in the billboard which was erected after the first heart transplants: "Drive Carefully. Christiaan Barnard Is Watching You." The relationship of trust between the physician and patient is not only an instrumental value in the sense of being an important factor in the patient's treatment. It is also to be endorsed because of its intrinsic worth as a relationship.

Thus the related values of individual dignity and trust are best maintained in selection by chance. But other factors also buttress the argument for this approach. Which criteria and procedures would men agree upon? We have to suppose a hypothetical situation in which several men are going to determine for themselves and their families the criteria and procedures by which they would want to be admitted to and excluded from SLMR if the need arose.[22] We need to assume two restrictions and then ask which set of criteria and procedures would be chosen as the most rational and, indeed, the fairest. The restrictions are these: (1) The men are *self-interested*. They are interested in their own welfare (and that of members of their families), and this, of course, includes survival. Basically, they are not motivated by altruism. (2) Furthermore, they are *ignorant* of their own talents, abilities, potential, and probable contribution to the social good. They do not know how they would fare in a competitive situation, e.g., the competition for SLMR in terms of social contribution. Under these conditions which institution would be chosen—letting all die, utilitarian selection, or the use of chance? Which would seem the most rational? the fairest? By which set of criteria would they want to be included in or excluded from the list of those who will be saved? The rational choice in this setting (assuming self-interest and ignorance of one's competitive success) would be random selection or chance since this alone provides equality of opportunity. A possible response is that one would prefer to take a "risk" and therefore choose the utilitarian approach. But I think not, especially since I added that the participants in this hypothetical situation are choosing for their children as well as for themselves; random selection or chance could be more easily justified to the children. It would make more sense for men who are self-interested but uncertain about their relative contribution to society to elect a set of criteria which would build in equality of opportunity. They would consider selection by chance as relatively just and fair.[23]

An important psychological point supplements earlier arguments for using chance or random selection. The psychological stress and strain among those who are rejected would be greater if the rejection is based on insufficient social worth than if it is based on chance. Obviously stress and strain cannot be eliminated in these borderline situations, but they would almost certainly be increased by the opprobrium of being judged relatively "unfit" by society's agents using society's values. Nicholas Rescher makes this point very effectively:

> A recourse to chance would doubtless make matters easier for the rejected patient and those who have a specific interest in him. It would surely be quite hard for them to accept his exclusion by relatively mechanical application of objective criteria in whose implementation subjective judgment is involved. But the circumstances of life have conditioned us to accept the workings of chance and to tolerate the element of luck (good or bad): human life is an inherently contingent process. Nobody, after all, has an absolute right to ELT [Exotic Lifesaving Therapy]—but most of us would feel that we have "every bit as much right" to it as anyone else in significantly similar circumstances.[24]

Although it is seldom recognized as such, selection by chance is already in operation in practically every dialysis unit. I am not aware of any unit which removes some of its patients from kidney machines in order to make room for later applicants who are better qualified in terms of social worth. Furthermore, very few people would recommend it. Indeed, few would even consider removing a person from a kidney machine on the grounds that a person better qualified *medically* had just applied. In a discussion of the treatment of chronic renal failure by dialysis at the University of Virginia Hospital Renal Unit from November 15, 1965 to November 15, 1966, Dr. Harry Abram writes: "Thirteen patients sought treatment but were not considered because the program had reached its limit of nine patients."[25] Thus, in practice and theory, natural chance is accepted at least within certain limits.

My proposal is that we extend this principle (first come, first served) to determine who among the medically acceptable patients shall live or that we utilize artificial chance such as a lottery or randomness. "First come, first served" would be more feasible than a lottery since the applicants make their claims over a period of time rather than as a group at one time. This procedure would be in accord with at least one principle in our present practices and with our sense of individual dignity, trust, and fairness. Its significance in relation to these values can be underlined by asking how the decision can be justified to the rejected applicant. Of course, one easy way of avoiding this task is to maintain the traditional cloak of secrecy, which works to a great extent because patients are often not aware that they are being considered for SLMR in addition to the usual treatment. But whether public justification is instituted or not is not the significant question; it is rather what reasons for rejection would be most acceptable to the unsuccessful applicant. My contention is that rejection can be accepted more readily if equality of opportunity, fairness, and trust are preserved, and that they are best preserved by selection by randomness or chance.

This proposal has yet another advantage since it would eliminate the need for a committee to examine applicants in terms of their social value. This onerous responsibility can be avoided.

Finally, there is a possible indirect consequence of widespread use of random selection which is interesting to ponder, although I do *not* adduce it as a good reason for adopting random selection. It can be argued, as Professor Mason Willrich of the University of Virginia Law School has suggested, that SLMR cases would practically disappear if these scarce resources were distributed randomly rather than on social worth grounds. Scarcity would no longer be a problem because the holders of economic and political power would make certain that they would not be excluded by a random selection procedure; hence they would help to redirect public priorities or establish private funding so that life-saving medical treatment would be widely and perhaps universally available.

In the framework that I have delineated, are the decrees of chance to be taken without exception? If we recognize exceptions, would we not open Pandora's box again just after we had succeeded in getting it closed? The direction of my argument has been against any exceptions, and I would defend this as the proper way to go. But let me indicate one possible way of admitting exceptions while at the same time circumscribing them so narrowly that they would be very rare indeed.

An obvious advantage of the utilitarian approach is that occasionally circumstances arise which make it necessary to say that one man is practically indispensable for a society in view of a particular set of problems it faces (e.g., the President when the nation is waging a war for survival). Certainly the argument to this point has stressed that the burden of proof would fall on those who think that the social danger in this instance is so great that they simply cannot abide by the outcome of a lottery or a first come, first served policy. Also, the reason must be negative rather than positive; that is, we depart from chance in this instance not because we want to take advantage of this person's potential contribution to the improvement of our society, but because his immediate loss would possibly (even probably) be disastrous (again, the President in a grave national emergency). Finally, social value (in the negative sense) should be used as a standard of exception in dialysis, for example, only if it would provide a reason strong enough to warrant removing another person from a kidney machine if all machines were taken. Assuming this strong reluctance to remove any-one once the commitment has been made to him, we would be willing to put this patient ahead of another applicant for a vacant machine only if we would be willing (in circumstances in which all machines are being used) to vacate a machine by removing someone from it. These restrictions would make an exception almost impossible.

While I do not recommend this procedure of recognizing exceptions, I think that one can defend it while accepting my general thesis about selec-tion by randomness or chance. If it is used, a lay committee (perhaps advi-sory, perhaps even stronger) would be called upon to deal with the alleged exceptions since the doctors or others would in effect be appealing the outcome of chance (either natural or artificial). This lay committee would determine whether this patient was so indispensable at this time and place that he had to be saved even by sacrificing the values preserved by random selection. It would make it quite clear that exception is warranted, if at all, only as the "lesser of two evils." Such a defense would be recognized only rarely, if ever, primarily because chance and randomness preserve so many important moral and nonmoral values in SLMR cases.

Notes

[1]George Bernard Shaw, *The Doctor's Dilemma* (New York, 1941), pp. 132–33.

[2]Henry K. Beecher, "Scarce Resources and Medical Advancement," *Daedalus* (Spring 1969), pp. 279–80.

[3]Leo Shatin, "Medical Care and the Social Worth of a Man," *American Journal of Ortho-psychiatry*, 36 (1967), 97.

[4]Harry S. Abram and Walter Wadlington, "Selection of Patients for Artificial and Trans-planted Organs," *Annals of Internal Medicine*, 69 (September 1968), 615–20.

[5]*United States v. Holmes* 26 Fed. Cas. 360 (C.C.E.D. Pa. 1842). All references are to the text of the trial as reprinted in Philip E. Davis, ed., *Moral Duty and Legal Responsibility: A Philosophical-Legal Casebook* (New York, 1966), pp. 102–18.

[6]*The Moral Decision* (Bloomington, Ind., 1955), p. 71.

[7]For a discussion of the higher suicide rate among dialysis patients than among the general population and an interpretation of some of the factors at work, see H. S. Abram, G. L. Moore, and F. B. Westervelt, "Suicidal Behavior in Chronic Dialysis Patients," *American Journal of Psychiatry* (in press). This study shows that even "if one does not include death through not following the regimen the incidence of suicide is still more than 100 times the normal population."

[8]I am excluding from consideration the question of the ability to pay because most of the people involved have to secure funds from other sources, public or private, anyway.

[9]Joseph Fletcher, "Donor Nephrectomies and Moral Responsibility," *Journal of the Ameri-can Medical Women's Association*, 23 (Dec. 1968), p. 1090.

[10]Leo Shatin, op. cit., pp. 96–101.

[11]For a discussion of the Seattle selection committee, see Shana Alexander, "They De-cide Who Lives, Who Dies," *Life*, 53 (Nov. 9, 1962), 102. For an examination of general selection

practices in dialysis see "Scarce Medical Resources," *Columbia Law Review,* 69:620 (1969) and Harry S. Abram and Walter Wadlington, op. cit.

[12]David Sanders and Jesse Dukeminier, Jr., "Medical Advance and Legal Lag: Hemodialysis and Kidney Transplantation," *UCLA Law Review,* 15:367 (1968) 378.

[13]"Letters and Comments," *Annals of Internal Medicine,* 61 (Aug. 1964), 360. Dr. G. E. Schreiner contends that "if you really believe in the right of society to make decisions on medical availability on these criteria you should be logical and say that when a man stops going to church or is divorced and loses his job, he ought to be removed from the programme and somebody else who fulfills these criteria substituted. Obviously no one faces up to this logical consequence" (G. E. W. Wolstenholme and Maeve O'Connor, eds. *Ethics in Medical Progress: With Special Reference to Transplantation,* A Ciba Foundation Symposium [Boston, 1966], p. 127).

[14]Helmut Thielicke, "The Doctor as Judge of Who Shall Live and Who Shall Die," *Who Shall Live?* ed. by Kenneth Vaux (Philadelphia, 1970), p. 172.

[15]Ibid., pp. 173–74.

[16]Ibid., p. 173.

[17]Thielicke, *Theological Ethics,* Vol. 1, *Foundations* (Philadelphia, 1966), p. 602.

[18]Cahn, op. cit., p. 71.

[19]Paul Freund, "Introduction," *Daedalus* (Spring 1969), xiii.

[20]Paul Ramsey, *Nine Modern Moralists* (Englewood Cliffs, N.J., 1962), p. 245.

[21]Charles Fried, "Privacy," In *Law, Reason, and Justice,* ed. by Graham Hughes (New York, 1969), p. 52.

[22]My argument is greatly dependent on John Rawls's version of justice as fairness, which is a reinterpretation of social contract theory. Rawls, however, would probably not apply his ideas to "borderline situations." See "Distributive Justice: Some Addenda," *Natural Law Forum,* 13 (1968), 53. For Rawl's general theory, see "Justice as Fairness," *Philosophy, Politics and Society* (Second Series), ed. by Peter Laslett and W. G. Runciman (Oxford, 1962), pp. 132–57 and his other essays on aspects of this topic.

[23]Occasionally someone contends that random selection may reward vice. Leo Shatin (op. cit., p. 100) insists that random selection "would reward socially disvalued qualities by giving their bearers the same special medical care opportunities as those received by the bearers of socially valued qualities. Personally I do not favor such a method." Obviously society must engender certain qualities in its members, but not all of its institutions must be devoted to that purpose. Furthermore, there are strong reasons, I have contended, for exempting SLMR from that sort of function.

[24]Nicholas Rescher, "The Allocation of Exotic Medical Lifesaving Therapy," *Ethics,* 79 (April 1969), 184. He defends random selection's use only after utilitarian and other judgments have been made. If there are no "major disparities" in terms of utility, etc., in the second stage of selection, then final selection could be made randomly. He fails to give attention to the moral values that random selection might preserve.

[25]Harry S. Abram, M.D., "The Psychiatrist, the Treatment of Chronic Renal Failure, and the Prolongation of Life: II" *American Journal of Psychiatry* 126:157–67 (1969), 158.

Allocating Resources to the Elderly

In the introduction to this section, it was suggested that factors such as race and sex were morally irrelevant to making allocation decisions. Daniel

Callahan defends the view that age is not morally irrelevant in allocation decisions. Indeed, he argues that age is so relevant that there ought to be a cutoff point beyond which no elderly person ought to expect anything but supportive care. Callahan recognizes that this is a view that conflicts with much of what appear to be gains made recently by the elderly.

His argument, in brief, is two-fold. First, he argues that our medical system will not be able to stand the economic strain of attempting to lengthen the life of the elderly. Second, he argues that his goal is to improve the quality of life of the elderly through prevention of as much illness as is possible and through reduction of suffering and pain. The overall effect of Callahan's program, he thinks, is increased autonomy for the aged, because fewer will be forced to spend their final years debilitated and humiliated.

Callahan's position can be analyzed in different ways. How much of his argument depends on facts? If those facts were to change, would his argument have to be amended? Which facts are most crucial to his view? Callahan seems to think that it is reasonable to make the early eighties an upper limit on a natural life span. Would a program like Callahan's actually turn out to enforce this upper limit, at least in part by seeing that research aimed primarily at extending life would not be undertaken? Is the concept of quality of life one that should be decided by society for individuals? Or, is this concept so important that it should be left, if at all possible, to individuals to decide for themselves? Moreover, does Callahan's proposal assume the continuation of current national priorities? What if those priorities changed and major funds were reassigned from defense spending to national health care? Would age then become irrelevant or perhaps less relevant in the allocation of medical resources?

Taking another approach to Callahan, what do you think are his views on euthanasia? Does the sort of program he envisions imply a position on euthanasia? How would Callahan have responded to the patient Dr. Hilfiker ·saw in the nursing home (Chapter 2)?

SETTING LIMITS

Daniel Callahan

Age or Need?

The use of age as a principle for the allocation of resources can be perfectly valid.[1] I believe it is a necessary and legitimate basis for providing health

Source: *Setting Limits: Medical Goals in an Aging Society* by Daniel Callahan. (New York: Simon and Schuster, 1987), pp. 138–53. Copyright © 1987 by Daniel Callahan. Reprinted by permission of Simon and Schuster, Inc.

care to the elderly. It is a necessary basis because there is not likely to be any better or less arbitrary criterion for the limiting of resources in the face of the open-ended possibilities of medical advancement in therapy for the aged.[2] Medical "need" can no longer work as an allocation principle; it is too elastic a concept. Age is a legitimate basis because it is a meaningful and universal category. It can be understood at the level of common sense, can be made relatively clear for policy purposes, and can ultimately be of value to the aged themselves if combined with an ideal of old age that focuses on its quality rather than its indefinite extension.

This may be a most distasteful proposal for many of those trying to combat ageist stereotypes and to protect the deepest interests of the elderly. The main currents of gerontology (with the tacit support of medical tradition) have moved in the opposite direction, toward stressing individual needs and the heterogeneity of the elderly. That emphasis has already led to a serious exploration of the possibility of shifting some old-age entitlement programs from an age to a need basis, and it has also been suggested that a national health-insurance program which provided care for everyone on the basis of individual need rather than age (as with the present Medicare program) would better serve the aged in the long run.[3] Thus while age classifications have some recognizably powerful political assets, a consensus seems to be emerging—clearly contrary to what I propose—that need is a preferable direction for the future. "Perhaps," as the Neugartens have written, "the most constructive ways of adapting to an aging society will emerge by focusing, not on age at all, but on more relevant dimensions of human needs, human competencies, and human diversity."[4] While that is an understandable impulse, I think it cannot for long remain possible or desirable in the case of allocating health care to the aged.

The common objections against age as a basis for allocating resources are varied. If joined, as it often is, with the prevalent use of cost-benefit analysis, an age standard is said to guarantee that the elderly will be slighted; their care cannot be readily justified in terms of their economic productivity.[5] The same can be said more generally of efforts to measure the social utility of health care for the old in comparison with other social needs; the elderly will ordinarily lose in comparisons of that kind. By fastening on a general biological trait, age as a standard threatens a respect for the value and inherent diversity of individual lives. There is the hazard of the bureaucratization of the aged, indifferent to their differences.[6] Since age, like sex and race, is a category for which individuals are not responsible, it is unfair to use it as a measure of what they deserve in the way of benefits.[7] The use of an age standard for limiting care could have the negative symbolic significance of social abandonment.[8] Finally, its use will run counter to established principles of medical tradition and ethics, which focus on individual need, and will instead, in an "Age of Bureaucratic

Parsimony. . . . be based upon institutional and societal efficiency, or expediency, and upon cost concerns—all emerging rapidly as major elements in decision making."[9]

These are weighty objections, and the hazards perfectly plausible. But all of them fail, or are sharply neutralized in their power, if the grounds for the use of age as a criterion for allocation are respect for the fundamental need of the elderly only to live out an adequate life span, and a recognition that medical need as a standard is utterly unworkable in any case in the face of technological advances. My principle of age-based rationing is not founded on the demeaning idea of measuring "productivity" in the elderly. The use of age as a standard treats everyone alike, aiming that each will achieve a natural life span, productive or not. Far from tolerating social abandonment, it will aim at improving care for the elderly, though not life-extending care. A standard of allocation rooted not in dehumanizing calculations of the economic value or productivity of the elderly, but in a recognition that beyond a certain point they will already have had their fair share of resources does not degrade the elderly or lessen the value of their life. It is only a way of recognizing that the generations pass and that death must come to us all. Nor does it demean the aged as individuals, or signal indifference to the variations among them, to note that they share the trait of being old. It is only if society more generally devalues the aged for being aged—by failing, most notably, to provide the possibility of inherent meaning and significance in old age (as is the case with the modernizing project)—that their individual lives are treated as less valuable. There is nothing unfair about using age as a category if the purpose of doing so is to achieve equity between the generations, to give the aged their due in living out a life-span opportunity range, and to emphasize that the distinctive place and merits of old age are not nullified by aging and death.

That a society could be mature enough to limit care for the aged with no diminution of respect, or could recognize the claims of other age groups without an implication that the elderly are less valuable than they are, seems rarely to be considered. By contrast, the motives I have been advancing reject not the elderly, but a notion of the good of the elderly based on pretending that death and old age can be overcome or ignored, that life has value only if it continues indefinitely, and that there is nothing to be said for the inherent value and contributions of the elderly as elderly. A society that adopts a wholly modernizing approach to old age must necessarily find the possibility of any limitation on care for the elderly a threat. It has robbed old age of all redeeming significance, and only constant efforts to overcome it are acceptable. To pick on the aged for "bureaucratic parsimony," to use Mark Siegler's term, would surely be wrong if done because they were perceived as weak and defenseless, a nice target-of-opportunity for cost containment. That is a very different matter from a societal decision that the overall welfare of the generations, the proper function of medicine, and a fitting understanding of old age and death as part of the life cycle justify limitation on some forms of medical care for the elderly.

Setting Priorities

There is no task in the fashioning of health policy more intimidating than establishing priorities; yet that is close to the essence of even having a policy. A policy might most concisely be defined as a set of priorities for action and the allocation of resources oriented toward achieving a goal. In this case, we are looking for a policy of allocating resources to the elderly consistent with acceptable and appropriate goals for their health and welfare. I want to present the outline of an allocation policy and priority system. It will be based on age as a legitimate principle of allocation, and will focus— in setting health-care goals for the elderly—on the averting of a premature death and the relief of suffering. This will be an "outline" only, not merely because my purpose here is more to think through the broad implications of a new and different vision of health care for the aged than to present a blueprint, but also because time and experience will be needed to determine what it would mean in practice. A full policy plan would include detailed directions, for example, for determining priorities within basic biological research, within health-care delivery, and between research and delivery. That I will not try to provide. I can only sketch a possible trajectory—or, to switch metaphors, a kind of likely general story. But if that at least can be done in a coherent fashion, avoiding the most flagrant contradictions, it might represent some useful movement. I will, however, take up some implications of this scheme in my next chapter.

There are four elements in my outline, three of which I shall examine in the remainder of this chapter. The first is the need for an antidote to the major cause of a mistaken moral emphasis in the care of the elderly and a likely source of growing high costs of their care in the years ahead. That cause is constant innovation in high-technology medicine relentlessly applied to life-extending care of the elderly; it is a blessing that too often turns into a curse. Unless an antidote is effective, and can be found, no alternative to the present arrangement is likely to take hold. The second element is a need to focus on those subgroups of the elderly—particularly women, the poor, and minorities—who have as yet not been well served, for whom a strong claim can be entered for more help from the young and society more generally. The third is a set of high-priority health and welfare needs—nursing and long-term care, prevention—which would have to be met in pursuit of the goals I have proposed. The fourth element, to be taken up in the next chapter, is the withholding or withdrawal of life-extending care from some groups of elderly patients.

1. High-Technology Medicine: Finding an Antidote. The great advances in health care in recent years have come from developments in high-technology medicine. Once the infectious diseases had been controlled or eliminated, further improvements in health have heavily depended upon technology (although changes in lifestyle, particularly in the case of heart disease, have made a contribution also). If any strong reins are to be put on the costs of health care for the elderly, high-technology medicine is one important place to begin. Most of the technological advances of recent decades have come to benefit the old comparatively more than the young (as an instance, dialysis) and the older segment of the old more than any other (as an instance, critical-care units).[10] Those same advances have also been heavily responsible for the increase in life expectancy that developed after the 1960s and continues to the present—and for the steady increase in chronic disease that has accompanied that increase. Technology has also had an important role in the rise in health-care costs. In analyzing the 8.9-percent increase in the cost of health care in 1985, the Department of Health and Human Services traced one-fourth of it to an "increased intensity of care," a combination of greater use of technology and a higher proportion of aged patients. The other sources of the increase were basic inflation in the economy and additional inflation in the cost of medical items above the national inflation rate.[11] Thus even if medical and other forms of inflation had been controlled, intensified use of technology would still have increased costs.

Where there is now a powerful bias in favor of innovative medical technology, and a correspondingly insatiable appetite for more of it, that will have to be replaced by a bias in the other direction where the aged are concerned. The alternative bias should be this: that no new technologies should be developed or applied to the old that are likely to produce only chronic illness and a short life, to increase the present burden of chronic illness, or to extend the lives of the elderly but offer no significant improvement in their quality of life. Put somewhat differently, no technology should be developed or applied to the elderly that does not promise great and inexpensive improvement in the quality of their lives, no matter how promising for life extension. Incremental gains, achieved at high cost, should be considered unacceptable. Forthright government declarations that Medicare reimbursement will not be available for technologies that do not achieve a high, very high, standard of efficacy would discourage development of marginally beneficial items.

While it would now be cruel to terminate federal kidney-dialysis support for the elderly, dialysis represents precisely the kind of technology that should not be sought or developed in the future. It does not greatly increase the life expectancy of its users (an average of only five years), and for most, that gain is at the price of a doubtful or poor quality of life and an inability to achieve earlier levels of functioning.[12] That it was originally developed with younger patients (aged 15 to 50) in mind, but soon saw an age creep of great proportions (with some 30 percent—25,000—of those on dialysis now over 65), is another part of the story to be remembered for the future.[13] The appeal to the Congress that in 1972 underwrote the costs of dialysis was that it would save lives and at a relatively modest cost (the estimate was for a maximum expenditure of $400 million). It has surely saved lives, but not for long, and the more than 80,000 users now cost well over $2 billion a year.[14] More generally, as a result of third-party reimbursement systems (up through 1983 at least, prior to the Medicare Prospective Payment System enacted by Congress in that year) there was, in the words of two analysts, "a near-maximum growth rate in the demand for new technologies to treat the elderly."[15]

The attraction of new and improved technologies remains as powerful now as it was in 1972, and their use gradually spreads from the younger to the older patient. That phenomenon is now visible in the cases of mechanical ventilation, artificial resuscitation, antibiotics, and artificial nutrition and hydration, four technologies singled out by the Congressional Office of Technology Assessment (OTA) in its important 1987 study of life-extending technologies and the elderly. While each of them is obviously of potential benefit for any age group, the greater likelihood of a life-threatening illness among the elderly means that they will be the primary candidates for their use. A reasonable estimate is that between 1980 and the year 2000, there will be an increase in the number of elderly of 9.5 million. That is a powerful incentive to continue improving those technologies, improvements that will almost certainly—on the basis of the historical pattern—extend their application to ever-sicker categories of patients at ever-increasing costs.

Consider some of the technological developments in this context. Antibiotics that can, at relatively low cost, be taken orally or given by injection are at present joined by those which can be given intravenously, a more expensive procedure. Eventually they will also be joined by those which can be infused by an implantable pump, a far more expensive procedure still. The provision of food and water can now go from the spoon and fork to the nasogastric tube, and then to the relatively new and very costly total parenteral nutrition (TPN), the last at a cost of $50,000 to $100,000 a year. Mechanical ventilation, a mainstay in the care of many elderly dying suffering from pulmonary insufficiency, is no less an area of advancing technology, ever able to sustain more people by ever-more-sophisticated means— high-frequency ventilation (HFV), extracorporeal-membrane oxygenation (ECMO), and—still in the theoretical stage—peritoneal oxygenation and carbon dioxide removal, and an implantable artificial lung. Since removal from a respirator is among the most common life-sustaining-treatment decisions, an increase in the efficacy of this technology alone is likely to intensify the moral dilemmas in the care of the elderly dying; and it is hardly likely to reduce the costs of caring for such patients.

Much of the use of these technologies would be devoted not just to the most desperately ill, at great cost and the frequent perpetuation of chronic disability, but also to any patient who could benefit from them. That is the common pattern with new technologies. An obvious dilemma here is that most technologies will benefit the young as well and are developed with them often primarily in mind. If technological development is discouraged, will that not damage the health interests of the young, even their chances to avoid a premature death? That is a hazard, but its effects could be lessened by a technology assessment that examined whether, if it were developed for the young, its primary or disproportionate use might be among the elderly, and whether alternative means could be found to meet the needs of the young. I leave these as difficult problems for the trajectory I am proposing.

However important though admittedly hard it would be to inhibit the development of marginally beneficial technologies, the larger problem lies not so much in what have been called the "big ticket" items as in the high costs of much more routine diagnostic and therapeutic procedures. "Ordinary" medical care, which accounts for most of the high costs of the elderly, is in great part driven by the routine use of what are by now routine technologies. That some 33 to 50 percent of the costs of medical care can be traced to technology suggests that a sharp focus on them in the case of the elderly is in order. Unless they can promise a high efficacy also, their routine employment should be discouraged. A telling commentary on present practice is the statement that "High quality acute care is necessary for the successful health of elderly [oldest-old] patients. Indeed, 44 percent of all present health care expenditures for the elderly arise from acute-care settings."[16] The value of this acute care, the authors emphasize, is to save on long-term-care expenditures, although they do not present any evidence that this result is usually achieved. If it is true that the road to hell is paved with good intentions, it is no less true that the road to higher long-term costs is paved with claims of the eventual savings to be achieved by the use of expensive technologies. A policy of systematic skepticism toward technology-driven expenses in the care of the elderly would serve a useful dampening effect.[17]

2. Providing Equitable Security. The greatest fear about old age seems to be not death but frailty, the loss of independence and self-direction, declining mental capacities, and impoverishment. The failure of present entitlement programs to cope with the fear of impoverishment as a result of old age and attendant ill health remains as a major flaw in the system.[18] While the elderly as an age group are now relatively well off, with only some 12 to 14 percent below the poverty line, a figure of that kind needs to be looked at closely. Those who live alone, the very old, and minority groups are much more likely to be in or only slightly above the poverty category than other aged people. In 1984, more than 1 in 3 black women 65 and over lived in poverty, and more than 1 in 5 Hispanic women. Women as a group constituted 71 percent, about 2.3 million, of the elderly poor; and women at all ages are twice as likely as men to be poor.[19] That is an intolerable situation.

A point not often sufficiently stressed is the insecurity that the present system breeds, even for those who are at the start better off. Though only a minority of the elderly are now in the poverty or near-poverty group, no younger person can be sure he or she will not be in that group, and no older person, even if well off at the moment, can be assured that some medical catastrophe will not put him or her into the group as well. Stories of the economic devastation wrought by catastrophic illnesses—or simply chronic illnesses that last for many expensive years—can be found in almost any family now. In general, also, the elderly are under pressure to reduce their use of hospital care. The Medicare deductible of about $500 is now twice what it was in the early 1980s, and general out-of-pocket medical expenses now take a larger portion of the income of the elderly than they did before Medicare went into effect in the mid-1960s.[20] Of the average $4,202 per capita consumption of health care by the aged in 1984, some 75 percent was paid by third parties (Medicare, Medicaid, or private plans), with the remaining 25 percent being paid directly. That latter proportion seems bound to grow. The Medicaid requirement of impoverishment—and thus a forced spending down of income and divestiture of resources—as a condition for qualifying for nursing-home or long-term care is a nasty threat to a lifetime of work and savings and a perfect symbol of government-imposed dependence.

The elderly (both poor and middle-class) can have no decent sense of security unless there is a full reform of the system of health care.[21] It may well be that reforms of the sweeping kind implied in these widely voiced criticisms could more than consume in the short run any savings generated by inhibitions of the kind I am proposing in the development and use of medical technology. But they would address a problem that technological development does nothing to meet. They would also reassure the old that there will be a floor of security under their old age and that ill health will not ruin them financially, destroy their freedom, or leave them dependent upon their children (to the detriment of both). It is, in any event, almost certain that unless the costs of technology are controlled, this reform has little chance of succeeding. Full or improved coverage for the elderly poor has historically competed badly against escalating reimbursements for high-technology care to existing beneficiaries.

Many years will be required to bring about the kind of shift in values needed to change attitudes and practices pertinent to the provision of life-extending technologies to the elderly. That is the long-term solution. In the meantime, while we are working toward that goal, an intensified effort to provide better basic health-care coverage for the elderly will most effectively demonstrate that there is no lessening of commitment to their well-being. It is that move—and no other—which will neutralize the kind of threat posed by a restriction of life-extending care. I cannot responsibly propose to limit that kind of care without simultaneously proposing to improve other forms of care. I will be the first to object to any effort to deny life-extending care before the other reforms are well under way and assured of success. A denial of the one without the flourishing of the other would indeed be a grave threat to the elderly.

3. Priorities for Care. A societal decision deliberately to limit life-extending high-technology care for those who have lived out a natural life span is not meant to be a recipe for, or symbol of, abandonment. It is meant to be an affirmation of the diverse needs of different age groups and an acceptance of the inevitable place of death at the end of life. It can be a tolerable basis for social policy only if that policy strikingly seeks to provide the elderly with an honorable and bearable life in their remaining years. This will entail first working to avert a premature death, and then seeking to minimize pain and suffering.

Any attempt to specify a "premature death" must have a certain arbitrary quality. I define it as a death prior to the living out of a natural life span, something that would ordinarily occur in the early 70s but could extend through the late 70s to early 80s. It is the latter range I will use as the basis for my discussion here. This is actually a more liberal standard than that used by the federal Centers for Disease Control (CDC), which uses the concept of "years-of-life-lost" prior to age 65 in determining premature death. That concept came into use during the 1970s and was incorporated into the CDC's *Morbidity and Mortality Weekly Report* in 1982. A focus on conventional death rates, by simply counting deaths in the population, emphasizes deaths occurring in older age groups. The "years-of-life-lost" calculation, by contrast, highlights the potentially preventable mortality occurring earlier in life and permits a more precise focus for health-care goals. A variant of that method has shown, for example, that accidents are the leading cause of premature death, while cancer and heart disease (affecting older people) fall into second and third places. Heart disease, which remains the leading cause among all deaths, thus falls by this calculation to a lower place because it is not as significant a cause of premature death. Using 1979 as the base year for its calculations, one important study determined that the rank order of causes of years lost is: accidents, cancer, heart disease, perinatal abnormalities, homicide, suicide, congenital abnormalities, cerebrovascular disease, cirrhosis and chronic liver disease, and pneumonia and influenza.[22] Whether this or some similar method of reckoning is used, the first goal in care for the aged will be to go after the causes of premature death.

Beyond avoiding a premature death, what do the elderly need from medicine to complete their lives in an acceptable way? They need to be as independent as possible, freed from excess worry about the financial or familial burdens of ill health, and physically and emotionally positioned to seek whatever meaning and significance can be found in old age. Medicine can only try to maintain the health which facilitates that latter quest, not guarantee its success. That facilitation is enhanced by physical mobility, mental alertness, and emotional stability. Chronic illness, pain, and suffering are all major impediments and of course appropriate targets for medical research and improved health-care delivery.

Major research priorities should be those chronic illnesses which so burden the later years and which have accompanied the increase in longevity. They encompass, in addition to a number of physical problems (particularly multiple organic diseases), a variety of major mental disorders, including schizophrenia, affective disorders, various senile brain diseases, arteriosclerosis, and epilepsy. The OTA study of aging and technology centered on five chronic conditions endemic among the elderly, of which only the first receives any great public attention (or, for that matter, sympathy): dementia, which characterizes Alzheimer's disease—a source first of humiliation, then of a loss of basic human potentials, then death; urinary incontinence—also a humiliating condition and a malodorous symbol of the loss of physical control; hearing impairment— embarrassing, isolating, and frustrating; osteoporosis (thinning of the bones)—because of the greatly enhanced incidence of fractures, a source of constant fear and danger for the old-old in particular; osteoarthritis— painful, sometimes disabling, and pervasive (affecting 16–20 million elderly).

As with the correction of inequities in health care for the elderly, there is no guarantee that the necessary research and future amelioration of such conditions would be inexpensive. Even low-technology approaches to non-curable chronic problems can be enormously expensive if used by enough people; and some of the therapeutic solutions to some of the conditions are clearly of the high-technology variety (e.g., hip and joint replacement at an average cost of $50,000 to victims of osteoarthritis). The most troubling problems in that respect may well be posed by advances in rehabilitation. Even now, rehabilitation for stroke is labor-intensive, difficult, and often of uncertain outcome, and the moral dilemma of choosing those patients most likely to benefit often wrenching. While rehabilitation has in the past been thought of as a low-technology, a caring rather than curing, field, it is also moving in a technological direction and, simultaneously, working to rid itself of the reputation of indifference to and pessimism about rehabilitation for the elderly.[23] The ongoing development of sophisticated prosthetic devices and computer-assisted methods of helping the partially paralyzed, paraplegic and quadriplegic do not promise to lower costs, and neither does their likely extension to use among the elderly. If such developments as these are even to be possible, it is hard to envision how they can financially coexist with continuing investment in life-extending treatments.

The prevention of illness has long been promoted as the best way in the long run to improve the health of the elderly (along with the health of everyone else) and to reduce health-care costs. Its primary virtue from any perspective is that it can help avoid a premature death and enhance physical well-being through an ordinary life span; illness and death would be pushed beyond the normal lifetime-opportunity-range boundary. That it will actually reduce costs is not, however, necessarily true as a flat generalization. Whether the sum total of the direct costs (to mount and implement a program of prevention) and the indirect expenses (time and other social resources) will equal the savings will vary from one disease category to another.[24] In some cases, moreover, it will be no more expensive to cure a disease than to prevent it—for example, the choice between bypass surgery and a preventive regimen for the hypertension that would have led to it.[25] "This means," Louise Russell has written, "that choosing investments in health is more difficult than some of the claims for prevention would suggest. Sometimes prevention buys more health for the money; sometimes cure does. . . . the issue most often is what mix of prevention and therapy is best. It is a rare preventive measure that, like smallpox vaccine, eradicates the condition altogether."[26] Yet even if economic savings are uncertain in each case, prevention programs can have many health benefits, helping to avoid some conditions altogether (cancer most notably through such changes in behavior as the cessation of smoking) and ameliorating the impact of others (as in a reduction of obesity among diabetics). A caution should also be mentioned. That some forms of prevention could impinge upon the freedom of the old, thus robbing them of one thing they prize, autonomy, in order to obtain something else they value, health, poses an evident dilemma.[27]

I have stressed some of the problems of reducing pain and suffering and attempting to maintain a decent quality of life. They should not be minimized. There will be some acute struggles about how much we can afford for them also, even if of demonstrable value to the health and well-being of the elderly. Their value, however, is that to give them priority over life-extending technologies would signal a change in thinking about the elderly and about the goals of medicine in caring for the elderly. This will be particularly true of the last category of issues I want to mention, that of long-term care, nursing care, and home care. For there is little doubt that the combination of longer life, particularly for those over 85, and accompanying chronic illness poses a special challenge to our ways of caring for the old.

Between 1985 and 2000 the estimate is that the nursing-home population will increase by 47 percent, from 1.5 to 2.1 million.[28] There will be a

corresponding increase in the number and proportion of the elderly requiring some degree of daily assistance and surveillance outside an institution. Both the number of people and the potential costs of adequate care
are enormous.[29] The trend has already worked a distorting effect on the
Medicaid program, one originally designed to help the poor in general but
which now supports more than half of all nursing-home care for the elderly.
As a result, only about 40 percent of Medicaid now goes to the non-elderly
poor. Medicare provides support for home care only in the form of short-
term critical nursing attention in the aftermath of serious health episodes,
not long-term home care. Nowhere is the national bias toward acute-care
medicine more obvious than in these policies. The lives of the elderly are
saved, often at great cost, but there are then scant federal resources to respond to the chronic illness or disability that may be the long-term result.
The afflicted can neither remain for long in acute-care facilities, eager to
discharge them to reduce costs under DRG pressure, nor easily find community facilities to carry on the needed continuing care.

As have others in recent years, I have become impressed with the philosophy underlying the British system and the way it meets the needs of the
old and chronically ill. It has, to begin with, a tacit allocation policy. It
emphasizes improving quality of life through primary-care medicine and
well-subsidized home care and institutional programs for the elderly rather
than life-extending acute-care medicine. An undergirding skepticism
toward technology makes that a viable option. That attitude, together with
a powerful drive for equity, "explains why most British put a higher value
on primary care for the population as a whole than on an abundance of
sophisticated technology for the few who may benefit from it."[30] That the
British spend a significantly smaller proportion of their GNP (6.2 percent)
on health care than Americans (10.8 percent) for an almost identical outcome in health status is itself a good advertisement for the British set of
priorities. Infant mortality is 11.5 percent in the United States and 11.1
percent in Great Britain. Life expectancies are, for men, 70.0 years in the
U.S. and 70.4 years in Great Britain; and, for women, 77.8 in the U.S. and
76.6 in Great Britain.[31]

No less important is the different orientation toward aging and death
that the British system appears to express. They are more readily accepted,
and it is understood that the consequences of a desperate struggle to save
the lives of the elderly cannot fail to have a distorting consequence for
health-care priorities and allocations generally. It is a system that works far
better to equalize across the generations the "normal opportunity range"
than does our own: it reflects a known and accepted allocation policy that
provides incentives for political self-restraint on interest-group demands
which our system does not.[32] That our present system fails to meet so many
health needs of the elderly, and particularly fails to cope with the emergence of chronic illness as their main burden, would surely suggest the

value of a change in priorities.[33] That it could also be an acceptable policy orientation for American elderly is possible, although American individualism and love of technology indicate an important difference in ethos. But the British direction has not been tried and provides the single most promising change in perspective to break the monopoly of high-technology medicine and the endless struggle against aging and death that has been its most willing partner. That the British themselves are tending toward the recreation of a private health-care system does not disprove the value of their traditional priorities, only the failures of a National Health Service beset by chronic national near-depression conditions.

Notes

[1]One of the first articles to explore the idea of an age basis for allocation was Harry R. Moody's "Is It Right to Allocate Care Resources on Grounds of Age?" in Elsie L. Bandman and Bertram Bandman, *Bioethics and Human Rights* (Boston: Little, Brown, 1978), pp. 197–201.

[2]For a good general discussion of age as an allocation principle, see Leslie Pickering Francis, "Poverty, Age Discrimination, and Health Care," in George R. Lucas, Jr., ed., *Poverty, Justice, and the Law* (Lanham, MD: University Press of America, 1986), pp. 117–29.

[3]Bernice L. Neugarten, ed., *Age or Need?: Public Policies for Older People.* (Beverly Hills: Sage Publications, 1982); see Douglas W. Nelson, "Alternative Images of Old Age as the Bases for Policy," in *Age or Need*, ed. Neugarten.

[4]Neugarten and Neugarten, "Age in the Aging Society," p. 47.

[5]Jerome L. Avorn, "Benefit and Cost Analysis in Geriatric Care: Turning Age Discrimination into Health Policy," *New England Journal of Medicine* 310 (May 1984), pp. 1294–1301.

[6]Carole Haber has written well on this problem in *Beyond Sixty-Five: The Dilemma of Old Age in America's Past* (New York: Cambridge University Press, 1983), especially pp. 125–29.

[7]"Life-Sustaining Technologies and the Elderly: Ethical Issues," Chapter 4 of U.S. Congress, Office of Technology Assessment, Biological Applications Program, *Life-Sustaining Technologies and the Elderly* (Washington, D.C.: OTA, July 1987).

[8]James F. Childress, "Ensuring Care, Respect, and Fairness for the Elderly," *Hastings Center Report* 14 (October 1984), p. 29.

[9]Mark Siegler, "Should Age be a Criterion in Health Care?" *Hastings Center Report* 14 (October 1984), p. 25.

[10]Jerome L. Avorn, "Medicine, Health, and the Geriatric Transformation," *Daedalus* 115 (Winter 1986), p. 213.

[11]Summarized in *The Washington Post* (July 30, 1986), p. A6, and forthcoming in *Health Care Financing Review* in 1987. See also George E. Thibault *et al.*, "Medical Intensive Care: Indications, Interventions, and Outcomes," *New England Journal of Medicine* 302 (April 1980), pp. 938–42; and Edward W. Campion *et al.*, "Medical Intensive Care for the Elderly: A Study of Current Use, Costs, and Outcomes," *Journal of the American Medical Association* 246 (November 1981), pp. 2052–56.

[12]Richard B. Freeman, "Treatment of Chronic Renal Failure: An Update," *New England Journal of Medicine* 312 (February 1985), pp. 577–79; see also Roger Evans *et al.*, "The Quality of Life of Patients with End-Stage Renal Disease," *New England Journal of Medicine* 312 (February 1985), pp. 553–59.

[13]Arthur L. Caplan, "Organ Transplants: The Costs of Success," *Hastings Center Report* 13 (December 1983), pp. 23–32.

[14]Alonzo L. Plough, *Borrowed Time: Artificial Organs and the Politics of Extending Lives* (Philadelphia: Temple University Press, 1986). For an example of "age creep" in the use of technology see "Cardiac Surgery in High Risk Octogenarians," *Journal of the American Medical Association*

256 (November 1986), p. 2669. In 1986, a liver transplant was carried out on a 76-year-old patient. "As Liver Transplants Grow More Common, Ethical Issues Multiply," *Wall Street Journal* 208 (October 14, 1986), p. 1. See also Karen Davis and Diane Rowland, *Medicare Policy,* p. 26.

[15]Louis P. Garrison, Jr., and Gail R. Wilensky, "Cost Containment and Technology," *Health Affairs* 5: (Summer 1986), p. 50.

[16]Kenneth L. Minaker and John Rowe, "Health and Disease Among the Oldest Old: A Clinical Perspective," *Milbank Memorial Fund Quarterly* 63:2 (Spring 1985), p. 343.

[17]For an analysis of the problem of encouraging appropriate technologies while controlling costs, see *Technology and Aging in America* (Washington, DC: Congressional Office of Technology Assessment, OTA-BA-264, June 1985); and Garrison and Wilensky, "Cost Containment and Technology."

[18]*Aging America: Trends and Projections,* 1985–86 Edition; John L. Palmer and Stephanie G. Gould, "The Economic Consequences of an Aging Society." *Daedalus* 115 (Winter 1986), pp. 295–323.

[19]Older Women's League, *Report on the Status of Midlife and Older Women in America* (1986).

[20]Rice, "Past Trends and Future Projections," p. 55.

[21]See Karen Davis and Diane Rowland, *Medicare Policy* (Baltimore: Johns Hopkins Press, 1986).

[22]Janet D. Perloff *et al.,* "Premature Death in the United States: Years of Life Lost and Health Priorities," *Journal of Public Health Policy* (June 1984), pp. 167–84. See also John W. Rowe, "Health Care of the Elderly," *New England Journal of Medicine* 312 (March 1985), pp. 827–834.

[23]I am particularly indebted for that information to Janet F. Haas, M.D. and other colleagues who were part of a Hastings Center project on ethical issues in rehabilitation medicine 1985–87.

[24]Louise B. Russell, *Is Prevention Better than Cure?* (Washington, DC: The Brookings Institution, 1986).

[25]*Ibid.,* p. 111.

[26]*Ibid.*

[27]For a good discussion of coercion and prevention, see Childress, "Ensuring Care, Respect, and Fairness for the Elderly"; Daniel I. Wikler, "Persuasion and Coercion for Health: Ethical Issues in Government Efforts to Change Life Styles," *Milbank Memorial Fund Quarterly* 56:3 (Summer 1978), pp. 303–38; and a special section, "Voluntary Health Risks," in the *Hastings Center Report,* 11:5 (October 1981), pp. 26–44.

[28]*Aging America,* p. 98. See also Anne R. Somers, "Long-Term Care for the Elderly and Disabled," *New England Journal of Medicine* 307 (July 1982), pp. 221–26; and Terrie Wettle, "Long Term Care: A Taxonomy of Issues," *Generations* 10 (Winter 1985), pp. 30–34.

[29]Dorothy P. Rice and Jacob J. Feldman, "Living Longer in the United States: Demographic Changes and Health Needs of the Elderly," *Milbank Memorial Fund Quarterly* 61:3 (Summer 1983), pp. 362–96.

[30]Frances H. Miller and Graham A. H. Miller, "*The Painful Prescription:* A Procrustean Perspective?" *New England Journal of Medicine* 314 (May 1986), p. 1385; cf. Aaron and Schwartz, *The Painful Prescription.* I should emphasize that the British health-care system seems in considerable trouble at present, in great part because of the financial difficulties of the country and diminishing resources allocated to the National Health Service. More people are opting to buy additional private care, and resources for the elderly are in particular in danger. See Keith Andrews, "Demographic Changes and Resources for the Elderly," *British Medical Journal* 290 (April 1985), pp. 1023–24.

[31]Iglehart, "Canada's Health Care System," p. 205.

[32]Daniels, "Family Responsibility Initiatives," p. 57.

[33]*Cf.* W. Andrew Achenbaum, *Shades of Gray: Old Age, American Values, and Federal Policies Since 1920* (Boston: Little, Brown, 1983), p. 125; Paul T. Menzel, *Medical Costs, Moral Choices: A Philosophy of Health Care Economics in America* (New Haven: Yale University Press, 1983), pp. 193*ff.*

Allocation Attempted

The state of Oregon is trying to create a plan for allocating state funds for health care. Its state legislature began in 1987 by eliminating Medicaid funds for organ transplants. The state went on to devise a method for setting priorities among medical needs. Into the hopper went cost of treatment, probability of success, years of benefit to the patient, and "quality of well-being" after treatment. Out came a computer generated list giving low priority to varicose veins, impacted teeth, and viral herpes but high priority to bacterial meningitis and help with stopping thumb sucking. There was an emphasis on preventive medicine with a focus on prenatal care.

The ranking used an assumption: that for every medical treatment there is a way to measure the benefits against the costs. This is clearly a utilitarian kind of assumption. Indeed, data for the list of rankings came from physicians who had to know the fact of the conditions in question (treatment, likelihood of recovery, and cost) and interviews with Oregonians. This was a case of the greatest number (at least a random sample of them) helping to decide how to distribute an important good.

One of the results of cutting off payments for organ transplants was the death of a young boy whose parents could not afford a marrow transplant. Thus, it may well be the case that someone whose condition gets a low ranking, and therefore can get little if any state financial aid, might die as a result of these rankings. How different is this—how far are we in this case—from the committee at the Swedish Hospital that made life and death decisions? That some may die as a result of allocation decisions may seem unfair; but without a total restructuring of our society and many of its values, it may be inevitable. This is an underlying assumption of Callahan's argument in the previous reading.

OREGON PUTS BOLD HEALTH PLAN
ON ICE

Virginia Morell

"I looked at the first two pages of that list and threw it in the trash can," said Harvey Klevit, a Portland, Oregon, pediatrician and member of the Oregon Health Services Commission. "That list" should have been a proud achievement in Oregon. After all, it was a first—and very bold—step toward

Source: "Oregon Puts Bold Health Plan on Ice" by Virginia Morell. *Science*, vol. 249 (August 3, 1990), pp. 468–71. Copyright © 1990 by the American Association for the Advancement of Science. Used by permission.

rationing Medicaid dollars in an era when one patient with little hope of survival can soak up millions simply because no mechanism exists for making hard choices in allocating funds. Indeed, the problem of providing the greatest benefit without increasing taxes is now plaguing every government agency, national or local, that funds health care.

Oregon's commission thought it had the solution. And so did all the newspapers, magazines, and television stations that covered the commission's announcement last May. A means had been found, the stories went, to assign a cost-benefit rating to nearly 2000 medical procedures. The basis of the list was a mathematical formula. All that had to be done was to feed piles of data into a computer, and the machine would respond with a list of procedures, carefully ordered according to their cost-benefit ratios.

Sounds great. But the list the computer actually spit out last May left the 11 commissioners reeling. Take thumb-sucking and acute headaches. Treatments for these problems ranked higher than those for cystic fibrosis and AIDS. Immunizations for childhood diseases did not appear. Deeply embarrassed, the commissioners hastily withdrew the list, and 3 months later Oregon appears to be no closer to a second version. The current prognosis: a revised list is not expected until some time in the fall.

While commission members dismiss the first draft's failure as unimportant ("Anything you do the first time isn't perfect," says Klevit, "it's like Edison's light bulb."), it does indicate the complexity of the problem they face. Few people disagree with the idea of providing some form of basic health care to all. But in an era of shrinking financial resources and soaring medical costs, the question becomes just how basic is "basic"? And who decides? The traumatic Oregon experience might serve as an object lesson for the entire nation in the complexities of trying to simultaneously achieve equity and contain health care costs.

Today, Americans spend nearly $540 billion a year, or 11.1% of the gross national product, on medical treatments. As the price tag climbs, programs like Medicaid suffer. Its costs have risen 10% annually over the last 10 years. Last year alone, $61.3 billion went to Medicaid, $34.6 billion in federal funds, $26.7 billion in state monies. Not surprisingly, many states are seeking ways to cut those expenditures. But Oregon is the first to actually suggest a concrete reform plan, and from California to Washington, D.C., health care professionals—and politicians—are keeping a close watch to see how the Oregon experiment turns out.

Oregon's search for a better way to deliver health care began in 1987 after its cash-strapped legislature halted Medicaid funding for most organ transplants, arguing that they were a high-cost procedure that benefited only a very few. The money was funneled instead into prenatal care, a move that two other states, Virginia and Arizona, have also taken. Initially, the legislature's decision received little attention. But its first victim was a 7-year-old named Coby Howard. Ineligible for state funds for a bone marrow transplant, he died while his parents were pleading for contributions to finance the operation.

At least four other children and one adult who might have been saved by organ transplants have died since the legislature's decision. As a result, the Oregon legislators have been faced with angry advocates for the poor, lobbyists for transplant patients, and citizen groups favoring socialized medicine—all demanding a new way of distributing the Medicaid dollars. In the president of the Oregon Senate, John Kitzhaber—himself an emergency room physician—they found a sympathetic ear.

Arguing that "there must be universal access for the state's citizens to a basic level of health care," Kitzhaber drafted three bills, which the legislature passed last June. One bill addressed the health care of Oregon's poorest citizens; the second made the private sector responsible for the health care of people whose income was higher than the federal poverty level; and the third established an insurance pool to provide coverage for people unable to qualify for private insurance. Together, the three bills were designed to weave a health-care safety net assuring every Oregonian of basic medical care. At the same time, physicians and hospitals were promised full reimbursement for the services they render—putting an end to a practice which often sees providers receiving 70% or less of their fees.

But the quid pro quo here was that the state would no longer finance all medical procedures—only the ones that had the highest ratio of costs to benefits. Which is where the first version of the famous list came in. "It's a step from an inequitable position to one that is more equitable," says Kitzhaber. "What we're doing now, nationally, is rationing poor people, so that some have access to health care and others do not. But then you have situations where 35 people die from measles. To me, that is outrageous." Instead of limiting the number of people who are eligible for Medicaid, Kitzhaber would reduce the services that each recipient gets. "We need to change the debate from who is covered to what is covered."

Congress created Medicaid in 1965 to provide health care to the poor; the federal and state governments would share its cost and operation. But millions of poor Americans do not qualify because each state sets its own eligibility standards, adjusting them annually to match their budgets. Alabama currently has the most stringent standards: a family of two qualifies only if it earns less than $88 a month, or 13% of the federal poverty level of $700 a month for one parent and one child. In Oregon, a family is eligible if it earns less than 58% of the federal poverty level, or approximately $400 a month. Because eligibility requirements can be raised, a family can be supported by Medicaid one year and dropped the next—subjecting citizens to a devastating medical roller coaster.

Under the new system, this practice of "forcing more and more people under the table," as Kitzhaber calls it, would come to an end. Instead, Oregon would enroll everyone eligible for Medicaid but restrict access to treatments at the bottom of the list: those that are, according to some measure, most expensive and least effective. State officials estimate that this will add 77,000 people to the current 130,000 now receiving Medicaid benefits. Another 300,000 people would be covered by the private sector. The Health Services Commission list—in its final form—will serve as the guideline for deciding which treatments are funded and which are not, for both Medicaid and private insurance recipients.

But as the commission, along with Kitzhaber and his allies, discovered, deciding how to rank health care treatments is no simple task. The procedure Oregon hit on combined community values—as described by Oregonians themselves—with a mathematical technique for estimating costs and benefits. "We attempted to assess what value a community places on health, what types of care it deems important," said Michael Garland, a bioethicist at the Oregon Health Sciences University and president of Oregon Health Decisions. OHD held 47 public meetings throughout the state, and conducted a telephone survey, asking participants to rank a variety of health situations in terms of "quality of well-being."

These feelings—which indicated that Oregonians generally favor preventive health care—were then mathematically correlated with cost-benefit data for various medical procedures to produce the controversial list. The ranking method clearly needs revision. How much revision is needed is a matter of debate, however. Some commissioners favor keeping the mathematical formula, while others believe the list needs a human touch and should be done by hand. Nevertheless, says Harvey Klevit, "We can make it work. It's just going to require some more time."

Yet complex as they are, the problems with the list are only part of the political, ethical, and financial quagmire in which the state of Oregon now finds itself. None of Oregon's Medicaid reforms can be implemented until the state receives a federal government waiver that would allow the state to cut some types of care for the "categorically needy" in order to add more people to the program. The state has sought the approval of the U.S. Department of Health and Human Services and Congress.

In so doing, it has run headlong into Washington's lobbying process and found itself outflanked and outgunned. Several groups, notably the Children's Defense Fund, the American Academy of Pediatrics, and the National Association of Community Health Centers, have spoken strongly against granting the waivers. The state does not have funds for a full-time lobbyist, and Kitzhaber's own trip to Congress was, he says, "one of the most depressing experiences" of his life. His opponents, he says, were "more interested in berating Oregon for not raising taxes" than they were in discussing the problems besetting Medicaid.

Ironically, the plan's critics argue that the scheme will work against exactly those whom it is intended to help, the poorest and most defenseless part of society—in particular, poor women and children. "Whether or not it's Oregon's intention, the only people who will have prioritized, rationed health care are the women and children who are currently covered by Medicaid," claims Molly McNulty, a health specialist at Children's Defense Fund. According to CDF and other critics, this is because one of the federal waivers would allow Oregon to redirect its Medicaid monies, except for those funds spent on the elderly, handicapped, and blind. The services these people now receive would remain the same. But 70% of the state's Medicaid dollars go to those three groups. The remaining 30% go mostly to women and children. Rationing the Medicaid dollars of women and children to expand the program to include another 77,000 people is, say the critics, grossly unfair.

The critics think that along with the rationing program a tax increase of some sort is necessary—an idea that raises difficulties in a state where there is tremendous resistance to new taxation. "The Oregon politicians want you to believe that they can give health care to all the poor, pay the providers for the cost of doing this, and not raise taxes. But in reality, you can't do all these things, and it's disingenuous to say so," says Maxwell J. Mehlman, director of the Law Medicine Center at Case Western Reserve University, where a special conference was held in June to discuss the Oregon proposals.

In Mehlman's eyes, the Oregon plan will simply take services from the poorest people, "people at the bottom of the barrel," in order to give to people who are only slightly better off. "It's a zero-sum game," he claims. Kitzhaber disagrees, arguing that to him "the most vulnerable people in our society are the uninsured." and those are the folks that the plan would cover. Unlike the critics, he expects women and children to benefit most because of the emphasis on preventive care. Nor does he worry about finding additional funds. He believes that once all Oregonians are involved in health care policy—through voting and participation in formulating the list—they will be more willing to increase funding if necessary.

"Health care will no longer be just a line item in the budget, where you can throw people out of the system to balance the bottom line, and then hold no one responsible for what happens to them." Under his plan, Kitzhaber sees citizen advocacy groups pressuring the legislature to increase funds for health care if the budget provides only skimpy coverage. He is also optimistic enough to think that wasteful spending in medical services will be identified by the Oregon rationing plan and eliminated.

Yet until the commission produces the final version of its much criticized list and the waivers from Washington come through, much of this debate will remain academic. Without the list, no one can predict just how Oregon's plan will affect the health, or pocketbooks, of its citizens. Nor are there any promises that situations like Coby Howard's won't occur again. Overall, Oregon's exercise in rationing may be seen as either a grand experiment or a crazy aberration. But if nothing else, it has stirred the pot in a national debate that won't go away: health care reform.

5

MEDICAL ETHICS
AND
THE LAW

FIRST SURGEON: What is black and tan and looks good on a lawyer?
SECOND SURGEON: What?
FIRST SURGEON: A doberman pinscher.

This joke reflects the fact that many physicians have come to view the law as less of a watchdog and more of a menace. The reason is simple. Malpractice cases have burgeoned. Malpractice insurance rates are prohibitive to many physicians. Many practitioners in specialties such as obstetrics and gynecology and orthopedic surgery are taking early retirement because their malpractice insurance rates are so high. Some physicians tend to feel that if they are less than perfect, then their patients will sue. To many doctors, it seems as though they are being dogged by profit-hungry lawyers.

Considering that there was a time when lawsuits were relatively rare, when patients would trust, without a second thought, whatever a doctor said, something must have happened. Precisely why we are such a litigious society is hard to say, except (to restate the point) that we have come to value freedom (autonomy) and to question authority. This, combined with the advances of medicine, which seem to promise just about limitless health, would at least lead us to expect that a physician who seemed to a patient overly self-assured and abrasive might well be sued if the results were not what the patient expected.

There is another aspect to the increase in lawsuits. In order to be reasonably sure that a physician's treatment has in fact been less than adequate, one needs more than just a bad result. One needs evidence that the physician should have done a better job. This information is difficult to get. First, it is highly technical information. Second, the people with the information, other physicians, are reticent, at best, to say that another physician has made a mistake. This is nothing new. It has been true in this country for at least the past one hundred years or so.

Until recently it seemed as though the profession of medicine was a closed shop. Access to and policing of the profession was limited by the profession itself. Moreover, to many it seemed a policing with little bite. When a healthy disrespect for entrenched authority clashed with the historical autonomy of the medical profession, there had to be a change. The closed-shop attitude conflicted with what many saw as a right to due process (roughly, everybody's right to their day in court). In such cases, the law can be used to step in and say: If you will not police yourself, then we will do it for you by finding for the plaintiff in malpractice cases. An overriding question to keep in mind is whether the law ought to serve this social function.

The aim of this chapter is not to pursue these broad sociological observations about law and medicine; nor is it to examine, in detail, malpractice law. Rather, what we want to highlight is the interplay among legal reasoning, social philosophy, and ethics as they all apply to medical issues.

In previous chapters we have discussed the issues of autonomy, competence, and paternalism as they arise in medical contexts. Medical ethics is a relatively new field. Law and philosophy of law are not. Given that law has a practical side to its theory, and given that these same issues have a long history within law, it only makes sense to examine legal thought on these topics. Remember that philosophers use thought experiments to help create and then fine-tune their theories. Law cases and court decisions are ready-made thought experiments.

Before looking at some cases, a brief overview of the law will be helpful.

Laws are meant to codify and regulate many of the actions of people. Does the codification and regulation mean that all will be treated equally under the law? Does law insure fairness? This is, in part, a factual question and clearly depends on the laws in question. But the issue can be restated: Should laws insure fairness? What should be the relationship between law and morality?

There are two traditional answers to these questions. *Legal positivism* holds that law and morality are two totally separate realms and that the two need never overlap. The law is the law. *Legal naturalism* holds that part of what it means to be a law is that it be in accord with moral fundamental standards. There are three different ways of interpreting legal naturalism.

1. The law should reflect current morality.
2. The law should take the lead in suggesting morality.
3. The law should lag behind in suggesting changes in morality.

Morality may be taken to be current standards in the sense of what most people believe at any given time is morally binding. Conversely, morality may be found in some more absolute set of standards. For example, it is possible to ground morality by appeal to general principles, which seem to go far beyond any particular set of social beliefs. As an example of how positivism and naturalism can clash, consider the following case, taken from West German law. Trying to construct a carefully worked out position on this case will show how difficult it can be to decide between positivism and naturalism.

In 1944, a woman denounced her husband for remarks that he made against Hitler. There was no legal obligation to turn him in but his comments violated the law that there should be nothing bad said about the Third Reich. He was arrested and sentenced to death. Instead of execution, he was sent to the front. The wife was tried in 1949, under an 1871 statute that made it a crime to deprive a person illegally of freedom. She argued that what she did was in accord with Nazi statutes and therefore could not be considered a crime. At the very least, the two laws (of 1871 and of the Third Reich) conflicted, making a decision just about impossible.

The courts, however, held that the statute that "protected" her was "contrary to the sound conscience and sense of justice of all human beings" and, therefore, not a true law at all. This appeal to a more fundamental law was the basis for condemning Nazi war criminals for their "crimes against humanity."

However we decide the positivist–naturalist dichotomy, the law is meant to help us to right wrongs in a civilized, nonviolent manner. Tort law is the set of laws created to right noncriminal wrongs. Malpractice law comes under the heading of tort law. In the case of the doctor–patient relationship, where the patient is often at a disadvantage, it seems reasonable that the wronged patient ought to have some recourse against a physician who has caused harm through negligence.

Obviously there are concepts here that have to be clearly spelled out: *cause, harm, damage,* and *negligence.* These crucial ingredients in the definition of malpractice just cry out for philosophical analysis.

To do this, we shall focus on three cases. *Curlender* v. *BioScience Laboratories,* in which negligence and wrongful life is claimed against the laboratory that erred in its genetic testing of the Curlenders. *Helling* v. *Carey,* in which a woman sues her ophthalmologists for not diagnosing glaucoma sooner than they did, even though they acted in accord with the usual standard of care. As an example of another kind of case, a woman is legally maneuvered into a cesarean that she really does not want.

Now we have reached the cash value of jurisprudence. How should these cases be argued; what are just findings?

Review the *Roe* v. *Wade* decision. Does it have the seeds of a defense of women's liberty; or does it give the state the right to intervene on behalf of the fetus? What is the relation between the concepts of liberty and privacy? Is it possible that the law created by such decisions (case law, which is appealed to by courts as necessary) makes it too easy to infringe on other liberties? Perhaps, in other words, we are willing to say that a pregnant woman loses the right to smoke and drink because we feel that the rights of the fetus outweigh her rights, but why not also enforce a good diet and exercise? (This slippery slope-type argument is often used by courts.) Can we gain some insights into the concepts of paternalism and competency from these cases?

Review the distinction between legal positivism and legal naturalism. Should we continually change our interpretation of malpractice to suit our consciences? Do physicians and judges have a better sense of what is right than the rest of us? Even if they do, should their sense of right be made into law?

It is easy to see that our sense of justice can be taken to its limits. We want to help those whose fortunes are starcrossed whether they are adults or fetuses, and yet to do so within the confines of much of our present law often seems both dangerous in terms of precedent and unfair to at least some of the parties involved. Remember that some claim that the integrity of the medical profession is being challenged by overzealous use of the courts. Remember also that the medical profession itself has fallen back on the courts, as we will see in the cases of forced Caesareans.

We can use our legal system to make whatever is unfortunate also unfair and, therefore, deserving of some restitution. But is this use of the legal system a misuse that might indeed undermine its ability to protect us all?

Wrongful Life

Traditionally, four elements are needed to show negligence: (1) A duty must be owed to the plaintiff either to act in a certain way or to refrain from acting in a certain way. (2) There must be a clear breach of that duty. In many clinical cases, the duty is to act according to an accepted standard of care. (3) The breach of duty must be the cause of the plaintiff's injury. (4) The injury or harm should be compensatable by money. Remember that malpractice is a form of negligence. With these four conditions as elements of negligence claims, it is easy to see the puzzle presented by the wrongful life suit brought by the Curlenders against BioScience Laboratories.

The facts in the case of *Curlender* v. *BioScience* are as follows. The Curlenders were tested by BioScience laboratories for the presence of the recessive Tay-Sachs gene. They were told that neither of them carried the gene.

Therefore, when Mrs. Curlender became pregnant, there seemed to be no need for amniocentesis to check the genetic status of the fetus for Tay-Sachs. But the laboratory had been negligent; the Curlenders did carry the gene, and their child Shauna was born with Tay-Sachs disease.

The courts had to deal with a new concept of harm. Can one claim that being born is a harm? The California Court also had to deal with two related questions. Is it even reasonable to claim that harm has occurred when the only way to have avoided the harm is never to have been conceived or never to have been born alive? Put another way, is it reasonable to claim that nonexistence is preferable to existing with a harm? Related to these questions: Can damages (usually money) be affixed to the harm, if indeed it is a harm, of being born, especially when the alternative would be nonexistence?

George Annas, in his article, "Righting the Wrong of 'Wrongful Life'," tries to account for the fact that the California court did not throw out the claim for damages by Shauna Curlender. She sought damages based on losing approximately 72 years of life (at the time the average age expectancy for females was 76, as opposed to her 4) as well as punitive damages against BioScience on the grounds of negligence. To some, even allowing the claim to come to court, which was all the judges did allow, was a surprising finding, because a New York court had recently not allowed such a wrongful life claim to come to trial.

The California Court argued that there ought to be at least a chance for recovery of damages when there is negligence. Moreover, since abortion is a legal right of women and since genetic information is increasing all the time, we have the ability to avoid certain genetic disasters. When we don't and the reason is negligence, then someone ought to pay. Important for our purposes is the court's comment that "the understanding [is] that the law reflects, perhaps later than sooner, basic changes in the way society views such matters." Annas thinks that this is reasonable.

What he finds difficult to understand is the court's comment that "we need not be concerned with the fact that had defendants not been negligent, the plaintiff might not have come into existence at all." To Annas, this is the crux of the wrongful life sort of case. For him, it is clear that for Shauna Curlender imagined in a state of nonexistence, there are no rights, which of course means no recovery of damages for Shauna Curlender. Stated differently, what could it possibly mean, especially in a court of law, to talk about a plaintiff who could only be better off by never having been given the chance to become the plaintiff? Wrongful life seems to involve a self-contradiction.

The California court allowed a chance for recovery based on Shauna Curlender's actual life expectancy of about four years. Again, Annas thinks that this is acceptable if one is going to allow recovery at all. But he finds the court too quick to accept a logical implication of their finding. If the child may sue for negligence on its own, independent from its parents, then a child ought to be able to sue its parents for negligence. Annas thinks that such suits should not be allowed for two reasons.

First, in the long run, it is better to let parents make good-faith judgments for their children without the law looking over their shoulders.

Second, there is no right (legal or moral) to be born healthy. Claiming that there is such a right might lead to all sorts of restrictions on the liberty of pregnant women.

These implications of allowing recovery for wrongful life are so distasteful to Annas that he sees them as reason to reject recovery in these cases. Notice that this article was written in 1981 and correctly foresees a spate of actions taken against pregnant women on behalf of their fetuses. These sorts of cases are the subject of the third reading of this section.

RIGHTING THE WRONG
OF "WRONGFUL LIFE"

George J. Annas

A lower court in California has taken what might turn out to be a major step in remedying what Alexander Capron has termed "the wrong of 'wrongful life'"—denying compensation to a genetically defective child whose birth would have been prevented had proper information been made available to the parents. Previous courts had ruled against such children because they believed that there was no way to comprehend nonexistence, thus making it impossible to calculate damages based on a comparison of it to a defective existence, and that it seemed illogical to permit a child to recover for something he or she would not even be able to sue for if he or she had not been born.

Professor Capron has argued eloquently that neither of these arguments is persuasive. As to the first, we permit judges and juries to make similar distinctions and measurements—for example, in wrongful death cases—all the time. And as to the second, there is nothing illogical in the plaintiff saying, "I'd rather not be here suffering as I am, but since your wrongful conduct preserved my life I am going to take advantage of my regrettable existence to sue you" (Alexander M. Capron, "The Wrong of 'Wrongful Life'" in Aubrey Milunsky and George J. Annas, editors, *Genetics and the Law II*. New York: Plenum, 1980, pp. 81, 89).

While the California case has been interpreted as against the weight of judicial authority and as creating a new cause of action against genetic

Source: "Righting the Wrong of "Wrongful Life'" by George J. Annas. *Hastings Center Report,* vol. 11, no.1 (February, 1981), pp.8–9. Used by permission of the author.

counselors and obstetricians, it can be seen as simply rectifying a legal anomaly that has up to now prevented a person who was severely injured, due to the negligence of another, from recovering damages from the negligent party. Why did the California court permit recovery on the part of the child while the highest court in New York would not? My conclusion, in a previous column about the New York cases, that "the issue of 'wrongful life' is dead in the courts," now seems premature (see "Medical Paternity and 'Wrongful Life,'" *Hastings Center Report,* June 1979, pp. 15–17).

The *Curlender* Case

One can only guess why the California court did what it did. The courts were moving toward permitting recovery by the child (both parents and the child were initially denied recovery by the courts; and now parental claims are almost universally acknowledged). And the facts made it especially difficult to deny the child an opportunity to present her case to a jury. Specifically, the plaintiff, Shauna Tamar Curlender, was born with Tay-Sachs disease. Her parents had previously retained the laboratories named as defendants to administer tests to determine whether or not they were carriers of recessive Tay-Sachs genes. The tests were reported to have been negative. The parents relied upon these tests. Because of the alleged negligence in the laboratory's performance, their daughter was born defective, subject to severe suffering, and had a life expectancy of only approximately four years (*Curlender* v. *BioScience Laboratories,* 165 Cal. Rptr. 477 [Ct. App. 2d Dist. Div. 1, 1980]).

The child's lawsuit sought damages for emotional distress and the deprivation of 72.6 years of life. She sought an additional $3 million in punitive damages on the grounds that the defendants knew their testing procedures were likely to produce a substantial number of false negatives and yet proceeded to use them "in conscious disregard of the health, safety, and well-being of the plaintiff. . . ." Since the complaint did not allege the date of the plaintiff's birth, the court could not determine whether the parents relied upon the test to conceive a child or to forego amniocentesis; nor does the court seem to care.

The court begins its inquiry with a worthwhile excursion through the history of so-called "wrongful life" cases. As Professor Capron has noted, this term is unfortunate and misleading: the plaintiff is not attempting to recover because it has been born. "The wrong actually being complained of is the failure to give accurate advice on which a child's parents can make a decision whether not being born would be preferable to being born deformed." The court understands this, and quotes with favor the dissenting opinion in a 1979 New Jersey case in which the majority granted the right to recover to the parents of a Down syndrome child, but denied recovery to the child itself: "To be denied the opportunity—indeed the right—to apply one's own moral values in reaching that decision [concerning the child's future], is a serious, irreversible wrong" (*Berman v. Allan*, 80 N.J. 421, 404 A2d 8, 18, dissenting opinion).

It also agrees with a Pennsylvania court that held, in a case involving the negligent performance of amniocentesis that failed to detect a fetus affected with Tay-Sachs disease, that "Society has an interest in insuring that genetic testing is properly performed and interpreted" (*Gildiner v. Thomas Jefferson Univ. Hospital*, 451 F. Supp. 692 [E.D. Pa. 1978]).

On the basis of this history, and the court's own view of what the law should be, it makes three important observations concerning the handling of "the 'wrongful life' problem" by previous courts:

1. There is a major difference between a child who is unwanted or illegitimate, but healthy (the type of children involved in the original cases in which the courts first coined the term "wrongful life"), and a child who is born with a severe deformity or disease. Unlike a severe deformity, illegitimacy is simply not an *injury*.

2. There is a trend in the law to recognize that there should be recovery when an infant is born defective and its "painful existence is a direct and proximate result of negligence by others." In this regard the court notes especially that abortion is currently a woman's legal right, and that there has recently been a "dramatic increase in ... the medical knowledge and skill needed to avoid genetic disaster."

3. The injured parents and children have continued to sue for "wrongful life," in spite of past decisions against them, because of the seriousness of the wrong, the increasing understanding of its causes, and "the understanding that the law reflects, perhaps later than sooner, basic changes in the way society views such matters."

Given these observations, the court is determined to recognize the right of the child to sue for the negligent acts of others that led to her birth:

The reality of the "wrongful life" concept is that such a plaintiff both *exists* and *suffers*, due to the negligence of others. It is neither necessary nor just to retreat into meditation on the mysteries of life. We need not be concerned with the fact that had defendants not been negligent, the plaintiff might not have come into existence at all. The certainty of genetic impairment is no longer a mystery ... a reverent appreciation of life compels recognition that the plaintiff ... has come into existence as a living person with certain rights (at 488; emphasis in original).

This remarkable statement deals with the major imponderable in wrongful life cases by dismissing it with the phrase "We need not be concerned" about it. And this *is* the key to wrongful life recovery *by the child*. All the court's major concerns can be addressed by permitting the parents to recover damages. Certainly they have been injured: expecting a normal child, they must deal with an abnormal one. There are both emotional and monetary costs. But what about the child? He or she expected nothing, not even birth. He or she *never* had the possibility of being born healthy—only the chance to be either aborted or not conceived at all. From one way of looking at it, the child *could not* be damaged by the testing laboratory's negligence, because without the negligence the child would not have existed at all. The argument is *not* that any life is better than none, no matter what the suffering; but rather that to be damaged one needs to be worse off after the negligent act complained of than before it. It cannot be said, in this sense, that the child is worse off existing than not existing if one assumes that nonexistence is a state in which there are no rights and no rightful expectations.

On the other hand, for policy reasons we may want to ignore this troublesome issue and deal with the "reality" of the existence of a defective child who needs care and attention. It is correct to say that the testing laboratories did not cause the child's disease—but it is also correct that the child would not be in existence, suffering from the disease, but for the negligence of the testing laboratories. The court's position seems no less difficult to sustain than the more traditional one.

Concerning damages, the court denies recovery based on a seventy-year life expectancy, and instead requires damages to be based on the plaintiff's actual life expectancy of four years. Though one can quarrel a bit with this, it seems a fair compromise. After all, the child *never* would have had any opportunity for a seventy-year life span: it was no life or a four-year life. Under these circumstances, limiting damages for medical expenses and pain and suffering for her actual life span seems reasonable. This may be especially so in light of the court's decision to permit the plaintiffs to proceed with their $3 million claim for punitive damages. It should be stressed, however, that the court did not find that the plaintiff did or should win this case, only that the plaintiff was entitled to try to prove in court what she alleged in the pleadings.

Marching into Muddier Waters

The court should have stopped here; instead it marches on into much muddier waters. It correctly notes a concern that recognizing the child's right to sue physicians and laboratories for negligence might logically lead to some courts recognizing the right of children to sue their own parents for allowing them to be born. While calling this fear "groundless," the court goes as far as any court ever has in approving the notion in principle. It specifically talks about a hypothetical case in which the parents have been properly warned of the probability of having a defective child, and yet decide to go ahead with the pregnancy. In such a case the court suggests no action could be brought against the physician or testing laboratory (of course), but remarkably it sees "no sound public policy which should protect those parents from being answerable for the pain, suffering, and misery which they have wrought upon their offspring" (at 488).

In a similar vein, Margery Shaw, a geneticist and lawyer, has suggested that women who "abandon their right to abort" upon being informed that their fetus is defective, should incur a "conditional prospective liability" for negligent acts toward their fetus should it be born alive. She would permit such a defective child to sue its mother for negligence, and would also permit children harmed by fetal alcohol syndrome or drug addiction during pregnancy to sue their mothers. She might even go further:

> Withholding of necessary prenatal care, improper nutrition, exposure to mutagens and teratogens, or even exposure to the mother's defective intrauterine environment caused by her genotype, as in maternal PKU, could all result in an injured infant who might claim that his right to be born physically and mentally sound had been invaded (Margery Shaw, "Preconception and Prenatal Torts," in, *Genetics and the Law II,* pp. 225, 229).

The court and Dr. Shaw are not alone, and their position is a *logical* extension of permitting the child to sue on its own behalf. But there are policy objections to this notion, the laudable purpose of which is to protect the unborn child. The most fundamental objection is that there is no "right to be born physically and mentally sound" and should not be. Such a "right" could almost immediately turn into a duty on the part of potential parents and their caretakers to make sure no defective, different, or "abnormal" children are born. As Alexander Capron has argued, "The enforcement of such a rule by the state, through the courts and other agencies of social control, might even lead to unprecedented eugenic totalitarianism." It could also lead to severe deprivations of liberty of pregnant women during the third trimester. One can envision confining certain women to ensure "proper nutrition" or withdrawal from alcohol or drug addiction, or to ensure a "healthful environment" for their fetuses. This seems absurd now but could seem reasonable in a world that viewed "normal" birth as an ultimate value.

Parents should be permitted—as they now are—to make good-faith judgments. Some children will suffer, but this seems a less onerous result than the massive curtailment of liberty implicit in the "right to normalcy" notion. Caretakers have the legal obligation to provide parents with accurate information on which to base decisions; they do not have the right to make decisions for them. Only by keeping this distinction firmly in place can we help to assure that increases in genetic knowledge will lead to increases in human autonomy rather than to its destruction.

The Standard of Care

In *Helling* v. *Carey*, we see the courts struggling with the fact that according to a strict interpretation of malpractice law, the physicians should not be held responsible for the harm incurred by Ms. Helling. She had been fitted for contact lenses by Dr. Carey in 1959. From that time until October 1968, she saw Dr. Carey with various complaints, all of which he attributed to the contact lenses. But during that October 1968 visit, he tested her field of vision and eye pressure. He discovered that she had glaucoma; that indeed she had probably had it for quite some time.

The physicians had carried out their duty to act within the accepted standard of care used by current ophthalmologists. They did not, in any direct way, cause her condition. Yet the harm could have been avoided if only the physicians had acted differently. Are they, therefore, in some sense, the cause of her harm? If they are the cause, then can a case be made that they are legally responsible? Should such a case be made and enforced? How would such a finding affect the crucial concept, standard of care? Is there a policy of recompense being used by the judges that transcends the written law?

Notice how the judges are careful to say that they are setting, by law, the standards needed to protect patients. The court is holding that the standards of ophthalmology should have been different from what they were. But even if this is so, can the physician be found negligent? The associate justice points out that the physician is liable, but liable without fault. He goes on to appeal to the principle that where a careful person has through no real fault caused harm, social justice demands that reparation be made by whomever is in the best position to do so. This is sometimes facetiously called the Deep Pockets Theory of Justice.

HELLING V. CAREY

Supreme Court of Washington
83 Wash. 2d 514, 519 P.2d 981 (1974)

HUNTER, Associate Justice.

This case arises from a malpractice action instituted by the plaintiff (petitioner), Barbara Helling.

The plaintiff suffers from primary open angle glaucoma. Primary open angle glaucoma is essentially a condition of the eye in which there is an interference in the ease with which the nourishing fluids can flow out of the eye. Such a condition results in pressure gradually rising above the normal level to such an extent that damage is produced to the optic nerve and its fibers with resultant loss in vision. The first loss usually occurs in the periphery of the field of vision. The disease usually has few symptoms and, in the absence of a pressure test, is often undetected until the damage has become extensive and irreversible.

The defendants (respondents), Dr. Thomas F. Carey and Dr. Robert C. Laughlin, are partners who practice the medical specialty of ophthalmology. Ophthalmology involves the diagnosis and treatment of defects and diseases of the eye.

The plaintiff first consulted the defendants for myopia, nearsightedness, in 1959. At that time she was fitted with contact lenses. She next consulted the defendants in September, 1963, concerning irritation caused by the contact lenses. Additional consultations occurred in October, 1963; February, 1967; September, 1967; October, 1967; May, 1968; July, 1968; August, 1968; September, 1968; and October, 1968. Until the October 1968 consultation, the defendants considered the plaintiff's visual problems to be related solely to complications associated with her contact lenses. On that occasion, the defendant, Dr. Carey, tested the plaintiff's eye pressure and field of vision for the first time. This test indicated that the plaintiff had glaucoma. The plaintiff, who was then 32 years of age, had essentially lost her peripheral vision and her central vision was reduced to approximately 5 degrees vertical by 10 degrees horizontal.

Thereafter, in August of 1969, after consulting other physicians, the plaintiff filed a complaint against the defendants alleging, among other things, that she sustained severe and permanent damage to her eyes as a proximate result of the defendants' negligence. During trial, the testimony of the medical experts for both the plaintiff and the defendants established that the standards of the profession for that specialty in the same or similar circumstances do not require routine pressure tests for glaucoma upon patients under 40 years of age. The reason the pressure test for glaucoma is not given as a regular practice to patients under the age of 40 is that the disease rarely occurs in this age group. Testimony indicated, however, that the standards of the profession do require pressure tests if the patients's complaints and symptoms reveal to the physician that glaucoma should be suspected.

The trial court entered judgment for the defendants following a defense verdict. The plaintiff thereupon appealed to the Court of Appeals, which affirmed the judgment of the trial court. The plaintiff than petitioned this Court for review, which we granted.

In her petition for review, the plaintiff's primary contention is that

under the facts of this case the trial judge erred in giving certain instructions to the jury and refusing her proposed instructions defining the standard of care which the law imposes upon an ophthalmologist. As a result,
the plaintiff contends, in effect, that she was unable to argue her theory of
the case to the jury that the standard of care for the specialty of ophthalmology was inadequate to protect the plaintiff from the incidence of glaucoma,
and that the defendants, by reason of their special ability, knowledge and
information, were negligent in failing to give the pressure test to the plaintiff at an earlier point in time which, if given, would have detected her
condition and enabled the defendants to have averted the resulting substantial loss in her vision.

We find this to be a unique case. The testimony of the medical experts
is undisputed concerning the standards of the profession for the specialty
of ophthalmology. It is not a question in this case of the defendants having
any greater special ability, knowledge and information than other ophthalmologists which would require the defendants to comply with a higher duty
of care than that "degree of care and skill which is expected of the average
practitioner in the class to which he belongs, acting in the same or similar
circumstances." The issue is whether the defendants' compliance with the
standard of the profession of ophthalmology, which does not require the
giving of a routine pressure test to persons under 40 years of age, should
insulate them from liability under the facts in this case where the plaintiff
has lost a substantial amount of her vision due to the failure of the defendants to timely give the pressure test to the plaintiff.

The defendants argue that the standard of the profession, which does
not require the giving of a routine pressure test to persons under the age
of 40, is adequate to insulate the defendants from liability for negligence
because the risk of glaucoma is so rare in this age group. The testimony of
the defendant, Dr. Carey, however, is revealing as follows:

Q. Now, when was it, actually, the first time any complaint was made
to you by her of any field or visual field problem? A. Really, the first
time that she really complained of a visual field problem was the August 30th date. (1968) Q. And how soon before the diagnosis was that?
A. That was 30 days. We made it on October 1st. Q. And in your opinion, how long, as you now have the whole history and analysis and the
diagnosis, how long had she had this glaucoma? A. I would think she
probably had it ten years or longer. Q. Now, Doctor, there's been some
reference to the matter of taking pressure checks of persons over 40.
What is the incidence of glaucoma, the statistics, with persons under
40? A. In the instance of glaucoma under the age of *40*, is less than
100 to one percent. The younger you get, the less the incidence. It is
thought to be in the neighborhood of one in 25,000 people or less. Q.
How about the incidence of glaucoma in people over 40? A. Incidence

of glaucoma over 40 gets into the two to three per cent category, and hence, that's where there is this great big difference and that's why the standard around the world has been to check pressures from 40 on.

The incidence of glaucoma in one out of 25,000 persons under the age of 40 may appear quite minimal. However, that one person, the plaintiff in this instance, is entitled to the same protection, as afforded persons over 40, essential for timely detection of the evidence of glaucoma where it can be arrested to avoid the grave and devastating result of this disease. The test is a simple pressure test, relatively inexpensive. There is no judgment factor involved, and there is no doubt that by giving the test the evidence of glaucoma can be detected. The giving of the test is harmless if the physical condition of the eye permits. The testimony indicates that although the condition of the plaintiff's eyes might have at times prevented the defendants from administering the pressure test, there is an absence of evidence in the record that the test could not have been timely given.

In The T. J. Hooper, 60 F.2d 737, on page 740 (2d Cir. 1932), Justice Hand stated:

(I)n most cases reasonable prudence is in fact common prudence; but strictly it is never its measure; a whole calling may have unduly lagged in the adoption of new and available devices. It never may set its own tests, however persuasive be its usages. *Courts must in the end say what is required; there are precautions so imperative that even their universal disregard will not excuse their omission.* (Italics ours.)

Under the facts of this case reasonable prudence required the timely giving of the pressure test to this plaintiff. The precaution of giving this test to detect the incidence of glaucoma to patients under 40 years of age is so imperative that irrespective of its disregard by the standards of the ophthalmology profession, it is the duty of the courts to say what is required to protect patients under 40 from the damaging results of glaucoma.

We therefore hold, as a matter of law, that the reasonable standard that should have been followed under the undisputed facts of this case was the timely giving of this simple, harmless pressure test to this plaintiff and that, in failing to do so, the defendants were negligent, which proximately resulted in the blindness sustained by the plaintiff for which the defendants are liable.

(Reversed and remanded on issue of damages only.)

UTTER, Associate Justice (concurring).

I concur in the result reached by the majority. I believe a greater duty of care could be imposed on the defendants than was established by their profession. The duty could be imposed when a disease, such as glaucoma, can be detected by a simple, well-known harmless test whose results are definitive and the disease can be successfully arrested by early detection, but where the effects of the disease are irreversible if undetected over a substantial period of time.

The difficulty with this approach is that we as judges, by using a negligence analysis, seem to be imposing a stigma of moral blame upon the doctors who, in this case, used all the precautions commonly prescribed by their profession in diagnosis and treatment. Lacking their training in this highly sophisticated profession, it seems illogical for this court to say they failed to exercise a reasonable standard of care. It seems to me we are, in reality, imposing liability, because, in choosing between an innocent plaintiff and a doctor, who acted reasonably according to his specialty but who could have prevented the full effects of this disease by administering a simple, harmless test and treatment, the plaintiff should not have to bear the risk of loss. As such, imposition of liability approaches that of strict liability.

Strict liability or liability without fault is not new to the law. Historically, it predates our concepts of fault or moral responsibility as a basis of the remedy. As noted in W. Prosser, *The Law of Torts* sect. 74 (3d ed. 1964) at pages 507, 508:

> There are many situations in which a careful person is held liable for an entirely reasonable mistake. . . . In some cases the defendant may be held liable, although he is not only charged with no moral wrongdoing, but has not even departed in any way from a reasonable standard of intent or care. . . . There is "a strong and growing tendency, where there is blame on neither side, to ask, in view of the exigencies of social justice, who can best bear the loss and hence to shift the loss by creating liability where there has been no fault."

If the standard of a reasonably prudent specialist is, in fact, inadequate to offer reasonable protection to the plaintiff, then liability can be imposed without fault. To do so under the narrow facts of this case does not offend my sense of justice. The pressure test to measure intraocular pressure with the Schiotz tonometer and the Goldman applanometer takes a short time, involves no damage to the patient, and consists of placing the instrument against the eyeball. An abnormally high pressure requires other tests which would either confirm or deny the existence of glaucoma. It is generally believed that from 5 to 10 years of detectable increased pressure must exist before there is permanent damage to the optic nerves.

Although the incidence of glaucoma in the age range of the plaintiff is approximately one in 25,000, this alone should not be enough to deny her a claim. Where its presence can be detected by a simple, well-known harmless test, where the results of the test are definitive, where the disease can be successfully arrested by early detection and where its effects are irreversible if undetected over a substantial period of time, liability should be imposed upon defendants even though they did not violate the standard existing within the profession of ophthalmology.

Whose Rights?

Veronika Kolder discusses cases of pregnant women being forced to undergo unwanted, invasive procedures on the grounds that the state is only trying to protect the rights of the fetus. The following (actual) case of a court-ordered cesarean is an example.

> An angry, uncooperative, and fearful woman is in the last stages of labor, having been admitted through the emergency room in a Denver, Colorado hospital. Fetal monitoring indicates that the fetus is very likely to be in distress, but labor has stopped. A cesarean is definitely in order, according to the physicians, who explain this to the woman. She refuses the surgery. A hospital psychiatrist examines her and finds that she is competent. The physicians call a judge, who holds a hearing in the hospital. He finds that the fetus counts as a juvenile under Colorado law and tells the woman that unless she consents to the surgery, she will be found guilty of child neglect. She consents to the surgery.

It is easy to see that forced surgery is an infringement of a woman's liberty. But it is just as easy to claim that a fetus ought to have a right to as healthy a life as the courts can ensure.

Kolder supplies us with data about the number of cases of court-ordered obstetrical procedures. She also supplies us with some interesting medical opinions. Forty-six percent of heads of fellowship programs in maternal–fetal medicine felt that mothers who risked their fetuses' lives by refusing advised procedures ought to be kept in hospitals in order to see that the appropriate procedures are done.

She argues that the crucial question is whether the state may override the decision-making of competent patients in order to help a second party. Is this the only crucial question? After all, to some obstetricians, it certainly must seem that the crucial question might be: Who is the primary patient? Even if the courts seem to go in one direction, should this change the way that a physician feels and acts? This sort of situation is the hallmark of a difficult moral situation. Each person involved is trapped with no easy answer and, worse, each answer hurts some party.

What often intensifies this sort of issue is the press for time. Medical facts must be evaluated quickly, decisions must be made quickly, and where compliance is needed, it must come quickly. But physicians do make errors. Sometimes fetuses turn out not to have been in nearly as much distress as the doctors feared. Bringing a judge into a hospital during an apparent emergency or trying to get a decision from a judge under pressure of a time limit may very well defeat the way that our legal system was meant to function. To some, this indicates that the liberty of women must be the first concern of the courts. Yet the well-being of future children does hang in the balance.

COURT-ORDERED
OBSTETRICAL INTERVENTIONS

Veronika E.B. Kolder, M.D., Janet Gallagher, J.D.,
and Michael T. Parsons, M.D.

In 1981 the Georgia Supreme Court ordered a cesarean section to be performed on a woman with placenta previa at term who had refused to allow an abdominal delivery.[1,2] A lower-court order had been obtained and appealed. However, immediately after the Georgia Supreme Court upheld the lower-court ruling, ultrasonography revealed that the placenta had shifted; the woman later delivered vaginally.

Since this decision, isolated reports have documented court orders for cesarean sections in three additional states (Colorado,[3] Illinois,[4] and South Carolina[5]). Forced obstetrical procedures have received attention in the popular, medical,[6] obstetrical,[3,7–12] medical-ethics,[13,14] and legal[15–20] literature. However, no national survey has addressed the subject.

In this study, we investigated the scope and circumstances of court-ordered obstetrical procedures and solicited obstetricians' opinions about this subject. A questionnaire format was selected because court decisions in this area are often unpublished or sealed and not readily accessible for research. Copies of the original survey are available on request from the authors.

Methods

In February 1986, a questionnaire was sent to two groups of obstetricians. The first group consisted of all 76 current heads of fellowship programs listed in the *1985–1986 Directory of Fellowship Programs in Maternal–Fetal Medicine.*[21] This group represented 31 states (Alabama, Arizona, California, Colo-

Source: "Court-Ordered Obstetrical Interventions" by Veronika E.B. Kolder, Janet Gallagher, and Michael T. Parsons, *The New England Journal of Medicine,* vol. 316, no. 19 (May 7, 1987), pp. 1192–96. Used by permission.

rado, Connecticut, Florida, Georgia, Illinois, Indiana, Louisiana, Massachusetts, Maryland, Michigan, Missouri, Mississippi, North Carolina, New Jersey, New Mexico, New York, Ohio, Oklahoma, Oregon, Pennsylvania, Rhode Island, South Carolina, Tennessee, Texas, Utah, Virginia, Washington, and Wisconsin) and the District of Columbia. To obtain information from as many additional states as possible, the questionnaire was also sent to a second group of obstetricians consisting of directors of maternal–fetal medicine divisions in residency programs in obstetrics and gynecology. One director (from a university-based program whenever possible) was selected from each of the following 14 states: Arkansas, Delaware, Hawaii, Iowa, Kansas, Kentucky, Maine, Minnesota, Nebraska, New Hampshire, Nevada, South Dakota, Vermont, and West Virginia. Five states (Alaska, Idaho, Montana, North Dakota, and Wyoming) were not represented in the survey.

Three mailings of the questionnaires, modified cover letters, and self-addressed envelopes were followed by at least one attempt to reach nonresponders by telephone. The objective data from all respondents are reported here, but in tabulating the opinions, we used only the responses of the heads of fellowship programs in maternal–fetal medicine.

Results

Response Rates

Sixty-one of 76 heads of fellowship programs in maternal–fetal medicine (80 percent) and 14 of 14 directors of divisions of maternal–fetal medicine responded. This gave a net response rate of 83 percent, with at least one response from each of 45 states and the District of Columbia.

Objective Data

Institutions in 18 states (Alabama, California, Colorado, Hawaii, Illinois, Kentucky, Maine, Michigan, Minnesota, Nebraska, New Mexico, New York, Ohio, Pennsylvania, South Carolina, Tennessee, Texas, and Wisconsin) and the District of Columbia reported 36 attempts to override a maternal refusal of therapy during the previous five years. Institutions in an additional six states (Louisiana, Massachusetts, Maryland, Missouri, New Jersey, and Oregon) reported that a maternal refusal of therapy had been successfully overridden at an institution other than their own.

After exclusion of court orders that were sought after delivery or for maternal transfusions, detailed descriptions of 21 court orders sought at the respondents' institutions within the previous five years remained. Since the respondents did not always answer all the questions on the questionnaire, the denominators in our calculations vary.

Fourteen of 18 cases (78 percent) involved women aged 20 to 30 years, and 12 of 17 women (71 percent) were multiparous. Seventeen of 21 women (81 percent) were black, Asian, or Hispanic. Seven of 16 (44 percent) were unmarried, and 5 of 21 (24 percent) did not speak English as their primary language. All 20 women were seen at a teaching-hospital clinic or were receiving public assistance. All received prenatal care—10 of 18 (56 percent) at the institution where the court order was sought. Maternal competency was established by a psychiatrist in 3 of 20 cases (15 percent) and was not investigated in the rest.

In 14 of 20 cases (70 percent), hospital administrators and lawyers were aware of the situation for a day or less before a court order was pursued. In five cases (25 percent), they were aware for two to seven days, and in one case, for more than seven days. Once a court order was deemed necessary, it took six or fewer hours to obtain it in 14 of 16 cases (88 percent). In three of these cases (19 percent), the court orders were actually obtained in an hour or less; at least one order was granted by telephone. Fetal custody was sought in juvenile court in four of nine cases. Probate court was petitioned for guardianship of the mother in three cases, and family court was petitioned in two cases. Eighteen of 21 petitions (86 percent) were granted. In 4 of 12 cases, custody or guardianship was conferred on a hospital administrator. In the remainder, it was conferred on a hospital lawyer, the hospital and doctor, the medical staff, the doctor alone, or a guardian ad litem. The next of kin were not given custody or guardianship in any of the cases described.

Cesarean Sections. Fifteen court orders for cesarean sections were sought in 11 states (Colorado, Hawaii, Illinois, Maine, Michigan, Minnesota, Ohio, Pennsylvania, South Carolina, Tennessee, and Texas) and were obtained in all except Maine. Two of 13 court orders were not enforced because the patient finally agreed to the procedure.

Eleven of 12 women involved were aged 20 to 30 years, and 8 of 11 were multiparous. Seven of 15 (47 percent) were black Americans, and 5 (33 percent) were African or Asian. Only 3 (20 percent) were white Americans. Five of 10 (50 percent) were unmarried, and 4 of 15 (27 percent) did not speak English as their primary language.

In 2 of 15 cases (13 percent), the court order was pursued at 31 to 33 weeks' gestation. In five cases (33 percent), the orders were sought at 34 to 36 weeks, and in the remainder, at or beyond term. The obstetrical diagnosis was fetal distress in 7 of 15 cases (47 percent), previous cesarean section in 3 cases (20 percent), and placenta previa in 2 cases (13 percent). There was one case each of Rh sensitization with an amniotic-fluid change in optical density at 450 nm in Liley zone III, maternal idiopathic thrombocytopenic purpura, and toxemia with breech presentation of the first of triplets.

No important maternal morbidity or mortality was reported. A Nige-

rian man, who, along with his wife, refused surgery for weeks before delivery and was physically removed from the hospital when his wife went into
labor, committed suicide a few months after her court-ordered cesarean
section. Only 2 of 14 infants (14 percent) had important morbidity; one
required multiple exchange transfusions for Rh disease, and the other had
intrauterine growth retardation and acidosis after cesarean delivery for fetal distress. No fetal deaths occurred.

Hospital Detentions. Three court orders for hospital detentions were
sought in two states (Colorado and Illinois). In two cases—one from each
state—court orders were obtained.

Two women were aged 16 to 19 years and were primigravidas. Two
were black Americans, and one was unmarried. The court orders that were
obtained involved women with diabetes at 31 to 33 weeks' gestation who
refused therapy. A court order was not granted (in Illinois) for a 20- to 30-
week gestation complicated by bleeding.

Intrauterine Transfusions. Three court orders were sought in two states
(Colorado and Michigan) for intrauterine transfusions. Both orders sought
in Colorado were obtained, whereas the order sought in Michigan was denied.

All three cases involved Rh sensitization in multiparous women at 20
to 30 weeks' gestation. Two women were between 20 and 30 years of age,
and one was unmarried. Two of the three women were black Americans,
and one was Hispanic American. No important maternal morbidity or mortality was reported. Both the infants who received transfusions required
prolonged neonatal care; in one, this was necessary despite three intrauterine transfusions. Maternal and fetal outcomes in the third case were not
known because the woman left the hospital system.

Opinions

The heads of fellowship programs in maternal–fetal medicine were
asked to agree or disagree with a number of statements. Twenty-six of 57
(46 percent) thought that mothers who refused medical advice and thereby
endangered the life of the fetus should be detained in hospitals or other
facilities so that compliance could be ensured. Twenty-seven of 57 (47 percent) thought that the precedent set by the courts in cases requiring emergency cesarean sections for the sake of the fetus should be extended to
include other procedures that are potentially lifesaving for the fetus, such
as intrauterine transfusion, as these procedures come to represent the standard of care. Finally, 15 of 58 (26 percent) advocated state surveillance of
women in the third trimester who stay outside the hospital system.

The future legality of home birth may depend partly on how issues of fetal versus maternal rights are resolved. Respondents were asked to choose the statement that best approximated their opinion about home birth. Twelve of 54 (22 percent) thought that home birth carried some inherent increase in risk and that every viable fetus had the right to live. Therefore, they concluded, home birth should be illegal. Eighteen (33 percent) thought that home birth might carry some increased risk but that the consequences of outlawing it might cause more harm than good, and therefore, home birth should be legal. Finally, 20 respondents (37 percent) thought that competent adults, including pregnant women with viable fetuses, were autonomous and might refuse medical care, and therefore, home birth should be legal. Interestingly, 7 of these 20 had advocated court-ordered hospital detentions, intrauterine transfusions, or state surveillance earlier in the questionnaire. This effectively reduced the number of respondents who consistently upheld a competent woman's right to refuse medical advice to 13 (24 percent).

No respondent was aware of any case in which a doctor had been sued for failure to seek fetal custody or maternal guardianship. Only 2 of 57 were aware of a case in which the woman sued for assault after a court-ordered procedure (in California and Michigan). However, the outcomes of these cases were not known.

Discussion

Among the most harrowing experiences for obstetricians is the refusal of therapy by a pregnant woman. For physicians who are specially trained in monitoring fetal well-being, such refusals may appear callous or irrational.[8,10] However, court-ordered interventions may ultimately cause more problems than they solve. They rest on dubious legal grounds, may expand rather than limit physicians' liability, and could adversely affect maternal and infant health. Our 83 percent response rate, representing obstetricians in 45 states and the District of Columbia, allows us to draw substantial conclusions.

Attempts to override maternal refusals of therapy have occurred in 26 states and the District of Columbia. Attempts in 24 states are reported here, and three additional instances have been reported elsewhere.[1,22,23] Courts have denied orders in at least six instances—three described here (those in Illinois, Maine, and Michigan) and three others,[22,23] including a case in Washington State that was reported to us by the patient's attorney. It should be noted that decisions made by lower-court judges do not necessarily represent the settled law of the state, and unpublished trial-court decisions are not binding on other judges. Of the two court orders that were reviewed by the highest courts in their respective states, one was upheld[1] and the other was overruled.[22]

Although some cases may involve procedures of limited invasiveness, courts in 11 states (Colorado, Georgia,[1] Hawaii, Illinois, Michigan, Minnesota, Ohio, Pennsylvania, South Carolina, Tennessee, and Texas) have ordered cesarean sections. Furthermore, hospital detentions have been ordered in two states (Colorado and Illinois), and intrauterine transfusions in one (Colorado). Presumably, these courts are invoking fetal rights against pregnant women who refuse therapy.

Proponents of forced treatment have focused on the legal status of the fetus. They interpret the statement in *Roe* v. *Wade*[24] that the states may assert a compelling interest in potential fetal life by barring certain abortions after the fetus is viable as authorizing court-ordered surgery on pregnant women. Moreover, the recent expansion of liability for wrongful fetal death and prenatal injuries is viewed as supporting claims to legal personhood on behalf of the fetus.[25]

But as the most recent Supreme Court ruling on abortion made clear,[26] any state interest in the potential life of even a viable fetus must be subordinated to the health and safety of the pregnant woman. Although judges frequently interpret wrongful-death statutes to include the loss of a pregnancy through negligence, especially if the pregnancy is far advanced, such decisions represent efforts to compensate prospective parents for their loss rather than recognition of the fetus as a person.[27,28] In recent cases allowing negligence and malpractice suits for prenatal injuries, great care has been taken to condition the legal recovery of damages on live birth, so that the right to recover damages belongs not to a fetus but to a live-born, independent person.[29] Decisions allowing suit for injuries received before conception also undercut the claim that allowing suit for prenatal injuries reflects enhanced fetal status, since such cases concern events involving not the fetus but one of its parents.[30]

Although such discussions of fetal status are interesting, they distract attention from the central legal question posed by treatment refusals during pregnancy. The question is really whether doctors or the government may usurp patients' decision-making rights and appropriate or invade their bodies to advance what they perceive to be the therapeutic interests of a second patient, the fetus. The closest legal analogy would be an organ "donation" ordered over the explicit refusal of a competent adult, and such an order would be profoundly at odds with our legal tradition.[31,32] As one judge in Washington State said in refusing to order a cesarean section, "I would not have the right to require the woman to donate an organ to one of her other children, if that child were dying.... I cannot require her to undergo that major surgical procedure for this child."

A number of commentators have assumed that authority for court-ordered surgery could be derived from the blood-transfusion cases involving Jehovah's Witnesses, especially *Raleigh Fitkin-Paul Morgan Memorial Hospital* v. *Anderson,*[33] a New Jersey case involving a pregnant woman, and

Application of the President and Directors of Georgetown College Hospital.[34] However, both these cases were decided in 1964, and neither reflects the current emphasis on respect for individual self-determination and bodily integrity in medical decision making. In the view of the judges, court-ordered treatment allowed the patient to abide by the prescripts of her religion while accepting a relatively noninvasive procedure that they thought she really wanted for the preservation of her own life. Whatever relevance these cases may retain in the context of transfusions, they provide little authority for the much more invasive, risky, and painful cesarean sections and intrauterine procedures at issue today.

Patients possess rights to bodily integrity and self-determination that are grounded in common-law principles[35] and that have played a key part in recent cases involving treatment refusal and the "right to die."[36] These rights are most explicitly articulated in the doctrine of informed consent. As Judge Benjamin Cardozo declared in *Schloendorff* v. *Society of New York Hospital,*[37] medical treatment given without consent constitutes assault. Deliberate disregard of a patient's refusal may constitute assault, battery, or both, depending on the law of the particular state. Exceptions to the informed-consent rule for emergencies or in cases of implied consent are specifically not applicable when there is an explicit refusal by a competent adult.[38]

Competency is assumed by the law, and even a medically "irrational" decision does not necessarily allow an inference of incompetency.[39] In the 21 cases described here, no patient was deemed incompetent by a psychiatrist. Clearly, court orders force women to assume medical risks and forfeit their legal autonomy in a manner not required of competent men or nonpregnant women. Thus, basic constitutional and common-law rights are at issue.

Among the patients ordered to undergo treatment in our survey, women more likely to be subject to various forms of discrimination predominated. Eighty-one percent were black, Asian, or Hispanic. Forty-four percent were unmarried, and 24 percent did not speak English as their primary language. All the patients were seen in teaching-hospital clinics or were receiving public assistance. This may reflect a sampling bias, since all the respondents were affiliated with teaching hospitals. However, it seems reasonable to assume that physicians treating private patients at smaller hospitals would be less inclined and less able to perform court-ordered procedures.

When a pregnant woman refuses advice, physicians are concerned about maternal and fetal well-being. They also fear liability. If the child that is born is proved to have been injured, doctors may be liable for malpractice. If, on the other hand, a woman's refusal is forcibly overridden without a court order, doctors are liable for assault or battery on the woman. In such difficult situations, obtaining a court order may appear to be in a doctor's best interest. However, when obtaining an order becomes an objective in itself, an incentive to overemphasize the consequences of nonintervention may exist. This places an even greater burden on the judge who must sort out the physician's claims.

Our data confirm that hospital administrators and lawyers often have little forewarning of impending conflicts. Judges, unfortunately, have even less time for deliberation. In 88 percent of the cases in our survey, court orders were obtained within six hours. In 19 percent, the orders were actually obtained in an hour or less, at times by telephone. The time required to weigh complex relative medical risks and benefits for both mother and fetus and then to balance these against the woman's rights is rarely, if ever, available. Impulsive and inconsistent judicial decisions are undesirable,[13,18] and the court is unlikely to provide a meaningful review of the medical facts. Furthermore, time pressure makes it unlikely that the pregnant woman will have adequate legal representation.

Uncertainty is intrinsic to medical judgments. The prediction of harm to the fetus was inaccurate in six cases in which court orders were sought for cesarean sections,[2,3,13,23,40,41] including the case in Washington State mentioned earlier. Despite the appointment of interdisciplinary committees to represent fetuses at some institutions,[42] any such representation inevitably rests partly on medical judgment. Although we are quick to accept medical uncertainty as justification for our errors, we are less quick to recognize its implications for patient self-determination.[43]

The decisions being made now have serious ramifications. For women, there are many potential intrusions. Will forgoing an abortion be interpreted as a waiver of maternal autonomy?[12,16] Will forced interventions occur earlier and earlier during pregnancy as fetal viability is pushed back by technical advances? Writers on both sides of the issue point out that viability represents a problematic,[19,44] if not meaningless,[20] cutoff point in the fetal-rights context.

Acceptance of forced cesarean sections, hospital detentions, and intrauterine transfusions may trigger demands for court-ordered prenatal screening, fetal surgery, and restrictions on the diet, work, athletic activity, and sexual activity of pregnant women. It could be argued that court orders regarding such factors might be less invasive and burdensome than an operation. Already, a 16-year-old pregnant girl in Wisconsin has been held in secure detention for the sake of her fetus because she tended "to be on the run" and to "lack motivation or ability to seek prenatal care."[45]

Forced obstetrical procedures may also have important consequences for physicians. Relationships with patients may be jeopardized. Will physicians be required to report all maternal refusals as cases of suspected fetal neglect or abuse? California authorities jailed a woman whose baby was born brain-dead, on charges that she took drugs during pregnancy and "willfully disregarded" doctors' instructions.[46] A judge dismissed those charges, but a bill to allow such prosecutions was immediately introduced in the California legislature.[47] In Michigan, the court allowed a suit against a mother whose son's teeth were discolored because she had taken tetracycline during pregnancy.[48] None of our respondents knew of a case in which a doctor had been sued for failure to seek a court order. Still, 46 percent of them supported hospital detentions, and 47 percent endorsed court-ordered intrauterine transfusions. Ironically, such an interventionist professional climate may give rise to a new standard of care and expand liability.

Such developments could also prove to be counterproductive to public policy goals for maternal and infant health. If court-ordered obstetrical procedures become more common, the public image of hospitals may be adversely affected and women may choose to deliver elsewhere.[13] The groups that are most in need of prenatal care may be driven away from it. If we can extrapolate from our respondents' opinions on home birth, most might agree with the pragmatic view that more harm than good would result.

Notes

[1]Jefferson v. Griffin Spalding County Hosp. Auth., 247 Ga. 86, 274, S.E. 2d 457.

[2]Berg RN. Georgia Supreme Court orders caesarean section—mother nature reverses on appeal. J Med Assoc Ga 1981; 70:451-3.

[3]Bowes WA Jr, Selgestad B. Fetal versus maternal rights: medical and legal perspectives. Obstet Gynecol 1981; 58:209-14.

[4]Illinois hospital given temporary custody of fetus. Am Med News. February 19, 1982:23.

[5]Holder AR. Maternal-fetal conflicts and the law. Female Patient 1985; 10(6):80-90.

[6]Fletcher JC. The fetus as patient: ethical issues. JAMA 1981; 246:772-3.

[7]Elias S. Annas GJ. Perspectives on fetal surgery. Am J Obstet Gynecol 1983; 145: 807-12.

[8]Lieberman JR, Mazor M, Chaim W, Cohen A. The fetal right to live. Obstet Gynecol 1979; 53:515-7.

[9]Shriner TL Jr. Maternal versus fetal rights—a clinical dilemma. Obstet Gynecol 1979; 53:518-9.

[10]Jurow R. Paul RH. Cesarean delivery for fetal distress without maternal consent. Obstet Gynecol 1984; 63:596-8.

[11]Raines E. Editorial comment. Obstet Gynecol 1984; 63:598-9.

[12]Engelhardt HT Jr. Current controversies in obstetrics: wrongful life and forced fetal surgical procedures. Am J Obstet Gynecol 1985; 151:313-8.

[13]Annas GJ. Forced cesarean sections: the most unkindest cut of all. Hastings Cent Rep 1982; 12(3)16-7, 45.

[14]Ruddick W., Wilcox W. Operating on the fetus. Hastings Cent Rep 1982; 12(5):10-4.

[15]Manner RL. Family law—court ordered surgery for the protection of a viable fetus. West N Engl Law Rev 1982; 5:125-48.

[16]Robertson JA. The right to procreate and in utero fetal therapy. J Leg Med (Chicago) 1982; 3:333-66.

[17]Hubbard R. Legal and policy implications of recent advances in prenatal diagnosis and fetal therapy. Women Rights Law Rep 1982; 7:201–18.

[18]Hallisey PL. The fetal patient and the unwilling mother: a standard for judicial intervention. Pac Law J 1983; 14:1065–94.

[19]Lenow JL. The fetus as a patient: emerging rights as a person? Am J Law Med 1983; 9:1–29.

[20]Johnsen DE. The creation of fetal rights: conflicts with women's constitutional rights to liberty, privacy, and equal protection. Yale Law J 1986; 95:599–625.

[21]Society of Perinatal Obstetricians. 1985–1986 Directory of fellowship programs in maternal-fetal medicine. For reprints contact Thomas J. Garite, M.D., Women's Hospital, Memorial Medical Center, 2801 Atlantic Ave., Long Beach, CA 90801.

[22]Taft v. Taft, 388 Mass. 331, 446 N.E. 2d 395 (1983).

[23]Gallagher J. The fetus and the law—whose life is it anyway? Ms. September 1984; 13(3):62–6, 133–4.

[24]Roe v. Wade, 410 U.S. 113 (1973).

[25]Robertson JA. Procreative liberty and the control of conception, pregnancy and childbirth. Virginia Law Rev 1983; 69:405–64.

[26]Thornburgh v. American College of Obstetricians and Gynecologists, 106 S. Ct. 2169 (1986).

[27]Roe v. Wade, 410 U.S. 113, 162 (1973).

[28]Dunn v. Roseway, 333 N.W. 2nd 830 (IA 1983).

[29]Keeton WP, Dobbs D, Keeton R, Owen D. Prosser and Keeton on the law of torts. Section 55 at 368. 5th ed. St. Paul: West Publishing. 1984.

[30]Jorgensen v. Meade Johnson Laboratories, Inc., 483 F. 2d 237 (10th Cir. 1973).

[31]McFall v. Shimp. No. 78-17711 in Equity (C.P. Allegheny County, Pa. July 26, 1978).

[32]Regan D. Rewriting Roe v. Wade. Mich Law Rev 1979; 77:1569–646.

[33]Raleigh Fitkin-Paul Morgan Memorial Hosp. v. Anderson, 42 N.J. 421, 201, A. 2d 537, cert. denied, 377 U.S. 984 (1964).

[34]Application of the President and Directors of Georgetown College Hosp., 331 F. 2d 1000 (1964).

[35]Clarke AM. The choice to refuse or withhold medical treatment: the emerging technology and medical-ethical consensus. Creighton Law Rev 1980; 13:795–841.

[36]In the matter of Eichner, 52 N.Y. 2d 363, 438 N.Y.S. 2d 266, 420 N.E. 2d 64 (1981).

[37]Schloendorff v. Society of New York Hospital. 211 N.Y. 125, 105 N.E. 92 (1914).

[38]Rozovsky F. Consent to treatment. Sect. 1.14.3 at 70 (1984).

[39]Lane v. Candura, 6 Mass. App. Ct. 377, 376, N.E. 2d 1232 (1978).

[40]Flanagan B. Mom follows belief, gives birth in hiding. Detroit Free Press. June 28, 1982:3a.

[41]Medical ethics case conference: ethical and legal issues in a court-ordered cesarean section. Med Hum Rep (Michigan State University), Winter 1984.

[42]Clewell WH, Johnson ML, Meier PR, et al. A surgical approach to the treatment of fetal hydrocephalus. N Engl J Med 1982; 306:1320–5.

[43]Shultz MM. From informed consent to patient choice: a new protected interest. Yale Law J 1985; 95:219–99.

[44]Fost N, Chudwin D, Wikler D. The limited moral significance of "fetal viability." Hastings Cent Rep 1980; 10(6):10–3.

[45]Girl detained to protect fetus. Wis State J. August 16. 1985:Section 3:2.

[46]Fetal abuse charged in son's death. Chicago Tribune. October 2, 1986; Section 1:3.

[47]Bill offered based on Pamela Rae Stewart baby case. San Diego Union. March 7, 1987:A-3.

[48]Grodin v. Grodin, 102 Mich. App. 396, 301 N.W. 2d 869–71 (MI 1980).

6

CONSENT,
CONFIDENTIALITY,
AND
TRUTH TELLING

Consent, confidentiality, and truth telling comprise a triad of issues. One usually speaks of *informed* consent. The force of the word informed is that one has been told (and understands) all the relevant information, i.e., that one has been told the truth. Often in taking a history from a patient, very personal and embarrassing information has to be requested. What makes patients feel comfortable giving this information is the belief that it will be held in confidence. A few examples will show how intertwined these three issues are.

George Smith, a seventy-year-old patient at University Hospital, is dying of cancer. The chief of internal medicine at the hospital asks Mr. Smith to participate in the testing of a drug that is still an experimental therapy for cancer patients. The drug has been cleared by the Food and Drug Administration for use on patients in an experimental mode. The physician tells Mr. Smith that the treatment may slow the development of the tumor, thereby prolonging his life.

Jerry Bunson, a seminary student, needs a job and is attracted to an advertisement by a local drug company offering to pay students $500 to participate in drug tests. The company likes to use seminary students for this because they generally have a healthy life style and are not users of illegal drugs that would bias the tests. The purpose of the tests is to determine how quickly certain drugs enter the bloodstream and whether they produce undesirable side effects in normal, healthy adults. Bunson agrees to participate in the experiments, especially when he discovers that all he has to do is to take the drug and then agree to have blood samples taken at regular intervals. He will spend the night in the hospital but can use the time for studying for his courses.

Ronda Walker, a twenty-five-year-old woman, is in the hospital for surgery to correct a ruptured disc. The evening before the surgery, her doctor reads her a list of the risks of surgery. The risks range from a small scar to death. She is more frightened now than ever. The doctor hands her the consent form and says, "Now please sign here."

Mr. Herman, a fifty-three-year-old man with hypertension, has stopped taking his antihypertension medication. "I would never even have started if you had told me that it would make me impotent," he tells his physician. "You should have told me."

This last case shows how difficult it is to separate one issue in medical ethics from the others. What appears to be an issue of truth telling may involve much more. The physician intentionally withheld significant information that would have been important to the patient. But the doctor did it to be certain that Mr. Herman would take his medicine. After all, not all men experience impotence as a side effect of this medication.

The doctor acted in a paternalistic way toward Mr. Herman. Because of this paternalism, we can say that Mr. Herman never really consented to take the medicine, because true agreement to treatment depends on a patient's being fully informed. Although consent can take different forms, a case can be made that it is valid only when the individual is fully apprised of all relevant information, including the risks involved, the benefits anticipated, and the likelihood of success. But what information counts as relevant? When is a risk so improbable that it need not be mentioned? What exactly is a benefit, and who decides? What alternatives are there, if any, to the recommended treatment? Finally, how should all the information be given so that it is reasonable to assume that the patient has truly understood the information?

Truly informed consent also implies freedom from coercion and duress. In practice, however, it is not always clear when coercion and duress are present. For example, is a patient scheduled for major surgery really free from duress? Is a terminal patient truly free? Is a student in need of money not pressured in some way when confronted with an easy way to make $500? Usually coercion and duress work to undermine patient autonomy and thereby call into question the validity of a consent to treatment.

If consent is to be judged valid, then not only must patients receive the relevant information and be free from coercion and duress, they must also be competent enough to understand and to use the information given them. Competence, however, and a related concept, rationality, are extremely difficult concepts to define with precision. Given this imprecision, an appropriate strategy would be to proceed on a case-by-case basis and to distinguish those cases in which competence is clearly present from those cases in which competence is clearly absent. Then, in the remaining unclear cases, it is probably fairer to err on the side of patient autonomy, which means on the side of assumed competence. For example, infants, young children, comatose patients, and those afflicted with certain types of dementia would be deemed incompetent. Under these circumstances, valid consent could not be obtained from the patient. Others, such as parents, spouses, relatives, and even the courts, could be called upon to provide substitute competence.

Consent is a matter of concern both in therapy and in experimentation. The readings on consent focus on consent in both contexts without losing sight of the setting of the problems, namely, what the doctor-patient relationship should be. Is it compromised when the physician is also a researcher? The first reading on consent deals in detail with the issue of competency to give consent. The second reading describes several case studies involving the consent (or lack thereof) of human participants in research. The third article on consent deals with the issues surrounding consent to therapies used in medical treatments, as seen from the perspectives of different models of the doctor–patient relationship.

In this chapter we begin with consent, move on to confidentiality, and conclude with a general discussion of truth telling.

Competency
to Give Consent

One of the ethical principles that guides our decisions affecting others is respect for them as individuals. This principle can be stated in different ways, but one of the clearest is the following: "A person has respect or is shown respect when his or her interests are taken into account and when his or her rights are honored. What these claims and rights are is contentious, but they include claims concerning life and health, claims to be dealt with honestly, and claims to be dealt with in a manner befitting the dignity of mankind."[1]

Note that central to respect is taking the individual's interest into account. But while easy to say this, it is much harder to do.

For example, who should decide what the best interests are for the patient? A patient may think that the best thing to do is to get out of the hospital and be home with family and friends, whereas the physician believes that the patient's best interest is to stay in the hospital. The grounds for the physician's having the final say in such matters might be the exper-

---

[1]The report from the Committee for Education in Business Ethics. Reproduced in Donald M. Borchert and David Stewart, *Exploring Ethics* (New York: Macmillan, 1986), p. 333.

tise and experience the physician brings to the treatment of an illness. Why go to an expert if the expert's advice is going to be ignored? But should the expert have all the authority and power? Why can't we be allowed to make mistakes, even costly mistakes?

There are arguments in favor of letting the decision procedure be tilted in favor of the physician. There are also arguments for honoring the patient's freedom and rationality that would allow the patient to decide after being given full information. Supporting this is the view that the individual patient has rights that should not be abridged except in the most extreme circumstances. If the patient does not consent to a treatment, that should be the end of the matter. For those arguing this point of view, the patient's rights are almost absolute. And for them, the decision procedure should be tilted in favor of the patient. Who is right in this debate? If consent is an important ethical principle, what grounds are there, if any, for ever doing something to a patient for which the patient withholds consent?

Consider the following case. Mabel Brown, a twenty-five-year-old woman, is admitted to a hospital emergency room with a perforated ulcer. She has lost a great deal of her blood supply through internal bleeding. Without blood transfusions, she will most certainly die. With transfusions she has a better than fifty-percent chance of survival. But because of religious beliefs, Ms. Brown refuses the transfusions. Lawyers for the hospital petition the district court to order the blood transfusions over Ms. Brown's objections. One of the arguments the lawyers use is that by coming to the hospital Ms. Brown effectively gave her consent to treatment that would save her life. In addition, they argue that she has a dependent child who will be left orphaned if Ms. Walker dies. The court orders the transfusions over the patient's objections.

There are also extreme cases when the patient cannot give consent. Children, the severely mentally retarded, and those in persistent vegetative states are three classes of persons who could be said to be unable to give consent in any meaningful sense of that term. But even with the retarded, some level of consent is possible for many; and how old does a child have to be before consent could be legitimately given? At one extreme would be the view that a child must be legally an adult before consent is necessary; others would say that children merely need to be old enough to understand the consequences of their decision. The same continuum exists for the retarded: A person need not have completely developed powers of reason and analysis to be able to give or withhold consent to a treatment.

These issues are explored with precision in the following article. As you read it, ask yourself under what circumstances, if any, patients should receive treatment for which they have not given consent. And how much must they know for such consent to be "informed"?

COMPETENCY
TO GIVE AN INFORMED CONSENT:
A MODEL FOR MAKING CLINICAL ASSESSMENTS

James F. Drane, PhD

In January 1980, as one more indication of the growing importance of medical ethics, a presidential commission was formed and began work on the moral questions posed by the practice of contemporary medicine. After three years of intense work, the commission published a separate volume on 11 different ethical problems in the hope of stimulating thoughtful discussion. Some broad principles were uncovered that apply to any and every bioethical issue, such as the principle of patient respect and its concrete application in the right of informed consent. But there were also recurring perplexities, one of which was competency or, in the language preferred by the commission, the patient's capacity to choose.[1]

Respect for patients means ensuring their participation in decisions affecting their lives. Such participation is a basic form of freedom and stands at the core of Western values.

But freedom, participation, and self-determination suppose a capacity for such acts. No one, for example, assumes that an infant has such a capacity and, time and again, doubts arise about the capacity of some older patients. Not to respect a patient's freedom is undoubtedly wrong. But to respect what may be an expression of freedom only in appearance would be a violation of another basic principle of ethical medicine: promotion of the patient's well-being.

Although the commission's report referred many times to competency or capacity to choose, commissioners and staff members privately expressed frustration and disappointment about their conclusions. The commission reports spelled out what are considered to be the components of competency: the possession of a set of values and goals, the ability to communicate and understand information, and the ability to reason and deliberate. In addition, the commission criticized some standards for determining competency that either were too lenient and did not protect a patient sufficiently or were too strict and in effect transferred decision making to the physician. But the commission did not come up with its own standard and left unsettled the question of how to decide whether a particular patient's decision should be respected or overridden because of incompetency. Incompetency is not the only reason for overriding a patient's refusal

Source: "Competency to Give an Informed Consent" by James F. Drane. JAMA, vol. 252, no. 7 (August 17, 1984), pp. 925–27. Copyright © 1984, American Medical Association. Used by permission of the American Medical Association and the author.

or setting aside a consent, but it is the most common reason for doing so. Defining incompetency or establishing standards of competency is a complex problem because it involves law, ethics, and psychiatry.

Competency Assessment

Competency assessments focus on the patient's mental capacities, specifically, the mental capacities to make an informed medical decision. Does the patient understand what is being proposed? Can the patient come to a decision about treatment based on an adequate understanding? How much understanding and rational decision-making capacity are sufficient for this particular patient to be considered competent? Conversely, how deficient must this patient's decision-making capacity be before he is declared incompetent? A properly performed competency assessment should eliminate two types of error: (1) preventing a competent person from participating in treatment decisions and (2) failing to protect an incompetent person from the harmful effects of a bad decision.

Model for Making the Assessment

The President's commission did not recommend a single standard for determining competency because any one standard is inappropriate for the many different types of medical decisions that people face. What is proposed here is a sliding standard, ie, the more dangerous the medical decision, the more stringent the standards of competency. The basic idea, following a suggestion of Mark Siegler,[2,3] is to connect determination of competency to different medical situations (acute or chronic, critical or noncritical), and next to take this idea a step further by specifying three different standards or definitions of what it means to be competent. These standards are then correlated with three different medical situations, each more dangerous than the other. Finally, the sliding standards and different medical situations are correlated with the types of psychiatric abnormalities that ordinarily undermine competency. The interrelationship of all these entities creates a model that can aid the physician faced with a question about a patient's capacity to choose. This model brings together disparate academic disciplines, but its goal is thoroughly pragmatic to provide a workable guide for clinical decision making.

Standard 1

The first and least stringent standard of competency to give a valid consent applies to those medical decisions that are not dangerous and objectively are in the patient's best interest. If the patient is critically ill because of an acute illness that is life threatening, if there is an effective treatment available that is low in risk, and if few or no alternatives are available, then consent to the treatment is prima facie rational. Even though patients are seriously ill and thereby impaired in both cognitive and conative functioning, they are usually competent to consent to a needed treatment.

The act of consent to such a treatment is considered to be an informed consent as long as the patient is aware of what is going on. *Awareness* in the sense of orientation or being conscious of the general situation satisfies the cognitive requirement of informed consent. *Assent* alone to what is the rational expectation in this medical context satisfies the decisional component. When adult patients go along with needed medical treatment, then a legal presumption of competency holds even though the patients are obviously impaired. To insist on higher standards for capacity to give a valid consent in such a medical setting would amount to requiring surplus mental capacities for a simple task and would result in millions of acutely ill patients being considered incompetent. Such an absurd requirement would produce absurd consequences. Altogether rational and appropriate decisions would be set aside as invalid, and surrogate decision makers would have to be selected to make the same decision. For what purpose? To accomplish what objective? To protect what value? None of the values and objectives meant to be safeguarded by the competency requirement is disregarded or set aside by a lenient standard for this type of decision.

Considering as competent seriously ill patients, even the mentally ill, who are aware and assent to treatment eliminates the ambiguity and confusion associated with terms such as *virtually competent, marginally competent,* and *competent for practical purposes* that are used to excuse the commonsense practice of respecting the decisions of patients who would be judged incompetent by a more demanding single standard of decision-making capacity. Refusal by a patient dying of a chronic illness of treatments that are useless and only prolong the dying requires the same modest standard of competency.

Infants, unconscious persons, and the severely retarded would obviously fall short even of this least demanding standard. These persons, and patients who use psychotic defenses that severely compromise reality testing, are the only ones who fail to meet this first definition of decision-making capacity. Children who have reached the age of reason (6 years or older), on the other hand, as well as the senile, the mildly retarded, and the intoxicated, are considered competent.

The law considers 21 and sometimes 18 years to be the age below which persons are presumed incompetent to make binding contracts, including health care decisions. The President's commission, however, endorses a lower age of competency, and so do many authors who write about children and mental retardation. In this model, we are discussing ethical standards, but the physician cannot ignore the law and must obtain consent from the child's legal guardian.

Standard 2

If the illness is chronic rather than acute, or if the treatment is more danger-ous or of less definite benefit (or if there are real alternatives to one or another course of action, eg, death rather than lingering illness), then the risk-benefit balance is tipped differently than in the situation described in the previous section. Consequently, a different standard of competency to consent is required. The patient must be able to *understand* the risks and outcomes of the different options and then be able to *choose* a decision based on this understanding. At this point, competency means capacity to understand the real options and to make an understanding decision, a higher standard than that required for the first type of treatment choice.

Ability to understand is not the same as being able to articulate con-ceptual or verbal understanding. Some ethicists assume a rationalist epis-temology and reduce all understanding to a conceptual or verbal type. Many, in fact, require that patients literally remember what they have been told as a proof of competence. Understanding, however, may be more af-fective than conceptual. Following an explanation, a patient may grasp what is best for him with strong feelings and convictions, and yet be hard pressed to articulate his understanding/conviction in words.

Competency as capacity for an understanding choice is also reconcil-able with a decision to let a trusted physician decide what is the best treat-ment. Such a choice (waiver) may be made for good reasons and represent a decision in favor of one set of values (safety or anxiety reduction) over another (independence and personal initiative). As such, it can be consid-ered as informed consent and creates no suspicion of incompetency.

Ignorance or inability to understand, however, undermines compe-tency. The same is true of a severe mood disorder or severe shock, which may either impair thought processes or undermine capacity to make an understanding choice. Short-term memory loss, delusion, dementia, and de-lirium would also render a patient incompetent. On the other hand, mature adolescents, the mildly retarded, and persons with some personality disor-ders would be competent to make this type of decision.

Standard 3

The most stringent and demanding standard of competency is reserved for those decisions that are very dangerous and fly in the face of both profes-sional and public rationality. When diagnostic uncertainty is minimal, the available treatment is effective, and death is likely to result from treatment refusal, a presumption is established against refusal of consent to treatment. The medical decision now is not a balancing of what are widely recognized as reasonable alternatives. Any decision other than the one to be treated seems to violate basic reasonableness. A decision to refuse treatment, then, is apparently irrational, besides being harmful. Yet, according to this model, such decisions can be respected as long as the patients satisfy the most demanding standard of competency.

Competency in this context requires a capacity to appreciate the nature and consequences of the decision being made. *Appreciation* is a term used to refer to the highest degree of understanding, one that grasps more than just the medical details of the illness and treatment. To be competent to make apparently irrational and very dangerous choices, the patient must be able to come to a decision based on the medical information and to appreciate the implications of this decision for his life. Competency of this type requires a capacity that is both technical and personal, both cognitive and affective.

Since the patient's decision flies in the face of objective standards of rationality, it must at least be subjectively critical and *rational*. A patient need not conform to what most rational people do to be considered competent, but the competent patient must be able to give reasons for his decision. The patient must be able to show that he has thought through the medical issues and related this information to his personal value system. The patient's personal reasons need not be medically or publicly accepted, but neither can they be purely private, idiosyncratic, or incoherent. Their intelligibility may derive from a set of religious beliefs or from a philosophical view that is shared by only a small minority. This toughest standard of competency does, however, demand a more rationalistic type understanding: one that includes verbalization, argumentation, and consistency.

The higher-level mental capacities required for competency to make this type of decision are impaired by less severe psychiatric abnormality. In fact, much less serious mental affliction suffices to create an assumption of incompetency to refuse a needed and effective treatment. On the other hand, however, not any mental or emotional disturbance would constitute an impairment of decisional capacity. A certain amount of anxiety, for example, goes with any serious decision and cannot make a patient incompetent. Some mild pain would not impair decisional capacity, but severe pain might do so. Even a slight reactive depression may not render a patient incompetent for this type of decision. But intense anxiety associated with mild or severe shock, and/or a mild endogenous depression, would be considered incapacitating. In fact, any mental or emotional disorder that compromises appreciation and rational decision making would make a patient incompetent. For example, persons who are incapable of making the effort required to control destructive behavior (substance abusers and sociopaths), as well as neurotic persons, hysterical persons, and persons who are ambivalent about their choice, would all be incompetent to refuse life-saving treatment. The same standard applies to consent to experiments not related to one's own illness.

Conclusion

Radical advocates of patient rights and doctrinaire libertarians will worry that this model shifts power back toward physicians who make competency determinations and away from patients whose choices ought to be re-spected. But only in situation 3 does the physician's power increase, and then only for the patient's welfare. Moreover, this loss in the patients' power never reaches the point where patients' self-determination is set aside. Pa-tients can insist on their decision to refuse a treatment even when the physi-cian knows that the outcome will be certain death, as long as every precau-tion is taken to ensure that such a decision is not the product of a pathological state.

A balancing of values is the cornerstone of a good competency assess-ment. Rationality is given its place throughout this model. Maximum auton-omy is guaranteed for patients because they can choose to do what is not at all beneficial (a nontherapeutic experiment) or refuse to do what is most beneficial. Maximum benefit is also guaranteed because patients are pro-tected against harmful choices that are more the product of abnormality than of their self-determination. All the values, in fact, on which compe-tency requirements were originally based are guaranteed in this model.

No one proposal will settle the question of which standard or stan-dards of competency are appropriate for medical decisions. More empirical research is required on the issue, and more physicians who have valuable practical experience with complex cases need to be heard from. After much more study and discussion, perhaps the medical profession itself, through its ethics committees, will take a stand on the issue. In the meantime, this proposal is meant to be a contribution to the discussion.

This investigation was supported in part by grant ED 0652-78 from the National Endow-ment for the Humanities.

Notes

[1]President's Commission for the Study of Ethical Problems in Medicine and Biomedical and Behavioral Research: *Deciding to Forego Life-Sustaining Treatment.* Washington, DC, US Gov-ernment Printing Office, 1983.

[2]Siegler M. Goldblatt AD: Clinical intuition: A procedure for balancing the rights of patients and the responsibilities of physicians in Spicker SF, Healey JM, Engelhardt HT (eds):

The Law–Medicine Relation: A Philosophical Exploration. Dordrecht, the Netherlands, D Reidel Publishing Co, 1981, pp 5–29.

[3]Jonsen AR, Siegler M, Winslade WJ: *Clinical Ethics.* New York, Macmillan Publishing Co Inc, 1962, pp 36–83.

Consent
in Experimentation

Consent to experimental procedures is vital if experimentation is to be allowed. Experimentation can be performed on either healthy or ill persons and on either adults or children. Of the four possibilities, experiments on well children seem to be the most difficult to defend. Experiments on ill adults, especially those with terminal illnesses, may seem morally more acceptable. Experiments on ill children and healthy adults raise their own set of issues. The use of prisoners, soldiers, and students also creates problems concerning freedom.

The following list of experiments spans the gamut from the morally outrageous to the morally acceptable. As you read through them, ask yourself in what respects the acceptable experiments differ from the unacceptable ones. It is also interesting to note that many of these experiments, some of which date from the 1960s, would no longer be allowed in any program receiving federal grant support. As you read through these cases, compare them to the following rules from the Code of Federal Regulations dealing with the protection of human subjects. This code was in force at the time this book went to press.[1]

> Except as provided elsewhere in this or other subparts, no investigator may involve a human being as a subject in research covered by these regulations unless the investigator has obtained the legally effective informed consent of the subject or the subject's legally authorized representative. An investigator shall seek such consent only under circumstances that provide the prospective subject or the representative sufficient opportunity to consider whether or not to participate and that minimize the possibility of coercion or undue influence. The information that is given to the subject or the representative shall be in language understandable to the subject or the representative. No informed consent, whether oral or written, may include any exculpatory language through which the subject or the representative is made

[1]From the Code of Federal Regulations, Title 45 Public Welfare, Part 46—Protection of Human Subjects. Department of Health and Human Services National Institutes of Health Office for Protection from Research Risks.

to waive or appear to waive any of the subject's legal rights, or releases or appears to release the investigator, the sponsor, the institution or its agents from liability for negligence.

(a) Basic elements of informed consent ... the following information shall be provided to each subject:

1. A statement that the study involves research, an explanation of the purposes of the research and the expected duration of the subject's participation, a description of the procedures to be followed, and identification of any procedures which are experimental;

2. A description of any reasonably foreseeable risks or discomforts to the subject;

3. A description of any benefits to the subject or to others which may reasonably be expected from the research;

4. A disclosure of appropriate alternative procedures or courses of treatment, if any, that might be advantageous to the subject;

5. A statement describing the extent, if any, to which confidentiality of records identifying the subject will be maintained;

6. For research involving more than minimal risk, an explanation as to whether any compensation and an explanation as to whether any medical treatments are available if injury occurs and, if so, what they consist of, or where further information may be obtained;

7. An explanation of whom to contact for answers to pertinent questions about the research and research subjects' rights, and whom to contact in the event of a research-related injury to the subject; and

8. A statement that participation is voluntary, refusal to participate will involve no penalty or loss of benefits to which the subject is otherwise entitled, and the subject may discontinue participation at any time without penalty or loss of benefits to which the subject is otherwise entitled.

The increasing moral sensitivity shown by these recent guidelines concerning the use of human subjects in medical experiments is evidence of progress made in ethics. Yet there are still issues for which the correct course of action is not clear. There is a group of problems raised by experimental design itself. To appreciate these issues requires a brief discussion of the design of experiments.

Experimental results can be confounded by a number of factors. Suppose there is a new drug, D, to treat condition C. We want to test the effectiveness of D and at the same time convince ourselves that it is at least as good as the old treatment, 0. In doing this, we have to guard against at least five sorts of problems:

1. The patients who get D might be different enough from the patients who get O so that we cannot really compare the two groups. Suppose, for example, that the physicians choosing who got which treatment

made the choice by putting all the patients with morning appointments in one group. It might turn out that many of these patients
wanted to come in the morning because they were feeling too ill to
wait until the afternoon. Thus this group would be biased toward being sicker than the afternoon group. To avoid this sort of bias researchers *randomize* patients into groups.

2. Suppose the researchers feel that patients who risk getting the new
   treatment are altruistic and brave. They might therefore treat them
   better, and give them better care in ways that are difficult to evaluate
   but which might account for what otherwise appears to be the effectiveness of the new drug. To avoid this sort of bias researchers *blind*
   the study. That is, researchers do not know which patient is getting
   which treatment.

3. Now suppose that the patients who choose to try the new drug also
   feel that they are altruistic and brave. They are feeling good about
   themselves. Somehow, in ways that are yet to be understood, this can
   translate into better all-around health. So if the new drug gets good
   results, it may be because of the subjects' psychology and not because
   of the drug's pharmacology. To help avoid this sort of bias the experiment is *double blinded.* That is, neither the subjects not the researchers
   know which group is getting what.

4. But now we have reminded ourselves of another source of bias: the
   beliefs of the subjects. It is a well-known fact that just believing that
   one is getting medical treatment often serves to make people better.
   Experiments have shown that subjects who believe they are getting
   effective treatment, but who in fact are getting nothing but sham treatment, to a surprising degree show the same results as subjects who are
   in fact getting the actual treatment. This is sometimes referred to as
   the *placebo effect.* Whenever a therapy is tested, we have to be able to
   know how much of the positive result is due to the action of the drug
   and how much is due to the action of the placebo effect. Our fear, of
   course, is that the real treatment is at best no better than the sham.
   To control this bias researchers use a group of patients who get a sham
   treatment. But in keeping with points 2 and 3 just cited, they and the
   researchers are blind to this fact.

5. The last important factor is knowing when to end the experiment.
   This is a technical question that turns on some of the fine points of
   statistics. Intuitively, however, the point is fairly simple. If we do not
   use enough subjects we may have by chance gotten only those subjects
   who would give just the results we found. Perhaps we got an overabun-
   dance—by chance—of somewhat sicker subjects, of noncompliant
   subjects, of pharmacologically odd subjects. To defend against this
   sort of bias, researchers use statistical methods to fix a safe endpoint
   for the experiment.

Points 1 through 4 make up what is called a *randomized double blind* study. Such a study is experimentally sound, but, for some, ethically questionable. Is it right for a physician to give up control of therapy choice? Even when there is a question of which therapy is better, should not the choice be left to the patient and the physician? This question becomes most urgent when the difference in treatment modalities is great, as in using surgery as opposed to medicine, and leads to the larger questions of if it is ever right for a physician to ask a patient to enter an experimental protocol. Can the patient say no without feeling that treatment from the physician will be less than it would have been? Both physician and patient are in a double bind.

Although there are cases when no one is at all certain which of two treatments is better, they are rare. Specialists often have clinical intuitions, based in part on their following the medical literature, as well as on their clinical experience, that suggest which of two therapies is to be preferred. What should such a physician do in this situation? Should part of the informed consent be a statement to the effect that one therapy is believed better than another?

Should subjects be asked to take the risk of getting no treatment by being put in the placebo group? Although great care is taken to minimize danger to those in this group, is it not a contradiction for a physician to ask a patient to risk getting no treatment for a disease?

Sometimes as a study progresses the results become clear. When people are being obviously injured—a rare occurrence—the study is of course, stopped. But when the results are favorable, the study continues until the endpoint is reached. But if the results are favorable and if the condition under study is serious (for example, coronary artery disease), should not the results be disseminated as quickly as possible? And should not the new treatment be made available as soon as possible?

These are some of the persisting ethical issues involving informed consent in experiments involving human subjects. As you read the following article, make a list of other issues that emerge from the reading.

HUMAN EXPERIMENTATION:
THE ETHICAL QUESTIONS PERSIST

Robert M. Veatch, Sharmon Sollitto

In 1966 a Harvard anesthesiologist shocked the biomedical research community by publishing in the *New England Journal of Medicine* the methods

Source: "Human Experimentation—The Ethical Question" by Robert M. Veatch and Sharmon Sollitto. *The Hastings Center Report,* vol. 3 (June 1973). Used by permission. Copyright © The Hastings Center.

used in twenty-two experiments on human subjects. The material presented below, a summary of the research designs of 11 studies selected from a collection of 43 questionable experiments, suggests that the problem is still vast.

The tragic fact is that less than 25% of the studies in our file claim that consent was obtained from the participants in the research and not one paper documented the nature of the information given to the subjects in conjunction with their consent. It is a very rare scientific article which explains the nature of the consent procedure, a deficiency which must be corrected. Nevertheless, we have in no instance used the lack of consent as a criterion for inclusion in our set of articles. They must have raised more provocative ethical questions. It is impossible to say for sure that each of the studies mentioned is an example of unethical research. We believe, though, that "reasonable men" would agree that each raises disturbing questions.

All these studies have been published in reputable medical journals or professional proceedings since 1966. In all cases the research was done in the United States or the funding came from this country. Experimenters are not mentioned by name. Excluded from these cases are all those published before 1966 and those which have previously received public attention.

Grave Risks to Subjects

Experiment 1.   Researchers in this experiment were seeking a way to evaluate anti-arrhythmic drugs. Epinephrine was injected in nine normal female patients to attempt to produce abnormal heart beat in order to test this new drug. In every case the production of an abnormal beat was repeated at least once. The researchers note that the production of arrhythmias experimentally had previously been avoided because of the belief that it was hazardous. They also tell the reader that although the procedure was explained to the subjects, they believe that "informed consent cannot be obtained for a study of this type." They claim that instead they "accepted the role of guarantor of the patient's rights and safety...."

Experiment 2.   In a second study researchers sought to study plasma renin levels in patients with both kidneys removed. Ten patients, who had had their kidneys removed as recently as two weeks prior to the experiment, were hospitalized for the eight-day period of the study. A few days prior to the beginning of the study they were transfused "in anticipation of blood loss due to repeated sampling." On the third day, "all subjects were clinically dehydrated. Serum samples were limited to the supine position since severe hypotension and near syncope rapidly developed in standing." On one day measurements were taken after standing quietly for two hours. According to the researchers, "to accomplish two hours of quiet standing, it was necessary to have most of the patients lean on a chest-high supporting table and to be frequently encouraged."

Experiment 3. The third study involved giving LSD to 24 subjects who had answered an advertisement for experimental subjects to be paid at a rate of $2 per hour. The purpose was to study the long-range "personality, attitude, value, interest, and performance change. . . ." Researchers claimed explicitly that no mention was made to subjects of possible personality or other changes, although 15 percent reportedly had never heard of LSD and another 73 percent had "only casual knowledge" of it.

Risks to Incompetent and Incarcerated Subjects

Research involving risks to incompetent subjects—children and mental patients—raises even more serious ethical difficulties.

Experiment 4. Nine children from $11\frac{1}{2}$ to 16 years of age suffering from asthma were intentionally subjected to "challenge doses" of antigens known to produce asthmatic attacks in order to test the effectiveness of cromolyn sodium in blocking these attacks. The nine children were subjected to a total of 55 antigen challenges. Every child experienced at least one reaction described by the researcher as "severe." In addition, delayed asthmatic reactions 6 to 12 hours after the challenge were reported in five of the nine children. It is reported that these delayed reactions "tend to be followed by increased, and repeated asthma for a further day or two." Although seven of the nine children required regular bronchodilator medication, this was withheld for a period of 18 hours prior to the study.

Experiment 5. In another experiment 48 subjects ages 7 to 12 with findings confirming or suggesting the presence of hematologic disease were subjected to simultaneous dual-site bone marrow aspirations. Bone marrow samples were removed with an 18-gauge needle. The researchers point out that there are "physical and psychological problems in performing multiple-site, concomitant bone marrow aspirations in the pediatric patient."

Experiment 6. Similar ethical questions arise in research on mental patients and prisoners where the quality of consent, even it it is obtained, is questionable. At a maximum security facility for treating the criminally insane 90 male patients were "used in an exploratory study to determine the effectiveness of succinylcholine as an agent in behavior modification."

This drug causes temporary muscle paralysis including inability to breathe. During the period when breathing is impossible, positive and negative suggestions are made to the subject which, according to theories of psychological conditioning, are then associated with the experience. The experience in this case is apparently not physically painful, but the subjects describe the inability to breathe (which according to design lasts between 1.25 and 2 minutes) as a terrible, frightful experience akin to that of drowning. The criteria for selection of subjects for the study, according to the researchers, included "persistent physical or verbal violence, deviant sexual behavior, and lack of cooperation and involvement with the individual treatment program prescribed by the patient's ward team."

Experiment 7. Another experiment in operant conditioning was reported by an American psychiatrist working at a mental hospital in Viet Nam. He initiated a program in which 130 chronic male Vietnamese patients (mostly schizophrenics) were offered the chance to be discharged if they proved that they could work and support themselves. Only 10 volunteered to work. The remainder were told that if they were too sick to work, they needed treatment. The "treatment" was unmodified electroconvulsive shock. Whether from actual therapeutic effects of ECT or from the patients' fear and dislike of the treatments, a majority were working at the end of this phase. Next, the test was repeated in a group of 130 female patients, but after each had received 20 ECT treatments, only 15 of the women were working. At this point, all treatments were discontinued and men and women not working were told, "After this, if you don't work, you don't eat." Food was withheld for periods of up to three days at which time all patients were working. Upon their discharge form the hospital, the work provided for these former patients was tending crops for Green Berets in Vietcong territory "under the stress of potential or actual VC attack or ambush."

The Rights of Subjects in Research with a Placebo Group

There is one class of experiments for which, even today, there are no clear guidelines. A well-designed experiment often requires a placebo group for purposes of comparison.

Shocking as it may seem, no established principle of medical ethics requires that subjects be informed that one of the "risks" of an experimental procedure is that there is a control group included in the research design. Even the new and rigorous HEW guidelines do not mention this specifically. We see no reason why this should not be one of the minimal requirements of informed consent. Likewise, there is no clearly-established right to effective therapy for those in the control group.

Experiment 8.   One such study was a 14-year prospective study of the value of hyposensitization therapy for children with bronchial asthma. Of 130 children still under observation at the time of their sixteenth birthday, 91 received ineffective treatment for periods apparently lasting up to 14 years. This included a group who "received injections of buffered saline according to an elaborate 'injection schedule.'" The authors point out that "No mother or child in the study knew that any sort of study was under way."

Responsibility for Harm to Subjects

Another principle which is not now recognized is that of the responsibility of the researcher, the researcher's institution, or the funding agency for harm done to subjects during the course of an experiment. Current DHEW guidelines do specify that

> the agreement, written or oral, entered into by the subject, should include no exculpatory language through which the subject is made to waive, or to appear to waive, any of his legal rights, or to release the institution or its agents from liability for negligence.

They do not go on, however, to require that the subject be informed of an institutional obligation for harm done to subjects and do not even make clear that any such obligation exists. For research not done under HEW guidelines, no requirements vis-a-vis harm to subjects are established.

Experiment 9.   Much of the research done on new contraceptives raises such questions. In one study, conducted in Latin America but funded by an American agency, 262 women had megestrol acetate capsules implanted in their forearms to test the long-term effectiveness of this drug as a contraceptive. The results were 48 unwanted pregnancies—six of them ectopic.

We have in our files published reports of hundreds of similar experimental pregnancies which raise the question of the researcher's obligation. We propose for consideration that as a matter of policy the funding agency or highest level of institutional sponsorship be clearly obligated for such consequences and that this be clearly made known to subjects of research during the consent procedure.

Experiment 10.   Another study may not have involved physical harm to patients, but may well have subjected them to legal and psychological risks without their consent. Researchers at an open-ward voluntary psychiatric hospital were interested in the extent to which young patients were engaged in covert drug abuse. In 332 patients serial urine analyses were performed weekly for an average of 27 weeks "under the guise of a statistical survey of urinary creatinine." The researchers state that "the urine analytic data were kept completely secret from all other members of the staff, and at no time were the patients or staff aware that the urine samples were being monitored for abusable drugs." This research was supported in part by a grant from the National Institute of Mental Health.

The Pervasiveness of Human Experimentation

The highly publicized experiments involving human subjects may give the erroneous impression that such procedures raising ethical questions are rare and involve only bizarre procedures. A final study indicates that this is not the case.

Experiment 11. In this research, 41,119 patients enrolled in a major group health plan were given a test for pain tolerance as part of their regular checkup. The subjects were told it was a test for "pressure tolerance." Each subject placed his heel in a vise-like machine and was instructed to stand the pressure as long as he could. Researchers then compared age, sex, and racial differences in pain tolerance.

This is a relatively simple procedure. Similar simple tests are conducted in clinical settings, at times without formal review. In some cases experimenters may not even conceive of what they are doing as an experiment.

The problem, then, is one of developing mechanisms for consent and review which give greater assurance to the subject that his rights and interests will be protected. These experiments strongly suggest that the mechanisms now available are inadequate to the problem. The typical researcher may well be benevolently motivated and indeed do a good job of getting reasonably informed consent from his subject and protecting the subject's interests. That simply is not good enough, however. That experiments such as those described here can be performed and be published within the last few years means that we simply must intervene to guard the welfare of the citizens. We can no longer tolerate a situation in which a citizen, altruistically motivated to participate in research, may be subjected to grave and undisclosed risks.

The immediate establishment of a governmental committee to formulate rigorous procedures to insure reasonably informed consent and review is the minimum that is called for. This might well be one of the functions of the proposed National Advisory Commission on Health Science and Society. Even more effective would be a special committee with this as its sole task. The committee should include a substantial majority of individuals who are in no way associated with biomedical research.

The first priority of this committee ought to be the refinement of consent procedures discussed above including the requiring of information on: (1) the possibility of receiving placebos, (2) institutional responsibility for harm done, and (3) commitment to provide effective therapy to members of control groups. This committee ought to develop procedures requiring such informed consent from all subjects or their guardians—not simply those falling under HEW guidelines.

The committee also ought to develop new mechanisms for research review. One of the great problems of peer review as we know it today is that even when it is used in a serious way (which happens all too rarely), it is the peers of the researchers and not the peers of the subjects who are asked to evaluate the ethical acceptability of the proposed research. It is simply too much to ask individuals uniquely committed to the importance of medical research to judge the ethical acceptability of their colleagues' work in a disinterested manner. New and more public mechanisms are needed to assure subjects that their ethical and legal rights will not be violated by the minority of researchers who are misguided or irresponsible in their judgment of a person's welfare.

Consent in Therapy

The relationship between the philosophical study of ethics and the making of decisions is itself of interest to philosophers, and the following article by the philosopher Alan Donagan begins by explaining what this relationship is. Philosophers have never claimed that they had a privileged access to moral thinking. Certainly one does not have to be a philosopher to make moral decisions any more than one has to be a grammarian in order to speak a language. Philosophers who have thought about their role have described it as giving a reasoned account of moral thinking in order to focus on what specifically makes an action moral. In other words, they have looked at examples of moral behavior and then tried to explain what made that behavior moral. This is the transition, to use the words of Immanuel Kant, from the popular to the philosophical account of morality.

Donagan points out that leadership in the movement to require informed consent has come not from philosophers but from physicians. Long before the issue became a popular one, physicians were insisting on better flow of information between patient and physician. There are at least three models for the relationship between physician and patient. The parent–infant relationship is one in which the physician has all the power to decide what is best for the patient and has only the best interests of the patient/infant at heart. A more enlightened model is that of a parent and an adolescent child. Here, again, the physician is the primary decision maker, with the patient playing a minor role. The third model is that of mutual partici-pation, a relationship between adults in which one, the physician, provides information and recommendations to the other, the patient. Both are re-sponsible for the acceptance and outcomes of the treatment. This relation-ship is more like that of an attorney and client.

The importance for discussing these models, Donagan asserts, is that the role of informed consent directly depends on which of these models one accepts as the preferred one for medical treatment. There are, of course, situations in which the physician alone is in a position to make a decision, such as when a patient is undergoing surgery under general anesthetic. But in most therapeutic situations, a mutual participation model leads directly to the demand that the patient be fully informed and may freely consent to any therapy that is administered.

As you read through the following article, ask yourself whether the kind of informed consent based on a mutual participation model is really possible. Is this the relationship most individuals want with their physician? And is it immoral for a physician to relate to another human being in the patronizing fashion suggested by the parent–infant model?

INFORMED CONSENT IN THERAPY

Alan Donagan*

I. A Case Study in the Transition from Common Rational Moral Knowledge to Philosophical

At Helsinki in 1964 the World Medical Association solemnly declared that, in using a new therapeutic measure in which clinical research is a secondary purpose, "if at all possible, consistent with patient psychology, the doctor should obtain the patient's freely given consent after the patient has been given a full explanation"; and that, in clinical research with no therapeutic purpose, nothing whatever may be done to a human being "without his full

*My research has been supported by the John Simon Guggenheim Memorial Foundation, by a grant from the National Science Foundation to the Center for Advanced Study in the Behavioral Sciences, and by the University of Chicago, to all of whom I offer my gratitude. I desire to thank Gerald L. Perkoff, M.D., for advice on philosophical as well as on medical topics; and also James M. Gustafson, Brian Barry, Albert R. Jonsen, and Robert L. Simon. Two excellent anthologies were much used in preparing this paper, namely, Katz (1972) and Ladimer and Newman (1963).

Source: "Informed Consent in Therapy" by Alan Donagan, Journal of Medicine and Philosophy, 2 (December 1977), pp. 289–305. Copyright © 1977 by D. Reidel Publishing Company. Reprinted by permission of Kluwer Academic Publishers.

consent, after he has been fully informed" (Katz 1972, pp. 312–13). Not all physicians welcomed the Helsinki Declaration, although it was arrived at only after an extensive debate in the medical profession throughout the world, which sprang from disclosures before the U.S. Military Tribunal at Nuremberg of crimes committed upon human beings in the name of medical research. Of those who did not welcome it, some distrusted moral codes as such; others complained that the Helsinki formulations were unclear, and still others that they were impracticable and even hypocritical.

And yet, with little attention from the pubic, biomedical research was transformed in the decade that followed. In institutions engaged in such research, it is now standard practice that all experiments on human subjects be sanctioned by a supervisory committee charged, among other things, with seeing to it that nothing is done to such a subject without his informed consent. And, following a proposal of Henry K. Beecher (Beecher 1966b), a number of medical journals now refuse papers based on experimentation on human subjects if they do not supply adequate evidence of those subjects' informed consent.

This professional consensus emerged out of professional discussions, in which every point was thoroughly debated, and some acrimoniously. Its emergence is a vivid example of what Kant took to be the first and crucial stage in constructing a philosophy of morals, a stage which he described, with a pomposity I find endearing, as "the transition from common rational moral knowledge to philosophical" (Kant 1786, p. 1). Only a very arrogant philosopher, and probably a very silly one, would claim as a philosopher to instruct his fellows as to how they ought to conduct themselves. With the exception of Plato, all the great moral philosophers have taken their task to be to identify what is sound and coherent in the practical moral thinking that goes on around them, and to investigate its rational structure. As grammarians and logicians know to their sorrow, the structure of intellectual operations which even unsophisticated folk carry out with ease may be very complex, and its character will then be difficult to discern just because those operations are familiar and habitual. That, I think, is why only the greatest moral philosophers—an Aristotle, an Aquinas, a Kant—have been able to penetrate the familiarity of everyday thinking about right and wrong, and to disclose its deeper structure.

From time to time, however, the process of social change confronts a society with situations of unforeseen kinds which call for a moral response, but to which the application of the moral principles held by that society is not evident. When this happens, given that those situations are not such as to expose to a flaw in the society's fundamental moral principles, the application of those principles must become a matter of debate; and since *ex hypothesi* the issue debated will have a rational solution, a consensus will be reached when controversy has made clear what that solution is. In order to reach it, members of the society will have to articulate what their moral principles are, and to work out how the newly accepted solution may be derived from them. At the same time, they will become aware of the errors that hindered acceptance of that solution, whether they were defective formulations of principles, or inadequate interpretations, or invalid derivations. Hence they will themselves have made the transition from common rational moral knowledge to philosophical—even though the philosophy is at the stage Kant called "popular" (Kant 1786, pp. 30–34).

Historical debates and resolutions of this kind—for example, that occurring over the legitimacy of usury as modern commerce developed, and that over the legitimacy of slavery—furnish academic philosophers with actual cases of popular moral philosophy they would do well to study. And because of its direct bearing on a number of issues in contemporary academic philosophy—most obviously, the controversy over utilitarianism—no such case of recent occurrence promises to be a more rewarding study than the acceptance by the medical profession of the requirement of informed consent.

No comprehensive history of the controversies that led to that acceptance is likely to be written; and for want of it, an outsider studying the evidence will miss much of historical and human significance. From one point of view, the debate was part of a process of self-regulation by which the medical profession forestalled the intrusion of public authority into certain of its activities. From another point of view, the latter phase of the debate, at least in the United States, can be regarded as an interchange in the medical profession on defensive strategy against a new kind of malpractice lawsuit. However, chronology shows that such interpretations are incomplete and superficial. That patients and experimental subjects not be acted on without their informed consent was demanded by a substantial body of physicians long before there were threats either from public authority or private litigants. Both prosecutors and tribunal at Nuremberg were guided throughout by medical advice. Even the Jewish Chronic Diseases Hospital Case of 1963–65, which appears to have been an unstated bone of contention in many professional exchanges in the late sixties, would not have occurred but for the protests of physicians in charge of some of the patients involved.

The truth appears to be that, before the public at large thought of it at all, the problem of informed consent became a matter of controversy in the medical profession because of changes in the relations of physicians to patients, and of experimental medicine to clinical medicine, of which physicians naturally became conscious before the public. The contribution of laymen to defining some of the issues cannot be denied. But the doctrine of informed consent as we now have it is principally the achievement of the medical profession: lawyers and politicians entered the field late, and their contribution has been secondary. Philosophers, in good Hegelian fashion, for the most part arrived to take stock after the work had been done.

II. Related Issues

In philosophy of science, a historical example of scientific thinking is normally chosen for a case study only if what it exemplifies is judged scientifically sound. In the same way, if I had not judged philosophically sound the grounds on which the doctrine of informed consent came to be accepted, I should not have chosen the development of that doctrine for a case study in moral philosophy. This judgment, however, extends only to the core of the doctrine: to what it lays down about the consent of responsible adults to what is done to themselves. Outside that core, a number of related questions remain unsettled. Two should be mentioned.

The first is whether consent is required for therapy or experimentation carried out upon human beings who are not adults, or are not responsible—either briefly, or for a long time, or permanently. If consent is required for what is done to such persons, who is to give it? If parents, legal guardians, or near relatives, does their consent have the same range and force as that of a responsible adult to the same treatment or experiment carried out upon himself? In view of the extraordinary things some people have proved to be willing to consent to for others, in particular for their deformed or retarded children, it has been forcibly argued that nobody should have the right to consent to the performing of a nontherapeutic experiment upon another, and least of all, upon a child (see Ramsey 1970, pp. 26–35).

The second is whether there are limits to what even a fully informed and responsible adult can allow a physician to do to him by way of therapy or experiment. As Pope Pius XII pointed out, in a much-quoted address, nobody can by his consent entitle another to do to him what he is not entitled to do to himself (Pius XII 1952). Most physicians would agree that in most circumstances suicide is wrong, and that therefore a responsible adult could not, by his informed consent, entitle a physician to carry out a lethal experiment on him in those circumstances. And yet, while nearly all physicians hold that there are other limitations as well upon what an informed, responsible adult's consent can entitle a therapist or an experimenter to do to him, there is much dispute as to what specifically they are.

Both these questions are very difficult, and occupy much of the discussion of consent that goes on today. But neither would arise at all unless it were regarded as settled that the informed consent of a responsible adult is necessary to any therapeutic or experimental procedure carried out upon him. The development of that doctrine is the sole case to be studied in what follows.

III. Informed Consent to Therapy

It has never been disputed that a necessary condition of the coming into existence of the relation between himself and his patient that is the source of a physician's professional responsibilities is that the patient have sought treatment from him, or that a sufficient condition of that relation's ceasing to exist is that the patient communicate to the physician his decision to terminate it. Except in emergencies, that a prospective patient asks for treatment does not suffice to make him a patient: physicians have always maintained that, as provided in the fifth section of the American Medical Association's *Principles of Medical Ethics,* "A physician may choose whom he will serve" (AMA 1964; from Katz 1972, p. 313). However, it has never been questioned that a patient's consent is necessary to his being a patient, and consequently that withdrawal of that consent terminates his being one.

Once a physician–patient relationship exists, what responsibilities to the patient does the physician incur by virtue of it? The Hippocratic oath, in its various forms,[1] lays down only one comprehensive responsibility, which is formulated as follows in the version reproduced by Katz: "I will follow that system of regimen which, according to my ability and judgment, I consider for the benefit of my patients, and abstain from whatever is deleterious and mischievous" (Katz 1972, p. 311). Taken strictly, this binds the physician, as long as the physician–patient relationship endures, to treat his patients for their benefit, but according to what he, not they, judge that benefit to be, and to what he, not they, judge will most promote it.

When the bulk of his patients have little power, influence, or education, that is how a physician will tend to conduct himself toward them. But it is now a long time since a physician could claim that he ought so to treat his patients without being unintentionally comic.

Consider the following exchange in a case heard as late as 1961 (*Moore v. Webb,* 345 S.W. 2d, Mo. 1961). A patient had consulted a surgeon about toothache. He was advised that extractions would be necessary, and he consented to that, but claimed at the same time to have insisted that they should be only partial. After X-ray examination, the surgeon decided that a complete extraction would be beneficial; and, without any further consultation, when the patient presented himself for the operation, extracted all his teeth. The patient sought to recover damages for an operation to which he had not consented. At the trial this passage occurred between surgeon and plaintiff's attorney:

... I think you should strive to do for the patient what is the best thing over a long period of time for the patient. We tried to abide by that.

Q: Isn't that up to the patient? A: No, I don't think it should be. If they go to a doctor they should discuss it. He should decide ...

Q: Isn't this up to the patient? ... If I want to keep these teeth, can't I do it? A: You don't know whether they are causing you trouble.

Q: That is up to me, isn't it? A: Not if you came to see me it wouldn't be. [Katz 1972, p. 649]

That this dialogue seems to belong in the captions of a silent movie shows how out-of-date is the conception of the physician–patient relation it presents. But in what ways is it out of date?

In an influential paper published in 1956, the psychiatrists Thomas Szasz and Marc Hollender distinguished three basic models of the physician–patient relation, more than one of which may be combined in any actual specimen of it. The first, or "activity–passivity" model, they describe as "the oldest conceptual model," and characterize it as "based on the effect of one person on another in such a way and in such circumstances that the person acted upon is unable to contribute actively, or is considered inanimate." According to it, a patient resembles a helpless infant, and a physician an active parent. The second, or "guidance–cooperation" model, they describe as underlying much of medical practice, and characterize it as one in which both patient and physician are active, but in which "the patient is expected to 'look up to' and to 'obey' his doctor" and is "neither to question nor to argue or disagree with the orders he receives." The prototype of this model is the relation between "the parent and his (adolescent) child." The third, or "mutual participation" model, is characterized as "predicated on the postulate that equality among human beings is desirable," and as an "interaction" in which physician and patient" (1) have approximately equal power, (2) [are] mutually interdependent (i.e., need each other), and (3) engage in activities that will be in some ways satisfactory to both." Sometimes relations satisfying this model are "overcompensatory," but sometimes they are medically necessary, as for example in the treatment of most chronic illnesses, where "the patients' own experiences provide valuable and important clues for therapy" and the program of treatment "is principally carried out by the patient" (Szasz and Hollender 1956; from Katz 1972, pp. 229–230).

Although profoundly suggestive, the Szasz–Hollender models partly obscure the change from which the informed consent requirement has grown by confounding two distinct generic physician–patient relations, which I shall call the treatment relation and the choice of course of treatment relation. For our purposes, it is the latter that counts.

The Szasz–Hollender models largely hold for the treatment relation: that is, the therapeutic relation between physician and patient as treatment is actually going on. This relation appears to have three specific kinds: (1) physician active and patient wholly passive, as in surgery under a general anaesthetic; (2) patient active as well as physician, but merely in following the physician's specific instructions; and (3) patients active as well as physician, and deciding many substantive questions of treatment for himself. By contrast, there seem to be only two specific kinds of choice of course of treatment relation: (1) physician chooses the patient's course of treatment until either terminates the physician–patient relation; and (2) physician proposes, patient decides. The Szasz–Hollender triad obscures the fact that each of the two kinds of choice of course of treatment relation is compatible with each of the three kinds of treatment relation. For example, a choice of course of treatment relation in which the physician chooses is perfectly compatible with a treatment relation in which the patient, a diabetic say, decides for himself many therapeutic questions. Likewise, a choice of course of treatment relation in which a patient, having rejected his physician's first recommendation, and, after inquiring about alternatives that are medically acceptable to his physician, chooses another is perfectly compatible with his choosing a course of treatment in which he will be in the most passive of all treatment relations—surgery under a general anaesthetic.

There are, of course, cases in which there is no distinction between course of treatment and treatment, as when a patient agrees to have a flu shot. But there will be a distinction wherever a course of treatment is complex. Advancing a claim to decide on the course of treatment one is to undergo in no way encroaches upon the physician's authority over how that course of treatment is to be carried out.

The express requirement of informed consent to therapy, I suggest, is no more than the formal recognition of a change taking place in the predominant form of physician–patient relation: a change from a "physician decides" kind of choice of course of treatment relation to a "physician proposes, patient decides" kind. And physicians who exhibit the deepest understanding of the physician–patient relation have seen in this change a realization of something present in it all along. Consider the following statement by Otto E. Guttentag: "the *original* and, indeed, the basic justification for our profession [is that] . . . one human being is in distress, in need, crying for help; and another fellow human being is concerned and wants to assist him. The cry for help and the desire to render it precipitate the relationship. Here *both* the healing and the sick persons are subjects, fellow-companions, partners to conquer a common enemy who has overwhelmed one of them. Theirs is a relationship between two 'I's . . . I have called it 'mutual obligation of equals'" (Guttentag 1953; from Ladimer and Newman 1963, p. 65).

In the majority of the writings known to me in which the requirement of informed consent is accepted (I had almost said "all," but I have made no systematic count), that requirement is grounded upon one or another of three principles, which, although not identical, are nevertheless connected, namely: (1) that in nature as it is known to us, human beings have a dignity and worth that is unique; (2) the Kantian principle that a human being is never to be used merely as a means, but always at the same time as an end; and (3) a principle laid down in the Declaration of Independence, which, as we shall see, is far from merely political, that every human being is endowed with an inalienable right to life, liberty, and the pursuit of happiness. In many of those writings, as in Guttentag's paper, these principles are explicitly or implicitly acknowledged to have been transmitted, in Western societies, largely through the Judaeo-Christian religious tradition, in which it is held that, unlike the innocent beasts, man is "created in the image of God, and tempted by the devil" (Guttentag 1953; from Ladimer and Newman 1963, p. 69). Of course, despite their historical connection, the conception of man expressed in this doctrine is logically separable from any belief in God or the devil.

In an important and justly influential statement on the ethics of consent, Paul Ramsey has shown that the requirement of consent is connected with the fidelity human beings owe one another in their interactions: "The principle of an informed consent [he wrote] is a statement of the fidelity between the man who performs medical procedures and the man on whom they are performed. . . . Fidelity is between man and man in these procedures. Consent expresses or establishes this relationship, and the requirement of consent sustains it" (Ramsey 1970, p. 5). But connecting the requirement of consent with "the faithfulness that is normative for all the . . . moral bonds of life with life" is only the first stage in its justification: Ramsey correctly went on to derive faithfulness itself from the unique dignity of man: "A human being is more than a patient or experimental subject; he is a *personal* subject—every bit as much a man as the physician–experimenter" (Ramsey 1970, p. 5). And that, of course, returns us to the first of the three principles above.

Recognition of every human being as having a unique dignity as human, and as therefore being an end in every relation in which others may morally stand to him, entails that no human being may legitimately be interfered with in pursuing his conception of his happiness in whatever way seems best to him, provided that in doing so he does not himself violate human dignity. A man is not deprived of his right to life, liberty, and the pursuit of happiness by preventing him from taking away the lives and liberty of others, or interfering with their pursuit of happiness, even if that can only be done at the cost of his life or liberty. An inalienable right may be forfeited. Nor does one violate another's human dignity by forcibly preventing him from killing himself, or destroying his own capacity to lead a human life. But no human being has the right to impose on another his view of that other's happiness, or of how that other's happiness may best be promoted. Paul Ramsey has drawn the corollary for medical practice, by adapting a saying of Lincoln: "no man is good enough to cure another without his consent" (Ramsey 1970, p. 7).

For this reason, no physician in the Western moral tradition has ever questioned that for a physician to lay hands on a patient's body (to "touch" him, in legal parlance) in any way to which that patient has not consented is wrong. Common lawyers call that wrong "assault and battery." The legal principle was stated in a celebrated opinion of Chief Judge Cardozo: "Every human being of adult years and sound mind has a right to determine what shall be done with his own body; and a surgeon who performs an operation without his patient's consent, commits an assault, for which he is liable in damages" (*Schloendorff* v. *New York Hospital* 105 N.E. 92; N.Y. 1914). As Marcus L. Plant has put it, in a magisterial article, "It is the patient's prerogative to accept medical treatment or take his chances of living without it" (Plant 1968, p. 650).

Yet although physicians seem never to have disputed this important principle, as the case of *Moore* v. *Webb* discussed above shows, some of them were slow to grasp its implications. By merely consulting a physician, and not discontinuing treatment, a patient does not confer on that physician the right to administer whatever treatment he judges best. Before embarking on any course of treatment, a physician must secure his patient's consent to it; and he cannot secure consent unless he informs his patient, in words that patient can understand, of the nature and character of the course of treatment proposed. The most frequent complaints of patients in civil actions against physicians for battery have not been that treatment was administered without consent, or that their consent was obtained by outright misrepresentation, but rather that they were not informed of important parts of what would be done (e.g., that the patient was informed of what would be done to his prostate, but not that, in order to do it, his spermatic cords would be severed and tied off), or that they were informed in technical or ambiguous language they did not understand (e.g., that the patient was told that a mastectomy would be performed, but did not understand that mastectomy is the removal of a breast). It is now generally conceded that, if any such complaint is true in fact, the physician has committed a grave wrong. And a physician is simply not competent if he is unable to describe, in words intelligible to his patients, everything that could matter to them as patients about the character of any course of treatment he proposes.

Avoidance of battery, however, is not enough to satisfy the principle of consent. For, in deciding whether or not to consent to a proposed course of treatment, a patient will certainly want to take into account any hazards that may be collateral to administering the proposed treatment. But here a difficulty arises. Nobody questions that good medical practice may require a physician to be reticent in discussing a patient's condition with him, if telling the full truth may disturb the patient needlessly and perhaps jeopardize his recovery. Many physicians conceived this duty of reticence to extend to what they should tell certain patients, especially those liable to be very disturbed by it, of hazards collateral to treatments proposed. And when Plant wrote on the subject, medical and legal opinion were in agreement that what information about collateral hazards a physician is called upon to divulge to a patient is a matter of expert medical judgment (see Plant 1968, p. 656; Mills 1974, p. 307).

A very little reflection will show that, in a physician–patient relation in which the patient decides upon the course of treatment proposed by the physician, this agreed opinion was muddled. Having conceded that, except in emergencies, it is for a responsible adult patient to decide whether or not he is to receive any proposed course of treatment, it is inconsistent to allow that he may be refused information essential to forming an intelligent judgment on the question. Indeed, for a physician to assume the right to conceal a certain hazard is to make that hazard count for nothing in the patient's deliberations, and so in part to usurp the prerogative to decide. Unless a physician is prepared to maintain that his patient is no longer responsible, and the public is rightly becoming reluctant to accept a physician's word on that, the patient has a right to all the information he needs to make a judgment.

Nor is it for the physician to decide what that information is. It is true, and as far as I know undisputed, that only a medical expert is qualified to judge what benefits are to be hoped for from a proposed treatment, and their probability, and what evils are to be feared, and their probability. Having reached a scientific conclusion on these questions, he will then try to judge what values and disvalues his patient would reasonably assign to the respective probabilities that those hopes and those fears will be realized, and will recommend a course of treatment accordingly. However, the judgment he makes as to what values and disvalues a patient ought to assign to those probabilities is patently not an exercise of his medical expertise. The surgeon general is within his medical province in informing us that cigarette smoking imperils our health; but he would not be if he were to add that we ought to account that peril of more weight than satisfying our craving to smoke. Again, simplifying a set of cases that have been litigated: a physician is within his medical province in advising his patient that while a serious prostate ailment can be cured by a certain treatment with 90 percent probability, there is a 20 percent probability that a collateral result will be infertility or diminished sexual capacity; but it is as a man, and not as a medical expert, that he proceeds to judge that the high probability of the cure hoped for should outweigh the low probability of the collateral harm that is feared. It is for the patient, not for the physician, to decide such questions, although most patients give a good deal of weight to their physicians' advice.

It follows that, as a U.S. Appellate Court ruled in *Canterbury* v. *Spence*

(464 F 2d 772, CA DC 1972): "The test for determining whether a particular peril may be divulged is its materiality to the patient's decision: all risks potentially affecting the decision must be unmasked" (quoted in Simonaitis 1973*a;* 1973*b,* p. 91). What is material to a patient's decision depends upon what values and disvalues *he* assigns to the respective probabilities of various possible outcomes of a proposed course of treatment, and not on those his physician thinks ought to be assigned to them. For example, different patients will assign very different disvalues to slight chances of death or serious disability, and they have the right to act on those they assign.

As these complexities became apparent, even physicians who advocated the principle of informed consent began to speak of "the fallacy [of] ... uncritically accepting [informed consent] as an easily attainable goal, whereas it is often beyond our full grasp" (Beecher 1962, p. 145). Those less favorable to the principle derided it as irksome, superfluous, and often gratuitously distressing (e.g., Burnham 1966), and even as calculated to empty surgeons' consulting rooms (Irvin 1963). Both reactions agree that the principle of informed consent cannot be a binding practical principle, but at best is an ideal to be approximated. To the extent that a principle is morally binding, it must be capable of being observed.

But can the principle of informed consent not be so formulated as to be capable of being observed? Is it not a logical development of the perfectly orthodox doctrine of the physician–patient relationship set out by Guttentag?

That an exact and applicable doctrine of informed consent is possible was soon demonstrated by the activities of courts in developing one. And so, in part from investigations of their problems with malpractice suits, physicians began to work out a practicable professional principle. Sober discussions such as those of Mills have largely established that there is "a line of reasonable disclosure ... that is consistent with good medical practice and that affords reasonable legal safety" (Mills 1974, p. 307; cf. Meisel 1975, Mills 1975). And this line is morally as well as legally obligatory. The principal difficulty discerned by Beecher in requiring informed consent is that the physician often does not know all the collateral risks incurred in undergoing a certain treatment. Experimenters are necessarily even more in the dark than therapists. Since physicians can only be required to do what they can do, the principle of informed consent cannot be interpreted as requiring them to provide all the information whatever that would be material to a patient's decision, but only all the information at the disposal of a competent practitioner, and any special knowledge they may have acquired themselves. They can also be required to inform their patients that, medicine being an inexact science, there is a small chance in any radical treatment of grave unforeseeable collateral effects, and that there may also be unforeseeable contingencies with harmful results.

In twenty years time it is predictable that cases such as *Canterbury* v.

Spence will be perceived as no more than registering a logical development in medical practice arising from a distinction physicians had already drawn between their province as scientific practitioners and their province as medical advisers. It has, after all, been in no small part through the educative efforts of physicians that patients have been learning that they must accept ultimate responsibility for whatever courses of treatment they undergo, and that they cannot blame their physicians when risks they decide to take become realities.

A recently reported "clinicosociologic" conference perhaps allows us a glimpse of the view that will prevail in the future. The case was discussed of an eighty-six-year-old lady, who was able to communicate with her physicians and supply an accurate medical history, but who because of failures of memory had assigned legal responsibility for her affairs to a guardian. She was found to have an asymptomatic abdominal aortic aneurysm. The rupture of such an aneurysm is immediately fatal, if complete, and fatal within hours to days if partial. Often, however, it can be prevented surgically, by elective aneurysm replacement. The physician, after telephoning a surgeon, decided that the risks of such surgery were too great and recommended against it. His recommendation was discussed with the guardian and accepted, but not with the patient. Six months later the aneurysm partially ruptured, and, in the emergency room, a different surgeon discussed with her what should be done, making clear the risks of surgery, now very much greater. Despite those risks, she chose it. The guardian could not be reached. Thirty hours after surgery she died. Two remarks on the case by Dr. Gerald Perkoff are of great interest. On the initial decision not to operate, he said: [I]t was a mistake not to have operated earlier when she was well. . . . Had this patient interacted personally with the surgeon at the time of her first visit, it clearly would have been preferable. . . . Either the internist or the surgeon, or both, should have insisted upon a consultation visit" (Cryer and Kissane 1976, p. 918). What matters here is less Perkoff's disagreement with the original physician's recommendation than his insistence that the patient should have been given the opportunity to decide. And on the second, and fatal, decision to operate, he said: "[T]he question I asked myself . . . is "Can a physician do other than treat a patient if the patient is completely informed and desires treatment?" The answer I gave was that there is no other choice but to treat such a patient" (Cryer and Kissane 1976, p. 918). . . .

Note

[1]The ancient text of the Hippocratic oath, in which, e.g., the physician forswears surgery, differs from later Christian versions of it (see Sigerist 1961, 2:301–430). Ludwig Edelstein (1943) has established that its origin was Pythagorean. The heart of all versions of it, however,

is that the physician is to act "in purity and holiness" solely for the benefit of the sick, and never to their harm.

References

American Medical Association. *Opinions and Reports of the Judicial Council.* Chicago: American Medical Association, 1964. In Katz (1972), pp. 313–14.

BEECHER, HENRY K. "Some Fallacies and Errors in the Application of the Principle of Consent in Human Experimentation." *Clinical Pharmacology and Therapeutics* 3 (1962): 141–45.

BEECHER, HENRY K. "Ethics and Clinical Research." *New England Journal of Medicine* 274 (1966): 1354–60. *(b)* Reprinted in *Biomedical Ethics and the Law,* edited by J. M. Humber and Robert F. Almeder. New York: Plenum Press, 1976. Page references to the latter. Excerpts in Katz (1972), pp. 307–10.

BURNHAM, PRESTON, J. "Medical Experimentation in Humans." *Science* 152 (1966): 448–50. Excerpts in Katz (1972), pp. 658–59.

CRYER, PHILIP E., and KISSANE, JOHN M., eds. "Clinicosociologic Conference: Decisions regarding the Provision or Withholding of Therapy." *American Journal of Medicine* 61 (1976): 915–23.

EDELSTEIN, LUDWIG. *The Hippocratic Oath.* Baltimore: Johns Hopkins Press, 1943.

GUTTENTAG, OTTO E. "The Problem of Experimentation on Human Beings: The Physician's Point of View." *Science* 117 (1953): 206–10. In Ladimer and Newman (1963), pp. 63–69. Excerpts in Katz (1972), pp. 918–19.

IRVIN, WILLIAM J. "Now, Mrs. Blare, about the Complications. . . ." *Medical Economics* 40 (1963): 102–8. Excerpts in Katz (1972), pp. 393–94.

KANT, IMMANUEL. *Grundlegung zur Metaphysik der Sitten.* 2d ed. Riga: J. F. Hartknoch, 1786.

KATZ, JAY. *Experimentation with Human Beings.* New York: Russell Sage Foundation, 1972.

LADIMER, IRVING, and NEWMAN, ROGER W. *Clinical Investigation in Medicine.* Boston: Law-Medicine Research Institute, Boston University, 1963.

MEISEL, ALAN. "Informed Consent—the Rebuttal." *Journal of the American Medical Association* 234 (1975): 615.

MILLS, DON HARPER. "Whither Informed Consent?" *Journal of the American Medical Association* 229 (1974): 305–10.

MILLS, DON HARPER. "Informed Consent—the Rejoinder." *Journal of the American Medical Association* 234 (1975): 616.

PIUS XII. "Address to the First International Conference on the Histopathology of the Nervous System, September 14, 1952." *Acta Apostolicae Sedis* 44 (1952): 779. Translated in Ladimer and Newman (1963), pp. 276–86.

PLANT, MARCUS L. "An Analysis of 'Informed Consent.'" *Fordham Law Review* 36 (1968): 639–72. Excerpts in Katz (1972), pp. 599–600.

RAMSEY, PAUL. *The Patient as Person: Explorations in Medical Ethics.* New Haven, Conn.: Yale University Press, 1970.

SIGERIST, HENRY E. *A History of Medicine.* New York: Oxford University Press, 1961.

SIMONAITIS, JOSEPH E. "More about Informed Consent, Part I." *Journal of the American Medical Association* 224 (1973): 1831–32. *(a)*

SIMONAITIS, JOSEPH E. "More about Informed Consent, Part II." *Journal of the American Medical Association* 225 (1973): 91. *(b)*

SZASZ, THOMAS S., and HOLLENDER, MARC H. "A Contribution to the Philosophy of Medicine—the Basic Models of the Doctor–Patient Relationship." *Archives of Internal Medicine*. vol. 97 (1956). Excerpts from pp. 585–87 in Katz (1972), pp. 229–30.

Confidentiality and the Duty to Warn

The case discussed in the next reading is usually credited (or blamed) for establishing a duty to warn for physicians, especially psychiatrists. What is so odd about a duty to warn? Is it not the case that we all have such a duty? If I see a tree limb about to fall on unsuspecting picnickers, surely I have a moral obligation to shout, "Watch Out!" It would be wrong of me, other things being equal, not to shout a warning. But this is a moral obligation and not a requirement of the law. I break no law by keeping silent. One of the reasons I would be considered particularly vicious for keeping silent is that no harm is done by the shouting and great harm is done by the silence.

But this is not quite the case with a physician in the doctor–patient relationship, which thrives only in an atmosphere of respected privacy and confidentiality. If patients feared that their most intimate thoughts and physical problems would be used for cocktail-party talk by their physicians, very little would be trusted to them. It is this trust that allows us to bare ourselves (literally and physically) to our physicians.

There have always been exceptions to the general rule of confidentiality. When the public well-being is at stake, physicians have a duty to allow the public to protect itself. For example, if a patient has a sexually transmitted disease, physicians have a legal duty to inform public officials so that the contact of the person involved can be notified and so choose treatment. If a patient has a medical condition that affects that patient's ability to perform a job where the public safety may be compromised, then the physician involved again has a legal duty to make the appropriate officials aware of the problem (e.g., a bus driver who develops a seizure disorder).

A more difficult case is when a physician, usually a psychiatrist, feels that patients present a danger to themselves or to others. Here the tradition has been to commit the patient. In the best of conditions, this was done voluntarily, i.e., with the patient's consent. (This avoids the interesting question of whether such a patient is capable of giving true consent.) The next-best condition has the consent of family or friends; the most difficult situation is involuntary commitment.

The case about to be discussed, *Tarasoff* v. *Regents of the University of California,* focuses on the problems that a psychiatrist faced trying to balance his desire to keep a confidence with his fear that his patient might harm a third party. Alan Stone argues that the ultimate court decision stating that the psychiatrist had a legal duty to warn is based on erroneous logic and will have a detrimental effect on the practice of psychiatry. His solution is to use involuntary commitment rather than to breach a confidence.

THE *TARASOFF* DECISIONS: SUING PSYCHOTHERAPISTS TO SAFEGUARD SOCIETY

Alan A. Stone

In this comment on the decisions of the California Supreme Court in Tarasoff v. Regents of the University of California, *Dr. Stone argues that if society wishes to introduce greater safeguards into involuntary civil commitment procedures, it must be willing to accept an increased risk from those of the mentally disturbed who are potentially violent. Although there are circumstances in which it will be appropriate for the psychotherapist to warn the police of danger posed by his patient, it is counterproductive to impose upon psychotherapists a duty to provide additional or alternative protection by warning potential victims. Such a duty, he explains, is incompatible with an effective therapeutic relationship and would deter both patients and therapists from undertaking treatment, thereby further increasing the risk of violence to which society is exposed.*

On October 27, 1969, Prosenjit Poddar, a citizen of India studying naval architecture at the University of California at Berkeley, shot and stabbed to death Tatiana Tarasoff, a young woman who had rejected his love. Poddar was convicted of voluntary manslaughter and confined to the Vacaville facility.[1] He has since been released from prison, has returned to India, and by his own account is now happily married.[2] The remedies of the criminal justice system have been exhausted, but the tragedy of Miss Tarasoff's death has set off a legal imbroglio in the civil courts that may long be with us.

The Supreme Court of California twice considered the issue of liability posed by the facts surrounding Miss Tarasoff's death. Vacating its origi-

Source: "The Tarasoff Decisions: Suing Psychotherapists to Safeguard Society" by Alan A. Stone. *Harvard Law Review* 90:358 (1976). Used by permission.

nal decision[3] after the quite unusual step of rehearing the case, it held that
a psychotherapist has a duty to protect third parties from a threat of serious
danger posed by a patient under his care.[4] The fundamental problem with
this decision, as with many other recent decisions in the malpractice area,
is that in an effort to create causes of action for the cases at hand the court
has placed legal constraints on clinical practice and treatment which have
adverse effects for the general public. The holding will, for several reasons,
have adverse consequences for the treatment of potentially dangerous patients. Two of those reasons should be noted at the outset. The mentally ill
who are thought to be dangerous are for a variety of reasons rarely provided adequate treatment. The California Supreme Court has erected new
barriers to that treatment by creating a vaguely defined liability that will
deter all those who attempt to provide such psychotherapy,[5] as well as the
many private and public agencies which employ them. Further, by restricting the assurance of confidentiality available when treatment is given, the
court's holding limits the effectiveness of that treatment. It thereby not only
reduces the opportunity of the seriously mentally disturbed to obtain effective treatment, but fails to serve the court's primary purpose of reducing
the danger that such patients pose to the public.

The facts of *Tarasoff v. Regents of the University of California*,[6] which have
been repeatedly distorted in published reports,[7] seem to be as follows. Poddar sought psychiatric assistance as an outpatient at the student health facility at Berkeley and was evaluated by a psychiatrist, who referred Poddar to
a psychologist for psychotherapy. The psychologist subsequently decided
that Poddar was dangerous. This judgment was based in part on Poddar's
pathological attachment to Tatiana Tarasoff and evidence that he intended
to purchase a gun. The psychologist therefore, quite responsibly, first consulted with psychiatric colleagues and then notified the campus police at
Berkeley both orally and in writing that Poddar was dangerous and should
be taken by the campus police to a facility authorized under California's
civil commitment statute to commit him. These steps are envisioned under
the provisions of California's civil commitment statute,[8] which, unlike those
of most other states,[9] now limits the legal authority of private psychiatrists
in authorizing emergency involuntary confinement.

The police interviewed Poddar at length and concluded that he was
rational and not dangerous. They released him after he promised to stay
away from Miss Tarasoff, who was at any rate then in Brazil, and reported
their actions to the clinic. The psychiatrist in charge of the clinic, who had
been absent during these events, returned and apparently decided that his
staff had overreacted. In the name of confidentiality, he requested that the
police return the correspondence about Poddar and ordered that it and
other records of the therapy be destroyed. He also directed that no further
action be taken to detain or commit Poddar.

Much of this account is based on allegations, and much is left to conjecture. It is unclear whether the director of the clinic simply put more faith in the judgment of the police than in that of his own staff, and why he felt it necessary to destroy the records.[10] At any rate, Poddar, understandably, never returned for psychotherapy.

While Tatiana Tarasoff was out of the country during the summer, Poddar broke his promise to the police and established a relationship with her brother, who, not having been warned, was unaware of the danger Poddar posed. On Miss Tarasoff's return to the country some two months after Poddar's encounters with the psychotherapist and the campus police, he went to her home and killed her.

Miss Tarasoff's parents attempted to sue the Regents of the University of California, the therapists involved, and the police. The trial court dismissed the complaint, holding that, despite the tragic events, there was no legal basis in the law of California for a claim against them.[11] After the dismissal was affirmed by the court of appeal, the parents appealed to the Supreme Court of California, arguing that the defendants had a duty to warn Miss Tarasoff or her family of the danger and that they also had a duty to bring about Poddar's confinement under the provisions of California's Lanterman-Petris-Short civil commitment statute.[12]

In the first of its two decisions, the supreme court reversed,[13] finding that the special relationship of the therapists to the patient had given them a duty to warn Miss Tarasoff. In addition, the court held that the police might be liable for a failure to warn on the theory that their abortive attempt to commit Poddar involuntarily had deterred him from seeking further therapy and aggravated the danger to Miss Tarasoff.

The defendants, joined by several amici curiae, petitioned for a rehearing, which the court, in an unusual step, granted.[14] The court in its second decision, without attempting to explain, or even mentioning, its original opinion, abandoned its position on the liability of the police. The opinion stated only that the police did not have a special relationship with either Poddar or the victim sufficient to give rise to a duty to warn. The second opinion formulated the duty of the therapists more broadly, however, holding that the relationship between a therapist and patient imposes on the therapist a duty to use reasonable care to protect third parties against danger posed by the patient. Whether this duty takes the form of a duty to warn, a duty to call the police, or some other form, will depend, in a way the court did not attempt to clarify, on the circumstances. In the circumstances of *Tarasoff,* the court held, the plaintiffs might allege that the duty to protect took the form of a duty to warn. These duties in *Tarasoff II* are all predicated on the *special relationship* of therapist to patient.

Both *Tarasoff* decisions were strongly influenced by an article by John Fleming and Bruce Maximov,[15] published while the case was on appeal to the California Supreme Court, which is typical of much recent law review literature in its critical assault on psychiatric decisionmaking. The neutral tone of the article is deceptive, for its legal conclusions rely heavily on the evaluation of the psychiatric profession by a small group of radical critics of psychiatry led by Thomas Szasz. Dr. Szasz, a psychiatrist, has argued that mental illness is a myth[16] created by psychiatrists, whom he has compared to the doctors in the concentration camps in Nazi Germany.[17] He opposes all involuntary psychiatric intervention and has characterized such intervention as the "manufacture of madness."[18]

It is against this perspective that Fleming and Maximov consider the dilemma faced by a therapist who believes that a patient under his treatment poses a serious threat to a third party. The origin of their conception of the therapist's affirmative duty is indicated by the title of their article, *The Patient or His Victim: The Therapist's Dilemma.*

The authors believe that, on the one hand, the therapist has an obligation to maintain the patient's confidences given in therapy, and that the patient has an interest in privacy, liberty, and due process. These factors argue against the therapist acting to protect third parties by committing the patient. But concern for public safety makes some action imperative. Since the special therapeutic relationship is sufficient under the principles of tort law to overcome the rule of nonfeasance and so allow policy considerations to determine the duty of the therapist, the dilemma is to be resolved by balancing the interests of society and of the patient. The therapist cannot be trusted to perform that balancing, for it cannot be assumed that he will sufficiently safeguard the interests of the patient. Indeed, Fleming and Maximov see the gravest risks to the patient as coming from the coercive legal decisions of the therapist. In following the normal course of involuntarily committing a patient, "the psychiatrist in many instances serves not only as arresting officer, but as prosecutor, judge, and jailer as well."[19] Relying on the radical critics of psychiatry, they assume that commitment is the worst thing that the psychiatrist can do to his patient. It deprives him of liberty, stigmatizes him, destroys his will to resist, and breaches confidentiality.

Thus the dilemma faced by the conscientious therapist, according to Fleming and Maximov, is how to protect the public without abusing psychiatry's awesome preemption of legal authority through involuntary commitment. Their resolution is to place on the therapist the duty to protect society in the manner least harmful to the interests of the patient.[20] That duty, they believe, will vary from case to case and will often take the form of a duty to warn potential victims. The breach of confidentiality required by a duty to warn such parties is, the authors imply, far preferable to the abusive and customary alternative of confining the patient. They make no attempt to consider the protective value to victims of a telephone warning from a psychotherapist or to argue that such warnings protect society as much as would confinement of the patient. The duty they impose is designed as much to protect patients from the power of psychiatrists as to protect the public from dangerous patients.

While the legal and social policy arguments made by Fleming and Maximov have serious shortcomings, the authors at least make a coherent attempt to balance the interests of patient and society. Despite the influence of the article on the two *Tarasoff* decisions, however, there is little evidence in either of them of any recognition of the policy of protecting the rights of patients. The court in *Tarasoff II* focused almost entirely on the issue of public safety. The governing factor seemed to be Justice Tobriner's admonition that "[i]n this risk-infested society we can hardly tolerate the further exposure to danger that would result from a concealed knowledge of the therapist that his patient was lethal. . . . The containment of such risks lies in the public interest.". . .[21]

The court rejected the argument, presented by the American Psychiatric Association as amicus, that a psychiatrist cannot predict dangerousness with sufficient reliability to make reasonable a duty to protect others from dangerous conduct.[22] The court's response was simple: the therapist will be expected to display only "that reasonable degree of skill, knowledge, and care ordinarily possessed and exercised by members of [that professional specialty]."[23] The court did not stop to inquire what sense this test makes when no member of the profession can reliably predict dangerousness.[24] Nor did it consider whether the kind of breach it endorsed would accord with the legitimate expectations of the patient or what its consequences might be for the nature of the therapist-patient relationship and ultimately for the safety of the public. Indeed, Fleming and Maximov's basic concern for the rights of the dangerous patient and their emphasis on the duty to warn as often being the least restrictive alternative for the patient was reduced by the court to little more than a footnote.[25]

The *Tarasoff* decisions are the product of a court unwilling to admit the consequences for public safety of the recent general trend, in which it has played a substantial role,[26] toward increasing recognition of the rights of the mentally ill and the resulting change in civil commitment procedures. The California legislature was in the vanguard of these developments. In passing the Lanterman-Petris-Short Act[27] it made civil commitment more difficult to initiate and even more difficult to prolong.[28] Indeed, the Poddar case is an example of these new difficulties of initiating commitment. And on the basis of my understanding of common practice in California, I am willing to speculate that an element in the decision of the campus police not to take Poddar to an L.P.S. detention facility was their experience that someone like him would be back on the street in a few days, resentful of police intervention. These sweeping changes mean that society must tolerate greater disturbance in the community and greater risks of harm to the public. Attempts like that of the *Tarasoff* court to avoid these results by exposing therapists to greater liability are self-defeating for, because of its effect on both therapists and patients, the imposition of a duty to warn third parties will result in a lower level of safety for society.

Even before reaching this conclusion on the basis of considerations that depend on an appreciation of the therapeutic relationship, one can see that Fleming and Maximov's analysis of tort law does not provide a legal foundation for their position. They and the court argue that the therapist-patient relationship is sufficiently "special" to justify overriding the usual presumption that there is no duty to control the conduct of a third person so as to prevent him from causing harm to another. Focusing on cases in which the defendant had control over someone who was dangerous as a result of a "social or mental maladjustment,"[29] they rely in particular on cases in which hospitals have been held liable for suicides or violence against others resulting from negligent control of suicidal or homicidal patients.[30] They admit that the distinguishing factor in the cases in which liability has been found is that the defendant had a right to control in addition to de facto control over the conduct of another, but suggest that such a right should not be necessary for the imposition of a duty to protect third parties. Turning to other jurisdictions for support, they cite a case in which a hospital was held liable for failure to render emergency care[31] and one in which a state mental hospital was held liable for an assault by a patient whom it negligently failed to admit, although the clinical director on standby was aware of his homicidal state.[32] "[A]n even more compelling duty to protect a foreseeable victim would arise a fortiori," they assert, "once the *culprit* had actually been *admitted* for therapy and a doctor–patient relationship established."[33] This misconceives both the ground for the imposition of the duty in the cases they cite and the nature of the therapeutic relationship. The language "admitted for therapy" is particularly misleading in its implications about the nature of the therapeutic relationship. The imposition of the duty in these cases was based not on the closeness of the relationship but on the fact that it was one of control (or, in one case,[34] on the fact that no relationship at all was established when, the court held, the hospital was under a duty to establish control). The authors' attempt to exploit the distinction between a right to control and de facto control, unsatisfactory in itself, simply ignores the fact that the therapist seeing an outpatient in a clinic or office has no control over the patient. Indeed, lack of control is the end sought by much recent mental health case law and legislation, an end Fleming and Maximov strongly support.[35] Moreover, even if a court saw fit to impose on a private psychotherapist, as well as on a state mental hospital, a duty to *treat* a patient whom he knows to have homicidal proclivities, that does not determine the issue of *how* the therapist ought to treat the patient or deal with the confidences divulged in the course of that treatment.

Once the suggestion of control is eliminated, there is nothing in the nature of the relationship between a psychiatrist and his patient to support an exception to the tort law presumption. . . .

Analyses of statutes bearing on confidentiality, however, do not reach the cardinal point, which both the *Tarasoff* court and Fleming and Maximov fail to appreciate, that the imposition of a duty to protect, which may take the form of a duty to warn threatened third parties, will imperil the therapeutic alliance and destroy the patient's expectation of confidentiality, thereby thwarting effective treatment and ultimately reducing public safety. The nature of the illness and treatment of the kind of dangerous person who voluntarily comes to therapy makes the imposition of such a duty particularly destructive. Such a person is typically not a hardened criminal but rather one whose violence is the product of passion or paranoia.[36] The object of that passion or paranoia is most often a person of intense significance to the patient.[37] Such, of course, was the case with Poddar. When a therapist tries to deal with the potential for violence of such patients, he must enter into a therapeutic alliance in which feelings are acknowledged at the same time that the impulses to act them out are discouraged. To maintain this attitude of respect for and acceptance of the patient's feelings while discouraging any violent action is often the central task of the therapist. If all goes well, the patient whose feelings are accepted will come to trust the therapist and be able to explore and understand his violent impulses and consider meaningful alternatives to them.[38] Given the special significance of the potential victim to those whose violence is the product of passion and paranoia, nothing could be more destructive of the tenuous therapeutic alliance than the patient's perception that there exists a significant relationship between the therapist and the potential victim. Nothing is more likely to give a patient the impression that such a significant relationship exists than being told by the therapist that he has a legal duty to protect, and perhaps to warn directly, the potential victim. . . .

Fleming and Maximov characterize as unsubstantiated the claim that patients in general, and dangerous patients in particular, will be alienated from therapy by a Miranda-type warning by the psychiatrist of his duty to breach therapeutic confidences in order to protect third parties. It is true, as they note,[39] that such consequences have not been demonstrated in an empirical study. But it is also true to my knowledge that no one has shown in any empirical study that confidentiality between lawyer and client is essential to good legal services. Nonetheless, lawyers are convinced of its necessity on the basis of their own clinical experience. In the absence of a reliable empirical study, a judgment based on clinical experience is obviously preferable to a judgment that contradicts such experience. Anyone who has worked in a therapeutic program serving drug addicts, prisoners, parolees, probationers, or juvenile delinquents can attest that the duty to breach the patient's privacy as required by *Tarasoff II* would eviscerate whatever possibility of treatment exists with these difficult patients.

A duty to warn potential victims will, therefore, often not be the alternative least harmful to the patient's general welfare. Moreover, although the argument for the least restrictive alternative may be powerful and convincing as it has been applied to civil commitment cases in which the commitment was patently serving a parens patriae function,[40] it loses its force in the critical situation when it is necessary to control someone whom the therapist has decided presents a serious danger to others. The overriding goal at that point is to protect those threatened, and the duty to warn may in fact increase the likelihood of violence.

Most patients will tolerate a variety of other protective forms of crisis intervention by the therapist with much less damage to the therapeutic alliance and with much less rage towards both the therapist and the potential victims because their psychological implications are much less sinister to the patient. For example, one typical pattern of violence involves male paranoid jealousy with profound ambivalence toward the potential female victim and suspicion of all her male relationships.[41] If the male therapist must prevent violence, he will do better to seek the assistance of the police or invoke civil commitment rather than give the patient the idea that he, the therapist, has a relationship with the woman. The therapist who, following a legal duty, warns the potential victim, not only endangers the therapeutic relationship but may also increase the risk to her and may even become a victim himself. Conversely, many violent patients are reassured when controlled by persons not directly implicated in their psychopathology. Although there are obvious differences in the two contexts, every policeman knows the potential danger of direct intervention in a domestic squabble. Many policemen are also aware that if they can deal with a violent husband alone he can much more readily be reassured and calmed. The important psychological point is that the police not be seen as the agent of the wife.[42]

As disturbing as the California Supreme Court's decision to impose a duty to warn third parties is its holding that the therapist's prediction of dangerousness is to be examined under the ordinary malpractice criterion of "conformity to standards of the profession."[43] One can only wonder what it means to apply standards to skills which do not exist. As Justice Mosk noted, dependence on such standards "will take us from the world of reality into the wonderland of clairvoyance."[44]

Although the requirement is without meaningful content, its practical consequences are obvious: it opens the door to lawsuits claiming negligent failure to predict dangerousness and protect the public. Psychotherapists have always been reluctant to treat dangerous patients. Not only must therapists deal with their own personal distress and fearful reactions as they become involved in the patient's violent predilections, but also those who are both mentally ill and dangerous are, because of the nature of their psychopathology, notoriously difficult to treat.[45] The new legal constraints imposed by the *Tarasoff* court will make effective treatment more difficult and so increase this reluctance. Nor, of course, can psychotherapists ignore the personal consequences of malpractice liability. Physicians everywhere have become wary of treating the type of patients who generate malpractice claims. Techniques for avoidance include refusal to accept the patient and referral to public clinics or to other specialists. Patients who are bounced around in this way often lose whatever motivation for treatment they have. One can only assume that this will be the experience of the dangerous mentally ill person in California with increasing frequency.

Liability will have the additional consequence of aggravating the inevitable tendency to overpredict dangerousness. The therapist, aware of the unreliability of his predictions and the fact that, if he fails to protect a third party who is harmed by his patient, he must trust to the hindsight judgment of a jury, can be expected to err on the side of caution. There are, moreover, few personal adverse consequences of overprediction for the therapist which might counteract this tendency. This is particularly true for therapists attached to clinics and prepaid group treatment programs who do not have to be concerned about the size of their practice. Since the acknowledged unreliability of psychiatric predictions of dangerousness makes standards of competence virtually nonexistent, there is little to retard the gradual erosion of the assurance of confidentiality.[46]

The California Supreme Court's willingness in *Tarasoff* to require confidential information to be disclosed directly to threatened parties on the basis of an unreliable prediction contrasts sharply with its position in *People v. Burnick*,[47] decided between *Tarasoff I* and *Tarasoff II*. There it held that proof beyond a reasonable doubt is necessary for the involuntary commitment of a mentally disordered sex offender.[48] Although that decision was based in part on the deprivation of liberty which commitment involves, the court repeatedly stressed the unreliability of psychiatric prediction as an additional factor, finding it "so inherently untrustworthy that [the court] would permit confinement even in a so-called civil proceeding only upon proof beyond a reasonable doubt."[49] The *Burnick* court made it quite clear that the jury need not be bound by psychiatric opinion. Since a jury may well decide that a psychotherapist's judgment that a mentally disordered sex offender is dangerous does not establish dangerousness beyond a reasonable doubt, *Burnick* and *Tarasoff II* may in combination produce the strange result of making it impossible for a therapist to commit, under California's law for mentally disturbed sex offenders,[50] someone whom he believes to be dangerous, and yet subsequently impose on him a duty to warn third parties of the danger! The state thereby avoids taking responsibility for someone the therapist believes to be a menace to society while requiring the therapist, as an independent citizen, to attempt to provide protection by divulging confidential information.[51] Indeed, the predictions required by *Tarasoff* are even less reliable than those questioned in *Burnick*, for they must be made on the class of all office patients who might be dangerous, a group with a much lower base rate than the class of sex offenders.[52]

Nothing I have said should suggest that therapists have no moral duty when third parties are endangered by their patients. I have argued rather that the duty which the *Tarasoff* court imposes will reduce rather than increase public safety because it will diminish the ability and motivation of therapists to treat effectively mentally disturbed and potentially dangerous people. Public safety may nonetheless be served, and the moral duty of the therapist fulfilled, in more traditional ways: the therapist who believes that his patient poses a serious danger to third parties should attempt to have that person committed or, if that fails, should call the police when he is convinced that such action will protect both the victim and his patient. That has been the traditional moral and prudential view, and I believe it is still valid. The requirement of confidentiality does not prevent either alternative. The Canons of Ethics of physicians make it clear that there is a moral duty to breach a patient's confidence should it be necessary in order to protect the community.[53] Those who advocate absolute confidentiality of the therapist–patient relationship either ignore this canon or fail to consider its implications. For example, no psychiatrist who believed his patient intended to assault some member of his treatment staff would fail to seek police or other assistance because that would breach confidentiality. If protecting the staff is an appropriate excuse for breach of confidentiality, then protecting others surely must be. However, the Canons of Ethics wisely leave it to clinical judgment to determine how the psychiatrist should go about protecting the community. . . .

[T]he primary inadequacy of the court's holding is not that it does not give serious thought to protecting the public, but rather that the duty it would impose is self-defeating, increasing, rather than reducing, the overall risk. It is highly disruptive of the patient–therapist relationship and a less appropriate way of protecting those threatened by dangerous patients than the traditional alternatives of commitment or simply informing the police.

Neither the court nor Fleming and Maximov recognize that the tragedy of Tatiana Tarasoff is the price society pays for restraints on the "coercive power" of psychiatrists. Their unwillingness to recognize that fact leads them to a result that will reduce the ability of the mentally ill in California to obtain effective therapy and consequently will diminish public safety. The decision is counterproductive of the goal of public safety it professes. It is a disservice to the citizens of California.

Notes

[1]Poddar's original conviction for second degree murder was reversed for failure to give adequate instructions concerning a defense of diminished capacity. *See* People v. Poddar, 10 Cal. 3d 750, 518 P.2d 342, 111 Cal. Rptr. 910 (1974).

[2]Personal communication.

[3]Tarasoff v. Regents of Univ. of Cal., 529 P.2d 553, 118 Cal. Rptr. 129 (1974) [hereinafter *Tarasoff I*].

[4]Tarasoff v. Regents of Univ. of Cal., 551 P.2d 334, 131 Cal. Rptr. 14 (1976) [hereinafter *Tarasoff II*].

[5]One of several ambiguities of the court's holding concerns who will be subject to the liability it introduces. Many mental health professionals and paraprofessionals, including social workers, psychiatric social workers, psychiatric nurses, occupational therapists, pastoral counselors, and guidance counselors, provide some form of therapy. Indeed, many parole and probation officers hold advanced degrees in one of the mental health specialties and claim to be doing therapy with the convicted felons who are their clients. How many of these millions of therapist-patient contacts each year are intended to be covered by the court's decision is unclear.

[6]551 P.2d 334, 131 Cal. Rptr. 14 (1976).

[7]*See*, e.g., Annas, *Law and Psychiatry: When Must the Doctor Warn Others of the Potential Dangerousness of his Patient's Condition?*, Medico-Legal News (April, 1975); People v. Poddar, 10 Cal. 3d 750, 753–54, 518 P.2d 342, 344–45, 111 Cal. Rptr. 910, 912–13 (1974).

[8]California's civil commitment procedures are governed by the Lanterman-Petris-Short Act, Cal. Welf. & Inst. Code §§ 5000-5404.I (West 1972 & Supp. 1976). The statute provides that [w]hen any person, as a result of mental disorder, is a danger to others . . . a peace officer, member of the attending staff, as defined by regulation, of an evaluation facility designated by the county, or other professional person designated by the county may, upon probable cause, take, or cause to be taken, the person into custody and place him in a facility . . . for 72-hour treatment and evaluation. *Id.* § 5150 (West Supp. 1976).

[9]Most states permit any licensed physician to initiate emergency confinement. *See* S. Brakel & R. Rock, *The Mentally Disabled and the Law* 36, table 3.2 (1971).

[10]Since the letter to the police in fact survives, it is not even certain that an order to destroy it was given. Brief or Respondent Moore at 168, *Tarasoff I*.

[11]Tarasoff v. Regents of Univ. of Cal., 108 Cal. Rptr. 878 (Ct. App. 1973), *vacated and remanded*, 529 P.2d 553, 118 Cal. Rptr. 129 (1974).

[12]Cal. Welf. & Inst. Code § 5150 (West Supp. 1976).

[13]Tarasoff v. Regents of Univ. of Cal., 529 P.2d 553, 118 Cal. Rptr. 129 (1974).

[14]13 Cal. 3d 205 (1974).

[15]Fleming & Maximov, *The Patient or His Victim: The Therapist's Dilemma*, 62 Calif. L. Rev. 1025 (1974) [hereinafter cited as *Fleming*]. Fleming is a Professor of Law at the University of California, Berkeley, where Maximov was a student at the time the article was written.

[16]*See generally* T. Szasz, *The Myth of Mental Illness* (1961).

[17]*See* Szasz, *The Danger of Coercive Psychiatry*, 61 A.B.A.J. 1246, 1248 (1975). A reply to that article appears in Stone, *Hanging the Psychiatrists*, 62 A.B.A.J. 773 (1976).

[18]*See generally* T. Szasz, *The Manufacture of Madness* (1970).

[19]*Fleming, supra* note 15, at 1046 (footnote omitted).

[20]*See id.* at 1065.

[21]551 P.2d at 347–48, 131 Cal. Rptr. at 27–28.

[22]This unreliability on the side of overprediction of dangerousness, resulting in a large number of "false positives," stems from the combination of the inevitable element of error involved in psychological predictions with the low "base rate" (i.e., rarity) of violent behavior among the mentally ill. One source illustrates the problem as follows:
Assume that one person out of a thousand will kill. Assume also an exceptionally accurate test is created which differentiates with ninety-five percent effectiveness those who will kill from those who will not. If 100,000 people were tested, out of the 100 who would kill, 95 would be isolated. Unfortunately, out of the 99,900 who would not kill, 4,995 people would also be isolated as potential killers.
Livermore, Malmquist & Meehl, *On the Justifications for Civil Commitment*, 117 U. Pa. L. Rev. 75,

84 (1968) (footnote omitted). *See also* A. Stone, *Mental Health and Law: A system in Transition* 25–40 [hereinafter cited as Stone].

[23]551 P.2d at 345, 131 Cal. Rptr. at 25 (quoting Bardessono v. Michels, 3 Cal. 3d 780, 788, 478 P.2d 480, 484, 91 Cal. Rptr. 760, 764 (1970)).

[24]Since the primary cause of overprediction is the low base rate of violent behavior among the mentally ill, even the therapist who is unusually accurate in his predictions will face essentially the same problem as his less accurate colleagues, as the example in note 23 *supra* illustrates.

[25]*See* 551 P.2d at 346, 347 & n.14, 131 Cal. Rptr. at 26, 27 & n.14.

[26]*See, e.g.,* Thorn v. Superior Court, I Cal. 3d 666, 464 P.2d 56, 83 Cal. Rptr. 600 (1970); *In re* Lambert, 134 Cal. 626, 66 P. 851 (1901).

[27]Cal. Welf. & Inst. Code §§ 5000–5404.I (West 1972 & Supp. 1976).

[28]*See* note 8 *supra;* Stone, *supra* note 23, at 60–65.

[29]*Fleming, supra* note 15, at 1028 (quoting Harper & Kime, *The Duty to Control the Conduct of Another,* 43 Yale L.J. 886, 898 (1934)).

[30]*See, e.g.,* Merchants Nat'l Bank & Trust Co. v. United States, 272 F. Supp. 409 (D.N.D. 1967) (homicide); Meier v. Ross Gen. Hosp., 69 Cal. 2d 420, 445 P.2d 519, 71 Cal. Rptr. 903 (1968) (suicide).

[31]Wilmington Gen. Hosp. v. Manlove, 54 Del. 15, 174 A.2d 135 (1961).

[32]Greenberg v. Barbour, 322 F. Supp. 745 (E.D. Pa. 1971).

[33]*Fleming, supra* note 15, at 1030 (emphasis added).

[34]Greenberg v. Barbour, 322 F. Supp. 745 (E.D. Pa. 1971).

[35]*See, e.g., Fleming, supra* note 15, at 1055.

[36]*See* Lion, Bach-y-Rita, & Ervin, *Violent Patients in the Emergency Room,* 125 Am. J. of Psych. 1706 (1969).

[37]*See* American Psychiatric Association, Task Force Report 8, Clinical Aspects of the Violent Individual 7–9, 28 (1974).

[38]*See generally* J. Lion, *Evaluation and Management of the Violent Patient* (1972).

[39]*See Fleming, supra* note 15, at 1039.

[40]*See e.g.,* Lake v. Cameron, 364 F.2d 657, 660 (D.C. Cir. 1966).

[41]*See* R. Mowat, *Morbid Jealousy and Murder* (1966); Lanzkron, *Murder and Insanity: A Survey,* 119 Am. J. Psych. 754 (1963); Shepherd, *Morbid Jealousy: Some Clinical and Social Aspects of a Psychiatric Symptom,* 107 J. Mental Sci. 687 (1961).

[42]Barocas, *Police Crisis Intervention and the Prevention of Violence,* 32 Am. J. Psychoanalysis 211 (1972).

[43]*Tarasoff II,* 551 P.2d at 354, 131 Cal. Rptr. at 34 (Mosk, J., concurring and dissenting).

[44]*Id.*

[45]*See* Stone, *supra* note 23, at 36–37.

[46]If Justice Clark's interpretation of section 5328 of the Lanterman-Petris-Short Act, *see* note 46 *supra,* is correct, then section 5330 of the Act exposes the therapist to liability for disclosure of confidential information acquired in even an unsuccessful attempt to commit a patient involuntarily.

More generally, a therapist may be liable for breach of the patient's right of privacy or for defamation, if his breach of the patient's confidence cannot be justified by a higher duty to protect threatened parties. *See* Berry v. Moench, 8 Utah 2d 191, 331 P.2d 814 (1958). Given the unreliability of predictions of dangerousness and the difficulty of supporting an assertion that a patient posed a threat which did not materialize, the defense of truth to a claim of defamation may be difficult to establish. Although the importance of the interests being protected by a warning given in good faith by a therapist to threatened third parties might suggest that the therapist need not fear tort liability for such a disclosure, the lack of any standard of skill in predicting dangerousness under which the therapist's decision to disclose may be judged makes his position a difficult one. Although the possibility of tort liability for disclosure may tend to reduce slightly the tendency to overpredict dangerousness, the primary result of putting therapists in the awkward situation of being forced to choose between two sorts of liability imposed under a chimerical standard will simply be greater reluctance on their part to treat potentially dangerous patients.

[47]14 Cal. 3d 306, 535 P.2d 352, 121 Cal. Rptr. 488 (1975).

[48]Such commitment is governed not by the Lanterman-Petris-Short Act but by separate provisions governing the treatment of mentally disordered sex offenders, Cal. Welf. & Inst. Code §§ 6300–6330 (West 1972 & Supp. 1976).

[49]*Tarasoff II*, 551 P.2d at 354, 131 Cal. Rptr. at 34 (Mosk, J., concurring and dissenting).

[50]Cal. Welf. & Inst. Code § 6300–6330 (West 1972 & Supp. 1976).

[51]Since the therapist in making the disclosure would run the risk of tort liability, *see* note 62 *supra*, the result of the transfer of responsibility is to replace due process safeguards by the therapist's exposure to liability for ill-considered disclosure.

[52]*See* note 23 *supra*.

[53]American Medical Association, *The Principles of Medical Ethics* § 9 (1973).

Truth Telling

Informed consent and the duty of a health-care provider to tell the truth are so intimately connected that it is difficult to discuss one topic without discussing the other. It is impossible for patients to make informed choices unless truthfully informed of all relevant aspects of their situation—the disease they suffer, treatments available, likely outcomes. At first sight, it is hard even to imagine a situation when it would be defensible for a physician or health-care provider to withhold information or to lie deliberately to a patient.

In her book, *Lying* (New York: Pantheon Books, 1978), Sissela Bok examines three arguments often given in support of lying to patients. The first is that no one really knows what is true anyway; the whole truth is always elusive. In reply to this, she points out that telling what one believes is the truth does not require that one be correct about what is the truth. Moreover, it certainly does not require that one be able to define "truth" well enough to satisfy a philosopher. Her definition of a lie makes it clear that this skeptical attack on truth telling will not work. She says that a lie is any intentionally "deceptive message in the form of a statement." (p. 15)

The second argument in favor of lying is that patients really do not want bad news. The third is that the truth can indeed hurt. The second and third arguments are based on facts: what patients do want and what does in fact hurt patients. Bok cites other facts to counter these arguments. She cites the results of studies that show that "over 80 percent of the persons asked indicated that they would want to be told [whether they had a serious illness such as cancer]" (p. 229). Bok goes on to challenge the view that bad news, more often than not, harms patients. Again citing evidence from studies, Bok makes it clear that this argument against truth telling lacks support.

Bok concludes that these arguments will not support the general contention that physicians may lie to patients. She does allow for deception for the good of the patient, but only in rare cases. In those cases, she insists that the burden of justification for deception falls squarely on the physician. Without strict adherence to truthfulness, there will be no way to ensure either the trust in physicians or the autonomy of patients so necessary for good medical care.

In the next reading, Joseph Ellin suggests that Bok overlooks an important moral distinction between deception, which falls short of lying, and lying itself. Deception is not so bad as lying. (If a patient addresses a medical student as "Doctor" and the medical student says nothing to the contrary, then that medical student has deceived the patient without actually lying to the patient. If a patient asks the medical student, "Are you a doctor?" and the student replies "Yes" then the medical student has lied.)

Ellin characterizes the doctor–patient relationship as one aimed at furthering the health interests of the patient. One visits a physician usually out of an interest to maintain, improve, or return to health. Getting good care is a health interest. Not being deceived, Ellin claims, is a moral interest. His point is that if the doctor–patient relationship is seen as fiduciary, in that the doctor is responsible for the patient's health, then there is no obvious reason that the relationship should, in general, rule out deception, since not being deceived is a moral interest.

Ellin concludes by examining the effect of lying on the doctor–patient relationship. Here he takes the strong position that if the doctor–patient relationship is a fiduciary one in which trust is a necessary condition for its very existence and survival, then where there are no alternatives except truth telling and lying, it is a doctor's duty to tell the truth.

As you read through the Ellin article, ask yourself if you are convinced of the value of the distinction between lying and deception. Also, decide whether deception can be a useful medical therapy.

The everyday saying, "The truth hurts," has some truth to it. We usually know when to go easy on the truth and even have some idea how to go easy on the truth. (When your best friend says "How do you like my new hairstyle?" and you think it looks absurd, you know better than to say so in those words.) Try to understand just what makes truth telling in the medical context so puzzling.

LYING AND DECEPTION:
THE SOLUTION TO A DILEMMA
IN MEDICAL ETHICS

Joseph S. Ellin

Should doctors deceive their patients? Should they ever lie to them? Situations arise in the practice of medicine in which it appears that a medically desirable course of treatment cannot be undertaken, or cannot succeed, unless the patient is deceived; or that a patient's health or state of mind would be damaged unless some information is concealed from him, at least temporarily. Sometimes medical personnel feel justified in practicing deceit for reasons which do not directly benefit patients; for example, Veatch's case of the medical students who are instructed to introduce themselves to hospital patients as "Doctor Smith" (instead of "Medical Student Smith") so as to overcome more quickly the anxiety they feel as they begin the transformation from layperson to physician.[1] Since in such cases most writers concede that patients ought not to be deceived unless something more important than truth is at stake, the problem is typically analyzed as determining the relative weight of the rights and interests involved: the patient's interest in the truth versus his or her interest in health and peace of mind, or perhaps the patient's right to the truth versus someone else's right to or interest in something else. When, however, the problem is posed in this way, the patient's right to the truth seems relatively unimportant, especially compared to an interest as obviously important as health, so that it seems evident that deception is justified, or even obligatory. The principle of not deceiving patients seems to have little weight when deception is thought necessary to achieve some desirable end.

The alternative, however, would seem to be to adopt the rigorist position that the duty of veracity is absolute, and this seems even less attractive. Most writers concede that the duty of veracity is prima facie only, at least as a principle of medical ethics where life and suffering are at stake; it does not appear plausible to adopt an ethic in which it is made obligatory to inflict avoidable anguish on someone already sick, especially where hope and good spirits, in addition to being desirable in themselves, may promote healing and help prolong life. One could hope to avoid this dilemma by holding that the duty of veracity, though not absolute, is to be given very great weight, and may be overridden only in the gravest cases; but this line conflicts with many of our intuitions about actual cases and will probably

Source: "Lying and Deception: The Solution to a Dilemma in Medical Ethics" by Joseph S. Ellin. *Westminster Institute Review*, vol. 1 (May 1981), pp. 3–6. Used by permission of the author.

prove useless because ad hoc. There is a temptation to deceive, or at the very least to conceal information and blur the truth, not only to prevent anxiety and stimulate hope and good spirits, but to make possible the use of placebos, to persuade patients to abandon harmful habits, to generate confidence in the medical team and the like. The whole problem is to determine what counts as a sufficiently important end to justify an exception to the veracity principle. Hence the dilemma: either we say that veracity is an absolute duty, which is too strict; or we admit that it is prima facie only, which seems ad hoc, useless, and mushy.

I would like to suggest that the solution to this dilemma is to be found in the simple distinction between lying and deception. Writers on medical ethics do not seem to acknowledge this distinction, though it is commonly made in ordinary morality. But if we allow it, assuming also that we adopt a certain conception of the doctor–patient relationship, we can say that the duty not to lie is indeed absolute, but that there is no duty at all not to practice deception. Deception, on this view, is not even wrong prima facie, but is simply one tool the doctor may employ to achieve the ends of medicine. The conception of the doctor–patient relationship which allows us to reach this result is that of a fiduciary relationship, and the argument I wish to make is that two principles, the one prohibiting lying and the other allowing deception, may be defended through this conception.

A little reflection will make clear that in ordinary morality we do distinguish between lying and deception. Most of us would not lie, but we are much less scrupulous about deceiving. We might even make it a point of honor not to actually lie when we feel justified in planting false ideas in other people's minds. You ask me how my book is coming. I have done nothing on it in a month. I reply, "The work is very difficult." This is not a lie (the work *is* very difficult); but I have managed to convey a false impression. I prefer such evasion even to a white lie or harmless fiction ("Very well." "Slowly."). Countless examples suggest themselves. An amusing story is told of a certain St. Athanasius. His enemies coming to kill him, but mistaking him for another, asked, "Where is the traitor Athanasius?" The Saint replied, "Not far away."[2]

One reason we do not distinguish between lying and deception in the medical context is that deception is sometimes used for unacceptable ends. An example of such malignant deception is given by Marsha Millman. A doctor performs a liver biopsy (a procedure not without risk) under circumstances in which the procedure is probably not justified. He avoids telling the patient the results for some days. Finally he says, "Don't worry, the biopsy didn't show anything wrong with your liver." When the patient after much agitation is allowed to read her chart, she discovers that the report on the biopsy reads, "No analysis, specimen insufficient for diagnosis."[3]

When doctors deceive for self-interested motives, to cover up their bad judgment or their failures, we are apt to think the distinction between lying and deception is mere hair-splitting. Millman asserts that the doctor "had evasively lied." Though strictly speaking inaccurate, this characterization is correct from the moral point of view, since because of the doctor's bad motive, the evasion may be considered morally no different from a lie. But the situation is different when the motives are benevolent. James Childress gives the interesting case of a patient who, due to constant pain caused by chronic intestinal problems, injects himself six times daily with a strong (but allegedly non-addictive) pain-killer. When the patient is admitted to the hospital with another complaint, the staff decides to wean him from the drug by gradually diluting the dosage with saline solution. After a time, when the pain does not recur, the patient is told that he is no longer receiving the medication.[4]

Here we have a treatment plan that can work only through deception; if the patient knows he is not receiving the usual dosage, his pain will recur. Hence the staff does not have the option of simply telling him what they intend to do and then doing it over his objections. The staff's alternatives therefore are: comply with the patient's wishes and administer medication they believe to be unnecessary and harmful; promise to do what he wants and then follow their withdrawal plan anyway, i.e., lie; avoid telling him what they are doing without actually lying about it. If it were not possible to carry out the plan without lying, if for example the patient asked direct questions about his medication, the choice thus posed between abandoning the plan and lying to him would seem far more difficult than the choice between abandoning the plan and simply deceiving him. It seems preferable to carry out the plan without actually lying; so much so that we are tempted to say that if the staff could not avoid lying, it would be better to abandon the plan, whereas employing the plan using deception is quite justifiable, given the alternative.

The distinction between lying and deception may, however, seem unjustified from what Sissela Bok has called "the perspective of the deceived." As far as the deceived is concerned, deception can be just as bad as a lie. Both give rise to resentment, disappointment and suspicion. Those deceived, as Bok says, "feel wronged; . . . They see that they were manipulated, that the deceit made them unable to make choices for themselves . . . unable to act as they would have wanted to act."[5] The deceived has been led to have false beliefs, has been deprived of control of a situation, has been subjected to manipulation, and so suffers a sense of betrayal and wounded dignity. Like lying, deception harms many interests. We have an interest in acquiring true beliefs, in having the information needed to make wise decisions about our lives, in being treated as trustworthy and intelligent persons, in being able to trust those in whom we put our trust. The deceiver, either intentionally or inadvertently, harms these interests. To the person whose interests are harmed by deceit, it is small comfort that the deceit did not involve an actual lie.

Those who find the lying/deception distinction objectionable are probably thinking of the harm each does to the deceived. Their argument is that if it is equally harmful to deceive and to lie, then no distinction between the two should be allowed. However, such a view oversimplifies the moral situation, as analysis of deception will reveal ... it is possible to take the view that intentional deception is no moral wrong at all. No less a moralist than Kant writes: "I can make believe, make a demonstration from which others will draw the conclusion I want, though they have no right to expect that my action will express my real mind. In that case, I have not lied to them ... I may, for instance, wish people to think that I am off on a journey, and so I pack my luggage."[6] Kant evidently sees nothing wrong with this; his view seems to be that he has every right to pack his luggage if he chooses and if others draw certain conclusions (however reasonable) which turn out to be false, they have only themselves to blame. This, however, is too lenient on deceivers. If a person says or does something, knowing or believing that others are likely to draw false conclusions from it, and if the person refrains from providing them information he knows would prevent the false conclusions from being drawn, then he is at least in part responsible for the deception. But though he is partly responsible, he is not as responsible as he would be were he to present the false conclusion himself. Even when there is a lie, of course, the victim must bear some of the blame for being deceived, since he has imprudently trusted the liar and failed to confirm the statements made. But when a victim is deceived without a lie, he is more to blame, since he has not only failed to investigate a situation, but has also drawn or jumped to a conclusion which goes beyond the statements made to him. Even where the conclusion is a very natural inference from the statements or actions, the fact that it is an inference shows that the deceived participates in his own deception.

However, this is not the only reason why deception is considered less bad than lying. When I lie, I tell you something which, since it is false, ought not to be believed; this harms your interest in having true beliefs. When I deceive, however, I merely give you grounds for an inference which does not actually follow; this harms your interest in having good grounds for inferences, but does not directly harm your interest in having true beliefs.

The third reason why deception is not as bad as lying is that lying violates the social contract in a way that deception does not. In a sense, the social contract is renewed by every act of speech (more properly by every assertion), since to speak is implicitly to give an assurance that what one says is true. Every statement implies a promise or certification of its truth. A lie, which with a single act both implies a promise and violates it, thus involves a self-contradiction. It could be said that the social contract prohibits deception generally, on the rule-utilitarian ground that social life would be unduly burdened if, as in a spy novel, every apparently innocent action were a potential source of misinformation. But though deception may be a violation of the rules (lying, too, is a violation of the rules in this sense), it is not at the same time a reaffirmation of the rules, and hence is not an implicit self-contradiction. We can understand this when we see that although the social contract may prohibit deception, it cannot prohibit deceptive statements, since deceptive statements which are not lies are true, and the social contract cannot prohibit true statements. The contract does prohibit making true statements with the intent to deceive, or in circumstances such that the speaker does or should realize that the statement is likely to deceive. But an intention is not a promise, not even an implicit promise, hence there is nothing self-contradictory about deception. To the extent that the deceiver affirms the contract by his statement, he also obeys the contract, since his statement is true.

This analysis has an important consequence for the theory of professional morality I am defending here, since it enables us to see the difference between lying and deception with regard to trust. In everyday life we have the feeling that the liar is less trustworthy than the deceiver. Why is this, since they both intend to mislead? The conceptual basis of this perception is that the liar reaffirms the promise of the social contract in the very act (the lie) by which he violates that promise. The deceiver may violate the social contract but does not promise to obey it in the very act of violation. Doubtless a deceiver should not be trusted, but it seems reasonable that we would be even more wary, more on guard against a person who not only deceives, but breaks a promise in the very act of reaffirming it. The significance of this distinction for professional morality I shall explain shortly.

So far I have argued that morality draws a distinction between lying and intentional deception. Now I must address the more controversial question of what the doctor's obligations are with respect to the duty of veracity. I will argue that if we conceive the doctor–patient relationship as a fiduciary relationship, then the doctor has an absolute duty not to lie, but not even a prima facie duty not to deceive. This is different from the view of ordinary morality which condemns both lying and deception, holds both wrong prima facie only, but holds lying morally worse. My defense of the above propositions as principles of medical ethics rests partly on conceptual points, and partly on contingent psychological facts having to do with the conditions of trust. It is because trust is more important in the doctor–patient relationship, conceived as fiduciary, than in ordinary life, that there is a difference between ordinary and professional morality.

As is well-known, there are many conceptions of the doctor–patient relationship. One can think of doctors as priests, friends, engineers, business partners, or partners in health. One can think of the relationship with patients as contractual, philanthropic, collegial, even exploitive. Doubtless there is merit in each of these points of view; each represents some significant truth about some doctor–patient relationships. Such conceptions or models are useful because they illuminate ethical principles; there are connections between the model of the relationship and the ethical principles which should govern it. A doctor who thinks of himself as a body mechanic will have different views about providing information to patients than one who thinks of himself as engaged with the patient in a partnership in healing. (It is unlikely that the doctors in the previous examples thought of themselves as engaged in a partnership with their patients.) Similarly, a doctor who imagines himself to be a patient's friend takes a different view of how much time he should spend with a patient than one who believes he is merely fulfilling a contract for services.

Undoubtedly many medical personnel think of themselves as having a fiduciary relationship, or something like it, with their patients or clients. The fiduciary conception is based on the legal notion of someone, the fiduciary, who has certain responsibilities for the welfare of another, the beneficiary. It is important to recognize that a fiduciary's responsibilities are limited to the specific goals of the relationship. A lawyer, for example, has responsibility for the client's legal affairs (or some of them), an accountant for his financial affairs, etc. Every beneficiary will have many interests which are external to the responsibilities of the fiduciary. This is not to say that these other interests might not impinge on the content of that relationship, but only that since the relationship was established for certain purposes relative to the specific competencies of the professional, the professional's responsibilities stop at the edges of these purposes.

If I seek legal assistance, it is because I want my legal interests to be protected; I do not expect my lawyer to take responsibility for my emotional stability, the strength of my marriage, how I use my leisure time, etc., though of course these other interests of mine might be affected by my legal condition. Where my legal interests conflict with some of my other interests, it is up to me, not my lawyer, to make the necessary choices. Those who expect their lawyer or doctor to look after a broad range of their interests, perhaps even their total welfare, obviously do not have a fiduciary conception of the professional relationship; they think of the professional as priest, friend, or some similarly broad model.

Since a fiduciary relationship is limited by specific defining goals, it is not a contractual relationship, although a legal contract may be the instrument that binds the relationship. A contractual relationship is more open, in that the parties may write anything they please into the contract. The responsibilities of the professional are exactly those stated in the contract, neither more nor less. In a contractual relationship, the professional's decisions will be guided by his interpretation of what the contract requires. Thus if a doctor believes he has agreed with the patient to do everything possible to restore the patient's health and preserve the patient's life, he will take one course of action. If, however, he believes he has also agreed to protect the patient's family from prolonged worry and exhaustion of resources, though these are not strictly speaking medical goals, he may well do or recommend something else.

Now in addition to one's interests in health, financial condition, etc., a person has moral interests. I have an interest not to be lied to, not to be manipulated, not to be treated with contempt. There is no theoretical reason why these moral interests could not conflict with other interests such as health. But since under the fiduciary conception a professional's responsibility is to foster only those interests which define the relationship, the professional is not obligated to foster the client's moral interests. Normally, of course, there will not be a conflict, and no doubt in certain professions, such as law, opportunity for conflict is small. But such conflicts do arise in the practice of medicine (the Childress example is a clear case). The fiduciary conception imposes no professional obligation on the doctor to be concerned with these interests. This is not to say that a doctor ought not to be concerned with such interests. But if he should be, this is either because the doctor–patient relationship ought not to be construed as fiduciary, or because under certain circumstances, the commands of ordinary morality ought to override the commands of medical ethics.

Since a patient's interest in not being deceived is a moral interest and not a health interest, the doctor–patient relationship, construed as fiduciary, does not even prima facie exclude deception. To argue that it does, is to construe the relationship as priestly, friendly, contractual or something else. One could hold that if general moral obligations take precedence over professional obligations, the doctor has a general moral obligation not to deceive, even if he has no such professional obligation. That general moral obligations take precedence over professional obligations is a proposition many professionals would dispute, however; lawyers for example will argue that their general moral obligation not to harm or pain innocent people is overridden by their professional obligation to do everything possible to protect their client's legal interests.[7]

It may seem to follow from this that doctors also have no obligation to avoid actual lying when, in their best judgment, a patient's health might be injured were he to learn some truth. To see why this is not the case we have to distinguish between the obligations *of* the doctor–patient relationship, and the obligations which make the relationship possible. In a fiduciary relationship, the only obligation *of* the relationship is to do whatever is necessary to further the goals by which the relationship is defined. But it might be the case that the relationship could not be established unless other obligations were respected. If this is the case, it follows that obligations which make the relationship possible override, in cases of conflict, obligations *of* the relationship, since the latter could not exist without the former (if the relationship is not established, then neither are any of its obligations). Hence, if the obligation not to lie is an obligation which makes the relationship possible, it follows that this obligation overrides even the obligation to protect health, and is thus an absolute.

The argument that lying destroys the doctor–patient relationship, conceived as fiduciary, is partly a conceptual argument, partly an argument based on judgment and experience. It is often said that the doctor–patient relationship depends heavily on trust. The patient puts himself (often literally) in the hands of his doctor. Although this could be true to an extent of any interpretation of the relationship, it is less true of some interpretations than others. Contracts, for example, do not depend on trust so much as on an understanding of mutual self-interest; a contractual relationship succeeds when each party understands that it is not in either party's best interest to violate the contract. Even the priest or friend roles do not require trust as their foundation, though they do generate trust. A priest is someone who has a special calling or vocation; his entire life is dedicated to an ideal of service. We trust him because his life witnesses his trustworthiness.[8] A friendship relation is based on personal satisfactions and mutual compatibility; these generate trust but do not rest on it. It is the fiduciary relationship which depends heavily on trust. A fiduciary must be trusted to act with the true interests of the beneficiary in view; the law recognizes this by defining trust as "a fiduciary relationship."[9] If, however, we were to allow the fiduciary to lie, the trust basis of the relationship would be undermined and the relationship itself jeopardized. A lie, it will be recalled, violates a kind of implicit assurance we give when we speak, namely, that our words will be used to state the truth. Deception through evasive or misleading statements which are nonetheless true, does not violate such an assurance but accords with it. The deceiver can thus be trusted at least to speak the truth, while the liar violates the very assurance he is giving with his speech. ... I maintain that the tendency of lying to destroy trust is considerably greater than the tendency of deception to destroy trust, and this I argue partly on the basis of the conceptual difference between lying and deception, partly on the basis of experience. Lying is more destructive to trust than deception because lying is a greater violation of the social contract. The liar by his false speech violates the very promise that he makes in speaking, the promise to speak the truth. And it is for this reason, as I think experience reveals, that we find ourselves less trusting of someone who has lied to us, than of someone who has misled us or created a false impression.

Given this threat to trust, it seems plausible to hold that lying is too dangerous ever to be allowed in a relationship founded on trust. Suppose we adopted a rule which made lying only prima facie wrong, and thus permitted lying in certain very serious cases. The patient would know that the doctor could not be trusted to tell the truth, even in response to a direct question, when the doctor deemed it unwise to do so; and therefore the patient would know that the doctor could never be believed, since even an apparently trivial matter might in fact be serious enough for the doctor to feel justified in lying about. Of course the fact that the patient would know this does not necessarily mean that the patient would not trust the doctor anyway. But a patient who has been lied to has been given very strong grounds to conclude that the doctor is not to be trusted, so that even a single justified lie is likely to undermine the patient's trust.

Let us test the prohibition of lying against a case where our intuitions seem to lead us to the opposite conclusion. Gert and Culver give the following case: "Mrs. E is in extremely critical condition after an automobile accident which has taken the life of one of her four children and severely injured another. Dr. P believes that her very tenuous hold on life might be weakened by the shock of hearing of her children's conditions, so he decides to deceive her for a short period of time."[10] According to these authors, a rational person would choose to be deceived in such circumstances, so there is nothing wrong with the doctor's decision to deceive her. As is typical of the medical ethics literature, the authors do not distinguish between lying and deception. On our principles, there is nothing even prima facie wrong with the doctor's use of evasive or misleading statements to conceal the truth. But suppose Mrs. E demands a straight answer from which evasion offers no escape. Gert and Culver seem to propose that the question to be answered is whether a rational person would want to be lied to in these circumstances, but as there does not seem to be any way to arrive at an answer to this question, their proposal does not really advance beyond our intuitions. In this case, our intuitions strongly suggest that lying would be justified in order to protect the woman's health, but on the principles advanced in this essay, lying is not permitted, since if Dr. P lies in response to Mrs. E's direct question, she will eventually discover that he cannot be trusted, and that therefore they cannot enjoy a relationship based on trust. Of course this is not to say that the doctor must tell her the truth in the bluntest or most painful way, but only that he must not lie. Where a harmful truth cannot be concealed, it is up to the doctor to reveal it in a way least damaging to the patient. To take a different view is to hold that the doctor–patient relationship is not a fiduciary relationship based on trust, but something else, friendship perhaps, or maybe some form of paternalism, in which the doctor has the responsibility of balancing all of the patient's interests and making decisions in light of his conception of the patient's total welfare. If, however, these conceptions of the relationship seem unattractive to us (and I have not argued that they should seem unattractive) we will have to take the view, intuitions to the contrary notwithstanding, that even in the situation just described, the doctor's duty is to tell the truth.

Notes

[1]Robert Veatch, *Case Studies in Medical Ethics* (Cambridge: Harvard University Press, 1977), pp. 147f.

[2]I found this example in an unpublished paper by James Rachels, "Honesty." Rachels evidently borrowed it from P. T. Geach. *The Virtues* (Cambridge: Cambridge University Press, 1977), p. 115.

[3]Marcia Millman. *The Unkindest Cut* (New York: William Morrow and Co., 1977), pp. 138f.

[4]James Childress. "Paternalism and Health Care." in *Medical Responsibility*, ed. Wade L. Robison and Michael S. Pritchard (New York: Humana Press, 1979), pp. 15–27.

[5]Sissela Bok, *Lying* (New York: Pantheon Books, 1978), Ch. 2.

[6]Immanuel Kant. *Lectures on Ethics*, trans. Louis Infeld (New York: Harper and Row, 1963), pp. 147–154.

[7]The contention that, as a general rule, professional obligations override ordinary moral obligations, is critically examined and disputed by Alan H. Goldman. *The Moral Foundations of Professional Ethics* (Totowa. N.J.: Littlefield, Adams and Co., 1980).

[8]On the idea of medicine as a calling founded on "covenant" which transforms the doctor, see William F. May, "Code, Covenant, Contract or Philanthropy," *Hastings Center Report* 5, 6 (December, 1975):pp. 29–38.

[9]"Trust. Noun: a fiduciary relationship; a matter of confidence." *Ballantine's Law Dictionary*, 3rd ed.

[10]Bernard Gert and Charles Culver, "The Justification of Paternalism" in Robison and Pritchard, *Medical Responsibility*, p. 7.

7

GENETICS
AND
MEDICINE

Infectious diseases are caused by germs, but some people seem to have more immunity to infectious diseases than others. Stress seems to be a cause of duodenal ulcers, but some people seem better at handling stress than others. Emergency rooms often deal with victims of trauma. Usually, accidents just happen to people. But some people just seem to fare better than others; they have stronger constitutions. Germs, stress, and accidents appear to be countered to some extent by certain inborn characteristics, namely our hereditary makeup. Unfortunately, it is also true that there are many diseases that are caused by our inherited genetic tendencies. The more we look into genetics, the more of a role we find that our genes play. It is not that they are the final determinants of what we are, but rather that they are too important for medicine to ignore. Therefore, medicine has turned to human genetics for a fuller understanding of health and disease. Genetic counseling, screening, and engineering are becoming increasingly integrated into the practice of medicine.

Genetic Counseling

The following cases may typically be seen by a genetic counselor.

A 22-year-old woman in the 14th week of pregnancy asks for counseling because she has a mentally retarded brother.

A couple in their early 30's seeks counseling because their first child had Down's syndrome.

A newly engaged couple seeks counseling because one of them has a brother with cystic fibrosis.

A couple has been referred to a genetic counselor by their pediatrician because their newborn son does not look quite normal, nor is he developing at a normal rate. If there is an underlying problem, is it genetic?

A young man wants to know if his skeletal and muscular problems are a form of muscular dystrophy, which is genetic.

A genetic counselor has three main tasks.

1. To determine if there is a medical problem at all.
2. To determine if the problem, when it does exist, has a genetic component, and if so, its mode of inheritance. In practical terms, what are the chances of reoccurrence?
3. To relay this information to the parents or patients in an understandable manner so that free and informed decisions can be made.

The tradition in genetic counseling has always been to counsel in a nondirective, value-free manner. In this, it has differed from much of clinical medicine, where, until fairly recently, physicians tended to tell patients what they ought to do. There is a reason for this difference.

Part of the reason has to do with the history of genetics. Genetics was misused by supporters of the Restrictive Immigration Act of 1924. Some argued that genetics showed that the current immigrants seeking admission to the United States were genetically inferior to previous immigrants. The Nazi regime used genetics to support their view that there was a master race. Thus, human genetics seemed a politically explosive discipline. The details of this part of the history of genetics are given by Mark Haller's book, *Eugenics*. (See the bibliography at the end of the book.) We shall now stress another reason.

Much of medicine deals with the desire to be free of diseases, conditions no truly rational person would want, except under very special circumstances. For example, some people might prefer an attack of the flu to having to take a calculus exam. When we speak of a genetic disease, we mean some condition, which no rational person would want except under special circumstances, that is caused by a genetic defect. (Genetic defects include chromosomal aberrations either in structure or number, as well as genes that are mutations. Conditions caused by the resultant effect of many genes are called polygenic. Still other conditions are caused by a combination of genetic and environmental factors, and are referred to as multifactorial.)

Obviously, not every variation from the average that has a genetic cause is a genetic disease. Nor does every genetic defect result in a disease as we have characterized disease. Indeed, some variations from average—the grace of Nureyev, the talent of Mozart—are very much worthwhile. Genes may contribute to the abilities of dancers and composers, but these abilities can hardly be considered genetic diseases. We value ballet and music.

We do not value cancer, ulcers, arthritis, influenza, or broken limbs. There are paradigms of generally unwanted conditions. They come about as close as anything can to being intrinsically bad. They are worth eradicating. Certainly it would be difficult to argue that the world would *not* be a better place if cancer, along with the other members on the list, were eliminated.

Many genetic diseases do not easily fit on our list of intrinsically bad things. Hemophilia is treatable. Many children with Down's syndrome lead happy and fulfilled lives. The outlook for cystic fibrosis is improving. Physical therapy is able to do more and more, as are medicine and surgery in general. There is no reason to think that the advances will stop.

What this points to is that the directive counselor who suggests that a parent ought not to have children because of genetic reasons may very well be espousing more than the physician who assumes that patients want their cancers eliminated. In genetic cases there is much more social philosophy involved. It is to avoid contaminating medical information with social philosophy that genetic counselors have tended to the nondirective side of counseling.

The problem with nondirective counseling is that it assumes that the facts speak for themselves. It assumes that when the facts are clearly presented the people involved will be able to make what they feel is a correct decision. But, as any genetic counselor knows, this is an oversimplification. It is difficult to present information in a manner that does not reveal personal biases. It is difficult to present complex information to people to whom the information represents the worst of dashed dreams. Moreover, for whatever the reason, it is the rare patient who does not at least ask, "What should I do?" or "What would you do, if you were in my position?"

There are clever techniques for deflecting such questions. In essence, however, they seem artificial, sometimes almost dishonest. They seem to take the "counselor" out of "genetic counselor."

Genetic Screening

Genetic screening is a procedure used to identify those with, or at risk of, genetic disease. Screening can also identify carriers of a genetic condition, even if they will never manifest the condition themselves. Genetic screening is usually done on a large scale: All newborns in the United States are screened for phenylketonuria (PKU). Jews can be screened for Tay-Sachs disease; blacks for sickle-cell anemia; pregnant women over 35 for fetuses with Down's syndrome. Screening in general is aimed at groups known to be at high risk for specific conditions.

It is generally agreed that screening programs should

1. Observe confidentiality
2. Offer high-quality counseling
3. Offer some therapeutic gain, as opposed to being pure research
4. Be accurate
5. Be inexpensive and cost effective.

Screening makes counseling efficient. It is much easier on the counselor when the presumptive diagnosis has, in effect, already been made by the elimination process of screening. It is much easier on the people involved to be assured that there is less chance of error. It is clear that values play a role in screening. We will not screen for conditions unless we want to give people a chance to get rid of them, through (2) and (3) of the list. Put another way: When we screen, we imply that these conditions are worth eliminating.

Let us take an example. Neural tube defects (multifactorial) are the result of improper closing of the spinal cord during fetal development. Defects range from barely noticeable to spina bifida with hydrocephaly. It has been possible for some time to screen all pregnant women for neural tube defects. The screening procedure, had it been implemented, would have been relatively inexpensive and would have offered therapeutic gain; that is, abortion would have been an option offered to women carrying affected fetuses. Two considerable problems arose with the screening program: The accuracy of the testing would have been very difficult to monitor, and every obstetrician would have had to have learned how to counsel women about the nature of the test and about neural tube defects. Because these requirements were felt to be unrealistic, large-scale screening was never undertaken. (Many obstetricians feared legal action as a result of what some patients might have perceived as poor counseling.)

A more successful screening involves Down's syndrome. Because of the prevalence of Down's syndrome in pregnant women over 35, offering prenatal diagnosis of this condition is considered the standard of care. Suppose that a pregnant woman discovers that her fetus has Down's syndrome. Her counseling will consist at least of being informed of the facts about Down's syndrome and the quality of life of the average child with Down's syndrome. She might also get some information about how raising a retarded child may affect other members of the household. She may be interested in costs associated with a Down's child. Her options are to have the child or to abort the fetus. In this context, abortion is often called selective abortion. Whatever moral problems are associated with abortion are also to be found here.

Notice that screening with the option of selective abortion can give the appearance of a policy or program of elimination. After all, a condition is targeted for the screening. Suppose your younger brother had Down's syndrome or spina bifida. How would you feel about a program that might seem dedicated to the elimination of children like your brother? Don't these programs carry with them the implication that children like your brother aren't really worth very much? Moreover, as noted earlier, screening programs tend to focus on particular groups at high risk for certain conditions. It is to avoid any appearance of bias toward a particular group that genetic counseling continues to be as nondirective as interpersonal relations allow.

Genetic Engineering

If genetic disease is treated only symptomatically, then no matter how much pain and suffering is alleviated in the present or near future, the genetic conditions that are the underlying cause of the disease will be untouched. Attempts to change the actual genetic material or to affect gene frequencies in the population are considered genetic engineering. Changes can be effected through genetic counseling and choices not to procreate, or through new techniques of gene therapy, in which defective genes are changed to normal genes. Recombinant DNA techniques that allow for the creation of new sorts of microorganisms or new kinds of frost-resistant fruits or vegetables are also the results of genetic engineering. Here we shall focus on the uses of genetic techniques in humans.

Two techniques of importance are artificial insemination and in vitro fertilization. Artificial insemination introduces sperm from husband or donor directly to the woman. In vitro fertilization is much newer and more advanced technologically than artificial insemination, which is a very old technique. Briefly, with in vitro fertilization, eggs are extracted from the ovary of a woman, mixed with sperm, fertilized, and then implanted either in the woman's uterus for the rest of the gestation or in the uterus of a willing surrogate mother. Notice that there are some possible further variations. The sperm can be from the husband, a specific donor, or an anonymous donor. The eggs can be from the woman who will gestate the fetus or from another woman.

There is no question that these methods provide solutions that help satisfy some of our most deeply felt desires, but they do so only at some cost. Not all the fertilized eggs used with the in vitro technique develop. Some people consider each fertilized egg lost a life destroyed. Even those who see this as too strong a claim argue that dealing with fertilized human eggs as though they were just things to be flushed if not usable works to cheapen our view of life. Moreover, legal and moral problems arise if surrogate mothers refuse to give up the children they have borne (as in the case of *Baby M*). Also, not all husbands react favorably to having their wives inseminated with the sperm of other men.

One asks where these methods might lead in a social context. Will such fertilizations and pregnancies become the norm? If so, what will happen to the institutions of marriage and family as we now know them? Perhaps having such a strong desire to pass on one's genes that one would resort to these techniques is a sign of psychological problems. Perhaps these problems will later be manifested in poor parenting.

Are we contradicting what some have called the wisdom of evolution? Evolution has made it impossible for some women to have children naturally. We are circumventing evolution. Will there be a price to pay sometime in the future? What exactly is the force of the word *natural*?

Why do we treat the inability to have a child as if it were a medical condition? Isn't it just the luck of the draw? Is every keenly felt desire worth medical treatment? Perhaps we feel that the desire to have children of one's own is among the most worthwhile of all desires. Surely, what is operating here is a philosophy of life, which should not be surprising, since medicine treats our most human needs.

A Use for Genetics?

H. J. Muller was awarded the 1946 Nobel Prize in Medicine and Physiology for his 1927 work in genetics. Muller was a very politically minded scientist. He always felt that science ought to be the conscience of humankind. He believed that geneticists, medical geneticists, and physicians were obligated to oversee the long-term well-being of the human race. His background in biology, much of which centered around genetics and evolution, convinced him that there was a sense in which medicine was running down the quality of the gene pool.

Muller noted that before great advances were made by medicine, many people with chronic and debilitating illnesses did not have children. They were not attractive marriage candidates, and often died at an early age. As medicine advanced, these people were kept alive and well enough to marry and work. They had children, many of whom had the genetic defects that were in part responsible for their own illnesses. Even if the illnesses were not present, the genetic defects were. Ultimately, Muller feared, these illnesses and constitutional weaknesses would show up, all at once, creating a tremendous drain on society. They might even signal the end of society. He suggested eugenic programs as a remedy.

Instead of playing what he liked to call the irrational game of seminal roulette, Muller advocated using only the best sperm and egg available. By *best* Muller meant more than just *healthy*. He meant from the best intellects society had to offer. Clearly, Muller had a social philosophy, a picture of a society worth striving for, and some beliefs about what in fact was controlled by genetics. Muller made these claims despite the fact that no one knows how much of intelligence is based on genetics and how much is produced by environmental influences. Indeed, it is not clear just what intelligence might mean. But even if we were to decide on a definition for intelligence and to discover that a good portion of it is genetically controlled, nothing about social policy would follow without further assumptions about what is worth having and what is worth doing to get what one wants.

Muller would certainly have been a directive genetic counselor. He would have tried to instill in his patients a desire to act as stewards for the future gene pool of society.

GENETIC PROGRESS
BY
VOLUNTARILY CONDUCTED GERMINAL CHOICE

Hermann J. Muller

The Negative Feedback Established by Modern Culture

Modern technologies and social organization, working in combination, have altered the manner of operation of selection much more drastically than this in those typical industrial societies in which the increase in the means of subsistence has been greater than the increase in the size of population. Not only is there in these societies an ever more rapid disappearance of that genetic isolation between small groups which underlies natural selection for truly social propensities; there is also a disappearance of the circumstances that have favored the survival and multiplication of individuals genetically better fitted to cope with difficulties and that, conversely, have led to the dying out of lines deficient in these faculties. For society now comes effectively to the aid of those who for whatever reason, environmental or genetic, are physically, mentally, or morally weaker than the aver-

Source: "Genetic Progress by Voluntarily Conducted Germinal Choice" by Hermann J. Muller, in *Man and his Future*, Gordon Wolstenholme, ed. (Boston: Little and Brown, 1963) pp. 247–62. Used by permission of Little, Brown and Co. and Churchill Livingstone Medical Division of Longman Group UK Limited. All rights reserved.

age. True, this aid does not at present afford these people a really good life, but it does usually succeed in saving them and their children up to and beyond the age of reproduction.

It is probable that some 20 per cent, if not more, of a human population has received a genetic impairment that arose by mutation in the immediately preceding generation, in addition to the far larger number of impairments inherited from earlier generations. If this is true, then, to avoid genetic deterioration, about 20 per cent of the population who are more heavily laden with genetic defects than the average must in each generation fail to live until maturity or, if they do live, must fail to reproduce. Otherwise, the load of genetic defects carried by that population would inevitably rise. Moreover, besides deaths occasioned by circumstances in which mutant genes play a critical rôle, there is always a large contingent of deaths resulting from environmental circumstances. Consequently, the number of individuals who fail to "carry along" must considerably exceed 20 per cent, if genetic equilibrium is to be maintained, and *merely* maintained. Yet among us today, in industrialized countries, the proportion of those born who fail to reach maturity has fallen to a small percentage, thanks to our present high standards of medicine and of living in general. This situation would, other things being equal, spell genetic deterioration, at a roughly calculable rate.

However, it has sometimes been surmised that the present excess of genetically defective adults—those whose lives have been saved by modern techniques—may somehow be screened out, after maturity, through the automatic operation of an increased amount of reproductive selection, in that these additional defectives (or an equivalent excess of others) fail to have offspring. However, it would be wishful thinking to suppose this to be the case. There is no evidence of an over-all positive correlation today between effective reproductive rate and soundness of body, mind, or temperament, aside from cases of extreme defect too rare to influence the trend to an important extent.

On the contrary, negative partial correlations have repeatedly been found between reproductive rate, on the one hand, and the rank of the parents in such social classifications as economic status or education, on the other hand. This has been the case not only in the Western world but even in the U.S.S.R. Now educational and economic status, although certainly not genetic categories, do have important genetic contingents, especially in societies not having very rigorous class divisions. Moreover, it is hardly credible that the factors that give rise to the observed negative correlations would be able to distinguish between the differences that depend on environmental influences and those that depend on genes, so as to allow the environmental differences but not the genetic ones to be responsible for all of the negative correlations found. We therefore return to the con-

clusion that genetically based ability and reproductive rate are today nega-
tively correlated. . . .

The Human Genetic Predicament

This is an ironical situation. Cultural evolution has at long last given rise
to science and its technologies. It has thereby endowed itself with powers
that—according to the manner in which they are used—could either wreck
the human enterprise or carry it upward to unprecedented heights of being
and of doing. To steer his course under these circumstances man will need
his greatest collective wisdom, humanity, will to cooperate, and self-control.
Moreover, he cannot muster these faculties in sufficient measure collec-
tively unless he also possesses them in considerable measure individually.
Yet in this very epoch cultural evolution has undermined the process of
genetic selection in man, a process whose active continuance is necessary
for the mere maintenance of man's faculties at their present none-too-
adequate level. What we need instead, at this juncture, is a means of *enhanc-
ing* genetic selection.

True, there are specialists who believe that equivalent or even better
results than selection could provide may be obtained by direct mutagenic
operations on the genetic material. In addition, some of them think that
much could be done by modifying development and physiology, and by
supplying much more sophisticated, more or less built-in, artificial aids.
Others, disgusted with the limitations and the patchwork constitution of all
natural organisms, boldly say that completely artificial contrivances can
and should be built to replace mankind.[6]

Let all these enthusiasts try their tricks, the more the merrier. But I
find myself a conservative on this issue. It seems to me that for a long time
yet to come (in terms of the temporal scale of human history thus far), man
at his present best is unlikely to be excelled, according to any of man's own
accepted value systems, by pure artifacts. And although artificial aids
should become ever better developed, and integrated as harmoniously as
possible with the human organism, it is more economical in the end to have
developmental and physiological improvements of the organism placed on
a genetic basis, where practicable, than to have to institute them in every
generation anew by elaborate treatments of the soma.

Finally, as regards changes in the genetic constitution (genotype) itself,
there is certainly enormous room for improvement. However, the genetic
material of man is so transcendently complex in its make-up and workings
that for some centuries, at least, we should be able to make genetic progress
on a wider front, with better balance, and more rapidly, by selecting among
the genotypes already on hand, whose physical (phenotypic) expressions

have been observed, than by intervening with what I call nano-needles to cause pre-specified changes in them. At any rate, we will be much more likely some day to attain such finesse if we are forthright enough to make use, in the meantime, of the cruder methods that are available at present.

Man as a whole must rise to become worthy of his own best achievements. Unless the average man can understand and appreciate the world that scientists have discovered, unless he can learn to comprehend the techniques he now uses, and their remote and larger effects, unless he can enter into the thrill of being a conscious participant in the great human enterprise and find genuine fulfillment in playing a constructive part in it, he will fall into the position of an ever less important cog in a vast machine. In this situation, his own powers of determining his fate and his very will to do so will dwindle, and the minority who rule over him will eventually find ways of doing without him. Democratic control, therefore, implies an upgrading of the people in general in both their intellectual and social faculties, together with a maintenance or, preferably, an improvement in their bodily condition.

Proposed Ways Out of the Predicament

Most eugenists of the old school believed they could educate the population so as to lead the better endowed to have larger than average families and the more poorly endowed to have smaller ones. However, people are notoriously unrealistic in assessing themselves and their spouses. Moreover, the determination of the size of a family is, as we have seen, subject to strong influences that tend to run counter to the desiderata of eugenics. In view of this social naïveté on the part of the eugenists in general, as well as the offensively reactionary attitude flaunted by that vociferous group of eugenists who were actuated by race and class prejudices, it is not surprising that some three-quarters of a century of old-style eugenics propaganda has resulted in so little actual practice of eugenic principles by people in general.

It is true that heredity clinics have recently made some headway and are in themselves highly commendable. However, the matter of choice of marriage partners, with which they concern themselves so much, has little relation to the eugenically crucial matter of gene frequencies. And so far as their advice concerning size of family is concerned, it is for the most part confined to considerations arising from the presence of a gene for some rare abnormality. For any individual case such a matter is of grave importance. Yet for the eugenic pattern as a whole the sum of all such cases is insignificant in relation to the major task of achieving a high correlation between the over-all genetic endowment and the rate of reproduction. However, counsellors would understandably hesitate to be so cavalier as to assign people over-all ratings of so comprehensive a nature, and if they did so their advice would probably be resented and rejected.

Similarly, the public in a democratic society would probably be unwilling to adopt social or economic rearrangements that were known to have as their purpose the encouragement of large families on the part of certain occupational groups, whose members were considered eugenically more desirable, and the making of reproduction less attractive for other occupational groups, considered genetically inferior. Moreover, the public's objections to the introduction of such programs would probably remain even if the people concerned were allowed the deciding voice in their choice of occupation.

Perhaps such considerations as these have played a part in leading Dr. P. B. Medawar[7] and some others to conclude that consciously directed genetic change in man could only be carried out under a dictatorship, as was attempted by Hitler. As they realize, a dictatorship, though it might hoodwink, cajole and compel its subjects into participation in its program, would try to create a servile population uncomplainingly conforming to their rulers' whims. That would constitute an evolutionary emergency much more immediate and ominous than any gradual degeneration occasioned by a negative cultural feedback.

If all these proposed means of escaping our genetic predicament are impracticable, insufficiently effective, or even positively vicious, what other recourse is available for us? To consider this problem we must rid ourselves of preconceptions based on our traditional behavior in matters of parentage, and open our minds to the new possibilities afforded by our scientific knowledge and techniques. We shall then see that our progress along certain biological lines has won for us the means of overcoming the negative feedback with which we are here concerned. We can do so by bringing our influence to bear not on the number of children in a family but on their genetic composition.

The method that first brought this possibility into view is of course that of artificial insemination with semen derived from a donor, "AID". Unlike what occurs in the usual practice of AID, however, the germinal material here is to be chosen and applied primarily with a view to its eugenic potentialities. Preferably it should be selected from among banks of germ cells that have been subjected to long-term preservation (see, for example, reference 2, 4b, 4c, 5, 8, 9).

It was long ago found that human semen will recover from freezing, even from deep-freezing, and that in the latter state it can probably be preserved indefinitely. Glycerol and other additives have been found by Drs. Polge, Parkes, Sherman and others to aid the process. Such preservation will allow the accumulation of larger, more diverse stores, their better appraisal, and the fading away of some of the personal biases and entanglements that might be associated with the donors. At first sight the most unrealistic of the proposals made, this method of *eutelegenesis* or *germinal choice*, turns out on closer inspection to be the most practical, effective, and satisfying means of genetic therapy. This is especially true, the more reliable and foolproof the means of preventing conception are.

The Advantages of Germinal Choice

The Western world is a chrysalis that still carries, over its anterior portion at least, a Victorian-looking shell, but wings can be discerned lying latent beneath the surface. Despite the protests of some representatives of traditional ways and doctrines, a little searching shows that a considerable section of the educated public, including outstanding leaders in law, religion, medicine, science and education, is prepared to take a sympathetic interest in the possibilities of germinal choice. As for the public at large, that of the United States, which has on the whole been more bound than that of Europe to old-fashioned ways, is now taking in its stride the practice of AID for the purpose of circumventing a husband's sterility. In fact, it is estimated[10] that five to ten thousand American children per year are now being engendered in this way, and the number is growing rapidly. In addition, an increasing number of couples are applying for AID in cases where the husband carries or has a strong chance of carrying some grave genetic defect, or some constitutional trait (of an antigenic nature, for instance) that may be incompatible with a trait of his wife's. Moreover, a few of the practitioners of AID are already making it a point to utilize, where feasible, germinal material from donors of outstanding ability and vigor, persons whose genuine merits have been indicated in the trials of life. Studies of the family life in AID cases have shown it to be, in general, unusually well adjusted.

When to these developments we add the fact that several banks of frozen human semen are even now in operation, in widely separated localities, we see that a thin line of stepping stones, extending most of the way to germinal choice itself, has already been laid down. It is but a short step in motivation from the couple who wish to turn their genetic defect to their credit by having, instead, an especially promising child, to the couple who, even though they are by no means subnormal, are idealistic enough to *prefer* to give their child as favorable a genetic prospect as can be obtained for it. There are already persons who would gladly utilize such opportunities for their families. These are persons who, as my friend Calvin Kline has put the matter, take more pride in what they can purposively create with their brains and hands than in what they more or less reflexly produce with their loins, and who regard their contribution to the good of their children and of humanity in general as more important than the multiplication of their own particular genetic idiosyncracies. Once these pioneers have been given the opportunity to realize their aspirations, and to do so without subterfuge, their living creations of the next generation will constitute a sufficient

demonstration of the worth of the procedure, both for the children themselves, for their parents, and for the community at large.

There are, however, several requirements still to be met before germinal choice can be undertaken on even a pilot scale. A choice is not a real
one unless it is a multiple choice, one carried out with maximum foreknowl-
edge of the possibilities entailed, and hampered as little as possible by irrational restrictions and by direct personal involvements. Moreover, to
keep as far away as possible from dictation, the final decision regarding the
selection to be made should be the prerogative of the couple concerned.
These conditions can be well fulfilled only after plentiful banks of germinal
material have been established, representing those who have proved to be
most outstanding in regard to valuable characteristics of mind, heart, and
body. In addition, such storage for a person's own germ cells should be a
service supplied at cost to anyone wishing it. Catalogued records should
be maintained, giving the results of diverse physical and mental tests and
observations of all the donors, together with relevant facts about their lives,
and about their relatives.

The couple making a choice should have access to these records and
the benefit of advice from physicians, psychologists, geneticists, and specialists in the fields in which the donors had engaged. The germinal material
used should preferably have been preserved for at least twenty years. Such
an undertaking by a couple would assume the character of an eminently
moral act, a social service that was in itself rewarding, and the couple who
engaged in it would be proud of it and would not wish to conceal it.

We have not here touched upon any of the more technical genetic
matters that would ultimately be involved in human betterment, because at
this stage the important task is to achieve the change in *mores* that will make
possible the first empirical steps. When the choices are not imposed but
voluntary and democratic, the sound values common to humanity nearly
everywhere[4b] are bound to exert the predominant influence in guiding the
directions of choice. Practically all peoples venerate creativity, wisdom,
brotherliness, loving-kindness, perceptivity, expressivity, joy of life, forti-
tude, vigor, longevity. If presented with the opportunity to have their children approach nearer to such goals than they could do themselves, they
will not turn down this golden chance, and the next generation, thus benefited, will be able to choose better than they did. The broadness of the base
constituted by the population of choosers themselves will ensure that they
also perpetuate a multitude of special faculties of mind and body, which
they severally regard especially highly. This will promote a salutary diversity.

Undoubtedly further techniques are in the offing that will radically
extend the possibilities of germinal choice. Among these are, perhaps, the
storage of eggs. Still more important is the working out of methods for
obtaining normal development of germ cells outside the body, using imma-
ture germ cells a supply of which can be stored in deep-feeze, to be tapped

and multiplied at will. Clonal reproduction, as by the transfer of unreduced nuclei to eggs, would be another milestone.[11] Beyond all that are of course more delicate methods of manipulating the genetic material itself—what I have termed the use of nano-needles. Yet long before that we must do what we can. One could begin by laying up plentiful stores of germ cells for the future. Their mere existence will finally result in an irresistible incentive to use them. Man is already so marvellous that he deserves all our efforts to improve him further.

Summary

Modern civilization has instituted a negative feedback from cultural progress to genetic progress. This works by preventing the genetic isolation of small groups, by saving increasing numbers of the genetically defective, and by leading the better endowed to engage more sedulously than others in reproductive restraint. Yet the increasing complications, dangers, and opportunities of civilization call for democratic control, based on higher, more widespread intelligence and cooperative propensities.

The social devices and the individual persuasion regarding family size advocated by old-style eugenics are inadequate to meet this situation, except in extreme cases of specific defects. For the major problem, concerned with quantitative characters, the more effective method and that ultimately more acceptable psychologically is germinal choice (Brewer's *eutelegenesis*). Artificial insemination, now used for circumventing sterility, can, by becoming more eugenically oriented, lay a foundation for this reform. For this purpose it must become increasingly applied in cases of genetic defect, genetic incompatibility, suspected mutagenesis, postponed reproduction, and finally, in serving the ardent aspiration to confer on one's children a highly superior genetic endowment.

For realizing these possibilities extensive germ-cell banks must be instituted, including material from outstanding sources, with full documentation regarding the donors and their relatives. Both lengthy storage and donor distinction will promote the necessary openness and voluntariness of choice, and aid the counselling. The idealistic vanguard, and those following them, will foster sound genetic progress by their general agreement on the overriding values of health, intelligence, and brotherliness. Their different attitudes regarding specialized proclivities will foster salutary diversities.

Bibliography and Notes

[1]Dobzhansky, T. (1962). *Mankind Evolving: The Evolution of the Human Species.* New Haven and London: Yale University Press.

[2]Huxley, J. S. (1940). *The Uniqueness of Man.* London: Chatto & Windus.

[3]Huxley, J. S. (1943). *Evolutionary Ethics.* London: Oxford University Press.

[4]Tax, S. (ed.). (1960). *Evolution after Darwin:* (1) **1,** Evolution of Life, (b) **2,** Evolution of Man, (c) **3,** Issues in Evolution. Chicago: University of Chicago Press.

[5]Muller, H. J. (1935). *Out of the Night: A Biologist's View of the Future.* New York: Vanguard Press. (Fr. trans. J. Rostand, Paris: Guillemard, 1938).

[6]Clarke, A. C. (1961). *Industrial Research* 3, No. 5, 30.

[7]Medawar, P. B. (1960). *The Future of Man.* New York: Basic Books.

[8]Huxley, J. S. (1962). *Eugenics in Evolutionary Perspective.* London: Eugenics Society.

[9]Hoagland, H., and Burhoe, R. W. (eds.). (1962). *Evolution and Man's Progress.* New York and London: Columbia University Press.

[10]Guttmacher, A. F. (1961). *Babies by Choice or by Chance.* New York: Avon Books.

[11]Rostand, J. (1959). *Can Man Be Modified?* New York: Basic Books, Inc.

Directive and Nondirective Counseling

The two articles on genetic counseling that follow differ as dramatically as the medical literature allows. One is a standard general account of genetic counseling; the other is a very nontraditional account.

In a general survey of genetic counseling in 1975, A. E. H. Emery reiterates the nondirective philosophy of genetic counseling: Patients should be helped to reach an informed decision; nothing else. He stresses the need to expunge feelings of guilt that parents of an affected child usually have, thereby showing sensitivity to the belief that a physician has an obligation to treat more than just physical conditions. Where there is suffering, it must not be ignored. Despite the fact that genetic screening is the only way to use counseling to affect large populations, Emery emphasizes the fact that the counselor's main role should be that of helping individual families. Thus he has no problem treating genetic disease symptomatically.

On the other hand, Phillips, Newton, and Gosden argue in "Procreative Instinct as a Contributory Factor to Prevalence of Hereditary Blindness" that many blind families are making inappropriate decisions regarding having children. The authors feel that these blind parents are bringing more blind children into the world, a situation the authors feel is unfair to society at large and to the children themselves. They say that while they are still nondirective, they have taken to persuasive counseling. They put the word persuasive in scare quotes as a warning that they are using the word in a special way. But they never say what that way is. Notice that at the end of their article they discuss genetics from a population standpoint. This is the hallmark of directive counseling, as we saw with Muller.

The article "Procreative Instinct as a Contributory Factor to Prevalence of Hereditary Blindness" was such a departure from popular philosophy that *The Lancet* published an editorial on the topic of directive genetic counseling. The editorial asked whether directive or persuasive counseling actually worked in getting people to make the appropriate decisions. Their findings, however tentative, are that directive counseling is no better at getting results than is nondirective counseling. The editors conclude that often it is more important to offer support than advice.

GENETIC COUNSELLING

A. E. H. Emery

Until the early 1960s little genetic counselling was done, and few people appreciated its value or even its need. But the situation has changed and nowadays almost every medical school and teaching hospital supports a genetic counselling unit. Before considering the problems of genetic counselling perhaps we should first be clear exactly what we mean by "genetic disease."

There are essentially three categories of genetic disease. Firstly there are the *unifactorial* disorders, each of which is due to a single (Mendelian) gene which may be dominant, recessive, or X-linked. These disorders are individually rare but the risks to relatives are usually high. Secondly, there are the *chromosomal* disorders such as Down's syndrome (mongolism) and certain disorders associated with male infertility (Klinefelter's syndrome) or primary amenorrhoea (Turner's syndrome). Thirdly, there are the *multifactorial* disorders which result from the effects of many genes plus environmental effects. They include many congenital malformations (anencephaly, spina bifida, hare-lip, and cleft palate), diseases of "modern society" (hypertension, coronary artery disease, peptic ulcer, diabetes mellitus), and certain psychiatric disorders (schizophrenia and probably manic-depressive psychosis).

Extent of Problem

With advances in medicine and surgery and the concomitant decline in infectious diseases and nutritional deficiencies, the proportion of morbidity and mortality due to genetic disease has increased. In fact at present roughly 1 in 20 children admitted to hospital have a unifactorial or chromosomal disorder, and such disorders account for about 1 in 10 of childhood

Source: "Genetic Counselling" by A. E. H. Emery. *British Medical Journal* (July 26, 1975), pp. 219–21. Used by permission.

deaths. In contrast only about 1 in 100 adult inpatients has a unifactorial or chromosomal disorder, but then many of these disorders lead to early death, or if they are compatible with survival to adulthood they usually do not warrant hospital admission.

The prevention of genetic disorders depends on ascertaining those individuals in the population who are at risk of having affected children and providing them with genetic counselling. Unfortunately only a relatively small proportion of those at risk are referred for genetic counselling. Some might argue that the ascertainment of those at risk should not be left to chance. For this reason it has been suggested that a confidential, computerized register of families with genetic disorders might prove valuable as a means of ascertaining and following up individuals at risk. Such a Register has been started in Edinburgh under the acronym RAPID (*R*egister for the *A*scertainment and *P*revention of *I*nherited *D*isease).

Changing Patterns in Genetic Counselling

Whereas at one time the majority of people seen for genetic counselling were married and in the higher social classes and were usually referred by a consultant interested in the disorder in question, this is no longer so. Recent follow-up studies indicate that an increasing proportion are referred by family doctors, and increasingly requests come from individuals themselves, often as a result of articles they have read or programs they have seen on television. There is no longer a preponderance of professional couples, and increasingly more individuals seek advice before marriage. It is clear therefore that an awareness of genetic disease and the importance of genetic counselling is extending into the general population.

Genetic Risks

In attempting to define the risk of recurrence the first prerogative is a precise diagnosis. When the diagnosis is well established and the mode of inheritance is clear, genetic counselling is straightforward. However, a serious complication is the existence of genetic heterogeneity. This term refers to disorders which are clinically similar but are inherited in different ways, and the individual's family history often gives no clue to this. In such cases the patient is best advised by a specialist genetic counsellor. . . .

In Down's syndrome the risks of recurrence depend on the cause. Most cases are due to an extra chromosome 21 (trisomy 21). In these cases the risks of recurrence in future children may be as high as 1 in 100 in women who have previously had an affected child, and 1 in 50 in women over the age of 40. Occasionally (no more than 3% of cases) the disorder is due to an inherited chromosomal translocation, in which case the chances

of recurrence are greater than 1 in 20 depending on the type of translocation and whether the mother or the father is the translocation carrier. It is
therefore important in all cases of Down's syndrome to check first the
child's chromosomes and, if a translocation is found, to check the parents'
chromosomes. . . .

Philosophy of Genetic Counselling

At the outset it must be emphasized that parents should never be told
what to do. Ideally they should be provided with all the information, within
the framework of their educational background, necessary to help them
arrive at an informed decision. When the diagnosis of a serious genetic
disorder is first made is not the time to give genetic counselling, as parents
are often upset and confused. They are more likely to welcome advice later
on. Whenever possible genetic counselling should be given when both parents can be present at the same time.

The first step is to remove the parents' feelings of guilt and self-
recrimination which often accompany the realization that a child has a genetic disorder. Next, the nature of the disease itself should be discussed
and, in the simplest of terms, what is meant by saying that it is "genetic."
The prognosis and the availability of treatment need to be made clear. Finally the risks of recurrence are presented, again within the framework of
the parents' educational background. Parents often find mathematical
probabilities difficult to comprehend, and in such cases it is better to emphasize the risks in less precise terms.

If a person is found to be at high risk (usually defined as greater than
1 in 10) of having and affected child, various possibilities may have to be
discussed, such as family limitation, sterilization, and antenatal diagnosis.

A problem which often arises is whether parents should be told that
they are at risk of having an affected child if they have not requested this
information—for example, after the diagnosis of Huntington's chorea in
the father or mother of a would-be parent. I feel that parents have a right
to know these risks if it might prevent the birth of an affected child. A
doctor who decides to withhold such information from a family assumes a
heavy responsibility. The family doctor is a good guardian of the individual's interest in this regard. I have found that in situations like this it is best
to discuss the genetic risks and their implications with the family doctor in
the first instance.

Value of Genetic Counselling

Since most genetic counselling is provided only *after* the birth of an
affected child, because only then is the need in any particular family recognized, it can prevent only some cases of genetic disease. For example, the

proportion of cases which could be prevented by genetic counselling is about 20% in the case of recessive and severe X-linked disorders and at most 5% in the case of multifactorial and chromosomal disorders. In dominant disorders it depends on the fertility of affected individuals. The closer this is to normal the greater the proportion which might be prevented by genetic counselling in families with an affected individual. If parents were screened *before* having children, a much greater proportion of genetic disease could be prevented, but in fact at present this is scientifically and economically possible only in a very few cases—for example, Tay-Sachs disease in Ashkenazi Jews. However, though these figures indicate that genetic counselling might not have a profound effect on the frequencies of genetic disorders in the population, this completely ignores the value to the individual family in providing reassurance for those who prove not to be at risk and in presenting various possibilities, such as antenatal diagnosis in the fetus, to those found to be at high risk. . . .

Response to Genetic Counselling

The individual's response to genetic counseling depends on the severity of the disorder, the availability of effective treatment, the risks of recurrence, religious attitudes, and socio-economic factors, probably in this order.

When faced with a high risk of having a child with a serious genetic disorder experience shows that many parents accept the risk and plan future pregnancies if the disorder is very severe and likely to be a "burden" for only a limited period. An example is Werdnig-Hoffmann disease, or progressive spinal muscular atrophy. In other situations the possibilities open to a couple are family limitation with therapeutic abortion if this fails, sterilization of one of the partners, artificial insemination by donor (AID) if both parents carry the same rare recessive gene or if the husband has a dominant disorder, and antenatal diagnosis.

In our studies we have been disturbed to find that contraceptive measures failed in as many as 1 in 10 couples who wished to avoid further pregnancies because of the risks involved. There is also no doubt that the fear of having another affected child has seriously impaired marital harmony in some families we have studied, with resulting separation and divorce. For these reasons if a couple is at high risk of having a child with a serious genetic disorder and therefore they do not wish to have further children, expert contraceptive advice should be provided. Not only this; couples must be given ample opportunities to discuss related anxieties, perhaps the most important of which will involve their marital relationships. Such problems may not be obvious at a casual interview—for example, in a busy outpatient clinic—and the physician may have to ask directly about such matters. In our experience these problems have sometimes come to light only when a social worker has made a home visit. Sterilization may be considered the best answer in some cases, but a little caution is required because increasing numbers of disorders can now be diagnosed in utero in early pregnancy, and if the fetus is found to be affected the parents can be offered selective abortion. In any disorder which cannot yet be diagnosed in utero this possibility at some time in the future has to be balanced against the risks of pregnancy in the intervening period. Adoption is no longer an obvious answer because of the decreasing number of babies which are available for adoption.

Role of the Family Doctor

The help and advice of a family doctor are of great assistance in genetic counselling. In straightforward cases he is best equipped to give such counselling himself. He can help the parents make their decision, which the specialist may find difficult because he usually has little idea of a couple's economic and social background. Our follow-up studies have repeatedly shown that genetic counselling in many cases is best given, or at least reinforced, in the home environment. Even with more complex problems, in which the geneticist has been asked to determine the risks —perhaps having to base such calculations on the results of special tests on the parents— the role of the family doctor is important. He can reinforce the advice given by the geneticist and probably enable the parents to understand it better.

Management of a Family with a Genetic Disorder

The first step in the management of a family with a genetic disorder is to establish the precise diagnosis. This may mean soliciting the advice of a hospital specialist and having access to death certificates and pathology reports. Secondly, the risks of recurrence have to be established. Here several publications can be helpful[1-5] If expert advice is required, it may be obtained from one of the genetic advisory centers listed in a publication entitled "Human Genetics" from the Health Department.[6] In many straightforward cases there is no doubt that genetic advice can be and is perhaps best given by the family doctor. In giving such advice, however, all doctors should bear in mind the complications, such as genetic heterogeneity, that may exist in a particular case, and the profound effect such advice may have on the social as well as the sexual life of parents.[7] Genetic counselling should therefore never be given lightly.

Notes

[1]Motulsky, A. G., and Hecht, F., *American Journal of Obstetrics and Gynecology*, 1964, 90, 1227.
[2]Emery, A. E. H., *Scottish Medical Journal*, 1969, 14, 335.
[3]Stevenson, A. C., and Davison, B. C. C., *Genetic Counselling*. London. William Heine-mann, 1970.
[4]McKusick, V. A., *Mendelian Inheritance in Man*, 3rd edn. Baltimore and London, Johns Hopkins Press, 1971.
[5]Emery, A. E. H. (ed.), *Antenatal Diagnosis of Genetic Disease*. Edinburgh, Churchill Living-stone, 1973.
[6]Standing Medical Advisory Committee, *Human Genetics*. Department of Health and So-cial Security, 1972.
[7]Emery, A. E. H., *Elements of Medical Genetics*, 3rd edn. Edinburgh, Churchill Livingstone, 1974.

PROCREATIVE INSTINCT
AS A CONTRIBUTORY FACTOR TO PREVALENCE
OF HEREDITARY BLINDNESS

Calbert I. Phillips
Marjorie S. Newton
Christine M. Gosden

Summary   The same, or different, autosomal dominant disease in both parents puts a child at 75% risk of having one or both diseases. The risk of hereditary disease is even higher (100%) when both parents have the same autosomal recessive disease. The blind tend to marry the blind, partly because of the bond of shared affliction and partly because they are usually segregated in blind schools and blind workshops. The propor-tion of those with hereditary blindness in these institutions is now high. Couples in which both partners have hereditary disease often take high risks of having children with "hyperendemic institutional genetic blind-ness"—perhaps because those with congenital or infantile blindness value sight less than do those who lose their sight later on, and perhaps because the power of the procreative instinct is strong enough to override more objective risk assessment. The procreative instinct is also an impor-tant cause of the exponential growth in world population.

Introduction

There is probably a tendency for the blind to marry the blind, and the deaf to marry the deaf,[1] and in general the handicapped to marry the handi-

Source: "Procreative Instinct as a Contributory Factor to Prevalence of Heredi-tary Blindness" by Calbert I. Phillips, Marjorie S. Newton, and Christine M. Gos-den. *Lancet*, vol. 1 (May 22, 1982), pp. 1169–72. Used by permission.

capped. Part of the reason may be shared affliction, but an important factor in many cases is their segregation in mixed-sex blind schools and blind workshops. In blind schools the high proportion (about 50%) of children with a hereditary disease[2] has probably been gradually rising over the past few decades, since environmental causes of blindness, e.g., retrolental fibroplasia, and have become less common. Accordingly "hyperendemic institutional genetic blindness" is probably increasing in frequency.

We present here some family-histories to illustrate the risks parents take of passing on their handicap(s) to their children. These risks can be easily worked out and are already known to geneticists, but it is time for clinicians in general to become aware of an increasing problem. A penalty of (super-) specialism in medicine can be the lack of concern of a specialist about aspects of his specialty which overlap with those of another: the clinician, preoccupied with immediate problems of life or death, vision or blindness, often tends to regard genetic as well as social, preventive, and other aspects of a patient's disease as irrelevant.

The term "blind" is used throughout to mean "so blind as to be unable to perform any work for which eyesight is essential" (usually visual acuity < 3/60)—i.e., the definition for certification of blindness for social welfare purposes in the U.K. "Partially sighted" means "substantially and permanently handicapped by defective vision".

Family Histories

Dominant × Dominant

Family 1. In generation II three cousins are blind from a rare, progressive, dominant choroidoretinal dystrophy.[3] II_1 has married a blind man from a large family with dominant retinitis pigmentosa. Their first child has the mother's disease; the twins from the second pregnancy are too young to be assessed accurately. The husband of II_2 is also blind from dominant congenital cataracts (associated with small eyes, small corneas, and nystagmus), despite operations, and their only child is blind from both diseases. It is probably no coincidence that II_3 has married another blind member of the family with congenital cataracts. Of their three children, the first has both diseases, the second has probably escaped entirely, while the third has inherited her mother's disease.

Family 2. The husband is blind from dominant retinitis pigmentosa while his wife is almost blind from a curious, dominant retinal condition (ectasia of the optic disc region plus congenital retinal fold), variants of which have caused blindness in a brother and sister but only impaired vision in her mother. The couple have been warned of the 75% risk of probable blindness in their children. The first pregnancy was terminated. The second produced a girl blind from the mother's disease. The father then wanted to be sterilized but his wife dissuaded him, because she wanted another child.

Autosomal Recessive × Same Autosomal Recessive

Family 3. A young man had been told that his blindness was due to buphthalmos for which operations in childhood had failed. He is illegitimate, and his mother subsequently married another man and had normal children. At the blind school he met a lady who had been told that her blindness was due to congenital glaucoma; operations in childhood had also been unsuccessful. Neither proband has affected relatives or consanguineous parents. It was only at the counselling session that they realized that they had the same disease. Very probably they are homozygous for the same defective autosomal recessive gene, which means that all their children would also be homozygous for the same gene. However, as was explained to the couple, the disease can have a low penetrance, down to 40%; males are more commonly affected than females, and only one eye is affected in around one-third of patients.[4-7] Moreover, microsurgical techniques have improved the operative prognosis. Also, the same hereditary "disease", in the sense of identical clinical manifestation, may not have the same genetic cause, as exemplified in a couple, each with albinism, who had normally pigmented children.[8] However, the young man decided on sterilization.

Autosomal Recessive × Different Autosomal Recessive

Family 4. A young man has very poor vision because of congenital cataracts, despite operations in early childhood, and nystagmus. One sister but no other family member is similarly affected. His wife is a partially sighted albino with two affected brothers but no other affected relative. Accordingly each has a different hereditary eye disease due to different autosomal recessive genes, although neither set of parents is consanguineous. They have been reassured from the genetic point of view that their children would be little more likely to have either disease than any child of normal parents.

Autosomal Dominant × Recessive

Since a parent with autosomal recessive disease is unlikely to have affected children (but all will be carriers) the risk to children will be that from the dominant disease in the spouse—viz, 50%.

Family 5. A mother with Marfan's syndrome and poor vision due to dislocated lenses brought her similarly affected daughter for counselling. (The mother has probably inherited her disease from her deceased mother.) Her husband, the girl's father, is blind from, quite possibly, congenital hereditary non-attachment of retina due to autosomal recessive genes, because he has one affected sister and no other affected family members;[9,10] their eyes are small and have opaque corneas. (A dominant mutation in the germ-line is a remote possibility.[11]) The daughter's children are at 50% risk of Marfan's disease but at no significant risk of her father's disease, provided her future husband is not consanguineous.

X-linked × Autosomal Dominant

Family 6. The wife had bilateral enucleations in childhood for bilateral retinoblastomas, inherited (dominant) from her bilaterally affected father who had also passed his disease on to a son, but not to two other children. The husband is blind from retinitis pigmentosa inherited as an X-linked recessive disease from his partially affected carrier mother and grandmother;[12] he has one blind maternal uncle, and three blind male cousins who inherited their disease from his two partially affected carrier aunts. His mother also has a blind half brother.

Difficulties Faced by Blind Families

Blindness in one or both parents must pose considerable problems in bringing up children, whether blind or sighted. For example, blind parent(s) must have difficulty in protecting the child from the common dangers such as boiling pans and traffic, and there must be some risk of economic difficulties since choice of occupation becomes very restricted and unemployment likely. However, grandparents or other relatives are often willing to help, and children of such marriages are often unusually mature. Many families seem to cope with their predicament, though our home visits show that the difficulties can be very great.

The realization that a child is blind is a very much greater shock to sighted than to blind parents, especially if no other family member is affected. However, sighted parents can cope better in the social and economic sense.

Factors Affecting Epidemiology of Hereditary Blindness

Sporadic cases must often be due to autosomal recessive genes but the hereditary nature of the condition may not be realized until a second affected child is born.[13] (An occasional dominant mutation, or even a "germ-line mutation" should also be considered.) Hyperendemic institutional genetic blindness is largely due to social factors, but preventive measures are difficult. Mixed sex institutions for the blind and for the deaf are difficult to dispense with because skilled intensive teaching is required; however, education in the general community would benefit both the handicapped and normal individuals, at least socially. Mixed handicap institutions would be less satisfactory than "normal" schools. However, there are considerable obstacles to obtaining wider social contact for the blind as we learned from a sad mother of a blind teenage daughter who had only blind boyfriends.

The marriage of two individuals, each with a "dominant" cause of blindness, would actually produce fewer blind children than if each had married a sighted spouse, all other factors being equal: one out of four children would "absorb" two causes of dominant blindness.

Attitudes to Blindness

Patients who have been blind from birth or early life value sight less highly than those who can remember the loss of this faculty and seem to be more willing to risk the transmission of their handicap to their children; they sometimes volunteer the information that they miss the sense much less than a sighted person would expect them to. The blind are rightly encouraged to live as normal a life as possible despite their visual handicap, and most are remarkably successful in doing so, albeit with support from parents, other relatives, and/or the welfare state and charity. It may only be on leaving the sheltered, and obviously happy, life among their similarly affected peers in the blind school that they realize their great problems in the harsher outside world.

In contrast, sighted people may perhaps overvalue sight—for example, the ophthalmologist who tries to alleviate poor vision in the elderly who face few man-years or woman-years of blindness compared with those faced by children in blind schools; or adoption agencies, which are reluctant to allot children to couples one of whom is blind.

Most of these considerations apply to hereditary disease of any sort. Children at high risk of hereditary handicap are "hostages to misfortune", to adapt a well-known phrase from Francis Bacon's essay "Of Marriage and Single Life."

Genetic Counselling

The patient's assessment of his own handicap due to blindness will vary and will affect his decision to put his child(ren) at risk. However, we have the impression that blind parents who pass on their blindness to their off-spring do not consider sufficiently how children feel when they realize that their parents were aware of the risks, yet decided to have children. The parents may make light of blindness in themselves and their children as a defense against criticism from within and without the family. Such attitudes are important factors in the passing on of a dominant cause of blindness from one parent only, through many generations. What is very surprising is the willingness to take the higher risks (75% in families I and II) which apply when both parents have hereditary blindness. The restrictions on the blind patients' occupational, social, and recreational life may increase their wish to procreate, so as to demonstrate their normality in an important area of life. The very challenge to overcome difficulties is probably also an attraction.

Our genetic counselling is only informative and never "directive." We provide a form of health education about the nature of their disease process and the risks of transmission (sometimes with difficulty, since they cannot see diagrams) without any indication of our personal conclusions. However, we are tending towards "persuasive," though not "directive," counselling. Emery[14] noted that an increasing proportion (41%) of couples at high risk of transmitting hereditary disease are undeterred by genetic counselling, and the option of antenatal diagnosis followed by termination of pregnancy partly accounts for this. Some families decide on a compromise and choose to limit the prevalence of their disease to some extent by having only one child. The willingness of general practitioners to provide contraception to prevent the transmission of a disease causing blindness and his support to the family with hereditary blindness are essential for this aspect of preventive medicine.

Parents' attitudes tend to be optimistic despite information to the contrary.[15] They may attribute to environmental causes diseases which are obviously inherited (rubella contact in pregnancy is sometimes blamed). Those who already have an affected child may believe the next has a higher chance of normality; they also tend to yearn for a normal child. Those who start by having a normal child may interpret this as evidence that the hereditary disease is disappearing from the family. It is surprising that the higher risk of genetic disease when parents are consanguineous is not universally known—although such information would be easy to disseminate widely.

Another source of optimism is the confident expectation of a cure by the time the next generation is growing up. Parents also do not realize sufficiently that only a small proportion of hereditary eye diseases can be detected early enough for terminations of pregnancy—for example, fetal sexing in X-linked retinitis pigmentosa could allow abortion of a male fetus at 50% risk when the mother is a carrier of the X-linked gene; and fetoscopy could detect the telltale polydactyly in the Bardet-Biedl syndrome that causes blindness from retinal aplasia. Even so, the option of embarking on a pregnancy which will probably have to be terminated is probably acceptable only when the procreative instinct is very strong, as is the option for artificial insemination (by donor) when it is appropriate, e.g., in family 3.

Social Values Which Contribute to Prevalence of Hereditary Blindness

Ophthalmologists are fortunate in rarely having to make life-and-death decisions concerning their patients. However, they share the interest and concern of the general public in the dilemmas facing other specialists. These dilemmas arise partly from inconsistencies in current "moral" attitudes: for example, "allowing" someone to die "naturally" without treatment—dysthanasia rather than euthanasia; or countenancing termination of pregnancy (another euphemism), yet condemning euthanasia of a multiply handicapped newborn baby.

Part of the difficulty in medical practice arises because the remedies we have are all-or-none, whereas the conditions we see—for example, hypertension and osteoarthritis—have a very wide spectrum of severity. Likewise in social therapeutics, society's laws take sudden leaps, usually belatedly, after the summation of the continuous variable of individual attitudes has reached a certain threshold—the introduction of (more) permissive legislation on termination of pregnancy in 1967 is an example.

The Procreative Instinct: A Biological Imperative

> Discovery of twinned helplessness
> Against the huge tug of procreation
> Robert Graves

The increasing recognition of the strength of the sex instinct may have obscured the realization that the reproductive or procreative instinct is at least as powerful and probably more so in the female than in the male (as shown by family 2 in which the wife would not allow her husband to be sterilized). The free availability of contraception has had a much smaller effect on population trends than many foresaw in its early stages. The instinct to have young is so very potent, and it is particularly obvious in blind parents who take high risks of passing on their diseases to their children—for example, in families 1 and 2. Another very strong instinct is the grandparental instinct, especially the grandmaternal. Perhaps it would be artificial to differentiate a "parental" instinct—the largely protective instinct of a parent for her or his child—from the procreative (reproductive) instinct.

The procreative instinct (which we are distinguishing from the sex instinct) may be associated with several factors: the intrinsic attractiveness of young animals of any sort, the fulfillment of parents in feeling needed, the female animal's usual state of well-being in pregnancy (despite the discomfort of parturition), and the emotional and economic security which children provide for the elderly, especially in poor societies.

Effect of Procreative Instinct on World Population

The opinion that spaceship earth already has too many (normal) people on it is increasingly prevalent. A possible, small, factor in the reproductive behavior of the blind is that they receive no visual impact of our overcrowded environment. However, most of the rest of us unthinkingly accept our present environment as normal, although there are many who suspect that too great a density of population, especially in cities, is an important factor leading to social evils ranging from wars and riots to environmental pollution.

Man has been too successful a species, from the point of view of his numbers.[16] His reproductive capacity represents a serious threat to civilization. . . . It is surprising that even in advanced countries there are only few and intermittent apocalyptic warnings.[16-18] It is probably already too late to prevent disaster, yet Dawkins[19] emphasizes the only hope: "We alone on earth can rebel against the tyranny of the selfish replicators."

References

[1]Nance WE, Rose SP, Conneally PM, Miller JZ. Opportunities for genetic counseling through institutional ascertainment of affected probands. In: Lubs HA, de la Cruz F, eds. Genetic counselling. New York: Raven Press, 1977: 307-29.

[2]Phillips CI, Stokoe NL, Hughes HE. An ophthalmic genetics clinic. Trans Ophthal Soc UK 1975; 95: 472-76.

[3]Douglas AA, Waheed I, Wyse CT. Progressive bifocal chorio-retinal atrophy. Br J Ophthal 1968; 52: 742-51.

[4]McKusick VA. Mendelian inheritance in man. 5th ed. Baltimore and London: Johns Hopkins University Press, 1978: 515.

[5]Peyman GA, Sanders DA, Goldberg MF (eds.). Principles and practice of ophthalmology, vol. I. Philadelphia: WB Saunders, 1980: 723.

[6]Duke-Elder S. System of ophthalmology vol III, part 2. London: Henry Kimpton, 1964: 558-59.

[7]Goldberg MF (ed.) Genetic and metabolic eye disease. Boston: Little, Brown, 1974: 99 and 252-53.

[8]Trevor-Roper PD. Marriage of two complete albinos with normally pigmented offspring. Proc Roy Soc Med 1963; 56: 21-24.

[9]Phillips CI, Leighton DA, Forrester RM. Congenital hereditary non-attachment of retina: a sibship of two. *Acta Ophthal* 1973; **51:** 425–33.

[10]Ohba N, Watanabe S, Fujita S. Primary vitreo-retinal dysplasia transmitted as an autosomal recessive disorder. *Br J Opthal* 1981; **65:** 631–35.

[11]Stern C. Principles of human genetics. 3rd ed. San Francisco: WH Freeman, 1973: 575.

[12]Lyon M. Sex chromatin and gene action in the mammalian X chromosome. *Am J Hum Genet* 1962; **14:** 135–48.

[13]Phillips CI, Newton MS. Beware recessive genes. *Lancet* 1981; ii: 293–97.

[14]Emery AEH. Changing patterns in a genetic counseling clinic. In: Lubs HA, de la Cruz F, eds. Genetic counselling. New York: Raven Press, 1977: 113–20.

[15]Godmilow L, Hirschhorn K. Evaluation of genetic counselling. In: Lubs HA, de la Cruz F, eds. Genetic counselling. New York: Raven Press, 1977: 121–30.

[16]Loraine JA. The global population. *Lancet* 1976; ii: 621–22.

[17]Loraine JA. Doctors and the global population crisis. *Br Med J* 1977; ii: 691.

[18]Editorial. *Br Med J* 1980; **280:** 3–4.

[19]Dawkins R. The selfish gene. Oxford: Oxford University Press, 1976: 224.

Counseling, Screening, and Engineering

The following article by Zucker and Patriquin points out some of the ethical dilemmas that arise from the usual sorts of cases seen by genetic counselors. After examining the dichotomy between directive and nondirective counseling, they conclude that the major differences between genetic counseling and many other specialties in clinical medicine are that genetic counseling can have a long-run future orientation, the question of who is the primary patient is often unclear (we have seen this in obstetrics), and profound suffering is often at the center of the patient's true concerns.

The discussion of genetic engineering focuses on techniques commonly used to alleviate infertility. These techniques, such as in vitro fertilization, raise moral and legal problems. Legal problems, as we have seen, get solved without settling the moral issues. For example, the New Jersey Supreme Court ruled that surrogate mother contracts were not legally enforceable. Even so, surrogate motherhood may answer a legitimate need on the part of some couples. The New Jersey finding does not render the use of surrogates immoral. It is characteristic of the moral dimension that it remains open to debate, even when some of the legal questions have been decided.

Zucker and Patriquin analyze the concept "natural," showing that it is vague, in need of clarification, and, therefore, very easily misapplied. They also attempt to clarify some appeals to the theory of evolution in medical contexts. Specifically, they deal with the claim that some medical techniques violate the dictates of evolution.

Concerning the newest molecular genetic techniques, they point out that it may soon become theoretically possible to perform therapy on the level of genes. Although they do not pursue this issue, we should ask: If this ability passes from extraordinary treatment to ordinary, everyday medicine, how will people use it? For example, some couples have used prenatal diagnosis to choose the sex of their child, aborting a fetus of the undesired sex. Might not some couples insist on gene therapy to ensure blue eyes, or musical or athletic ability? Would private companies appear to answer these desires? Is there enough possibility for abuse that gene therapy ought to be strictly limited? Indeed, how should abuse be defined? Who should create and enforce those limits?

Finally, we are reminded that genetic screening combined with genetic counseling and the right to abortion has the effect of what is called negative eugenics, the effective breeding out of unwanted conditions. This is another sense of genetic engineering. Is this the way that medicine ought to be used?

This last question is one that goes beyond the arena of genetic engineering. To ask if this is the way that medicine ought to be used is to question the potential allocation of medical resources. Do new and powerful (and often expensive) medical techniques belong to everyone or should there be a limit on their use? Is it the right or the obligation of the medical profession to be the gatekeepers against misuse?

MORAL ISSUES
ARISING FROM GENETICS

Arthur Zucker and David Patriquin

Gene therapy, prenatal diagnosis, genetically altered bacteria, patenting new life forms: these are all outgrowths from the development of genetics. Our focus will be on the moral issues engendered by some of the genetic techniques which are now so well integrated into clinical medicine. The section on genetic counseling is meant to show the most frequent moral problems encountered as they might really occur. Genetic screening is presented as a mix of preventive medicine and aid for genetic counseling. Genetic engineering is discussed in the context of evolution and human needs and desires.

Source: Moral Issues Arising from Genetics" by Arthur Zucker and David Patriquin. *Listening: Journal of Religion and Culture*, vol. 22, no. 1 (Winter 1987), pp. 65–85. Used by permission of the authors.

Introduction

The relatively recent interest in medical ethics has spurred an analysis of two crucial concepts: privacy and paternalism. Briefly, we tend to assume that competent adults should be left alone to make their own decisions, even bad ones. Intervention, violating privacy, can only be justified if 1) we are reasonably sure the person is not competent; 2) the decision is so bad that either (a) it is *prima facie* reason for assuming incompetence, or (b) it is *prima facie* reason for assuming that important aspects of the decision have been overlooked or misunderstood; or 3) the decision affects (many) other people directly and adversely. In all of this, of course, we assume that our use of the value terms, "bad" and "adversely" are not eccentric or idiosyncratic.

In keeping with the general rule, leave others alone, there is a model of the doctor–patient relationship. According to this model, the physician gives facts to the patient. The decision, often laden with value implications, is made by the patient. Naturally, the facts must be correct and relevant and they must be presented neutrally if there is to be no influence from the physician. This model proposes that information from physician to patient be value-free and nondirective. Such a model is an ideal. Perhaps best stated, the goal should be to be as value free and nondirective as possible.

Another model is based on the premise that few if any patients (even physicians when they are patients) are capable of properly understanding and coolly deciding on a difficult course of action. On this view, value-laden direction is not only allowed, but called for in many cases. Anything less is seen as an abrogation of professional responsibility. Usually the goal of this sort of doctor–patient relationship is the health of the patient. But, sometimes the goal is also the health of the family, another family member, or, as we shall see, society.

None of the above is digression. To understand many of the ethical issues that arise in the practice of clinical genetics, we must have *at least* this much background on these two approaches to the practice of clinical medicine.

Case 1. A 25-year-old woman has just given birth to a child with Down's Syndrome. She wants to know about future pregnancies.

Factual information, we have seen, is plentiful. The traditional nondirective counselor can offer reassurance in the form of prenatal diagnosis (amniocentesis and karyotyping). Should there be an affected fetus in future pregnancies, there is the possibility of abortion. But there is more for the counselor to consider. The information about possible measures should the next pregnancy result in a fetus with Down's syndrome can be taken by the parents to mean "You should not have had this child." "You should not keep this child." "If you consider aborting another Down's child, doesn't it mean that you really don't love the child you have?" Each of these implications must somehow be avoided by the counselor. There is no easy formula-like way to do this. The counselor must be sensitive to those times when such messages have been picked up, however incorrectly. It is perhaps the strength of the directive approach that it avoids this particular sort of issue, for a directive counselor would say something like "There is absolutely nothing to worry about." The directive counselor must have the stylistic ability to carry off such an approach. Developing such a style is probably no harder than learning to be sensitive to mixed messages.

There can be another counseling issue when dealing with Down's Syndrome. Sometimes the condition is due to a balanced translocation. Where this is the form of inheritance, the translocation will be carried by one of the parents about 30% of the time. There is a sense in which this information about the form of inheritance belongs to the parents. But will they make good use of it? That is, will they want to know who is responsible; perhaps for further attempts at pregnancy? If it is the father, then artificial insemination might be desired. Or, will there inevitably be guilt and recrimination? Is any of this for the counselor to judge? This situation also has implications for privacy. Some counselors feel that it is their obligation to trace the translocation to its source in the family so that other family members at risk can be notified. This is almost a public health slant on the doctor–patient relation.

Yet another counseling problem may occur. Suppose the parents do not want to raise the child. Instead, they feel that the child's quality of life, as retarded, is just not worth all their time and effort. Is it the obligation of the counselor to take the part of the child and to point out (how strongly?) that with infant stimulation programs, etc., many children with Down's Syndrome can certainly be happy and lead reasonable, if somewhat sheltered, lives. Shouldn't the decision of the parents be final? The question obviously becomes when should it be accepted as final when it seems to be harming the innocent child?

One of the assumptions of nondirective counseling is that the facts speak for themselves. When the facts are clearly presented, the right decision will be made. This is, of course, an oversimplification which is implicitly recognized by the directive approach. The directive counselor knows that sometimes (often?) parents just don't know how to use information. Thus, where some decisions are clearly better than others, directive counselors will feel that they are right to see that these decisions get made.

Risk figures play a large role in genetic counseling. To the counselor, risk is given as probability. It is the patient who interprets the probability as risk. This can be seen in the case of a young woman whose youngest brother had Down's Syndrome. She always saw her brother as a great burden and grew up knowing that she would never be able to handle such a child. Now that she is pregnant, she wants prenatal diagnosis. Her risk (probability) of carrying a fetus with Down's Syndrome is less than one percent. The probability of morbidity or mortality from the prenatal diagnosis is greater than one percent, yet she elects to have the amniocentesis. Is she unreasonable? To her, the idea of a retarded child is so horrendous that not knowing is unacceptable. A patient's interpretation of probability is something that every counselor must learn to understand, if not fully accept.

Case 2. A man in his late thirties is diagnosed as having Huntington's disease. He knew he had a chance of having the disease because his father had the disease. He chose not to tell his wife until well into their marriage. They have two teenage daughters. He does not want the children to know. His wife thinks they ought to know. They ask the counselor: "What should we do?"

On the traditional nondirective model, the counselor can say only "It is your decision." Opening up a discussion by asking for reasons, "Why don't you want them to know?" is certainly reasonable and may not clearly violate the "code" of nondirectiveness. Yet, doesn't even the hint that further discussion is needed, imply that the counselor sees a problem with the decision? Indeed, suggesting a visit to another, more specialized counselor, e.g., psychologist or clergyman, also carries this implication. Lurking in the background is another issue. Is the genetic counselor, most likely trained in pediatrics and genetics, truly competent to be leading a discussion of family dynamics?

A directive approach would very likely be based on the presumption that Huntington's disease is a bad thing, an evil, which the world could certainly do without. As a simple, Mendelian dominant, the occurrence of the disease could be reduced to its mutation rate if all at risk for the disease did not have children. (Until there is prenatal diagnosis this is the only way.) Thus the directive counselor would certainly advise telling the daughters and indeed strongly suggest to them that they have no children of their own.

This presumption of directive counseling would also justify a social program to educate people with Huntington's disease: Do not fail to tell your children. Don't have children if you are at risk. Such programs if ever instituted, in any way, would likely not be welcome for they sound like the beginning of an ugly slippery slope. Who next would be told not to have children? In the case of a disease such as Huntington's disease, it seems to be good and well intentioned advice. Yet aiming at the future good of the population seems to overlook short term rights and privacy of individuals. Sometimes this is necessary. But the burden, at least in our society, falls on those who suggest violating privacy rights of individuals. With infectious diseases, we have come to believe that individual rights do in general take a second place to the general welfare of the public. An interesting question is how analogous is genetic disease to infectious disease.

Truth telling plays a central role in creating ethical issues for genetic counselors.

Case 3A.   A genetic counselor discovers, during her work-up of a family, that the "father" of the children is not the biological father, although he thinks he is.

3B.   The afternoon before a clinic visit, a genetic counselor gets a call from the mother of a woman whose family is to be seen for a child with dysmorphic features. The mother says that her daughter has been having an incestuous affair with her brother for a number of years. Probably the child to be examined is the result of the incest.

3C.   While examining a child suspected of having fetal alcohol syndrome, the mother of the child admits that she is a recovered alcoholic who lost control while pregnant and went on a "binge." But she begs, "Please don't tell my husband. He thinks I don't drink for religious reasons."

These cases highlight problems. There is no straightforward answer to any of them. The best one can do is to understand how to approach the issues. Is the goal of counseling to say everything that is true about the case to all involved? Is the goal to give relevant information for decision making? Is the goal of information giving secondary to doing no harm; secondary to the wishes of one of the patients? Case 3B may present an extra problem if the husband is not present. Does he care at all? Does he want more (normal) children? Does the counselor's obligation to inform extend to the husband even if he is not present? Should the counselor even hint to the mother that there is suspicion of incest or, like all gossip, should the phone call be totally dismissed? Case 3C is difficult if the child does have fetal alcohol syndrome, for then it would seem that the father would have to be told. Would it be acceptable for the counselor to use another *name* for the condition in order to protect the mother on the grounds that no harm is thereby done, so long as *only* the name and not the prognosis of the condition is changed? Hidden is perhaps a distinction between truth telling, lying, and deception. Or are these distinctions mere semantic categories reflecting only a wish that the problems go away?

Abortion is another problem that arises in genetic counseling. Much of the efficacy of counseling turns on the availability of abortion. Some parents are totally opposed to abortion and use prenatal diagnosis only to allay fears or to gain time to prepare for a bad outcome. Some institutions offer genetic counseling only for these reasons and never suggest abortion as an option. In the setting of genetic counseling the decision to abort is rarely unfelt. That is, even in parents for whom the decision "if the fetus is affected, we will abort" is a foregone conclusion, the abortion is still a sad event, one which recalls lost hopes and dreams. Yet there do seem to be some striking exceptions.

Case 4.   A 38-year-old woman with 4 boys is pregnant. She and her husband desperately want a girl and want only one more child. She asks for prenatal diagnosis for sex, i.e., is the fetus a female? She makes her case very clear. If the fetus is a male, she will abort it. If you deny her the prenatal diagnosis, she will also abort. These cases do exist and show how, in the eyes of some, medical advances created to answer medical needs can be used to fulfill personal desires. This sort of situation can be avoided by specifically regulating it out of existence: No prenatal diagnosis for sex alone where sex-linked disease is not involved. One justification is a straightforward moral abhorrence of this use of amniocentesis and selective abortion. Another justification can be that sex selection is not an economical use of a resource such as amniocentesis and karyotyping. A "reply" is that medical resources are not owned by physicians. Rather they are the "property" of all. Physicians by virtue of their medical training are no better at being moral gatekeepers to therapy than anyone else.

Where sexlinked disease, e.g., hemophilia, is involved, a variation of the abortion problem arises.

Case 5.   A woman who is a carrier for hemophilia is pregnant. Half of her sons (on average) will have hemophilia, the other half will be normal. She may want to abort any male because her perception of the disease is so bad. Here abortion is being used to ensure this woman's idea of a reasonable quality of life for her children, herself and her husband. The problem, of course, is that until there is prenatal diagnosis for hemophilia, she will, if she chooses to abort all males, have (on average) a probability of one-half of aborting normal males. From the public health perspective, this may be a justifiable risk, especially from the economic viewpoint. On the other hand, should the public perspective *ever* be used? Furthermore, should the counselor be an advocate for the possible normal male fetuses being put at risk?

Case 6.   A couple, whose first child recently died because of multiple genetic anomalies, are anxious to have another child as soon as possible. Many workers who study grief and grief reactions are convinced that after the death of a child, a period of at least one year should go by before a couple tries to "replace" that loss. How strongly, if at all, should a counselor suggest a waiting period? This may seem to be a clear issue: at most, a suggestion, but nothing more. After all, what are the counselor's credentials for deciding how long this particular couple should wait? Is their grief any part of the counselor's obligation? Surely the nondirective view would hold that a factual mention of grief responses is more than enough. Yet even the most nondirective counselor is quick to point out, usually without having to be asked, "What happened is not your fault. Nothing you could have done would have avoided what happened, etc." Self-blame is fairly common and it seems to be just a normal human reaction to want to help someone through these feelings. The directive counselor could point out that these human feelings are also the well-springs of directive counseling, i.e., giving direction to others is not necessarily a mere need to invoke power over others who are relatively helpless.

Summary of Genetic Counseling

Genetic counseling differs, but only in degree, from much of clinical medicine in four ways. (1) It is usually the case that there is no one patient to be considered. (2) Abortion is an important aspect of genetic counseling. (3) Guilt and self blame are almost always present. (4) Often there is nothing to offer but reassurance, through the force and style of one's personality.
. . .

Let us turn now to some of the techniques of genetic engineering.

In Vitro Fertilization (IVF)

Many couples are infertile. When the problem is a blocked fallopian tube, or any problem which does not compromise a woman's ability to carry a fetus to term, it is now possible to fertilize an egg outside the body and subsequently to implant it in the uterus. Yet IVF is not worry free.

Not all fertilized eggs develop. Some people consider each fertilized egg that does not develop a life destroyed. We are, therefore, presented with issues of abortion. Also, couples who insist on high technology, risking abortion instead of accepting adoption, may be poor risks for parenthood. Are we being tricked by our technological ability into treating desires and not true medical problems?

When IVF was first begun, it was argued that *in vitro* fertilization was just the first step. Once *in vitro* fertilization with implantation in the mother is accepted, why not *in vitro* fertilization and the use of surrogate mothers? Why not *in vitro* gestation? (*In vitro* fertilization does not mean test-tube baby, i.e., the development of the fertilized ovum in a test tube.) Critics saw this progression as unavoidable and either intrinsically immoral or as a danger to socially accepted and proven values and institutions. Whether intrinsically immoral or not, these critics were right to predict that surrogate mothers were the next step.

One often-made claim is that *in vitro* fertilization is not natural. It is easy to point out that medicine has always strived to break out of the hold of "the natural." To say that something is natural, however, is vague. One use of "natural" is to mark off things that are not supernatural. In a way, then, everything we are familiar with can be considered natural. Another purpose in calling something natural is to set it apart from man-made or man-interfered with. Although this is relatively clear, it presupposes a distinction between nature without man and nature with man, as if somehow man is not a legitimate part of nature. Another possible sense for "natural" is traditional. On this view, to say that *in vitro* fertilization is not natural would be similar to saying, in 1902, that the horseless carriage is not natural. The question, as always, is whether the break with tradition is worth making.

Sometimes it is held that *in vitro* fertilization may contradict the wisdom of evolution; that infertile women ought to be left that way. Strictly speaking, evolution teaches us that to prosper, we must fit our environment. This fit is most easily measured by focusing on number of progeny. But number of progeny must be in accord with environmental resources. Studies have shown that there is no evolutionary pressure merely to maximize number of progeny. Rather, progeny number is kept at optimal levels given the resources.

In controlling the environment, we should plan changes so that our genes are not "surprised." If we are considering evolution as a teacher, we must, at the very least, consider how we are affecting the environment and how this might affect our genes' ability to keep us fit. The concept of fit can take into account quality of life. Indeed, the analogue for this is the above-mentioned fact that number of progeny is a function of the environment's ability to support a certain population size. There is no reason to think, for example, that evolution and compassion for the problems of others are in any way at odds with each other.

Another charge is that *in vitro* fertilization may undermine social institutions and important human values. Values and social institutions do change with new technologies. If the changes cannot easily be cut off, then at least we should have some idea of what they are and what they mean. Trying to undermine change simply because it is change, without a full understanding of the issues, is politically as well as ethically naive. The instant demand for *in vitro* fertilization makes this plain.

Artificial Insemination by Husband (AIH) and Artificial Insemination by Donor (AID)

Objections to AIH are based on two approaches. One is the wisdom-of-evolution argument: We are attempting to countermand evolution, which has determined that some males are not meant to have progeny. Another approach takes its force from the concept of tradition. It is not natural (traditional) for a woman to conceive in this fashion. Furthermore, this sort of break with tradition will tend to undermine values, e.g., marriage, sex, etc. by pushing us down the slippery slope to (a) deciding who can procreate and (b) eliminating "mistakes" by infanticide. We have previously discussed these sorts of objections based on natural, tradition, and evolution.

The slippery-slope argument is difficult to assess. "Who can procreate?" is still answered by "whoever wants to." However, the Baby Doe cases can be taken as evidence that society is beginning to condone infanticide. Yet even the Supreme Court ruling that Baby Doe regulations are unconstitutional only keeps the decision in the hands of the parents. It still remains to be seen what this may mean in the long run.

Another set of objections we have mentioned in another context. Are we treating legitimate medical conditions or just human desires? Are these desires unworthy since so many young children are available for adoption? Are these desires symptomatic of unstable and less than adequate future parents? Is anyone capable of deciding any of these questions? These are in large part empirical questions.

More controversial than AIH is AID, where the sperm is donated by someone other than the husband or the social father to be. The focus here is on (1) the naturalness of AID and (2) its wisdom from a moral and social standpoint. AID undercuts any evolutionary argument because presumably only the "best" donors are used. A remaining question is: Are we wise enough to know who the best donors are? There are two sorts of answers. From the evolutionary standpoint, we probably are not wise enough, but can likely do better than random, which is the usual way sperm are "chosen." From a social standpoint, this decision can be made by understanding what society values and what it will likely value in the not too distant future.

Of course the spectre of AID blossoming into some kind of oppressive society still looms. H. J. Muller foresaw that AID would not work on a large scale without much public education and a change in attitude. Naturally to an opponent of institutionalized AID, "public education" means propaganda. What this shows is that how one sees AID is a function of whether one sees a need for it on an institutionalized basis. One can be for it on a case-by-case basis without arguing that it become a recognized part of society.

The discussion so far has been general. There are some specific problems that exist for us now. What is the legal status of a child born of AID? Who is the father? How is legal inheritance to work, especially if there is a previous or subsequent child either adopted or had in the traditional manner? Does AID and confidentiality increase the risk for future in-breeding between a couple who, unknown to them, have the same father? Are we ready for AID psychologically? What is the reaction of parents of children born of AID? What is the reaction of the children if they find out? Can research be done to find out? If not, then are we risking too many psychological problems for too many people? If there is some evidence that some parents react differently to AID children, will there be a special obligation to identify those who will react badly so that we can refuse the service to them? Is it likely that this identification will be done with accuracy and precision? And if not, should it and AID not be done at all? Many of these questions apply to children born of surrogate mothers.

Although *in vitro* fertilization, AIH, and AID all have eugenic implications and are methods of genetic engineering in the sense that they are nontraditional ways of changing the gene pool, there is no way to separate them from other techniques of clinical medicine. What they have in common is alleviation of pain and suffering in the short run; pain and suffering as reported by the patient. They stress compassion in the short-run while basically ignoring long-run implications. This is the hallmark of clinical medicine.

Recombinant DNA

The final technique for genetic engineering we shall only mention: the use of recombinant DNA. Briefly, it is now possible to insert DNA pieces from one type of organism into the DNA of another. This technique has many benefits.

1. We are learning a great deal about genetics.
2. Organisms (such as *E. coli* bacteria which naturally live in the human gut) can be "tricked" into producing chemicals of use to humans, e.g., insulin and interferon.
3. Conceivably, if research continues, we could reach the point of removing human genes (e.g., the gene for Huntington's chorea) and replacing it with its normal allele. This is referred to as gene therapy.

Controlling Our Destiny
with Genetic Engineering

Genetic counseling, genetic screening, and genetic engineering are techniques which give us some measure of control over the effects that genes have on us as individuals and as a population. Theoretically, through control, comes freedom—not just a philosophical sense of freedom, but a freedom from disease and ill health. All these techniques contribute to eugenics if they are used properly. We can breed out (negative eugenics) and breed in (positive eugenics). But given our penchant for dealing with the present, we may be basically building up a store of deleterious genes. We do this by treating genetic disease symptomatically and by not making a real attempt to get at the cause, namely, the genes. Thus, the incidence of many genetically related diseases will increase. In 1950, H. J. Muller, a 1946 Nobel Laureate for his work in genetics, argued in "Our Load of Mutations," that geneticists in general and medical geneticists in particular had an obligation to oversee the quality of the human gene pool. Muller, as did others before him, suggested a program of eugenics which would reach long into the future.

Do we ever have obligations long into the future? We often chastise children for not considering the long-term effects of their decisions; for thinking only of the pleasures of the here and now. To grow morally, we must reach out beyond the pleasures and safety of the present. Only by being future directed are we being truly moral. This is the view exemplified by the argument of H. J. Muller.

We certainly feel justified in worrying about the environment in general and how we will affect it. But is this just because (1) we are closely related in a causal way to what happens to the environment in the next, say 30 years; (2) we feel obligated to supply minimum requirements for life and health to near future generations? We may feel responsible for providing our children and even grandchildren with the best possible life, not just a minimal life. Yet how good a life are we obligated to provide for untold numbers untold generations from now? If value judgments are as complex and as eccentric as some believe, then perhaps the entire enterprise of trying to provide more than minimal health requirements is folly. Certainly on a value-free model of counseling, we should hesitate to choose values for future generations. Yet, when we decided that building a dam was less important than preserving the snail darter, we did impose values on the future. At the very least we restricted the future for coming generations. We do this sort of thing more often than we realize.

An interesting way to generate reasons for believing that there are, and ought to be, obligations into the future is by doing a thought experiment. Imagine a time when all the persons who will ever exist get together (before they do "really" exist) to decide whether there should be instilled in us a feeling of obligation for the future. If no one knew when he or she were to live, but did know that ultimately the world would run down in quality, then it would seem to be rational to want to be assured that those who came before would make provision for those who came after. In a sense, this is like saying "if I were to live 2500 years from now, I would like to know that someone had made appropriate plans for the society 2500 years from now."

Returning to the practice of genetic counseling, we have a new perspective: sometimes the counselor may feel obligated to consider the effect of certain decisions on society and very likely on yet unborn generations. The value-free model, which some believe most resembles the traditional doctor–patient relation, emphasizes care in giving proper information and support to the patient; there is a short-run focus.

Conclusion and Prospects

Four questions capture the conclusions.

1. Who is the best person to be a medical geneticist? Who should do genetic counseling? Should there be two specialties—one primarily research (the medical geneticist); the other, the practitioner? Need the counselor be a physician? What kind of training should the counselor have: part medicine, part genetics, part psychologist, pastor, philosopher, lawyer?

2. Can genetic screening be separated from treatment in the practice of medical genetics? It is more efficient (and ultimately more accurate) to limit the population to be treated by initially screening for those at risk. Where funding calls for efficiency, this will become especially important. This has already manifested itself in the massive screening programs in Great Britain for neural tube defects.

3. The public has in effect paid for much of the development of genetic techniques. Naturally the public should profit from the results of recent genetic technology. But can use lead to over-use and then to misuse? Will the public ultimately be led to believe in the right to utilize medical resources in order to ensure "the perfect baby"? What will happen to babies less than perfect?

4. Genetic counseling followed by a choice for selective abortion amounts to *de facto* negative eugenics, the elimination of undesirable traits. Issues such as the morality of abortion, the psychological effects of abortion, the moral, social, and political consequences of eugenics must be faced squarely.

These issues are no longer mere philosophical questions of interest, they have become crucial to the practice of medicine and to the well being of society.

Cases and Survey Results

J. C. Fletcher, D. C. Wertz, J. R. Sorenson, and K. Berg, under the auspices of The National Institutes of Health, undertook a survey to "see how medical geneticists in different cultures respond to situations that require ethical decision making."

Geneticists from seventeen countries were asked to respond to ethical scenarios that represent typical ethical dilemmas seen by geneticists. The results of the survey indicated that there is not a clearly "dominant moral approach . . . in the practice of medical genetics when considered in a cross-cultural perspective." There was a greater consensus "within individual nations than among nations, although for a few problems, very strong consensus exists in all respects, e.g. voluntary genetic screening, protection of the mother's confidentiality in false paternity findings related to recessive disease, and full disclosure of conflicting diagnostic findings." The following conclusion to their article, "Ethics and Human Genetics: A Cross-Cultural Study in 17 Nations" (*Human Genetics,* 1987) is worth citing in full.

> Societal problems tend to sneak up on medicine and catch physicians unaware. The outlook on ethical problems among medical geneticists reflects a general confidence about resolving moral conflicts at the individual-familial level and a lack of preparedness to make a contribution at the societal-political level, especially in terms of questions that involve society's interests. One explanation for this situation is that many geneticists avoid any appearance of eugenic considerations and shy away from societal issues. The emergence of even more powerful scientific and diagnostic tools will not allow medical geneticists any place to hide from the social implications of medical genetics. In our view, medical geneticists need to consolidate their best insights of the past, so that they can be better prepared to contribute to the process of discovering new ethical guidance for the more complex problems of the future.
>
> A dominant moral approach may be evolving, however. The results reported here may be the beginning of greater consensus about appropriate choices of action. Certainly they point to the need for discussion in professional organizations and for consideration of bodies of guidance for medical geneticists in the areas of greatest concern. As technology becomes more complex and presents more difficult moral choices, medical geneticists from different cultures may be drawn together to face these complex problems. In other words, the diffusion of technology may lead to greater consensus across cultures.

The following scenarios are some of those used in the survey. The "Discussion" lists the six ethical issues that geneticists identified as especially important. The authors discuss the ethical problems within the context of social and political approaches. They are anxious to point out that genetics (medicine in general, we would emphasize) cannot be disassociated from its social implications.

GENETIC COUNSELLING SCENARIOS

D. C. Wertz and J. C. Fletcher

You identify a parent of a Down syndrome child as having a balanced translocation. What is your approach to disclosure of this information to the parents? Select the *one* that best describes your response. I would choose to:

a. Before drawing the parents' karyotypes, ask them if they want to know who is the carrier, and if they say they want to know, tell them
b. Ask the parents whether they want to know *everything* about the source of the child's abnormality, including their own carrier status, and if they say yes, tell them which parent carries the extra chromosomal material. If they say "no," I would not tell them
c. Wait for the parents to ask which of them is the carrier, and if they ask, tell them
d. Provide full disclosure whether or not they ask for it
e. Not disclose information about carrier status even if asked
f. Tell them they are *both* carriers
g. Tell them that *one* is a carrier, then give them the choice of whether or not they wish to be told which one

WHY did you select this course of action?

A woman of 25 with no family history of genetic disorders and no personal history of exposure to toxic substances requests prenatal diagnosis. There are no genetic or medical indications for its use in this case. Nevertheless, she appears very anxious about the normalcy of the fetus, and persists in her demands for prenatal diagnosis even after being informed that in her case the potential medical risks for the fetus, in terms of miscarriage, may outweigh the likelihood of diagnosing an abnormality. Your clinic has no regulations that would prevent your doing prenatal diagnosis for her. What would you do, as a professional?

a. Perform prenatal diagnosis
b. Refuse to perform prenatal diagnosis
c. Do amniocentesis and have analysis done by whichever lab in the region could do a "low priority" sample

Source: The counseling scenarios have been incorporated by Dorothy C. Wertz and John C. Fletcher in the Appendix of their forthcoming book *Ethics and Human Genetics: A Cross-cultural Perspective* (Heidelberg: Springer-Verlag). Used by permission.

WHY did you select this course of action?

Repeated MSAFP [maternal serum alpha fetoprotein] tests reveal a value that is *below* the norm. Although some studies have found low MSAFP values to be associated with Down syndrome, geneticists are not in agreement about how a low value should be interpreted. What do you tell the family?

   a. Tell them that the tests indicate a possible Down syndrome fetus and urge them to have PDX [prenatal diagnosis]
   b. Tell them that the MSAFP value is low, but that research on this topic is so new that we do not know how to interpret the test results
   c. Tell them that geneticists are not in agreement about the interpretation of test results, but that some geneticists think there may be a possibility of Down syndrome, and then let then decide whether or not to have PDX
   d. Not tell them about the test results

WHY did you select this course of action?

Assume that in the near future a test is developed that is sufficiently sensitive to predict susceptibility to brown lung and other occupationally-related diseases affecting factory workers exposed to dust. You are a member of an advisory group that will develop guidelines for mass screening of workers in your country. Do you believe that mass genetic screening of workers and prospective employees in potentially dangerous industries should be

   a. Mandatory for all who would be occupationally exposed
   b. Voluntary

WHY did you select this course of action?

Discussion

In their contributions to *Ethics and Human Genetics,* our contact geneticists in the 18 nations identified six ethical problems that are most likely to receive attention in the future, in the following order: (1) fairness of access to scarce genetic services; (2) protecting or establishing rights of choice, especially

Source: The discussion has been incorporated by Dorothy C. Wertz and John C. Fletcher in Chapter One of their forthcoming book *Ethics and Human Genetics: A Cross-cultural Perspective* (Heidelberg: Springer-Verlag). Used by permission.

with regard to abortion, in cases of fetal malformations; (3) protecting the privacy of genetic information; (4) disclosing psychologically sensitive information to patients; (5) requests for prenatal diagnosis without medical indications (e.g., for sex selection); and (6) directive versus nondirective counseling. The first three especially involve societal interests and will require attention by policy-makers.

The issue with the widest social ramifications is disclosure of personal information. Geneticists around the world agreed that third parties such as insurance companies and employers should not have access to personal genetic data without consent. Realizing the potential power of institutions to engineer consent by denying employment or insurance, a substantial minority of geneticists believed that third parties should have no access at all. In the future, discrimination on genetic grounds in the workplace, in schools, or in insurance promises to be one of the thorniest policy problems arising from advances in genetics. Balancing individual rights to privacy, protection of health, and, in some nations, the legitimate interests of institutions, will be matters for legislation and public debate that go beyond the doctor–patient encounter.

Other types of disclosure—to family or patient—are closer to the usual practice of clinical genetics. Most patients, including those in the United States, are in effect scientifically illiterate. Few know enough about genetics to suspect what types of personal information tests may reveal, and therefore few will request information on their own initiative. The geneticist must therefore decide whether and what to disclose. Nondisclosure and selective disclosure are forms of directiveness. On the other hand, disclosure to an unsuspecting person who does not ask and may not wish to know, for example, an XY female or a person at risk for HD, does not respect the "right not to know," and may also cause harm. Geneticists in our survey would disclose some types of information, such as ambiguous, conflicting, or controversial test results, but would withhold other types of information, such as false paternity. In deciding what to disclose and what to withhold, many apparently weighed benefits against harms of disclosure. Few saw any harm in revealing test results, while almost all saw great harm—and no benefit—in telling a husband that he was not the child's biological father. In some cases geneticists were divided about which course of action would lead to the least harm. This explains the lack of consensus almost everywhere about disclosing which parent was a translocation carrier, XY genotype in a female, or risks for HD or hemophilia A. To some extent, disclosure depends on individual characteristics of the patient. Some said that they would more likely disclose to well-educated patients or to those well versed in genetics, because such patients would experience less harm. In the future, as genetic knowledge becomes more widespread among the public, the balance will probably tip in favor of full disclosure, including disclosure to relatives at risk. False paternity will likely remain an exception; geneticists are not clinical psychologists, and few clinics—or patients—have the resources that would be necessary to heal the wounds from revelation of marital secrets.

Geneticists' approaches to individual cases have social ramifications. Two examples are prenatal diagnosis for maternal anxiety and for sex selection. Many clinicians want to respect patients' wishes and want to avoid paternalism. Indeed, in nations where abortions are available on request and where prenatal diagnostic services are in adequate supply, it might seem reasonable to respond to all patient requests. On the other hand, giving individual patients what they want also has social consequences, and clinicians must become aware of these. For example, what if many families wanted their first-born to be a boy—a strong preference in the United States—and achieved this family constellation through prenatal diagnosis? This would change children's socialization and self-images, and tip the balance of power between the sexes because first-borns have material and social advantages.

There seems to be a developing trend in some nations toward acceding to patient requests for sex selection. Responses from the United States and Canada contrast markedly with findings from surveys conducted in 1973–74 and 1975, when only 1% and 21% of geneticists were willing to perform prenatal diagnosis for sex selection only. Since chorionic villus sampling is done before quickening, the demand for prenatal sex selection may increase as the procedure becomes widely available. The geneticists' reasons for facilitating sex selection mention little about its social consequences or the potential harm to the practice of medical genetics itself. To some, sex selection appeared to be an extension of families' right to determine the number, spacing, and quality of their children. Others mentioned how easily patients desiring sex selection could claim, for example, that they had toxic exposure that required prenatal karyotyping. Although it would be possible to withhold information about fetal sex, this contravenes the practice of full disclosure and respect for patients' rights to know.

What of the future? Would a survey five years from now reveal greater consensus around the world? Possibly—especially with regard to situations where there is already a strong consensus, such as belief in nondirective counseling or disclosure of test results. On the other hand, some differences will be inevitable. For example, the strength of the workers' movement, legal protection for employees, and job opportunities in individual nations will affect policies about mandatory or voluntary screening; there is no universal "right" answer. Requests for sex selection must be seen in the context of the entire range of parental choices and the limits that a society chooses to set on such choices. If prenatal sex selection unrelated to X-linked disease becomes prevalent, we cannot help but wonder if demands for selection on other nonmedical characteristics will follow.

As genetic technology and services become more complex and present more difficult moral dilemmas than in the past, medical geneticists around the world may be drawn together to face these problems. At present, there are impressive cross-national differences of opinion.

8

ETHICAL ISSUES
RELATING TO AIDS

There are traditional ethical principles that are often used in making ethical decisions. For example:

Do not hurt individuals
Help individuals
Let individuals make their own important decisions
Do not hurt (endanger) society
Help society to improve itself
Treat all individuals equally to the extent that this is possible

We have seen these maxims clash as we have delved into many medical–ethical issues; this should not have come as a surprise. The ethical questions raised by the practice of medicine are the questions raised by the difficulties of life—they are merely brought into sharper focus by the immediacy of medical needs. Where these needs run the gamut from individual to social needs; where the obligations of professionals seem to go beyond the obligations of others; where pain and suffering are unavoidable, easy answers must be false answers.

Nowhere is this seen more readily than with AIDS. Indeed, AIDS touches just about every issue raised in this book, in part because AIDS is now everyone's concern. No longer a disease solely of homosexuals and drug addicts, AIDS affects heterosexuals, women, infants, and a large proportion of some Third World nations.

What are some of the relevant medical facts about AIDS?

AIDS was first delineated as a disease entity in 1981. It is characterized by malaise, high fever, and diarrhea. It often leads to death from a form of pneumonia (Pneumocystis carinii) or a previously rare form of skin cancer (Kaposi's sarcoma). By 1983, it had been found among intravenous drug users, homosexual males, Haitians, persons receiving blood transfusions, central Africans, and heterosexual partners of patients with AIDS and infants whose mothers were in the previously mentioned risk groups. AIDS was found to be transmitted by a virus, which was named the human immunodeficiency virus; HIV, for short.

Studies so far indicate that there are three main routes of transmission: sexual (exchange of fluids, especially semen, during contact); contact with infected blood; and intrauterine (from affected pregnant woman to fetus). Not yet shown to be involved in transmission are nonintimate personal contact, e.g. living in the same household with an AIDS patient; health-care activities not involving exposure to blood; and insects. Blood and semen are definite carriers of the virus and have seen shown to have transmitted AIDS. Breast milk and vaginal fluid are likely transmitters of the virus. HIV has also been found in tears and saliva as well as in urine, serum, cerebrospinal fluid, and alveolar fluid. But there is yet no evidence that these fluids have ever transmitted the disease.

Contact with the virus can be confirmed with a positive seroconversion (ELISA) test. Some people who have been in contact with the virus fail to give a positive result (false negative). Some people who have never been in contact with the virus give a positive result (false positive). There is a period of unknown length between (1) the time of contact and the time of conversion to seropositivity; and (2) the time of seroconversion and onset of disease symptoms. Not every seropositive person has yet had clinical symptoms of AIDS, and it is possible that some never will.

However, to this date, once the symptoms of AIDS do appear, death due to some aspect of AIDS is a certainty. (Ninety percent of patients with AIDS will not survive beyond four years from the onset of symptoms.) There is a related syndrome, AIDS-related complex (ARC), which is a less serious form of the AIDS symptoms. Of patients with ARC, it is now felt that about twenty-five percent will progress to AIDS within three years.

In brief, these are the facts about AIDS. How does AIDS differ from other diseases? Why is it such a morass of problems?

Although we have learned a great deal about AIDS, there still remains *uncertainty.* For example, how long is the incubation period (the time between infection and the onset of symptoms of AIDS); or does it differ so much from case to case that there is no reasonable answer to this question?

AIDS is one hundred percent *fatal,* once the symptoms appear. But getting AIDS is actually rather difficult without intimate sexual contact or inoculation with affected blood. Thus it is safer to deal with AIDS patients than with patients with meningitis, since this disease is much easier to get than

AIDS. Yet the "death sentence" that comes with AIDS means to some that nothing justifies even the smallest risk of catching AIDS, especially where children might be involved.

It is tempting to say that such fear is understandable even if it is irrational. But is it even irrational? While it is just plain wrong to think that AIDS is easier to catch than meningitis, it would not be irrational to be more afraid of catching AIDS than of catching meningitis, since there are no recoveries from AIDS. A person with this perspective might value his or her life more than whatever good might come from helping others with AIDS, which may be a selfish perspective, but it is not irrational.

Even if the fear is not considered irrational, should it be excused? Health professionals, it might be argued, should treat patients in need, and treat them equally. Doctors have been told by medical associations, hospitals, and medical schools that patients are to be treated appropriately whether they have AIDS or appendicitis. Physicians and other health-care professionals are not allowed to refuse to treat patients with AIDS or with positive tests for the antibody. If we hold these people to a "higher" standard in the case of AIDS, we may in effect be forcing this higher standard on the families (and other patients) of physicians. Is this unfair? Is the only answer, "Yes—but life is unfair. No one forced you to be a physician."

Many books and articles on AIDS point out that homosexuality is still a stigma to many people. It is bad enough to have a fatal disease, but to have a disease that brands one, in the eyes of many, as an undesirable is certainly worse. The claim has been made that research on AIDS was slowed because no one in authority believed that a disease of homosexuals was worth the time and money needed for a fuller understanding.

These factors—the uncertainties of the disease process itself, the fears attached to the one-hundred percent mortality of the disease, the negative social worth attached by many to the disease—give a unique twist to what otherwise might be no more than another outbreak of a serious disease. For example, if Legionnaire's disease had not been contained so well and had spread as AIDS has spread, it is unlikely that the ethical and social problems raised by Legionnaire's disease would approach those raised by AIDS.

Let us turn now to some of the traditional areas of medical ethics that have been invaded by the issue of AIDS.

A patient tells you that he is bisexual and that he has engaged in high-risk behavior. He is about to be married but has no plans to tell his future wife about his previous behavior. Is there an implied morally binding agreement to keep a patient's confidences? Suppose the patient, before telling you of his impending marriage, had asked you to test him for AIDS and he tested positive for the virus. He had asked you to keep the results of the test confidential and you said "Of course." You then found out through a third party that he is about to get married. What are the physician's professional responsibilities in these cases? What are the physician's moral obligations in these cases? Are there differences between professional and moral obligations? Suppose the patient had some clinical manifestations of the disease. Should there be some legal guidelines here to follow?

This case and its variations are based on an old example, "Don't tell my wife that I have contracted gonorrhea (from a prostitute)." The issues raised are the same. The difference is the urgency felt. Gonorrhea is treatable. All sorts of wrongs may be committed in the case of gonorrhea, but almost certainly no one will die. With AIDS and its one hundred percent mortality, the temptation to keep the confidence is much smaller than it is concerning gonorrhea.

In which glossary, one of medical terms or of ethical terms, should the expression, "high-risk (sexual) behavior" appear? It is clearly a value-laden term. To some it is an explosive term. Sometimes clinical medicine is given the look of a value-free discipline: Physicians are to identify the disease causing problems and then cure it. But, as our examples show, such a picture of medicine is misleading at best. Certainly, with AIDS, we see the merging of virology, medicine, social needs, and personal desires.

It seems that now all patients have to be educated about AIDS. Young adults who may be considering becoming sexually active definitely have to be told something (about AIDS, about "safe" sex, about becoming sexually active). Confidentiality can become an issue here again. Suppose a teenager confides "I am gay." One doesn't need much of an imagination to see how such a comment might put a family physician in a bind.

We have already read Daniel Callahan's argument from his book *Setting Limits*. From the economic standpoint the health-care system just cannot take much more financial strain. The elderly, especially the elderly ill, are just going to have to make do with less health care even if theoretically there is enough to cure them of whatever it is that they have at the moment.

Perhaps we shall have to say the same to AIDS patients. There is more than money involved here. As teaching institutions take on more AIDS patients, more resident time will have to go into the care of these patients. Will this put too much strain on the medical educational system? AIDS will cut into what is considered good, balanced medical education. It has been suggested that, at least at the end stages, AIDS patients need home care and hospice care. They really do not belong in traditional hospital settings. Is this view just self-serving?

What do we do with recalcitrant AIDS sufferers? There are people with AIDS who continue their high-risk behavior for a variety of reasons. Ought we to make such actions crimes? Should we jail such people on the grounds that they constitute a public menace?

Is AIDS itself such a public menace that mandatory testing should be required? This is partly a factual question. So long as the tests give enough false positives in a low-risk (large) population, testing is probably not worthwhile. What makes it a bad idea is that there would be emotional distress caused to the people with false positives. But perhaps that is just the price that a few people have to pay to keep the rest of us safe. But who is to count as "us"?

Preventive medicine has always yielded uneven results, especially in cases for which data are unclear and valued parts of a lifestyle are called into question. In the case of AIDS, homosexuals seem to have changed their high-risk behaviors quickly and with good results. But drug users (needle users) and prostitutes (many of whom are also drug users) have not. What rights do we have against these two groups? What sorts of educational efforts do we owe these groups? AIDS may well force us to negotiate between force and reason.

We often hear the comment, "Life is unfair." This is especially highlighted by AIDS. When an infant is born with AIDS or when a child with hemophilia develops AIDS because of contaminated blood, we think to ourselves, "That's unfair." When gays develop AIDS because of behavior that they had no reason to believe would lead to fatal illness, they also think "How unfair." No matter what the behavior that leads to AIDS, if the treatment of the AIDS victim only adds to the suffering, something has gone wrong somewhere. But are these truly medical issues? Are these social issues? Are these religious issues best left untouched by those of us trying to get a clear conceptual understanding of medicine in all its facets?

In much of the literature on AIDS, we see over and over the theme that the AIDS patient can become a kind of outcast. As a society, we think that we have come a long way since the time of shunning leper colonies. We think that we are much more sensitive to the needs of victims of disease. We are, and what this shows is that the easing, and therefore the understanding, of suffering so often necessary for healing *is* a legitimate part of medicine, for medicine is really just a part of being human and offering help to those in need.

AIDS: Prevention
in Health-Care Workers

Guidelines from the Centers for Disease Control (CDC) illustrate the measures needed to insure the safety of health-care workers. The safety measures are not new to workers in the fields of microbiology or infectious diseases. Now, however, such precautions must become second nature to just about all health-care workers.

PRECAUTIONS TO PREVENT
TRANSMISSION OF HIV

Universal Precautions

Since medical history and examination cannot reliably identify all patients infected with HIV or other blood-borne pathogens, blood and body-fluid precautions should be consistently used for *all* patients. This approach, previously recommended by CDC (*3,4*), and referred to as "universal blood and body-fluid precautions" or "universal precautions," should be used in the care of *all* patients, especially including those in emergency-care settings in which the risk of blood exposure is increased and the infection status of the patient is usually unknown (*20*).

  1. All health-care workers should routinely use appropriate barrier precautions to prevent skin and mucous-membrane exposure when contact with blood or other body fluids of any patient is anticipated. Gloves should be worn for touching blood and body fluids, mucous membranes, or non-intact skin of all patients, for handling items or surfaces soiled with blood or body fluids, and for performing venipuncture and other vascular access procedures. Gloves should be changed after contact with each patient. Masks and protective eyewear or face shields should be worn during procedures that are likely to generate droplets of blood or other body fluids to prevent exposure of mucous membranes of the mouth, nose, and eyes. Gowns or aprons should be worn during procedures that are likely to generate splashes of blood or other body fluids.

  2. Hands and other skin surfaces should be washed immediately and thoroughly if contaminated with blood or other body fluids. Hands should be washed immediately after gloves are removed.

  3. All health-care workers should take precautions to prevent injuries caused by needles, scalpels, and other sharp instruments or devices during procedures; when cleaning used instruments; during disposal of used needles; and when handling sharp instruments after procedures. To prevent needlestick injuries, needles should not be recapped, purposely bent or broken by hand, removed from disposable syringes, or otherwise manipulated by hand. After they are used, disposable syringes and needles, scalpel blades, and other sharp items

Source: "Precautions to Prevent Transmission of HIV." *Morbidity and Mortality Weekly Report,* vol. 36, no. 2s (August 21, 1987), pp. 1s-18s.

should be placed in puncture-resistant containers for disposal; the puncture-resistant containers should be located as close as practical to the use area. Large-bore reusable needles should be placed in a puncture-resistant container for transport to the reprocessing area.

4. Although saliva has not been implicated in HIV transmission, to minimize the need for emergency mouth-to-mouth resuscitation, mouthpieces, resuscitation bags, or other ventilation devices should be available for use in areas in which the need for resuscitation is predictable.

5. Health-care workers who have exudative lesions or weeping dermatitis should refrain from all direct patient care and from handling patient-care equipment until the condition resolves.

6. Pregnant health-care workers are not known to be at greater risk of contracting HIV infection than health-care workers who are not pregnant; however, if a health-care worker develops HIV infection during pregnancy, the infant is at risk of infection resulting from perinatal transmission. Because of this risk, pregnant health-care workers should be especially familiar with and strictly adhere to precautions to minimize the risk of HIV transmission.

Implementation of universal blood and body-fluid precautions for *all* patients eliminates the need for use of the isolation category of "Blood and Body Fluid Precautions" previously recommended by CDC (7) for patients known or suspected to be infected with blood-borne pathogens. Isolation precautions (e.g., enteric, "AFB" [7]) should be used as necessary if associated conditions, such as infectious diarrhea or tuberculosis, are diagnosed or suspected.

Precautions for Invasive Procedures

In this document, an invasive procedure is defined as surgical entry into tissues, cavities, or organs or repair of major traumatic injuries 1) in an operating or delivery room, emergency department, or outpatient setting, including both physicians' and dentists' offices; 2) cardiac catheterization and angiographic procedures; 3) a vaginal or cesarean delivery or other invasive obstetric procedure during which bleeding may occur; or 4) the manipulation, cutting, or removal of any oral or perioral tissues, including tooth structure, during which bleeding occurs or the potential for bleeding exists. The universal blood and body-fluid precautions listed above, combined with the precautions listed below, should be the minimum precautions for *all* such invasive procedures.

1. All health-care workers who participate in invasive procedures must routinely use appropriate barrier precautions to prevent skin and

mucous-membrane contact with blood and other body fluids of all patients. Gloves and surgical masks must be worn for all invasive procedures. Protective eyewear or face shields should be worn for all invasive procedures. Protective eyewear or face shields should be worn for procedures that commonly result in the generation of droplets, splashing of blood or other body fluids, or the generation of bone chips. Gowns or aprons made of materials that provide an effective barrier should be worn during invasive procedures that are likely to result in the splashing of blood or other body fluids. All health-care workers who perform or assist in vaginal or cesarean deliveries should wear gloves and gowns when handling the placenta or the infant until blood and amniotic fluid have been removed from the infant's skin and should wear gloves during post-delivery care of the umbilical cord.

2. If a glove is torn or a needlestick or other injury occurs, the glove should be removed and a new glove used as promptly as patient safety permits; the needle or instrument involved in the incident should also be removed from the sterile field.

Precautions for Laboratories

Blood and other body fluids from *all* patients should be considered infective. To supplement the universal blood and body-fluid precautions listed above, the following precautions are recommended for health-care workers in clinical laboratories.

1. All specimens of blood and body fluids should be put in a well-constructed container with a secure lid to prevent leaking during transport. Care should be taken when collecting each specimen to avoid contaminating the outside of the container and of the laboratory form accompanying the specimen.

2. All persons processing blood and body-fluid specimens (e.g., removing tops from vacuum tubes) should wear gloves. Masks and protective eyewear should be worn if mucous-membrane contact with blood or body fluids is anticipated. Gloves should be changed and hands washed after completion of specimen processing.

3. For routine procedures, such as histologic and pathologic studies or microbiologic culturing, a biological safety cabinet is not necessary. However, biological safety cabinets (Class I or II) should be used whenever procedures are conducted that have a high potential for generating droplets. These include activities such as blending, sonicating, and vigorous mixing.

4. Mechanical pipetting devices should be used for manipulating all liquids in the laboratory. Mouth pipetting must not be done.

5. Use of needles and syringes should be limited to situations in which there is no alternative, and the recommendations for preventing injuries with needles outlined under universal precautions should be followed.

6. Laboratory work surfaces should be decontaminated with an appropriate chemical germicide after a spill of blood or other body fluids and when work activities are completed.

7. Contaminated materials used in laboratory tests should be decontaminated before reprocessing or be placed in bags and disposed of in accordance with institutional policies for disposal of infective waste (24).

8. Scientific equipment that has been contaminated with blood or other body fluids should be decontaminated and cleaned before being repaired in the laboratory or transported to the manufacturer.

9. All persons should wash their hands after completing laboratory activities and should remove protective clothing before leaving the laboratory.

Implementation of universal blood and body-fluid precautions for all patients eliminates the need for warning labels on specimens since blood and other body fluids from all patients should be considered infective.

References

1. CDC. Acquired immunodeficiency syndrome (AIDS): Precautions for clinical and laboratory staffs. MMWR 1982;31:577–80.
2. CDC. Acquired immunodeficiency syndrome (AIDS): Precautions for health-care workers and allied professionals MMWR 1983;32:450–51.
3. CDC. Recommendations for preventing transmission of infection with human T-lymphotropic virus type III/lymphadenopathy-associated virus in the workplace. MMWR 1985;34:681-6, 691–95.
4. CDC. Recommendations for preventing transmission of infection with human T-lymphotropic virus type III/lymphadenopathy-associated virus during invasive procedures. MMWR 1986;35:221–23.
5. CDC. Recommendations for preventing possible transmission of human T-lymphotropic virus type III/lymphadenopathy-associated virus from tears. MMWR 1985;34:533–34.
6. CDC. Recommendations for providing dialysis treatment to patients infected with human T-lymphotropic virus type III/lymphadenopathy-associated virus infection. MMWR 1986;35:376–78, 383.
7. GARNER JS, SIMMONS BP. Guideline for isolation precautions in hospitals. Infect Control 1983;4 (suppl) :245–325.
8. CDC. Recommended infection control practices for dentistry. MMWR 1986; 35:237–42.

9. McCRAY E. The Cooperative Needlestick Surveillance Group. Occupational risk of the acquired immunodeficiency syndrome among health care workers. N Engl J Med 1986;314:1127–32.

10. HENDERSON DK, SAAH AJ, ZAK BJ, et al. Risk of nosocomial infection with human T-cell lymphotropic virus type III/lymphadenopathy-associated virus in a large cohort of intensively exposed health care workers. Ann Intern Med 1986;104:644–47.

11. GERBERDING JL, BRYANT-LEBLANC CE, NELSON K, et al. Risk of transmitting the human immunodeficiency virus, cytomegalovirus, and hepatitis B virus to health care workers exposed to patients with AIDS and AIDS-related conditions. J Infect Dis 1987;156:1–8.

12. McEVOY M, PORTER K, MORTIMER P, SIMMONS N, SHANSON D. Prospective study of clinical, laboratory, and ancillary staff with accidental exposures to blood or other body fluids from patients infected with HIV. Br Med J 1987;294:1595–97.

13. Anonymous. Needlestick transmission of HTLV-III from a patient infected in Africa. Lancet 1984;2:1376–77.

14. OKSENHENDLER E, HARZIC M, LE ROUX JM, RABIAN C, CLAUVEL JP. HIV infection with seroconversion after a superficial needlestick injury to the finger. N Engl J Med 1986;315:582.

15. NEISSON-VERNANT C, ARFI S, MATHEZ D, LEIBOWITCH J, MONPLAISIR N. Needlestick HIV seroconversion in a nurse. Lancet 1986;2:814.

16. GRINT P, McEVOY M. Two associated cases of the acquired immune deficiency syndrome (AIDS). PHLS Commun Dis Rep 1985;42:4.

17. CDC. Apparent transmission of human T-lymphotropic virus type III/ lymphadenopathy-associated virus from a child to a mother providing health care. MMWR 1986;35:76–79.

18. CDC. Update: human immunodeficiency virus infections in health-care workers exposed to blood of infected patients. MMWR 1987;36:285–89.

19. KLINE RS, PHELAN J, FRIEDLAND GH, et al. Low occupational risk for HIV infection for dental professional [Abstract]. In: Abstracts from the III International Conference on AIDS. 1–5. June 1985. Washington, DC: 155.

20. BAKER JL, KELEN GD, SIVERTSON KT, QUINN TC. Unsuspected human immunodeficiency virus in critically ill emergency patients. JAMA 1987;257:2609–11.

21. FAVERO MS. Dialysis-associated diseases and their control. In: Bennett JV, Brachman PS, eds. Hospital infections. Boston: Little, Brown and Company, 1985:267–84.

22. RICHARDSON JH, Barkley WE, eds. Biosafety in microbiological and biomedical laboratories, 1984. Washington, DC: U.S. Department of Health and Human Services, Public Health Service. HHS publication no. (CDC) 84-8395.

23. CDC. Human T-lymphotropic virus type III/lymphadenopathy-associated virus: Agent summary statement. MMWR 1986;35:540–42, 547–49.

24. Environmental Protection Agency. EPA guide for infectious waste management. Washington, DC: U.S. Environmental Protection Agency, May 1986 (Publication no. EPA/530-SW-86-014).

25. FAVERO MS. Sterilization, disinfection, and antisepsis in the hospital. In: Manual of clinical microbiology. 4th ed. Washington, DC: American Society for Microbiology, 1985;129–37.

26. GARNER JS, Favero MS. Guideline for handwashing and hospital environmental control, 1985. Atlanta: Public Health Service, Centers for Disease Control, 1985. HHS publication no. 99-1117.

27. SPIRE B, MONTAGNIER L, BARRÉ-SINOUSSI F, CHERMANN JC. Inactivation of lymphadenopathy associated virus by chemical disinfectants. Lancet 1984;2:899-901.

28. MARTIN LS, McDOUGAL JS, LOSKOSKI SL. Disinfection and inactivation of the human T-lymphotropic virus type III/lymphadenopathy-associated virus. J Infect Dis 1985; 152:400-403.

29. McDOUGAL JS, MARTIN LS, CORT SP, et al. Thermal inactivation of the acquired immunodeficiency syndrome virus-III/lymphadenopathy-associated virus, with special reference to antihemophilic factor. J Clin Invest 1985;76:875-77.

30. SPIRE B, BARRÉ-SINOUSSI F, DORMONT D, MONTAGNIER L, CHERMANN JC. Inactivation of lymphadenopathy-associated virus by heat, gamma rays, and ultraviolet light. Lancet 1985;1:188-89.

31. RESNIK, L, VEREN K, SALAHUDDIN SZ, TONDREAU S, MARKHAM PD. Stability and inactivation of HTLV-III/LAV under clinical and laboratory environments. JAMA 1986;255:1887-91.

32. CDC. Public Health Service (PHS) guidelines for counseling and antibody testing to prevent HIV infection and AIDS. MMWR 1987;3:509-15.

33. KANE MA, LETTAU LA. Transmission of HBV from dental personnel to patients. J Am Dent Assoc 1985;110:634-36.

34. LETTAU LA, SMITH JD, WILLIAMS D, et al. Transmission of hepatitis B with resultant restriction of surgical practice. JAMA 1986;255:934-37.

35. WILLIAMS WW. Guideline for infection control in hospital personnel. Infect Control 1983;4 (suppl) :326-49.

36. CDC. Prevention of acquired immune deficiency syndrome (AIDS): Report of inter-agency recommendations. MMWR 1983;32:101-103.

37. CDC. Provisional Public Health Service inter-agency recommendations for screening donated blood and plasma for antibody to the virus causing acquired immunodeficiency syndrome. MMWR 1985;34:1-5.

AIDS: Counseling Test Subjects

In some ways, the counseling technique discussed here is business as usual: Give information; use open-ended questions, and be nonjudgmental. Much of this should remind you of the points made about nondirective genetic counseling. Notice, however, that the HIV counseling style recommended here is different in important ways. There is an insistence on a postcounseling session with those who do test positive. Physicians are told that they "must" make an attempt to change any high-risk behavior of their counselees. What would be the analogous "must" for a genetic counselor?

COUNSELING
THE HIV-TEST SUBJECT . . .

Robert C. Rinaldi and John J. Henning

The impact of human immunodeficiency virus (HIV) disease on the health-care system is increasing. Specialized centers alone are unable to provide all required services. Physicians and other health professionals will encounter a growing number of concerned individuals and family members who need counseling about possible exposure to HIV.

Although counseling related to HIV antibody testing has been widely recommended,[1-3] the medical literature contains little in the way of specific guidelines to conduct this counseling. The following provides a brief outline of some essential elements required to conduct HIV antibody blood test counseling.

Pretest Procedures

During the pretest session the physician must provide information about HIV, AIDS and the test, conduct a sex and drug history, and provide counseling. The patient should be told about the virus, HIV-related diseases, routes of transmission and methods of reducing the risk of infection. This can be accomplished through a variety of mediums including videotape, audiotape, printed matter, group lecture and one-to-one interaction.[4]

The pretest session also must include a patient history of sexual behavior and drug use. The physician should use frank, nonjudgmental, open-ended questions to determine the patient's risk of HIV infection. The physician must be sure that the patient understands the words being used.

Discussing sexual behavior is difficult for many patients and physicians. The interview style and terminology used should be tailored to suit the comfort of the individual patient and physician. The patient's sexual orientation is less important than the specific sexual practices in which he or she engages.

Discussing drug use with patients also may be difficult. However, information on intravenous drug use and needle sharing is essential. A full drug use history including substances such as alcohol and marijuana can also be helpful.

Pretest counseling should include discussion of medical, psychological and social implications of the HIV antibody blood test. Specific recom-

Source: "Counseling the HIV-Test Subject" by Robert C. Rinaldi and John J. Henning. Ohio Medicine, vol. 86, no. 2 (February 1990), pp. 100–102. Used by permission.

mendations for behavior change must be based on the physician's assessment of risk. Finally, the physician can assist the patient in deciding whether or not to be tested.

Essential elements of the pretest counseling session include:

- Ask directly why the patient believes he/she needs to be tested.
- Explain that the test determines the presence or absence of antibodies to the virus.
- Discuss the meaning of a positive test result: The individual is infected and assumed contagious but does not necessarily have AIDS.
- Discuss the meaning of a negative test result: An individual is not currently demonstrating infection but is *not* "protected" against the virus.
- Discuss the possibilities of false-positive or indeterminate results.
- Discuss ways to modify behavior to reduce risks.
- Discuss the confidentiality of test results in relation to office/clinic procedures and state reporting requirements.
- Discuss potential benefits of anonymous testing.
- Discuss the stress often related to waiting for test results and possible reactions to learning results (e.g., depression and anxiety).
- Discuss potential negative social consequences of being tested and/ or being seropositive (employment, housing, insurance and personal relationship ramifications).
- Assist the patient in making a decision about testing.
- Obtain consent before voluntary testing is conducted (local statutes pertaining to adults and minors should be consulted).
- Make an appointment for a return face-to-face visit to give and discuss test results.

Post-test Counseling

Disclosure of the test result is best done at the beginning of the post-test session in a direct manner. Many patients anxiously anticipate the test result and are eager to learn the findings. After the result is disclosed, the patient should be encouraged to express feelings. Repeating the patient's remarks and labeling his or her underlying feelings is often helpful.

Reporting a positive result can be difficult. If the patient had predicted a positive result during the pretest counseling session, the physician might say, "Well your prediction was right. Your tests show that you have the virus." Although it is important to be honest and straightforward in reporting a positive result, it is equally important to give the seropositive patient hope. Quoting the annual percentage of seropositive individuals who actually become ill (approximately 7% to 10% per year) and mentioning the ongoing scientific search for effective treatments and vaccines might prove helpful.

The physician must assess the patient's understanding of the result by asking a question such as "Now that you know you are antibody positive (or negative), what does this test result mean for you?" The physician must help the patient understand and assimilate the information. A review of the information conveyed in the pretest session should be conducted.

When the result is negative, the patient's understanding of how to prevent future infection must be assessed. When the result is positive, the patient must be advised on how to avoid infecting others. He or she must understand that infection is probably lifelong but that having a positive antibody test alone does not mean one has AIDS. It is also important to communicate to seropositive individuals that they are probably infectious to others by the established routes of transmission and that there is currently no way to predict with certainty when and if clinical symptoms will develop. Antibody-positive persons should be told:

- Do not donate blood, semen or body organs.
- Employ what have come to be known as "safer sex practices."
- Do not share personal hygiene items (e.g., razors, toothbrushes).
- Inform physicians and dentists of serologic status.
- Encourage sexual partners and needle contacts to seek evaluation and serologic testing.

The physician must be sensitive to the wide range of psychological reactions possible when the test result is given. For seronegative patients, an immediate reaction of surprise and relief may occur, followed by an overall reduction of psychological distress and anxiety. Seropositive individuals may react with expression of disbelief, anger, fear, guilt or self-recrimination. Clinical depression often occurs among those testing positive for HIV antibody.[5-6] In some, the depression may lead to suicidal thoughts or attempts.[7]

Seropositive patients sometimes require repeated sessions, supportive services and monitoring of psychological functioning. A psychiatric referral should be made for patients who require assistance in adapting to current conditions or managing feelings of depression or anxiety beyond what the primary care physician can offer. A patient may also benefit from counseling hotlines, HIV support groups and/or psychotherapy. A schedule to monitor medical status must be determined as well.

The post-test session also should include an assessment of the patient's commitment to altering high-risk behaviors. The physician must work with the patient to promote behavior change by reiterating routes of transmission, discussing risks and highlighting methods of risk reduction.

In summary, essential elements of the post-test counseling session include:

- Provide the test result.
- Allow the patient to express feelings and reactions.
- Assess the patient's understanding of the test results.
- Review routes of transmission.
- Assess the patient's psychological condition.
- Recommend psychiatric follow-up when appropriate.
- Assess risk behavior and commitment to risk-reduction strategies.
- Recommend medical follow-up.
- Recommend additional support services as needed.

Conclusion

The need for HIV antibody blood test counseling has been widely acknowledged. Physicians must be prepared to provide such services for their patients. The brief guidelines presented here serve as an outline for HIV antibody blood test counseling to patients.[8]

Notes

[1]Board of Trustees: (Report LLL) Progress in the prevention and control of AIDS. Annual meeting, American Medical Association, Chicago, IL, June 1988.

[2]Perry SW, Markowitz JC: Counseling for HIV testing. *Hosp Comm Psychiatry* 1988;39:731–738.

[3]Henry K, Maki M, Crossley K: Analysis of the use of HIV antibody testing in a Minnesota Hospital. *JAMA*. 1988;259:229–232.

[4]*AIDS counseling and HIV-antibody testing: A position paper.* Coalition for AIDS prevention and education. Washington, DC, American Psychological Association, 1987.

[5]Faulstich ME: Psychiatric aspects of AIDS. *Am J Psychiatry* 1987;144:551–556.

[6]Miller D: HIV counseling: Some practical problems and issues. *JR Soc Med* 1987;80:278–280.

[7]Marzuk PM, Tierney H, Tardiff K, et al: Increased risk of suicide in persons with AIDS. *JAMA* 1988;259:1333–1337.

[8]Rinaldi RC: *HIV blood test counseling: AMA physician guidelines.* Chicago, IL, American Medical Association, 1988.

The Rights of Persons with AIDS

Gostin and Curran examine the moral and legal implications of some measures which, if legally enforced, might help to control the spread of AIDS.

Each of the measures examined would also have the effect of curtailing some personal liberty. The authors recognize that the public might be in favor of turning to the law for help in dealing with AIDS. After an analysis of the various possibilities, Gostin and Curran conclude that such measures would be either counterproductive or so clearly unfair that they should not be undertaken.

THE LIMITS OF COMPULSION
IN CONTROLLING AIDS

Larry Gostin
and
William J. Curran

AIDS poses an unparalleled challenge for health policy makers seeking methods to reduce its spread and to help ensure public safety, consistent with the protection of individual rights. Pressure is mounting on public health officials to consider compulsory infection control strategies. Many see the use of compulsion as necessary to counter the epidemic. The United States Assistant Secretary for Health asked us to examine legal and regulatory methods for controlling the spread of AIDS.[1] This article is an outgrowth of that study.

The classic public health response to communicable disease, developed in the late nineteenth and early twentieth centuries, is to identify those who harbor the virus by casefinding (testing and screening); to report infectious individuals to public health officials, who keep a register; and to treat or to modify the behavior of those capable of transmitting the infection. A full assessment of compulsory casefinding and reporting appears elsewhere.[2] In that article we put forward a five-tier test for assessing screening programs: (1) the selected population should have a significant reservoir of infection so that there are no disproportionate numbers of uninfected persons having to submit to intrusive testing procedures; (2) the environment within which the population operates must pose a significant risk of communication of the infection; (3) knowledge of the results of testing should enable the authorities to take precautions to reduce the spread of infection which would be effective and which would not otherwise be taken without that knowledge; (4) the critical consequences of the testing and precautions should not be disproportionate to the benefits; and (5) no less restrictive or intrusive means of achieving the public health objective of screening are available. In that article, we also assess the constitutionality and public health efficacy of reporting requirements for positive tests to antibodies for the Human Immunodeficiency Virus (HIV).

Here, we will examine control measures that directly impinge on individual liberty, including sexual contact tracing, quarantine, and the use of the criminal law.

Contact Tracing

Programs of contact notification can occur on two levels: voluntary notification by the client or statutory notification by the public health department. The U.S. Centers for Disease Control (CDC) has recommended the first level of notification by the client in recent guidelines to reduce the transmission of HIV infection.[3] The CDC recommends that serologic testing to detect the presence of antibodies to HIV should be routinely offered to all persons at increased risk of contracting HIV infection. Infected persons should then be counseled to "inform previous sexual partners and any persons with whom needles were shared of their potential exposure to HIV and encourage them to seek counseling/testing." This first level of contact notification is the least intrusive, for it takes place within the confidential health care professional/client relationship, and relies upon the client's voluntary cooperation.

Notification of sexual partners by seropositive individuals can be beneficial, since its objective is to inform the partners that they have been exposed to the infection. The notification provides an opportunity to seek further diagnostic information, including serologic testing; to be counseled; and to modify reproductive, sexual, or drug-using behavior.

CDC guidelines, however, do not address a number of troubling matters: (1) there have been few studies designed to answer the critical question of whether knowledge of sero-status actually influences behavior and, if so, in what direction; (2) there are insufficient resources and services to ensure that testing, public health information, and counseling are provided in a reliable and professional manner; and (3) there are insufficient statutory protections of confidentiality for the client and his or her contacts.

The second level of notification of contacts is more properly termed contact tracing, a form of medical surveillance in which public health officials seek to discover the sexual partners of an index case (a known infected person) and then seek to prevent further spread of the disease, if possible, by treating those contacts. Contact tracing is specifically authorized in many venereal disease statutes across the country. The health care professional reports his or her client's name to the public health department; the name is entered on a register, and the public health officer then has a statutory power or duty to inquire about the person's previous and current sexual partners.

Although the public health officer is authorized to interview the index case in order to identify his or her sexual contacts, it is questionable whether there is authority to compel the person to provide the information. Public health statutes do not specifically empower the public health department to force the individual to cooperate in an interview. There is, for example, no power to cite the patient for contempt. Compelling a person to disclose intimate matters may legally invade the right to privacy both of the patient and the contact. Further, where there are criminal penalties for intentional transfer of infection (see below), compelling the disclosure of names may be a form of self-incrimination proscribed by the U.S. Constitution.

Once a sexual contact has been located, public health officers generally do have statutory power to order a physical examination and treatment. Public health officers must, however, have reasonable grounds for believing that the contact is infected and is refusing treatment.

In most states there is no clear statutory authority for the public health department to trace the sexual contacts of persons with HIV infection. The foundation of contact tracing is a statutory or regulatory requirement to report carriers of the disease. Our survey revealed only five states with an explicit legal requirement to report positive HIV antibody tests (Arizona, Colorado, Idaho, Montana, and Wisconsin). Further, contact tracing is applicable only to venereal disease under most state statutes, and AIDS is not usually classified as a venereal disease.

There are strong reasons against statutory contact tracing as a public health response to the AIDS epidemic. First, the direct public health benefits would be marginal; and, second, the introduction of intrusive measures would seriously undermine other existing public health efforts to contain the spread of the disease.

From a public health perspective, the major question is what use would be made of the data collected from a program of sexual contact tracing. Investigation of sexual partners is most effective when there is a preventive vaccine or therapy. There is an undisputed public health benefit of locating persons potentially exposed to an infectious agent when an effective medical intervention is possible. The availability of penicillin to treat gonorrhea or syphilis, for example, not only preserves the health of the infected person, but also prevents that person from transmitting the disease unless he or she becomes reinfected. Because no such medical intervention exists in relation to AIDS, use of the data would be restricted to education and counseling; public health educational programs and counseling should be available irrespective of any program of compulsory contact tracing. Moreover, education as part of a compulsory program has never been demonstrated to be effective.

AIDS and syphilis also have quite different incubation periods. The first symptoms of syphilis—a chancre followed by slight fever and other constitutional symptoms—appear after an incubation period of twelve to thirty days. Symptoms related to HIV infection may not appear for many years, if at all. In most cases, therefore, transmission of HIV infection will very likely have taken place a considerable time before the index case has been identified and his or her contacts have been located.

Despite these obvious limitations, contact tracing might still be a viable policy option if it did not seriously undermine other public health strategies for controlling the spread of AIDS, and if it did not fundamentally affect the rights and dignity of persons vulnerable to HIV infection. Current public health policy is based upon encouraging persons at high risk of contracting HIV infection to voluntarily seek testing to determine their serological status, to have that information reported to public health departments, and then to modify their behavior. The cooperation of persons vulnerable to HIV infection is critical to the achievement of public health objectives.

The introduction of contact tracing would significantly interfere with these voluntary strategies for controlling the spread of AIDS. At the heart of voluntarism is trust that the physician/patient relationship will remain confidential and that cooperation will not trigger any form of coercion. The specter of the state interviewing the individual to obtain names and addresses, and then tracing sexual partners and informing them of the person's health status would be regarded as highly intrusive and objectionable. Sexual contact tracing in relation to any disease represents a deep intrusion into individual rights of privacy. But the social dimensions of AIDS are unique in the recent history of disease epidemics. Disclosure by the state that a person has HIV infection can lead to social opprobrium among family and friends, and to loss of employment, housing, and insurance.

The probable outcome of statutorily mandated investigation of sexual contacts, therefore, is that individuals vulnerable to HIV infection would not come forward for testing, impeding epidemiologic and public education efforts; they would not seek counseling, care, and treatment in sexually transmitted disease (STD) and drug dependency clinics, harming these vital public health programs; and they might even refrain from seeking therapeutic treatment for physical illness caused by HIV infection, creating human hardship.

The justification for sexual contact tracing is based on the right of the state to enter the realm of private affairs for a clear public health benefit, which could override the deep intrusion into individual privacy. Where sexual contact investigation is of marginal public health benefit, or worse, where it may be seriously counterproductive to the achievement of public health goals, it cannot be justified.

General Isolation or Quarantine

The terms "isolation" and "quarantine" are often used interchangeably in public health statutes and in common parlance; indeed, *Stedman's Medical Dictionary* (1982) circuitously defines quarantine as the isolation of persons with a contagious disease. The two terms, in fact, have different meanings. Historically, quarantine referred to a period (originally forty days) of detention for vessels coming from an area where infectious disease was prevalent. In modern usage quarantine is the restriction of freedom of movement for healthy persons who may have been exposed to a communicable disease in order to prevent contact with unexposed persons; the period of time the quarantine lasts equals the longest usual incubation period for the disease. Isolation is the separation of infected persons from others during the period of communicability so as to prevent transmission of the infectious agent.

The distinction, therefore, is that quarantine affects healthy individuals who may have been exposed to the infectious agent but who are not yet known to be infected; isolation applies to those already known to be infectious, either suffering from the disease or carrying the infectious agent. Since the discussion of confinement in the context of AIDS tends to focus on people who are HIV-positive, whether or not they manifest symptoms of immunosuppression, we will use the term isolation.

In our survey of all fifty states, we found that isolation is the most common personal control measure provided for in public health statutes. It is authorized for a large number of common diseases, in all of the states.[4] Yet state statutes would not currently authorize isolation of persons with AIDS or HIV infections because most state statutes classify AIDS as a communicable or reportable disease, and not as a venereal or sexually transmitted disease. Venereal disease classifications automatically authorize compulsory state interventions, including isolation. At the same time, they provide stricter protections of confidentiality. Communicable disease classifications, including AIDS, do not authorize isolation unless state regulations are specifically amended. No state has specifically amended its legislative or regulatory structure to put AIDS or HIV infection in this category. A recent proposal to do this in Texas failed to be enacted. One reason states have been reluctant to pass specific regulations making persons with AIDS subject to confinement is that regulatory action might be interpreted as an intention actually to use those powers.

While isolation of persons with AIDS is not within the current authority of public health officials at the state or local level, it has been advocated as the only truly effective public health measure available to control the disease. In March 1986 the *American Spectator* said:

> From what we know now, the only alternative available until cures or vaccines, or, both, are developed is to prevent the spread of the disease by making it physically impossible. This implies strict quarantine as has always been used in the past when serious—not necessarily lethal—infections have been spreading.[5]

Isolation is the most serious form of deprivation of liberty that can be utilized against a competent and unwilling person. It is based upon what a person *might* do in future rather than what he or she has done; there is no clear temporal limitation; and it is not subject to the same rigorous due process procedures as in a criminal charge.

Given its impact on freedom of movement, isolation is likely to trigger the strictest level of judicial scrutiny.[6] A general isolation of all those who test positive for HIV antibodies or all those with the disease would, in our judgment, be unconstitutional. For every individual who, in fact, poses a danger to public health, many more nondangerous people would be isolated. It is prudent to assume that persons who are seropositive harbor the virus. Yet only a small proportion of this population would be likely intentionally to engage in unsafe sexual behavior or the shared use of contaminated needles, which are the only two efficient mechanisms for HIV transmission. Consequently, isolation would needlessly confine many individuals who are nondangerous.

For many reasons general isolation is not a feasible public health measure to control the spread of HIV infection. First, isolation of the seropositive population would require widespread compulsory public action to reliably locate, identify, and periodically screen persons in high-risk populations. This would involve public resources and invasions of privacy of unacceptable magnitude.

Second, isolation of persons with AIDS or HIV infection would have no finite time limit, because the retrovirus may persist in humans for life. Since there is no therapeutic treatment available, those whose liberty is infringed would have no way to restore themselves to a normal condition in order to rejoin society.

Third, the sheer number of people who harbor the virus, which is estimated at one to two million and rising, would make a general isolation wholly unmanageable.

Finally, since isolation is a civil action that is not intended as a punishment, punitive or unsafe environments would not be legally supportable.[7] Isolated individuals would have to be cared for, treated, fed, and clothed in humane facilities, which currently do not exist. Moreover, reinfection within the segregated facility might be a danger. While scientists do not yet know the factors that cause progression from seropositivity to AIDS, it is possible that repeated exposure to the virus can increase the risk of developing the disease. Isolation in segregated facilities, therefore, may actually pose a danger to the health of those confined.

Modified Isolation Based upon Behavior

The more serious proposals for isolation do not focus on a person's health status as having a disease or infection, but upon his or her future behavior leading to viral transmission.

A modified isolation statute could require a due process determination that a viral carrier will not, or cannot, refrain from engaging in conduct likely to spread the virus. The 1985 amendment to the Connecticut Public Health Statute, for example, authorizes a local health director to order the confinement of an individual if he has reasonable grounds to believe that the person is infected with a communicable disease and is unable or unwilling to act so as not to expose other persons to infection.

The tension between public health and civil liberties is most apparent when a decision must be taken whether to restrict the freedom of a "recalcitrant" individual, one who intentionally and continuously refuses to comply with reasonable public health directives. The most obvious illustration is a male prostitute with AIDS who reappears at an STD clinic with rectal gonorrhea, despite education and counseling as to the serious consequences of sexual transmission of HIV. Similar situations occur with IV drug users who have to support their dependency by prostitution.

A strong theoretical case can be made for the limited use of powers of isolation. The courts would probably support isolation if the subject were infectious and highly likely to engage in behavior leading to viral transmission. The measure would not be overinclusive, because it would be possible to demonstrate a strict relationship between the restriction to be applied and a compelling public health purpose. Courts have repeatedly recognized the right of the state to confine specific dangerous individuals, in both the public health[8] and civil commitment[9] context. It is difficult to envisage a court striking down a narrowly conceived order for isolation where there was clear evidence established at a fair hearing that an individual was likely to engage in behavior leading to transmission of a potentially lethal virus.

Health officials have a public duty to protect against transmission of a potentially lethal disease agent. Wherever possible, voluntary, or less restrictive compulsory, measures should first be used. But if less restrictive measures were not successful, public health officials would, arguably, be remiss not to exercise the power of limited isolation. Public policy must protect the welfare of those at risk of contracting HIV as well as the civil liberties of those who are infected. Failure to intervene effectively to prevent a serious health hazard does a disservice to those vulnerable to HIV infection.

Nevertheless, a limited use of isolation would prove to be an essentially ineffective and invidious public policy if widely implemented. Proponents see it as an effective method of impeding the spread of the AIDS epidemic. But the invocation of limited isolation does not go to the heart of the epidemic, which cannot be impeded by concentrating on the occasional recalcitrant individual, no matter how dangerous his or her conduct may seem.

Overall, any widespread use of isolation is likely to be counterproductive to the strategy of obtaining voluntary compliance by risk group members. As stated previously, any obvious use of coercive measures would tend to discourage persons who are vulnerable to HIV infection from seeking diagnostic testing or treatment, or speaking honestly to counselors concerning their future behavioral intentions.

Given a population of one to two million people infected with HIV, the decision about whom to confine is likely to be highly discriminatory. It is difficult to frame objective statutory criteria and psychological parameters to determine who is most dangerous.[10] Individuals who declare an intention to engage in unsafe behavior could not be reliably distinguished from those who foreswore such conduct. Further, those who came to the attention of public health officials as candidates for isolation would likely be the poorest, least articulate of those infected with the virus. The vast majority of instances of transmission would continue to go unnoticed by the authorities. This could make even the most carefully selective isolation a lottery affecting primarily the most vulnerable persons, with a negligible impact on the epidemiology of the disease. Finally, a limited isolation program based upon preventing intimate personal behavior between two consenting individuals has serious monitoring and enforcement difficulties; it could be viewed as a broad license for public health and law enforcement officials to intrude into the private lives of people vulnerable to HIV infection.

Criminal Law Deterrence

The personal control measures discussed thus far are part of the civil law, and are concerned with preventing future dangerous behavior. Legal options for controlling behavior, however, extend to the criminal law. The criminal law is often thought to be based upon a model of retribution for past behavior and is, therefore, considered inappropriate in the public health context. Yet one of the principal objectives of the criminal law is prevention. By establishing clear penalties, the criminal law seeks to deter individuals from engaging in certain well-specified behaviors.

What role might the criminal law play in identifying behavior resulting in transmission of HIV? It could specifically proscribe behavior likely to communicate HIV infection when a person knows that he or she is infected and appreciates the threat to health or life posed by the behavior, and when he or she does not inform sexual partners of those risks. The knowing or reckless transmission of a potentially lethal infection is just as dangerous as other behavior that the criminal law already proscribes.

This approach cannot be considered unfair to groups at high risk of contracting AIDS, because it serves as a measure of protection for them against the spread of infection. Nor can it be considered unfair to the potential subjects of criminal penalties, for it is better to give clear forewarning of unacceptable conduct than to confine a person who might engage in that behavior in the future.

The civil liberties advantages of the criminal law are well known: it is based upon behavior that is objectively stated in the statute; it requires proof beyond a reasonable doubt of a specific dangerous act; it requires the highest level of procedural due process and appeal; and the period of confinement is usually finite and proportionate to the gravity of the offense. The criminal law offers the "tightest fit" between means and a public health objective. Each person convicted of the offense has demonstrably failed to comply with behavioral standards set by the law; conversely, prospective public health control measures almost invariably have an impact on individuals who will not pose an actual risk to the public health.

Clarity, objectivity, and sufficient safeguards make the criminal law an attractive candidate for consideration in the public health context. A number of jurisdictions (for example, Texas, New York, California, Pennsylvania, Colorado, and Florida) identify "public health crimes." These statutes make it a crime (usually a misdemeanor) for an individual who knows he has an infectious venereal disease to have sexual intercourse with another. Many of these statutes apply only to venereal diseases and, consequently, do not apply to AIDS. They do, however, provide a precedent for the use of criminal law penalties in a public health context. Indeed, as a matter of general criminal law theory, it probably is already an offense to knowingly (battery) or recklessly (reckless endangerment) harm another through viral transmission;[11] moreover, consent is probably not a defense to a crime involving serious physical injury.

Objection can be made to the use of the criminal law to penalize private sexual activity, particularly when the behavior involves two consenting adults. Yet sexual acts are *not* wholly consensual if the infected person fails to inform his partner of the substantial risk to health; nor is the behavior wholly private because of the public risk inherent in increasing the reservoir of infection. A decision to assume the risk of transferring or contracting a lethal infection clearly concerns members of the public who may become affected. It may be reasonable, therefore, for society to establish clear parameters to behaviors it will not tolerate. By drawing a clear line around the behaviors that pose serious health risks, the law gives notice of the conduct that will be subject to criminal penalty.

However, we do not place any undue reliance upon the criminal law as a mechanism for impeding the spread of HIV infection in the population. Moreover, we have significant reservations about the use of the criminal law in the private realm. First, it would be virtually impossible to achieve any consistency in application of the criminal law to high-risk behaviors. Variable law enforcement and prosecutorial discretion would result in arbitrary decisions.

Second, highly intrusive policing of the private activities of sexual minorities might be encouraged. Any use of the criminal law to control intimate behavior can be construed as an invitation to law enforcement officers to use surveillance in relation to places where there is some expectation of privacy, such as restrooms, hotels, or even private homes. This already occurs, for example, in the enforcement of sodomy laws.

Finally, there would be great difficulty in proving beyond a reasonable doubt that a person intentionally or recklessly transmitted the infection. A conviction would have to depend upon the uncorroborated evidence of the person contracting the infection. While similar evidence is used in cases of rape, the person contracting HIV infection would usually not realize that a former sexual partner exposed him or her to the infection until months or years later. It would also have to be demonstrated that the partner was not informed of the risk and that "safe" or "protected" sex, encouraged by CDC, had not taken place. It would be nearly impossible to prove in a courtroom that specific behavior had occurred some time earlier.

The Failure of Compulsion

In the absence of successful behavioral alteration, or scientific intervention, society is beginning to look to the law. There is increasing pressure on public health officials to mark the gravity of the AIDS epidemic by introducing more coercive measures. When dispassionately examined, however, most legal and regulatory proposals would have little, or even a counterproductive, impact on the spread of the HIV infection. They also impose disproportionate restrictions on the liberty, autonomy, and privacy of persons vulnerable to HIV infection. The only conclusion that can be drawn, therefore, is that compulsory legal interventions will not provide a fair and effective means of interrupting the spread of the AIDS epidemic.

Notes

[1]William J. Curran, Larry Gostin, and Mary Clark, *Acquired Immunodeficiency Syndrome: Legal, Regulatory and Policy Analysis* (Washington, Department of Health and Human Services, 1986). Available from the National Technical Information Service, U.S. Department of Commerce, 5285 Port Royal Road, Springfield, VA 22161.

[2]Larry Gostin and William J. Curran, "The First Line of Defense in Controlling AIDS: Compulsory Casefinding—Testing, Screening and Reporting," *American Journal of Law and Medicine* 12 (1986) in press. Larry Gostin and William S. Curran, "The Applications of Legal Control Measures to AIDS, Part 2: Compulsory Screening for HIV in Selected Populations," *American Journal of Public Health,* (in press).

[3]Centers for Disease Control, "Additional Recommendations to Reduce Sexual and Drug-Related Transmission of Human T-lymphotropic Virus Type III/Lymphadenopathy-Associated Virus," *Morbidity and Mortality Weekly Reports* 35 (10) (March 14, 1986) 152–55.

[4]Frank P. Grad, *Public Health Law Manual: A Handbook on the Legal Aspects of Public Health Administration and Enforcement,* (Washington, D.C., American Public Health Association, 1978).

[5]J. Grutsch and A. D. Robertson, "The Coming of AIDS: It Didn't Start with Homosexuals and It Won't End with Them," *American Spectator* 19 (1986), 12–15.

[6]*Shapiro v. Thompson,* 394 U.S. 618 (1969).

[7]*Kirk v. Wyman,* 83 S.C. 372, 65 S.E. 387 (1909).

[8]See *dicta* and cases cited by the United States Supreme Court in *Jacobson v. Massachusetts,* 197 U.S. 11 (1905).

[9]*O'Connor v. Donaldson,* 422 U.S. 463 (1975).

[10]Difficulties of predicting dangerousness have been extensively documented in the mental health context. R. Kirkland Gable, "Prediction of Dangerousness and Implications for Treatment," In *Forensic Psychiatry and Psychology,* eds. William J. Curran, A. Louis McGarry, and Saleem A. Shah (Philadelphia: F.A. Davis, 1986).

[11]See, for example, prosecutions pending against defendants with HIV infection who spit at or bit police officers. *People v. Richards,* 85-1715 FH (Flint, Michigan); *People v. Prairie Chicken,* CRE-77357 (El Cajon, California).

Limiting the Activity of Physicians with AIDS

In "HIV-Infected Physicians and the Practice of Seriously Invasive Procedures," Gostin continues the analysis of controlling AIDS by controlling those with AIDS. He deals with the personal freedom of physicians versus the need to know of patients whose physicians have AIDS. Gostin discusses relevant legal decisions, the concept of reasonably foreseeable risk, and the wisdom of screening physicians as a general rule. Gostin's conclusion is in his last sentence. "Given these special societal burdens on the physician [the expectation that a physician will treat those with AIDS even given the health risks], it is reasonable to protect his [i.e., the physician's] personal rights and livelihood."

HIV-INFECTED PHYSICIANS AND THE PRACTICE OF SERIOUSLY INVASIVE PROCEDURES

Lawrence Gostin

AIDS is increasingly being viewed as an occupational disease for physicians despite the evidence that human immunodeficiency virus (HIV) is exceedingly hard to transmit in health care settings.[1] Physicians who carry out seriously invasive procedures claim the "right to know" whether their patients are infected with HIV, including the right to screen patients for the virus.[2] Some hospitals, irrespective of what the law may allow, already screen their patients without specific informed consent.[3]

Conversely, patients undergoing seriously invasive procedures claim the right to know if their physician is infected with HIV. Eighty-six percent of a Gallup Poll sample taken in 1987 said patients should be told if their physician has AIDS.[4] Most patients would choose not to receive treatment from an infected physician. Their case has been buttressed by a policy statement from the American Medical Association that "a physician who knows that he or she is seropositive should not engage in any activity that creates a risk of transmission of the disease to others."[5] Presumably this advice would extend to other health care workers involved in performing seriously invasive procedures. If it is wrong for infected physicians to treat patients invasively, does this create a correlative duty on the part of hospitals to screen physicians before they carry out such treatment? The prospect of a "right to know" the health status of both doctor and patient, with calls for screening on both sides, together with the potential of litigation for avoidable transmission of HIV, undermine trust within the health care system.

The concept of a "right to know" the serologic status of physician or patient is misplaced. Information that a patient is HIV positive is of very limited use to the physician. Physicians have a professional,[6] if not a legal,[7] responsibility to treat infected patients. It is usually not possible to utilize *different* methods for treating HIV-positive patients to reduce the risk of contracting the infection; and in some cases different methods could result in prolongation of operative time, potentially having an adverse effect on the patient. Further, the Centers for Disease Control recommends,[8] and the Occupational Health and Safety Administration requires,[9] the universal application of barrier protection in all cases of exposure to blood. Information that a patient is HIV-positive should not significantly affect the precautions taken in most cases.[10]

Patients, on the other hand, clearly would act upon the knowledge that their physicians were infected with HIV, and when they could choose many would not opt for a physician who is infected with HIV. However, it is not always reasonable for the patient to expect this information. The certain consequence of informing patients that their physician is HIV-positive would be the abandonment of the physician's practice.

This article, therefore, does not make a case for a patient's "right to know." Rather, it argues that the risks inherent in seriously invasive procedures are sufficient for the profession to take patient safety seriously, even before the first case of HIV-transmission to a patient occurs. Professional guidance is required to identify the circumstances where a physician should withdraw from performing certain seriously invasive procedures. This conclusion is based upon the doctrine of informed consent and evolving standards of professional care. Failure to take appropriate preventive action now may result in policies that are overly restrictive. For example, Cook County Hospital already has a policy of allowing patients to refuse to be treated by HIV-positive physicians who "routinely provide direct patient care."[11] The policy would appear to put the careers of infected physicians at risk even if they do not perform seriously invasive procedures. This article also makes the case for protecting the privacy of infected physicians and safeguarding against discrimination by their employers and others.

Risks of HIV Transmission in Health Care Settings

There has been no scrutiny of transmission of HIV from physicians to patients, and there is no recorded case where it has occurred.[12] This is not surprising since there has been no systematic attempt to discover which physicians are HIV positive. But there has been careful examination of transmission from patient to health care worker,[13] and some indication of the level of risk in both directions can be ascertained. The possibility of transmission in health care settings has been demonstrated by approximately sixteen cases where health care workers seroconverted from occupational exposure to HIV.[14]

The sixteen reported cases of occupational exposure to HIV appear insignificant given the frequency of contacts between health care workers and HIV-infected patients. Several prospective studies show there is a risk in the range of 0.03 to 0.9 percent that a health care worker will contract HIV following a documented case of percutaneous or mucous membrane exposure to HIV-infected blood.[15] This is relatively low compared to the risk of 12 to 17 percent seroconversion after accidental percutaneous injection from patients with hepatitis B, even after passive immunization of recipients by immune serum globulin.[16]

Physicians performing seriously invasive procedures, such as surgeons, have a potential to cut or puncture their skin with sharp surgical instruments, needles, or bone fragments. Studies indicate that a surgeon will cut a glove in approximately one out of every four cases,[17] and probably sustain a significant skin cut in one out of every forty cases.[18] Given these data, it has been calculated that the risk of contracting HIV in a single surgical operation on an HIV-infected patient is remote—in the range of 1/130,000 to 1/4,500.[19]

It is impossible accurately to calculate the level of risk of HIV transmission from surgeon to patient. Surgeons who cut or puncture themselves do not necessarily expose the patient to their blood, and even if they do the volume is extremely small. A small inoculum of contaminated blood is unlikely to transmit the virus.[20] This suggests that the risk of infection from surgeon to patient is much lower than in the opposite direction. Nonetheless, the fact that the surgeon is in significant contact with the patient's blood and organs, together with the high rate of torn gloves, makes it reasonable to assume that the risk runs in both directions, as is the case with the hepatitis B virus. The cumulative risk to surgical patients, arguably, is higher. While an HIV-infected patient is likely to have relatively few seriously invasive procedures, the infected surgeon, even if the virus drastically shortens his surgical career, can be expected to perform numerous operations. Assuming that the surgical patient's risk is exceedingly low (1/130,000), the risk that one of his patients will contract HIV becomes more realistic the more operations he performs—1/1,300 (assuming 100 operations) or 1/126 (assuming 500 operations). Patients, of course, cannot expect a wholly risk-free environment in a hospital. But there does come a point where the risk of a detrimental outcome becomes sufficiently real that it is prudent for the profession to establish guidelines.

Patient Treatment Decisions

The doctrine of informed consent can help clarify the physician's duties toward his patient. In many jurisdictions, the law of informed consent lays down a patient-oriented standard for the information that must be disclosed by the physician.[21] It is for the patient to assess the risk and to determine where his or her interests lie. If the risk would be intolerable for the reasonably prudent patient he or she is entitled to make that judgment, however unwise the assessment of relative risk is in the eyes of the medical profession.[22] Courts, therefore, require the physician to provide all information that a reasonable patient would find relevant to make an informed decision on whether to undergo a medical procedure.[23] Risks that are relevant or "material" depend upon their severity, the probability that they would occur, and the circumstances under which they would be endured.[24] As the severity of a potential harm becomes greater the need to disclose improbable risks grows, though courts have yet to assign a threshold for the probability of a grave harm beyond which it must be disclosed.[25]

A reasonably prudent patient would find information that his physician is infected with HIV material to his decision to consent to a seriously invasive procedure because the potential harm is severe and the risk, while low, is not negligible. Moreover, he can avoid the risk entirely without any adverse consequences for his health: By choosing another equally competent physician (where available) he can obtain all the therapeutic benefit without the risk of contracting HIV from his physician. The patient, then, can demonstrate not only that the information is material to his decision, but that he would have made a *different* decision had he been given the facts.

Courts have usually been concerned with risks inherent in the treatment, rather than risks associated with a physician's physical condition or skill. Although courts have required disclosure of risks as low as 1 percent or less,[26] they have not required disclosure of risks that are simply unforeseeable—because no case has ever occurred, or the risk is minute (on the order of 1 in 100,000).[27] The risk of transmission of HIV in the ordinary physician/patient relationship where exposure to large amounts of blood is unlikely is too remote to be foreseeable. Nonetheless, the risks inherent in seriously invasive treatments may well reach the threshold where they become relevant to a rational assessment by the patient.

Courts have been highly consistent in elucidating valid reasons for nondisclosure, all ostensibly for the patient's therapeutic benefit.[28] Relevant information may be withheld when the treatment is necessary in an emergency[29] or is nonelective; the patient is incompetent[30]; or disclosure would be harmful to his psychological state.[31] Nondisclosure of a physician's seropositive status is not founded upon the patient's interests, however, but expressly on the physician's, particularly with respect to rights to privacy and confidentiality.

In *Piper v. Menifee* the court held that a physician was liable to the patient and his family when he failed to inform them that he was attending another patient infected with smallpox. The court held that "if a physician, knowing he has an infectious disease, continues to visit his patients without apprising them of the fact ... [he] is guilty of a breach of duty."[32]

While few cases affirm the holding in *Piper,* there is ample judicial authority that a physician has a duty to notify third parties who might be exposed to his patient's contagious disease.[33] If a physician has a duty to inform and protect third parties, he owes at least as great a duty toward his own patients.

Yet the right to be informed of a physician's seropositive status requires a finely balanced assessment. There are limits to what society reasonably can expect of a physician in disclosing remote risks. The *Piper* case and more recent duty-to-inform cases involved more substantial risks of contracting disease. There are, moreover, many risks posed by the physician himself, such as inexperience in performing highly technical operations, that are not traditionally disclosed in modern medicine. Nevertheless, the increasing focus of modern law on the patient's rights should require a seropositive physician to withdraw from performing seriously invasive procedures if there is a significant risk to the surgeon's patients.

The Evolving Standard of Professional Care

A physician is expected in law to exercise the care ordinarily used by members of the medical profession in his specialty. Failure to exercise that standard of care is negligence, and a physician will be liable to his patient if harm results.[34] Most cases of medical negligence involve lack of due professional care in providing treatment, but in addition to *Piper* a few demonstrate that a physician may be negligent for continuing to practice when he knows, or reasonably should know, that his physical condition may pose a risk to the patient.

An oral surgeon paid a substantial settlement for transmission of hepatitis B to his patient, and through her to her husband and her child in utero.[35] The employing hospital of a potentially dangerous physician can also be held liable for allowing an infectious or incompetent physician to treat patients.[36]

Both the physician and hospital, therefore, may be negligent for treating a patient in circumstances where the professional standard of care is to refrain from practicing. There is little doubt that a malpractice case would succeed if adequate infection control guidelines had not been followed and, as a result, HIV was transmitted to the patient.[37]

What if HIV is transmitted even though all reasonable infection control procedures are followed? The outcome of a malpractice case would be uncertain. A court might well take cognizance of the fact that there has been no documented case of transmission of HIV from health care worker to patient,[38] and that Boards of Registration in medicine and individual physicians have made conflicting statements of principle.[39]

Nevertheless, the evolving standard of professional care is for an HIV-infected physician to refrain from performing seriously invasive procedures. Physicians have a special responsibility in practicing their profession because of the guardianship of their patients' health. The American Medical Association states that a

> physician who knows that he or she has an infectious disease should not engage in any activity that creates a risk of transmission of the disease to others ... [P]atients are entitled to expect that their physicians will not increase their exposure to the risk of contracting an infectious disease, even minimally.[40]

The U.S. Public Health Service also recommends an individual assessment to determine whether an HIV-infected health care worker "can adequately and safely be allowed to perform patient care duties or whether their work assignments should be changed ..."[41]

The American Hospital Association, state hospital associations and state public health departments have likewise acknowledged the risk of transmission of HIV from health care worker to patient in performing invasive procedures.[42] Each group has recognized the legitimacy of an individual determination limiting the practice of invasive procedures by HIV-infected physicians.

While the Public Health Service and professional medical associations have indicated that HIV-infected physicians may pose unacceptable risks for patients when they perform medical procedures, they have not identified those procedures. In each case HIV-infected physicians are told to seek advice and counseling from their personal physician, employing hospital, and colleagues to determine any restrictions on their practice of medicine. The AMA Board, for example, has said that "the decision must be determined on an individual basis founded on the opinions of the worker's personal physician and those of the medical directors and personnel health service staff of the employing institution."[43]

There is a need for national guidance on which procedures should be avoided by infected physicians. Clear guidance would help set a uniform standard of practice across the country; reduce the burden on individual physicians and hospitals to make difficult assessments of risk; prevent inconsistent practice in different hospitals and geographic regions leading to loss of patient confidence; and reduce the possibility of legal liability for infected physicians and hospitals that countenance allowing an infected physician to continue performing seriously invasive treatment. The absence of prospective guidelines issued by the medical profession could well result in undesirable retrospective standards laid down by the courts.

Physician Screening

If legal and public health policy require the HIV-infected physician to refrain from performing certain seriously invasive procedures, does the hospital have an obligation to screen physicians? The law holds physicians and hospitals accountable, not only for what they know, but for what they reasonably should know. If a physician has engaged in high risk behavior such as homosexual activity or sharing of needles, and failed to be tested or to make any disclosure to the hospital, the courts probably would put him in the same position as if he knew he were seropositive. Any other rule of law would provide an incentive for physicians to avoid being tested and counseled. The prudent course, then, is for physicians who are at increased risk for HIV to obtain confidential testing and counseling, and to inform the health care facility of a positive test result, before performing seriously invasive medical procedures.[44]

Physicians who are not at increased risk for HIV or those who do not perform seriously invasive procedures have no legal or ethical obligation to be tested; and there should be no duty on health care facilities to screen them routinely. In such cases, the social, personal, and financial costs of a comprehensive screening program outweigh the public health benefit. The disadvantages of mandatory physician screening are similar to those in other low risk populations, and have been explicated elsewhere.[45]

A positive test result in a health care professional who is not in fact

infected could have devastating personal consequences. A negative test result, moreover, does not guarantee that a physician is free from infection.
There is a period of up to twelve weeks or longer before antibodies are
produced and detectable after infection; or the physician could contract the
virus at some future time, necessitating periodic retesting at considerable
expense to the health care facility.

Systematic collection of highly sensitive health care data would place
considerable burdens on hospitals. They would be required to keep the
information confidential and could be liable for intentional or negligent
disclosure.[46] Hospitals would also have to decide whether to disclose the
information to patients or third parties under a duty to warn theory.[47]

The legal and ethical quandaries, therefore, posed for the hospital by
systematic collection of the HIV status of all physicians would be disproportionate to any public health benefit. The medical literature is replete with
documented cases of transmission of hepatitis B in health care settings,[48]
and there are some one hundred health care worker deaths each year attrib-
utable to HBV. The risk of transmission and cumulative morbidity and mortality associated with HBV are greater than for HIV. Yet there is no systematic
screening for HBV, and restrictions on the practice of invasive procedures
often occur only after a physician has transmitted HBV (sometimes repeatedly).[49] If the case for screening for hepatitis B has never been sustained,
what new facts or data mandate screening for the AIDS virus?

Finally, a systematic program of screening for HIV among physicians
might well violate constitutional protection of a person's right to be free
from "unreasonable search and seizures." A blood test for HIV with important personal consequences, like a test for drugs or alcohol,[50] may infringe
upon a person's "expectation of privacy."[51] In *Glover v. Eastern Nebraska Community Office of Mental Retardation,* a federal district court held that screening
for HIV among certain employees in a mental retardation facility constituted unreasonable search and seizure because the risk to clients "is extremely low and approaches zero."[52] It is possible that the courts may find
a greater public health interest in a screening program more narrowly focused on health care workers involved in seriously invasive procedures; yet
any widespread screening policy is likely to be found unconstitutional.

An effective argument could be made that, once it is determined that
HIV-positive physicians should refrain from seriously invasive treatment, it
necessarily follows that they should be screened before performing such
procedures. I do not accept, however, that screening is a logically necessary
result. There are many well-accepted situations in modern medicine where
legally and ethically it is advisable for physicians to restrict their medical
practice but which do not require systematic screening. A surgeon with HBV,
TB or who is drug or alcohol impaired should not continue to practice without the hospital's knowledge and review. It does not necessarily follow (nor
might it even be constitutionally permitted) systematically to screen all sur-

geons for HBV, TB, drugs, and alcohol. Rather, I argue that a physician who knows, or ought to know, that he or she is HIV-positive, should voluntarily refrain from practicing seriously invasive procedures. The cost of such a professional rule is not prohibitive and can be ameliorated by transfer to other duties and by equitable compensation programs. However, the sheer social and personal burdens of systematic screening on physicians, hospitals, and the entire health care system substantially outweigh its public health benefit.

Consequences for the Physician

The standards developed thus far for HIV-infected physicians are strict and based upon prevention of even a minimal risk of transmission. If the physician is expected voluntarily to disclose his serological status to the patient and/or to refrain from performing certain seriously invasive procedures, he is entitled to protection from the consequences of his good faith actions. The right to practice medicine is "sufficiently precious to surround it with a panoply of legal protections."[53] Any public health policy on HIV-infected physicians, therefore, must ensure confidentiality and nondiscriminatory treatment including reasonable accommodation.

    Confidentiality. HIV-infected physicians, like other seropositive individuals are concerned with maintaining confidentiality. Because the majority of physicians infected with HIV are members of risk groups subject to persistent prejudice and discrimination, unauthorized disclosure of their serological status can lead to social opprobrium among family and friends, and to loss of employment, housing and insurance. Consequently, physicians have strong grounds for desiring personal privacy and confidentiality of medical information. Their cooperation with the hospital in protecting against the spread of infections relies upon their trust that their serological status will be kept confidential.

    Physicians have a right to confidentiality of intimate health care information based upon a number of legal grounds. First, physicians with HIV are treated by a personal physician and are entitled to the protection of confidentiality inherent in the physician/patient relationship. Second, employees have the right to expect that sensitive health care information will not be disclosed by their employers without their permission.[54] While health care employers may have a legitimate interest in knowing if a physician is HIV positive, they have no legitimate interest in disclosing this information to patients, other employees, or individuals or organizations outside of the hospital. Third, statutes in several states and municipalities specifically protect the confidentiality of HIV-positive test results. These statutes generally provide civil liability for disclosing the result of a serological test without the individual's written informed consent.[55]

Two cases establish the importance of confidentiality for the physician, at least against media disclosure to the general public. In *X. v. Y.* the British High Court issued a permanent injunction against a national newspaper publishing confidential information about a physician with AIDS. The court held that "the public interest in the freedom of the press and informed debate on AIDS was outweighed by the public interest in maintaining the confidentiality of actual or potential AIDS sufferers."[56]

In a similar case the *Miami Herald* filed suit against the Dade County Health Department and the hospital to gain access to the medical records and death certificate of a urologist. The newspaper's intention was to confirm that the urologist had practiced medicine for several years while he had AIDS. The court did not allow release of this confidential information,[57] basing its decision upon the state Public Records Act, which regards such information as confidential unless the person claiming the information has a "direct and tangible" interest in it.

Confidentiality for the HIV-infected physician not only safeguards his personal rights, but also is in the public interest.[58] The right to confidentiality will encourage physicians to disclose their serological status to their employers, and to seek counseling, treatment, and peer review of the safety of their continued medical practice.

Antidiscrimination.   Discrimination against a physician because of his HIV status is just as repugnant as discrimination on other morally irrelevant grounds such as race or gender. The United States Supreme Court in *School Board of Nassau County v. Arline* condemned irrational prejudice based upon a person's infectious condition noting that:

> Society's accumulated myths and fears about disease are as handicapping as are the physical limitations that flow from actual impairment. Few aspects give rise to the same level of public fear and misapprehension as contagiousness.[59]

AIDS has been held to be a handicap within the meaning of section 504 of the Federal Rehabilitation Act of 1973 and similar state statutes.[60] The Civil Rights Restoration Act 1988 states that section 504 is applicable to a person with a contagious disease if he does not pose "a direct threat to the health or safety of other individuals or . . . who is unable to perform the duties of the job." The congressional history of the 1988 Act shows that the language "direct threat" embodies the standard of "significant risk of transmission" articulated by the Supreme Court in *Arline.*[61]

Physicians, then, have a right under federal and state handicap laws not to be denied the right to practice medicine or to be reassigned to an administrative position unless there is a significant risk of HIV transmission. Any limitation on the right of a physician to practice must be reasonably related to the achievement of greater patient safety. Narrow limitations on the practice of seriously invasive procedures may thus be found not to be discriminatory.

In *Doe v. Cook County Hospital* U.S. District Court Judge John A. Nordberg required the signing of a consent decree to protect an HIV-infected neurologist from unreasonable limitations placed on his right to practice.[62] The physician agreed to special surveillance; to double glove before performing invasive procedures; and not to perform three procedures—muscle biopsy, sural nerve biopsy and cerebral arteriography—formally a part of his credentialing, but which he had not performed in recent years. The judge, in language mirroring the *Arline* decision, held that future alterations in clinical practice could be permitted only if the physician posed "a significant health or safety risk to himself or others"; and, except in an emergency, the neurologist received seven days' notice of any alteration.

The Cook County Hospital case establishes the need for balance between a physician's rights and a patient's safety. Yet the concept of "significant risk" needs further clarification. "Significant risk" should be based upon epidemiologic evidence of the gravity of the harm and the probability of it occurring. A risk is significant if: the mode of transmission is well established, even if the risk is small; the potential harm is serious; and the public health intervention is efficacious and does not pose disproportionate burdens on individual rights. Withdrawal of an HIV-infected physician from performing seriously invasive procedures, provided the information can be kept confidential, does not pose an unbearable burden on the physician or the health care system. Reassignment to noninvasive procedures virtually eliminates any risk of harm.

The Cook County case also shows the futility of a case-by-case determination by courts of which medical procedures are sufficiently safe for an HIV-infected physician to perform. It is not the proper function of the courts to list a detailed set of allowed and prohibited medical procedures. The court's decision simply underlines the need for forwardlooking professional guidelines to assess which medical procedures pose a risk to the health of patients.

The federal Rehabilitation Act requires employers to make reasonable accommodation for handicapped workers. Health care facilities should ensure that HIV-infected physicians have the opportunity for a wide-ranging clinical practice that is both professionally rewarding and remunerative. The professional guidance called for in this essay should reflect the rich variety of clinical practice infected physicians could safely engage in, ranging from internal medicine and psychiatry to pediatrics and neurology.

The right to confidentiality and antidiscrimination including reasonable accommodation for physicians should be viewed as a *quid pro quo* for the physician's good faith fulfillment of his or her special professional and ethical obligations. The physician has made a substantial human and financial investment in medical education. He is expected to provide treatment for HIV-infected patients despite the occupational risks. Given these special societal burdens on the physician, it is reasonable to protect his personal rights and professional livelihood.

Notes

[1]See for example, Centers for Disease Control, "Recommendations for Prevention of HIV Transmission in Health-care Settings," *Morbidity & Mortality Weekly Report* 36:2S (1987), 3S-18S.

[2]The Surgeon General, for example, has advocated HIV screening of all preoperative patients. Dennis L. Breo, "Dr. Koop Calls for AIDS Tests Before Surgery," *American Medical News,* 26 June 1987, 1, 21-25.

[3]Keith Henry, Karen Willenbring and Kent Crossley, "Human Immunodeficiency Virus Antibody Testing: A Description of Practices and Policies at U.S. Infectious Disease Teaching Hospitals and Minnesota Hospitals," *Journal of the American Medical Association* 259:12 (1988), 1819-22.

[4]*Medical Staff News* (August 1987), 2.

[5]Council on Ethical and Judicial Affairs, American Medical Association, "Ethical Issues Involved in the Growing AIDS Crisis," *Journal of the American Medical Association* 259:9 (1988), 1360-61.

[6]Council on Ethical and Judicial Affairs, "Ethical Issues."

[7]George J. Annas, "Not Saints, But Healers: The Legal Duties of Health Care Professionals in the AIDS Epidemic," *American Journal of Public Health* 78:17 (1988), 844-49.

[8]Centers for Disease Control, "Recommendations."

[9]Department of Labor and Department of Health and Human Services, "Joint Advisory Notice: Protection against Occupational Exposures to Hepatitis B Virus (HBV) and Human Immunodeficiency Virus (HIV)," *Federal Register* 52:10 (1987), 41818-23.

[10]J. Louise Gerberding and the University of California, San Francisco Task Force on AIDS, "Recommended Infection Control Policies for Patients With Human Immunodeficiency Virus Infection: An Update," *New England Journal of Medicine* 315:24 (1986), 1562-64.

[11]"Chicago Patients Gain Curb on AIDS Carriers," *New York Times,* 22 September 1988, A34.

[12]Centers for Disease Control, "Recommendations," 65-75.

[13]James R. Allen, "Health Care Workers and the Risk of HIV Transmission," *Hastings Center Report* 18:2 (1988), Special Supplement, 2-5.

[14]Deborah M. Barnes, "Health Care Workers and AIDS: Questions Persist," *Science* 241 (1988), 161-62.

[15]Centers for Disease Control, "Recommendations"; Gerald H. Friedland and Robert S. Klein, "Transmission of the Human Immunodeficiency Virus," *New England Journal of Medicine* 317:18 (1987), 1125-35.

[16]Barbara G. Werner and George F. Grady, "Accidental Hepatitis B-Surface-Antigen-Positive Inoculations: Use of e Antigen to Estimate Infectivity." *Annals of Internal Medicine* 97:3 (1982), 367-9.

[17]Peter J. E. Cruse and Rosemary Foord, "The Epidemiology of Wound Infection," *Surgical Clinics of North America* 60:1 (1980), 27-40.

[18]Michael D. Hagen, Klemens B. Meyer and Stephen G. Parker, "Routine Pre-Operative

Screening for HIV: Does the Risk to the Surgeon Outweigh the Risk to the Patient?", *"Journal of the American Medical Association* 259:9 (1988), 1357–59.

[19]Hagen *et al.,* "Routine Pre-Operative Screening."

[20]Friedland and Klein, "Transmission of the Human Immunodeficiency Virus."

[21]See for example, *Harnish v. Children's Hospital Medical Center,* 387 Mass. 152, 439 N.E.2d 240 (1982).

[22]*Wikinson v. Vesey,* 110 R.I. 606, 624 (1972).

[23]*Canterbury v. Spence. Cobbs v. Grant,* 8 Cal. 3d 229 (1972).

[24]*Precourt v. Frederick,* 395 Mass. 689, 694–95 (1985).

[25]See *Precourt v. Frederick,* 395 Mass. 689, 697 (1985). The development of law as to which risks are too remote to require disclosure must await future cases.

[26]*Salis v. United States,* 522 F. Supplement 989 (Md. and Pa. 1981).

[27]See for example, *Precourt v. Frederick. Henderson v. Milobsky,* 595 F.2d 654 (D.C. Cir 1978). It is difficult to predict how the courts would respond in a case of an HIV-infected surgeon, since the risk to any *single* patient is highly remote.

[28]See *Mroczkowski v. Staub Clinic and Hospital,* 732 P.2d 1255 (Hawaii App. 1987).

[29]*Keegan v. Holy Family Hospital,* 95 Wn.2d 306, 622 P.2d 1246 (1980).

[30]See A. Meisel, "The 'Exceptions' to the Informed Consent Doctrine: Striking a Balance Between Competing Values in Decisionmaking," *Wisconsin Law Review* (1979), 413.

[31]*Harnish v. Children's Hospital Medical Center.*

[32]*Ben Monroe's Reports,* Winter Term 465 (Winter Term 1851).

[33]See generally, Lawrence Gostin, William Curran, and Mary Clark, "The Case Against Compulsory Casefinding in Controlling AIDS: Testing, Screening and Reporting," *American Journal of Law and Medicine* 12:1 (1986), 7–53; Lawrence Gostin and William Curran, "AIDS Screening, Confidentiality and the Duty to Warn," *American Journal of Public Health* 77:3 (1987), 361–65.

[34]See for example, *Cross v. Huttenlocher,* 440 A.2d 952 (Conn. 1981).

[35]*Ruffin v. Harris,* No 80-00627835, New London, Conn., August 1983.

[36]See *Opithorne v. Framingham Union Hospital,* 401 Mass. 860 (1988); *Penn Tanker Company v. United States,* 310 F. Supplement 613 (1970).

[37]See for example, *LaRoche v. United States* 730 F. 2d, 538 (8th Cir. 1984).

[38]Jeffrey J. Sacks, "AIDS in a Surgeon," *New England Journal of Medicine* 313:16 (1985), 1017–18. [One dentist is now known to have infected five of his patients with AIDS. —*Ed.*]

[39]J. H. Morton, "One More Article About AIDS," *Federation Bulletin* 75:2 (1988), 62–64; Cf. R. J. Feinstein, "When Should the Sick Doctor Stop Caring for Patients, And Who Will Make That Decision?," *Journal of the Florida Medical Association* 73:1 (1986), 43–45.

[40]Council on Ethical and Judicial Affairs, "Ethical Issues."

[41]Centers for Disease Control, "Recommendations," 16S.

[42]American Hospital Association, AIDS Task Force, AIDS *and the Law: Responding to the Special Concerns of Hospitals* (Chicago: AHA, 1987), 52–54; Massachusetts Hospital Association, AIDS*: Administrative Reference Manual* (1987), 64; Massachusetts Department of Public Health, *Governor's Task Force on* AIDS *Policies and Recommendations* (1987), 4–9.

[43]Mary M. Devlin, "Ethical Issues in the AIDS Crisis: The HIV-Positive Practitioner," *Journal of the American Medical Association* 260:6 (1988), 790.

[44]A related issue is presented by the case of a physician who is stuck with a needle from an HIV-infected patient. Should he refrain from doing invasive procedures for the time it takes to learn whether he seroconverted? In such a case the risk might fall below a reasonable range for concern (a small probability that the surgeon became positive multiplied by a small probability that he could transfer the infection).

[45]Paul Cleary, *et al.,* "Compulsory Premarital Screening for the Human Immunodeficiency Virus: Technical and Public Health Considerations," *Journal of the American Medical Association* 258:13 (1987), 1757-62; Lawrence Gostin, "Screening for AIDS: Efficacy, Cost, and Conse-

quences," AIDS & *Public Policy Journal* 2:4 (1987), 14–24; Ronald Bayer, Carol Levine, Susan M. Wolf, "HIV Antibody Screening: An Ethical Framework for Evaluating Proposed Programs," *Journal of the American Medical Association* 256:13 (1986), 1768–74.

[46]Many state supreme courts have held that disclosure of confidential health care information can result in liability; see for example, *Alberts v. Devine*, 395 Mass. 59 (1985). Moreover, several jurisdictions have now enacted statutes prohibiting unauthorized disclosure of an HIV test. See Larry Gostin and Andrew Ziegler, "A Review of Aids-Related Legislative and Regulatory Policy in the United States," *Law, Medicine and Health Care* 15:1-2 (1987), 5–16.

[47]Gostin and Curran, "AIDS Screening."

[48]Frederic E. Shaw, Charles L. Barrett and Robert Hamm, "Lethal Outbreak of Hepatitis B in a Dental Practice," *Journal of the American Medical Association* 255:23 (1986), 3260–64; Robert J. Gerety, "Hepatitis B Transmission Between Dental or Medical Workers and Patients," *Annals of Internal Medicine* 95:2 (1981), 229.

[49]W. W. Williams, "Guidelines for Infection Control in Hospital Personnel," *Infection Control* 4:4 (1983), 326–49; Ludwig A. Lettau *et al.*, "Transmission of Hepatitis B with Resultant Restriction of Surgical Practice." *Journal of the American Medical Association* 255:7 (1986), 934–37.

[50]See *Schmerber v. California*, 384 U.S. 757 (1966).

[51]*O'Connor v. Ortega*, 107 S. Ct. 1492, 1497 (1987) (quoting *United States v. Jacobsen*, 466 U.S. 109, 113 (1984)).

[52]*Glover v Eastern Nebraska Community Office of Mental Retardation*, 686 F. Supp. 243 (D. Neb. 1988).

[53]*Grannis v. Board of Medical Examiners*, 96 Cal. Rptr. 863, 870, 19 Cal. App. 3d 551, 561 (1971).

[54]See *Bratt v. International Business Machine Corporation*, 785 F. 2d 352 (1st Cir. 1986).

[55]See Gostin and Ziegler, "A Review of AIDS-Related Legislative and Regulatory Policy."

[56]Diana Brahams, "Confidentiality for Doctors Who are HIV Positive," *The Lancet*, 21 November 1987, 1221–22.

[57]*Yeste v. Miami Herald Publishing Company*, 451 So.2d 491 (Fla. App. 3 Dist. 1984). See Feinstein, "When Should the Sick Doctor Stop Caring for Patients."

[58]Gostin and Curran, "AIDS Screening."

[59]107 S. Ct. 1123 (1987).

[60]*Chalk v. Orange County Department of Education*, 832 F.2d 1158 (9th Cir. 1987); *Shuttleworth v. Broward County*, 639 F. Supplement 654 (S.D. Fla. 1986).

[61]134 *Congressional Record* S1738–1740, (daily ed. March 2, 1988) (statement of Sen. Harkin).

[62]No. 87 C 6888, Consent Decree filed 21 February 1988, N.D. Illinois.

Treating AIDS

In the previous article, Gostin assumed that physicians will bear the burden of treating those with AIDS. He is assuming that treating patients with AIDS is a clear obligation of physicians.

Ezekiel Emanuel asks, "What are the obligations of the medical profession; is there an obligation to treat patients with AIDS?" He discusses four factors that are said to limit the obligations of doctors. Emanuel says that even if there are no absolute obligations, it may still be that physicians have special obligations that make up the essence of being a physician.

It is a mistake, he contends, to see medicine as a purely commercial undertaking. "Heal the sick" is a moral principle that underlies, indeed creates, the very profession of medicine as we know it. Whatever conditions may limit the obligations of physicians, they are morally obligated to ". . . care for patients with AIDS."

The replies to Emanuel ask some hard questions. Doesn't the 100% mortality make AIDS a special case? What does one do when treating AIDS patients will endanger other patients? If a physician has no "competence" in dealing with AIDS, isn't there less of an obligation? Doesn't honest and outright fear of AIDS at least save a physician from being condemned for not treating patients with AIDS?

Emanuel replies to these (and other) comments. Does he defend his position well or should he change his views in light of some of the criticism?

DO PHYSICIANS HAVE AN OBLIGATION TO TREAT PATIENTS WITH AIDS?

Ezekiel J. Emanuel

Are physicians obligated to treat patients with the acquired immunodeficiency syndrome (AIDS)? This is clearly an important question for practicing physicians, but its scope extends beyond AIDS and matters of clinical care. It raises fundamental questions about the medical profession itself, about the social and professional understanding of the purpose of medicine. In analyzing the physician's obligation to patients with AIDS, two issues must be considered—the nature of the obligation, and what factors, if any, serve to limit it.

The Obligation to Treat Patients with AIDS

Our investigation of physicians' obligation should begin with the acknowledgment that unless they have a familial or other special relationship with the patient, ordinary citizens have no obligation to care for patients with AIDS; for unrelated persons to provide any such care is supererogatory. This point is important: if there is nothing unique about being physicians, if medicine is not a profession, if patients are accurately described as consumers, and if health care is a "marketplace product line,"[1] then physicians have the same responsibilities as ordinary citizens, with no obligation to care for patients with AIDS. If society values medicine as a trade, subject to

Source: "Do Physicians Have an Obligation to Treat Patients with AIDS?" by Ezekiel J. E. Emanuel. *The New England Journal of Medicine,* vol. 318 (June 23, 1988), pp. 1686–90. Copyright © 1988 Massachusetts Medical Society. Used by permission.

the laws and policies of commerce, then it is hard to defend a unique obligation of physicians. In this sense, the physician's obligation is relative; it depends on the concept of medical practice espoused by physicians and society. As yet no polity, not even the United States, has completely accepted
the view of medicine as commerce, so physicians cannot summarily deny
their obligation to care for patients with AIDS.

If physicians have an obligation to treat such patients, it is derived
from the concept of medicine as a profession and from the physician's particular professional role. The objective of a commercial enterprise is the
pursuit of wealth; the objective of the medical profession is devotion to a
moral ideal—in particular, healing the sick and rendering the ill healthy
and well. The physician is committed to the help and betterment of other
people—"selflessly caring for the sick,"[2] as the president of the American
College of Physicians has put it. When a person joins the profession, he or
she professes a commitment to these ideals and accepts the obligation to
serve the sick. It is the profession that is chosen. The obligation is neither
chosen nor transferable; it is constitutive of the professional activity.

There are some qualifications to this professional obligation. Physicians are not obliged, of course, to treat patients whose ailments fall beyond
their expertise. Oncologists are not expected to operate on patients. Furthermore, medical professionals are neither expected to seek patients nor
obligated to treat everyone who appears at their offices for help. With the
understanding that medicine is a profession committed to the ideal of caring for the sick, physicians can deny nonemergency care, but not simply
because of a person's disease, the inability to pay, or the physician's personal dislike; physicians cannot discriminate against people in accepting
nonemergency patients.[3] This position overrides the conventional view,
that physicians are absolutely free to choose whom they will serve.[4] For if a
physician can freely refuse to accept people with AIDS as patients, the obligation to treat patients with AIDS has no force. Sickness presents an urgent
need for care, whatever the person's race, religion, or life style. Care can be
denied, but only for moral reasons. A patient's illness claims the physician's
attention and constrains—but does not eliminate—the physician's grounds
for refusing treatment.

In fulfilling the obligation to treat patients with AIDS, physicians are
expected to accept some personal risk, since risk is in the nature of work
with sick people who have communicable diseases. In the past, physicians
have accepted risks both in caring for patients with communicable diseases,
such as hepatitis and tuberculosis, and in seeking cures through research.
Indeed, we know that in treating the sick, many physicians, especially surgeons and pathologists, face up to five times the normal risk of contracting
hepatitis B.[5] In this respect, medicine is no different from other occupa-
tions in which one is expected to accept some personal risk in pursuit of
one's aim. Thus, it is expected that firefighters will risk burns, even death,

to fight blazes, and that lifeguards will risk injury to rescue drowning people. Taking such risks is part of joining the profession and affirming its objective to help the needy.

Accordingly, each physician is obligated to treat patients with AIDS if he or she has the professional competence to do so. This obligation derives from the more inclusive obligation to care for all sick people. It is a view the American Medical Association's Council on Ethical and Judicial Affairs endorses: "A physician may not ethically refuse to treat a patient whose condition is within the physician's current realm of competence solely because the patient is seropositive [for the human immunodeficiency virus, HIV]."[6] The American College of Physicians advocates a similar position:

> [Physicians] must provide high-quality non-judgmental care without regard to their own personal risk, real or perceived. Physicians and nurses alike are charged by the ethics of their healing profession to treat patients with all forms of sickness and disease [including AIDS].[7]

Those uneasy with this view have put forward a weaker interpretation of professional obligations, according to which the medical profession in toto has an obligation to minister to patients with AIDS, but individual physicians may ethically refuse to care for them as long as they refer them to a competent physician for treatment. This is the position of the Texas Medical Association's Board of Councilors:

> A physician shall either accept the responsibility for the care and treatment of a patient with AIDS, HIV, antibodies to HIV, or infection with any other probably causative agent of AIDS, or refer the patient to an appropriate physician who will accept the responsibility for the care and treatment of the patient.[8]

Similarly, the Arizona State Board of Medical Examiners maintains that the refusal to care for patients with AIDS may be deemed unprofessional only when unaccompanied by reasonable efforts to find another physician.[9]

This weaker interpretation attempts to combine the marketplace view of medicine with the ideal of medicine as a profession. It is not a principled view. Rather, it is an attempt to rationalize opinions, and it produces a conceptual contradiction. A physician's obligations are defined by the professionally and culturally accepted ideals of the profession. Leaving them to the individual practitioner implies that there are no professional obligations, only personal choices. Such a view undermines the professional status of medicine, making it more like business. In addition, there could be serious practical effects. Many physicians would probably refuse to care for patients with AIDS, and the profession as a whole might be unable to fulfill its obligation to care for such patients. Such a hybrid view of professional obligations could compromise the effort to persuade physicians of their obligation by allowing individual physicians to determine their own obligations and suggesting that it is ethical not to treat patients with AIDS.

We can conclude that if medicine is properly viewed as a profession committed to curing and ameliorating the ailments of sick people, then the obligation to treat patients with AIDS, even at some personal risk, is a particular case of the physician's general obligation to treat the ill. Accepting this obligation is not a matter of individual choice, for it constitutes an essential element of the medical profession.

Limiting Factors

Like individual rights, obligations cannot be absolute. Too frequently, those who correctly argue for the physician's professional obligation to care for patients with AIDS minimize or even fail to acknowledge this reality.[6, 7] At least four factors may limit the physician's professional obligation to treat patients with AIDS: excessive risk, minimal or questionable benefits, competing obligations to other patients, and competing obligations to self and family. In refusing to treat patients with AIDS, many physicians justify their view by citing these factors. To determine the physician's obligation, each factor must be evaluated carefully.

Excessive Risks

What risk does AIDS pose to physicians? Consider a related case. Firefighters are not normally considered obligated to enter a blazing house to rescue the inhabitants if such an attempt would almost certainly result in serious bodily injury. A rescue attempt clearly against the odds is considered supererogatory, even for the professional. Similarly, the (American) military does not send soldiers on suicide missions, and for high-risk operations it requests volunteers.

Because HIV infection is not a legally reportable disease in all states, statistics about health care workers who have become HIV positive after a work-related exposure are imprecise. According to an informal tabulation of the Centers for Disease Control, only a handful of health care workers, probably less than 20, have become HIV positive from such exposures—a low estimate, probably, since as Kelen et al. point out,[10] many physicians may be stuck by needles that they do not realize are contaminated; therefore, they do not suspect HIV infection and do not test themselves. Nevertheless, given the thousands of physicians and health care workers who have treated patients with AIDS, the overall risk to physicians appears low. But we must distinguish subgroups of physicians, since for some the risk may be excessive.

Three factors determine the cumulative risk for HIV infection among health care workers: the risk of becoming HIV positive from a single contaminated needle stick, the proportion of patients treated who are HIV positive, and the frequency of needle-stick injuries and other exposures. The Centers for Disease Control have concluded that the risk of becoming HIV positive after a single HIV-contaminated needle stick is 1 percent or less.[11] A study of the risk of HIV infection among laboratory workers reached similar conclusions.[12] In addition, seroconversion has been reported after exposure to HIV through the skin and mucous membranes (but not by means of needle sticks), although the risk from such exposures is much lower.[13] The proportion of patients treated who are infected with HIV varies among physicians. According to Kelen et al.,[10] "4.6 percent of the patients who required emergency major surgery in the operating suite" at Johns Hopkins had an unrecognized HIV infection. Dr. Lorraine Day, chief of orthopedics at San Francisco General Hospital, stated that as many as a third of her patients were at high risk for HIV positivity (an estimate, since routine HIV testing is prohibited). Finally, the frequency of needle sticks varies among physicians. Among internists, who perform relatively few complex, invasive procedures, the frequency of puncture wounds is relatively low. For surgeons, the frequency of needle or instrument punctures is high. The precise number is hard to quantify, but Dr. Day maintained that surgeons who follow proper infection-control precautions will inevitably contaminate themselves, and added that she "may get stuck 20 times in the next six months."[14]

Do these factors represent an excessive risk that limits the obligation to treat? Of course, there is no precise point at which risks become excessive; this is a matter of judgment and consensus. It also depends on what risks the polity expects such workers as firefighters, law-enforcement officials, and soldiers to incur in performing their jobs. Internists may have a high proportion of patients infected with HIV, but they perform few procedures with needles and sharp instruments. If one makes a high estimate of the frequency of HIV-contaminated needle punctures, which are likely to occur among medical house staff about once every two years, internists have an overall annual risk of becoming HIV positive of about 0.5 percent. (Since so few physicians have become HIV positive when thousands are treating patients with AIDS, this estimate represents a high upper limit.) This appears to be a high, but not excessive risk—not one that would limit the internist's obligations to patients with AIDS. One way to confirm this intuition would be to compare it with the risk taken by someone in a different occupation—a firefighter, for instance. Although a firefighter's risk is calculated retrospectively, not as an estimate of future events, it is a useful standard. Recently, firefighters on the front line in Boston have faced a risk of death of about 0.5 percent during each of the worst years, and of 0.2 percent in normal years (there are approximately 1600 firefighters and 1 to 9 deaths per year).

For surgeons who operate on a large number of patients with AIDS and incur frequent, unavoidable punctures, the risks are much higher. For the sake of argument, we may determine the risk for two types of surgeons. If we assume 40 sticks per year, the emergency department surgeons in the study by Kelen et al.[10] have a 2 percent annual risk of contracting an HIV infection from performing major surgical operations (40 sticks per year, with 4.6 percent infected with HIV and a 1 percent risk of HIV infection from each HIV-infected stick). The risk may be higher still if, in addition to major operations, the surgeon is involved in invasive procedures that could result in needle-stick injuries—thoracostomy, central-line placement, and the like. Similarly, the surgeon's actual risk may be higher or lower, depending on the actual number of sticks per year. Next, let us consider Dr. Day's experience, which probably represents the upper limit of the risk to surgeons. Her risk of contracting HIV infection from a work-related puncture is 12 percent per year, with a five-year cumulative risk of 49 percent (40 sticks per year, of which 33 percent carry HIV infection at a risk of 1 percent with each puncture). Are these risks excessive? Certainly that of Dr. Day has crossed the line into the excessive-risk category, in which the obligation of surgeons to patients with AIDS is limited. The risk taken by surgeons in the emergency department is high and probably bordering on the excessive. It can be compared with the risk faced by soldiers. At the height of the Vietnamese War, in 1968, a soldier's annual risk of dying in combat was less than 3 percent (January 1968, 1202 deaths among a total of 498,000 troops).[15]

Although excessive risk limits the physician's obligation to treat patients with AIDS, it does not eliminate all obligations to them. One way to combine the recognition of an abiding obligation to treat patients with AIDS with an affirmation of reasonable limits to the risks would be to have physicians perform emergency procedures on patients with AIDS but forgo elective interventions. It is incumbent on society and the medical profession to reduce the risk to these practitioners. All physicians should adopt universal blood and body-fluid precautions, but these and other safety precautions cannot eliminate all needle punctures. Consequently, the necessary remedies may include reducing the number of patients with AIDS treated by a single physician by requiring other competent physicians to treat them.

It is important to remember that the validity of the ethical considerations of risks depends on the particular facts—the frequency of puncture wounds and the number of patients with AIDS—and on social judgments of excessive professional risk. The analysis presented here cannot be taken as a blanket excuse to retreat from obligations to treat patients with AIDS, especially for physicians likely to treat only a few patients with HIV infection and to perform few invasive procedures.

Questionable Benefits

Again, consider a related case. Firefighters are normally expected to risk bodily injury to save humans from a fire, but they are usually not expected to risk injury to rescue a person known to be dying. Likewise, it is unethical for a physician to treat a patient, with AIDS or not, if no benefit is anticipated; there can be no obligation to provide valueless care. Conversely, when the treatment is lifesaving, when the patient is expected to survive for a period of time, and when the treatment would be given to every other patient in similar clinical circumstances, then there is a clear obligation to provide it to patients with AIDS. Furthermore, there is an obligation to provide tests and interventions that meet established standards of proper medical care and provide a clear and distinct medical benefit. However, when a choice must be made among several beneficial interventions for the same purpose—for instance, between an open surgical biopsy of lymph nodes and a fine-needle aspiration biopsy[16]—the evaluation of options should include concern about minimizing the risk of HIV exposure to health care workers. Finally, there is an obligation, especially in the case of patients with AIDS, to provide therapies that relieve suffering.

There are certain interventions that physicians are not obligated to provide to patients with AIDS because the treatments are medically inessential. One type of such treatment involves care that does not affect the patient's longevity, bodily function, or degree of physical pain but that the patient desires—cosmetic surgery, bunion removal, or the like. Even though physicians perform these procedures, many commentators doubt whether they form a legitimate part of medical care, because they do not contribute to curing or ameliorating ill health.[17] A second type of inessential treatment is elective interventions that are not absolutely required to benefit the patient—for example, elective surgical repair of a nonincarcerated hernia. With both types of inessential treatment—treatments to satisfy a patient's desires and elective interventions—the benefits to the patient, in terms of restoring the body's normal function, are not clear. The physician's obligation to render such treatments is open to evaluation on a case-by-case basis.

Obligations to Other Patients

To consider a related example once again: firefighters are expected to fight fires even at risk of personal injury; they are expected to minimize risks, but not to avoid present risks in order to be able to combat future blazes. Indeed, it would be deemed a specious excuse for shirking professional duties if firefighters justified failure to combat a blaze with the claim that an injury would render them unable to fight future fires. So, too, with physicians who suggest that obligations to other patients eliminate their obligation to treat patients with AIDS. First, assuming that a physician has competing obligations to other patients, it requires a stronger reason to demonstrate that these obligations outweigh the physician's obligation to serve patients with AIDS. Identifying competing duties does not itself determine which one has a greater claim. Second, in an era of physician oversupply, when every patient can choose among many competent physicians, when the talents of no single physician are irreplaceable, no physician's services are so essential to patients that they confer a moral obligation to avoid activities, including the provision of medical care to other needy patients, that might prevent the physician from rendering medical care in the future. Finally, the argument of competing obligations tries to deny the physician's obligation to patients with AIDS by entangling it with obligations to other patients. This thinking runs counter to that of the medical profession, which has consistently and vigorously opposed policies, such as cost containment, which it sees as forcing individual physicians to balance a patient's best interests against a reduction in costs, society's needs, or another patient's need for the same services. Such balancing, it is argued, should occur through political deliberations, not at the bedside or in the physician's office.[18] If proper medical ethics preclude an individual physician's balancing the interests of society and other patients in clinical judgments concerning patient care, consistency requires that it should also preclude such balancing in the case of patients with AIDS.

Obligations to Self and Family

Obligations to self seem specious grounds for refusing to treat patients with AIDS. If such obligations are not "fraudulent items"[19] but designate something important, then they must mean that a person has a right to pursue a chosen vocation and other major projects. With this understanding, a person who feels called to a profession that involves assuming some routine personal risk, and yet shrinks from accepting that risk, is being inconsistent. Properly understood, obligations to self actually require physicians to treat patients with AIDS, even at some reasonable personal risk. Only thus can they realize the true ideal of a physician; only thus can they fulfill the obligations associated with the professional practice of medicine that they see as their vocation. If a physician genuinely feels that he or she cannot accept a reasonable personal risk in caring for patients, then it is time not to evade a professional obligation, but to wonder whether medicine is that physician's true vocation.

Obligations to family are more complex. The choice to become a physician and to have a family entails certain personal risks, to which the family is subjected in consequence. But some members of the family, notably the children, cannot give informed consent to the profession and its attendant risks. Nor can the family be expected to accept all the consequences of the risks a physician has taken. Therefore, a person who is both a physician and a parent does have genuine conflicting obligations; that person faces a moral dilemma. This conflict, it should be stressed, is not limited to caring for patients with AIDS, but extends to many other areas. The family's claims for time and attention frequently conflict with a physician's obligations to patients, and too often are displaced by these professional obligations.

How are these competing obligations to be resolved? Another society might treat physicians with families differently. In the Israeli military, for instance, a married man cannot be a commando. But in our society, a distinction between the married and the unmarried is untenable; the married physician is expected to fulfill the same obligations as the unmarried one. In the past, familial obligations have not overwhelmed a parent's professional obligations or vice versa. Consistency requires that AIDS be treated in the same manner. A balancing of obligations is required. Yet there is no simple rule: the balancing depends on actual risks entailed in the practice of medicine. Furthermore, the balancing cannot simply be a matter for the individual conscience; professional and social expectations constrain acceptable resolutions of this dilemma. As a general rule, when the risks of contracting AIDS are not excessive by accepted social standards, the professional obligation must be fulfilled, regardless of the physician's marital status—just as firefighters and soldiers with families must still risk their lives to fulfill their professional obligations when those risks, although real and high, are not deemed excessive. There may be one exception: pregnant physicians. The threshold of excessive risk should be lower for pregnant physicians because contracting AIDS also places the unborn child at a high risk—50 percent chance—of being infected with HIV. Thus, concern for the future child's health may limit the professional obligations of a pregnant physician.

In conclusion, three points about the physician's obligation to treat patients with AIDS need emphasis. First, this obligation depends on viewing medicine as a profession, not as a commercial enterprise. Second, it follows that physicians who join the profession assume an obligation to care for the ill even at some reasonable personal risk. Because of this inclusive obligation, physicians have a specific obligation to patients with AIDS. Third, this obligation can be limited by several factors, especially excessive personal risk. It appears that a few physicians are assuming excessive risk in treating their patients with AIDS. The recognition of limiting factors, however, does not eliminate the obligations of every physician to treat such patients. Medicine is committed to caring for the sick, and thus physicians must care for patients with AIDS.

[3]Schwartz H, Gray A. Can you say no? Can a doctor legally withhold treatment from a patient with AIDS? Mass Med 1987; 2(5):39–43.

[4]The Council on Ethical and Judicial Affairs. Current opinions of the Council on Ethical and Judicial Affairs of the American Medical Association. Chicago: American Medical Association, 1986:33.

[5]Denes AE, Smith JL, Maynard JE, Doto IL, Berquist KR, Finkel AJ. Hepatitis B infection in physicians: results of a nationwide seroepidemiologic survey. JAMA 1978; 239:210–12.

[6]Report of the American Medical Association's Council on Ethical and Judicial Affairs: ethical issues involved in the growing AIDS crisis, Report A. Chicago: American Medical Association, 1987.

[7]Health and Public Policy Committee, American College of Physicians; Infectious Diseases Society of America. The acquired immunodeficiency syndrome (AIDS) and infection with the human immunodeficiency virus (HIV). Ann Intern Med 1988; 108:460–96.

[8]Second Supplemental Report of the Texas Medical Association Board of Councilors, November 20, 1987.

[9]Ariz. MDs can refuse AIDS patients. American Medical News. November 6, 1987:37.

[10]Kelen GD, Fritz S, Qaqish B, et al. Unrecognized human immunodeficiency virus infection in emergency department patients. N Engl J Med 1988; 318:1645–50.

[11]Recommendations for prevention of HIV transmission in health-care settings. MMWR 1987; 36:Suppl 2S:3S–18S.

[12]Weiss SH, Goedert JJ, Gartner S, et al. Risk of human immunodeficiency virus (HIV-1) infection among laboratory workers. Science 1988; 239:68–71.

[13]Update: human immunodeficiency virus infections in health-care workers exposed to blood of infected patients. MMWR 1987; 36:285–89.

[14]Orthopod urges HIV testing: decision in San Francisco sparks debate. American Medical News. December 4, 1987:1, 36–7.

[15]Lewy G. America in Vietnam. New York: Oxford University Press, 1978:147.

[16]Bottles K, McPhaul LW, Volberding P. Fine-needle aspiration biopsy in patients with acquired immunodeficiency syndrome (AIDS): experience in an outpatient clinic. Ann Intern Med 1988; 108:42–45.

[17]Kass LR. Toward a more natural science: biology and human affairs. New York: Free Press, 1985:157–86.

[18]Levinsky NG. The doctor's master. N Engl J Med 1984; 311:1573–75.

[19]Williams B. Ethics and the limits of philosophy. Cambridge, Mass.: Harvard University Press, 1985:182.

Correspondence: Do Physicians Have an Obligation to Treat Patients with AIDS?

To the Editor: Dr. Emanuel writes with thoroughness, thoughtfulness, and conviction on the issue of physicians' obligation to treat patients with acquired immunodeficiency syndrome (AIDS) (June 23 issue).* I agree with his premise that physicians do have such an obligation, but I recognize several unique features of this epidemic that can lead to understandable differences of opinion among physicians, hospitals, and health care providers.

Patients with AIDS will die of AIDS. Virtually no one will survive. By contrast, not all patients with poliomyelitis, tuberculosis, or even bubonic plague died of their illness.

If a physician contracts AIDS as a consequence of treating a patient with AIDS, then he or she will die also. That was not the inevitable fate of the physician in any of the epidemics or plagues throughout medical history.

Because of these two facts, I believe the role of physicians, hospitals, and health care providers is arguably different from that in the past.

Richard Lennihan, Jr., M.D.
Wilmington, DE 19803   1701 Augustine Cut-off

*Emanuel EJ. Do physicians have an obligation to treat patients with AIDS? N Engl J Med 1988; 318:1686–90.

To the Editor: Dr. Emanuel's interesting and thoughtful discussion does not address one aspect of the problem that I have found puzzling. To what extent are physicians obliged to treat patients infected with the human immunodeficiency virus (HIV) when that decision may place their other patients at risk?

Children and adolescents admitted to psychiatric inpatient facilities often present with histories that include such factors as intravenous drug use, unprotected sexual intercourse with multiple partners, or sexual abuse, which raise concern about HIV infection. Despite the best efforts of an alert and competent nursing staff, it is not always possible to prevent sexual encounters between teens, to keep very aggressive younger children from inflicting serious bite wounds on others, or to enforce strict blood and body-fluid precautions in the case of a confused, uncooperative child. In evaluating children for admission who may be infected with HIV, our staff has struggled with the ethical dilemma of whether it is right to refuse treatment to one patient because of the potential harm that patient's behavior may cause another patient. Although this problem may be beyond the scope of Dr. Emanuel's paper, I would be interested in his comments.

Robert S. McKelvey, M.D.
Houston, TX 77030   Baylor College of Medicine

To the Editor: The recent essay by Dr. Emanuel contains several statements with which I disagree. The author states, "The threshold of excessive risk should be lower for pregnant physicians." His last sentence on this subject states that "concern for the future child's health may limit the professional obligations of a pregnant physician." I see no reason why this fallacious reasoning should not apply to both current and future pregnancies. Any young physician, male or female, who is planning to have a family runs a risk of having those plans altered if the physician becomes infected with HIV. An infected woman's 40 to 50 percent risk of transmitting HIV to her offspring probably applies whether she becomes infected before or during a pregnancy, current or future. One could take this argument of excessive risk for current and future pregnancies and use it to negate one's obligation to take care of any patients with HIV infection.

For pregnant health care providers, the concerns expressed about HIV infection are no different from those about any other potential blood-borne pathogen. Although most infections do not carry such high mortality rates, the infectivity rates may be higher. At our hospital's labor-and-delivery unit, we do not allow pregnant nurses to decline to take care of patients with infectious diseases. I see no reason to permit physicians to be relieved of their professional obligations toward similar patients.

George D. Wendel, M.D.
Dallas, TX 75235-9032   Parkland Memorial Hospital

To the Editor: Several recent discussions, including the Sounding Board article by Emanuel, have concluded that physicians have an obligation to care for patients with AIDS.[1,2] Although I agree with that message, I am concerned that the depth of support by health care agencies for health care workers who take care of patients with AIDS is shallow and without much substance. Concern and fear about caring for patients with AIDS or HIV infection still run far and deep among health care workers.[3,4] Although issues such as homophobia contribute to the reluctance of health care workers to care for patients with AIDS,[4,5] there are a number of practical issues that have not been addressed. Can health care workers keep their jobs if they seroconvert to HIV positivity at work? Who will pay for their disability and health insurance if health care workers become ill after HIV seroconversion? Who will pay for prophylactic zidovudine if a health care worker receives a needle stick?[6] Will health care workers have to pay higher insurance premiums if they care for patients with HIV? Commentaries detailing the duty of health care workers to care for such patients do not pay the bills or address adequately the concerns of those providing such care.

I would propose that federal agencies establish criteria for work-related HIV infection. If HIV infection that meets such criteria develops in a health care worker, then that health care worker should have disability and health insurance coverage guaranteed in the event the worker becomes ill with AIDS and loses standard insurance coverage. The affected health care worker should also be protected against premium increases on the basis of work-acquired HIV infection or exposure. Funding for such programs should be made available from a variety of hospital, insurance-industry, and governmental agencies. Not to provide such financial protection sends a message that society expects health care workers to care for patients with HIV but is unwilling to back that expectation with direct support for the health care workers themselves. Such a program would somewhat ameliorate the stress arising from concern about HIV infection in the workplace and would help to maintain a professional approach to the care of patients with HIV by health care workers.

Keith Henry, M.D.
St. Paul, MN 55101-2595   St. Paul–Ramsey Medical Center

Notes

[1]Zuger A, Miles SH. Physicians. AIDS, and occupational risk: historic traditions and ethical obligations. JAMA 1987; 258:1924–28.

[2]Kim JH, Perfect JR. To help the sick: an historical and ethical essay concerning the refusal to care for patients with AIDS. Am J Med 1988; 84:135–38.

[3]Henry K., Maki M, Crossley K. Analysis of the use of HIV antibody testing in a Minnesota hospital. JAMA 1988; 259: 229–32.

[4]Henry K, Campbell S, Willenbring K. AIDS-related knowledge, attitudes and behaviors among employees at a U.S. hospital. Presented at the Fourth International Conference on AIDS, Stockholm. June 12–16. 1988. abstract.

[5]Kelly JA, St. Lawrence JS, Smith S Jr, Hood HV, Cook DJ. Stigmatization of AIDS patients by physicians. Am J Public Health 1987; 77:789–91.

[6]Staver S. New study to offer zidovudine to HIV-exposed health workers. American Medical News, June 10, 1988:1, 11.

To the Editor: The excellent paper by Dr. Emanuel overlooks one very important issue that requires discussion. Which physicians satisfy the requirements for the "current realm of competence" (in the words of the American Medical Association's Council on Ethical and Judicial Affairs[*]) that would obligate care of patients with AIDS? And who decides? Certainly, everyone would agree that board-eligible infectious disease consultants are under such an obligation. But what about general internists and other primary care providers?

AIDS is a complex disease, resulting in rare and unusual infections with which the general internist has little experience. Would anyone disagree with the statement that no internist or primary care provider should assume the care of a patient with AIDS without at least a considerable amount of reading? Which raises the challenging question of whether physicians are "off the hook" in their obligations to patients with AIDS simply by failing to maintain up-to-date knowledge. And yet primary care providers will have to become heavily involved, since the numbers of patients with AIDS anticipated in the future will easily overwhelm the capacity of infectious disease consultants.

Lester J. Kobylak, M.D.
Detroit, MI 48202   Henry Ford Hospital

To the Editor: Pious statements from higher-ups like the Surgeon General and Dr. Emanuel about the treatment of patients with AIDS do not cut it. It is one thing to treat a patient who has AIDS and quite another to come into direct contact with that patient's blood. My guess is that that never happens to either Dr. Emanuel or Dr. Koop, which is why their position is so objectionable.

You cannot command people not to be afraid. Fear is not logical and does not take orders. If a resident or medical student—a member of the group at highest risk—is afraid to work with the blood of patients with AIDS, he or she could say, "I am afraid to get HIV-infected blood on me. I can't help it, I'm afraid."

No one, from the Surgeon General on down to the most liberal human-rights lawyers, can condemn a doctor for not taking on a patient with AIDS (abandonment is a different issue) if that action truly stems from fear. It does not matter whether the belief is rational or irrational, as long as it is true.

James Kalivas, M.D.
University of Kansas
Medical Center

Kansas City, KS 66103

The above letters were referred to Dr. Emanuel, who offers the following reply:

To the Editor: Dr. Lennihan's comparison of AIDS with other epidemic diseases is inaccurate. Limits on the physician's obligation to care for patients are determined by the overall risk of a fatal outcome from an occupational exposure to an infection. The risk to physicians from HIV infection is probably smaller than that from smallpox, tuberculosis, and other past infectious epidemic diseases, because both the number of patients infected with such diseases and the transmission rate of such infections were higher.

There is no simple formula for dealing with the risks Dr. McKelvey describes. The physician must evaluate the likelihood of the patient's transmitting HIV to others and compare it with the likelihood of exposing patients to hepatitis B or other infections. The physician must also recognize that by sexual abuse and the like, some dangerous patients can affect others in ways that may not be life-threatening but can be irreversibly damaging. Finally, the physician must consider whether the obligation to care for potentially harmful patients with HIV infection can be fulfilled by arranging for the patient's care in another facility where there is a lower possibility of the patient's harming others.

A pregnant physician has an obligation to treat patients infected with HIV. The justification for limiting her risk of HIV infection is not, as Dr. Wendel seems to think, concern for her health, family plans, or career but rather concern for her fetus's health when the fetus has not assumed a duty that might justify endangering its health.

In response to Dr. Henry's concern, I certainly support initiatives that would ensure not only guarantees of disability and health insurance, but also professional respect and dignity for health care workers infected because of job-related HIV exposure. Nevertheless, the current absence of such guarantees does not obviate the obligations of physicians and others to care for patients with AIDS. Furthermore, we should not forget that our society already grants physicians fairly large compensations, financial and otherwise, for performing their job and assuming its risks.

The response to Dr. Kobylak's query is that ignorance cannot legitimize the denial of care to patients with AIDS. Surely any physician, whether gastroenterologist or general internist, who fails "to maintain up-to-date knowledge" of clinical diseases, including AIDS, cannot possibly provide competent care and should not be practicing medicine. It should also be emphasized that properly caring for patients with AIDS does not require becoming an infectious disease specialist. Many such patients receive excellent care in primary care clinics.

Finally, in reply to Dr. Kalivas' letter: Although I cannot speak for Surgeon General Koop, I can certainly affirm that I am no "higher-up" spouting "pious statements." My regular medical duties include drawing blood from patients infected with HIV, performing lumbar punctures in such patients, and introducing central venous and arterial lines in them. I recognize the risks attendant on such procedures. Hence, I do them with some fear. But fear cannot cripple us and prevent us from fulfilling our duty. To be morally responsible persons, we must be able to do what is right despite our instincts and fears.

Ezekiel J. Emanuel, M.D., Ph.D.
Boston, MA 02215   Beth Israel Hospital

A Physician with AIDS

"When a House Officer Gets AIDS" reminds us of what it means to treat a patient humanely by showing how the health-care profession itself treated one of its own shabbily. There is no self-pity in Dr. Aoun's account. Rather, he is using his experience to highlight some of the frailties of the medical profession in general. His hope is that when these weaknesses are realized, faced, and corrected, medicine and all patients will be the better for it. He makes many of the points about the nature of medicine that we, and many of the other authors, have been stressing throughout this book.

WHEN A HOUSE OFFICER
GETS AIDS

Hacib Aoun

I am a physician who contracted the acquired immunodeficiency syndrome (AIDS) from a young patient while working as a resident at a well-known teaching hospital. Almost three years have passed since the diagnosis—a terrible three years for my wife, my small daughter, and me. Because I am convinced that my situation is not unique and that the tragedy that affects us now will affect other physicians in times to come, I want to share it with you.

In February 1983, I was a second-year resident in medicine rotating through the bone marrow-transplantation unit. Pat, a patient, was a courageous teenager who had received a transplant after running out of other options for the cure of his leukemia. His course in the unit had been fairly stormy, with infections, failure to graft, fevers, and multiple episodes of massive gastrointestinal bleeding. He had received at least 100 units of blood and blood products.

One evening in mid-February, Pat had another episode of gastrointestinal bleeding. Again he was given a transfusion, and again I went to the lab with some of his blood to perform a hematocrit, a test that I had performed hundreds of times since leaving medical school. This time, however, the capillary tube containing his blood shattered as I tried to seal it against the clay, lacerating my index finger. I was worried. Pat was so sick, so febrile and jaundiced, and I dreaded contracting hepatitis. And who knew how many other infections Pat might have? AIDS, however, was not even a consideration. The virus had not yet been discovered, there were no tests for AIDS, and the illness had been reported in only two cities. Transmission through blood at the workplace was unknown.

When Pat's condition became stable, I went home and tried unsuccessfully to sleep. I was tremendously relieved to find out the next day that his serologic tests for hepatitis were negative. As the days passed, Pat's condition continued to deteriorate, and he bled repeatedly. For me, life went on as usual.

Suddenly, three weeks after the accident with the shattered capillary tube, I became acutely ill. A strange rash covered my face and trunk; a dry cough and sore throat bothered me continuously. Fever, myalgias, and malaise made it almost impossible to work. The feelings of dread returned.

Were these symptoms an unusual presentation of hepatitis or some other illness contracted at the time of the capillary-tube accident?

Working became more difficult as the days went by. The fever continued; the cough and sore throat failed to improve like those of the usual cold. My chief resident examined me and ordered an initial battery of tests that included a complete blood count, blood chemistry tests, a test for mononucleosis, adenovirus and rubella titers, chest radiography, and blood and throat cultures. All the test results were normal, except the blood counts which revealed marked leukopenia and thrombocytopenia that could have been caused by any ordinary viral infection. I was sent home to rest.

Over the next 10 days I visited the clinic daily for more tests. Slowly, most of the symptoms subsided, but the rash persisted, and over the next several weeks generalized lymphadenopathy developed. The persistent leukopenia and thrombocytopenia earned me a marrow aspiration, and eventually the lymphadenopathy led to the performance of a cervical-node biopsy. The results of both tests were normal.

Since I slowly regained my energy and the negative test results provided the assurance that everything was all right, my physician and I attributed the illness to "some virus." Little did we know how correct we were. And life went on.

Several months after the onset of my mysterious illness, I was back to normal, even playing racquetball three times a week. I worked long hours as a resident, did some clinical research, participated in the work of several hospital committees, and prepared talks. My hospital accepted me as a fellow in cardiology, and I was given the honor of being named assistant chief of service for 1985–1986. I met, fell in love with, and married a young woman who had just graduated from the medical school associated with my hospital. Together we started many professional and personal projects.

Except for the treatment of a varicocele and a visit to a dermatologist for my persistent facial rash, I did not see a physician for the next three years. I did not need one, because I was feeling very well. However, by the middle of my year as assistant chief of service I started feeling a bit tired, and getting up in the morning became more difficult. At first, I attributed these changes to my schedule: I made rounds every night until midnight or later, prepared conferences for residents every week, and participated in clinical research. In addition, there was a beautiful newborn baby at home who did not agree with our sleeping schedule and who had her own firm opinions about playtime.

I had been sure that my fatigue would disappear with the end of that busy academic year, but it did not. I also started to lose weight—more than 10 lb (4.5 kg) by November 1986. At the end of November, I went to see the physician who had taken care of me during my acute illness in 1983; he was now on the faculty of another local teaching hospital.

We realized immediately that my condition was serious, as evidenced by severe pancytopenia and a fairly high sedimentation rate. The fears of a grave process returned. Lupus was a possibility, and I secretly hoped it was the answer. Lupus was something I could live with; it was certainly better than a leukemia or aplastic anemia. But once again all the tests failed to yield a diagnosis. Deeply puzzled, my physician obtained copies of the records of my 1983 illness. In these records he had compulsively recorded every finding, along with a description of the capillary-tube accident.

In the $3\frac{1}{2}$ years that had passed, medical news had been dominated by one horrifying story: AIDS. In that time, as the death toll mounted, it had been firmly established that AIDS was caused by a virus transmissible through blood. The memory of that accident with Pat's blood sent a wave of fear washing over me. And Pat had had over 100 transfusions in the days just before the accident that sent his blood spilling into my own. He had died shortly afterward.

The lack of any answer from my medical evaluation led to testing for the human immunodeficiency virus (HIV). A couple of days later, my physician came to see me at work. The personal visit could only mean bad news. And it did: the HIV test had been run twice, and twice it was positive. The illness that I had had three weeks after the accident with the capillary tube had been an acute HIV infection, a syndrome now well recognized. The mystery was solved, and the nightmare began.

How can I describe what I felt? It was not only the horror of dying from a terrible illness, but also the horrifying possibility that I had infected my wife and therefore our daughter. Telling my wife was as painful as being told myself. We cried together but tried to believe that the test was a false positive. After all, I had no risk factors other than my exposure to the patient's blood. In addition, we were reassured by data from the Centers for Disease Control (CDC) about the likelihood of being infected with HIV in the workplace: virtually impossible, according to the CDC. So we waited two weeks for the result of the Western blot test to come back from the state laboratory—two weeks in which we prayed constantly and did not sleep. There had been times when I, like any other house officer, had been drenched with blood, but the accident with the capillary tube, because of the depth of the cut and the illness that followed, was the main suspect. It would be a cruel irony if one of the patients to whom I had devoted myself at the beginning of my career had unknowingly given me a fatal illness.

On Christmas Eve, 1986, the Western blot result came back positive. With that, the nightmare became reality. What would happen to my job? How long would I live? How would my family manage? Like most physicians in training, I had no disability insurance and no life insurance. I would probably die soon and leave my family with nothing but our debts.

The decision to test my wife was agonizing. One of the few things that could make this unbearable tragedy worse was the spread of the infection to her or our daughter. We developed the necessary strength to have my wife tested in January 1987. The only good news we had had for a long time were the two independent negative results of her blood tests.

Meanwhile, my physician requested and obtained a sample of Pat's serum. (Serum samples from all patients admitted to the oncology center were routinely stored for future research.) Two separate enzyme-linked immunosorbent assays and Western blot tests (done at another teaching hospital in town and at the state laboratory) were positive, confirming that I had been infected in the accident.

We had to decide whom to tell right away and whom not to tell. Such an illness, with its stigma and its repercussions in every aspect of our lives, was certainly not to be made public. It was our tragedy, to be shared only with family members and a few close friends who we knew would feel it with us. However, I desperately needed to obtain employee benefits, so I went to see a hospital official.

What followed was nearly as painful as the illness itself. News of my illness spread rapidly through the hospital community. For many months, hospital officials refused to acknowledge that I had contracted AIDS while caring for an infected patient. In addition, no job assurance was provided, and my contract was not renewed. After six months of bitter dispute, we sued the hospital to defend my reputation and obtain appropriate benefits. After months of legal battling, the hospital offered a settlement three weeks before the trial date.

This horrible experience has taught my wife and me sad lessons about the weaknesses of medicine and of some of the people who manage and practice it. AIDS affects patients in every aspect of their existence—physically, personally, and socially. Even minor matters of daily living become major ordeals. Recently, for example, I broke a tooth. A trifling matter under normal circumstances, obtaining dental care became very complicated. Some dentists did not want to treat me because of the perceived risk, and most dental laboratories refused to handle the material from the dental impression. In this way, many otherwise trivial problems become big issues. More disturbing are the social changes. People you considered your friends suddenly vanish. I remember the friend and fellow physician who came to me for support when his father died but who disappeared after learning of my illness. I remember many of my younger colleagues who seemed to forget that I had counseled them during their personal and professional rough times. I remember some physicians from whom I requested help, who expressed their sympathy but chose to bury their heads in the sand. The disappearance of these people was particularly painful to us because my wife and I had been members of this medical community for many years.

Only a handful of people from the medical community came forward to help us. They had the moral and ethical strength to see beyond their personal interests, and they will forever have a special place in our hearts.

There are also other, new and special friends, some of whom we knew barely or not at all before these events, and whose warmth and support were crucial during the difficult times.

Although the risk of contracting AIDS in the workplace is relatively small as compared with the risk of contracting hepatitis, it is very real, and when it happens it is devastating. All hospitals and medical institutions have a responsibility to make the workplace safe, ensuring that the CDC guidelines are not just posted but followed. However, a safe work environment also means one in which health workers are well protected economically, with appropriate health, disability, and life insurance. In addition, health workers must be assured continued employment for as long as they can work.

Workers' compensation works well to cover medical expenses and income lost because of occupational injuries that result in temporary or minor disabilities such as muscle tears or bone fractures. But these are not the accidents that a physician is likely to suffer at work. The main threats today are catastrophic, and workers' compensation is grossly inadequate for a catastrophic illness. In most states, it entitles workers to only two thirds of their income at the time of the injury, once they have become totally disabled. Thus, for a resident, nurse fellow, or technician earning $23,000 a year, disability income is about $15,300. And the ambiguous status of medical students, who are not employees, complicates the question of their compensation.

For the health worker, proof of causation should not be a stringent precondition of compensation. With AIDS, it is particularly easy for an employer to avoid responsibility by suggesting that the employee had a previous sexual contact that led to the infection. In one sense I was very fortunate; although Pat had died, his serum samples had been stored and could be tested, and my medical records thoroughly described the accident and the illness that followed. In most cases, however, a health worker may not recall the particular incident or patient that led to the infection, or there may not be any of that patient's serum available for testing. Furthermore, fear of facing an insulting challenge to one's character, in addition to the probable loss of one's job, will keep health workers from coming forward.

Just as the illness has changed the way physicians handle body fluids and practice medicine, so it must change the way we pursue our careers. Beyond its reputation, location, and the quality of its training, we must also examine how an institution cares for its workers and what benefits it provides. None of the 40 house officers I met during a recent visit to a medical school in the Northeast knew what their benefits were. At the same school I asked the graduating students, then interviewing for internships, how many had inquired about benefits; no one raised a hand. It is simply mind-boggling that a secretary working on a word processor, without any

major occupational health risk, would have a better knowledge of benefits—not to mention better benefits—than a health worker.

It has been almost three years since my illness was diagnosed; in that
time I have been hospitalized five times and have battled several of the
complications of AIDS. As a patient, I know that physicians can do much
more than just pursue a cure for this horrible illness. Compassion, concern,
and support are crucial for relieving some of the overwhelming pain of the
victims of AIDS, as well as for prolonging life and improving its quality.
What has helped me most during my hospitalizations is the fighting attitude
of my physician; the fact that he has never given up has helped me not to
give up. He has been at my side during the worst of times, during the unrelenting fevers and the unpleasant bronchoscopies. His kindness and compassion have been matched only by those of my wife, this strong and caring
person who has cried with me and fought at my side. Together we allow no
concessions to this illness or the cruelty it brings out in some people. It
gives me great sadness that many patients who have AIDS do not have this
kind of support. It is up to us, members of the most humane profession, to
fight against discrimination, to fight against our own natural fears, and to
see to it that these patients are not abandoned. Health workers must not
deny care to the victims of this complex human nightmare. But if we are to
be in the front lines, then we must make sure that we are better protected
in all respects. I am living proof that it can happen to any of us. And no
other health worker should have to go through what I have endured.

GLOSSARY
OF
PHILOSOPHICAL
AND
RELATED TERMS

Ab initio: Latin phrase meaning "from the beginning."

Act utilitarianism: The theory offered by utilitarians who insist that when contemplating *each act* we should choose to do that which will produce the greatest good or happiness.

Altruism: Actions characterized solely by concern for the welfare of others and in no way based on self-interest or concern for the welfare of the one doing the action. Unselfishly acting for the sake of others. *See* **Benevolence.**

Ambiguity: A situation resulting when the principles for decision are unclear or indistinct. Many observers find that abortion is filled with ambiguity.

Applied ethics: The analysis of ethical problems based on actual cases and events rather than the study of ethical terms and principles.

Autonomy: The term literally means *self-legislated.* For Kant, autonomy was a key notion for morality, since an act can have moral significance only if it is willed freely and without compulsion by a rational being.

Benevolence: Derived from Latin words meaning "good will"; a characteristic of actions freed from self-interest or personal considerations. *See* **Altruism.**

Bioethical principle: A principle for decision or action resulting from ethical considerations rather than considerations of medical acceptability or likelihood of success.

Bioethics: *See* **Medical ethics.**

Categorical imperative: For Kant, the unconditional moral law that can be expressed as the rule that we should act on that principle that we could make a universal law. If we cannot universalize our principle without contradiction, the action resulting from the principle is immoral.

Charity: Derived from the Latin term *caritas,* charity is self-giving love untainted by self-interest; benevolence, goodwill.

Consequentialist ethics: Ethics that assess actions as right or wrong on the basis of the consequences generated by those actions. *See* Teleological ethics.

Constitutive: Something is said to be constitutive if it has the power to enact or establish something. Reason could be said to be constitutive for ethics for those holding the deontological view.

Deontological: Derived from the Greek word for "duty" and referring to any ethical system that makes the morality of any action depend on one's acting out of a sense of duty. Kant's ethical system is deontological.

Egalitarian: Advocating equal political, economic, and legal rights for all citizens. Deontological ethics are egalitarian in that they argue that every human being has inherent dignity and deserves respect.

Egoism: The ethical view that self-interest is the rule of conduct. There are two types of egoism: **psychological egoism,** the claim that as a matter of fact people do act only out of self-interest, and **ethical egoism,** the claim that people ought to act only out of self-interest.

Emotivism: The doctrine that claims that moral judgments do not convey information about the world but rather express the emotions of the speaker and perhaps attempt to evoke similar emotions in the hearers.

En bloc: French phrase that means as a whole, entire, or as a mass.

Epicurean: Refers to followers of Epicurus (341–270 B.C.), who set forth a strategy for achieving truly human happiness by emphasizing the delights of the mind (over which a person has control) rather than the delights derived from material things (which are so often beyond one's personal control).

Epistemology: The theory of knowledge; an inquiry into the origin, validity, and limits of knowledge.

Equity: Related to the principle of fairness. Something that is done on grounds of equity is based on principles of equality and justice, not on grounds of self-interest or consideration of consequences. *See* **Justice.**

Ethical problem: An ethical problem occurs when we are faced with a conflict between ethical principles, both of which are values that we accept (for example, telling the truth and avoiding injury to others). An ethical problem can also arise when we are faced with a decision and do not know which ethical principle to use in making a decision. In some contemporary usage, an ethical problem is distinguished from a **moral problem.**

Ethical relativism: The view that there are no objective moral standards, and that the principles for conduct are relative to individuals or societies. Ethical relativists claim that there are no cross-cultural ethical norms by which to evaluate the conduct of persons in all societies.

Ethics: The philosophical investigation of the principles governing human actions in terms of their goodness, badness, rightness, and wrongness.

Existentialism: Existentialism is a philosophical view that emphasizes the centrality of human freedom and choice. When used in ethical discussions, it frequently refers to the necessity of making a choice even when one is not sure of the grounds for choosing. An **ethical problem** may present us with the need to make an existential decision.

Ex officio: Latin phrase that means "by reason of office." A person may be an ex officio member of a medical review committee by virtue of an administrative office held; for example, the hospital administrator may be an ex officio member of a committee that allocates scarce medical resources.

Hedonism: Derived from the Greek word for pleasure, hedonism is the ethical philosophy that holds the view that pleasure is the goal of life. Most philosophical hedonists have held, however, that intellectual pleasures are superior to sensual pleasures and that long-term considerations should enter into the choice of pleasures. **Utilitarianism** is a contemporary hedonistic view.

Heterogeneity: Diversity, dissimilarity. Sometimes used to refer to human diversity.

Humane: Characteristic of actions that show concern for other human beings.

Humanitarian: Concern for human welfare in general.

Instrumental good: That which is desirable for the sake of an intrinsic good or for the sake of another instrumental good which will in turn lead to the intrinsic good.

Intrinsic: That which characterizes the essential nature of a thing. One holding a deontological view would say that fairness is intrinsic to morality.

Intrinsic good: That which is desirable for its own sake, as distinct from the instrumental good, which is desirable because it leads to the intrinsic good.

Justice: A social ideal concerned with distribution of society's benefits and burdens. In contemporary philosophical writings, such as those by John Rawls, justice is treated as a principle of fairness. Discussions of justice can relate to various spheres of action, hence one can speak of economic justice, distributive justice, criminal justice, even cosmic justice.

Justifiable: In philosophy, something is justifiable if one can give good reasons for the action contemplated. Good reasons are those stemming from the application of rational principles or guidelines and are not based on feelings or emotions.

Legal naturalism: The view that laws enacted by human groups do not create what is good or ethical but reflect what we know on other grounds to be right or good. In the Middle Ages this view was referred to as the natural law view. A legal naturalist would say that an action may not be ethically correct even though it may be legally correct.

Legal positivism: The view that holds that laws themselves define what is good, just, or ethical, as opposed to legal naturalism.

Living will: A document expressing a person's decisions regarding the kind of medical treatment to be given when that person is unable to communicate such decisions. For example, a person in a coma may have expressed in a living will the desire not to receive life-prolonging therapy if the medical judgment is that there is little likelihood of recovery. Living wills are not considered valid legal documents in many states.

Medical ethics: Applied ethics that deals with ethical problems arising in the practice of medicine, medical research, or the use of experimental therapies. Sometimes referred to as bioethics.

Metaethics: A philosophical investigation of the terms and principles used in an ethical system, as opposed to an attempt to deal with an actual ethical problem. An example of metaethical analysis is the attempt to analyze how the term *right* functions in discourse or in an ethical theory. Metaethics is distinct from **applied ethics,** which deals with specific ethical problems.

Morality: In general usage, morality is synonymous with **ethics.** Some contemporary writers use the term to refer to one's personal ethics, hence it is possible to distinguish between a **moral problem** and an **ethical problem.**

Moral problem: In some contemporary usage, a moral problem is said to occur when we face a conflict between an ethical principle and our inclination or desire to do something that violates that principle; for example, wanting to steal money in violation of the principle that says stealing is wrong.

Omniscience: Having knowledge of all things, or perfect knowledge; a characteristic traditionally attributed to God. When applied to a human being, it refers to the erroneous belief that one knows everything.

Optimal: Relating to the best possible outcome.

Prima facie duty: W. D. Ross's term for a duty that a person recognizes at first glance to be a duty; closer scrutiny may confirm or deny it as one's actual duty.

Primum non nocere: Latin phrase meaning "first, do no harm."

Psychological egoism: A theory of human motivation, it claims that humans are so constituted that they always act selfishly.

Randomization: Making a choice based on random or chance selection. It is argued by some that the fairest way of allocating scarce resources is such random choices rather than basing the decision on calculations of utility. Those holding deontological ethical views would tend to favor randomization as the basis for allocating scarce resources since it treats everyone as inherently equal.

Rational guidelines: A feature of those ethical views holding that reason, not feeling or some kind of "moral sense," is the basis for determining the rightness or wrongness of an action. Kant's ethical view is an example of an ethics based on rational guidelines.

Rationale: The reasons given for a decision or action. Actions based on a rationale are thought to be based on rational considerations rather than on feeling or emotion.

Rationalism: The view that appeals to reason, not the senses, as the source of knowledge. In its most extreme form, rationalism insists that all knowledge is derived from reason. A *rationalist epistemology* would argue that reason is the *sole* source of knowledge. In ethics, rationalism is the view that human actions can be judged by rational principles, not by feelings or a moral sense.

Rule utilitarianism: That form of utilitarianism which holds that rather than apply the utility principle to each act, our actions should be guided by general rules which are derived from utilitarian consideration. *See* **Act utilitarianism.**

Slippery slope argument: Frequently a moral claim can be attacked by showing that if one accepts the claim, then one seems to be committed to accepting a series of additional claims which become increasingly offensive to one's moral sensibilities. One seems unable to draw a line and claim with justification that the implications of one's moral claim must stop here and go no further. It is as if one were on a slippery slope, sliding down into an objectionable situation without the capacity to arrest one's slipping.

Straw man: An informal fallacy wherein one substitutes for the opponent's position a simplistic caricature. By defeating the caricature (the straw man) the fallacious impression is created of having defeated the opponent's position.

An example of the straw man fallacy is the following: "Of course the Equal Rights Amendment must be defeated. Do you want men and women sharing the same toilets?"

Subjectivism: In ethics the view that ethical statements are descriptions of the way people feel about certain actions and involves the claim that moral values and principles represent the individual's subjective feelings and reactions which, in the absence of objective moral norms, cannot be assessed as true or false. According to subjectivism, there are no moral standards independent of human feelings. *See* **Ethical relativism.**

Teleological: From the Greek word for end or purpose; refers to that which is purposive. The teleological argument for God's existence is based on the claim that the world exhibits order and purpose, which can best be explained with reference to God.

Teleological ethics: Ethical positions that determine the rightness or wrongness of acts on the basis of their consequences. The term is derived from the Greek word telos, which means "end" or "purpose."

Theoretical: Relates to the study of principles underlying a practice or point of view, as opposed to *practical,* which relates to the application of the principles.

Utilitarianism: The ethical theory associated with the work of Jeremy Bentham, James Mill, and John Stuart Mill in the nineteenth century. Utilitarians hold that actions are moral if they aim at the general good, or the greatest good for the greatest number of people. *See* **Utility principle.**

Utility: The property in any object by which it tends to produce benefit, advantage, pleasure, good, or happiness to the party whose interest is considered.

Utility principle: The principle of utilitarianism that says that we ought to do what will produce the greatest good for the greatest number of people. Sometimes it is referred to as "the greatest happiness principle." *See* **Teleological ethics.**

Virtue: According to Aristotle, virtue is related to function. When a thing is performing its proper function well, virtue is present. The proper and distinctive human function involves reason. Moral virtue is present when the appetites are regulated by a rational regulating principle (the mean between the extremes of excess and deficiency directed toward a worthy goal). Aristotle distinguished between intellectual and moral virtues. Intellectual virtues (excellence in grasping the forms of truth) can be taught; moral virtues are learned through experience and through the development of right habits.

GLOSSARY
OF
MEDICAL TERMS*

Abortion, induced: Expulsion of the products of conception from the uterus of the mother, due to outside intervention.

Abortion, spontaneous: Expulsion of products of conception from the uterus of the mother, not due to outside intervention.

Alzheimer's disease: Dementia, occurring often under the age of 50, due to progressive pathological changes in the brain.

Amici: Amici's disk, "Z-line," cross striation in a muscle fiber.

Amniocentesis: A test done during pregnancy in which a needle is passed into the amniotic sac in the mother's uterus in order to obtain a sample of amniotic fluid which is tested to detect the presence or absence of many defects.

Amniotic fluid: The fluid inside the sac containing the fetus in the uterus.

Aortic aneurysm: An abnormal bulging in the large artery which goes from the heart down through the chest and abdomen.

Aphasic: Impaired or absent ability to communicate, more often referring to inability to speak.

Appendectomy: A surgical procedure by which the appendix is removed. The appendix is attached in the region of the junction of the large and small bowel.

Arteriosclerosis: Hardening of the arteries by sclerosis (fibrous thickening) or calcification.

Caesarian section: A surgical procedure by which a fetus is delivered. The incision is made in the abdomen of the mother.

Cervix: The portion of the uterus extending through the upper wall of the vagina in a female. Sperm must pass through the cervix to enter the uterus and the fetus passes out of the uterus through the cervix in a normal delivery.

*Compiled by David Patriquin, D.O.

Chorionic villi biopsy: A surgical procedure done on the pregnant female in which tissue is taken from the placenta for examination in the laboratory. Used to detect the presence or absence of many defects, this test can be performed much earlier in pregnancy than can amniocentesis.

Chronic liver disease: Any disease of liver tissue that has persisted for a time; often "chronic" is used to indicate a duration greater than six months.

Cirrhosis: Progressive disease in which generalized inflammation is followed by fibrosis and loss of function. Liver cirrhosis results in loss of liver function and death.

Clinicosociologic: Pertaining to application of sociology to a clinical (medical) subject.

Clonal reproduction: Asexual reproduction in which an organism arises from a single individual.

Congenital defects: Defects existing at the time of birth.

Contraception: Preventing pregnancy.

Cystic fibrosis: An inherited metabolic disorder usually appearing in children, characterized by a markedly shortened life span; lung, gastrointestinal and growth disturbances are commonly a part of this disease.

Debilitation: Wekaness such as that following starvation or disease.

Dementia: A general mental deterioration.

DNA: Deoxyribonucleic acid, genetic material.

Down's syndrome: A syndrome of mental retardation with a constellation of physical changes resulting from the presence of three chromosome 21s instead of the usual two; hence the name, Trisomy 21.

ECMO: Extracorporeal-membrane oxygenation; providing oxygen by transfer into the blood in a machine (outside of the body).

Ectopic implantation: Establishment of the fertilized ovum in a part of the mother's pelvis other than inside the uterus.

ELT (exotic lifesaving therapy):   Extreme measures taken to permit the survival of a patient.

Embryo: An organism in the early stages of development.

Epilepsy: A chronic disorder characterized by brain dysfunction often accompanied by alteration of consciousness; a seizure disorder.

Extrauterine life: Life outside the uterus.

Fetus: An unborn product of conception; usually referred to as such from the end of the eighth week of pregnancy.

Gametes: Any germ cell, either sperm or ovum.

Glaucoma: An eye disease characterized by increased pressure within the eye resulting in loss of vision.

Goldman applanometer: A device used to measure intraocular pressure by flattening the cornea of the eyeball.

Gynecology: The study of disease of women, especially of the female reproductive tract.

Hemodialysis, chronic: Continuing treatment by which blood is circulated outside the body through a machine that removes impurities; necessary when the patient's diseased kidneys are not functioning adequately.

Hemophilia: An inherited coagulation disorder of the blood marked by a permanent tendency to hemorrhage.

Huntington's chorea: A hereditary nervous-system disease characterized by irregular, involuntary movements of muscles and body parts.

Hydration, artificial: Provision of fluids to a patient other than by mouth, e.g., through intravenous or intraperitoneal routes.

Hydrocephaly: A condition marked by accumulation of excess fluid in the skull often resulting in pressure damage to the brain.

Hysterectomy: The surgical removal of the uterus.

Influenza: An acute infectious viral disease having severe respiratory and gastrointestinal effects.

In utero: Within the uterus.

In vitro fertilization: Fertilization of the ovum in the laboratory, outside of the body of the mother.

IUD: Intrauterine (contraceptive) device; device placed in uterus to prevent conception.

Karyotyping: A laboratory procedure performed on cells from a patient to identify the chromosomal characteristics of that person.

Mantoux test: An intracutaneous (within the skin) test for tuberculosis.

Maternal thrombocytopenic purpura: A disease inherited from the mother marked by bleeding into and under the skin resulting from abnormally small numbers of platelets in the circulating blood.

Mechanical ventilation: Machine assistance for patient respiration.

"Morning after" pill: A birth control pill that may be taken after sexual intercourse; it will cause the expulsion of any fertilized egg.

Myocardial infarction: A heart attack: acute loss of blood supply to heart muscle causes the muscle to waste; heart function is diminished.

Neonates: Newborn infants.

Nutrition, artificial: Provision of food by routes other than the mouth, e.g., intravenous feeding.

Obstetrician: A physician skilled in the care of pregnant women and childbirth.

Obstetrics: The medical care of pregnant women and childbirth.

Ophthalmology: The medical study of the eye.

Orthopedic surgery: Surgery of the muscles, bones, and joints of the body.

Osteoarthritis: A condition characterized by pain and stiffness of the joints due to wear and tear; chronic degenerative joint disease.

Ovum: The female sex cell (reproductive cell).

Peritoneal oxygenation: Providing oxygen to the patient by absorption from the peritoneal (intra-abdominal) spaces.

Placebo: An inert substance that has a therapeutic effect presumably through suggestion.

Pneumonia: Inflammation of the lungs with many causative agents including bacteria, viruses, and chemical exposure.

Postnatally: The time after birth.

Prognosis: The forecast of the outcome of the disease.

Prostaglandins: Physiologically active substances in tissues having varying effects.

Renal dialysis: A treatment often used for patients with kidney disease. The patient's arterial blood is circulated through an external machine that removes impurities.

Resuscitation, artificial: Restoration of life by externally applied means after apparent death.

Resuscitation, cardiopulmonary: Restoration of heart-lung function using externally applied means.

Retinitis pigmentosa: A hereditary disease of the eye marked by degeneration of the retina and progressive blindness.

Retrolental fibroplasia: A disease of the lens of the eye (the lens becomes fibrous) thought to result from application of high concentrations of oxygen in an incubator during the neonatal period.

Schiotz tonometer: A mechanical device used to measure intraocular pressure.

Schizophrenia: A group of mental disorders including delusions, hallucinations, and withdrawal from the outside world.

Scoliosis: A lateral curve of the spine.

Spina bifida: Incomplete covering of the spinal cord permitting membranes or spinal cord to protrude.

Tay-Sachs disease: An inherited disease characterized by failure to thrive, progressive paralysis, loss of vision, convulsions, and mental degeneration, associated with abnormal storage of lipids (fats) in the brain; death occurs between the ages of 2–5 years.

Toxemia: Illness caused by accumulation of toxins and other noxious substances elaborated by infectious agents or organ dysfunction.

Ultrasonography: Using sound waves (instead of X-rays) in diagnosis. This diagnostic method, when used to study the unborn child, helps to identify the presence of congenital anomalies.

Viability: Of a fetus; the ability to live (survive) outside the womb.

Viable: Capable of life.

Werdnig-Hoffman disease: Infantile muscular atrophy (wasting).

Zygote: The (diploid) cell resulting from the union of the ovum and the sperm.

BIBLIOGRAPHY

This bibliography runs the gamut from traditional philosophical journals through the newer hybrid medical ethics journals to some specialized medical journals. Of medical journals, *The Journal of the American Medical Association, Annals of Internal Medicine,* and *The New England Journal of Medicine* often have articles of clear ethical interest. Of the hybrid journals, *Hastings Center Report* and *The Journal of Medical Ethics* are probably the most useful. Of philosophy journals, *Ethics* and *Philosophy and Public Affairs* almost always have something directly relevant to medical ethics. Having the *Encyclopedia of Bioethics* near at hand is a definite plus.

Abortion

ANDRUSKO, DAVE. *The Triumph of Hope: A Pro-Life Review of 1988 and a Look to the Future.* Washington, D.C.: National Right to Life Committee, 1989.

BOK, SISSELA. "Ethical Problems of Abortion." *Hastings Center Studies* 2: 33–52 (January 1974).

BONDESON, WILLIAM B.; ENGELHARDT, H. TRISTRAM, JR.; SPICKER, STUART F.; and WINSHIP, DANIEL H., eds. *Abortion and the Status of the Fetus.* Norwell, Mass.: D. Reidel Publishing Co., 1983.

BOYD, KENNETH; CALLAGHAN, BRENDAN; and SHOTTER, EDWARD. *Life Before Birth: A Search for Consensus on Abortion and the Treatment of Infertility.* London: SPCK, 1986.

BRODY, BARUCH. *Abortion and the Sanctity of Human Life.* Cambridge, Mass.: MIT Press, 1975.

BROOKES, BARBARA. *Abortion in England, 1900–1967.* New York: Croom Helm, 1988.

BUTLER, J. DOUGLAS, and WALBERT, DAVID F., eds. *Abortion, Medicine, and the Law* (3rd ed.). New York: Facts on File Publication, 1986.

CALLAHAN, DANIEL. *Abortion: Law, Choice and Morality.* New York: Macmillan, 1970.

CALLAHAN, SIDNEY, and CALLAHAN, DANIEL, eds. *Abortion: Understanding Differences.* New York: Plenum, 1984.

CRIGGER, BETTE JANE. "Just What Does *Webster* Mean?" *Hastings Center Report* 20: 2–3 (January/February 1990).

CUDD, ANN E. "Sensationalized Philosophy: A Reply to Marquis's 'Why Abortion Is Immoral.'" *The Journal of Philosophy* 87 (May 1990).

DAVID, HENRY; DYTRYCH, ZDENEK; MATEJCEK, ZDENEK; and SCHULLER, VRATISSLAV. *Born Unwanted: Development Effects of Denied Abortions.* New York: Springer, 1988.

DAVIS, SUSAN E. "Pro-Choice: A New Militancy." *Hastings Center Report* 19: 32–33 (November/December 1989).

DEMARCO, DONALD. *In My Mother's Womb: The Catholic Church's Defense of Natural Life.* Manassas, Va.: Trinity Communications, 1987.

ELLIN, JOSEPH S. "Lying and Deception: The Solution to a Dilemma in Medical Ethics." *Westminster Institute Review* 1: 3–6 (May 1981).

ENGELHARDT, H. TRISTRAM, JR. "The Ontology of Abortion." *Ethics* 84: 217–34 (April 1974).

FAUX, MARIAN. *Roe v. Wade: The Untold Story of the Landmark Supreme Court Decision That Made Abortion Legal.* New York: Macmillan, 1988.

FOWLER, PAUL B. *Abortion: Toward an Evangelical Consensus.* Portland, Ore.: Multnomah Press, 1987.

FRANCOME, COLIN. *Abortion Practice in Britain and the United States.* Boston: Allen and Unwin, 1986.

FRANKOWSKI, STANISLAW J., and COLE, GEORGE F. *Abortion and Protection of the Human Fetus: Legal Problems in a Cross-Cultural Perspective.* Norwell, Mass.: Kluwer Academic Publishers (Nijhoff), 1987.

GARFIELD, JAY L., and HENNESSEY, PATRICIA, eds. *Abortion: Moral and Legal Perspectives.* Amherst: University of Massachusetts Press, 1984.

GLENDON, MARY ANN. *Abortion and Divorce in Western Law.* Cambridge, Mass.: Harvard University Press, 1987.

GOLDSTEIN, ROBERT D. *Mother-Love and Abortion: A Legal Interpretation.* Berkeley: University of California Press, 1988.

HARE, R. M. "Abortion and the Golden Rule." *Philosophy and Public Affairs* 4: 210–22 (Spring 1975).

HORAN, DENNIS; GRANT, EDWARD R.; and CUNNINGHAM, PAIGE, eds. *Abortion and the Constitution: Reversing* Roe v. Wade *Through the Courts.* Washington, D.C.: Georgetown University Press, 1987.

IMBER, JONATHAN B. *Abortion and the Private Practice of Medicine.* New Haven, Conn.: Yale University Press, 1986.

KENYON, EDWIN. *The Dilemma of Abortion.* Winchester, Mass.: Faber and Faber, 1986.

KEOWN, JOHN. *Abortion, Doctors and the Law: Some Aspects of the Legal Regulation of Abortion in England from 1803 to 1982.* New York: Cambridge University Press, 1988.

LOVENDUSKI, JONI, and OUTSHOORN, JOYCE. *The New Politics of Abortion.* Newbury Park, Calif.: Sage Publications, 1986.

McCARTNEY, JAMES J. *Unborn Persons: Pope John Paul II and the Abortion Debate.* New York: Peterlang, 1987.

McINERNEY, PETER K. "Does a Fetus Already Have a Future-Like-Ours?" *The Journal of Philosophy* 87 (May 1990).

MAESTRI, WILLIAM F. "Abortion in America: Public Faith, Public Policy." *Linacre Quarterly* 56: 50–60 (November 1989).

MARQUIS, DON. "Why Abortion Is Immoral." *The Journal of Philosophy* 86 (April 1989).

MASON, JOHN KENYON. *Human Life and Medical Practice.* Edinburgh: Edinburgh University Press, 1988.

MEILANDER, GILBERT. "Abortion: The Right to an Argument." *Hastings Center Report* 19: 13–16 (November/December 1989).

MELTON, GARY B., ed. *Adolescent Abortion: Psychological and Legal Issues.* Lincoln: University of Nebraska Press, 1986.

MESSER, ELLEN, and MAY, KATHRYN E. *Back Rooms: Voices from the Illegal Abortion Era.* New York: St. Martin's Press, 1988.

MILLER, HAL. *The Abandoned Middle: The Ethics and Politics of Abortion in America.* Kapuskasing, Ont.: Penumbra Press, 1988.

NATHANSON, BERNARD. "Operation Rescue: Domestic Terrorism or Legitimate Civil Rights Protest?" *Hastings Center Report* 19: 28–32 (November/December 1989).

NOONAN, JOHN T., Jr. "An Almost Absolute Value in History," in *The Morality of Abortion: Legal and Historical Perspectives,* ed. John T. Noonan. Cambridge, Mass.: Harvard University Press, 1970.

NORCROSS, ALASTAIR. "Killing, Abortion, and Contraception: A Reply to Marquis." *The Journal of Philosophy* 87 (May 1990).

OVERALL, CHRISTINE. *Ethics and Human Reproduction: A Feminist Analysis.* Boston: Allen and Unwin, 1987.

REARDON, DAVID C. *Aborted Women: Silent No More.* Chicago: Loyola University Press, 1987.

RODMAN, HYMAN, and TROST, JAN, eds. *The Adolescent Dilemma: International Perspectives on the Family Planning Rights of Minors.* New York: Praeger, 1986.

RODMAN, HYMAN; SARVIS, BETTY; and BONAR, JOY. *The Abortion Question.* New York: Columbia University Press, 1987.

ROSEN, NORMA. "Between Guilt and Gratification." *The New York Times Magazine* (April 17, 1977), pp. 70–71, 73–77.

RUBIN, EVA R. *Abortion, Politics, and the Courts: Roe v. Wade and Its Aftermath* (rev. ed.). Westport, Conn.: Greenwood Press, 1987.

SACHDEV, PAUL, ed. *International Handbook on Abortion.* Westport, Conn.: Greenwood Press, 1988.

SHANNON, THOMAS A., ed. *Bioethics: Basic Writings on the Key Ethical Questions That Surround the Major, Modern Biological Possibilities and Problems* (3rd ed.). Mahwah, N.J.: Paulist Press, 1987.

SHEERAN, PATRICK J. *Women, Society, the State and Abortion: A Structuralist Analysis.* New York: Praeger, 1987.

SHERLOCK, RICHARD. *Preserving Life: Public Policy and the Life Not Worth Living.* Chicago: Loyola University Press, 1987.

SLOAN, IRVING J. *The Law Governing Abortion, Contraception, and Sterilization.* Dobbs Ferry, N.Y.: Oceana Publications, 1988.

SZUMSKI, BONNIE, ed. *Abortion: Opposing Viewpoints.* San Diego, Calif.: Greenhaven Press, 1986.

THOMSON, JUDITH JARVIS. "A Defense of Abortion." *Philosophy and Public Affairs* 1: 47–66 (Fall 1971).

TOOLEY, MICHAEL. *Abortion and Infanticide.* New York: Oxford University Press, 1983.

U.S. Congress; Senate; Committee on the Judiciary; Subcommittee on the Constitution. *Abortion Funding Restriction Act; Hearings, 2 April and 22 July 1985.* Washington, D.C.: U.S. Government Printing Office, 1986.

WARREN, MARY ANNE. "The Abortion Struggle in America." *Bioethics* 3: 320–32 (October 1989).

WERTHEIMER, ROGER. "Understanding the Abortion Argument." *Philosophy and Public Affairs* 1: 67–95 (Fall 1971).

WINTER, EUGENIA B. *Psychological and Medical Aspects of Induced Abortion: A Selective, Annotated Bibliography, 1970–1986.* Westport, Conn.: Greenwood Press, 1988.

WOLF-DEVINE, CELIA. "Abortion and the 'Feminine Voice.' " *Public Affairs Quarterly* 3: 81–97 (January 20, 1990).

AIDS

ALTMAN, DENNIS. *AIDS in the Mind of America.* New York: Anchor Press/Doubleday, 1986.

ANNAS, GEORGE J. "FDA's Compassion for Desperate Drug Companies." *Hastings Center Report* 20: 35–37 (January/February 1990).

AVINS, ANDREW, and LO, BERNARD. "To Tell or Not to Tell: The Ethical Dilemmas of HIV Test Notification in Epidemiologic Research." *American Journal of Health* 79: 1544–48 (November 1989).

BADER, DIANA, and MCMILLAN, ELIZABETH. *AIDS: Ethical Guidelines for Healthcare Providers.* St. Louis, Mo.: Catholic Health Association of the United States, 1987.

BAYER, RONALD. *Private Acts, Social Consequences: AIDS and the Politics of Public Health.* New York: Free Press, 1989.

BLENDON, ROBERT J., and DONELAN, KAREN. "Discrimination Against People with AIDS: The Public's Perspective." *New England Journal of Medicine* 319: 1022–26 (October 13, 1988).

BRANDT, ALLAN M. "AIDS and Metaphor: Toward the Social Meaning of Epidemic Disease." *Social Research* 55: 413–32 (Autumn 1988).

COOKE, MOLLY, and SANDE, MERLE. "The HIV Epidemic and Training in Internal Medicine." *New England Journal of Medicine* 321: 1334–38 (November 9, 1989).

CURRAN, WILLIAM; GOSTIN, LARRY; and CLARK, MARY E. *Acquired Immunodeficiency Syndrome: Legal and Regulatory Policy.* Springfield, Va.: U.S. National Technical Information Service, 1986.

FALCO, MATHEA, and CIKINS, WARREN. *Toward a National Policy on Drug and AIDS Testing.* Washington: Brookings Institution, 1989.

GERBERT, BARBARA; MAGUIRE, BRYAN T.; HULLEY, STEPHEN B.; and COATES, THOMAS J. "Physicians and Acquired Immunodeficiency Syndrome: What Patients Think About Human Immunodeficiency Virus in Medical Practice." *Journal of the American Medical Association* 262: 1969–72 (October 13, 1989).

HUMBER, JAMES, and ALMEDER, ROBERT F. *Biomedical Ethics Reviews, 1988: AIDS and Ethics*. Clifton, N.J.: Humana Press, 1989.

HUMMEL, ROBERT F.; LEAVY, WILLIAM F.; RAMPOLLA, MICHAEL; and CHORST, SHERRY, eds. *AIDS: Impact on Public Policy—An International Forum: Policy, Politics, and AIDS*. New York: Plenum Press, 1986.

JONSEN, ALBERT R. "The Duty to Treat Patients with AIDS." *State of the Art Reviews: Occupational Medicine* 4: Special Issues 31–34 (1989).

JUENGST, ERIC T., and KOENIG, BARBARA A. *The Meaning of AIDS: Implications for Medical Science, Clinical Practice, and Public Health Policy*. New York: Praeger, 1989.

KERMANI, EBRAHIM J., and WEISS, BONNIE A. "AIDS and Confidentiality: Legal Concept and Its Application in Psychotherapy." *American Journal of Psychotherapy* 43: 25–31(January 1989).

KIRBY, MICHAEL. "AIDS and Law." *Daedalus* 118: 101–21 (Summer 1989).

LAUFMAN, JANET K. "AIDS, Ethics, and the Truth." *American Journal of Nursing* 89: 929–30 (July 1989).

MCKUSICK, LEON, ed. *What to Do About AIDS: Physicians and Mental Health Professionals Discuss the Issues*. Berkeley: University of California Press, 1986.

MECHANIC, DAVID, and AIKEN, LINDA H. "Lessons from the Past: Responding to the AIDS Crisis." *Health Affairs* 8: 16–32 (Fall 1989).

NELKIN, DOROTHY, and GILMAN, SANDER L. "Placing Blame for Devastating Disease." *Social Research* 55: 361–78 (Autumn 1988).

NOVICK, ALVIN. "Civil Disobedience in the Time of AIDS." *Hastings Center Report* 19: 35–37 (November/December 1989).

———. "Clinical Trials with Vulnerable or Disrespected Subjects." *AIDS and Public Policy Journal* 4: 125–30 (1989).

PANEM, SANDRA. *The AIDS Bureaucracy*. Cambridge, Mass.: Harvard University Press, 1988.

PARMET, WENDY E. "Legal Rights and Communicable Disease: AIDS, the Police Power and Individual Liberty." *Journal of Health Politics, Policy and Law* 14: 741–71 (Winter 1989).

PETERSON, LYNN M. "AIDS: The Ethical Dilemma for Surgeons." *Law, Medicine and Health Care* 17: 139–44 (Summer 1989).

PIERCE, CHRISTINE, and VANDEVEER, DONALD. *AIDS: Ethics and Public Policy*. Belmont, Calif.: Wadsworth, 1988.

PRICE, MONROE E. *Shattered Mirrors: Our Search for Identity and Community in the AIDS Era*. Cambridge, Mass.: Harvard University Press, 1989.

QUINTON, ANTHONY. "Plagues and Morality." *Social Research* 55: 477–89 (Autumn 1988).

RICHARDS, DAVID A. J. "Human Rights, Public Health, and the Idea of Moral Plague." *Social Research* 55: 491–528 (Autumn 1988).

RICHMAN, DOUGLAS D. "Public Access to Experimental Drug Therapy: AIDS Raises Yet Another Conflict Between Freedom of the Individual and Welfare of the Individual and the Public." *Journal of Infectious Diseases* 159: 412–15 (March 1989).

RIGA, PETER J. "The Health Care Professional and the Care of the Dying: The Crisis of AIDS." *Linacre Quarterly* 56: 53–62 (February 1989).

SAPOLSKY, HARVEY M. "AIDS, Bloodbanking, and the Bonds of Community." *Daedalus* 118: 145–63 (Summer 1989).

SHILTS, RANDY. *And the Band Played On: Politics, People and the AIDS Epidemic.* New York: St. Martin's Press, 1987.

SIEGHART, PAUL. *AIDS and Human Rights: A UK Perspective.* London: British Medical Association Foundation, 1989.

SONTAG, SUSAN. *AIDS and Its Metaphors.* New York: Farrar, Straus & Giroux, 1989.

SPIERS, HERBERT R. "AIDS and Civil Disobedience." *Hastings Center Report* 19: 34–35 (November/December 1989).

TAUER, CAROL A. "AIDS: Human Rights and Public Health." *Medical Anthropology* 10: 177–92 (March 1989).

WACHTER, ROBERT M.; LUCE, JOHN M.; HEARST, NORMAN; and LO, BERNARD. "Decisions About Resuscitation: Inequities Among Patients with Different Diseases but Similar Prognosis." *Annals of Internal Medicine* 111: 525–32 (September 15, 1989).

WITT, MICHAEL D. *AIDS and Patient Management: Legal, Ethical and Social Issues.* Owings Mills, Md.: National Health Publishing, 1986.

Allocation

AARON, HENRY, and SCHWARTZ, WILLIAM B. "Rationing Health Care: The Choice Before Us." *Science* 247: 418–22 (January 26, 1990).

AGICH, GEORGE J., and GEBLEY, CHARLES E., eds. *The Price of Health.* Norwell, Mass.: D. Reidel Publishing Co., 1986.

ARRAS, JOHN D. "Retreat from the Right to Health Care: The President's Commission and Access to Health Care." *Cardozo Law Review* 6: 321–45 (Winter 1984).

BASSON, MARC D. "Choosing Among Candidates for Scarce Medical Resources." *Journal of Medicine and Philosophy* 4: 313–33 (September 1979).

BAYER, RONALD, and CAPLAN, ARTHUR, eds. *In Search of Equity: Health Needs and the Health Care System.* New York: Plenum, 1982.

BELL, J. M., and MENDUS, SUSAN. *Philosophy and Medical Welfare.* New York: Cambridge University Press, 1988.

BERKOWITZ, EDWARD D. "Allocating Resources for Rehabilitation: A Historical and Ethical Framework." *Social Science Quarterly* 70: 40–52 (March 1989).

CAHN, EDMOND. "The First of Life," in *The Moral Decision.* Bloomington: Indiana University Press, 1966.

CALLAHAN, DANIEL. "Modernizing Mortality: Medical Progress and the Good Society." *Hastings Center Report* 20: 28–32 (January/February 1990).

CAPLAN, ARTHUR L. "Kidneys, Ethics and Politics: Lessons of the ESRD Program." *Journal of Health Politics, Policy and Law* 6: 488–503 (Fall 1981).

CHURCHILL, LARRY. *Rationing Health Care in America: Perceptions and Principles of Justice.* Notre Dame, Ind.: University of Notre Dame Press, 1987.

DANIELS, NORMAN. "The Biomedical Model and Just Health Care: Reply to Jecker." *Journal of Medicine and Philosophy* 14: 677–80 (December 1989).

———. *Just Health Care.* Cambridge: Cambridge University Press, 1985.

DANIELS, NORMAN, and MORREIM, E. HAAVI. "Cost Containment and Strains of Commitment." *Hastings Center Report* 19: 47–48 (September/October 1989).

ENGELHARDT, H. TRISTRAM, JR. "Shattuck Lecture: Allocating Scarce Medical Resources and the Availability of Organ Transplantation: Some Moral Presuppositions." *New England Journal of Medicine* 331 (July 5, 1984).

FRIED, CHARLES. "Rights and Health Care—Beyond Equity and Efficiency." *New England Journal of Medicine* 293: 241–45 (July 31, 1975).

FRIEDMAN, EMILY. "Just Deserts: Ethics, Costs, and Rationing," in *Decision Making in Long-Term Care: Factors in Planning,* eds. Ruth Dunkle and May L. Wykle. New York: Springer, 1988.

GUTMANN, AMY. "Equality and Rights in Medical Care." *Hastings Center Report* 6 (1976).

HAAS, JANET; CAPLAN, ARTHUR; and CALLAHAN, DANIEL. *Case Studies in Ethics and Medical Rehabilitation.* Briarcliff Manor, N.Y.: The Hastings Center, 1988.

HARRIS, JOHN. "The Survival Lottery." *Philosophy* 50: 81–87 (1975).

HIATT, HOWARD H. *America's Health in the Balance: Choice or Chance?* New York: Harper & Row, 1987.

IGLEHART, JOHN K. "The United States Looks at Canadian Health Care." *New England Journal of Medicine* 321: 1767–72 (December 21, 1989).

JAKE, DRY GULCH. "The Danes and Their Health Service." *Arizona Medicine* 30: 37–39 (1973).

JENNET, BRYAN. "Quality of Care and Cost Containment in the U.S. and U.K." *Theoretical Medicine* 10: 207–15 (September 1989).

KAPLAN, MORTON A. "Discussion: What Is a Life Worth?" *Ethics* 89: 58–65 (1978–1979).

KAPP, MARSHALL B. "Rationing Health Care: Will It Be Necessary? Can It Be Done Without Age or Disability Discrimination?" *Issues in Law and Medicine* 5: 337–51 (Winter 1989).

MOONEY, GAVIN. "QALYs: Are They Enough? A Health Economist's Perspective." *Journal of Medical Ethics* 15: 148–52 (September 1989).

MORREIM, HAAVI E. "Cost Containment: Issues of Moral Conflict and Justice for Physicians." *Theoretical Medicine* 6 (1985).

ORANDI, A. "Swedish Health Care? We Do Better in My Hometown." *Medical Economics* (April 18, 1977).

OUTKA, GENE. "Social Justice and Equal Access to Health Care." *Journal of Religious Ethics* 2: 11–32 (1974).

PENSLAR, ROBIN LEVIN, and LAMM, RICHARD D. "Who Pays for AZT?" *Hastings Center Report* 19: 30–32 (September/October 1989).

RAWLES, JOHN. "Castigating QALYs." *Journal of Medical Ethics* 15: 143–47 (September 1989).

SADE, ROBERT M. "Medical Care as a Right: A Refutation." *New England Journal of Medicine* 285: 1288–92 (December 2, 1971).

SCHWARTZMAN, KEVIN. "*In Vino Veritas?* Alcoholics and Liver Transplantation." *Canadian Medical Association Journal* 141: 1262–65 (December 15, 1989).

SHENKIN, B. "Change in Swedish Health Care." *New England Journal of Medicine* 302 (February 28, 1980).

STROSBERG, MARTIN; FELIN, I ALAN; and CARROLL, JAMES D. "Rationing of Medical Care for the Critically Ill." Washington, D.C.: Brookings Institution, 1989.

QUINN, WARREN S. "Actions, Intentions and Consequences: The Doctrine of Double Effect." *Philosophy and Public Affairs* 18: 334–51 (Fall 1989).

VEATCH, ROBERT M., and BRANSON, ROY. *Ethics and Health Policy.* Cambridge, Mass.: Ballinger, 1976.

Alternative Concepts of Medicine (Homeopathy, Ayurvedic)

DESAI, PRAKASH N. "Medical Ethics in India." *Journal of Medicine and Philosophy* 13: 231–55 (August 1988).
NUMBERS, RONALD, and AMUNDSEN, DARREL W. *Caring and Curing: Health and Medicine in the Western Religious Traditions.* New York: Macmillan, 1986.
PEEL, ROBERT. *Health and Medicine in the Christian Science Tradition: Principle, Practice, and Challenge.* New York: Crossroad, 1988.
SCHWARTZ, BARUCH. "Judicial Deflection of Scientific Questions: Pushing the Laetrile Controversy Toward Medical Closure," in *Scientific Controversies: Case Studies in the Resolution and Closure of Disputes in Science and Technology,* eds. H. Tristram Englehardt and Arthur L. Caplan. New York: Cambridge University Press, 1987.

Comparative Bioethics

BRAHAMS, DIANA. "Right to Know in Japan." *Lancet* 2: 173 (July 15, 1989).
CAPRON, ALEXANDER MORGAN. "Harmonies and Conflicts in Law and Biomedical Ethics," in *Biomedical Ethics: An Anglo-American Dialogue,* eds. Daniel Callahan and G. R. Dunstan. New York: New York Academy of Sciences, 1988.
HU, HU-HUAN, and FANG, NENG-YU. "Report from China [on the] Social and Ethical Influence of Some Pain: The Causes of Lower Incidences of Some Pain Syndromes in Chinese People." *Bioethics* 3: 236–44 (July 1989).
"International Perspectives on Biomedical Ethics." *Hastings Center Report* 18 (August/ September 1988), Suppl.
LABRUSSE-RIOU, CATHERINE. "Should There Be Governmental Guidelines in Bioethics? The French Approach." *Boston College International and Comparative Law Review* 12: 89–101 (Winter 1989).
LUTHER, ERNST. "Medical Ethics in the German Democratic Republic." *Journal of Medicine and Philosophy* 14: 289–99 (June 1989).
SHAW, JOSEPHINE. "Informed Consent: A German Lesson." *International and Comparative Law Quarterly* 35: 864–90 (October 1986).
VEATCH, ROBERT, ed. *Cross Cultural Perspectives in Medical Ethics.* Boston: Jones and Bartlett, 1989.
WOLF, SUSAN M., and STRATCHAN, DONNELLE. "Doing Ethics in Italy." *Hastings Center Report* 18: 207–15 (August/September 1988).

Competence

APPLEBAUM, PAUL S., and GRISSO, THOMAS. "Assessing Patients' Capacities to Consent to Treatment." *New England Journal of Medicine* 319: 1635–38 (December 22, 1988).

BRAHAMS, DIANA. "Incompetent Adults and Consent to Treatment." *Lancet* 1: 340 (February 11, 1989).

BUCHANAN, ALLEN. "Advance Directives and the Personal Identity Problem." *Philosophy and Public Affairs* 17: 277–302 (Fall 1988).

CHELL, BYRON. "Competency: What It Is, What It Isn't and Why It Matters," in *Medical Ethics: A Guide for Health Professionals*, eds. John F. Monagle and David C. Thomasma. Rockville, Md.: Aspen Publishers, 1988.

DRESSER, REBECCA, and ROBERTSON, JOHN A. "Quality of Life and Non-Treatment Decisions for Incompetent Patients: A Critique of the Orthodox Approach." *Law, Medicine, and Health Care* 17: 234–44 (Fall 1989).

DUNKIE, RUTH E., and WYKLE, MAY L., eds. *Decision Making in Long-Term Care: Factors in Planning*. New York: Springer, 1988.

EMANUEL, EZEKIEL J. "A Communal Vision of Care for Incompetent Patients." *Hastings Center Report* 17: 15–20 (October/November 1987).

Group for the Advancement of Psychiatry, Committee on Child Psychiatry. *How Old Is Enough? The Ages of Rights and Responsibilities*. Report no. 126. New York: Brunner/Mazel, 1989.

LOWY, CATHERINE. "The Doctrine of Substituted Judgment in Medical Decision Making." *Bioethics* 2: 15–21 (January 1988).

RHODEN, NANCY. "How Should We View the Incompetent?" *Law, Medicine and Health Care* 17: 264–68 (Fall 1989).

SPICKER, STUART F.; INGMAN, STANLEY R.; and LAWSON, IAN R., eds. *Ethical Dimensions of Geriatric Care: Value Conflicts for the 21st Century*. Norwell, Mass.: D. Reidel Publishing Co., 1987.

STRUDLER, ALAN. "Self-Determination, Incompetence, and Medical Jurisprudence." *Journal of Medicine and Philosophy* 13: 349–65 (November 1988).

WINSLADE, WILLIAM J. "Taken to the Limits: Pain, Identity, and Self-Transformation," in *Dax's Case: Essays in Medical Ethics and Human Meaning*, ed. Lonnie Kliever. Dallas: Southern Methodist University Press, 1989.

Confidentiality

Aberdeen Medical Group. "Drunken Drivers: What Should Doctors Do?" *Journal of Medical Ethics* 12: 151–55 (September 1986).

CURRAN, WILLIAM. "Protecting Confidentiality in Epidemiologic Investigations by the Centers for Disease Control." *New England Journal of Medicine* 314: 1027–28 (April 17, 1986).

FOX, DANIEL M. "From TB to AIDS: Value Conflicts in Reporting Disease." *Hastings Center Report* 16: 11–16 (December 1986).

KOTTOW, MICHAEL H. "Medical Confidentiality: An Intransigent and Absolute Obligation." *Journal of Medical Ethics* 12: 117–22 (September 1986).

MORRISSEY, JAMES; HOFMANN, ADELE D.; and THORPE, JEFFREY C. *Consent and Confidentiality in the Health Care of Children and Adolescents: A Legal Guide*. New York: Free Press, 1986.

SHELDON, MARK. "Truth Telling in Medicine." *Journal of the American Medical Association* 247: 651–54 (February 5, 1982).

STONE, ALAN A. "The *Tarasoff* Decisions: Suing Psychotherapists to Safeguard Society." *Harvard Law Review* 90: 358–78 (1976).

WINSTON, MORTON E., and LANDESMAN, SHELDON H. "AIDS and Duty to Protect." *Hastings Center Report* 17: 22–23 (February 1987).

Diagnostic Related Groups

BERENSON, ROBERT A. "A Physician's Reflections." *Hastings Center Report* 19: 12–15 (January/February 1989).

BROWN, E. RICHARD. "DRGs and the Rationing of Hospital Care," in *Health Care Ethics: A Guide for Decision Makers,* eds. Gary R. Anderson and Valerie A. Glenes-Anderson. Rockville, Md.: Aspen Publishers, 1987.

FLECK, LEONARD. "DRGs: Justice and the Invisible Rationing of Health Care Resources." *Journal of Medicine and Philosophy* 12: 165–96 (May 1987).

GLOVER, JACQUELINE J. "DRGs, Hospital Costs and the Right to Adequate Health Care: Case Study," in *Philosophical Issues in Human Rights: Theories and Applications,* eds. Patricia Werhane; A. R. Gini; and David T. Ozar. New York: Random House, 1986.

HARPER, THOMAS. "DRGs and the Idea of a Just Price." *Journal of Medicine and Philosophy* 12: 155–64 (May 1987).

HORN, SUSAN, and BACKOFEN, JOANNE E. "Ethical Issues in the Use of a Prospective Payment System: The Issue of a Severity of Illness Adjustment." *Journal of Medicine and Philosophy* 12: 145–53 (May 1987).

POWDERLY, KATHLEEN E., and SMITH, ELAINE. "The Impact of DRGs on Health Care Workers and Their Clients." *Hastings Center Report* 19: 16–18 (January/February 1989).

VEATCH, ROBERT. "DRGs and the Ethical Reallocation of Resources." *Hastings Center Report* 163: 32–40 (June 1986).

Euthanasia

Ad Hoc Committee of the Harvard Medical School to Examine the Definition of Brain Death. "A Definition of Irreversible Coma." *Journal of the American Medical Association* 205: 337–40 (August 5, 1968).

ANGELL, MARCIA. "Handicapped Children: Baby Doe and Uncle Sam." *New England Journal of Medicine* 309: 659–61 (September 15, 1983).

BERNAT, JAMES L.; CULVER, CHARLES M.; and GERT, BERNARD. "Defining Death in Theory and Practice." *Hastings Center Report* 12: 5–9 (February 1982).

BLACK, P. "Brain Death I & II." *New England Journal of Medicine* 299: 338, 393 (August 17, 24, 1978).

CURRAN, WILLIAM J. "The Saikewicz Decision." *New England Journal of Medicine* 298: 499–500 (March 2, 1978).

FEINBURG, JOEL. "Voluntary Euthanasia and the Inalienable Right to Life." *Philosophy and Public Affairs* 7: 93–123 (Winter 1978).

GERVAIS, KAREN GRANDSTAND. *Redefining Death.* New Haven: Yale University Press, 1986.

GREEN, MICHAEL, and WIKLER, DANIEL. "Brain Death and Personal Identity." *Philosophy and Public Affairs* 9: 105–33 (Winter 1980).

GRISEZ, GERMAIN, and BOYLE, JOSEPH M., JR. *Life and Death with Liberty and Justice: A Contribution to the Euthanasia Debate.* Notre Dame, Ind.: University of Notre Dame Press, 1970.

HACKER, CHRIS; MOSEBY, R.; and VAWTER, D. *Advanced Directives in Medicine.* New York: Praeger, 1989.

IMBUS, S., et al. "Autonomy for Burned Patients. . . ." *New England Journal of Medicine* 299: 308 (August 11, 1977).

In the Matter of Claire C. Conroy. Supreme Court of New Jersey. 98 N.J. 321, 486 A.2d 1209, Decided Jan. 17, 1985.

In the Matter of Karen Quinlan, an Alleged Incompetent. Supreme Court of New Jersey. 70 N.J. 10 355 A.2d 647.

KUHSE, HELGE. *The Sanctity of Life Doctrine in Medicine: A Critique.* Oxford: Darendo Press, 1987.

LAMB, DAVID. *Death, Brain Death and Ethics.* Albany: SUNY Press, 1985.

LO, B., et al. "Clinical Decision to Limit Treatment." *Annals of Internal Medicine* 93: 764 (November 1980).

LUXTON, R. "The Modern Hospice. . . ." *British Medical Journal* 8 (September 1979).

REED, E. A. "The Case of Brother Fox: Withdrawal of Life Support from the Incompetent Terminally Ill." *Legal Aspects of Medical Practice* 9: 1–2, 8 (May 1981).

SAUNDERS, CICELY, and BAINES, MARY. *Living with Dying: The Management of Terminal Disease.* New York: Oxford University Press, 1983.

STRAIN, JAMES E. "The American Academy of Pediatrics Comments on the 'Baby Doe II' Regulations." *New England Journal of Medicine* 309: 443–44 (August 18, 1983).

Superintendent of Belchertown State School v. Saikewicz. 373 Mass. 728, 370 N.E.2d 417 (1977).

General

ABRAMS, NATALIE, and BUCKNER, MICHAEL. *Medical Ethics.* Cambridge, Mass.: MIT Press, 1982.

BOK, SISSELA. *Lying.* New York: Pantheon Books, 1978.

BRANDT, RICHARD B. *Ethical Theory.* New York: Random House, 1958.

BURNS, CHESTER R. "Fictional Doctors and the Evolution of Medical Ethics in the United States, 1875–1900," in *Literature and Bioethics,* eds. Heyward Brock and Richard M. Ratzan. Baltimore, Md.: Johns Hopkins University Press, 1988.

CHRISTIE, RONALD. *Issues in Family Medicine.* New York: Oxford University Press, 1986.

COLEN, B. D. *Hard Choices.* New York: Putnam's, 1986.

DUNCAN, A. S.; DUNSTAN, G. R.; and WELBOURN, R. B. *Dictionary of Medical Ethics.* New York: Crossroad, 1981.

ENGELHARDT, H. TRISTRAM, JR. *The Foundations of Bioethics.* New York: Oxford University Press, 1986.

FLETCHER, JOSEPH. *Humanhood: Essays in Biomedical Ethics.* Buffalo: Prometheus Books, 1979.

FRANKENA, WILLIAM K. *Ethics* (2nd ed.). Englewood Cliffs, N.J.: Prentice Hall, 1973.

GABER, GLEEN. *Ethical Analysis of Clinical Medicine*. Baltimore: Durban and Schwatzewchy, 1985.

GERT, BERNARD. *Morality: A New Justification of the Moral Rules*. New York: Oxford University Press, 1988.

GEWIRTH, ALAN. *Reason and Morality*. Chicago: University of Chicago Press, 1978.

GOROVITZ, SAMUEL. *Doctor's Dilemmas: Moral Conflict and Medical Care*. New York: Macmillan, 1982.

HARMAN, GILBERT. *The Nature of Morality*. New York: Oxford University Press, 1977.

HARRN, FRANK. *Health and Human Values*. New Haven: Yale University Press, 1983.

JONSON, A., and SIEGEL, M. *Clinical Ethics*. New York: Macmillan, 1982.

KASS, LEON. *Toward a More Natural Science*. New York: Free Press, 1985.

KRUSCHWITZ, ROBERT B., and ROBERTS, ROBERT C. *The Virtues: Contemporary Essays on Moral Character*. Belmont, Calif.: Wadsworth, 1987.

LINDENTHAL, JACOB JAY, and THOMAS, CLAUDEWELL S. "Some Roots, Dilemmas, and Research into Confidentiality," in *Ethical Issues in Epidemiologic Research*, ed. Laurence R. Tancredi. New Brunswick, N.J.: Rutgers University Press, 1986.

MACINTYRE, ALASDAIR. *After Virtue* (2nd ed.). Notre Dame, Ind.: University of Notre Dame Press, 1984.

MACKLIN, RUTH. *Moral Choices: Bioethics in Today's World*. New York: Pantheon Books, 1987.

MAY, WILLIAM. *Human Existence, Medicine and Ethics*. Chicago: Frauescan Herald Press, 1977.

PELLEGRINO, E. *A Philosophical Basis of Medical Practice*. New York: Oxford University Press, 1981.

PELLEGRINO, E. and THOMASMA, D. *For the Patient's Good: The Restoration of Beneficence in Health Care*. New York: Oxford University Press, 1988.

PURTILLO, RUTH, and CASSELL, CHRISTINE. *Ethical Dimensions in the Health Professions*. Philadelphia: Saunders, 1981.

RAMSEY, PAUL. *Ethics at the Edges of Life*. New Haven, Conn.: Yale University Press, 1978.

REICH, WARREN T., ed.-in-chief. *Encyclopedia of Bioethics*. New York: Macmillan, 1978.

ROBISON, WADE, and PRITCHARD, MICHAEL S., eds. *Medical Responsibility*. Clifton, N.J.: Humana Press, 1979.

SMITH, HARMON L., and CHURCHILL, LARRY R. *Professional Ethics and Primary Care Medicine: Beyond Dilemmas and Decorum*. Durham, N.C.: Duke University Press, 1986.

VANDEVEER, DONALD. *Paternalistic Intervention: The Moral Bounds of Benevolence*. Princeton, N.J.: Princeton University Press, 1986.

VEATCH, ROBERT M. *Case Studies in Medical Ethics*. Cambridge, Mass.: Harvard University Press, 1977.

———. *Death, Dying, and the Biological Revolution: Our Last Quest for Responsibility* (rev. ed.). New Haven, Conn.: Yale University Press, 1989.

———. *A Theory of Medical Ethics*. New York: Basic Books, 1981.

WALTERS, LEROY, and KAHN, TAMAR JOY, eds. *Bibliography of Bioethics*. Washington, D.C.: Kennedy Institute of Ethics, Georgetown University, 1984.

WILLIAMS, BERNARD. *Morality: An Introduction to Ethics*. New York: Harper & Row, 1972.

WINSLADE, W. *Choosing Life or Death: A Guide for Patients, Families, and Professionals.* New York: Free Press, 1986.

YOUNGER, STUART. *Human Values in Cultural Care Medicine.* New York: Praeger, 1986.

Genetics

ALLEN, GARLAND E. "Genetics, Eugenists and Class Struggle." *Genetics* 79 (January/April 1975), Suppl.

ANDERSON, W. FRENCH, and FLETCHER, JOHN C. "Gene Therapy in Human Beings: When Is It Ethical to Begin?" *New England Journal of Medicine* 303: 1293–97 (November 27, 1980).

CAPRON, ALEXANDER M. "The New Reproductive Possibilities: Seeking a Moral Basis for Concerted Action in a Pluralistic Society." *Law, Medicine and Health Care* 192:12 (1984).

DONNAI, P., et al. "Attitudes of Patients After 'Genetic' Termination of Pregnancy." *British Medical Journal* 282: 621–22 (February 21, 1981).

ELIAS, SHERMAN, and ANNAS, GEORGE. *Reproductive Genetics and the Law.* Chicago: Year Book Medical Publishers, 1987.

FLETCHER, JOSEPH. *The Ethics of Genetic Control.* New York: Doubleday, 1974.

GLOVER, JONATHAN. *What Sort of People Should There Be?* New York: Doubleday, 1974.

GROBSTEIN, CLIFFORD. *A Double Image of the Double Helix: The Recombinant-DNA Debate.* San Francisco: W. H. Freeman, 1979.

HAGARD, SPENCER, and CARTER, FELICITY A. "Preventing the Birth of Infants with Down's Syndrome: A Cost Benefit Analysis." *British Medical Journal* 1: 753–56 (March 27, 1976).

HILTON, BRUCE, and CALLAHAN, DANIEL, eds. *Ethical Issues in Human Genetics: Genetic Counseling and the Use of Genetic Knowledge.* New York: Plenum, 1976.

HOLMES, HELEN B.; HOSKINS, BETTY B.; and GROSS, MICHAEL. *The Custom Made Child? Women Centered Perspectives.* Clifton, N.J.: Humana Press, 1981.

"In Vitro Fertilization: Four Commentaries." *Hastings Center Report* 8: 7–14 (October 1978).

JONES, HARDY. "Genetic Endowment and Obligations to Future Generations." *Social Theory and Practice* 4: 29–46 (Fall 1976).

JONES, MARSHALL B. "Years of Life Lost Due to Cystic Fibrosis." *Journal of Chronic Disorders* 33: 697–701 (1980).

JUENGST, ERIC T. "Patterns of Reasoning in Medical Genetics: An Introduction." *Theoretical Medicine* 10: 101–5 (June 1989).

KOLATA, GINA BARI. "Prenatal Diagnosis of Neural Tube Defects." *Science* 209: 1216–18 (September 12, 1980).

LAPPE, MARC. *Genetic Politics.* New York: Doubleday, 1979.

———. "The Limits of Genetic Inquiry." *Hastings Center Report* 17: 5–10 (August 1987).

LEWIS, RICKI. "Genetic-Marker Testing: Are We Ready for It?" *Issues in Science and Technology* 4: 76–82 (Fall 1987).

MAZUMDAR, PAULINE. "The Eugenists and the Residuum: The Problem of the Urban Poor." *Bulletin of the History of Medicine* 54 (Summer 1980).

MILUNSKY, AUBREY, and ANNAS, GEORGE, eds. *Genetics and the Law.* Vols. I (1976), II (1980), III (1985). New York: Plenum Press.

MULLER-HILL, BENNO. *Murderous Science: Elimination by Scientific Selection of Jews, Gypsies, and Others, Germany 1933–1945.* New York: Oxford University Press, 1988.

President's Commission for the Study of Ethical Problems in Medicine and Biomedical and Behavioral Research. *Screening and Counseling for Genetic Conditions: The Ethical, Social, and Legal Implications of Genetic Screening, Counseling, and Educational Programs.* Washington, D.C.: President's Commission, 1983.

President's Commission for the Study of Ethical Problems in Medicine and Biomedical and Behavioral Research. *Splicing Life: A Report on the Social and Ethical Issues of Genetic Engineering with Human Beings.* Washington, D.C.: President's Commission, 1982.

RAMSEY, PAUL. *Fabricated Man: The Ethics of Genetic Control.* New Haven, Conn.: Yale University Press, 1970.

———. "Shall We 'Reproduce'?" *Journal of the American Medical Association* 220: 1346–50 (June 5, 1972).

"Risk Taking and a Minor Birth Defect." *Hastings Center Report* 11: 25 (April 1981).

ROTHMAN, BARBARA KATZ. *The Tentative Pregnancy: Prenatal Diagnosis and the Future of Motherhood.* New York: Penguin, 1987.

SINGER, PETER, and WELLS, DEANA. *Making Babies: The New Science and Ethics of Conception.* New York: Scribner, 1985.

SINSHEIMER, ROBERT. "An Evolutionary Perspective for Genetic Engineering." *New Scientist* 73: 150–52 (January 20, 1977).

SORENSON, JAMES R.; SWAZEY, JUDITH; and SCOTCH, NORMAN A. *Reproductive Pasts, Reproductive Futures: Genetic Counseling and Its Effectiveness.* New York: Alan R. Liss, 1982.

SUZUKI, DAVID, and KNUDTSON, PETER. *Genetics: The Clash Between the New Genetics and Human Values.* Cambridge, Mass.: Harvard University Press, 1989.

Symposium on "Surrogate Motherhood." *Law, Medicine and Health Care* 16: 1–137 (Spring/Summer 1988).

THOMAS, S. "Ethics of a Predictive Test for Huntington's Chorea." *British Medical Journal* 284: 1383–84 (May 8, 1982).

WALTERS, WILLIAM, and SINGER, PETER, eds. *Test-Tube Babies: A Guide to Moral Questions, Present Techniques, and Future Possibilities.* Melbourne: Oxford University Press, 1982.

WARNOCK, MARY. *A Question of Life: The Warnock Report on Human Fertilization and Embryology.* Oxford: Blackwell, 1985.

WARREN, MARY ANNE. "IVF and Women's Interests: An Analysis of Feminist Concerns." *Bioethics* 2: 37–57 (1988).

ZANER, RICHARD M. "A Criticism of Moral Conservatism's View of In Vitro Fertilization and Embryo Transfer." *Perspectives in Biology and Medicine* 27 (Winter 1984).

Health Insurance

BAYER, RONALD; CALLAHAN, DANIEL; CAPLAN, ARTHUR L.; and JENNINGS, BRUCE. "Toward Justice in Health Care." *American Journal of Public Health* 78: 583–88 (May 1988).

BLENDON, ROBERT J. "What Should Be Done About the Uninsured Poor?" *Journal of the American Medical Association* 260: 3176–77 (December 2, 1988).

CALIFANO, JOSEPH A. *America's Health Care Revolution: Who Lives? Who Dies? Who Pays?* New York: Random House, 1986.

CASSCELLS, WARD. "Heart Transplantation: Recent Policy Developments." *New England Journal of Medicine* 315: 1365–68 (November 20, 1986).

ENTHOVEN, ALAIN, and KRONICK, RICHARD. "A Consumer-Choice Health Plan for the 1990s: Universal Health Insurance in a System Designed to Promote Quality and Economy" (first of two parts). *New England Journal of Medicine* 320: 29–37 (January 5, 1989).

ENTHOVEN, ALAIN, and KRONICK, RICHARD. "A Consumer-Choice Health Plan for the 1990s: Universal Health Insurance in a System Designed to Promote Quality and Economy" (second of two parts). *New England Journal of Medicine* 320: 94–101 (January 12, 1989).

EVANS, ROGER W. "The Heart Transplant Dilemma." *Issues in Science and Technology.* 2: 91–101 (Spring 1986).

GRAHAM, GORDON. "The Doctor, the Rich, and the Indigent." *Journal of Medicine and Philosophy* 12: 51–61 (February 1987).

GRUMET, GERALD W. "Health Care Rationing Through Inconvenience: The Third Party's Secret Weapon." *New England Journal of Medicine* 321: 607–11 (August 31, 1989).

HIMMELSTEIN, DAVID U., and WOOLHANDLER, STEFFIE. "A National Health Program for the United States: A Physician's Proposal." *New England Journal of Medicine* 320: 102–8 (January 12, 1989).

MENZEL, PAUL T. "Scarce Dollars for Saving Lives: The Case of Heart and Liver Transplants," in *Organ Substitution Technology: Ethical, Legal and Public Policy Issues,* ed. Deborah Mathieu. Boulder, Colo.: Westview Press, 1988.

OPPENHEIMER, GERALD M., and PADGUG, ROBERT A. "AIDS: The Risks to Insurers, the Threat to Equity." *Hastings Center Report* 16: 18–22 (October 1986).

RUSHING, WILLIAM A. *Social Functions and Economic Aspects of Health Insurance.* Norwell, Mass.: Kluwer Academic Publishers (Nijhoff), 1986.

SAGER, ALAN. "Making Universal Health Insurance Work in Massachusetts." *Law, Medicine and Health Care* 17: 269–82 (Fall 1989).

THORPE, KENNETH E., and SIEGEL, JOANNA E. "Covering the Uninsured: Interactions Among Public and Private Sector Strategies." *Journal of the American Medical Association* 262: 2114–18 (October 20, 1989).

Informed Consent

ALEXANDER, LEO. "Medical Science Under Dictatorship." *New England Journal of Medicine* 241: 39–47 (July 14, 1949).

ALFIDI, RALPH J. "Informed Consent: A Study of Patient Reaction." *Journal of the American Medical Association* 216: 1325–29 (May 24, 1971).

ANNAS, GEORGE; GLANZ, LEONARD; and KATZ, BARBARA. *Informed Consent to Human Experimentation.* Cambridge, Mass.: Ballinger, 1977.

APPELBAUM, PAUL, and GRISSO, THOMAS. "Assessing Patients' Capacities to Consent to Treatment." *New England Journal of Medicine* 319: 1635–38 (December 22, 1988).

APPELBAUM, PAUL; LIDZ, CHARLES W.; and MEISEL, ALAN. *Informed Consent: Legal Theory and Clinical Practice.* New York: Oxford University Press, 1987.

APPELBAUM, PAUL; ROTH, LOREN; LIDZ, CHARLES W.; BENSON, PAUL; and WINSLADE, WILLIAM. "False Hopes and Best Data: Consent to Research and the Therapeutic Misconception." *Hastings Center Report* 17: 20–24 (April 1987).

BAUM, MICHAEL; ZILKHA, KEVIN; and HOUGHTON, JOAN. "Ethics of Clinical Research: Lessons for the Future." *British Medical Journal* 299: 251–53 (July 22, 1989).

BEECHER, HENRY K. *Research and the Individual: Human Studies.* Boston: Little, Brown, 1970.

BICKNELL, JOAN. "Consent and People with Mental Handicap: Nobody but the Patient May Give Consent." *British Medical Journal* 299: 1176–77 (November 11, 1989).

BRACKBRILL, Y., et al. "Public Opinion on Subject Participation in Biomedical Research: New Views on Altruism, Perception of Risk, and Proxy Consent." *Clinical Research* 27 (February 1979).

BRODY, HOWARD. "Transparency: Informed Consent in Primary Care." *Hastings Center Report* 19: 5–9 (September/October 1989).

BUCHANAN, ALLEN. "Medical Paternalism." *Philosophy and Public Affairs* 7: 370–87 (Summer 1978).

CHILDRESS, JAMES. "The Place of Autonomy in Bioethics." *Hastings Center Report* 20: 12–17 (January/February 1990).

———. *Who Should Decide? Paternalism in Health Care.* New York: Oxford University Press, 1982.

CROSS, ALAN W. "Ethical and Cultural Dimensions of Informed Consent." *Annals of Internal Medicine* 96: 110–13 (1982).

DWORKIN, GERALD. "Autonomy and the Demented Self." *Milbank Quarterly* 64: 4–16 (1986), Suppl. 2.

———. "Paternalism." *The Monist* 56: 1 (January 1985).

"Electroshock Experiment at Albany Violates Ethical Guidelines." *Science* 198 (October 28, 1977).

ENGLEHARDT, H. TRISTRAM. "Information and Authenticity: Rethinking Free and Informed Consent." *Journal of General Internal Medicine* 3: 91–93 (January/February 1988).

FADEN, RUTH R., and BEAUCHAMP, TOM L. *A History and Theory of Informed Consent.* New York: Oxford University Press, 1986.

FOST, NORMAN. "Consent as a Barrier to Research." *New England Journal of Medicine* 300: 1272–73 (May 31, 1979).

GILLET, GRANT R. "Informed Consent and Moral Integrity." *Journal of Medical Ethics* 15: 117–23 (September 1989).

GOODFIELD, JUNE. *Playing God: Genetic Engineering and the Manipulation of Life.* New York: Random House, 1977.

GRUNDNER, T. M. *Informed Consent: A Tutorial.* Owings Mills, Md.: National Health Publishing, 1986.

HOLDER, ANGELA R. "Disclosure and Consent Problems in Pediatrics." *Law, Medicine and Health Care* 16: 219–28 (Fall/Winter 1988).

——. "Minor's Rights to Consent to Medical Care." *Journal of the American Medical Association* 257: 3400–402 (June 26, 1987).

INGELFINGER, F. J. "Informed (But Uneducated) Consent." *New England Journal of Medicine* 287: 465–66 (August 31, 1972).

IRB: A Review of Human Subjects Research. Hastings-on-Hudson, N.Y.: The Hastings Center.

"Is Serum Hepatitis Only a Special Type of Infectious Hepatitis?" Editorial from *Journal of the American Medical Association,* and "Viral Hepatitis," by S. Krugman and J. Giles. *Journal of the American Medical Association* 212: 1020 (May 11, 1970).

JONAS, HANS. "Philosophical Reflections on Experimenting with Human Subjects," in *Experimentation with Human Subjects,* ed. Paul Freund. New York: Braziller, 1970.

JONES, JAMES. *Bad Blood: The Tuskegee Syphilis Experiment, A Tragedy of Race and Medicine.* New York: Free Press, 1981.

KATZ, JAY, with CAPRON, ALEXANDER, and GLASS, ELEANOR SWIFT. *Experimentation with Human Beings.* New York: Russell Sage Foundation, 1972.

KING, NANCY M. P., and CROSS, ALAN W. "Children as Decision Makers: Guidelines for Pediatricians." *Journal of Pediatrics* 115: 10–16 (July 1989).

LAVIN, MICHAEL. "Ulysses Contracts." *Journal of Applied Philosophy* 3: 89–101 (March 1986).

LIDZ, CHARLES; APPELBAUM, PAUL; and MEISEL, ALAN. "Two Models of Implementing Informed Consent." *Archives of Internal Medicine* 148: 1385–89 (June 1988).

MACKLIN, RUTH, and FRIEDLAND, GERALD. "AIDS Research: The Ethics of Clinical Trials." *Law, Medicine and Health Care* 14 (December 1986).

MALCOM, JOHN GULTON. *Treatment Choices and Informed Consent: Current Controversies in Psychiatric Malpractice Litigation.* Springfield, Ill.: Charles C Thomas, 1988.

MAY, WILLIAM E. "Proxy Consent to Human Experimentation." *Linacre Quarterly* 43: 73–84 (May 1976).

MAZUR, DENNIS J. "What Should Patients Be Told Prior to a Medical Procedure? Ethical and Legal Perspectives on Medical Informed Consent." *American Journal of Medicine* 81: 1051–54 (December 1986).

MINOQUE, BRENDAN P.; TARASZEWSKI, ROBERT; ELIAS, SHERMAN; and ANNAS, GEORGE. "The Whole Truth and Nothing But the Truth." *Hastings Center Report* 18: 34–36 (October/November 1988).

MORRISSEY, JAMES M.; HOFMANN, ADELE D.; and THROPE, JEFFREY C. *Consent and Confidentiality in the Health Care of Children and Adolescents: A Legal Guide.* New York: Free Press, 1986.

National Commission for the Protection of Human Subjects of Biomedical and Behavioral Research. *Research Involving Children—Report and Recommendations.* Bethesda, Md.: DHEW Publication No. (OS) 77–0004 and 77–0005 (1977).

ORLOWSKI, JAMES P.; KANOTI, GEORGE A.; and MEHLMAN, MAXWELL J. "The Ethics of Using Newly Dead Patients for Teaching and Practicing Intubation Techniques." *New England Journal of Medicine* 319: 439–41 (August 18, 1988).

PERRY, CLIFTON. "Negligence in Securing Informed Consent and Medical Malpractice." *Journal of Medical Humanities and Bioethics* 9: 111–20 (Fall/Winter 1988).

ROSNER, RICHARD, and SCHWARTZ, HAROLD I. *Geriatric Psychiatry and the Law.* New York: Plenum, 1987.

ROZOVSKY, FAY A. *Consent to Treatment: A Practical Guide—1986 Supplement.* Boston: Little, Brown, 1986.

SCHAFER, A. "The Ethics of the Randomized Clinical Trial." *New England Journal of Medicine* 307: 719–24 (1982).

SCHAFFNER, KENNETH F., issue ed. "Ethical Issues in the Use of Clinical Controls." *Journal of Medicine and Philosophy* 11 (November 1986).

SCOFIELD, GILES. "The Calculus of Consent." *Hastings Center Report* 20: 44–47 (January/February 1990).

SILVERMAN, WILLIAM A. "The Myth of Informed Consent: In Daily Practice and in Clinical Trials." *Journal of Medical Ethics* 15: 6–11 (March 1989).

STRAUSSER, MARK. "Physicians, Battery, and the Duty to Give Consent." 6: 40–48 (March 1987).

SWENDER, PHILLIP. "Reflections on the New York Do-Not-Resuscitate Law." *New York State Journal of Medicine* 89: 57–58 (February 1989).

VANDEVEER, DONALD. "Experimentation on Children and Proxy Consent." *Journal of Medicine and Philosophy* 6: 281–93 (1981).

VAN EYS, JAN, ed. *Research on Children.* Baltimore: University Park Press, 1978.

VEATCH, ROBERT. *The Patient as Partner: A Theory of Human-Experimentation Ethics.* Bloomington: Indiana University Press.

VISSCHER, MAURICE B. *Ethical Constraints and Imperatives in Medical Research.* Springfield, Ill.: Charles C Thomas, 1975.

Law

CANTOR, NORMAN. *Legal Frontiers of Death and Dying.* Bloomington: Indiana University Press, 1987.

HART, H. L. A. "Positivism and the Separation of Law and Morals," in *Philosophy of Law,* ed. J. Feinberg and H. Gross. Encino, Calif.: Dickenson Publishing Co., 1975.

JOSEN, ALBERT R. "Transition from Fetus to Infant: A Problem for Law and Ethics." *Hastings Law Journal* 37: 697–701 (May 1986).

LASAGNA, LOUIS. "The Boston State Hospital Case (*Rogers* v. *Okin*): A Legal, Ethical and Medical Morass." *Perspectives in Biology and Medicine* 25: 382–403 (Spring 1982).

MATHIEU, THOMAS H. "Respecting Liberty and Preventing Harm: Limits of State Intervention in Prenatal Choice." *Harvard Journal of Law and Public Policy* 8 (Winter 1985).

NELSON, LAWRENCE J., and MILLIKEN, NANCY. "Compelled Medical Treatment of Pregnant Women: Life, Liberty and Law in Conflict." *Journal of the American Medical Association* 259: 1060–66 (February 19, 1988).

PALMER, LARRY I. *Law, Medicine, and Social Justice.* Louisville, Ky.: Westminster/John Knox Press, 1989.

PELLEGRINO, EDMUND, and SHARPE, VIRGINIA ASHBY. "Medical Ethics in the Court Room: The Need for Scrutiny." *Perspectives in Biology and Medicine* 32: 547–64 (Summer 1989).

REILLY, PAUL. *Genetics, Law and Social Policy.* Cambridge, Mass.: Harvard University Press, 1977.

STILLER, JENNIFER A. "A Practical Guide to Legal Considerations in Ethical Issues," in *Health Care Ethics: A Guide for Decision Makers,* eds. Gary R. Anderson and Valerie A. Glesnes-Anderson. Rockville, Md.: Aspen Publishers, 1987.

Women in Medicine

HOWARD, MARY C. "What Medical Schools Teach About Women." *New England Journal of Medicine* 291 (1974).

JUSSIN, JUDITH, and MULLER, CHARLOTTE. "Medical Education for Women: How Good an Investment?" *Journal of Medical Education* 50 (1975).

LEWIS, CHARLES E., and LEWIS, MARY ANN. "The Potential Impact of Sexual Equality on Health." *New England Journal of Medicine* 297 (1977).

MANTHORPE, CATHERINE. "Feminists Look at Science." *New Scientist* 1446 (March 7, 1985).

PERNICK, MARTIN S. *A Calculus of Suffering: Pain, Professionalism, and Anesthesia in Nineteenth-Century America.* New York: Columbia University Press, 1985.

"Women's Liberation and the Practice of Medicine." *Medical World News* (June 22, 1973).

Normality (*see also* Rationality)

STAFFORD, BARBARA M.; LA PUMA, JOHN; and SCHIEDERMAYER, DAVID L. "One Face of Beauty, One Picture of Health: The Hidden Aesthetic of Medical Practice." *Journal of Medicine and Philosophy* 14: 213–30 (April 1989).

Nursing Ethics

BENJAMIN, MARTIN, and CURTIS, JOY. *Ethics in Nursing.* New York: Oxford University Press, 1981.

CHAMORRO, TERRY, and APPELBAUM, JANET. "Informed Consent: Nursing Issues and Ethical Dilemmas." *Oncology Nursing Forum* 15: 803–8 (November/December 1988).

FOWLER, MARSHA D. M. "The Nurse's Role: Responsibilities and Rights," in *Biomedical Ethics Reviews, 1987,* eds. James M. Humber and Robert F. Almeder. Clifton, N.J.: Clifton Press, 1988.

FOWLER, MARSHA D. M., and LEVINE-ARIFF, JUNE, eds. *Ethics at the Bedside: A Source Book for the Critical Care Nurse.* Philadelphia: Lippincott, 1987.

FREEDMAN, BENJAMIN. "Health Professions, Codes, and the Right to Refuse HIV-Infectious Patients." *Hastings Center Report* 18: S20–S25 (April/May 1988).

FRY, SARA T. "The Role of Caring in a Theory of Nursing Ethics." *Hypatia* 4: 88–103 (Summer 1989).

HILLIARD, MARIE T. "Nursing, Ethics, and Professional Roles." *Hastings Center Report* 20 (January/February 1990).

JAMETON, ANDREW. *Nursing Practice: The Ethical Issues.* Englewood Cliffs, N.J.: Prentice Hall, 1984.

OMERY, ANNA. "Values, Moral Reasoning, and Ethics." *Nursing Clinics of North America* 24: 499–508 (June 1989).

PACKARD, JOHN S., and FERRARA, MARY. "In Search of the Moral Foundation of Nursing." *Advances in Nursing Science* 10: 60–71 (July 1988).

QUINN, CARROLL A., and SMITH, MICHAEL D. *The Professional Commitment: Issues and Ethics in Nursing.* Philadelphia: Saunders, 1987.

REISMAN, ELIZABETH C. "Ethical Issues Confronting Nurses." *Nursing Clinics of North America* 23: 789–802 (December 1988).

THEIS, E. CHARLOTTE. "Nursing Student's Perspectives of Unethical Teaching Behaviors." *Journal of Nursing Education* 27: 102–6 (March 1988).

WEGMANN, JO ANN. "Ethical Issues in Critical Care Nursing," in *Medical Ethics: A Guide for Health Professionals,* eds. John F. Monagle and David C. Thomasma. Rockville, Md.: Aspen Publishers, 1988.

Phenomenological

KESTERBAUM, VICTOR, ed. *The Humanity of the Ill.* Knoxville: University of Tennessee Press, 1982.

PELLEGRINO, EDMOND D., and THOMASMA, DAVID C. *A Philosophical Basis of Medical Practice: Toward a Philosophy of Ethic of the Healing Professions.* New York: Oxford University Press, 1981.

ZANER, RICHARD. *Ethics and Clinical Encounter.* Englewood Cliffs, N.J.: Prentice Hall, 1988.

Professionalism

APPELBAUM, DAVID, and LAWTON, SARAH, eds. *Ethics and the Professions.* Englewood Cliffs, N.J.: Prentice Hall, 1990.

BAUMRIN, BERNARD, and FREEDMAN, BENJAMIN, eds. *Moral Responsibility and the Professions.* New York: Haven Productions, 1983.

BLEDSTEIN, BURTON J. *The Culture of Professionalism.* New York: W. W. Norton, 1976.

BOISAUBIN, EUGENE V. "Defining the Limits of Housestaff Care." *Journal of Medicine and Philosophy* 13: 457–58 (November 1988).

CALLAHAN, JOAN C., ed. *Ethical Issues in Professional Life.* New York: Oxford University Press, 1988.

CAMPBELL, ALASTAIR V. *Professional Care: Its Meaning and Practice.* Minneapolis: Fortress Press, 1984.

CULLEN, JOHN. *The Structure of Professionalism.* New York: Petrocelli, 1978.

FREEDMAN, BENJAMIN. "A Meta Ethics for Professional Morality." *Ethics* 89: 1–19 (1978).

FREIDSON, ELLIOT. "Profession as Organization—Formal and Informal." *Profession of Medicine.* New York: Dodd, Mead and Co., 1973.

———. *Professional Powers: A Study of the Institutionalization of Formal Knowledge.* Chicago: University of Chicago Press, 1986.

GEWIRTH, ALAN. "The Professional Ethics: The Separatist Thesis." *Ethics* 96: 282–300 (1986).

GOLDMAN, ALAN H. *The Moral Foundations of Professional Ethics.* Savage, Md.: Rowman and Littlefield, 1980.

ILLICH, IVAN. "The Killing of Pain." *Medical Nemesis.* New York: Random House, 1976.

ILLICH, IVAN, et al. *The Disabling Professions.* London: Marion Boars, 1977.

LEBACQZ, KAREN. *Professional Ethics: Power and Paradox.* Nashville, Tenn.: Abington Press, 1985.

LIFTON, ROBERT JAY. *The Nazi Doctors.* New York: Basic Books, 1986.

MCKEON, THOMAS. "Introduction—Concepts of Health and Disease." *The Role of Medicine.* London: Nuffield Provincial Hospitals Trust, 1976.

PARSONS, TALCOTT. "Professions." *International Encyclopedia of the Social Sciences* XII, 536–46. New York: Macmillan, 1968.

RITCHIE, KAREN. "Professionalism, Altruism, and Overwork." *Journal of Medicine and Philosophy* 13: 447–55 (November 1988).

STARR, PAUL. *The Social Reformation of American Medicine.* New York: Basic Books, 1982.

SZASZ, T. "The Myth of Mental Illness." *The American Psychologist* 15 (February 1960).

VOLLMER, H. M., and MILLS, D. L., eds. *Professionalization.* Englewood Cliffs, N.J.: Prentice Hall, 1966.

WILLIAMS, JANICE, and SCHEIDERMAN, HENRY. "The Ethics of Impaired Physicians: Wolfe's Dr. McGuire and William's Dr. Rivers," in *Literature and Bioethics,* eds. D. Howard Brock and Richard Ratzman. Baltimore: Johns Hopkins University Press, 1988.

Rationality

CLOUSER, K. DANNER, and GERT, BERNARD, issue eds. "Rationality and Medicine." *Journal of Medicine and Philosophy* 11 (May 1986), Special ed.

MACKLIN, RUTH. "Philosophical Conceptions of Rationality and Psychiatric Notions of Competency." *Synthese* 57: 205–25 (November 1983).

MURPHY, EDMOND A. *The Logic of Medicine.* Baltimore: Johns Hopkins University Press, 1976.

WULFF, HENRIK R. *Rational Diagnosis of Treatment.* Oxford: Blackwell Scientific Publications, 1976.

Religious

ASHLEY, BENEDICT. *Health Care Ethics: A Theological Analysis.* St. Louis: Catholic Hospital Association, 1978.

CURRAN, CHARLES. *Politics, Medicine, and Christian Ethics: A Dialogue with Paul Ramsey.* Minneapolis: Fortress Press, 1973.

FELDMAN, DAVID. *Health and Medicine in the Jewish Tradition.* New York: Crossroad, 1986.

GUSTAFSON, JAMES. *The Contribution of Theology to Medical Ethics.* Milwaukee: Marquette University Press, 1975.

LEVEY, MARTIN. *Medical Ethics of Medieval Islam.* Philadelphia: American Philosophy Society, 1966.

McCORMICK, RICHARD. *Health and Medicine in the Catholic Tradition.* New York: Crossroad, 1985.

MAHONEY, JOHN. *Bioethics and Belief.* Westminster, Md.: Christian Classics, 1984.

SINCLAIR, DANIEL B. *Tradition and the Biological Revolution: The Application of Jewish Law to the Treatment of the Critically Ill.* Edinburgh: Edinburgh University Press, 1989.

"Theology, Religious Traditions, and Bioethics." *Hastings Center Report* 20 (July/August 1990), Suppl.

Truth Telling

GILLON, RAANAN. "Deciding Not to Resuscitate." *Journal of Medical Ethics* 15: 171–72 (December 1989).

RODWIN, MARC A. "Physician's Conflicts of Interest: The Limitations of Disclosure." *New England Journal of Medicine* 321: 1405–8 (November 16, 1989).

SCHADE, STANLEY G., and MUSLIN, HYMAN. "Do Not Resuscitate Decisions: Discussions with Patients." *Journal of Medical Ethics* 15: 186–90 (December 1989).

SPENCER, WALTER. "Suspicion of Multiple Sclerosis: To Tell or Not to Tell?" *Archives of Neurology* 45: 441–42 (April 1988).

SPIRO, STEVEN. "Clinical Oncology: Medical and Surgical Practice," in *Doctor's Decisions: Ethical Conflicts in Medical Practice,* eds. G. R. Dunstan and Elliot A. Shinebourne. New York: Oxford University Press, 1989.

INDEX